MEHMED II
THE CONQUEROR

And the Fall of the Franco-Byzantine Levant
to the Ottoman Turks:
Some Western Views and Testimonies

Medieval and Renaissance
Texts and Studies

Volume 302

MEHMED II
THE CONQUEROR

And the Fall of the Franco-Byzantine Levant
to the Ottoman Turks:
Some Western Views and Testimonies

*Edited, Translated,
and Annotated
by*

MARIOS PHILIPPIDES

ACMRS
(Arizona Center for Medieval and Renaissance Studies)
Tempe, Arizona
2007

© Copyright 2007
Arizona Board of Regents for Arizona State University

Library of Congress Cataloging-in-Publication Data

Philippides, Marios, 1950-
  Mehmed II the Conqueror and the fall of the Franco-Byzantine Levant to the Ottoman Turks : some western views and testimonies / edited, translated, and annotated by Marios Philippides.
    p. cm. -- (Medieval and Renaissance texts and studies ; v. 302)
  Includes bibliographical references and index.
  ISBN 978-0-86698-346-4 (alk. paper)
  1. Istanbul (Turkey)--History--Siege, 1453. 2. Mehmed II, Sultan of the Turks, 1432-1481. I. Title.

DF649.P39 2007
956'.015092--dc22

                                                                                          2007013638

∞
This book is made to last.
It is set in Adobe Jenson Pro,
smyth-sewn and printed on acid-free paper
to library specifications.
Printed in the United States of America

CONTENTS

Preface — ix

Abbreviations — xiii

CHAPTER I — 1
Introduction

CHAPTER II — 55
Nicolai Secundini
    de Familia Otthomanorum Epitome ad Aeneam Senarum Episcopum

An Epitome on the Family of the Ottomans for Aeneas, *the Bishop of Siena*
    by Nikolaos Sekoundinos

CHAPTER III — 93
Pii Secundi Pontificis Maximi
    De Captione Urbis Constantinopolis Tractatulus

A Brief Treatise on the Capture of Constantinople
    by Pope Pius II

CHAPTER IV — 121
Magister Henricus de Zomern
    Qualiter urbs Constantinopolis anno LIII° a Turcis depredata fuit et subiugata

The Fall and Sack of the City of Constantinople by the Turks in the Year [14]53
    by Master Henry of Soemmern

CHAPTER V — 133

Tetaldi
 Tractatus de Expugnatione Urbis Constantinopolis
Tetaldi: A Treatise on the Fall of Constantinople

CHAPTER VI — 219

Caso ruinoso della cittade di Negroponte inteso per mi
 Iacomo Rizzardo scrivan dello spettabil uomo Messer Lorenzo
 Contarini Sopracomito di una galia grossa di Fiandra

The Siege and Destruction of Negroponte
 by Giacomo Rizzardo, Secretary of the Reverend Lord Lorenzo
 Contarini, Commander of a Large Galley of Flanders

CHAPTER VII — 249

Perdita di Negroponte,
 scritta per Frate Iacopo dalla Castellana

The Loss of Negroponte
 by Brother Jacopo dalla Castellana

CHAPTER VIII — 261

Gu<g>lielmi Cao<u>rsi<n>i Rhodiorum vice cancelarii
 Obsidionis Rhodiae Urbis Descriptio

A Description of the Siege of Rhodes
 by Guillaume Caoursin, the Vice Chancellor
 of the Rhodians [Hospitallers]

CHAPTER IX — 315

I. Epistola ad Papam una cum vexillo Turchino
 missa 1480, die XVII Nov., de obsidione insulae, Rhodus, a Turcis

I. Letter to the Pope together with a Turkish Standard
 Captured from the Turks during the Siege of the Island of Rhodes,
 Sent on November 17, 1480

II. Frater Petrus Daubusson &c. & nos Conventus &c.
 universis & singulis prioribus, praeceptoribus,
 & fratribus Ordinis nostri ubilibet constitutis, ad quos
 nostrae praesentes literae pervenerint salutem in eo,
 qui est omnium vera salus.

II. Brother Pierre d'Aubusson etc. and we the Convent etc.
to all and to each individual prior, preceptor,
and brother of our Order, wherever they may be,
wherever they receive our letter:
health in Him who is the true salvation of all.

APPENDIX I 341
    Tetaldi's French Text

APPENDIX II 347
    The *Aman-name* of Mehmed II, Granted to Pera (1453)

APPENDIX III 351
    Extracts from Pietro Giustiniani,
    Rerum Venetarum ab Urbe Condita ad Annum M.D.LXXV
    (*Argentorati M. DC. XI*)

Bibliography   369

Illustrations   391

Index of Persons   413

Index of Places   421

Index of Scholars   427

PREFACE

The systematic study of the fall of Byzantine-Frankish Greece and the related expansion of the Ottoman Turks in southeastern Europe was pioneered by Constantine N. Sathas, Philippe A. Déthier, and Spyridon P. Lampros, in their numerous publications which spanned the latter half of the nineteenth century and the first quarter of the twentieth century. I have put this modest collection together partly in the belief that their work was never brought to a proper conclusion and that their studies and contributions to Medieval and Renaissance historiography remain largely inaccessible to English-speaking students of this period. In recent decades our understanding of the monumental events that involve the end of Byzantine Greece and the expansion of the Ottoman Turks into the Levant and southeastern Europe have been aided and enriched by new and interesting approaches, innovative lines of research, and fresh ways of looking at a fascinatingly complicated situation, but the sad fact remains that numerous sources still remain inaccessible to the majority of students and scholars. I therefore make no apologies for the unabashedly old-fashioned approach employed here.

I am, like all students of medieval Greek history, most of all indebted to three influential scholars, Agostino Pertusi, Kenneth M. Setton, and Speros Vryonis, Jr. Agostino Pertusi's Herculean series of three volumes of selected source material on the fall of Byzantium is far more comprehensive than this little book could hope to be; the first two volumes of his *opus* should be consulted at least for the narratives presented, even though often they are incomplete, selections appear arbitrary, and original texts are often absent, presenting only Italian translations; unfortunately, the third volume is marred by numerous typographical errors. Kenneth M. Setton's monumental work on the Levant, along with his numerous publications over the past forty years, has molded the present generation of medieval historians focusing on this geographical area and period. Speros Vryonis's magisterial work on the Islamization of medieval Greek culture and his subsequent work examining the interaction of Greeks and Turks in the Balkans comprise a major scholarly achievement of the twentieth century. Whatever interpretive skills I may possess I largely owe to the published works of these scholars.

One of the reasons that compelled me to produce a limited commentary to accompany the texts consists of my subjective notion that something should be said in connection with the narrative techniques of the writers, whose works,

opuscula, and essays have not been studied *in extenso* and in a systematic fashion previously. Although there have been many specialized studies on narrative in western-Byzantine-Turkish historiography in recent years, all of them have been based on the researches carried out by Sathas, Déthier, Lampros, and Nicolae Iorga, who discovered and published archival material along with other, major texts. The narratives and authors presented in this volume have been neglected and have not attracted major scholarly attention perhaps because they were overlooked by the nineteenth-century investigators. Thus the present collection is addressed to students, to fellow historians (in particular, those with philological interests), and to researchers of the period, who may not have found easy access to the sources and the surviving texts presented in this volume.

This is not a comprehensive textbook of Turkish expansion into southeastern Europe, for it deals with only a few texts. I see it as a collection of "test cases" for a future comparative study of historic narrative dealing with these themes. I have chosen texts that were mostly published in the form of incunabula in the Renaissance and narratives that have been neglected, for one reason or another, by scholars of the previous centuries. Although this book is the product of many years of studying pertinent material in regard to the fall of the Byzantine-Frankish Levant and the rise of Ottoman Turkey, the editing, translating, and actual writing itself have taken place during various visits to the Gennadius Library of Athens, whose incomparable holdings and expert staff are famous among scholars and bibliophiles alike.

I would like to express my gratitude to my friends and colleagues in the Department of Classics, who have created a supportive and most stimulating scholarly environment, and have endured my interests in the medieval Levant for almost one quarter of a century. In particular, I would like to thank Professor Brian Breed for observations in regard to the text of d'Aubusson; Professor Elizabeth Keitel for her help on numerous difficult points with the incunabula of Caoursin; Professor Kenneth Kitchell for comments on Tetaldi; and Professor Rex Wallace for his expertise on the peculiar orthography and the linguistic problems encountered in the Italian texts of Rizzardo and Castellana. Thanks are also due to Dr Constantine Hatzidimitriou for lending me his Giustiniani edition, and to my guide in modern Negroponte, Mr. Christos Galatenios, a lover of Khalkis, who managed, in good spirit, to handle my incessant requests to identify remains and structures from the Venetian period. I owe a debt to the two anonymous readers of the Press who clarified numerous points in my text. I am deeply indebted to Dr Leslie S. B. MacCoull, who edited a difficult manuscript with infinite patience, intelligence, and scholarly generosity, offered innumerable suggestions and corrections, and clearly improved this study. Needless to say, none of these individuals are responsible for the remaining infelicities and errors; they are my own.

Finally, I would like to take this opportunity to thank my wife, Corinne Lynam Philippides; I am indeed at a loss for words in expressing my immense

gratitude for her love of scholarship, her passion for antiquities and history, and her unqualified support of my research, punctuated by irrepressible optimism and thoughtful, challenging advice: σεῦ δ' ἐγὼ ἀρξάμενος μεταβήσομαι ἄλλον ἐς ὕμνον.

Marios Philippides
November 2004 University of Massachusetts, Amherst

ABBREVIATIONS

BSEB	*Byzantine Studies/Études byzantines*
BS	*Byzantinoslavica*
Byz	*Byzantion*
BZ	*Byzantinische Zeitschrift*
CC 1	A. Pertusi, *La Caduta di Costantinopoli*, vol. 1: *Le Testimonianze dei Contemporanei*
CC 2	A. Pertusi, *La Caduta di Costantinopoli*, vol. 2: *L'Eco nel Mondo*
CSHB	*Corpus Scriptorum Historiae Byzantinae*
DOP	*Dumbarton Oaks Papers*
EdO	*Echos d'Orient. Revue d'histoire, de géographie et de liturgie orientales*
FC	S. Runciman, *The Fall of Constantinople 1453*
LCB	D. M. Nicol, *The Last Centuries of Byzantium, 1261–1453*
MCT	F. Babinger, *Mehmed the Conqueror and his Time*
MP	J. W. Barker, *Manuel II Palaeologus (1395–1425): A Study in Late Byzantine Statesmanship*
NE 1–6	N. Iorga, *Notes et extraits pour servir à l'Histoire des Croisades au XVe siècle*, 6 vols.

NH	Νέος Ἑλληνομνήμων
NΣBE	P. D. Mastrodemetres, Νικόλαος Σεκουνδινὸς (1402–1464): Βίος καὶ Ἔργον
OCP	Orientalia Christiana Periodica
ODB	Oxford Dictionary of Byzantium
OGN	A. E. Vacalopoulos, Origins of the Greek Nation: The Byzantine Period, 1204–1261
PG	J.-P. Migne, ed. Patrologiae Cursus Completus, Series Graeca
PL 1	K. M. Setton, The Papacy and the Levant (1204–1571), vol. 1: The Thirteenth and Fourteenth Centuries
PL 2	K. M. Setton, The Papacy and the Levant (1204–1571), vol. 2: The Fifteenth Century
RdD 1–3	F. Thiriet, Régestes des délibérations du Sénat de Venise concernant la Romanie, 3 vols.
REB	Revue des études byzantines
RKOR	F. Dölger, P. Wirth, edd., Regesten der Kaiserkunden des oströmischen Reiches von 565–1453 [= Corpus der griechischen Urkunden des Mittelalters und der neuen Zeit], vol. 5: Regesten von 1341–1453
SOC	R. Schwoebel, The Shadow of the Crescent: The Renaissance Image of the Turk (1453–1517)
TIePN	A. Pertusi, A. Carile, edd., Testi Inediti e Poco Noti sulla Caduta di Costantinopoli
ZRVI	Zbornik Radova Vizantijloškog Instituta, Srpska Akademija Nauka

CHAPTER I:
INTRODUCTION

GENERAL REMARKS

At an exciting time, when the Italian Renaissance eagerly embraced the culture of ancient Greece and the rise of humanism disseminated a new spirit expressing itself in new forms of literature and art that created the foundations of modern European and western society, dark clouds appeared on this bright horizon. Humanists pointed out that the monumental struggle that had been played out in antiquity and had been often described by ancient writers in an obsessive fashion was undergoing a process of revival and was rising out of its ashes: the conflict between Occident and Orient. It no longer took the form of "Greek against Persian" or "Roman against Parthian." Its modern incarnation generalized Christian against Moslem and western, Latin Christendom versus Islamic, Ottoman Turkey. It amounted to a great deal more than a struggle over competing religions. Indeed it was seen as a fight for survival, a war between conflicting ideologies competing to eliminate established ways of life through aggressive military encounters. In the *quattrocento* the Turkish military machine engulfed, annexed, and absorbed all remnants of the old, tired empire of the Byzantine Greeks, which had survived for over one thousand years and had promulgated the fiction that Constantinople and her Caesars had been the only direct heirs and only legitimate successors of the Roman Empire. While this empire existed, it provided a buffer zone, sometimes a very thin buffer zone, and a demarcation line between Latin west and Islamic east. Finally, the fifteenth century witnessed the elimination of this buffer zone and Latin Europe came to face a depressing reality: sooner or later there had to be a direct conflict with the Ottoman Turks. Thus far the struggle had been played out in the Aegean and the southern Balkans. When the Turks launched raids deep into Hungary, Serbia, Transylvania, Bulgaria, and Albania, the Italians began to take serious notice, which translated into real concern and panic among the northern cities that had maintained ties with the Orthodox Christian states in the east and awaited an inevitable confrontation and an all-out war.

While Italy expressed sympathy and advanced aggressive moral support to the vanishing enclaves of the Byzantine Greeks against their Oriental foe, the actual military and economic aid came belatedly and in minute quantities; clearly, the West had been deceived by its hope that the situation would correct itself. Even when it came to the defense of Constantinople, which was mainly supervised by the Venetian residents of Constantinople and the Genoese mercenaries of the Greek emperor, aid to the beleaguered city never came in any substantial form. The Venetian armada, put together and equipped explicitly for the relief of the Greek capital, made its way through the Aegean in so painfully slow and so unconcerned a manner that it reached the neighborhood of the city well after the sack by the Turks on May 29, 1453. The disaster that made Constantinople the capital of the Ottoman sultan ignited outcries in the west; petitions were circulated and were directed to ecclesiastical leaders and secular lords, demanding the formation of a crusade to recover the ancient city. No actual attempts were made, however, in spite of the widespread anguish expressed in Christendom. By the middle of the summer of 1453 even the Venetians, who had forfeited so much property, who had sustained heavy casualties during the siege and sack, and who had lost prominent members of numerous noble families in the wave of executions that followed the disaster, initiated intense negotiations with the conqueror to recover some remnants of the previous privileges they had enjoyed under the Byzantine emperor. A peace treaty between the *Serenissima* and the Porte was indeed ratified as early as April 18, 1454. Nevertheless, the loss of Constantinople radically changed the situation and the west made plans for her recovery. Humanists disseminated various military projects, which were never embraced seriously by the secular powers and never advanced beyond the planning stage.

It was not just the loss of Constantinople that rang the alarm bell. The disaster underscored the reality that the Turks were already within the gates of Europe and that Islamic expansion would not evaporate. The following year, 1454, witnessed Sultan Mehmed II's incursions into the Serbian territories of Despot George Branković; Ottoman troops plundered the areas between the Save and the Danube. In the spring of 1455 Mehmed II, the conqueror of Constantinople, marched and took Novo Brdo, a city well known for its wealth in silver mines. In 1456 there appeared a ray of hope, as Sultan Mehmed II failed to seize Belgrade, in the face of the determined opposition organized and led by the monk Giovanni Capistrano and the legendary soldier John Corvinus Hunyadi of Transylvania. Once more Mehmed suffered a setback in Albania in 1457 but in 1458 Turkish forces marched into Serbia, while Mehmed himself led another army into Greece and annexed the despotate of the Morea ruled by the brothers of the last Greek emperor of Byzantine Constantinople. In 1459 the sultan personally directed his forces into Serbia and seized Smederevo. Thus he gained control of Serbia. In 1461 he easily annexed the Greek "empire" of Trebizond and turned his attention to Wallachia. Immediately after this campaign, and with

the mainland of Greece under his control, the sultan turned his attention to the Italian possessions in the Aegean. The Genoese island of Lesbos was the first to suffer: Turkish troops took over Lesbos in the fall of 1462. Venice's possessions did not remain safe for long. After a fierce siege, Mehmed seized the capital of the island of Euboea, Khalkis (or Negroponte, as it was then called by its Venetian lords), in 1470, and increased the number of raids into Albania, after the death of her heroic defender, George Kastriota Scanderbeg. By the late 1470s it was painfully clear that the Turks were focusing their attention on Italy. In fact, their forays brought them into the Veneto. Finally in 1480, the Ottoman Turks dispatched by sea an expeditionary force to Italy herself and seized Otranto, while at the same time a Turkish armada laid siege to the capital of the island of Rhodes, which was defended by the Knights of Saint John under the inspired leadership of the Order's Grand Master, Pierre d'Aubusson.

Thus the threatening circumstances of the *quattrocento* demanded that the west display some interest in the Turks, as they expanded westwards and encroached upon Christian territories. While the Ottomans inched closer and closer, Europeans became anxious to learn something about the Turks. While in popular literature the old ideas of chivalry, of the western concept of holy war, of the propagation of the faith, and of the heroic opposition to the Turkish peril became the stock motifs of romances, more scholarly-inclined readers wished to gather a few facts about the dread Turk. The response to this desire was mainly academic, as humanists began to compose ethnographic treatises based on genres that had been formed in antiquity. But before serious attempts were made, eyewitness accounts of the events had to be collected to provide the foundations for such academic exercises. Thus the West eagerly anticipated reports on the Turk's advance; these reports usually came in the form of letters written by ambassadors and by diplomatic emissaries and in the form of learned narratives and pamphlets composed by private individuals who possessed first-hand knowledge of the enemy. As material amassed, scholars began to compile "histories" and ethnographic accounts on the Turks. Since most scholars were humanists with a classical education, their approach to the subject had to be traditional and was handled in a manner that would have been approved by some historians in antiquity, such as Herodotus or Pausanias. Even Greeks joined the chorus of humanists in this endeavor. Laonikos (i.e., Nikolaos, in Christian form) Khalkokondyles wrote his famous *Historiarum demonstrationes* as a response to this demand. Following the slightly earlier example of Sekoundinos, Laonikos composed a lengthy inquiry into the origins of the Ottoman Turks and produced, in the process, a virtual περιήγησις, an old-fashioned tour, of the contemporary Orient and Occident, embedded in his history of the related themes of the fall of Byzantine Greece and the rise of the Turks. As a true humanist, he shapes his work under guidelines and methods that had so successfully been utilized by Herodotus in antiquity, while his linguistic idiom betrays immense influence from the style of the famous Athenian historian, Thucydides.

European humanists struggled to view the fall of Constantinople in a scholarly context. While the image of the Turk as a savage barbarian continued to be employed in popular literature, a few intellectuals attempted to bring the Turks into the humanistic sphere. And in time the Turk was rehabilitated in some circles and was even welcomed into a world familiar to humanists, as a long-lost relative. The Turks had already been viewed as descendants of the ancient Trojans. And this notion gained popularity after 1453. The assimilation of Turk into a descendant of the ancient Trojans had been created in the late fourteenth century when the West employed a Latinized term to designate a Turk, who thus became known as not only *Turcus* but also as *Teucrus*. And *Teucri* was the term the celebrated Vergil had used in antiquity for the Trojans in his *Aeneid*. The Italians were not unique in this scholarly transformation and assimilation of a newcomer into a familiar old group, a term designated by humanists as ἔθνος. In the Middle Ages the Byzantine Greeks themselves had employed classical terms, which made sense no longer, to indicate contemporary ethnic groups. Thus in medieval Greek literature, among educated Byzantine Greeks, the Turks were often styled "Persians," the Albanians "Illyrians," the Slavs "Thracians," "Sarmatians," or "Triballians," the Mongols "Scythians," and the Hungarians "Pannonians." While the term *Teucrus* gained momentum in the west, it should be emphasized that not all humanists accepted this equation. Francesco Filelfo and Nikolaos Sekoundinos, the brilliant Greco-Italian simultaneous translator of Latin into Greek and Greek into Latin during the Council of Florence, for instance, continued to use the more accurate phonetic approximation, *Turci*. The assimilation of Turk into Trojan became stronger after the fall of Constantinople in 1453, and it was in the very fall of Byzantium that some humanists found another connection. It was then said that in 1453 the Ottoman Turks avenged the sack of Troy that had taken place in antiquity and that Mehmed II, the Turkish sultan, rectified the murder of Priam and his family by the Achaean Greeks of the Bronze Age, when he plundered the capital of Byzantium.

It is quite possible that Mehmed himself took advantage of this Trojan fiction, as there are hints in our sources that he may have used the Trojan-Turk equation to his advantage. The tale must have reached the Levant and it may have had a limited circulation in the Porte. At least his Greek biographer, Kritoboulos, claims that the sultan had availed himself of this hypothesis and presented himself as the just avenger of the sack of Troy:[1]

---

[1] IV.11.5: καὶ ἀφικόμενος ἐς τὸ Ἴλιον κατεθεᾶτο τά τε τὰ ἐρείπια τοιούτου καὶ τὰ ἴχνη τῆς ... Τροίας καὶ τὸ μέγεθος καὶ τὴν θέσιν καὶ τὴν ἄλλην τῆς χώρας ἐπιτηδειότητα ... προσέτι δὲ καὶ τῶν ἡρώων τοὺς τάφους ἱστόρει, Ἀχιλλέως τέ φημι καὶ Αἴαντος καὶ τῶν ἄλλων, καὶ ἐπῄνεσε καὶ ἐμακάρισε τούτους τῆς τε μνήμης καὶ τῶν ἔργων καὶ ὅτι ἔτυχον ἐπαινέτου Ὁμήρου τοῦ ποιητοῦ· ὅτε λέγεται καὶ μικρὸν συγκινήσας τὴν κεφαλὴν εἰπεῖν· "ἐμὲ τῆς πόλεως ταύτης καὶ τῶν αὐτῆς οἰκητόρων ἐν τοσούτοις περιόδοις ἐτῶν ἐκδικητὴν ἐταμιεύετο ὁ θεός· ἐχειρωσάμην γὰρ τοὺς τούτων ἐχθροὺς καὶ

He [sc. Mehmed] arrived at Ilium and viewed its ruins and the traces of the ancient city of Troy, its size, its location, and the excellent arrangement of the rest of the region and the way it was situated in a proper spot between land and sea; in addition, he toured the tombs of the heroes (of Achilles, I mean, of Ajax, and of the others), whom he praised and counted them "blessed" because they had the luck to be memorialized, along with their deeds, by their praise-singer, Homer. It is said that he nodded his head slightly and then commented: "God had reserved me to be the avenger of this city and her inhabitants after the passing of so many years. I enslaved their enemies, I took their cities, and I gave their possessions as booty to the Mysians. Indeed those who sacked this city in antiquity were Greeks, Macedonians, Thessalians, and Peloponnesians; after the passing of so many years their descendants paid the penalty to me for their aggressive conduct towards the Asians and for their numerous acts of aggression against us."

Attempts to bring the Turks within the classical family of nations culminated in an epic poem composed by Giovanni Mario Filelfo, entitled the *Amyris* (i.e., the poem about the "emir" or sultan). The author of the poem's preface, Othman Lillo Ferducci, a member of a family that maintained good relations with the Porte (reflected in the choice of his first name), admitted that this work was meant both as a panegyric of Sultan Mehmed II and as a celebration of his conquests. The poet himself, the son of the famous humanist Francesco Filelfo, cited classical precedents in order to elevate his theme in the eyes of humanists and claimed that the deeds of its protagonist, the sultan, rivaled the careers of several illustrious individuals in antiquity: Philip of Macedon, Pyrrhus of Epirus, Hannibal of Carthage, and Cyrus of Persia. His work presented a new attitude towards the Turks, who were then assigned heroic dimensions. This panegyric amounted to an exception, however, in the literature of the period and the motivation of Ferducci and Filelfo was dictated, it turns out, by their mercenary desire to win trade concessions from the Porte. There is every reason to believe that Book IV was composed as an afterthought and was marked by a change of heart: the poem at this point was rededicated to Galeazzo Mario Sforza, the duke of Milan, whom the author urged to take up the cross and campaign in the east.

τὰς πόλεις αὐτῶν ἐπόρθησα καὶ Μυσῶν λείαν τὰ τούτων πεποίημαι. Ἕλληνες γὰρ ἦσαν καὶ Μακεδόνες καὶ Θετταλοὶ καὶ Πελοποννήσιοι οἱ ταύτην πάλαι πορθήσαντες, ὧν οἱ ἀπόγονοι τοσούτοις ἐς ὕστερον περιόδοις ἐνιαυτῶν νῦν ἐμοὶ τὴν δίκην ἀπέτισαν διά τε τὴν τότε ἐς τοὺς Ἀσιανοὺς ἡμᾶς καὶ πολλάκις γενομένην ἐς ὕστερον ὕβριν αὐτῶν." On the western perception of the Ottoman Turks, see now Nancy Bisaha, *Creating East and West: Renaissance Humanists and the Ottoman Turks* (Philadelphia, 2004), and, on Troy/Constantinople, see Marios Philippides, "History Repeats Itself: Ancient Troy and Renaissance Istanbul," İstanbul Üniversitesi 550. Yıl Uluslararası Bizans ve Osmanlı Sempozyumu (XV. Yüzyıl), 30–31 Mayıs 2003, ed. Sümer Atasöy (Istanbul, 2004), 41–69.

Giovanni Mario Filelfo belonged to the second generation of humanists to deal closely with the Turks. Giovanni Mario's father, the famous Francesco, provides a better case of a humanist dealing with the "Turkish menace." Francesco Filelfo had studied ancient Greek in Christian Constantinople for seven years and had married a member of the Chrysoloras family. In 1453, during the sack, his mother-in-law and some of her daughters were enslaved by the Turks and in time Filelfo secured their release by singing the praises of the sultan in one of his poetical compositions. Francesco spent the rest of his life assisting refugees from the Levant, in various ways, and promoting a crusade to liberate Greece from the Turks. While Sekoundinos wrote the Latin work presented in this volume for Aeneas Sylvius Piccolomini, who was soon to ascend the papal throne as Pius II, Francesco Filelfo commissioned a similar work from Theodore Gaza, a Greek humanist: *De origine Turcarum*; yet the work by Gaza was not easily accessible to most scholars in the west, as it was written in Greek and not in Latin.

It is indeed the generation of Francesco Filelfo and its response to the events in the east that will concern us in the present volume. By far, the individuals represented here were well aware of the events. After all, most accounts are relating events that their authors had witnessed with their own eyes. Thus these works provided Europeans with authoritative material on events in the Levant and their authors played the role that Cassandra had played in the literature of antiquity: they rang the alarm bell, warned the west of the expansionist policies of the Ottomans, and lamented the passing of the Byzantine Greek-Christian "empire." Individuals were sympathetic to their complaints and literary dirges but no one took them very seriously. Meanwhile, the enemy advanced closer and closer. The expansion of the Turks was halted after the lifetime of these individuals. Only the failure to seize Vienna and the defeat at the battle of Lepanto brought an end to Turkish aggression towards Europe. But all this was in the future. In the *quattrocento* the Europeans had to defend their way of life against a triumphant enemy; and in order to do so effectively, they had to learn about him and his ways. Some of the earliest responses to this real need are represented here.

Nikolaos Sekoundinos

In all probability Nikolaos Sekoundinos's short work on the Ottoman sultans was written in 1456, at the request of Aeneas Sylvius Piccolomini, the bishop of Siena, destined to become Pope Pius II in 1458. Sekoundinos and the future pope met in Naples in April 1456. On that occasion the bishop asked Sekoundinos to compose this opusculum, since he wished to become familiar with the nature of the enemy. Sekoundinos had first-hand knowledge of the situation in the Levant: he had been born in Negroponte/Euboea, had participated in numerous notable diplomatic occasions, and had been a member of the first western delegation to visit Sultan Mehmed II Fatih after the fall of Constantinople in 1453. Sekoundinos responded eagerly to the bishop's request and even wrote an encomium for him. This was not the only opportunity for Sekoundinos to take

up the pen and produce a historical work. He had already translated numerous ancient Greek works into Latin, had been the author of a voluminous corpus of letters (which, for the most part, have not found a modern editor and still remain in manuscript form), had expressed strong interest in philosophy and theology, and had produced several written accounts of his active diplomatic missions that had brought him all over the Levant and Italy.[2]

He was born either in 1402 or, less likely, in 1405.[3] The only evidence for the date of his birth is contained in an unpublished letter[4] that Sekoundinos wrote to his son in 1457 ("ex Neapoli IIII nonas Novembris MCCCCLVII," "from Naples, on 4th of the Nones of November, 1457"), in which he alluded to his own age: "I am already fifty-one years old." His early life is not well documented, but it has been reasonably conjectured that he had been educated in Constantinople for the most part, even though his fluency in Latin indicates that he must have received training in one of the Latin areas in Greece at some point; after all, he had been born in Khalkis, the capital of Negroponte/Euboea, which was administered by the Venetians. It should be emphasized that it was extremely unusual for an educated Greek of the period to be so well versed in Latin; in fact, he exhibited such admirable linguistic skills that he often found employment in the administrative services of the *Serenissima* as a ducal secretary and was entrusted with various important diplomatic missions throughout his life. His interests were scholarly, as becomes evident from his activities as a translator of ancient Greek authors (including Plutarch and Demosthenes) into Latin.

After 1430 testimonies about Sekoundinos begin to multiply, as his career progresses. He was in Thessalonica, probably in some capacity that involved him with the Venetian authorities, when Sultan Murad II seized the city on March 13, 1430. He was seriously wounded in the assault and sack and, together with his wife and children, became a prisoner for the next thirteen months, as it is stated in a document:[5] "Together with his wife and sons, he was captured by the Turks and remained thirteen months in captivity in the hands of the Turks." After his release he was sponsored by Nicolaus Memo and Petrus Bembo and

---

[2] The basic bibliography on Sekoundinos includes: *NΣBE*; Panagiotes D. Mastrodemetres, "Nicolaos Secundinòs a Napoli dopo la caduta di Costantinopoli," Ἰταλοελληνικά: *Rivista di cultura greco-moderna* 2 (1989): 21–38; Franz Babinger, "Nikolaos Sagountinos, ein griechisch-venedischer Humanist des 15. Jhdts.", in Χαριστήριον εἰς Ἀναστάσιον Ὀρλάνδον 1 (Athens, 1965): 198–212; Alice-Mary Talbot, "Sekoundinos, Nicholas," *ODB* 3: 1865; and James Hankins, "Renaissance Crusaders: Humanist Crusade Literature in the Age of Mehmed II," *DOP* 49 (1995): [= *Symposium on Byzantium and the Italians, 13th–15th Centuries*], 137 ff.

[3] "Quinquaginta iam et alterum annos natum." Detailed discussion in *NΣBE*, 19–29.

[4] The complete text remains unedited, in manuscript form: Codex Vaticanus Ottobonianus 1732, fol. 61ʳ, but some excerpts have been published.

[5] Quoted in *NΣBE*, 30: "fuit captus a Teucris cum uxore et filiis et stetit menses XIII in captivitate in manibus Teucrorum."

further enjoyed the patronage of Alvise Polani and Marcus Consareno to secure some undefined position in the administration of the *Serenissima*, which he held until 1437. During this period he met the famous antiquarian and father of epigraphy, Cyriacus of Ancona, for whom Sekoundinos copied seven lines from the *Odyssey*.[6]

The next stage of his career is well documented, as he was selected for the position of official translator of Greek into Latin and of Latin into Greek during the Council of Florence, a post that had been first offered to the humanist Francesco Filelfo, who had declined the responsibility. Sekoundinos traveled to Constantinople in 1437, but he does not seem to have been involved with the early stages of the planned council/synod in any official capacity. Later, at Ferrara and Florence, he discharged his difficult duties with distinction and earned high praise for his spectacular linguistic skills. It was probably at this time that he came to the attention of Aeneas Sylvius Piccolomini, who noted his abilities:[7] "In these affairs and after many debates, the interpreter Nicholas Sagundinus, an expert in both languages [Latin/Italian and Greek], won an illustrious name for himself." Pope Eugenius IV also recognized the fact that Sekoundinos discharged his Herculean labor with distinction during the proceedings of the Council and, after the conclusion of the union in 1439, he offered him the post of papal notary, *secretarius apostolicus*. Again in February 1441, Pope Eugenius IV promoted him to the post of *nuntius/nunzio*, papal legate, and soon afterwards dispatched him to Greece and to Genoa. Sekoundinos learned of the fall of Constantinople while he was in Negroponte in some unknown capacity (perhaps as a secretary to the Venetian *bailo*). He spoke of the event in a later letter (dated September 20, 1460) that he addressed to Cardinal Bessarion:[8] "Afterwards I traveled from the Roman Curia to Greece, and hoped to be offered a post that would transfer me permanently from Greece to Italy, to make a home for myself and a permanent base in Italy. Circumstances were dangerous in Greece for us and I felt I should not stay there. And so I tried everything and, as the saying goes, 'I left no stone unturned,' so I could leave and find comfort

---

[6] Franz Babinger, "Notes on Cyriac of Ancona and Some of his Friends," *Journal of the Warburg and Courtauld Institutes* 25 (1962): 321–23.

[7] *Cosmographiae Pii Papae in Asiae et Europae eleganti descriptione* (Paris, 1509), 134: "Post multas disputationes in quibus tanquam interpres Nicolaus Sagundinus, utraque lingua disertissimus ingenio facundiae iuxta promptus illustre nomen adeptus est."

[8] Codex Marcianus latinus, classe XIII, no. 62 (4418), fol. 11ᵛ; the entire text of this manuscript remains unpublished; the present extract is quoted in NΣBE, 52: "postea quam e Romana Curia in Graeciam redii, occasionem ullam mihi offerri, qua in Italiam e Graecia demigrare possem. In Italia figere domicilium, in Italia perpetuam mihi constituere sedem. Nam et calamitosae Graeciae nostrae conditiones, ut inde obsederem, animum invitabant. Tentavi proinde omnia, et, ut aiunt, omnem lapidem movi, ut illinc abire, huc venire per quam commode possem. Cecidit interea clades, et exitium Urbis regiae Constantini, quo casu exterritus."

here. Then came the disaster, the destruction of the imperial City of Constantine [Constantinople], and her fate terrified me."

His next important mission brought him to Constantinople in the summer of 1453; he accompanied the Venetian envoy Bartolomeo Marcello to the Porte in order to assist in the difficult negotiations involving the ransom of the Venetian warriors and citizens who had been captured by the sultan's janissaries in the sack of May 29, 1453, and in the thorny problem of resuming trade in the Levant. This was the first substantial mission that he undertook, but in the future and in his later years such missions became the rule rather than the exception. He probably spent about two months in Constantinople. Then he was dispatched by Marcello to Venice, and from there he traveled to Rome and to Naples in order to present his impressions of the new situation in the Levant. In fact, in one of his speeches pronounced on January 25, 1454, Sekoundinos produced a portrait of Mehmed II. Since this embassy must have given him occasion to observe the young sultan closely during the delicate negotiations, his eyewitness description supplies one of the earliest authoritative portrayals of the Conqueror in the west:[9]

> Most glorious prince: the king [= sultan] of the Turks, Mehmed by name, is twenty-three years old; he has a melancholy nature; he is average in stature, is presentable in appearance, and possesses the rudiments of kindness and mildness (notwithstanding his instincts), although he

---

[9] CC 1: 128–40, and NE 3: 316–23: "Rex ipse Teucrorum, gloriossime princeps, Mahumetus nomine, tertium et vigessimum annum agit aetatis; naturae est habitus melancholici, staturae mediocris, formae satis honestae, lineamenta prae se ferentis insitae profecto humanitatis atque dulcedinis, tametsi adversus Christianos acerrime saevire videtur. Quod equidem non naturae adscripserim hominis, ... sed odio, quo contra gentem nostram nomenque Christianum flagrare et vexari videtur. Ingenium habet peracutum et acre; nam ubi, mortuo patre, successit in regnum omnium regni conditionum minutim, ut ita dixerim, notitiam habere quam primum praestitit operam: curiae domusque regiae ministrandae modum diligentissime perquisivit, multa quae sibi viderentur vel damnosa vel parum utilia, sustulit et evertit, multa correxit et emendavit, multa deinceps instituit et servanda decrevit. Vita moresque eius, etsi non ea temperantia, ea modestia, ea gravitate sunt, quae a principe gravi et integerrimo exigi et praestari deberent, ad mores tamen gentiles et patrios, ad aetatem iuveniliter exultantem natura pronam et labilem ad voluptates et luxum, ad facultates regias libidinum explendarum non modo ministras atque pedisequas, verum etiam hortatrices incitatricesque, postremo ad legis potius corruptelae licentiam, ductu<m> cuius laxis habenis ad flagitia et praecipitum itur et, ut aiunt, manibus pedibusque ad perditionem irruitur; ad haec, inquam, vitam et mores ipsius si referres, continentem eum et sobrium appellare non admodum dubitaveris. Nam, sive de industria id et studio fiat, sive occupatione animi tam amplissimi tamque opulentissimi regni gubernaculis die noctuque intendentis, non luxu neque lascivia admodum delectari videtur, non ventri deditus, non venandi, aucupandi, saltandi cantandique studio occupatur, non scurrilitatem ridiculaque adamat, non epulis et ebrietati pro more gentis indulget, non otio, non segnitie marcescit

is apparently quite cruel to Christians. I would attribute it not to his character but to hatred, as he seems to express wrath towards our faith and the name of Christ vehemently. He is very clever and sharp. After the death of his father, he painstakingly took over the kingdom and, as I mentioned, he focused all his attention on its internal conditions: with great diligence did he educate himself about the court and the palace; he eliminated and canceled trivial affairs that seemed a waste of time to him, but he adjusted and corrected many conditions, before he chartered innovations and issued orders to attend to them.

His life and habits do not exhibit the temperance, the modesty and gravity, which should accompany a somber and responsible prince but they match the habits of his forefathers and are appropriate for a young man, proud by nature, addicted to pleasures and luxury, and accustomed to taking advantage of his royal power to fulfill his desires; instead of serving him under control, they urge and press him on, and result in corruption rather than legislation; they lead him headlong, "with free rein," as the saying goes, to crime and perdition. Yet I suggest that if you study his ways, you would conclude that he does exhibit self-control and sane judgment. Day and night he is energetically involved with the ship of such an extensive and rich state, avoiding the appearance of being eagerly addicted to pleasure, to sex, to food, to hunting, to fowling, to dancing, and to singing. He evades ridicule and superficiality, does not indulge in banquets and in drinking (an addiction of their race), and is not involved in such lazy games. Something always occupies him and he

---

et crapulis. Semper aliquid agit, aliquid molitur, semper in negotio est, vel excogitando, vel deliberando, vel mira celeritate incredibilique cura et diligentia ea exsequendo, quae quidem facienda statuisset. Nam, ubi de honore, de regni utilitate, de laude, de gloria quicquid agitur, incredibile homo utatur; non modo opibus regiis ministerioque subditorum, sed sibi ipsi vitaeque haud parcendo, ut plerumque, ubi res praesentiam desiderat principis et exposcit, nec difficultate itineris, nec inclementia caeli, nec inundatione aquarum, nec asperitate deterritus montium, non aestu, non frigore, non fame, non siti defatigatus non dicam currere, sed potius videatur volare. In tot tantarumque rerum perenni, ut ita dixerim, ministratione, et litteris et philosophia doctissimum lingua Arabem, qui cotidie certo tempore principem adeundi et aliquid auditu dignum ei legendi potestatem habet. Tenet praeterea duos medicos, quorum alter latine, alter graece est eruditus. Hic familiarissime utitur eorumque ductu veteris historiae cognitionem habere voluit, neque visus est Lacedaemoniorum, Atheniensium, Romanorum, Carthaginiensium aliorumque regum et principum rebus festis accommoda<vi>sse animum. Alexandrum Macedonem et Gaium Caesarem praecipue sibi imitandos delegit, quorum res gestas in linguam suam traduci effecit; in quibus legendis vel audiendis mirum delectatur in modum. Aemulationem enim gloriosa quadam illis se parem conatur ostendere, gloriaeque at laudis studio inflammari videtur atque ardere." Both editions contain sizable extracts but not the complete text of the speech. The complete text (with inaccuracies, as it is based on inferior manuscripts) is found only in Vikentii V. Makušev, *Monumenta Historica Slavorum Meridionalium Vicinorumque Populorum* (Warsaw, 1874), 1: 295–306.

is always on the move, planning, thinking out, and pondering how to carry out all designs he has decided upon, with admirable speed, incredible care, and diligence. This does not apply only to the royal resources and the management, but also in his own life: he is very frugal for the most part; he desires and demands to participate in everything, regardless of the difficulty of a march, of inclement weather, or of local floods; he is deterred by nothing: not by mountains, not by hot weather, not by cold, not by hunger, not by thirst; he seems not to run but to fly, in my opinion.

In spite of being busy with all administrative matters, as I was saying, he finds time for literature and philosophy: he is learned in Arabic. Daily, at a prescribed time, the prince devotes time to hear or read something worthwhile. In addition, he employs two physicians, one educated in Latin, the other in Greek. Under their attentive tutelage he wants to learn ancient history and he particularly pays attention to the deeds of the Lacedaemonians, of the Athenians, of the Romans, of the Carthaginians, and of kings and princes. He has particularly chosen to emulate Alexander of Macedon and Gaius Caesar, whose deeds he has arranged to be translated into his own language. He is delighted when he hears or reads about them. He is determined to challenge their fame and he seems to be ardently inspired by their glory and praises.

This description of the sultan made quite an impression, as we detect echoes from it in other contemporary western descriptions of Mehmed II. Languschi-Dolfin, for instance, employed similar phrases to produce a portrait of the young sultan:[10]

[10] "Et primo diro de la qualita, et natura dei Maumethei Ottomano come descriue D. Jacomo Langusto Ueneto, quanto die esser formidabile a tutta la nation Christiana cum tutti li descendenti. El signor Maumetho gran Turco, e zouene d anni 26, ben complexionato, et de corpo piu presto grande, che mediocre de statura, nobile in le arme, de aspetto piu presto horrendo, che verendo, de poco riso, solerte de prudentia, et predito de magnanima liberalita, obstinato nel proposito, audacissimo in ogni cosa, aspirante a gloria quanto Alexandro Macedonico, ogni di se far lezer historie Romane, et de altri da uno compagno d.º Chiriaco d Ancona, et da uno altro Italo, da questi se fa lezer Laertio, Herodoto, Liuio, Quinto Curtio, Cronice de i papi, de imperatori, de re di Franza, de Longobardi; usa tre lengue, Turcho, Greco, et Schiauo. Diligentemente se informa del sito de Itallia, et de i luoghi doue capitono Anchise cum Enea et Anthenor, doue e la sede del papa, del Imperator, quanti regni sono in Europa, la quale ha depenta cum li reami et prouincie. Niuna cosa cum magior aplauso, et uolupta che el sito del mundo aprende et la scientia di cose militar, arde di uolunta de signorizar, cauto exploratore de le cose. Cum tale, et cosi fato homo habiamo a far nui Christiani." See Georg M. Thomas, "Die Eroberung Constantinopels im Jahre 1453 aus einer venetianischen Chronik," *Sitzungsberichte der königl. bayer. Akademie der Wissenschaften zu München* 2 (1868): 1–41; TIePN: 169–87, has produced few extracts, with some typographical errors that render this account useless to the serious student. Some extracts have also been translated in John R. Melville Jones,

First I will speak of the quality and nature of the Ottoman Mehmed, as he has been described by Don Jacomo Langusco, the Venetian, in his demonstration that he and all his descendants will be formidable to the Christian world. Lord Mehmed, the Grand Turk, is a young man (twenty-six years old), of nice complexion, with a rather large body, and of average stature. He is well trained in weapons; his appearance causes more terror than respect; he seldom laughs, is quite prudent, is endowed with magnificent generosity, is stubborn in his undertakings, is most audacious in his projects, and aspires to equal the glory of Alexander of Macedon. Daily he has the histories of Rome and of other nations read to him by a companion of his, Cyriacus of Ancona, and by another Italian. He makes them read to him [Diogenes] Laertius, Herodotus, Livy, Quintus Curtius, the Chronicles of the popes, of emperors, of the king of France, and of the Lombards. He uses three languages: Turkish, Greek, and Slavic. With diligence he has learned about the geography of Italy, the points where Anchises with Aeneas and Antenor landed, where the seat of the pope and that of the emperor are, the number of kingdoms in Europe, which he has placed on a map that notes realms and provinces. Most of all he loves to study world geography and the science of warfare; he burns with desire to be lord and researches everything cautiously. Such is the man and such is his nature. And we Christians have to deal with him.

It should be noted, nevertheless, that Cyriacus of Ancona could not have been in the Porte at the time, even though Languschi-Dolfin made this claim. Cyriacus had died earlier, in 1452, at Cremona in Italy, as the Trotti manuscript 373, fol. 41, of the Ambrosian Library in Milan makes clear: "Kiriacus Anconitanus Cremone moritur anno Domini McCCCL secundo," "Cyriacus from Ancona died at Cremona in 1452 A.D." The confusion occurred because of a misreading in the Languschi-Dolfin manuscript. The manuscript abbreviation *d* was incorrectly read as *detto*, while, the true reading has recently been shown to be *di*.[11] Similar is the

---

The Siege of Constantinople 1453: Seven Contemporary Accounts (Amsterdam, 1972), 125–30. The relation of this chronicle to other contemporary documents is treated in Marios Philippides, "The Fall of Constantinople 1453: Bishop Leonardo and his Italian Followers," *Viator* 29 (1998): 189–227. The Italian passage quoted here has been translated by Melville Jones, *Siege*, 126. For a new edition of this document, with English translation and detailed commentary, see Marios Philippides and Walter K. Hanak, *The Pen and the Sword: Historiographical, Topographical, and Military Studies on the Siege and Fall of Constantinople in 1453*, forthcoming, ch. 5.

[11] Julian Raby, "Cyriacus of Ancona and the Ottoman Sultan Mehmed II," *Journal of the Warburg and Courtauld Institutes* 43 (1980): 242–46; *Vita Viri Clarissimi et Famosissimi Kyriaci Anconitani* by Francesco Salamonti (Transactions of the American Philosophical Society 86.4), edd. Charles Mitchell and Edward W. Bodnar, S.J. (Philadelphia, 1996), 19, n. 2; and Christos

description supplied by Adamo di Montaldo,¹² which is evidently based on Sekoundinos's earlier literary depiction. Adamo deals with Mehmed's appearance in an early section of his work, under the chapter heading *Nomen et aetas regis; forma et statura eius*, "Name and Age of the King [= sultan]; His Appearance and Stature":¹³

> It is agreed that the illegitimate king of the Turks [= sultan], by the name of Mehmed, is twenty-six years old; he has a melancholy nature; he is average in stature; his appearance is pleasant; and he is rather pale. A young man, gentle by nature, and sweet, with a sharp mind, who is ill-disposed and ferocious towards our people ... With his father dead and his brother murdered ... he assumed power over an unwilling nation through the violation of an oath ... and initiated an admirable way of governing the royal court in a dignified manner; he coerced each prince, duke, petty king, and governor of the several grades and ranks to acknowledge his majesty with formidable threats and an obedience so great that no prince has ever been able to boast of.

At the end of this opusculum di Montaldo returns to the sultan. In a speech he attributes to Mehmed II himself, di Montaldo tries to indicate the interests of the sultan after the fall of Constantinople; classical references appear again:¹⁴

G. Patrinelis, "Κυριακὸς ὁ Ἀγκωνίτης καὶ ἡ Δῆθεν Ὑπηρεσία του εἰς τὴν Αὐλὴν τοῦ Σουλτάνου Μωάμεθ τοῦ Πορθητοῦ καὶ ὁ Χρόνος τοῦ Θανάτου του," Ἐπετηρὶς τῆς Ἑταιρείας Βυζαντινῶν Σπουδῶν 36 (1968): 152–62.

¹² This account was first published by Carl Hopf, Philippe A. Dethier [*sic*], and Cornelio Desimoni, "Adae de Montaldo, *De Constantinopolitano Excidio*," *Atti della Società Ligure di Storia Patria* 10 (1874): 325–54; extracts were also published, with Italian translation, in *TIePN*: 190–209. Also see Hankins, "Renaissance Crusaders," 143.

¹³ "Regem Turcorum spurium, quem Mahometum vocant, sextum et vigesimum aetatis agere annum constat; naturae melancholicae, mediocris staturae et congruentis formae, albedinem prae se ferentis, insitae humanitatis iuvenem atque dulcedinis esse, ingenio callidissimum, contraque nostram gentem ... feroces vultus malosque animos habere. Nam, ubi, defuncto patre fratreque obtruncato ... invita gente et violato iure, successit, ... curiae regiae pro exigenti dignitate mirabilem modum constitutionemque; unumquemque in singulorum graduum principem copiarumve ducem et regulum aut praefectum, maiestati eius formidolosae gravi sub sententia coercuit, oboedientiae quantae nemo sibi unquam potuit princeps gloriari."

¹⁴ "Imprimis ut nomen meum immortale posteris reliquam, deinde Christianam abdicantes fidem, nostra sub caelo me duce sola excolatur. Alexandrum enim regis Philippi filium, tot regnorum atque imperatorum novimus parva cum manu victorias adeptum esse. Quis si admisso seniorum consilio desistere coeptis maluisset, non Alexandri Magni, ceterorum regum et ducum nomen tanta de se laude usurpa<vi>sset. Hannibalem Africanum praeclarum in armis ducem, aequatis cum populo Romano viribus ut plurimum victorem, quis ignorat, nisi Scipio in senatu Romanos salutem iam desperantes conterruisset, urbem sibi atque imperium vendica<vi>sse."

To begin with, I will leave my name immortal for posterity; secondly, under my leadership, our faith alone will be celebrated under the sky, with the abandonment of the Christian faith. We are aware that Alexander, the son of King Philip, won victories over so many territories and empires with a small army. Who, among our wise elders, would dare claim that Alexander failed to accumulate more praise for himself than all other kings and lords? Who has not heard of Hannibal, the excellent general from Africa, who rivaled the Romans and who would have conquered them, their city, and their empire, if Scipio had failed to offer safety to a desperate Roman senate?

Reports of this type, which purport to indicate the classical interests of Mehmed, also contributed to the legend that the sultan himself was a polyglot and a polymath. While Mehmed may have possessed the rudiments of Greek, as some of his own childhood notebooks reveal that the young prince copied the Greek alphabet in a neat hand typical of the fifteenth century, stories about his linguistic skills are undoubtedly exaggerated. The nucleus of such claims and earliest verbal western portraits of the Conqueror derive from, and can be traced back to, Sekoundinos's observations as an eyewitness at the Porte in the summer of 1453. It was through Sekoundinos's speech that Italy became familiar with the Conqueror as an individual.

After his stay in Naples Sekoundinos returned to Venice and then was sent to Naples once more; his second stay in Naples gave him the opportunity to make numerous contacts with notable humanists. At the request of King Alfonso he translated into Latin the Greek military treatise of Onesander. By the middle of August 1456 he was back in Venice, but the *Signoria* again dispatched him to Naples in April 1457 and from there he traveled extensively, to Rome and Siena. He returned to Venice in December 1458. At this time he sought a promotion, as his current post, *segretario ducale*, made too many demands on himself and his family. Sekoundinos wished to be appointed *cancellarius Cretae*, a post that he could hold until the end of his life, but his ambitious plans came to a halt when he was shipwrecked in July 1460; in this misfortune he lost his pregnant wife, two sons, one daughter, and all the family possessions. After this loss it seems that Sekoundinos turned down his appointment and did not go to Crete after all. The year 1461, however, brought him back to the Levant, as Venice dispatched him to Mehmed II to negotiate on behalf of the *Signoria*. In this mission Sekoundinos seems to have accompanied the Conqueror and his court to the Black Sea, and he must have witnessed the surrender of Trebizond, the last Greek enclave in an Ottoman sea, as it becomes clear in documents of the period:[15] "The Turk did not wish to have Uzun [Hasan] as his neighbor; he increased his army and personal-

---

[15] Guglielmo Berchet, *La Repubblica di Venezia e la Persia* (Turin, 1865), Documento I°, p. 97: "il Turco non volendo Ussun per vicino, aumentato il suo esercito andò in persona e prese Trebisonda, nel cui esercito fu Nicolò Sagondino segretario della Signori."

ly went to take Trebizond. In his army was Nikolaos Sekoundinos, the secretary of the *Signoria*." After his return, he traveled to Rome. While he was living in Venice he fell ill and died on March 23, 1463, as was reported by his son:[16] "This man wasted away with a disease of the chest [pleurisy?], and suffered a long time; finally, on the 10th of Kalends of April [= March 26] he succumbed to the affliction."

His historical opusculum, *De Otthomanorum Familia*, is translated here for the first time into a modern language. It has been preserved in nine manuscripts.[17] It seems that the first printed edition is the one by John Ramus (Johannes Baptista Rhamnusius, i.e., Giovanni Battista Ramusio [1485–1557]), which I have followed; this edition was likely based on the Codex 3522 [Rec. 1080], fols. 133^r–141^r, of the Bayerische Staatsbibliothek in Munich. Ramus also included Sekoundinos's essay in his subsequent edition of Laonikos Khalkokondyles, *De origine et rebus gestis Turcorum libri decem* of 1556. I consulted the 1551 edition, a copy of which is currently owned by the Gennadius Library in Athens.[18] The complete title of this edition is *Otthomanorum Familia, seu DE TURCORUM imperio historia, N. SECUNDINO AUTORE. addito commento Io. Rami, à capta Constantinopoli usque ad nostra tempora. Item, Elegiae et Hendecasyllaba quaedam, eiusque Rami. Cum gratia et privilegio Egidua Aquila, Anno M.D.LI.*

This opusculum exercised influence on the historians of the sixteenth century and it was extensively used by Andrea Cambini, Paolo Giovio, I. Cuspinianus, and Francesco Sansovino, among others.[19] It was clearly produced for Aeneas Sylvius Piccolomini, for whom Sekoundinos also penned an encomium, which has been recently edited on the basis of two codices.[20] In this encomium Sekoundinos alludes to the opusculum that he wrote for Aeneas Sylvius:[21]

---

[16] Codex Marcianus latinus, classe XIII, no. 62 (4418), fols. 151^v–152^r; the Roman-style date is also explained in the margin as 23 *Marzo*: "Is inquam cum morbo lateris correptus, aliquamdiu aegrotasset: tandem X Kal Ap eius morbi dolore consumptus est."

[17] A comprehensive and descriptive list of all manuscripts containing this work can be found in *NΣBE*, 169–70.

[18] *Catalogue of the Gennadius Library, American School of Classical Studies at Athens* 6 (Boston, 1968), 728^c.

[19] *NΣBE*, 177 ff.

[20] Marc. lat. XIII, no. 62 (4418), fols. 1^r–1^v and Vat. Ottob. lat. 1732a, fols. 24^r, and 1732b, fol. 63^v, in *NΣBE*, 173–74.

[21] *NΣBE*, 173–74: "Id enim tua singularis humanitas, tua egregia virtus, tua auctoritas, dignitas, doctrina, mores, ingenium, vitae nominisque celebritas, et in me praecipuus quidam amor et haud obscura caritas et benevolentia, honesto iure exigere ac efflagitare videntur. Quamobrem mihi magnopere gratulor. Quod id mihi ultro videtur oblatum, et sua sponte feliciter ortum. Quod ut eveniret vehementer optassem, et ad quod adipiscendum quosvis labores haud invitus sumere ne utiquam recusassem. Petiisti namque a me ut eorum tibi nomina darem, qui Machumetae, Turcorum regi, a primo domus et familiae auctore maiores fuissent. Ita cuiusque vite et nomine designaris, ut loco et ordine quis cui successisset, intelligere posses. Itaque ut paulo altius repetam, paucis tamen ne historiam contexere videar, ad te praesertim, cui, pro ea quae in te sita est doctrina et diligentia penitus, ista nota explorataque sunt."

> Your exceptional kindness, your distinguished virtue, your influence, your learning, your traits, your character, and the fame of your name, not to mention your affection and your magnificent generosity and good will towards me, urge me on. And greatly do I congratulate myself. The blessed opportunity offered itself spontaneously. What I had hoped for has happened, and I will now willingly undertake the task before me. You requested that I supply you with the names of the ancestors of Mehmed, the king of the Turks, from the founder of their dynasty on, as you wish to examine the lives and names of each one of them in succession and in proper order. And so I will go into it in detail (but I will not appear to be writing a history), so that my research may inform you, an educated and active scholar, on these matters.

This monograph on the Turks and their sultans demonstrates that Sekoundinos was a pioneer; it is only in the next century that Europe became interested in the Turks and various ethnological and historical accounts appeared, some of which (like Francesco Sansovino's) became bestsellers.[22] Other accounts were important also.[23]

Clearly Sekoundinos was a fascinating personality. He was an eyewitness to numerous significant events of the *quattrocento* and had personally interacted with notable dignitaries of the Levant. Endowed with uncommon talents, he was a linguist, a diplomat, a humanist, and a polymath, who left his mark in the culture of the period. Perhaps it is not an accident that one of the last artists to specialize in the dying art of the miniature, the Cretan George Klontzas, who had studied together with his childhood friend Domenikos Theotokopoulos (destined to become the famous *el Greco* of Toledo), also chose, in his voluminous and fascinating codex, to include a fictional "portrait" of this engaging Greco-Italian personality of the *quattrocento*.[24]

---

[22] Francesco Sansovino, *Historia universale dell'origine et imperio dei Turchi: nella quale si contengono la origine, le lege, l'usanze, i costumi, cose religiosi come mondani de' Turchi: oltre cio vi sono tutte le guerre che di tempo sono state fatte da quella natione cominciando da Othomano primo Re di questa gente fino al moderno Selim con le vite di tutti i principi di casa Othomana*, 3 vols. (Venice, 1564, 1568, 1571, etc); and idem, *Gl'Annali overo le vite de principi et signori della casa Ottomana ne quali si leggono di tempo tutte le guerre particolarmente fatte della natione de' Turchi in diverse provincie del mondo contra i Christiani* (Venice, 1571, with subsequent editions and various modifications of the title). On these works, see Philippides, "The Fall of Constantinople 1453."

[23] See, e.g., the work by the Renaissance French scholar Richer, *De Rebus Turcarum ad Franciscum Gallórum Regem Christianissimum libri quinque* (Paris, 1543); for details on the author and his work, cf. Marios Philippides, "*Urbs Capta*: Early 'Sources' on the Fall of Constantinople (1453)," in *Peace and War in Byzantium: Essays in Honor of George T. Dennis*, ed. Timothy S. Miller and John Nesbitt (Washington, D.C., 1995), 209–25.

[24] A miniature portrait of Sekoundinos by Klontzas, in the company of Pope Pius II (Aeneas Sylvius Piccolomini) and Francesco Filelfo, is included in the Klontzas codex, Marc. Gr. classe VII, no. 22, fol. 60ᵛ, and is further reproduced in *ΝΣΒΕ*, Plate I, and in Athanasios

Aeneas Sylvius Piccolomini (Pope Pius II) and Henry of Soemmern

It is not unreasonable to suppose that Aeneas Sylvius discussed the siege and fall of Constantinople in 1453 with Sekoundinos. Eventually, Aeneas Sylvius published the opusculum included here on the events of the conflict. While Aeneas Sylvius undoubtedly used other accounts, such as Bishop Leonardo's famous *epistula*, there is nothing to prevent us from assuming that he had received some facts from Sekoundinos also. After all, Sekoundinos, as we have seen, was one of the first western visitors to tour Constantinople in the summer of 1453. An early printed edition of his work, under the title *Tractaculus*, was at some point rather logically bound together with Sekoundinos's *Otthomanorum Familia*; this volume is currently housed in the Gennadius Library of Athens. The same work of Aeneas Sylvius was also published in the collection *Aeneae Sylvii Piccolominei Senensi, qui post adeptum pontificatum Pius eius nominis secundus appellatus est, opera quae extant omnia, nunc demum post corruptissimas aeditiones summa diligentia castigata & in unum corpus redacta. Quorum elenchum uersa pagella indicabit* (Basileae, sine anno [= 1571], ex officina Henrici Petrina; repr. Frankfurt, 1967), 400–3. The second edition is clearly later than the Gennadius pamphlet. The two printed texts are not identical: there are various differences in spelling, punctuation, and choice of words. I have followed both editions in my presentation of this text and have supplied an apparatus criticus to indicate the differences; readings and forms from the Gennadius pamphlet are indicated by [ ] and from the Basel edition by < >. Further variations in words and expressions are provided in the apparatus criticus.

While this work of Aeneas Sylvius is not well known to modern historians, it clearly exercised considerable influence on Renaissance accounts of the siege of 1453. Aeneas Sylvius had done his research. He had been well aware of the authoritative account of the siege by the pen of the eyewitness Genoese defender, Leonardo Giustiniani of Chios, archbishop of Lesbos, and he utilized his text. In particular, Aeneas Sylvius seems to echo a particular passage of Leonardo.[25] The passage in the Genoese bishop's *epistula* reads as follows:[26] "meanwhile Theophilus Palaeologus, a Catholic ... resisted the heavy attack of the Turks for a long time and in the conflict was killed with an ax. Then John Sclavus Illyricus ... killed many before his life ended." Pius echoes this passage

---

D. Paliouras, Ὁ Ζωγράφος Γεώργιος Κλόντζας *(1540 ci. – 1608) καὶ αἱ Μικρογραφίαι τοῦ Κώδικος Αὐτοῦ* (Athens, 1977), 112. Sekoundinos is portrayed in deep study, his body turning to the right as his head moves to the left; the composition is clearly one of the formulas in the depiction of humanists encountered in Klontzas' work. Sekoundinos is flanked by Raphael Volterranus on the left and Francesco Filelfo on the right.

[25] Details on this work by Aeneas Sylvius can be found in Philippides, "*Urbs Capta*," esp. 221–24.

[26] "Inter haec Theophilus Palaeologo, vir catholicus ... Theucrorum pondus aliquam diu sustinens et decertans securi discinditur. Ita Johannes Sclavus Illyricus ... multos prius mactat, deinde, gladio vitam finivit." The authoritative text of Leonardo still awaits a serious scholarly

in the following words:²⁷ "in this great crowd of warriors there were found only two individuals to show themselves as men: one was a Greek, Theophilus Palaeologus; the other was a Dalmatian, John Sclavus. They thought that it would be shameful to flee. They resisted the heavy attack of the Turks for a long time and put many to death. Finally they were overpowered by fatigue rather than by defeat and fell among the corpses of the enemy."

Another manuscript that was in circulation in the sixteenth century, usually entitled *Cronaca Magno* and attributed to the hand of Stefano Magno (1490–1557),²⁸ further presents a narrative written in a mixture of the vernacular

---

critical edition. In the fifteenth and sixteenth centuries, his epistola became famous through various renditions of his Latin text into the vernacular. As such it was first published by Francesco Sansovino in his immensely popular history (above, n. 22). The Latin text of Leonardo was first published by Philip Lonicer in volume 2 of his *Chronica Turcica* (Frankfurt-am-Main, 1584), 315–36; the same version was reprinted by Luigi T. Belgrano, "Prima serie di documenti riguardanti di colonia di Pera," *Atti della Società Ligure di Storia Patria* 13 (1877–1884): 233–57; in Izmail I. Sreznevskii's Slavonic text of Nestor-Iskander, Повѣсть о Царьградѣ (Saint Petersburg, 1855), as an appendix; in *PG* 159, cols. 923–941 (with the cautionary note in CC 1: 121); and by Philippe A. Déthier, *Monumenta Hungariae Historica* 21.1: 553–616 (see below, n. 42, for some details on this edition). Agostino Pertusi, in CC 1: 124–69, published only selections, with improved text, but with incomplete apparatus criticus, and with an Italian translation; unfortunately, Pertusi took into account neither the important Florentine codex of this work nor the valuable marginalia that accompany Leonardo's text in the Codex Mediol. Trivult. lat. N 641, fols. 11ʳ–21ʳ. Leonardo's work is extremely significant for our knowledge of the events of the siege of 1453. Clearly, a modern edition of his work, with a comprehensive apparatus criticus and the marginalia, has become imperative. The important *quattrocento* manuscripts of Leonardo that must be consulted in a future definitive edition of this account include: Ven. Marc. lat. 218 (no. 4677), fols. 46ᵛ–68ᵛ; Ven. Marc. lat. 397 (no. 1733), fols. 1ʳ–22ʳ; Mediol. Trivult. lat. N 641, fols. 1ʳ–21ʳ (not utilized in its entirety in CC 1); Mediol. Ambros. lat. C 145. fols. 25ᵛ–44ʳ; Vat. lat. 4137, fols. 172ʳ–206ᵛ; and Flor. lat. 660, fols. 44–50; the last two codices were unfortunately not consulted for the selections presented in CC 1. For additional manuscripts of the sixteenth century, cf. CC 1: 121.

²⁷ "In tanta multitudine pugnatorum, duo tantum reperti sunt, qui se viros ostenderint. Alter grecus, alter dalmata Theophilus Paleologus, Johannes Sclavus, qui fugire turpe putantes, cum diu Thurcorum impetum sustinuissent multosque obtruncassent, denique non tam victi quam vincendo fatigati, inter cadavera hostium occubuere."

²⁸ "... in tanta moltitudine de pugnanti che fù, che huomini si monstrorono, uno Theofilo Paleologo, Greco, l'altro Zuanne Schiavo, Dalmatino, quali a fuggir turpse pensando, longamente sostennero lo empito de Turchi, et cum multi havessero ottroncado, nella fine, non tanto vinti, quanto vincendo defatigati, infrà i cadaveri de nemici accumbeteno." For Magno, cf. CC 2, no. 112 (105). The entire text of this work remains unedited. Extracts pertaining to the siege of 1453 have been published in *NE* 3: 295–301. Magno is not included among the 38 entries of Agostino Pertusi's list of texts relating the events of the siege in "La Lettera di Filippo da Rimini, Cancelliere di Corfù, a Francesco Barbaro e i Primi Documenti Occidentali sulla Caduta di Costantinopoli (1453)," in Μνημόσυνον Σοφίας Ἀντωνιάδη, ed. idem [Βιβλιοθήκη τοῦ Ἑλληνικοῦ Ἰνστιτούτου Βενετίας Βυζαντινῶν καὶ Μεταβυζαντινῶν Σπουδῶν 6] (Venice, 1974),

with Latin and was based clearly on the text of Aeneas Sylvius, as the phraseology of the following extract reveals:

> ... in this crowd of warriors that was there, two men excelled. One was Theophilus Palaeologus, a Greek, and the other was John Schiavo, a Dalmatian, who thought that it would be shameful to flee. For a long time they resisted the heavy attack of the Turks and they put many to death; finally, they were overpowered by fatigue rather than by defeat and fell among the corpses of the enemy.

Nor was Stefano Magno the only scholar to have read and echoed Aeneas Sylvius's opusculum. There is another text, which used to be attributed to a supposed "Italian" eyewitness of the siege by the name of "Christoforo Riccherio." Since the nineteenth century scholars assumed that his work presented a valuable account of the events of the siege of 1453 and that it was based on the personal observations of an otherwise unknown participant in the defense.[29] I have demonstrated elsewhere[30] that this "Christoforo Riccherio" is really a known French courtier of the sixteenth century, whose name was actually Richer: *Christoforo Richerio Thorigneo Serone, Cubiculario Regio, & Cancellario Franciae à secretis*, who wrote a book on the origins and expansion of the Ottoman Turks to his own period, something more elaborate and more scholarly than Sekoundinos' *De Familia Otthomanorum*, and the section that Richer devoted to the siege, far from being an eyewitness account, is really a derivative piece relying on previous scholarly versions. Among the sources that Richer used was the *Tractaculus*

120–57. Furthermore, Magno is not mentioned by Eric Cochrane, *Historians and Historiography in the Italian Renaissance* (Chicago and London, 1981). The extract in our text can be found in *NE* 3: 297.

[29] The first scholar to make extensive use of "Riccherio" was Alexandros G. Paspates in his learned monograph, Πολιορκία καὶ Ἅλωσις τῆς Κωνσταντινουπόλεως ὑπὸ τῶν Ὀθωμανῶν ἐν Ἔτει 1453 (Athens, 1890; repr.: 1995), who provided the following information on this source: "Christoforo Riccherio: La presa di Costantinopoli, l'anno MCCCCLIII à XXIX di Maggio secondo l'edizione di Francesco Sansovino." Edwin Pears, *The Destruction of the Greek Empire and the Story of the Capture of Constantinople by the Turks* (London, 1903; repr. New York, 1968), xiii, also commented: "Christoforo Riccherio, 'La Presa di Costantinopoli,'... is a valuable and brightly written narrative." Steven Runciman, *FC*, 196, 197, believes "Riccherio" to have been "present in the siege." Melville Jones, *Siege*, 118–24, translated Riccherio's text, under the impression that he was an eyewitness, and considers the narrative "a brief and brisk account of the major events of the siege, by one who was himself present in it." Pertusi, "La Lettera," no. 38 (235), n. 64, states his belief that "Riccherio" was not an eyewitness and further states that he could find no information on this author. In addition Elizabeth A. Zachariadou, Τὸ Χρονικὸ τῶν Τούρκων Σουλτάνων (τοῦ Βαρβερινοῦ Ἑλληνικοῦ Κώδικα 111) καὶ τὸ Ἰταλικό του Πρότυπο (Thessalonica, 1960), 23, considers "Riccherio" to be one of the Italian sources for the composition of Ottoman history in the sixteenth century.

[30] Philippides, "Urbs Capta."

of Aeneas Sylvius. This becomes apparent when we consider Richer's rendition of the passage of Aeneas that Stefano Magno also echoed:[31]

> In this great number of warriors who had been guarding the city in the recent past, there were only two who fought to the very end for salvation, faith, and glory and fell victim to the enemy swords, preferring death over flight. One of them was Greek, Theophilus Palaeologus. The other was a certain John from Dalmatia, a slave. They ... alone resisted the heavy attack of the enemy, were surrounded by a countless crowd, and were overpowered by fatigue rather than by defeat. They put to death many but finally expired, in total exhaustion, in the midst of the enemy corpses.

It is apparent from the phraseology involved that Richer derived his information from Aeneas Sylvius's elaboration of Leonardo's text and not directly from Leonardo or from Leonardo's early translators in the vernacular such as Languschi-Dolfin. Thus both Richer and Magno are indebted to the *Tractaculus*, which apparently enjoyed greater popularity in the sixteenth century and was not as marginal as scholars have suspected thus far.

In addition to Aeneas Sylvius's work, I have also included the text of a letter written by Henry of Soemmern on the fall of Constantinople, or, to be more precise, about the adventures of the Greek Cardinal Isidore, who was the papal legate in the Greek capital during the siege. It is an interesting document as it deals with the aftermath of the military operations and the difficulties that refugees faced after the sack. It is more of a "personal" or even "oral" history than a formal composition. Unfortunately Pertusi in CC 2 failed to publish the entire text but instead offered extensive extracts. The entire text of this *epistula* had been earlier published by A. Vigna, "Codice diplomatico delle colonie Tauro-Liguri durante la signoria dell'Ufficio di S. Giorgio (MCCCCLIII–MCCCCLXXV)," *Atti della Società Ligure di Storia Patria* 6 (1868): 19–21, and by Nicolae Iorga (Jorga), *Notes et Extraits pour servir à l'histoire des Croisades au XVe Siècle*, 6 vols. (Paris and Bucharest, 1899–1902, 1916), 3: 292–95. I have included the entire text and further present the first English translation of this fascinating document in Chapter 5. As I have supplied full commentary on the siege, and on Cardinal Isidore, in the accounts of Aeneas Sylvius and Tetaldi, I felt that that there was no pressing need to supply notes to Henry's short epistle.

---

[31] "At in tanto propugnatorum numero qui nuper afflictae vrbi praesidio erant, duo solum reperti sunt, qui salute religioni ac famae postposita, viriliter ad extremum pugnando, strenuorum hostium gladiis configi atque internecari quam fugere maluerunt. Eorum unus, Graecus erat Theophilus Palaeologus: alter Ianus quidam natione Dalmata, seruus conditione. Qui ... inimicam irruptionem soli tantisper sustinuerunt, dum turba innumera circumeunti, non tam victi quam vincendo fatigati, caesis sua manu permultis, ipsi denique promiscue in stragem hostilem neruis deficentibus prolabentes expirarunt."

Giacomo Tetaldi

We possess very few facts about the individual who wrote this eyewitness account of the siege and fall of Constantinople. Even his name appears in doubt, as it is spelled variously. Thus his Christian name appears as Giacomo, Jacopo, or Jacques, while the versions of his last name include Tetaldi, Edaldy, Tetardi, Tedardi, Detaldi, and Tedaldi. The manuscript tradition of his account is also confused. His text has come down to us in a French and in a Latin version. The French text is contained in the following manuscripts: Paris. fr. 2691, fols. 264–271 (incorporated in the *Chronique* of Jean Chartier); Paris. fr. 15217, fols. 67ᵛ–72ᵛ; Paris. fr. 6487, ff. 18–21; Cambrai 1114, fols. 28–30; and Bruxell. fr. 19684, fols. 253–256 (as part of an anonymous Chronicle). It has been argued persuasively that our French text represents the amalgam of two different traditions, as the Cambrai manuscript bears little relationship to the other five French versions.[32] In addition to "confused" and contaminated French texts, Tetaldi's work has also survived in a single Latin version preserved in an abbey and currently housed in the National Library of Vienna, under the series number 12709.

The French text of this narrative is better known, as it has been translated into various modern languages. The Latin version remains virtually unexamined by scholars and has not been translated into a modern language thus far. The French and Latin versions are not identical. Furthermore, both the Latin and the French texts display evidence of contamination, as they include a coda containing a proposal for a crusade to recover Constantinople. Clearly, something has been added to the original text, as Chapter 22.1 refers to events that took place in Italy the next decade, such as the death of Pope Pius II. So there has been elaboration. This coda could not have been part of the original account by Tetaldi, who was a merchant and whose eyewitness account of the siege is concerned only with the defense operations and the events of the sack and whose original formulation could not have shown interest in future organized expeditions to the Levant for the liberation of the Greco-Byzantine capital.

In all likelihood Tetaldi's original account was dictated in Italian and its original form amounted to an *aviso* (perhaps resembling the report of Benvenuto,[33] the Anconitan consul in Constantinople in 1453) which was subsequently transformed into a Latinized scholarly account by the hand of a humanist and

---

[32] The manuscripts of Tetaldi have been studied by Marie-Louise Concasty, "Les 'Informations' de Jacques Tedaldi sur le siège et la prise de Constantinople," *Byz* 24 (1954): 95–110, but the conclusions are rather speculative, as it has been noted by Setton, *PL* 2: 111–112, n. 9. This article nevertheless remains the only modern scholarly study of this author.

[33] Benvenuto's *relazione* was discovered by Agostino Pertusi. See Agostino Pertusi, "The Anconitan Colony in Constantinople and the Report of its Consul, Benvenuto, on the Fall of the City," in *Charanis Studies: Essays in Honor of Peter Charanis*, ed. Angeliki E. Laiou-Thomadakis (New Brunswick, 1980), 199–218. The Latin text with Italian translation was reprinted in *TIePN*, 4, 5. For an English translation of this document, with brief discussion, see Marios

was then put into the French idiom. It has further been suggested that Tetaldi dictated his story when his Venetian saviors put in at Negroponte (Khalkis in Euboea) on their way to Venice;[34] at least this scenario would explain why a scribe, apparently not Tetaldi himself, consistently referred to the author in the third person. The following stages in the history of this account have been proposed, and they remain our best model for the evolution of this text:[35]

1. The original Italian account (an *aviso* of some sort?) dictated or written by the author himself.
2. The first scholarly translation into Latin.
3. The French renditions.
4. The Cambrai French version.

While an attempt has been made to show that the French versions were composed earlier than the Latin,[36] this hypothesis cannot be proven. At any rate, one French manuscript (to be cited presently) seems to have been produced early and the evidence indicates that it was in circulation as early as January 1454. This particular situation, however, does not invalidate the reasonable assumption that the Latin version precedes the French renditions; alternatively, both versions may be contemporary and may be based on the lost original account in Italian. The news of the siege and fall made quite an impact in Europe and all sorts of narratives found their way into circulation soon after the event. It is quite possible that both the French and Latin versions were created as soon as the original Italian redaction of Tetaldi's text appeared.

It appears probable that an early form of this account (either in Italian or in Latin) was translated and elaborated into French by someone called Jean Blanchin (or perhaps Blancet). The opening statement of the French version reveals that a "Jehan Blanchin" brought this account to the Cardinal of Avignon. Moreover, MS. Paris. fr. 6487 includes the following Latin note at the end of the text:[37] "Given on the last day of the month of December, 1453 A.D. It was entered and carried by me, John Columbi; also letters from Constantinople were brought by the hand of Johann Blanchin. Signature of Columbi." The same manuscript states that "Jacques Edaldy" was a Florentine merchant: "marchant Florentin."

Philippides, *Byzantium, Europe, and the Early Ottoman Sultans 1371–1513: An Anonymous Greek Chronicle of the Seventeenth Century (Codex Barberinus Graecus 111)*, Late Byzantine and Ottoman Studies 4 (New Rochelle, 1991), 197–99.

[34] Melville Jones, *Siege*, vii–viii.

[35] P. D. Pogodin, "Обзор источниковъ по историй осаду и взятия Византии Турками вь 1453 г.," *Журнал Министерства Народнаго Просвещения* 264.8 (August, 1889), 205 ff. (reviewed by Concasty, "Les 'Informations,'" 95–97).

[36] Concasty, "Les 'Informations.'"

[37] "Datum ultima die mensis decembris anno Domini M°CCCC°LIII°. Columpnatum est presens transumptum per me Johannem Columbi et apportate <sc. littere> fuerunt de Constantinopoli per manum Johannem Blanchin. Sic signatum Columbi."

Tetaldi's account of the siege is that of an eyewitness, a merchant/soldier, who was not a member of the High Command that oversaw the general strategy of the defense of Constantinople; apparently Tetaldi had no contacts with the court or with the Genoese mercenary band of the *condottiere* Giovanni Guglielmo Longo Giustiniani, who was in charge of the military operations. He seems to have been acquainted with the notable personalities such as the warlord Giustiniani and Cardinal Isidore by sight only. Tetaldi fought on the walls and included an account of his escape to the Christian ships after the Turks made their entry into the city. All information on his activities during the siege comes from this unique document.[38] Furthermore, there is every reason to believe that Tetaldi suffered loss of property in the sack, and the authorities in Venice eventually discussed his case and claim. The following document of Doge Francesco Foscari to the Venetian administrators of Crete survives in the archives of Venice[39] and confirms, among other matters, that Tetaldi was from Florence, in spite of the statement in the added section to his text that he was a *nobilis Venetus* (Ch. XX.2):

> Francesco Foscari, by the grace of God Doge of Venice, etc. to the noblemen [*sc.* the duke and his Council]:
> Case: The noble and good man, Jacopo Tedaldi from Florence, was in the City of Constantinople when the emperor [= sultan] of the Turks conquered it in war. Wishing to save himself, he jumped into the sea and swam to our galleys and thus escaped the attack and notice

---

[38] As we are about to see (cf. next note), the statement that "... Tetaldi, of whom we know nothing more than is said of him in the text" (Melville Jones, *Siege*, vii) may be a slight exaggeration, as there is at least one Venetian document that speaks of him.

[39] Archivio di Stato di Venezia, Duca di Candia, Ducali e letter ricevute, quaderno 27. This document was published by Nicolae Iorga in *NE* 4, no. 19 (99):
Franciscus Foscari, Dei gratia dux Venetiarum, etc., nobilibus [sc. Duci et Consilio]:
Exponunt nobilis vir prudens Iacobus Tedaldi de Florentia quod erat in civitate Constantinopolitana quando Imperator Turcorum eam expugnavit et vicit, et, volens servare personam suam, se in mari proiecit et ad galeas nostras transnatavit et evasit impetum et favorem infidelium. Similiter unus eius sclavus vocatus Valentinus, aetatis annorum XII vel circa, de genere Russorum, quem emerat a Iohanni Ghola et erat in Constantinopoli, natando ad navem quamdam Ialina Cretensis se reduxit et venit Candidam, ubi est, et ei detinetur et occupatur per dictum Cortaçi, indebite et iniuste. Ex quo subsidium nostrum implorabat. Volumus ergo et mandamus vobis quod, si constiterit vobis eundem sclavum esse ipsius Iacobi Detaldi, eum sibi aut suo legitimo nuntio subito restitui facere debeatis, quoniam non est iustum, nec honestum quod hoc modo perdat sclavum suum, et, si fortasis allegaretur quod respectu belli quod tunc habebamus cum Florentinis dictus sclavus bene accipi potuerit, dicimus vobis quod propter hoc non desistatis quomodo dictum sclavum ipsi Iacobo restitui faciatis, in quantum, ut praediximus, constituerit vobis quod suus sit, quoniam bene sufficit ei damnum quod passus est in comiserabili casu. Propter hoc volumus ut sclavus praedictus sibi retineatur.
Datum in nostro ducali palatio, die VI mensis Augusti, indictione II, M°CCCC°III. Recepta die V Septembris M°CCCC°IIII.

of the infidels. Similarly, one of his slaves, called Valentinus, a Russian twelve years old (or thereabouts), who was in Constantinople and had been purchased from John Ghola, also swam to the ship of the Cretan Hyalinas; thus he came to Candia, where he remains, as he is detained and held under the power of Khortatzes, unjustly and unduly. Consequently, he is begging for our assistance. Therefore we willingly order that you, if it is concluded that this is the slave of Jacopo Detaldi, restore him to him or his lawful representative without delay, since it is neither just nor equitable that he should lose his slave in this manner; if perhaps it is alleged that that the aforementioned slave is held justly because of our war with the Florentines, we state to you that you should not hesitate, on account of this, to restore the aforementioned slave to Jacopo (if indeed, as we stated earlier, you conclude that he is his property); he has endured a great deal and he has suffered in miserable circumstances. Therefore it is our wish that the aforementioned slave be returned to him.

Given in our ducal palace on the 7th day of August of the 2nd indiction, 1454. Received on September 5, 1454.

Thus confirmation in regard to Tetaldi's homeland comes through Venetian archives. Unfortunately, his name receives various spellings in this document. That the document is authentic cannot be doubted, as it also states that Hyalinas' ship escaped from the harbor of Constantinople, a fact that can be confirmed independently of this document. The escape of Hyalinas and his ship from Constantinople and his arrival in Crete are also recorded, with various spelling errors, by a scribe at the Monastery of Ankarathos in Crete:[40]

---

[40] ἔτε<ι> αυγ΄, ἰουνίου κθ΄, ἡμέρα ς, ἦλθαν ἀπὸ τὴν Κωνσταντινούπολιν καράβια τρία Κρητικά, τοῦ Σγούρου, τοῦ Ταλινᾶ, καὶ τοῦ Φιλομάτου· λέγοντες ὅτι τὴν κθ΄ τοῦ Μαΐου μηνός, τῆς ἁγίας Θεοδοσίας ἡμέρα τρίτη, ὥρα γ΄ τῆς ἡμέρας, ἐσέβησαν οἱ ἀγαρηνοὶ ἐς τὴν Κωνσταντινούπολιν, τὸ φωσάτον τοῦ Τούρκου τζαλαπῆ Μεεμέτ, καὶ εἶπον ὅτι ἐπέκτειναν τὸν βασιλέα τὸν κῦρ Κωνσταντῖνον τὸν Δράγασιν καὶ Παλαιολόγον. Καὶ ἐγένετο οὖν μεγάλη θλῖψις καὶ πολλὶς κλαυθμὸς εἰς τὴν Κρήτην διὰ τὸ θληβερὸν μήνυμα ὅπερ ἦλθε, ὅτι χεῖρον τούτου οὐ γέγονεν οὔτε γενήσεται. καὶ Κ<ύριο>ς ὁ Θ<εὸ>ς ἐλεήσαι ἡμᾶς, καὶ λυτρώσεται ἡμᾶς τῆς φοβερᾶς αὐτοῦ ἀπειλῆς. The text of this note was first published in Odysseus Arampatzoglou, *Η Φώτειος Βιβλιοθήκη* (Constantinople, 1933), 108. It was republished, with short discussion, by Robert Browning, "A Note on the Capture of Constantinople in 1453," Byz 22 (1953): 379–87, and, with Italian translation, in *TIePN*, 214. A document listing the names of noble refugees who reached Crete on a Venetian galley is provided in the manuscript *Miscellanea Gregolin* (Archivio di Stato di Venezia, no. 27: Testamenti); its text was published by Konstantinos D. Mertzios, "Περὶ Παλαιολόγων καὶ Ἄλλων Εὐγενῶν Κωνσταντινουπολιτῶν," in *Γέρας Κεραμοπούλου* (Athens, 1953), 355–72, and, again by idem, "Περὶ τῶν ἐκ Κωνσταντινουπόλεως Διαφυγόντων τὸ 1453 Παλαιολόγων καὶ

In the y<ear> 1453, June 29, a Tuesday, three Cretan ships arrived from Constantinople; they belonged to Sgouros, to Hyalinas, and to Philomates. They said that on the 29th of the month of May (the day of Saint Theodosia), a Tuesday, the descendants of Hagar [the Turks], the army of the Turkish *çelebi* [= prince] Mehmed, entered Constantinople. They also said that they killed the emperor, Constantine Dragaš, also called Palaeologus. There ensued much grief and a great deal of mourning in Crete, on account of this grievous piece of news; nothing worse than this has happened nor will happen. May the L<ord> our G<od> have pity on us and deliver us from His terrible threat.

Antonios Hyalinas who escaped with his ship and brought Valentinus to Crete lost almost his entire fortune in the sack and was subsequently beset by debtors; such was his plight that the Venetian Senate eventually took pity on him and, in view of his services during the siege, attempted to alleviate his condition with an official decree.[41]

We do not know the outcome of Tetaldi's petition to reclaim his slave and we have no further information on this author/warrior/merchant/refugee. Numerous editions of the French text have appeared over the last centuries, including: D. Godefroy, ed., *Histoire de Charles VII, roy de France; par Jean Chartier, Jacques Le Bouvier, dit Berry, Matthieu de Coucy, et autres autheurs. Mise en lumiére, & enrichie de plusieurs titres, mémoires, etc. par Denys Godefroy* (Paris, 1661), 271–79

'Ἀποβιβασθέντων εἰς Κρήτην," *Actes du XIIe Congrès International d'Études Byzantines, Ochride, 10–16 Septembre 1961* (Belgrade, 1964), 171–76. In general, see Manoussos Manoussakas, "Les derniers Défenseurs crétois de Constantinople d'après les documents vénitiens," *Actes des XL. Internationalen Byzantinischen Kongresses*. ed. Franz Dölger and Hans-Georg Beck (Munich, 1958), 331–40. For the timetable of the Christian ships and their departure from Constantinople, see *PL* 2: 131–32; *FC*, 141–42; Tetaldi also presents a general picture, in addition to Barbaro, 59, 60 [= *CC* 1, 34–37].

[41] Barbaro, 64 [= *CC* 1: 36, 37] refers to this captain as "el Galina": "la galìa de Candia patron misser Zacaria Grioni el cavalier, quela si fo prexa, poi driedo queste galìe si levò tre nave de Candia, le qual son, ser Zuan Venier, ser Antonio Filamati <e> el Galina, e tuti andasemo in conserva nave a galìe per infina fuora del streto . . . ." John R. [Melville] Jones, *Nicolò Barbaro: Diary of the Siege of Constantinople 1453* (New York, 1969), made an error in the translation of this passage, which he subsequently corrected: see Melville Jones, *Siege*, p. xii: "It was this Nemesis which inspired me, in the translation of Barbaro . . . to assume that 'el galina' was a Venetian nickname ('The Hen') for Antonio Filamati. It is, in fact, the name of a Cretan shipmaster, Yalinas."

For the documents dealing with the adventures of the captains after their escape, cf. *RdD* 3, no. 2950, and no. 3026. The Hyalinas family continued to make its home in Crete until the fall of the island to the Turks. Then the survivors migrated to Corfu. See Spyridon P. Lampros, "Κατάλογος τῶν Κρητικῶν Οἴκων Κερκύρας," *NH* 10 (1913): 449–65, esp. 451: the *Gialinà* family is included among the *nobili della città di Candia*, but, it is noted, the family ultimately stems from Constantinople.

(based on Paris. fr. 2691); and Valet de Virville, *Chronique de Charles VII, roi de France, par Jean Chartier. Nouv. éd. rev. sur les manuscrits, suivie de divers fragments, inédits, pub. avec notes, notices, et éclaircissemens par Velt de Virville*, vol. 3 (Paris, 1858), 20–35. The best edition remains that of E. Martène and U. Durand, *Thesaurus novus anecdotorum*, vol. 1 (Paris, 1717), cols. 1819 ff. (which was further reprinted[42] in P. A. Déthier and C. Hopf, *Monumenta Hungariae Historia. Ser. Scriptores* [*Második osztály irok*], vol. 22, part 1 [*sine loco* (Galatas/Pera), *sine anno* (1872?, 1875?), 891 ff.]. I have utilized this edition but have further arranged its text into numbered paragraphs in Appendix I). There has been only one translation of the French text into English: Melville Jones, *Siege*, 1–10. The Melville Jones translation is based on Paris. fr. 6487. Selections from the French Tetaldi translated into Italian have also appeared. The Latin version of Tetaldi has never been studied fully by scholars and has not been utilized in various modern studies of the siege and fall. It was published once: Martène and Durand, *Veterum scriptorum et monumentorum historicorum, dogmaticorum, moralium amplissima collectio*, vol. 5 (Paris, 1729), 175–89. I have utilized this edition and have further divided each chapter into paragraphs. I present the first translation of the Latin version into a modern language, along with a modest commentary (the only one in existence); such oversights and omissions in the scholarship of the siege are understandable, I suppose: while the narrative itself is informative and of interest to scholars investigating the events of the siege, it can hardly be said to have any literary merit.[43]

Giacomo Rizzardo and Frate Jacopo dalla Castellana

The fall of Constantinople in 1453 created panic in Christian Europe. Actual reports of the disaster followed all sorts of rumors that had been spreading throughout the Aegean. Eventually, refugees managed to escape from the

---

[42] This useful collection of sources on the siege and fall of Constantinople was not officially published for a simple, albeit legitimate, reason: an inordinate amount of printing errors had been detected in the galleys and the publication came to an abrupt halt, as the Hungarian Academy of Sciences withdrew its sanction; the project then reached a state of scholarly limbo. Officially the collection was not published but a number of advance copies had already been forwarded to a handful of investigators and libraries. These rare surviving copies have been widely sought and eagerly consulted ever since. Some of the texts included in this collection have not seen the light of print a second time and their manuscripts still await modern editors. Another two volumes were prepared but were never printed. This awkward situation was aptly summarized in Pears, *The Destruction of the Greek Empire*, xii: "The late Dr. Dethier [*sic*] ... compiled four volumes of documents relating to the siege ... Two of them were printed about 1870, but they can hardly be said to have been published and they are procured with difficulty ...." On this matter, see Philippides, "The Fall of Constantinople," 191–93.

[43] Cf. the remarks of Melville Jones, *Siege*, vii, in regard to the French version: "[Tetaldi's] account has no literary merit except that of brevity and, perhaps, the sense of of immediacy that it conveys."

carnage, boarded ships that had been present in the harbor of the hapless city, sailed away, and announced the sad news to western territories. In addition to the Venetian vessels, there had been seven Genoese and three Cretan ships that had participated in the defense. The captains of the vessels that escaped set a southward course through the Dardanelles to the Aegean archipelago. Like the proverbial bird-messengers of Greek folk poetry, these vessels were the bearers of ill tidings to the western world.

Even before these ships brought confirmation of the fall of Constantinople, rumors of doom had already spread throughout the Greek islands. Thus as early as June 11 the Paduan Paolo Dotti in Candia dictated a letter in which he outlined his suspicions that the Greek capital had been taken.[44] His premonition was confirmed exactly one month after the sack, when the three Cretan ships with the numerous refugees on board (including the slave of Tetaldi, as we have seen) finally reached Candia. Their story of unbelievable grief spread throughout the town. On the evening of the same day, Friday, June 29, a scribe at the Monastery of Ankarathos recorded his personal reaction to the event.[45] It is in short notes of this type that we are able to gauge the despair that spread throughout the Aegean.

The impact of the fall was felt deeply by the inhabitants of Candia. It is quite possible that Cardinal Isidore, another famous refugee who found his own way to Crete, gave an account of his impressions of the disaster to an assembly of the local magistrates. He may have even given a public recitation of the events of the siege and of his adventures. He then went on to compose a lengthy series of letters intended to communicate the sad news to western Christendom.[46] Meanwhile the local population went into heavy mourning. A formal lamentation on the sack, composed by a Jewish resident of Candia, Michael ben Shabettai Kohen Balbo, survives.[47] His sentiments match the universal grief that is detected throughout Europe immediately after the sack. As far away as London,

---

[44] Latin text in Spyridon P. Lampros, "Μονῳδίαι καὶ Θρῆνοι ἐπὶ τῇ Ἁλώσει τῆς Κωνσταντινουπόλεως," *NH* 5 (1908): 263–65 [= improved text in *CC* 2: 12–17, with Italian translation].

[45] The text of this interesting note has already been quoted, above: Greek passage and translation that are accompanied by n. 40.

[46] See the account of Isidore's adventures by Henry of Soemmern.

[47] The Hebrew text of Balbo's lamentation is quoted in Steven B. Bowman, *The Jews of Byzantium, 1204–1453* (University Park, 1985), 144–47, who further discusses the impact of the fall among the Jews of the Aegean. Quite different was the reaction of the Jews of Spain; see Sebastian Cirac Estopañan, *Byzancio y España. La caida del imperio byzantino y los Españoles* (Barcelona, 1954): 92: "... en un proceso del Santo Oficio de la Inquisición, instruído alrededor del año 1480 en Castilla la Nueva, se testificaba que *los judíos de Castilla habían celebrado con gran júbilo la conquista de Constantinopla por el Gran Turco*, a quien consideraban como el Mesías, que vendría también a conquistar España y echar de ella a los cristianos" (my emphasis).

the event is noted in chronicles: "Also in this yer, which was the yer of Ower Lord god MCCCCLiij was the cite of Constantyn the noble lost by the Cristen men, and wonne by the Prynce of the Turkes named Mahumet."[48]

The initial reaction in the west to the loss of Constantinople amounted to universal disbelief, which was gradually transformed into acceptance and public grief; at first the western world proved unable to comprehend the fact that Constantinople was sacked and that the buffer, however slight, which had separated Christian west and Islamic east has been eliminated.[49] Shock and initial suspicion in regard to the accuracy of reports announcing major disasters are characteristic human reflexes. It is only after the full impact of a radically new situation has been realized that such reports begin to find credence; only then do the new sets of circumstances and implications sink in. The news of the fall and sack reached Venice on Friday, June 29, 1453 (the very same day on which the three Cretan ships arrived in Candia), in the form of official dispatches from the castellan of Methone (Modon) in the Morea and from the *bailo* of Khalkis at Negroponte/Euboea. Rome learned of the disaster by July 8 from the Franciscan Roberto Caracciolo. Four days earlier the Venetian envoy Giovanni Moro personally informed the Greek humanist Cardinal Bessarion at Bologna. In spite of official dispatches and accurate reports, however, as late as July 10 and 11, the Florentine Nicolò Soderini observed that numerous individuals in Genoa still refused to accept the reality of the event, and he resigned himself to the impossibility of discovering what had actually occurred. Moreover, by July 19 optimistic rumors began to circulate, claiming that the Christians had miraculously recovered Constantinople.[50] On July 12 Emperor Frederick III at Graz in Styria was informed of the fall by travelers from Serbia: his court formed the impression that the Turks had massacred all inhabitants, forty thousand or more; inaccurate details about the fate of the Greek emperor were also

---

[48] *Chronicles of London*, ed. C. L. Kingsford (Oxford, 1905), 164. This monumental event, the fall of Constantinople, seems to have been overlooked in Russia, the other major Orthodox state in Europe, precisely because the Greek Church had accepted union with the Catholic Church in 1438–39 during the Council of Florence.

[49] The best modern analysis of the aftermath, with special emphasis on various reactions in the west, is provided in *SOC*, chap. 1, esp. 1–14, which establishes a timetable of the news spreading through Europe. A useful diagram of the various points of origin from which reports of the fall fanned out can be found in *CC* 1: xxvi.

[50] For the early reaction in Italy, cf. *PL* 2: 138, and n. 2. The official report on the defense and the fall of Constantinople was presented by Alvise/Aluvixe (Ludovico) Diedo, who led the Venetian flotilla with numerous refugees aboard away from the sack of Constantinople; he eventually found his way to Venice and made his *relazione* to the Senate on July 4, 1453; one would give much to read this report, written by an actual commander of the defense. Diedo's report, however, has vanished without a trace. For the votes of the Venetian Senate in conjunction with Diedo's report, see *TIeNP*, 8–9.

being presented.⁵¹ By August of the same year a bishop from Constantinople, named Samuel, brought a report of the events to Wallachia, to Transylvania, and to Hermanstadt.⁵² Letters from various cities in Italy were dispatched to Burgundy, Portugal, Spain, and Denmark.

After the initial shock the attitude of Venice, a city that had contributed much to the defense of the Greek capital in 1453, was more realistic than numerous romantic theatrics, like the Oath of the Pheasant, that were being staged elsewhere. Early in the summer of 1454, Venice quietly concluded a mutually satisfactory peace treaty with the Porte and with the conqueror of Constantinople himself, who during the sack had captured and had subsequently executed Venice's *bailo*, Girolamo Minotto; this treaty confirmed, in fact, the pact that had been negotiated with the sultan in 1451. Bartolomeo Marcello became the new Venetian *bailo* in Ottoman Constantinople and remained in this post until 1456 when Lorenzo Vitturi replaced him.⁵³ Yet the situation remained critical and the new peace treaty did not solve most of the problems. In 1459 the Turks initiated a series of raids directed at the Venetian possession of Negroponte/Euboea. The response of Venice was lukewarm and no strategic plan for the defense of this island was formulated. The raids and the failure of Venice to respond encouraged the Porte to prepare a major expedition against Negroponte/Euboea, which after a siege fell to the hands of the Turks; the population was subjected to a bloody sack.

Euboea, with its capital city of Khalkis, both generally known as Negroponte in the *quattrocento*, had come under Venetian control in 1205, one year after the sack of Constantinople by the crusaders; it was in 1209 that the first Venetian *bailo* established himself in Khalkis. Venetian control of Euboea became a firm reality in the period 1261–1304; by 1398 all other Latin areas of Euboea had come

---

⁵¹ Cf. the pertinent letters of Aeneas Sylvius Piccolomini (who became Pope Pius II on August 27, 1458, but at this time was the secretary of Frederick III), published in R. Wolkan, *Die Briefwechsel des Eneas Silvius Piccolomini* 3 [Fontes Rerum Austriacarum 68] (Vienna, 1918). The letter of July 12 is quoted in 189–202; extracts from the same letter are published in CC 2: 44–48 (with Italian translation). See, in particular, 199 [44–45]: "... Turchorum imperator magnis militum copiis Constantinopolim proximis his diebus obsidione terra marique cinxit atque admotis machinis et insultu ter facto expugnavit, populum omnem gladio extinxit, sacerdotes diversis tormentorum generibus excarnificavit neque sexui neque etati pepercit; quadraginta et amplius milia personarum illic occisa referuntur, qui res gestas ad nos ex Rascia venientes enarrant, Palaeologum qui apud imperavit, capite multatum filium ejus erectum fuga in Pera modo obsessum ajunt..."

⁵² The German text of the report of "Vladik" [= владыка, i.e., bishop] Samuel has been published in NE 4, 65–68; an Italian translation of this document can be found in CC 1: 228–31.

⁵³ Marcello was accompanied by a Porte official when he returned to Venice after completing the initial negotiations in Constantinople; for other individuals who assisted Marcello in his mission, see MCT, 111–12. For the treaty itself, see RdD 3: 186 ff. Also, see PL 2: 140.

under Venetian jurisdiction.⁵⁴ Numerous notable Venetian noblemen served in the post of *bailo*, indicating the island was indeed one of the most important possessions of Venice in the Levant; in the period before the conquest the notable individuals include:⁵⁵ Leonardo Calbo (1461); Fantin Zorsi (1463): "Fantinus Georgio intravit die XXX marti 1464;" Francesco Gradenigo (1465): "Franciscus Gradenigus intravit die XXVII iunii 1466;" and Paolo Erizzo (1468): "Paulus Erizo intravit die ultimo novembris 1468."

The basic cause for the fall of Khalkis, the capital of Euboea, it was universally concluded in the *quattrocento*, was Nicolo da Canale's hesitation, indecision, and lack of action;⁵⁶ he had been appointed Captain General of the fleet that made its approach from the north into the straits of Euboea, in plain sight of the besieged, but then failed to engage the enemy army and navy and took no action whatsoever to assist the beleaguered defenders; he simply stood by while the Turkish troops overran the fortifications and began the general massacre of the population. The news of the fall of Negroponte reached Venice on the last day of July and, once it was ascertained that the disaster was due to da Canale's incompetence, Pietro Mocenigo (who later became doge) was immediately appointed to the post of Captain General and was instructed to arrest and transport da Canale and his associates to Venice to stand trial, as we find out from the surviving legal document that proclaimed the heavy penalties that were imposed upon da Canale after his trial:⁵⁷ "The designated Captain General of

---

⁵⁴ A great deal of information on the Latin conquest of Euboea/Negroponte in these centuries is supplied in Marin Sanudo Torsello's work; see the recent edition, with modern Greek translation and commentary, by Eutychia E. Papadopoulou, *Marin Sanudo Torsello Istoria di Romania: Introduction, Edition, Translation, Commentary*, National Hellenic Research Foundation, Institute for Byzantine Research: Sources 4 (Athens, 2000).

⁵⁵ As is recorded in the Archives: *Segretario alle voci dal 1441 al 1490*, which notes the elections of all magistrates.

⁵⁶ Some modern authorities echo the general opinion about da Canale's incompetence. See, e.g., *PL* 2: 304: "The captain-general Canale, though he had served Venice well as a diplomat, was a loser, and certainly proved himself to be a timid and inept commander." However, the same modern authority also provides some mitigating remarks on this individual; see *PL* 2: 303: "Niccolò da Canale was a doctor of laws, more given to books than to battles. His election to the captaincy-general had been the Senate's mistake. If Canale was a failure in the high command, his galley commanders (*sopracomitti*) were also a sad lot."

⁵⁷ "Quod viro nobili <domino> Petro Mocenigo designato capitaneo generali maris loco praefati d<omini> Nicolai committeretur, et sic fuit commissum quod simul atque applicuisset ad classem nostram videret cum bono et dextero modo de retineri faciendo prefatum ser Nicolaum tam in havere quam in persona ac scripturis et illum mittere in una ex galeis sibi commissis Venetias, te similiter filium illius Petrum, ac Alovisium Sagundinum cancellarium, omnes in ferris et divisim, presentandos carceribus ad petitionem advocatorum et subsequenter procederet ad examinationem supracomitorum melius informatorum de progressibus dicti capitanei et amissionis civitatis predicat<a>e [Negropontis], et sic fuisset per ipsum dominum Petrum impigre et citissime executum." This document is dated "MCCCCLXX ind. XIII.

the Sea, Lord Pietro Mocenigo who replaced the aforementioned Lord Nicolo [da Canale], was instructed to use our fleet expertly in order to arrest the aforementioned Sir Nicolo [da Canale] and to dispatch him, in a galley entrusted to him, to Venice, along with his son Pietro and with Alvise Sagundino, his secretary; all were to be put in irons, apart from each other. They were to be brought, in accordance with the desire of the public prosecutors, to prison in order to be questioned by the captains of galleys about the actions of the aforementioned captain and the loss of the aforementioned city [of Negroponte]. And so the case was energetically pursued by the Lord Pietro himself who brought it to a swift conclusion."

It is interesting to note that the da Canale's secretary was "Alvise Sagundino," i.e., Sekoundinos, the son of Nikolaos Sekoundinos.[58] Alvise was also imprisoned with da Canale; in time, Sekoundinos proved his innocence and was recalled to his former position as secretary; perhaps it was then that he was promoted to the post of ducal secretary. He certainly had this position by 1480 when he was despatched to Dalmatia to announce a decision of the Senate. Numerous other diplomatic, naval, and military missions followed all over the Levant. In old age he was again despatched on a diplomatic mission to Egypt, but he fell ill on the way and eventually died in Cairo: "Alvise Sekoundinos, our secretary, died in Cairo on February 28 [1506]."[59] Like his father, he performed numerous services on behalf of the Venetian government throughout his life. Unlike his father, he was not an accomplished scholar and never authored any treatises or histories.

The same legal document recorded, in Latin, the penalty for dereliction of duty imposed on da Canale; this legal brief was published by Cicogna as an appendix to Rizzardo's text.[60] This document expresses no doubts as to da Canale's guilt and further describes da Canale in harsh terms. The charge against him was explicit: "... he was responsible, in dereliction of his duty, for the wretched destruction of the city Negroponte."[61] The document never doubts his

---

Die VII novembris" and bears the title *Bernardus Veneris Marcus Barbadicus Candianus Bolan. Advocatores Con. in Rogatis*. It is included in *Reggistro Raspe*, no. XIII and was published in its entirety by Emmanuele A. Cicogna as *Documento D* in his Appendix to Rizzardo's text, *La Presa di Negroponte fatta dai Turchi ai Veneziani describa da Giacomo Rizzardo* (Venice, 1844). The instructions to Mocenigo are included in a document: *Sen. Secreta, reg.* 24, fol. 130ᵛ [134ᵛ]; see PL 2: 303, n. 117; and Luigi Fincati, "La Perdita di Negroponte (luglio 1470)," *Archivio Veneto* 22 (1886): 267–307, esp. 300.

[58] On this son of Nikolaos Sekoundinos, see *NΣBE*, 106–8.

[59] "[A] di 28 fevrer al Chayro era morto Alvise Sagudino, secretario nostro." So it is reported in Marino Sanuto's Chronicle: *I Diarii* (<MCCCCXCV–MDXXXIII>) *dall' autografo marciano ital. cl. VII codd. CDXIX–CDLXXVII*), 58 vols. (Venice, 1879–1903), 3.1: 331.

[60] A comprehensive and descriptive list of all manuscripts containing this work can be found in *NΣBE*, 169–70.

[61] "... cujus culpa et machamentis esset secutus casus infelicissimae amissionis civitatis Negropontis."

guilt: "The oral and written testimony against Doctor Nicolo da Canale, who, while Captain General of the Sea, should and ought to have helped, with his great resources, the city of Negroponte, he did nothing neither on his own nor through anybody else after the fleet of the Grand Turk entered the Channel of Negroponte."[62] And further describes his activities in strong words: "... the territory itself had been ruined in many places and was in the most evident danger of being taken, unless it received help from the captain himself [da Canale]; nevertheless calmly he postponed all action to help ... even on the 11th day of July when the captain [da Canale] entered the channel of Negroponte with the fleet of ships and galleys entrusted to him, with a favorable wind, he endured, shamefully and pathetically, the capture occurring before his very eyes ...."[63] Further on he is again described as "unconcerned about the safety and preservation of that city."[64]

It is evident from this document that the prosecution based its case on seven questions that were submitted to da Canale. While the rest of the document is written in Latin, this section is composed in Italian, presumably so that the charges could be understood clearly; the first five questions deal with the military situation while the last two deal with the disappearance of grain. Here are the five questions that were directly concerned with his reluctance to assist actively in the defense of Negroponte:[65]

> 1st: Why did neither he nor anyone else come to the aid of the city of Negroponte, when the armada of the Turk entered the channel of Negroponte from the south and the Lord Turk with his army [came] overland?
>
> 2nd: Why did he deny his help, which he was able to give and should have given, after he was informed that the walls of the city were in ruins

---

[62] "... per ea que dicta et lecta sunt ... contra ... Nicolaum de Canali doctorem, qui dum esset capitaneus generali maris debuissetq<ue> ac maximum potuisset, tamen nec per se nec per alium non succurrerit civitati Negropontis post introitum classis magni turchi in canali Nigropontis."

[63] "... terra ipsa ob ruinas multiplices erat in evidentissimo periculo amissionis nisi quam citissime ab ipso capitaneo subveniretur, non solicitando distulit subsidium ... quique etiam tunc capitaneus dum ad diem XI mensis julii applicuisset in canali Nigropontis cum classe navium et galearum sibi commissarum cum vento prospero ... non investivit pontem inimicorum nec prestitit imploratum subsidium illi misere civitatis, quam turpiter et miserabiliter passus est ante oculos suos amitti."

[64] "immemor salutis et conservationis illius civitatis."

[65] 1.°: perche da poi che l'armada del turcho intro de sotto nel canal de Negroponte et el signor turco cum l' hoste da terra, ne per lui ne per altri el soccorse la cita de Negroponte=

2.°: perche poi hauti i advisi che le mure de la cita erano ruinate da molte parte, et in periculo evidentissim el non sollicito el suo soccorso, chome el dovea far et podea=

in numerous places, and it could be plainly seen that the city was in danger?

3rd: Why did he fail to attack the bridge and help the unfortunate territory after he reached, on the 11th day, the channel of Negroponte with the armada of ships and galleys entrusted to him, with a favorable wind of 15 miles per hour?

4th: Why did he fail to invest, break, and destroy the bridge when the enemy armada set sail and was patrolling the straits in numerous places?

5th: Why did he move towards Negroponte so unadvisedly and without consulting anyone after the fall of that city and thus endangered their lives of so many brave men along with the armada that had been entrusted to him?

Da Canale was found guilty, was sentenced to prison, and then was sent to internal exile; he never returned to Venice. Da Canale, who had been a well-known senator, also had been honored with the title of "doctor of laws," thus enabling him to wear an embroidered gown, a collar of fur, and a purple hood; he was even wearing these insignia in his official portrait exhibited in the hall of the Great Council in Venice. He had been more suited for scholarly pursuits than for an actual command in the Aegean;[66] yet he had been earlier entrusted with important posts in the service of the *Signoria*: special emissary to the duke of Milan (1444), special emissary to the king of Portugal (1445), emissary to the pope (1451), emissary to the diet of 1454 in Germany for the formulation of an alliance against the Turks, special emissary to the king of France (1464); and in 1467 he was elected *provveditore* of the fleet. His arrest after the fiasco at Negroponte made an impression in the Levant, as George Sphrantzes included the following note in his authentic Chronicle, the *Chronicon Minus*:[67]

3.º: perche sendo adì xi zonto nel canal de Negroponte cum larmada delle nave et gallie a si commesse cum vento prospero a mia XV per hora, el no investì el ponte, et soccorse quella misera terra=

4.º: perche usita larmada inimica per tornar in stretto in più luogi et diversi zorni et tempi, quella el non investì per romper et fracassur quella=

5.º: perche cussi imprudente et inconsultamente el se ne ando a Negroponte poi persu quella cita, mettendo in evidentissimo periculo tanto numero de valenti homini cum tuta larmada a lui commessa=

[66] *PL* 2: 303.
[67] *Chronicon Minus*, 46.8: Τὸν δὲ ῥηθέντα καπετάνιον Νικολῶ Ντεκανάλια, στείλαντες ἕτερον καπετάνιον τὸν Τομᾶ Μουτζενίγον, ἔπιασαν αὐτὸν καὶ τὸν υἱὸν αὐτοῦ καὶ τὸν γραμματικόν, καὶ σιδήροις δεσμεύσαντες ἔστειλαν εἰς τὸν αὐθέντην αὐτῶν εἰς τὴν ἀρχὴν τοῦ φθινοπώρου τοῦ οθ^{ου} ἔτους.

... They arrested their aforementioned admiral, Niccolo da Canale, ... his son, and his secretary; they were put in irons and sent to their lord in the beginning of the fall of the 79th year [1470].

After the fall of Constantinople, the loss of Negroponte was the second serious disaster suffered by Venice in the course of the *quattrocento*. It was through Euboea that Venice had been able to support its interests in the duchy of Athens, in the Morea, and in the islands of the Aegean.

The first "chronicle" by Giacomo Rizzardo is not, strictly speaking, a direct eyewitness account of the situation within the besieged city. Rizzardo served as the secretary of Captain Lorenzo Contarini, whose galley was included in the Venetian fleet that was despatched to the city's aid but failed to offer any assistance to the besieged. So Rizzardo is reproducing accounts of the siege that were circulating soon after the loss, and he must have based his account on the observations of survivors which had been communicated to him. That he did not wait very long after the fall to compose his account becomes evident in the text itself: Rizzardo mentions that no one, at the time immediately after the sack, knew the fate of Ser Marco Venier, the son of Antonio from Candia; yet from subsequent documents we know that he survived the carnage and wave of executions and married Diana Santin in 1472; he died in 1502. Rizzardo's ignorance about the fate of this individual indicates that his narrative was composed soon after the fall. His manuscript was eventually discovered by Emmanuele A. Cicogna, who published the account in Giambatista Merlo's printing establishment of Venice in 1844, under the title, *La presa di Negroponte fatta dai Turchi ai Veneziani nel MCCCCLXX descritta da Giacomo Rizzardo autore contemporaneo ed ora per la prima volta pubblicata con documenti e annotazioni*.

The second "chronicle" by Brother Jacopo/Giacomo dalla Castellana is in fact the work of an eyewitness from within the city. It was indeed composed soon after the sack, and was probably based on notes that the good brother had kept during the siege. His name has been erroneously recorded in the manuscript catalogues as "della Castellana" or as "Castellina." Jacopo can further be identified with a Fra Giacomo Pugliese. His text was edited and published, along with two poetical lamentations on the fall of Negroponte, by Filippo-Luigi Polidori, "*Due Ritmi e una narrazione in prosa di autori contemporanei intorno alla presa di Negroponte fatta dai Turchi a danno dei Veneziani nel MCCCLXX, con annotazioni ed una lettera proemiale*," as an Appendix to the journal *Archivio storico italiano* 9 (1853): 399–440 (Jacopo's account: 433–40). Polidori dedicated this work to the editor of Rizzardo: "Al Chiarissimo ed Eruditissimo Signor Cav. Emmanuele Antonio Cicogna."

Another survivor of the sack of Negroponte, Gian-Maria Angiolello (1451–1525), a native of Vicenza, who lost his brother in the siege, became a prisoner of the sultan and eventually composed a work usually entitled *Historia Turchesca, 1300–1514*. This work was published by I. Ursu (Bucharest, 1909), who, however,

attributed it erroneously to the pen of Donado da Lezze.⁶⁸ Both chronicles, by Rizzardo and by Brother Jacopo, are here translated into English for the first time.

Both chronicles bear the stamp of emotional turmoil; Rizzardo was an observer from afar, from the fleet that failed to provide any relief to the defenders, while Brother Jacopo, among the defenders, actually survived the siege and sack. Their emotional involvement in the events is evident in their colorful descriptions of the battles and assaults, composed in the difficult vernacular of the Venetian dialect (complicated by their idiosyncratic orthography) of the *quattrocento*. One may compare the dry, general account of Sphrantzes' note:⁶⁹

> ... there ensued intensive land and sea battles; on July 12 the emir [= sultan] stormed and seized the city. After this event the nearby small islands and cities were forced to surrender, willingly or unwillingly. The emir [= sultan] lingered in the area for a while and then departed for Constantinople in the beginning of August.

There are numerous mentions of the fall in the so-called "Short Chronicles," which are brief notes without details.⁷⁰ One note is more extensive and more informative than the rest:⁷¹

> In the year 6978 [= A.D. 1470], the 8th indiction, the emir [= sultan] came with a very large army, infantry, cavalry, and navy (360 large and small vessels) to Euripos [= Khalkis, Negroponte] and launched attacks day and night with many siege engines, from June 12 until July 12. And on July 12, a Thursday, the aforementioned emir [= sultan], Mehmed Çelebi [= prince], took it with much bloodshed after a mighty

---

⁶⁸ *MCT*, 45. n. 47. I understand that Professor Pierre MacKay is preparing a new edition, with English translation and extensive commentary, of Angiolello's text.

⁶⁹ *Chronicon Minus*, 46.6: . . . καὶ πολεμήσαντες σφοδρῶς ἀπό τε γῆς καὶ θαλάσσης τῇ ιβ ͏ͅ τοῦ Ἰουλίου μηνὸς ἀπῆραν τὸ κάστρον πολέμῳ. καὶ τούτου γενομένου, πάντα τὰ περὶ αὐτὸν νησύδρια καὶ καστέλλια ἐδουλώθησαν ἑκουσίως ἀκουσίως. ὁ δὲ ἀμηρᾶς προσκαρτερήσας μικρόν τι περὶ τὰς ἀρχὰς τοῦ αὐγούστου ἐξῆλθε καὶ ἀπῆλθεν εἰς τὴν Κωνσταντινούπολιν.

⁷⁰ Peter Schreiner, *Die byzantinischen Kleinchroniken* 3 vols. (Vienna, 1975), 1: 33.42, 65; 34.33; 36.25; 37.11; 38.16; 40.9; 53.24; 54.19 55.22; 56.4; 58.17; 59.2; 60.26; 61.9; 62.12; 63.24; 64.11; 65.5; 66.5; 67.6; 68.5; 69.12, 64; 70.28; 71.5 74.4; 75.3; 76.8; 77.5; 79.14; 102.8; and 107.18.

⁷¹ Schreiner, *Kleinchroniken*, 1, 33.62: τῷ ͵ϛϠοη΄ ἔτει, ἰνδικτιῶνος η΄, ἦλθε ὁ ἀμηρᾶς σὺν στρατοῦ πλείστου, ἱππέων καὶ πεζῶν καὶ πλοίων διὰ θαλάσσης, τριακοσίων ξ΄, μικρῶν καὶ μεγάλων, εἰς τὴν Εὔριπον, καὶ ἐπολέμιζεν αὐτὴν ἡμέραν καὶ νύκταν μετὰ μηχανημάτων πολλῶν ἀπὸ ιουνίου ιβ΄ ἕως ιουλλίου ιβ΄. καὶ τῇ ιβ΄ τοῦ ιουλίου, ἡμέρα ε΄, ἐπαρέλαβεν αὐτὴν ὁ αὐτὸς ἀμηρᾶς ὁ Μεεμέτης τζαλαπῆς μετὰ αἱματοχυσίας πολλῆς καὶ μάχης ἰσχυρᾶς. ἀπέθανε δὲ πλῆθος ἄπειρον ἐμφοτέρωθεν, καὶ οὕτως ἐπαρέλαβεν καὶ τὴν καθόλου νῆσον.

battle. Countless multitudes died from both sides. And so he seized the entire island.

Equally brief is the notice found in the early sixteenth-century Ἔκθεσις Χρονική:[72]

> In the year 978 [= A.D. 1470] he [= Mehmed II] fought against the Venetians. He attacked Euripos [= Negroponte/Euboea/Khalkis] by land and sea and seized it; it had refused to submit; he put all men, ten years or older, to death . . . brought the entire population to Constantinople . . . the women and children from Euripos.

Finally, mention should be made of the Anonymous Barberini Chronicle, which supplies some details in regard to the fall of Negroponte:[73]

> Then again he [= Sultan Mehmed II Fatih] started a war against the Venetians (1461) and went to the city Euripos [= Negroponte] which

---

[72] Translation from Marios Philippides, *Emperors, Patriarchs, and Sultans of Constantinople: An Anonymous Greek Chronicle of the Sixteenth Century* (Brookline, 1990), 62 (80); the original text reads as follows: Ἐν ἔτει ϡοη΄ ποιήσαντες μάχην μετὰ τῶν βενετίκων, πορευθεὶς ἐκ γῆς καὶ θαλάττης ἔλαβε τὴν Εὔριπον ἣ οὐκ ἠθέλησε προσκυνῆσαι αὐτόν· ἀπέκτεινε δὲ πάντας ἄνδρας ἀπὸ δεκαετοῦς καὶ ἀνωτέρω . . . πάντα τὸν λαὸν ἔφερεν ἐν Κωνσταντινουπόλει . . . καὶ τῆς Εὐρίπου γυναῖκάς τε καὶ παῖδας.

[73] The Greek text of this anonymous Chronicle was first published in separate pamphlets by the editor, Georgios T. Zoras; this particular section belongs to the *vita* of Mehmed II and was published separately, Ἡ Ἅλωσις τῆς Κωνσταντινουπόλεως καὶ ἡ Βασιλεία Μωάμεθ Β΄ τοῦ Κατακτητοῦ (κατὰ τὸν Ἀνέκδοτον Ἑλληνικὸν Βαρβερινὸν Κώδικα 111 τῆς Βατικανῆς Βιβλιοθήκης) (Athens, 1952), 61; Zoras eventually published the entire text in one volume: Χρονικὸν περὶ τῶν Τούρκων Σουλτάνων (κατὰ τὸν Βαρβερινὸν Ἑλληνικὸν Κώδικα 111) (Athens, 1958); see Philippides, *Byzantium, Europe, and the Early Ottoman Sultans*, 90, for this passage: Τότε πάλι ἐσήκωσε πόλεμον κατὰ τοὺς Βενετζάνους . . . καὶ ἐδιάβη εἰς τὴν Ἔγριπο, ὁποὺ τὴν ὡρίζανε οἱ Βενετζάνοι. Καὶ ἡ Ἔγριπο ἔναι κάστρο δυνατὸ καὶ καλὰ ἀρματωμένο, καὶ εἶχε καὶ πολὺν λαὸν μέσα, Φράγκους καὶ Ῥωμαίους. Καὶ ἔναι κοντὰ εἰς τὸν γιαλό. Καὶ ἐδιάβη ὁ σουλτὰν Μεχεμέτης μὲ τὰ φουσσάτα του ἀπὸ τὴν στερεὰ καὶ διὰ θαλάσσης ἔστειλε τὸν Ὀμὲρ πασὰ καπετάνιο μὲ τὴν ἀρμάδα του. Καί, ἐπειδὴ στέκει τὸ κάστρο κοντὰ - κοντὰ εἰς τὴν στερεὰ εἰς τὴν Ῥούμελη καὶ ἔναι στενὸς ὁ τόπος τὸ διάστημα, ἔφερε καράβια χαμηλὰ καὶ βάρκες καὶ τὰ ἔκαμε ὡσὰν γιοφύρι καὶ ἀπέρασε τὰ φουσσάτα του μέσα ΄ς τὸ νησί. Καὶ ἐτριγυρίσαν τὸ κάστρο καὶ ἐδίδαν πόλεμο μέρα καὶ νύκτα. Καὶ οἱ Ἐγριπιῶτες δὲν ἐθαρροῦσανε ὅτι νὰ τοὺς πολεμᾶ ἀπὸ κεῖνο τὸ μέρος . . . Καὶ οἱ Βενετζάνοι ἐστείλανε τὴν ἀρμάδα τους διὰ νὰ δώσῃ βοήθειαν. Αὐτὴ ἐπήγαινε ἔνθε καὶ κἀκεῖθεν καὶ ἔχανε καιρὸ καὶ ὕστερα ἦρθε κοντὰ εἰς τὸ κάστρο. Καὶ ὡς τὸ μάθανε ἀπὸ μέσα, ἐλάβανε μεγάλην χαρὰν τὸ πῶς ἦρθε βοήθειαν. Ἀμμὴ δὲν ἠμπόρεσαν νὰ δώσουνε βοήθειαν καμμίαν . . . Καὶ ὕστερο, ὡσὰν εἴδανε οἱ ἐλεεινοὶ Εὐριπιῶτες πῶς ἐδιάβη ἡ ἀρμάδα τους καὶ δὲν ἠμπόρεσε νὰ δώσῃ βοήθειαν, ἐπικράθηκαν πολλὰ καὶ ἦταν ἀποσταμένοι τοῦ πολέμου . . .

was ruled by the Venetians. Euripos is a strong city, well-fortified, and it had a large population, both Franks and Romans [= Greeks]. It is near the shore. Sultan Mehmed came with his armies by land while he sent by sea Captain Ömer Pasha with his armada. And since the city is situated very close to the mainland of Rumeli and the dividing gulf is narrow, he brought low ships and big boats, arranged them like a bridge, and his armies thus crossed into the island. They surrounded the city and fought day and night. The inhabitants of Euripos had not expected him to attack from that side . . . And the Venetians sent their armada to help. It kept sailing back and forth and wasted time; then it approached the city. When the defenders discovered this, they rejoiced greatly over the fact that help had come. But they were not able to help in the least . . . At last, when the pitiable inhabitants of Euripos saw that the armada left and that it had been unable to help, they became greatly sad; they were also exhausted by the war.

The same chronicle goes on to describe the fall and the atrocities that followed: "Then they all gathered in the middle of the forum [= *piazza*], where the palace [of the *bailo*] stands, and the countless army of the Turk entered through the breaches that had been created by artillery bombardment. They mingled and the battle with swords became hot; there was great slaughter and both sides lost a great deal of blood. Among the slain, armed women were found also, killed among the men; both unmarried and married women had also fought like brave men and had acted like the Amazons of antiquity."[74]

The anonymous author singles out the case of the *bailo*, Paolo Erizzo, and further reports the tale of his daughter's fate, perhaps the most famous incidents of the sack[75] (even though both Rizzardo and Fra Jacopo rather curiously omit them):

The lord [= *bailo*], Messer Paolo Erizzo, the Venetian nobleman, retreated with a number of noblemen to the inner citadel, the strong

---

[74] Zoras, Ἅλωσις, 61; idem, Χρονικόν, 117; see Philippides, *Byzantium, Europe, and the Early Ottoman Sultans*, 90: Τότε ἐμαζώκτησαν ὅλοι τους εἰς τὴν μέσην τοῦ φόρου, ὁπού στέκει τὸ παλάτι καὶ ἐμπῆκε μέσα τὸ ἀμέτρητο φουσσάτο τοῦ Τούρκου ἀπὸ τὶς χαλάστριες τῶν λουμπαρδῶν. Καὶ ἐσμείξανε καὶ ἄναψε ὁ πόλεμος εἰς τὸ σπαθί, καὶ ἐγίνη μεγάλη σφαγὴ καὶ πολὺ αἷμα ἔτρεχε ἀπὸ τὴν μίαν μερέαν εἰς τὴν ἄλλην. Καὶ εἰς τοὺς σκοτωμένους εὑρέθησαν καὶ γυναῖκες ἁρματωμένες σκοτωμένες μέσα εἰς τοὺς ἄνδρες καὶ ἐπολεμούσανε καὶ αὐτὲς ὡσὰν παλληκάρια, παντρεμένες καὶ ἀνύπαντρες, καὶ ἐκάμανε ὡσὰν τὶς ἀμαζῶνες τοῦ παλαιοῦ καιροῦ.

[75] Zoras, Ἅλωσις, 61; idem, Χρονικόν, 117; cf. Philippides, *Byzantium, Europe, and the Early Ottoman Sultans*, 90: Καὶ ὁ ἀφέντης ὁ μισὲρ Παῦλος Ἔριτζος, τζιντιλόμος Βενετζάνος, μὲ καμπόσους ἄρχοντες τοῦ κάστρου ἐμπήκανε εἰς τὸ παραμέσα καστέλλι τὸ δυνατὸ τοῦ κάστρου. Καὶ ὡσὰν ἐπαρελάβανε οἱ Τοῦρκοι τὸ κάστρο ἐπήρανε ὅλους καὶ τὶς Φράγκους

sector of the city. Once the Turks had taken over the city, they seized all; they impaled the Franks and some they even sawed alive. They enslaved the Romans [= Greeks] and sold them at the bazaar. They captured Lord Erizzo's daughter and gave her to Sultan Mehmed; she was very beautiful. Because she refused to yield to his wishes, she was slaughtered. Then he promised the lord and the noblemen in the citadel that, if they surrendered and gave him the keys of the citadel, he would take no action against them and would allow them to go free. So they believed him and surrendered. But the sultan did not keep his word and had them all beheaded.

The story involving this heroic "daughter" of Erizzo is interesting. Erizzo was not married and he is unlikely to have had a daughter. Yet in time she even acquires a name, Anna. Her story became a favorite tale and was used a number of times in the theater.[76] Apparently we are facing a widespread folk tale of the fifteenth century. A similar, equally fictitious, tale was told about the supposed daughter of Constantine XI during the sack of Constantinople in 1453.

Two refugees from the sack of 1453 gave a *relazione* of the event. Their names were apparently Thomas Eparkhos and Joseph Diplovatatzes (as we may restore these names behind the transmitted corrupted forms in the conclusion of the document)[77] and they reported a tale involving a fictitious daughter of the

τοὺς ἐσουγλίσανε καὶ καμπόσους ἐπριονίσανε ζωντανούς, καὶ τοὺς Ρωμαίους τοὺς ἐκάμανε σκλάβους καὶ τοὺς ἐπουλούσανε ᾽ς τὸ παζάρι. Καὶ τὴν θυγατέρα τοῦ ἀφεντὸς τοῦ Ἐριτζου τὴν ἐπιάσανε καὶ τὴν ἔδωσαν τοῦ σουλτὰν Μεχεμέτη. Καὶ ἤτονε ὄμορφη κατὰ πολλά. Καὶ διατὶ δὲν ἤθελε νὰ κάμη τὸ θέλημά του τὴν ἔσφαξε. Καὶ ὑστέρου ἔταξε τοῦ ἀφεντὸς καὶ τῶν ἀρχόντων ὁποῦ ἤτανε μέσα ᾽ς τὸ καστέλλι ὅτι νὰ παραδοθοῦνε καὶ νὰ τοῦ δώσουνε τὰ κλειδία τοῦ καστελλίου, καὶ αὐτοὺς νὰ μὴν τοὺς κάμη τίβοτα, μόνε νὰ εἶναι ἐλεύτεροι. Καὶ οὕτως τὸν ἐπιστέψανε καὶ ἐπαραδόθησαν. Ἀμμὴ ὁ σουλτάνος δὲν ἐστάθη εἰς τὸν λόγο του, μόνε τοὺς ἀποκεφάλισε ὅλους.

[76] On this interesting, albeit fictitious, personality, who becomes such an important heroine of numerous tales, see Spyridon Biazes, "Ἡρωὶς κατὰ τὴν Ἅλωσιν τῆς Χαλκίδος τῷ 1470," *Πανευβοϊκὸν Ἡμερολόγιον* 1 (1916): 8–11. The fall of Negroponte was also echoed in the literature of the period. Two poems entitled *Il Pianto de Negroponte* and *La Presa di Nigroponte* were published by Polidori, "Due Ritmi e una narrazione in prosa di autori contemporanei," 397–440; it is in the same publication, 433–40, that Castellana's original text was printed for the first time.

[77] The German text of this *relazione* was published in NE 2: 514–18. CC 1: 232–39 included an Italian translation of the report, but unfortunately he did not print the original German text, which remains available only in Iorga. The conclusion of the report speaks of the circumstances of the translation, of the eyewitnesses, and of the translators: "Disse Ding hat gesagt Herr Thomas Eperkus, ein Graf auss Constantinopel, und Josu Deplorentatz, eins Grafen Sun, und Thutro de Constantinopel, der ir Krichisch in Weilisch prach hat, und Dumita Exswinnilwacz, und Mathes Hack von Utrecht, der ir Welisch in Teutsch hat pracht."

Greek emperor, according to which Mehmed raped the daughter of the emperor on the altar of Santa Sophia.[78] The tale is also taken up in a letter composed a few months after the sack by Filippo da Rimini, who was the Venetian chancellor of the island of Corfu. At the end of 1453, da Rimini wrote a short account of the fall to a friend of his in Italy. His account[79] presents the bare facts of the siege. Yet in the section on the sack da Rimini reserves a few sentences to indicate that Mehmed II Fatih raped a virgin in Santa Sophia in order to avenge the rape of Cassandra by the Greeks during the sack of Troy.[80]

Da Rimini most probably was aware of the fact that Constantine XI had no daughters, and did not transform the "virgin" into a "princess." Yet other humanists in the west had no qualms about inventing, consciously or unconsciously, an imperial princess. Soon after the sack, Matthieu d'Escouchy, probably following rumors that escalated through Eparkhos' *relazione*, reported that the Turks committed numerous atrocities and that Sultan Mehmed II raped the daughter of Constantine. D'Escouchy goes on to supply graphic details, and states that Mehmed II did his utmost to persuade this Greek princess to convert to Islam, but she preferred death to apostasy. By his order she was then stripped and decapitated; her head was despatched to her surviving uncle.[81] There is further elaboration. Matthias Döring enters the following note in his continuation of Engelhaus' Chronicle, stating that the sultan raped the daughter of the emperor on the very altar of Santa Sophia:[82] "the emperor of the Turks ... seized it [Constantinople] and turned the population into slaves; he took the emperor, his son, and his daughter prisoners and conducted them to the great church of Santa Sophia, on whose altar, it is related, he raped the daughter under the eyes of her father and brother. Afterwards, he issued orders to slaughter father, son, and

---

[78] *NE* 2: 518: "Item: als er nu erfur daz der Keisser zu Constantinopel erslagen waz, do nam er den grossen herzogen der an des Keissers Stat was und slug seinem Kinden dem Knaben dis Kopf ab, dar nach im selber auch den Kopf ab. Dar nach, namer sein Tochter, gar eine schone, und legt sie auf dem hohen Altar Sant Sophia und ein Crucifix unter ir haubt, und lebt da mit unzuchtiglichen."

[79] Pertusi, "La lettera," 152–57 (text) extracts with Italian translation: *TIePN*, 127–41.

[80] Pertusi, "La lettera," 157: "Cum enim victoria tumens Teucrorum rex omnia quaereret quibus animum suum expleret ad obpropia omnis generis inferenda sanctae religioni nostrae, celeberrimum Sophiae fanum profanandum prae ceteris cum duxisset, ibi immitis bestia ab miti virgine pudorem extorquens golriatus est tum ultum Troianae virginis vicem in templo Palladis defloratae."

[81] M. d'Escouchy, *Chronique*, ed. G. du Fresne de Beaucourt, 3 vols. (Paris, 1863–1864), 2: 35. The report is briefly discussed in *SOC*, 27, n. 45.

[82] This entry is dated 1464; cf. *Codex diplomaticus Brandenburgensis* 41 (Berlin, 1862), 224; also quoted in *CC* 1: 431, n. 20: "Imperator Turcorum ... cepit eam [sc. Constantinopolim] et populum redegit in servitutem imperatoremque et filium et filiam captivos duxit ad ecclesiam magnam Sancte Zophie, in cuius altari, prout famabatur, filiam stupravit patre et fratre inspicientibus; quo facto et patrem et filium et filiam immaniter in frusta concidi iussit."

daughter in a savage manner." A similar report is also found in Leonardo Benvoglienti. In this report the most noble virgin is raped together with her young brother on the altar and then they are both put to death.[83]

Thus one more component is added to the dramatic narratives of sieges in the *quattrocento*: a folk motif that becomes very popular and attracts a great deal of attention, even though it has nothing to do with the historical events. The loss of Negroponte nevertheless was one of the setbacks for Venice. One further detects a note of regret over the loss in the conclusion to the siege section of Negroponte written by the anonymous author of the Barberini Chronicle:[84] "after he [Mehmed II] had taken over pitiable Euripos [= Negroponte] and, similarly, the entire island, which measures 300 miles in circumference, he established garrisons within the cities, which they guard to the present day."

Guillaume Caoursin and Pierre d'Aubusson

The Turkish-Venetian War formally ended in January, 1479. As a consequence of termination of hostilities and the resulting peace with Venice, the Porte, it was believed, was next going to move aggressively against the Knights of Saint John,[85] based on the island of Rhodes. For a long time the Hospitallers had carried on acts of piracy and been energetically involved in the slave trade. As their chief prey consisted of Moslem merchantmen, the sultan wished to eliminate

---

[83] CC 1: 431, n. 20: "Aiunt, qui praesentes fuere, spurcissimum illum Turchorum ducem ... apud summa aram sanctae Sophiae propalam videntibus omnibus nobilissimam virginem et fratrem eius adolescentem regalis sanguinis constuprasse ac deinde necari iussisse."

[84] Καὶ ὡσὰν τὴν ἐπερίλαβε τὴν ἐλεεινὴν Ἔγριπο καὶ ὁμοίως καὶ ὅλο τὸ νησὶ ὁποὺ γυρίζει τριακόσα μίλια ἔβαλε φυλάκτορες μέσα καὶ τὸ ἐφυλάγουνε ἕως τὴν σήμερο. Towards the end of 1478 Giovanni Dario, the secretary of the *Signoria*, was sent to the Porte with instructions to end the sixteen-year war, to secure a peace treaty, to protect Venetian commercial interests in the eastern Mediterranean, and to accept all other terms demanded by the sultan. The treaty was concluded on January 25, 1479. Venice ceded Scutari in Albania, the island of Lemnos, and the region of Mani in the Morea; furthermore,

Venice relinquished all claims to the island of Negroponte/Euboea. In return, the Porte undertook to restore the Venetian possessions that Ottoman troops had seized in Dalmatia, Albania, and the Morea. For these events, see *MCT*, 374–76, and Stanford J. Shaw, *History of the Ottoman Empire and Modern Turkey*, vol. 1: *Empire of the Gazis: The Rise and Fall of the Ottoman Empire, 1280–1808* (Cambridge, 1976), 69. The negotiations that eventually ended this war between the Porte and the Signoria are reviewed by Theoharis Stavrides, *The Sultan of Vezirs: The Life and Times of the Ottoman Grand Vezir Mahmud Pasha Angelović (1453–1474)* The Ottoman Empire and its Heritage 24 (Leiden, 2001), with emphasis on the role that Mahmud Pasha played in diplomacy, 208–34.

[85] The Knights of Saint John had enjoyed a special place among the *quattrocento* military orders. After all, they had been the avowed opponents of Islam, as they were a by-product of the First Crusade. In addition, they had always been able, through their numerous influential contacts in European courts, to secure a flattering picture of their military role in the Levant. Their

this thorn from the side of his empire; after all, Rhodes presented the only serious obstacle to turning the Aegean into an Ottoman lake. Skirmishes and diplomatic warfare had kept both sides busy since the election of Pierre d'Aubusson, prior of Auvergne, as Grand Master of the Order.[86] It was no surprise to him or to his fellow knights to hear that the Turkish army had been mobilized, that the Ottoman fleet was under sail by the spring of 1480, and that the primary target of this expedition would be the island of Rhodes.

The Knights had expected the attack and they had made adequate preparations, as far as their fortifications were concerned.[87] And the siege demonstrated that both the knights and their fortifications of Rhodes proved equal to the task. They were able to defend their city well and successfully, in sharp contrast to the fate of Greek Constantinople in 1453. During his tenure d'Aubusson had strengthened the defenses, amassed provisions, recruited warriors, and despatched appeals throughout Europe for help. In the diplomatic sphere, the Grand Master had concluded peace with Mamluk Egypt, had brought about a truce with Tunisia, and had even secured an agreement to buy considerable amounts of grain from Abu-'Amr 'Uthman, Tunisia's governor. As always, Europe was slow to react and the plight of the Knights was realized only after the siege began.[88]

---

appeals to popes, princes, and the nobility were loud, clear, and frequent. D'Aubusson was particularly active in the sector and his alarms had been distributed widely throughout Europe in the 1470s. His prose was full of hyperbolic rhetoric (echoed in Caoursin's work). Both the Grand Master and the Vice Chancellor of the Order referred to Sultan Mehmed II as a *tyrannus* and both exaggerated the numbers of the Porte's armed forces. While the Knights were outnumbered in resources and men, their estimates of their opponent's strength were an overestimation that possibly represents a calculated attempt to elicit sympathy for their plight and cause in Europe.

[86] The Knights had been sufficiently alarmed by the fall of Constantinople in 1453 to embark upon a vigorous campaign to strengthen their fortifications. In 1453 the Grand Master Jean de Lastic had summoned Florentine engineers to modernize his defenses: they widened the moat, added a second series of curtains, and reinforced the towers. De Lastic also sent the energetic Pierre d'Aubusson to secure funds in Europe; he returned from France with a considerable sum granted by Charles VII. Moreover, the key point in the defense in 1480, Fort Saint Nicholas on the quay, was completed under the direction of Grand Master Pedro Ramón Zacosta in 1461 at the expense of Philip of Burgundy. D'Aubusson remained active, and he seems to have represented the aged Grand Master Orsini before his death. Under Orsini and under the watchful eye of d'Aubusson three more towers were erected and a chain to block the harbor's entrance was prepared. On the completed work, see Eric Brockman, *The Two Sieges of Rhodes 1480–1522* (London, 1969), 33–35.

[87] See the concluding pages of Book III of Dominique Bouhours, *Histoire de Pierre D'Abusson-la-Feuillade grandmaître de Rhodes* (Paris, 1676) which deal with such matters; in addition, see *PL* 2: 348.

[88] *MCT*, 109–10, 126–28; and Elizabeth A. Zachariadou, "The First Serbian Campaigns of Mehemmed II (1454, 1455)," *Annali* 14 (1964): 837–40.

It was in July 1480 that the emissaries of the Grand Master reached Rome and alarmed Pope Sixtus IV. The pope then attempted to establish peace in Italy and bring an end to the "Tuscan War." At the same time a Turkish contingent seized Otranto in Italy, and the Italians became more alarmed by the immediate threat than by the news from the east. Pope Sixtus IV proposed to send two of his galleys to the Levant, while King Ferrante of Naples made his own preparations to aid Rhodes. The Venetian Republic had just established peace with the Porte and seemed unwilling to do anything that would anger the sultan; and so the *Serenissima* refused to participate in the plans to dislodge the Turks from Otranto or to help the Knights in Rhodes, with whom the Venetians had their own problems. So by the time the siege began, no help had arrived and Ferrante's ships reached the island only after the *certamen generale* had been fought and the outcome of the siege had been decided.

Since the occupation of Constantinople by the Turks in 1453 Europe had been the recipient of bad news from the Levant. The years 1454 and 1455 had seen Ottoman campaigns in Serbia and naval operations against the Genoese in the Black Sea. The siege of Belgrade in 1456 by Mehmed II had followed[89] and even though the Ottoman armies proved unable to overcome the spirited defense headed by the monk Giovanni Capistrano and the heroic Janos Corvinus Hunyadi, it had become alarmingly evident that Mehmed II was planning to extend his territories to Italy. In addition, the death of Hunyadi[90] occurred soon after the siege of Belgrade and the Balkans then lost one of its active champions against Turkish aggression. The 1460s saw the annexation of the Greek despotate of the Morea, the fall of Trebizond,[91] and the death of Albania's George Scanderbeg.[92]

---

[89] Robert N. Bain, "The Siege of Belgrade by Muhammad II, July 1–23, 1456," *English Historical Review* 7 (1892): 235–53; Franz Babinger, "Die Quellenwert der Berichte über den Einsatz von Belgrade am 21./22. Juli 1456," *Sitzungsberichte der bayerischen Akademie der Wissenschaften, philos.-hist. Klasse* 6 (1957): 1–69; *SOC*, 41–50; and *MCT*, 138–44.

[90] On this important figure of the *quattrocento*, see Joseph Held, *Hunyadi: Legend and Reality*, East European Monographs 178 (Boulder, 1985). Hunyadi fell victim to an epidemic, perhaps the plague, in Zemun (Semlin) on August 1, 1456; see *MCT*, 146.

[91] Trebizond, the last independent Greek despotate, surrendered to the Turks sometime around the middle of August 1461. On this event, see William Miller, *Trebizond: The Last Greek Empire* (London, 1926, repr. Chicago, 1968), 96 ff; Emile Janssens, *Trébizond en Colchide* (Brussels, 1969), 141 ff.; Spyridon P. Lampros, "Ἡ Ἅλωσις τῆς Τραπεζοῦντος καὶ ἡ Βενετία," *NH* 2 (1905): 324–33; J. F. Boissonade, *Anecdota Graeca e Codicibus Regiis*, vol. 5 (Paris, 1833), 389–401 (with the corrections supplied by S. P. Lampros, "Ἡ περὶ Ἁλώσεως Τραπεζοῦντος Ἐπιστολὴ τοῦ Ἀμηρούτζη," *NH* 12 [1915]: 476–78); *LCB*, chap. 18; *OGN*, 225 ff; and *FC*, 173 ff.

[92] On this personality, see among others Titos P. Giokhalas, Ὁ Γεώργιος Καστριώτης-Σκεντέρμπεης εἰς τὴν Νεοελληνικὴν Ἱστοριογραφίαν καὶ Λογοτεχνίαν, Ἴδρυμα Μελετῶν τῆς Χερσονήσου τοῦ Αἴμου 151 (Thessalonica, 1975); Fan S. Noli, *George Kastrioti Scanderbeg* (New York, 1947); Athanas Gegaj, *L'Albanie et l'invasion turque au XVe siècle* (Louvain, 1937); N. Drizari, *Scanderbeg: His Life, Correspondence, Orations, Victories, and Philosophy* (Palo Alto, 1968); and F. Pall, "Skanderbeg et Ianco Hunedoara," *Revue des études sud-est européens* 6 (1968): 5–21.

A long war between Venice and the Porte began in 1463.⁹³ To top it all, in that war Venice had lost the island of Negroponte/Euboea.⁹⁴ In the next decade the Turks raided Transylvania and the Crimea and even launched expeditions into Italy and within the borders of Venice.⁹⁵ It was only after a Turkish raid into Friuli that the *Serenissima* decided to conclude a peace treaty with the Porte on January 25, 1479.

At the conclusion of this war, the sultan immediately dispatched his *sancak beg* of Valona in Epirus to raid the Ionian islands; Leonardo III Tocco, the count of Leucas (Santa Maura), was forced to flee with his family to Italy. His islands, Leucas, Zacynthus, and Cephalonia, were raided extensively by the Turks and their populations were decimated. In the following spring the sultan sent his troops to seize Rhodes while he also directed an expeditionary force to Italy to seize Otranto.⁹⁶ Thus when the news of the victory of the Knights of Rhodes over the Turks reached Italy there was reason for celebration. It presented hope that the Turks could be stopped. Soon afterwards, with the death of Mehmed II, the Turkish expeditionary forces were forced to withdraw from Otranto. As a text of the early seventeenth century makes clear, Europe sighed with relief at this point. Reporting the death of the Conqueror (1481), the anonymous author of this seventeenth-century chronicle made reference to the Turkish attacks upon Italy and Rhodes: "And they brought the remains of the sultan

⁹³ Relations between the *Signoria* and the Porte reached their nadir during Mehmed's invasion of Bosnia. Hostilities broke out in the Morea, which was undoubtedly the true object of the dispute. The Turks seized Argos on April 3, 1463, while Ottoman contingents raided the Venetian districts of Naupaktos (Lepanto) and Methone (Modon). On these events, see Dorothy M. Vaughan, *Europe and the Turk: A Pattern of Alliances 1350–1700* (Liverpool, 1954), 79; and A. D. Andrews, "The Turkish Threat to Venice, 1453–1463" (diss., University of Pennsylvania, 1962).

⁹⁴ William Miller, *The Latins in the Levant. A History of Frankish Greece (1204–1566)* (London, 1892; repr. Chicago, 1968); Nicolas Cheetham, *Mediaeval Greece* (New Haven and London, 1981), 248–49; *MCT*, 280–84.; and *PL* 2: ch. 9 (271–311). In general, cf. Peter Lock, *The Franks in the Aegean 1204–1500* (London and New York, 1995).

⁹⁵ Ottoman troops from Bosnia overran a hastily fortified line between Goritzia and Aquileia and proceeded to plunder regions in the neighborhood of Venice; see Vaughan, *Europe and the Turk*, 79–80.

⁹⁶ For the Ottoman attempt to establish a bridgehead for the conquest of Italy, see E. Fossati, "Dal 25 luglio 1480 al 6 aprile 1481: l'opera di Milano," *Archivio storico lombardo* 36 (1909): 1–71; G. Panarco, "In terra d'Otranto dopo l'invasione turchesca," *Rivista storica salentina* 7 (1913): 35–56; P. Coco, *La Guerra contro i Turchi in Otranto. Fatti e persone, 1480–1481* (Lecce, 1945); and Alessio Bombaci, "Venezia e la impressa turca di Otranto," *Rivista storica italiana* 56 (1954): 159–203. The original objective of the Ottoman expedition had been Brindisi. After the capture of Otranto, the Turks launched raids into the territories of Lecce, Brindisi, and Taranto. Eventually, the duke of Calabria, Alfonso joined forces with his father, King Ferrante of Naples, and, with papal support, surrounded the Turks in Otranto. Eventually the Turks withdrew from Italian soil on July 10, 1481; see *PL* 2: 312–45; and *MCT*, 390–96.

to Constantinople and they buried them in the City; they wrote an epigram on top of this tomb: 'Rhodes and Italy: you have been liberated.'"[97] Of course, this attitude represented wishful thinking and not a historical event, as we hear of no such "epigram" on the tomb of Mehmed II recorded in reliable texts and archival material; his surviving *turbe* in Istanbul bears no trace of such an inscription. Yet the sentiments are representative of the westerners at the time. Indeed, for the time being, Rhodes and Italy felt liberated.[98]

The Knights of Saint John had established themselves as the defenders of the faith at the very edge of Christendom. They had been expecting the Turkish assault on their Order as early as 1477. In December 1479 Mesih Pasha had made an appearance with the Turkish fleet before Rhodes and Tilos, as a prelude to the actual siege. The Knights were able to beat the serious Turkish assault off when it finally came and their victory was publicized in the west (by the Knights themselves and by representatives and spokesmen of their Order) as the significant setback for the Turks of the period. However, during the actual siege, the situation was too chaotic to allow the formal drafting of public acts and no archival material was compiled.[99]

Soon after the withdrawal of the Turks from Rhodes, three accounts of the events were published in Europe. They were all by eyewitnesses and participants. While the original account by Mary Dupuis, *Le Siège de Rhodes: La defense de Rhodes contre les Turcs en 1480* (Lyon, 1480/81) seems to be lost, most of the work is still preserved embedded, under the title *Relation de siège de Rhodes en 1480*, in the *Histoire des Chevaliers Hospitaliers de S. Jean de Jerusalem*, vol. 2 (Paris, 1726), 598–616 by Abbé René d'Aubert de Vertot. Dupuis, a soldier in the Auvergne in all likelihood, described the method that he followed in the composition of his opusculum:[100] "... je Mary Dupuis gros et rude de sens et de entendement je veuille parler et descripte au plus brief que je pourray et au plus pres de la verite selon que jeu peu voir a lueil ... Mais seulement en gros le descripts

---

[97] The *Anonymous Barberini Chronicle 111*: Zoras, Ἡ Ἅλωσις, 65; idem, Χρονικόν, 122: Καὶ τὸ κορμὶ τοῦ σουλτάνου τὸ ἠφέρανε εἰς τὴν Κωνσταντινούπολι καὶ τὸ ἐθάψανε πρῶτον εἰς τὴν Πόλι καὶ ἐγράψανε ἐπίγραμμα ἀπάνω εἰς τὸ μνῆμα του καὶ ἔλεγε: "Ρόδο καὶ Ἰντάλια ἐλευτερώθητε". For a translation of and a commentary on this chronicle, see Philippides, *Byzantium, Europe, and the Early Ottoman Sultans*.

[98] On November 29, 1480, the king of France ordered celebrations to be held: "... et en faire feuz de joye, processions solennelles, sonner cloches et chanter loanges à Dieu, acostumées à faire en saincte eglise pour telles grandes et miraculeuse nouvelles." See *Lettres de Louis XI*, ed. Joseph Valsen and Étienne Charavay, vol. 3 (Paris, 1903), 318–19.

[99] As it is pointed out in *PL* 2: 347. The closest to archival material that we possess consists of D'Aubusson's compositions; he himself wrote a *De obsidionis urbis Rhodiae*, which was published in Mainz (1480), in Nuremberg (1480), and in Strasbourg (1480), and his various letters of appeals, as well as descriptions of the operations.

[100] Dupuis (in Vertot), 598. Nothing else is known about this soldier/author. It seems that Dupuis utilized in his composition the printed work of Caoursin; see *PL* 2: 347, n. 3.

selon que je le peu savoir pour en advertin ceulx les quieulx en vouloront savoir des nouvelles, et aussi les quieulx y predront plaisir de loir lire." A second account appeared, by Giacomo de Curti, and was entitled *De urbis Colossensis obsidione anno 1480 a Turcis tentata*; it was printed in Venice in 1480; an Italian translation of this work also appeared under the title *La Citta di Rodi assediata dai Turchi il di 23 maggio 1480*. This Italian text is available, under the title *Relazione*, in E. F. Mizzi, *Le Guerre di Rodi* (Turin, 1934), 68–87.

More popular than the works by either de Curti or Dupuis proved the brisk narrative by another participant in the defense, Guillaume Caoursin, the Vice-Chancellor of the Hospital.[101] After the siege Caoursin was sent as an ambassador to the pope and secured for the Knights immunity from taxation for five years. His reputation, as the author of this account, had preceded him. His original Latin text was published in Venice (1480) and then was reprinted an amazing number of times: in Parma (1480), in Bruges (1480), in Passau (1480), perhaps in Barcelona (1481), in Rome (1482), and in Odense (1482). It was also translated into German and published in Passau (1480/1481) and into Italian and published in Venice (1480). His narrative also attracted a contemporary, not very accurate, translator[102] into English: Edward IV's poet laureate John Kay: *The dylectable newesse and tithyngs of the glorious victorye of the Rhodyans agayenst the Turkes* (Westminster, c. 1490); it was printed by W. Caxton of Sir Thomas Malory fame. It should be pointed out that Caoursin's work is a landmark in the annals of printing, in the sense that his printed text appeared long before his manuscript; while the printed text circulated a few months after the withdrawal of the Turks, his notable manuscript illustrated with exquisite miniatures depicting the operations of the siege and the various councils of the Knights was completed after the publication of the printed pamphlet, an understandable delay since the miniatures could not be executed with a speed that could match that of the printer.[103]

I have followed the edition of Caoursin in the Gennadius Library of Athens, bearing the title *Guglielmi Caorsici* [sic] *Rhodiorum vicecancellarii obsidionis Rhodiae urbis descriptio*. This early printed work states neither place nor year of publication but it is clear that we are facing a copy of the 1480/81 Rome edition.[104] I have divided the text into paragraphs and have modernized the punctuation.

---

[101] Caoursin's career is summarized in G. S. Picenardi, *Itinéraire d'un chevalier de Saint-Jean de Jérusalem dans l'ile de Rhode* (Lille, 1900), 129–30.

[102] See *PL* 2: 347, n. 3.

[103] For some color photographs of the miniatures that accompany the text of Caoursin in various manuscripts, cf. Elias Kollias, *The Knights of Rhodes: The Palace and the City* (Athens, 1988), plates 2, 27, 28, 30, 33, 34, 41, 42, 43, 44, 45, and 46.

[104] The evidence cited in *PL* 2: 346, n. 2: "The copy of this work in the Gennadius Library in Athens contains 18 unnum. fols., with 26 lines per page, whence I assume . . . that it is the edition of Euchar. Silber, published in Rome shortly after the siege."

Nowadays Caoursin's Latin editions are rare and are eagerly sought by bibliophiles. Thus the Venice 1480 edition of his Latin text (bound together with a few other items from the sixteenth and seventeenth centuries) was recently in the market for a price of 25,000 Swiss francs.[105]

Next to Caoursin's detailed and rhetorical account, the most important documents dealing with the siege of Rhodes come from the pen of the Grand Master himself, Pierre d'Aubusson, who soon after the conclusion of the siege and after he had recovered from his wounds wrote several letters to European leaders. His formal letter, the official report of the Order, was dispatched to two individuals, Frederick III and Pope Sixtus IV. While the two reports to emperor and pope contain identical sections dealing with the events of the siege, they display different beginnings and different conclusions. The letter to Frederick III was dictated on September 13 and the letter to the pope on September 15.[106] In addition, a letter of the Grand Master appealing for aid is also published and translated here.[107] As the events covered in d'Aubusson's texts are also covered by Caoursin, no commentary is given in this section;[108] the salient points are sufficiently covered by the notes to the narrative of Caoursin.

---

[105] See Catalogue 549 of Hellmut Schumann entitled *The Orient* (Zurich, *sine anno*), item 64 (13–14).

[106] The letter to the pope has been published in J. P. Ludewig, *Reliquiae manuscriptorum omnis aevi diplomatum ac monumentorum ineditorum adhuc*, vol. 5 (Frankfurt and Leipzig, 1723), 290–99. *PL* 2: 353, n. 22, correctly points out that the editor made a mistake in his title of the piece: *Epistola ad papam . . . missa 1480 die XVIII. Nov.*; the actual date, as it is stated in the conclusion of the letter is, of course, September 15. Ludewig's edition contains numerous errors of transcription (see *PL* 2: 354, n. 23). This letter has been published in S. Pauli, *Codice diplomatico del Sacro militare ordine gerosolimitano, oggi di Malta, raccolto de varj documenti di quell' archivio, per servire alla storia dello steso ordine in Soria in Rodi ed in Malta, et illustrato con una serie chronologica di gran maestri, che lo governarono in quei tempi, con alcune notizie storiche, genealogiche, geographiche, ed altre osservazioni*, 2 vols., (Lucca, 1733–37), 2:149–153, no. CXXVI: *Lettera del G. M. Piero d'Aubusson all'Imperadore d'Occidente, dandogli in quella diligente contezza del tutto l'operato nella difesa di Rodi* (and reprinted in J. Taaffe, *History of the Holy, Military, Sovereign Order of St. John in Jerusalem, or Knights Templars, Knights of Rhodes, Knights of Malta*, 4 vols. [London, 1852], 4: cxv–cxxiii).

[107] Originally published in Pauli, *Codice diplomatico del Sacro militare ordine gerosolimitano*, as no. CXXV, 148, 149: *Lettera del G. M. e Convento di Rodi a tutti i Professori dell'Oriente, narrando loro il terribile ed ostinato assedio, con cui li travagliava Maometto, rimproverando la loro tardanza, e comandando loro l'accorrere quanto prima alla difesa della propria Religione pericolante*.

[108] The additional information in the Grand Master's letter comes at the end of his letter (dated September 15, 1480), when he informs us that he is dispatching the knight Anthony de Monteil (his own brother), the prior of Capua, and the "preceptor" (i.e., commander) D'Aliaga to the pope as his emissaries and bearers of his official dispatch. To do so was apparently decided in a council that took place three days after the Turkish withdrawal, which also decided to investigate the whereabouts of the enemy armada, as is evident in a document in the archives of Malta (Reg. 76, fol. 35ᵛ quoted in *PL* 2: 361, n. 43): "Die XXI Augusti MCCCCLXXX. Fuerunt

In the Appendices I supply the French text of the Tetaldi document for the purposes of comparison with the Latin and its translation into English provided here. I have not translated the French text, as it is readily available in an English translation.[109] However, because Agostino Pertusi, in his collection of contemporary evidence on the fall of Constantinople, provided only a partial Italian translation[110] of the narrative, without the original French text, I decided to include the French version, so that the original texts of the two versions of Tetaldi in the original languages become available for comparison purposes. In addition, I supply the *aman-name* that Zaganos, in the name of Mehmed, granted to Pera, the Genoese suburb of Constantinople, in both the Greek and the Italian versions. It should be recalled that in the Ottoman Empire of the fifteenth and sixteenth centuries, Greek was the accepted diplomatic language of the Porte[111]

---

electi oratores ad S.D.N. et Ec. D. regis Ferdinandi reverendus d. prior Capue et preceptor Daliage ad manifestandum victoriam habitam de Turcis et tractandum de succursu pro vere considerato quod inimicus proponit vere. Fuit deliberatum quod mittatur brigantinus ad sciendum de armata si recessit vel non."

[109] English translation by Melville Jones, *Siege*, 1–10.

[110] CC I: 175–89.

[111] Spyridon P. Lampros, " Ἡ Ἑλληνικὴ ὡς Ἐπίσημος Γλῶσσα τῶν Σουλτάνων," *NH* 5 (1908): 40–79; this article also contains valuable information on the *aman-name* granted by Mehmed II to the Perenses. It is a typical document of the Ottoman Porte and contains formulas that are encountered in other similar texts. The formulaic nature appears in the opening statement: Ὀμνύω εἰς τὸν θεὸν τοῦ οὐρανοῦ καὶ τῆς γῆς καὶ εἰς τὸν μέγαν ἡμῶν προφήτην τὸν Μωάμεθ καὶ εἰς τὰ ἑπτὰ μουσάφια ὅπου ἔχομεν καὶ ὁμολογοῦμεν, καὶ εἰς τοὺς ρκδ´ χιλιάδας προφήτας τοῦ θεοῦ, καὶ πρὸς τὴν ψυχὴν τοῦ πάππου μου καὶ τοῦ πατρός μου, καὶ πρὸς ἑαυτὸν καὶ πρὸς τὰ παιδία μου καὶ εἰς τὸ σπαθὶ ὅπου ζώνομαι, "I [sc. Mehmed II] swear by the God of heaven and earth, by our great prophet Mohammed, by the seven names [books] that we have and confess, by the one hundred and twenty-four thousand prophets of God, by the souls of my grandfather and father, by myself and by my children, and by the sword that I wear." The earlier treaty of Murad II's general, Sinan Pasha, issued to the metropolitan of Ioannina in regard to the city's surrender includes a very similar formula in its text: . . . ὀμνύω σας εἰς τὸν θεὸν τοῦ οὐρανοῦ καὶ τὸν προφήτην Μωάμεθ καὶ εἰς τὰ ἑπτὰ μουσάφια καὶ εἰς τοὺς ρκδ´ προφήτας τοῦ θεοῦ καὶ εἰς τὴν ψυχήν μου καὶ εἰς τὴν κεφαλήν μου καὶ εἰς τὸ σπαθὶ ὅπου ζώνομαι . . . . For a discussion of this treaty and the various editions of its text, see Lampros, " Ἡ Ἑλληνικὴ ὡς Ἐπίσημος Γλῶσσα," 59–65. Again, we encounter similar language and identical phrases in another document of Mehmed II granted to a number of Greek archons on December 26, 1454 (my thanks to Dr. Diana Gilliland Wright for this reference); see F. Miklosich and J. Müller, *Acta et Diplomata Graeca Medii Aevi Sacra et Profana* 3 (Vienna, 1865), 295 (with my corrections on the orthography and accentuation on the original text): καὶ ὀμνέγω [= ὄμνυμι/ὀμνύω] σας εἰς τὸν μέγαν μας προφήτην τὸν Μουάμεθ τὸν πιστεύομεν ἡμεῖς οἱ Μουσουλμάνοι καὶ εἰς τὰ ἑπτὰ μας μουσάφια καὶ εἰς τὰς ρκδ´ χιλιάδας προφήτας μας· καὶ εἰς τὸ σπαθὶ ὁποῦ ζώνομαι· καὶ εἰς τὴν ψυχὴν τοῦ πατρός μου. The same formula seems to have been in the mind of Bishop Leonardo, who gave a summary of the speech that Mehmed II pronounced to his troops at the last stage of the siege of 1453, promising

and the Greek version of this document provides the official text of Mehmed's court. The Italian translation would have been used by the Genoese of Pera. As there is a readily available translation of the Greek document,[112] I did not supply a translation of it into English but only the original texts, which cannot be obtained with the same ease as the translation.

In order to compare the eyewitness documents presented here, which were written for the most part under the emotional stress, depression, or elation of the events that they recount, I also decided to present something of the "official" version of these events, composed at a slightly later time: two extracts, and their first translation into English, on the fall of Constantinople and on the fall of Negroponte, respectively, written in the sixteenth century (and subsequently published in 1611) by the Venetian Pietro Giustiniani (who Latinized his name into Petrus Justinianus). Giustiniani presents, in Latin, a panoramic view of the history of Venice from its humble beginnings to the days after the battle of Lepanto (1571). Giustiniani used typical humanistic precepts to compare the Roman Empire to Venice, and the *Pax Romana* to a *Pax Italica* of the period. His work has been rather neglected by modern historians but it should be remembered that Giustiniani used, and actually quoted verbatim, numerous official documents, as he was also involved in the government of the *Serenissima*.[113] The edition from which[114] I have taken the extracts presented in the Appendix was printed in Germany and dates from 1611; its complete title is *Rerum Venetarum ab Urbe Condita ad Annum M.D.LXXV. Petri Justiniani Patricii Veneti Aloisi filii, Senatorii ordinis viri amplissimi. Ab eodem Autore denuo revisa & rerum memorabilium additione illustrata, cumque indice locupletissimo ornata. Cui haec Accesserunt Opuscula. Nunc primum in Germania typis excusa*, Argentorati [= Strasbourg] *Sumptibus Lazari Zenteri Bibliopolae M.DC.XI*. As with all the other texts, I have divided the extracts from Giustiniani into numbered paragraphs for easier reference.

* * * * *

a three-day sack of Constantinople; at the conclusion of this speech, Leonardo mentions that Mehmed took the following oath, which is strongly reminiscent (with a change in the numbers, perhaps reflecting a misunderstanding on the part of the bishop or a scribal error in the transmission of Leonardo's text), *PG* 159, col. 938 [this passage is not included among the selections offered in CC 1]: "Juratque rex [= Sultan Mehmed II] per Immortalem Deum, perque quatuor millia prophetarum, per Mahometum, per animam patris, per liberos, perque ensem quo cingitur, omnem depopulationem, omneque hominum utriusque sexus genus, omnemque pariter urbis thesaurum atque substantiam, libere bellatoribus donatam."

[112] English translation by Melville Jones, *Siege*, 136–37.

[113] For the few facts known about Giustiniani, see Cochrane, *Historians and Historiography*, 231–34.

[114] My thanks to Dr. Constantine Hatzidimitriou for bringing this work to my attention and for lending me his 1611 edition of this rare publication.

The last two centuries have witnessed an immense increase in our knowledge of the expansion of the Ottoman Turks in the Greco-Byzantine/Frankish Levant, as new or neglected manuscripts and contemporary testimonies have been steadily discovered.[115] Yet our views on this subject have hardly been modified, in spite of the new discoveries and the new sources that have become available to scholarship. And so if one were to read the story of the siege and fall of Constantinople, as it has been told and retold a number of times in the last two hundred years, one would be hard pressed to discover any new insights on this monumental event in the various studies of the event, aside from the literary talents of each author. Thus while Sir Steven Runciman composed a popular account on the siege of 1453 which has remained in print for almost forty years since its first edition, there are severe limitations to his approach[116] and

---

[115] Thus a significant number of important documents saw the light of print for the first time: (i) the eyewitness account of Angelo Giovanni Lomellino, the *podestà* of Pera/Galatas (the Genoese suburb of Constantinople), whose important *epistula* was written on June 2, 1453, while its author still felt the effects of the disaster and was in deep grief: S. de Sacy, "Pièces diplomatiques tirées des Archives de la Republique de Gênes," *Notices et extraits des manuscrits de la Bibliothèque du Roi* 11 (1827): 74–79 [reprinted, without attribution, by Luigi T. Belgrano, "Prima serie di documenti riguardanti la colonia di Pera," *Atti della Società Ligure di Storia Patria* 13 (1877–1884): 229–33]; (ii) Nicolò Barbaro, the Venetian physician, whose valuable diary was edited by Enrico Cornet, *Giornale dell'assedio di Costantinopoli 1453 di Nicolò Barbaro P.V. corredato di note e documenti* (Vienna, 1856); (iii) the section of Zorzi Dolfin's *Chronicle*, evidently copied, to a large extent, from Languschi's work (which will concern us presently); Languschi's opusculum was entitled *Excidio e presa di Costantinopoli nell'anno 1453* [Thomas, "Die Eroberung Constantinopels im Jahre 1453," 1–41]; although it is not mentioned by Thomas, the actual title of Dolfin's work is *Cronaca delle famiglie nobili di Venezia*; (iv) Adamo di Montaldo's *De Constantinopolitano Excidio ad nobilissimum iuvenem Melladucam Cicadam*, edd. Philippe A. Dethier [sic], Cornelio Desimoni, and Carl Hopf, "Della conquista di Costantinopoli per Maometto II," 289–354; (iv) the Greek text of Kritoboulos edited by C. Müller in *Fragmenta Historicorum Graecorum* 5 (Paris, 1883); and (v) Nestor-Iskander, Повѣсть о Царьградѣ first edited by Izmail I. Sreznevskii (St. Petersburg, 1855) and later by the Archimandrite Leonid, Повѣсть о Царьградѣ (его оснований и взятіи Турками в 1453 году) Нестора-Искандера XV Вѣка, in Памятники древней письменности и Искусства 11 (St. Petersburg, 1888). The most recent edition is *The Tale of Constantinople by Nestor-Iskander (of its Origin and Capture in the Year 1453)*, ed. and trans. Walter K. Hanak and Marios Philippides, Late Byzantine and Ottoman Studies 5 (New Rochelle, 1998). See Marios Philippides, "A 'New' Eyewitness Source and the Prosopography of the Defenders in the Siege of Constantinople (1453)," and Walter K. Hanak, "One Source, Two Renditions: *The Tale of Constantinople amd Its Fall in 1453*," in *Twenty-Eighth Byzantine Studies Conference, Abstracts* (Columbus, 2002), 90–91.

[116] The book is, of course, *FC*. Runciman complicated his narrative by using "forged" sources as his main guide; thus, even though he was aware of the unreliability of Pseudo-Sphrantzes (i.e., the sixteenth-century elaborator of the *Chronicon Minus* into the *Maius*, Makarios Melissenos/Melissourgos), he still followed the elaborator's narrative closely (but admitted his own "mixed"

his narrative does not differ in outlook and interpretation substantially from the earlier studies of numerous worthy predecessors, such as Mordtmann,[117]

---

feelings about the authenticity of this narrative), producing confusing statements; cf., e.g., 193: "Modern research has shownthat almost certainly the *Majus* was compiled in the following century by a certain Macarius Melissenus. The account of the siege is, however, contained in the original version." This statement amounts to a contradiction, as Sphrantzes never composed a siege section that can be identified with any degree of certainty. Research on the sixteenth-century forgery that turned Sphrantzes' authentic work, the *Chronicon Minus*, into the celebrated but inauthentic *Chronicon Maius* through the hand of Makarios Melissourgos-Melissenos has achieved Homeric proportions. On scholarly efforts to find a way through a labyrinth of primary, forged, and elaborated sources, see, among others, Jean B. Falier-Papadopoulos, "Phrantzès est-il réellement l'auteur de la grande chronique qui porte son nom?," in *Actes du IVe Congrès international des études byzantines, Bulletin de l'Institut Archéologique Bulgare* 19 (1935): 177–89. Franz Dölger, "Ein literarischer und diplomatischer Fälscher des 16. Jahrhunderts: Metropolit Makarios von Monembasia," in *Otto Glaunig zum 60. Geburtstag, Festangabe aus Wissenschaft und Bibliothek* (Leipzig, 1936), 25–36, and repr. in idem, *Byzantinische Diplomatik: 20 Aufsätze zum Urkundenwesen der Byzantiner* (Ettal, 1956), 371–83; Raymond-Joseph Loenertz, "Autour du Chronicon Maius attribué à Georges Phrantzès," in *Miscellanea G. Mercati*, Studi e Testi 123 (Vatican City, 1946), 273–311; Nikolaos B. Tomadakis, Περὶ Ἁλώσεως τῆς Κωνσταντινουπόλεως *(1453)* (Athens, 1953; repr. 1993), 137–66; Vasile Grecu, "Das Memoirenwerk des Georgios Sphrantzes," *Actes du XIIe Congrès international d'études byzantines* 1 (Belgrade, 1963): 327–41; idem, "Georgios Sphrantzes. Leben und Werk. Makarios Melissenos und sein Werk. Die Ausgaben," *BS* 26 (1965): 62–73; Ioannes K. Khasiotes, Μακάριος, Θεόδωρος καὶ Νικηφόρος οἱ Μελισσηνοὶ (Μελισσουργοί) (16ος-17ος αἰ.) (Thessalonica, 1966); Marios Philippides, "The Fall of Constantinople: Bishop Leonard and the Greek Accounts," *Greek, Roman and Byzantine Studies* 22 (1981): 287–300; idem, "Σύγχρονες Ἔρευνες στὰ Κείμενα τοῦ Σφραντζῆ," Παρνασσός 25 (1983): 94–99; idem, "An 'Unknown' Source for Book III of the *Chronicon Maius* by Pseudo-Sphrantzes," *BSEB* 10 (1983): 174–83; idem, "Patriarchal Chronicles of the Sixteenth Century," *Greek, Roman and Byzantine Studies* 25 (1984): 87–94; E. D. Dzhagatspanian, "Мировозрение Византийского Историка XV в. Георгия Сфрандзи," *Кавказ и Византия* 3 (1982): 45–63. In addition, see now R. Maisano, "Il manoscritto Napoletano II. E. 25 e la storia della tradizione dello pseudo-Sfranze," ʹΙταλοελληνικά: *Rivista di cultura greco-moderna* 2 (1989): 103–21; Thierry Ganchou, "Le Mésazon Démétrius Paléologue Cantacuzène a-t-il figuré parmi les Défenseurs du Siège de Constantinople (29 Mai 1453)?," *REB* 52 (1994): 245–72, esp. 245–58; and idem, "Sur quelques Erreurs relatives aux derniers Défenseurs grecs de Constantinople en 1453," Θησαυρίσματα: Περιοδικὸν τοῦ Ἑλληνικοῦ Ἰνστιτούτου Βυζαντινῶν καὶ Μεταβυζαντινῶν Σπουδῶν τῆς Βενετίας 25 (1995): 61–82.

[117] Andreas D. Mordtmann, *Belagerung und Eroberung Constantinopels durch die Türken im Jahre 1453 nach den Originalquellen bearbeitet* (Stuttgart and Augsburg, 1858). Mordtmann made good use of his familiarity with the Constantinopolitan topography; thus his study on the siege and fall was immensely enhanced by his vast knowledge of the remains and by his intelligent use of the terrain, even though his account ultimately suffers from the lack of original sources, which, at that time, still awaited discovery and publication.

Paspates,[118] Pears,[119] or Schlumberger.[120] The same observations apply to the book of D. Stacton/Dereksen,[121] who does not possess Runciman's familiarity with the sources, which he could not, and did not, read in the original languages but had to rely on the few available, albeit inaccurate and flawed, translations in existence. The only modern account that is aware of most of the available sources, and not of all by any means, remains that of Setton.[122] These modern accounts may differ in details, and in the literary talent that each author possesses, but they can hardly be said to offer new insights and new interpretations. Scholarship is always careful to move slowly in modifying transmitted pictures. As small changes, in the form of additions and corrections, accumulate, in time new syntheses become imperative. I would go so far as to submit that our basic conception of the siege, fall, and sack is still based on the interpretation that the nineteenth century placed on that monumental event.

The nineteenth-century investigators, researchers, and historians in general, one is reminded, were in many ways motivated by concerns that differ considerably from those of modern scholarship. Thus the scholars of that time could

---

[118] Paspates, Πολιορκία καὶ Ἅλωσις. In addition, Paspates effectively utilized his considerable topographical knowledge in the composition of a seminal study (which admittedly remains useful): Βυζαντιναὶ Μελέται Τοπογραφικαὶ καὶ Ἱστορικαὶ (Constantinople, 1874; repr. as Βιβλιοθήκη Ἱστορικῶν Μελετῶν 208, Athens, 1986). The scholarly community soon realized the value of topographical studies, as it already had done in the case of classical studies, and important investigations were soon carried out; one of the most popular accounts to appear in English was Alexander Van Millingen, *Byzantine Constantinople: The Walls of the City and Adjoining Historical Sites* (London, 1899).

[119] Pears, *The Destruction of the Greek Empire*.

[120] Gustave Schlumberger, *Le siège, la prise et le sac de Constantinople par les Turcs en 1453* (Paris, 1914) [= Ἅλωσις τῆς Κωνσταντινουπόλεως, trans. E. G. Protopsaltes (Athens, *sine anno*); and Κωνσταντῖνος Παλαιολόγος καὶ ἡ Πολιορκία καὶ Ἅλωσις τῆς Κωνσταντινουπόλεως ὑπὸ τῶν Τούρκων τῷ 1453, trans. Spyridon P. Lampros (Athens, 1914; repr. Thessalonica, 1991)]. The translation by Lampros is far superior to the one by Protopsaltes, both in terms of style and in terms of scholarship; in fact, Lampros tacitly corrected the various mistakes of Schlumberger and enriched the text with informative notes. Thus the Lampros translation is more valuable than the original work, which, at any rate, was heavily dependent on Pears, *The Destruction of the Greek Empire*.

[121] David Stacton, *The World on the Last Day. The Sack of Constantinople by the Turks on May 29, 1453: Its Causes and Consequences* (London, 1965); the same book was published in the United States under the pseudonym David Dereksen with the title *The Crescent and the Cross: The Fall of Byzantium, May 29, 1453* (New York, 1964). While the literary merits of Stacton's narrative are inferior to *FC*, his comments in regard to the military situation in 1453 are superior.

[122] *PL* 2: 108–38. The text of Setton, fortified by extremely valuable notes on primary sources (generally absent in most other modern accounts), make his thirty pages more valuable than most of the previous, massive analyses of the siege of 1453.

not break free from the bonds their own period had placed upon them. It was an era characterized by nationalistic ideas and sweeping generalizations, as the "new" nations in southeastern Europe, free at last from the Ottoman yoke, were struggling to survive and were desperate to discover and isolate, in the events of the past, historical precedents to justify and sanction their newly-found liberty. In addition, western European scholars still viewed Ottoman Turkey as "the sick man" of Europe. Furthermore, under the immense influence of Edward Gibbon, the Greco-Byzantine civilization of the Middle Ages was largely seen as a monolithic, theocratic state that showed some sparks of heroism in its final chapters, only when the inevitable decline to the Ottoman Turks came.[123] With such background, the "causation" of the fall was focused on the "degenerate" character of the Greeks who refused to fight against the Ottoman aggressor. At the same time, the triumphal victory of the Turks over Constantinople was attributed to advances in western technology imported to the Turkish army, such as the artillery and the enormous bombards of Mehmed II Fatih, that supposedly leveled the ancient fortifications of Constantinople and thus delivered the city to him.

I believe that the time has come to discard or radically to modify such simplistic views; scholarship is obligated to produce a new, authoritative analysis of such events that may produce a surprisingly fresh synthesis. While this is not the proper place to argue on behalf of such an approach, the texts presented in this volume would militate in its favor. For instance, even a cursory reading of our texts shows that the supposed ace of Mehmed II, i.e., his bombards operated by gunpowder, was a failure. The bombards, in fact, achieved very little in

---

[123] See Philippides, "The Fall of Constantinople 1453: Bishop Leonardo and his Italian Followers," esp. 189–92, with the accompanying notes. Pears, *The Destruction of the Greek Empire*, xiii and xiv, lists all the primary sources that had been recovered since the days of Gibbon: Languschi-Dolfin, the letter of Lomellino (which had wrongly been attributed, by the time Pears wrote his book, to "Ang. Johannis Zaccharia"), Adamo di Montaldo, Riccherio, the account of Nestor-Iskander, etc. A similar list had appeared earlier in Paspates, Πολιορκία καὶ Ἅλωσις, 21–32 (and was, in fact, more inclusive than Pears', as Paspates listed all the sources that had been available to him and not only those that were unknown to Gibbon or those that Gibbon had failed to use in spite of the fact that they were available to him). It should be recalled, nevertheless, that Gibbon's century had witnessed the discovery and subsequent publication of some of our precious sources on the siege of 1453 such as Tetaldi's French version. Gibbon did not know of either the Latin or the French version of Tetaldi's work. Some sources were published in the eighteenth and nineteenth centuries and in both cases the resulting editions were inferior; thus the eyewitness poet of the siege, Ubertino Pusculo, wrote an important work entitled *Constantinopolis libri IV*; this work was edited by G. Bergantini, *Miscellanea di varie operette*, vol. 1 (Venice, 1740); this edition utilized only one manuscript of Pusculo's poem, available in the Biblioteca Marciana of Venice, even though another four manuscripts were known to exist. The same Latin text was reprinted in A. S. Ellissen, *Analekten der mittel- und neugriechischen Literatur* 3.3: *Anecdota Graecobarbara* (Leipzig, 1857), 12–83. To this day there has appeared no complete, critical edition of this important work.

the siege of 1453,[124] played little part in the siege of Negroponte, and failed miserably in the siege of Rhodes. The Ottoman victory in 1453 must be attributed to other factors. The Ottoman bombards were too cumbersome, could not be aimed effectively, and failed to reduce the mighty fortifications of Constantinople to rubble. One should recall in this connection that the art of effectively deploying artillery pieces was still in its infancy and that the bombards of the *quattrocento* were used as battering rams or as stone-throwing catapults. The science of ballistics was still far in the future. The effect of the bombards was only psychological and was felt more by the non-combatants than by the professionals who must have observed, at least in the course of the siege, the strategic and tactical limitations of the Ottoman artillery. The immediate cause of the fall of Constantinople in 1453 consisted of the withdrawal of Giustiniani and his disciplined band of *condottieri* and of the ensuing panic among the rest of the defenders. The Turks did not breach the walls; the ancient fortifications were essentially abandoned by their defenders in the vicinity of the Gate of Saint Romanus. Consequently, this critical sector in the defense was overrun by the enemy troops.

Similarly, the fall of Negroponte can be reasonably attributed to the failure of the Venetian commander to provide effective aid to the besieged who probably perished more in bewilderment, in view of their fleet simply standing by and idly watching the conflict. Immensely more important, more significant, and more effective to operations during any siege in the Levant of the *quattrocento* were the activities of "renegades," spies, potential traitors, and the existence of fifth columns within cities under siege. This specific aspect of warfare has not been exhaustively investigated by modern scholarship and deserves a fresh look. Given the indisputable role played by such individuals as Halil, the grand vizier of Mehmed II's Porte, or of Loukas Notaras, the "prime minister" of the imperial administration of Constantine XI Dragaš Palaeologus in Constantinople, during the siege of 1453, of Tommaso Schiavo and of Luca da Curzola and of their cohorts in Negroponte, of Meister Georg and of Meligalos and of Sophianos in Rhodes, I believe that a modern investigation into the importance of intelligence and counter-intelligence operations in siege warfare of the period will produce rewarding results.

There is another oversight in the various investigations about this period, as I have pointed out elsewhere:[125] the compilation of the prosopography of the participants in the siege and sack of Constantinople has become imperative. There

---

[124] See Marios Philippides, "Urban's Bombard(s), Gunpowder, and the Siege of Constantinople (1453)," *BSEB* n.s. 4 (1999 [= 2002]): 1–67.

[125] See the concluding remarks in Marios Philippides, "Giovanni Guglielmo Longo Giustiniani, the Genoese *Condottiere* of Constantinople in 1453," *BSEB* n.s. 9 (1998 [= 2000]), 13–59, esp. 53.

has never been any systematic study of defenders, attackers, and survivors.[126] Such a project could provide us with a solid background to carry out an authoritative military study of the operations in 1453. A solid prosopography based on reliable texts and on archival material must be compiled before the definitive history of that important event of the *quattrocento* can be completed.

All this of course provides a fascinating field for further investigation, re-evaluation, and research. For the time being, I present these texts and their first translation into English (with modest commentary) in the hope that they will be of some assistance in our attempts to understand and re-evaluate the events of the past that transformed the Greco-Byzantine/Frankish civilization of southeastern Europe into the Ottoman Levant.

---

[126] Recent attempts at compiling information on individual participants include G. Olgiati, "Angelo Giovanni Lomellino: Attività politica e mercantile dell'ultimo podestà di Pera," *Storia dei Genovesi* 9 (1989): 139–96; Marios Philippides, "Some Prosopographical Considerations in Nestor-Iskander's Text," *Macedonian Studies* 6 (1989): 35–50; Ganchou, "Le Mésazon"; and idem, "Sur quelques Erreurs." A thorough compilation is provided in Philippides and Hanak, *The Pen and the Sword*, ch. 10.

CHAPTER II

**AN EPITOME ON THE FAMILY OF THE OTTOMANS
FOR AENEAS, THE BISHOP OF SIENA
BY NIKOLAOS SEKOUNDINOS**

NICOLAI SECUNDINI
DE FAMILIA OTTHOMANORUM EPITOME
AD AENEAM SENARUM EPISCOPUM

I.   Turcarum gens ab annis sexcentis et supra, a Scythicis (qui trans Tanaim Asiam versus, nulla stabili sede, nullis urbibus, nullis certis aut perpetuis domiciliis, campos patentes vage passimque incolere soliti sunt) originem traxit, et veluti rivulus quidam e fonte inde emana<vi>sse videtur. Huic argumento esse potest, quod primo per Pontum et Cappadociam transgressi ad reliquas inde finitimas partes sensim illapsi sunt. Accedit vit<a>e morumque similitudo, habitus cultusque corporis, equitandi sagittandique ratio, et omnino rei militaris communis quaedam et patria disciplina, et quod sine ulla dubitatione cuique probari possit, linguae ipsius ac usus loquendi cognatio. Hi parva manu primo latronum more, clandestinis quibusdam excursionibus, vires sibi vendicare conati, confluente subinde, ut sit, huiuscemodi generis hominum multitudine, occupatis opportunis quibusdam montibus claustrisque, unde per occasionem facile irruptiones fieri possent, usque adeo emerserunt, ac sublati sunt animis, ut palam tam, ac pari Marte adversus finitimos de agrorum possessionibus certare non vererentur.

II.   Denique // procedente tempore, sive negligentia Graecorum, quorum de re agebatur, sive fatali quadam necessitate ac rerum humanarum var<i>etate, sive permissu Deorum iam aliter de huiusmodi imperio prae<t>eribentium, ita celeri succrevere cursu ut opinione omnium citius, non modo Pontum et Cappadociam, verum etiam Galatiam, B<i>th<y>niam, Pamphyliam, Persiam utramque Phrygiam, Cilices, Cares, et eam Asiam quae Minor vocatur, ad oras usque Ioniae et littora Graeci nuncupati maris occupa<ve>rint et in suam

AN EPITOME ON THE FAMILY OF THE OTTOMANS FOR AENEAS, THE BISHOP OF SIENA BY NIKOLAOS SEKOUNDINOS

1.   Six hundred years ago and more the nation of the Turks originated from the Scythians [= Mongols], who had been accustomed to live across the Don, everywhere in Asia, in no specific capital, no cities, and no firm or long-term homes but wandered over the open fields; like a stream flowing from its spring, it seems to have spread. To illustrate the point, they first moved through the Pontus and Cappadocia and gradually infiltrated the other neighboring parts. In addition, the same point is argued by the similarity of [style of] life, customs, clothing, care of the body, way of riding horses and of using the bow, the identical way of waging war, their native discipline, and the greatest proof of all: the related languages and manner of speaking. At first they were a small band and operated like robbers, going on clandestine forays and trying to flex their muscles; they flocked together, as it were, and they occupied appropriate mountains and gorges, from which they could easily make sorties and, with inflated courage, they then waged war openly and were no longer afraid to compete with their immediate neighbors about the possession of fields.[1]

2.   Finally, with the passage of time, because the Greeks were careless about this matter, because Fate and the uncertainty of human affairs decreed it necessary, or because the Gods chose to command it otherwise, they succeeded with such amazing speed (in the opinion of all) that they occupied and subjugated not only the Pontus and Cappadocia but also Galatia, Bithynia, Pamphylia, Persia, farther Phrygia, the Cilicians, the Carians and that [part of] Asia that is known as Minor, all the way to the shores of Ionia and the coast of the

---

[1] For the rise of the Ottoman Turks and their early successes, see among others, Paul Wittek, *The Rise of the Ottoman Empire* (London, 1938); Ernst Werner, *Die Geburt einer Grossmacht — Die Osmanen (1300 bis 1481). Ein Beitrag zur Genesis des türkischen Feudalismus*, Forschungen zur mittelalterlichen Geschichte 13 (Berlin, 1966); Georgios Georgiades Arnakis, Οἱ Πρῶτοι Ὀθωμανοί, Texte und Forschungen zur byzantinischen-neugriechischen Philologie 41 (Athens, 1947); Speros Vryonis, *The Decline of Medieval Hellenism in Asia Minor and the Process of Islamization from the Eleventh through the Fifteenth Century* (Berkeley and Los Angeles, 1971); Norman Itzkowitz, *Ottoman Empire and Islamic Tradition* (Chicago, 1972); Halil Inalcik, *The Ottoman Empire: The Classical Age, 1300–1600* (New York, 1973); Stanford J. Shaw, *History of the Ottoman Empire and Modern Turkey*, vol. 1: *Empire of the Gazis: The Rise and Fall of the Ottoman Empire, 1280–1808* (Cambridge, 1976); and Rudi P. Lindner, *Nomads and Ottomans in Medieval Anatolia* (Bloomington, 1983). For a new, challenging interpretation on the rise of the Ottomans, see Heath W. Lowry, *The Nature of the Early Ottoman State* (Albany, 2003).

potestatem redegerint. Nec unum quendam principem sed alios alii duces et varia auspicia quasi per factiones secuti.

III.   Ex hac itaque gente quinquagesimum ab hinc et centesimum circiter annum, Otthomanus quidam exigui tantum census et obscuri inter privatos nominis, ex collecticio quodam et gregario milite, non ingenti manu propter seditionem conflata, grassari passim et quo vastare posset, praedabundus invadere, neque reliquos Christianos solum vexare atque prosternere, verum etiam homines ipsos suae gentis sine ullo discrimine armis infestis petere et qua daretur populari, et sibi subdere occepit. Iam enim Turcorum ipsi duces ac principes dominandi cupiditate et plura habendi libidine commoti, sese invicem infestare coeperunt et eo usque superandi studio ac vires hostiliter exercendi promoti sunt ut bellum domesticum intestinumque omnibus viribus gerere viderentur. Hanc Otthomanus ille nactus occa//sionem, quae moribus utique et libidini suae congrueret, ac idoneam videretur posse suppeditare materiam, ascitis undique omnibus, qui pro ingenio praedae rapinarumque percupidi essent, qui ve studio quovis opprimendi spoliandique flagrarent, au<ct>oritatem brevi adeptus est. Oppida quaedam per opportunitatem aggressus alia vi cepit, alia deditione subegit, nonnulla (ut metum incuteret) diripuit atque evertit, ut hinc futuri incrementi non admodum aspernanda iecisse videretur fundamenta.

sea named "Greek." They did not follow any one leader but there were various groups under numerous lords and commands, divided into factions.²

3. And so about one hundred and fifty years later a certain Osman of this tribe, born to a modest and undistinguished family, hastily assembled private soldiers and with this small band, brought together through sedition, he was able to move about widely and launch plundering and devastating raids at will; he indiscriminately harassed and ruined both Christians and members of his own tribe [Moslems] in war, spread destruction wherever he could, and began his annexations. Then the lords and princes of the Turks became upset by his desire to dominate and his passion to acquire riches and gradually turned against him; driven by their eagerness to prevail they stirred up so much trouble that they seemed prepared to enter upon an internal conflict and a civil war with all their might. Osman took advantage of this opportunity (which suited his customs and his desires), provided the suitable means, and, with the general approval of all those eager by nature to plunder and pillage and of those whose passion was to amass booty and spoils, he assumed power in a brief span of time. Some towns he seized by luck and others by force; some surrendered to him; quite a few he devastated and wiped out in order to create terror; thus he laid the foundations of a state that would grow and be envied in the future.³

---

² For the methods and tactics of the gazis, see Halil Inalcik, "Ottoman Methods of Conquest," *Studia Islamica* 2 (1954): 103–29; Peter Charanis, "The Strife among the Palaeologi and the Ottoman Turks 1370–1402," *Byz* 16 (1942/1943): 286–314; Herbert A. Gibbons, *The Foundation of the Ottoman Empire. A History of the Osmanlis up to the Death of Bayezid I, 1300–1403* (New York, 1916); and Franz Taeschner, "The Ottoman Turks to 1453," in *The Cambridge Medieval History*, 4: 753–75.

³ Osman's life became part of a potent legend and few historical facts can be salvaged. His reign was indeed accented by the rapid acquisition of land at the expense of the old empire of the Greeks. What seems certain is that he defeated the Greeks in the battle of Baphaion in 1302 and that he made the Greek city of Prousa his capital on April 6, 1326. Osman (d. 1326) became known as *Gazı*, because of the holy wars that he waged against the infidels, the Greek population of Asia Minor; the traditional view of the *gazı* ethos is now being reviewed by scholars and less emphasis is placed on it. See the views of Colin Heywood, *Writing Ottoman History: Documents and Interpretations. Collected Studies* (Aldershot, 2002). For the few details that we possess, see the literature cited above, n. 1, as well as the following older works: Joseph von Hammer-Purgstall, *Geschichte des osmanischen Reiches*, 10 vols. (Pest, 1827–1835); Johann W. Zinkeisen, *Geschichte des osmanischen Reiches in Europa*, 7 vols. (Gotha, 1908–1913); Paul Wittek, *Das Fürstentum Mentesche: Studien zur Geschichte Westkleinasiens im 13.–15. Jh.* (Istanbul, 1934); Mehmed F. Köprülü, *Les origines de l'empire ottoman* (Paris, 1934); and Halil Inalcik, "The Question of the Emergence of the Ottoman State," *International Journal of Turkish Studies* 2 (1980): 71–79. In addition, see the various publications of Halil Inalcik assembled in idem, *Collected Studies I: The Ottoman Empire: Conquest, Organisation, and Economy* (London, 1978), and in idem, *Collected Studies II: Studies in Ottoman Social and Economic History* (London, 1985); and Colin Imber, *The Ottoman Empire, 1300–1481* (Istanbul, 1990). Also, cf. *LCB*, chap. 9, 141–47.

IV. Et cum vita discessisset, Orchanes successit filius, qui ambitione et audacia patri non erat absimilis, ceterum rei militaris a disciplina longe peritior, copiis apparatuque opulentior et instructior; nam liberalitate animi, facilitate morum, dexteritate quadam ingenii, felicitate bene probeque imperandi, commoditatis opinione ingentem sibi undique multitudinem comparavit, quorum animos semel ad sequendum allectos atque conciliatos, populari deinceps facilitate quadam, comitate, consuetudine atque largitionibus mirum in modum in officio retinebat. Quo factum est, ut rem inchoatam a patre su<a> apt<a> ipse industria, diligentia, studio, cura, prudentia, commode prosecutus auxerit et longe evexerit ac propaga<ve>rit.

V. Eum mortuum Amurates filius secutus est, vir sane robore animi, laborum tolerantia, disciplina rei militaris, industria, et ambitione superioribus haud inferior. Porro vafritie quadam et caliditate longe superior; quippe qui simulandi // dissimulandique egregius esset artifex et fallendi magister. Forte ea tempestate inter Graecos ingens erat orta dissensio et intestinae acriter agitabantur discordiae. Duo enim fuere qui tametsi diversis au<c>toribus procreati ortique essent uterque tamen ea stirpe se natum asserebat, ut ad se ius imperii spectare et sibi competere affirmaret. Horum utru<m>que ceteri pro suo quisque studio et amore secuti pugnaciter dimicabantium alter quod se victum superatumque; iri arbitraretur, temeritati et studio suo obsecutus (adeo enim ulciscendi libidine caecus in praeceps, transversusque visus est agitari ut honeste ne et ex re sua an secus id faceret minime cogitaret) Amuratem ad partes suas tutandas pretio pollicitationeque facile illectum ex Asia arcessivit. Neque enim magni fuit negotii et persuadere, qui sponte sua ad hoc pronior iam diu inhiaret totoque pectore propenderet. Hunc itaque et copias eius mature in Thraciam per Hellespontum traduxit ea conditione, ut, consummato perfectoque bello, navigio rursus domum per Hellespontum reverteretur. Hoc pacto Turcarum gens Amurate principe Graecorum ductu et opera in Thraciam ex Asia cum armis traiecit. Sed quid sibi posset conducere, animo voluere, sagaciterque longe prospicere, consulto bellum protrahere, et in dies causando differe et procrastinare coepit, ratus hinc fore, ut Graecorum viribus diuturnitate belli et discordiarum

4. After he died, he was succeeded by his son Orhan who shared his father's ambitions and audacity but clearly surpassed him in waging war; he had more troops and made better preparations. His innate generosity, easy-going traits, flexible cleverness, ability to govern easily and well, and ability in speaking won him many followers from everywhere, who became ready to follow him; furthermore, he was eager to go on plundering expeditions and he governed admirably with friendliness, in accordance with custom, and with generosity. And so his appropriate actions enlarged, augmented, and extended his patrimony through diligence, zeal, and attentiveness. So it was done and he conveniently pursued, augmented, and extended the course indicated by his father with his own energy, enthusiasm, care, and good sense.[4]

5. His son, Murad [I], succeeded him after he died; he was a spirited man, who tolerated hard work, a good soldier, and an energetic individual; he matched his predecessors in ambition but clearly surpassed them in subtlety and cleverness; he was a specialist in pretense and masking and a master of deception. It so happened that at that time the Greeks faced extensive strife and civil war was widespread. Two men, put forth by various supporters, vied for the empire, and each man asserted that his lineage justly entitled him to be the emperor and to ascend the throne. Each one fought strongly in the pursuit of his goal and desire in his efforts to prevail and bring about the defeat of the other. One was ruled blindly by such passion to avenge himself that he even seemed to be moved back and forth so much that he could do nothing unless it advanced his cause; desire and rashness, it is thought, compelled him to summon Murad from Asia to his regions, whom he easily attracted with money and promises. It was not much of a challenge to persuade him because he had been rather inclined to do so himself willingly and he had been casting covetous eyes. So in time he brought him and his army to Thrace across the Hellespont under this condition: once the war would be completed and brought to an end he would sail back to his home via the Hellespont. Under this treaty, with the guidance and the assistance of the Greeks, the Turks took up arms and followed their lord Murad from Asia to Thrace. This contract was what he really desired and he carefully planned for the future by extending the war and began to postpone matters and to procrastinate, as he reckoned that the daily action and cruelty of war would weaken the

---

[4] Orhan minted the first Ottoman silver coins in Prousa (1327); defeated a Greek army in the battle of Pelekanon, once thought to have occurred in 1333 but now securely dated to 1329; and married Theodora, the daughter of the Greek emperor, John VI Kantakouzenos: see *LCB*, 167–69. For the early coinage of the Turks, see Halil Inalcik, "Bursa and the Commerce of the Levant," *Journal of Social and Economic History of the Orient* 3 (1960): 131–42. Orhan's most notable achievement was the extension of the Ottoman state into Europe, as he was the first Turkish emir to cross the straits and acquire a base on European soil, the Greek city of Kallipolis/Gallipoli/Gelibolu; he occupied this city on March 2, 1354, and thus he initiated the Turkish conquest of the Balkans. Also see Inalcik, *The Ottoman Empire*, 231–46.

atrocitate utrinque consumptis enervatisque ipse integer fractos iam // et defessos illos adortus facile opprimere. Ubi igitur diuturno bello mutuisque contentionibus deficere Graecos animadvertit, domesticis denique opibus penitus iam exhaustis nutare et sibi parum subsistere sensit, extemplo versis, ut aiunt, proris, arma in eos sine ullo discrimine per occasionem convertit. Occupato autem Calliopoli oppido, peropportune in Chersoneso ad Hellespontum fretum sita, cetera Graeca oppida armis infestis petere, agros vastare, praedam agere, cuncta passim invadere, nec iam amplius dissimulanter rem gerere sed palam sibi et posteris Graecorum imperium polliceri, et ad occupandum omnes cogitationes, consilia, opes et nervos intendere. Hinc effectum est, ut nullis ferme obsistere audentibus, facile et sine ullo negotio magnam Thraci<a>e partem ditioni suae subiecerit. Is vita defunctus duos reliquit filios ad capessendam rerum administrationem patriaeque expeditionis reliquias ex<s>equendas, tum aetate tum disciplina et ingenio peridoneos, quorum alteri Solmanus, alteri Baiazetes nomen erat.

Greeks; once their strength and spirit were down, he himself would rise up with all his forces and he would easily overcome the broken and exhausted men. When he observed that the Greeks were weakening because of the daily war and civil strife, that their resources had been wasted, and that they had reached their breaking point, he immediately reversed course, as the saying goes, and initiated hostile action against both sides, as the opportunity offered itself. He then seized the town of Kallipolis which occupies a strategic location in the Chersonese by the straits of the Hellespont, launched attacks upon other Greek towns, devastated the countryside, amassed booty, and invaded the entire territory; he abandoned all pretenses, publicly promised that the empire of the Greeks would become his property and that of his descendants, and turned all thought, plans, resources, and efforts to its conquest. As no one dared to offer any serious resistance, he easily and effortlessly subjugated and brought under his control a great part of Thrace.[5] When he died, he left behind two sons to seize the government of the state and to complete the expedition that he had initiated; their age and innate talent recommended them to the task: one was called Suleyman[6] and the other Bayezid.

---

[5] Sekoundinos is correct in his assessment of the effects of the civil wars in medieval Greece, which, as he noted, assisted the Turks immensely in their task of occupying Thrace in this early period. For the civil strife in fourteenth-century Greece, see among others, *LCB*, chaps. 14 and 15; Peter Charanis, "Internal Strife in Byzantium during the Fourteenth Century," *Byz* 15 (1940/1941): 208–30; and Raymond-Joseph Loenertz, "La première insurrection d'Andronic Paléologue," *EdO* 38 (1939): 342–45. Sekoundinos has failed to mention a number of important events in the reign of Murad I; his early reign was marked by expansion into Thrace and by conquests in Anatolia. He seized Philippopolis/Plovdiv/Filibe in 1363 and in the following year defeated the combined forces of Serbia and Hungary in the battle of Maritza. After the death of the Bulgarian tsar Alexander (1365) he availed himself of the confusion to seize effective control of Sofia and eventually reduced the tsar to the status of a vassal (1377). He conquered Serres, Drama, and Kavalla, and even seized Thessalonica in Greek Macedonia (1371–1375). Murad I was assassinated by a Serb immediately after the Ottoman victory over the Serbs at the battle of Kossovo. For this last campaign of Murad against Serbia's Lazar, Tvrtko (the prince of Bosnia), and Vuk Branković (the lord of Kossovo), see Harold W. V. Temperley, *History of Serbia* (London, 1917), 100 ff.; Gibbons, *The Foundation of the Ottoman Empire*, 173 ff.; C. Jireček, *Geschichte der Serben* (Gottha, 1911–1918), 2: 119 ff.; M. Braun, *Kossovo. Die Schlacht auf dem Amsefelde in geschichtlichen und epischen Überlieferung* (Leipzig, 1937); and *LCB*, 300. A fragmentary but accessible *vita* of Murad I is included in the Barberini Chronicle III; for English translation and commentary, see Philippides, *Byzantium, Europe, and the Early Ottoman Sultans*, 19–23. For evaluations of Murad I's reign, cf. Shaw, *History of the Ottoman Empire*, 17 ff., and *LCB*, 301 ff. In addition, see now Stephen W. Reinert, "From Niš to Kosovo Polje. Reflections on Murad I's Final Years," in *The Ottoman Emirate (1300–1389). Halcyon Days in Crete I: A Symposium Held in Rethymnon 11–13 January 1991*, ed. Elizabeth Zachariadou (Rethymnon, 1993), 169–211.

[6] This is an error; Bayezid's brother was called Yakub. His execution was one of the first orders issued by Bayezid after he ascended the throne. This execution initiated the well-known practice of imperial fratricide in the Ottoman dynasty, which was not given legal sanction, however, until the reign of Mehmed II (when it was justified by a statement in the Koran [Sura IV, 94] stating that assassination is preferable to sedition).

VI.   At Solmano extincto res universa ad Baiazetem venit, qui procaci fuit ingenio et rerum maximarum percupidus, in rebus arduis capessendis audax, in adversis solers, in laboribus perferendis infatigabilis, in occasionibus prospiciendis acutus et sagax, in ex<s>equendis celer, animo fortis, corpore strenuus, belli appetens, quietis impatiens, glori<a>e avidus, in periculis obeundis promptus, in hostibus fallendis mire // versutus. Is dolis instruendis et hoste insidiis opprimendo percallidus; contra in hisce praesagiendis evitandisque ac hostium consiliis praevertendis cautus ac providus. In omni renovanda pr<a>eferentia animi, laborum tolerantia, usu, exercitatione, consilio mirifice instructus atque imperio natus, hoc ingenio, hac disciplina, hoc usu, his moribus, prosperos praeterea fortunae afflatus adeptus, usque adeo novelli regni fines brevi temporis spatio produxit et extulit, ut Thraciam universam, Thessaliam, Macedoniam, Phociden, Boeotiam, Atticam occupa<ve>rit et sui iuris fecerit, Mysios quoque, Illyricos, Tr<i>ballos assiduis excursionibus, oppugnationibus ac proeliis deiecerit atque infirma<ve>rit, et alios quidem subegerit, aliis tributa quotannis exigenda indixerit, nonnullos, ut ad praescriptum milites et arma darent, coegerit et tot tantasque opulentas provincias patrio et avito regno adiecerit. Byzantium denique urbem regiam adeo omni agro suburbanisque deliciis spoliavit, tam longa et perdifficili obsidione vexavit ut iam imperator ipse cum omnibus ferme civitatis principibus auxilia fidelium emendicaturus profectus pere-

6.   After Suleyman was eliminated, Bayezid became the sole ruler; he was brash, had a passion to achieve greatness, and was bold in his hard tasks; he exhibited cunning in adversity and was indefatigable in bringing matters to completion; he was sharp and perceptive of advantageous situations, swift to action, courageous, strong, warlike, restless in peace, hungry for glory, ready to embrace danger, and admirably skilled in deceiving his enemy. His specialty was to wipe out his enemy by employing stratagems and ambush; by contrast, he could predict and evade his enemy's plans skillfully and wisely. His superior intellect, endurance, talent, discipline, way of life, habits, as well as fortune's favor so extended and magnified the boundaries of his new state in a brief span of time that he occupied and brought under his control all of Thrace, Thessaly, Macedonia, Phocis, Boeotia, and Attica; in addition, he reduced and weakened the Mysians [= Bulgarians], the Illyrians [= Albanians], and the Triballians [= Serbs] with frequent raids, sieges, and battles. He conquered some and exacted annual tribute from others; from others he demanded soldiers for his expeditions and weapons. He added so many rich provinces to the kingdom of his father and grandfather.[7] He finally plundered the countryside and the pleasant suburbs of Byzantium [Constantinople], the imperial city, which he tormented with such a long and cruel siege[8] that the emperor, with almost all the princes of the state, set out for a voyage abroad to seek help from the faithful [= Christians] in Italy and even

---

[7] It was with the support of the army that Bayezid I was able to take over the throne. He enjoyed the support of the *kapı kulları*, the Moslem converts of Christian origin, recruited through the *devşirme*, the "child tribute" collected from Christian subjects in the Balkans and Asia Minor to produce the dread janissary corps of the sultan, the *yeni çeri* or "new army." On this practice, see *OGN*, 73 ff.; Speros Vryonis, "Seljuk Gulams and Ottoman Devshirmes," *Der Islam* 41 (1965): 224–52; idem, "Isidore Glabas and the Turkish Devshirme," *Speculum* 31 (1956): 433–43 [repr. in idem, *Byzantium: Its Internal History and Relations with the Muslim World*, Collected Studies (London, 1971), Studies 12 and 13, respectively]; Basilike Papoulia, *Ursprung und Wesen der "Knabenlese" im osmanischen Reich* (Munich, 1964), and its review by Speros Vryonis, *Byzantium*, Study 14. Against Mircea, the prince of Wallachia, Bayezid I waged a campaign that culminated in the battle of Rovine (May 17, 1395); cf. *LCB*, 316; *MP*, 128; Dorothy M. Vaughan, *Europe and the Turk: A Pattern of Alliances 1350–1700* (Liverpool, 1954), 23; Dorde S. Radojičić, "La Chronologie de la bataille de Rovine," *Revue historique du sud-est européen* 5 (1928): 136–39; and Franz Babinger, *Beiträge zur Frühgeschichte der Türkenherrschaft in Rumelien (14.–15. Jahrhundert)*, Südost-europäische Arbeiten 34 (Munich, 1944), 14–15. The most thorough study of Bayezid I's reign remains that of Gibbons, *The Foundation of the Ottoman Empire*.

[8] Early on in the 1390s, the Greek emperor of Constantinople concluded that there could be no understanding between emperor and emir, as the latter had been planning the murder of the former. So Emperor Manuel II Palaeologus refused to attend his emir-overlord in person. The policy of appeasement and accommodation that had been pursued by the Greek court for so long came to an end and Bayezid initiated a series of raids that brought his irregulars as far south as the Peloponnese. At the same time Bayezid began a seven-year blockade of Constantinople but, as he possessed no fleet, he could not prevent the inhabitants from receiving aid from

gre in Italiam et usque in Superiorem Galliam accesserit. Reliqui vero cives omni praesidio destituti, fame valida supra modum urgente et bello atrocissimo in dies acrius ingruente et hostibus undique frementibus, desperata salute, de ditione agere coeperunt peri<i>ssentque nimirum ac in hostis saevissimi potestatem // venissent, ni Tamerlanus ille Scytharum praepotens rerum instar torrentis ipso incursu impetu cuncta prosternendo atque vastando Baiazetem ipsum omni

went so far as to reach Upper Gaul [= France]. Abandoned, unprotected, and driven by extreme famine and the most cruel war which increased daily as the enemy pressed his advantage on all sides, the citizens began to negotiate a surrender; they would have incurred widespread death and would have become subjects to a most cruel enemy,[9] if that renowned Tamburlaine, the overlord of the Scythians [= Mongols], had not appeared like a torrent which destroys and devastates everything in its forceful path,[10] sweeping along its path Bayezid himself

....

the west. The blockade was granted a respite when Bayezid became the target of the crusade of Nicopolis but he was able to turn his full attention to the siege after he defeated the westerners on September 25, 1396. Soon after the Christian defeat, Emperor Manuel II attempted to cede Constantinople to Venice, as he felt that he could not effectively defend the capital against the Turks. Venice declined his offer and Manuel renewed his appeal to western powers for aid. At long last in 1399 a small contingent from France under the command of the heroic Jean le Maingre, Maréchal Boucicaut, came to Constantinople and assumed control of the defense operations. For this siege, cf. *MP*, chap. 3; *LCB*, 315–24; Dionysios Bernicolas-Hatzopoulos, "The First Siege of Constantinople by the Ottomans (1394–1402) and its Repercussions on the Civilian Population of the City," *BSEB* 10 (1983): 39–51; and *PL* 1: chap. 15.

[9] At the suggestion of Boucicaut, Manuel II left for western Europe on December 10, 1399; he was accompanied by Boucicaut himself, while the defense of Constantinople was entrusted to Jean de Chateaumorand, Boucicaut's second-in-command. Manuel stopped at the Peloponnese and then proceeded to Venice, Ferrara, and Milan via Pavia and Vicenza. On June 3, 1400 Charles VI received the Greek emperor at Clarenton and then proceeded to Paris. Manuel then visited England and was entertained in London by Henry IV on December 21, 1400. He was back in Paris by February 1401. After he was informed of the battle of Ankara and of the capture of Bayezid he started on the long way home and reached Genoa on January 22, 1402. He entered Constantinople on June 9, 1402. There is extensive secondary literature on this famous journey, as no other Greek emperor had traveled such great distances in the Middle Ages. See, among others, Gustave Schlumberger, *Un Empereur de Byzance à Paris et Londres* (Paris, 1916); Martin Jugie, "Le voyage de l'empereur Manuel Paléologue en Occident (1399–1403)," *EdO* 15 (1912): 322–33; Donald M. Nicol, "A Byzantine Emperor in England. Manuel II's Visit to London in 1400–1401," *University of Birmingham Historical Journal* 12 (1971): 204–25; Marija Andreeva, "Zur Reise Manuels II Palaiologos nach West-Europa," *BZ* 34 (1934): 37–47; and *MP*, 170 ff. Sekoundinos is quite correct when he states that Constantinople was ready to surrender. Indeed he is one of the very few authors of the fifteenth century to mention that the surrender of the Greek capital was imminent; the initial negotiations in regard to this cession may go as far back as the summer of 1401; see *RKOR*, no. 3195 (74); the detailed discussion in *MP*, 200 ff.; and the contemporary evidence cited in *MP*, 207 and n. 14.

[10] While in Greece and in the west the general impression was that Timur-i-lenk ("Tamburlaine") appeared suddenly and unexpectedly, the Mongol warlord had been attracted to Anatolia by Bayezid's campaigns: in 1390 Bayezid overwhelmed the emirates of Aydın, Germiyan, Tekke, and Hamit, went on to threaten Karaman and Ikonion, and then concluded a treaty with Karaman, which, by 1391, effectively extended his borders as far the river Çarflanba Suyu; in 1392 he attacked Al ad-Din and Isfendiyar of Kastamonia and even annexed Sinope. Timur-i-lenk (c.1336–1405)

apparatu et copiis occurrere, et reluctari conantem in Asiam revoca<vi>sset, ubi instructa acie, collatis signis celeberrima illa pugna utrinque fortiter dimicatum

with all his troops and forces; he [Tamburlaine] summoned him [Bayezid] to fight in Asia [Minor];[11] the battle lines were formed; there were many standards; and the two sides fought courageously during that famous battle. Bayezid had less strength and his courage proved lacking; he lost the battle, was defeated in an

---

claimed descent from Genghis Khan and was in the process of building a Mongol empire centered around Samarkand; he had conquered Iberia-Georgia and Armenia, had penetrated India and Afghanistan, and had launched raids againts the Golden Horde in Russia. Tahartar, the emir of Erzindzan, became a vassal of the Mongols in order to avoid subjection to Bayezid, who demanded tribute from him in 1399; Tahartar refused to pay and summoned the Mongols to his side. In 1400 Timur plundered the Ottoman city of Sebasteia/Sivas and then withdrew into Syria. In the spring of 1402 Timur advanced into Anatolia. Cf. Hilda Hookham, *Tamburlaine the Conqueror* (London, 1962); *LCB*, 326 ff.; for Turkish literature on the events, see Shaw, *History of the Ottoman Empire*, 307; and Gibbons, *The Foundation of the Ottoman Empire*, 245. For the Greek contacts with Timur and for the activities of their diplomats to negotiate with the Mongols, cf. *MP*, Appendix 18; and *LCB*, 327.

[11] Sekoundinos is referring to the battle of Ankara, which in fact resulted in the defeat of Bayezid and granted the Greek capital a life of another half century. The battle was fought on July 28, 1402. See Gibbons, *Foundation of the Ottoman Empire*, 250 ff.; Hookham, *Tamburlaine*, passim; Edwin Pears, *The Destruction of the Greek Empire and the Story of the Capture of Constantinople by the Turks* (London, 1903; repr. 1968), 133–44; G. Roloff, "Die Schlacht bei Angora," *Historische Zeitschrift* 161 (1943): 244–62; and Werner, *Die Geburt einer Grossmacht*, 170–79. Bayezid was taken prisoner and subsequently died at Ak Şehir on March 9, 1403; the causes of his death remain obscure. It may have been brought about by apoplexy or it may have been a suicide. For the aftermath of the battle and the reaction in the Christian world, cf. *LCB*, 329–330, and *MP*, 216 ff. Already by the early sixteenth century tales were accumulating to form what became known in the west as "the tale of Tamburlaine and his captive, Sultan Bayezid," which became the subject of plays and operas. Thus the Greco-Venetian Theodorus Spandugnino (or, more accurately, Spandounis/Spandounes) included a section on Bayezid's "passion" in his *De la origine deli imperatori Ottomani ordini de la corte, forma del guerreggiare loro religione rito, et costumi de la nationes*, ed. Constantine N. Sathas, in Μνημεῖα Ἑλληνικῆς Ἱστορίας: *Documents inédits relatifs à l'histoire de la Grèce au moyen âge* 9 (Paris, 1890; repr. Athens, 1972), 147–48: "... et tenne questo Ildrim Baiasit di continuo incatenato con cathene d'oro et conducevalo seco per tutto dove lui andava in una gabbia di ferro, et ogni volta che voleva ascendere o à cavallo o sopra il carro, faceva cavar di gabbia Ildrim Baiasit, et era condotto alla presentia sua incathenato et japandoli sopra le spalle montava a cavallo. Et tornato che fu Sachatai in Scytia fece uno bellissimo triompho et della havuta vittoria de Ildrim Baiasit et fece uno grande convito ove si trovorso quasi tutti li signori et principi de Scytia, et fu condotta la gabbia onde stava Ildrim Baiasit dentrò onde fece uno atto non conveniente alla sua grandezza et nobilità, fece conduire la moglie de Ildrim Baiasit, laqual havea presa con lo marito, fece Sachatai tagliari li panni a quella apresso all' ombelico, di dorte che ella mostrava tutte le sue vergogne, et vuolse quella servire et portasse le vivande alli convitati ...." Then Spandugnino relates the death of Bayezid, 148: "Et vedendo Ildrim Baiasit la moglie in tanto opprobrio et vergogna, dolendosi della perservera fortuna, et volendosi amazzar se stesso, et non travondo coltello o altro expediente, percosse tanto con la testa in quella gabbia che era di ferro che amazzò miserabilmente."

est. At Baiazetes ipse impar profecto viribus etsi animus minus deerat, infeliciter proeliatus est ingenti strage superatus, captus, tandem dimissus, paulo post diem obiit.

VII. Post hanc cladem acceptam omnes paene filii eius, qui complures erant, in potestatem et manus Graecorum venere. Cum enim ex Asia ob calamitatem patris, calamitatem evasuri, in Thraciam traiicere contenderent, in naves Graecorum inciderunt, quibus fretum et transitum custodiebant. Calepinus itaque ceteris natu maior, emissus a Graecis patrium regnum obtinuit; adversus quem, rebus iam Turcarum cassatis ac p<a>ene fractis, Sigismundus inclytus eo tempore Pannoniae Superioris rex, post vero diademate et corona pro more a pontifice maximo insignitus imperator, ingenti conflato exercitu, Danubium amnem traiecit, verum priusquam universis copiis instructa ex ordine acies, signis collatis cum

enormous slaughter, was captured, was finally released, and died shortly thereafter.¹²

7.   After they heard about this battle, almost all his sons (who were many) fell into the hands of the Greeks and became their vassals. As a result of their father's disaster in Asia, they tried to escape destruction themselves and hurried to cross over to Thrace and came upon the ships of the Greeks, which were guarding the straits and the ferrying place. And so the eldest of the sons, <Suleyman> Çelebi, was released by the Greeks and took over his father's kingdom.¹³ As the affairs of the Turks were by now in ruins and in total disarray, against him moved the renowned Sigismund, who at that time was the king of Upper Pannonia [= Hungary], after he was crowned [Holy Roman] emperor with the customary diadem and crown by the highest priest [= pope]; he mustered a huge army and crossed the river Danube, but before he could in an orderly fashion form his battle line with all his troops, battle was joined with a fearful

---

¹² After the battle of Ankara began the period that is known as the *Interregnum* or "the Turkish Times of Troubles," so aptly dubbed in *MP*. Numerous contenders for the Ottoman throne appeared. Musa had been the only son of Bayezid to remain with his father and so he secured the support of Timur. Mehmed established himself at Amasya, while Suleyman (Sekoundinos' "prince" or, in Turkish, çelebi; the same "name" is also employed by John Ramus, whose epitome is appended at the end of Sekoundinos' epitome) assumed control of the European territories and moved to Adrianople. Suleyman pursued a policy of reconciliation with the Greeks of Constantinople, as it is reflected in the treaty that he struck with the Greeks early on in his reign. For this treaty, see George T. Dennis, "The Byzantine-Turkish Treaty of 1403," *OCP* 33 (1967): 72–88; *MP*, 224 ff.; and *LCB*, 335. For the *Interregnum*, see *MP*, 220 ff.; *LCB*, 334 ff.; Paul Wittek, "De la défaite d'Ankara a la prise de Constantinople," *Revue des études islamiques* 12 (1938): 1–34. In addition, see Klaus-Peter Matschke, *Die Schlacht bei Ankara und das Schicksal von Byzanz. Studien zur spätbyzantinischen Geschichte zwischen 1402 und 1422* (Weimar, 1981).

¹³ This is a reference to the crusade of Nicopolis (above, n. 8), which Sekoundinos has erroneously placed at this time; the same mistake is repeated by John Ramus; the campaign took place earlier, during the reign of Bayezid I. In the aftermath of the battle of Rovine (above, n. 7), the Turks moved into Dobrudja and their rapid expansion alarmed Sigismund, who, with the blessing of Pope Boniface IX, allied himself with the French; a coalition of German, Hungarian, and French troops under the command of Jean, comte de Nevers, the son of the duke of Burgundy, moved against Bayezid in the Balkans; at the same time the cooperation of the Genoese and the Hospitallers from Rhodes was sought and they pledged to guard the Black Sea and the mouth of the Danube. On this crusade, see Aziz S. Atiya, *The Crusade of Nicopolis* (London, 1934); idem, *The Crusade in the Later Middle Ages* (London, 1938), esp. 435 ff.; the old, reliable work of Joseph Aschback, *Geschichte Kaiser Sigismunds I: Sigismunds frühere Geschichte bis auf die Eröffnung des constanzer Conciliums* (Hamburg, 1838); Gibbons, *The Foundation of the Ottoman Empire*, 201 ff.; and *MP*, 129 ff.

¹⁴ The battle took place on September 15, 1396. The crusaders had underestimated the strength of the Turks and further misjudged their tactics. On the morning of the day, the French contingent engaged the Ottoman cavalry under the impression that they were facing the entire army of Bayezid; they were led into an ambush and were massacred. Sigismund rallied heroically

hoste iam pavitante proelium iniretur, levitate petulantiaque Gallorum et praeripiendae pugn<a>e insolenti cupiditate, tumultuose fusus castra et impedimenta reliquit et hostibus acriter insequentibus in fugam conversus, vix per Danubium lacrimanda rei Christian<a>e // calamitate, parvo navigio, turpem sibi salutem invenit. Haec tam ingens clades, tam grandis no<x>a, tam t<a>etra ignominia, magnas profecto vires et ingens robur hostium animis visa est addidisse et hinc instauratis viribus audaciores efficacioresque effecti ad maiora patranda induxerunt animum. Calepino posthaec mortuo Orchane filio tenella aetate adulescentulo quorundam principum ductu, regnum occupare conanti Moyses patruus armis infeste occurrit et magis proditione quam pugna adulescentem oppressum extinxit. Haud multo post et ipse nullo superstite filio desidera-

enemy;[14] because of the lack of seriousness, arrogance, and insolent desire of the Gauls [= French] to enter battle prematurely, he left his camp and his baggage train in disorder and turned to flight with the enemy hard at his heels; the lamentable Christian expedition hardly made it to the Danube, and he sailed the short distance across to seek safety in shame.[15] The news of this enormous disaster, of such great injury, of such execrable shame actually created great strength and immense confidence to the morale of the enemy; hence, with their confidence and morale restored, they became more audacious and achieved more, as they turned their attention to bigger things. After the death of <Suleyman> Çelebi, Orhan,[16] his very young son attempted to take over the kingdom with the help of certain lords, but his paternal uncle Musa attacked him and, through betrayal rather than battle, eliminated the young man.[17] Shortly thereafter, he himself

---

to launch a counter-attack, failed, and was forced to flee to the Hospitallers' boats. On board their vessels he was mocked by the Turks who were massacring their prisoners in cold blood. Those who could afford to pay high ransom were spared and so were those under the age of twenty, who were taken to Anatolia. In later times a survivor wrote his impressions of his captivity: Johann Schiltberger, *The Bondage and Travels of Johann Schiltberger*, trans. J. B. Telfer (London, 1879). Among Bayezid's prisoners were Jean, comte de Nevers; Jacques Bourbon; Philippe de Barr; Boucicaut; and Guy de la Tremouille.

[15] In Anatolia Mehmed had managed to secure the support of Musa, whom he encouraged to attack Suleyman in Thrace. In 1404 Musa declared war and received aid from Mircea the Old (1386–1418), the voivode of Wallachia, and from Serbia's Stephen Lazarević. Even though Suleyman enjoyed some successes at first and even managed to seize Prousa in Anatolia, Musa launched an invasion and inflicted a defeat on Suleyman's *beglerbeg* of Rumeli on February 10, 1410. Musa then confronted Suleyman in the vicinity of Constantinople. On June 15, 1410, Musa was defeated; again he suffered another military setback on July 11, 1410; he then took advantage of the winter of 1410/11 to strengthen his forces. In February, 1411, Suleyman's troops deserted to Musa and Suleyman was eliminated.

[16] Sekoundinos is one of the few authors of the fifteenth century to mention Orhan, the son of Suleyman, who is erroneously said by most contemporary authors to be the son of Bayezid. Sphrantzes, in his authentic *Chronicon Minus* (3.1), states that Orhan was blinded in Thessaly:. . . καὶ τῆς περὶ τὰ μέρη τῆς Λαρίσσου ἐκτυφλώσεως Ὀρχάνη, τοῦ υἱοῦ τοῦ Μουσουλμάνου [= Suleyman].

[17] Mehmed had been courted by the imperial administration of Constantinople. He was first defeated by Musa (July, 1412), withdrew to Anatolia, regrouped, and formed an alliance with Manuel II and Serbia's Stephen Lazarević. On June 15, 1413, Greek vessels transported Mehmed's army to Europe. A battle was fought in Jamurlu in Serbia (July, 1413); Musa's troops deserted to his brother and he was captured and executed. Mehmed became the sole ruler of the Ottoman state and thus the *Interregnum* came to an end. Mehmed I abandoned the aggressive policies of his predecessors; consequently, both the Turkish sultan and the Greek emperor were granted a respite to turn their attention to their pressing internal problems. On these events, see *MP*, 258–288, and *LCB*, 341 ff..

tus est. Hunc Mahumetes frater subsequitur, regnum incruente adeptus. Is tum armis et diligentia, tum dolo et astu, regnum terra marique non modo incolume tenuit, verum etiam auxit vehementer. <B>lacciis ferocissimis et bellicosissimis gentibus trans Danubium versus mare Euxinum late dominantibus bello prius et crebris incursionibus labefactatis atque attritis, tributa gravia imperavit, nonnullos regulos Turcos, in Asia vi armisque oppressos regnis penitus spoliavit.

VIII.   Eo exinde mortuo Amuratem filium, qui per id tempus in Asia morabatur, cum patris audita morte per Hellespontum in Thraciam traiicere conaretur, reliquum regnum occupaturus, imperator Graecorum triremibus et maritimo apparatu diu prohibuit. Mustapham quoque reliquum ex Baiazete filium, ut eorum potiretur, emisit et summa ope eum prosecutus est. At pugna superato Mustapha ac interempto Amu//rates victor, universum regnum iam consecutus, patriis fretus opibus, fortuna quoque propitia usus omnia incepta eius mirifice fecundante clara facinora edidit. Thessalonicam illustrem Graeci<a>e

perished and left no surviving son.[18] His brother Mehmed [I] followed him and took over the kingdom without shedding any blood. He guided his realm with such force and energy, such cleverness and subtlety, that he suffered no setbacks over land and sea and even greatly enlarged it. He ordered the Wallachians to pay a heavy tribute; in the past these most warlike and ferocious tribes had dominated the regions across the Danube towards the Euxine, but they had been weakened and exhausted by numerous raids; from them he commanded heavy tribute and he even plundered quite a few Turkish petty kings, whose principalities in Asia his armies overwhelmed.

8. After his death,[19] the emperor of the Greeks prevented, for a long time, with his galleys and his naval forces, his son Murad [II] (who was in Asia at the time and had heard of his father's death) from crossing to Thrace through the Hellespont and from taking over the rest of the realm. Instead he released Mustafa,[20] Bayezid's son left in Byzantium [Constantinople], and gave him a great deal of aid to assume control over them. But Mustafa was defeated in a battle and was killed; Murad emerged victorious and took over the entire realm; relying on the resources of his father and taking advantage of his good fortune who smiled with favor upon all his projects, he performed heroic deeds. He besieged and devastated Thessalonica,[21] the city in Greece, which was famous

---

[18] Mehmed died of apoplexy on May 14, 1421 (*MP*, 355, n. 101) or on May 26, 1421 (Anthony D. Alderson, *The Structure of the Ottoman Dynasty* [Oxford, 1956], Tables 15 and 25). In addition, see Franz Taeschner, "Beiträge zur frühosmanischen Epigraphik und Archäologie," *Der Islam* 30 (1932): 109–86, esp. 147–48, and Sokrates Kougeas, "Notizbuch eines Beamten der Metropolis in Thessalonike aus dem Anfang des XV. Jahrhunderts," *BZ* 23 (1914–1919): 143–63, at 151–52, no. 80.

[19] The Greek court had been divided in its opinion in regard to the succession in the Ottoman realm. The peace faction led by Manuel II was ready to accept the legitimacy of Murad II, but Manuel's son John VIII was more aggressive and wished to revive the policies that had been in effect during the *Interregnum* in order to weaken the Ottoman realm. For these events, see *MP*, 355 ff.

[20] Mustafa, who claimed to be Bayezid's son, appeared c. 1416. At first he received support from the Venetians, who brought him to Thrace. He fell into the hands of the Greeks, who sent him to Lemnos and kept him under guard. It is not certain that he was an actual son of Bayezid; he may have been a pretender. The validity of his claim has never been authenticated. See Nicolae Iorga, "Sur le deux prétendants Moustafa du XVe siècle," *Revue historique du sud-est européen* 10 (1933): 10 ff. For his early career, see Sphrantzes, *Chronicon Minus*, 4.4; *MP*, 340 ff.; and *LCB*, 344–45. After the death of Mehmed, Mustafa was released by the Greeks to create trouble for Murad. Mustafa reached Anatolia in late January 1422; his Anatolian campaign was a failure and he was forced to retreat to Thrace. He was eventually captured and executed by Murad. On the fall of Mustafa, see Pears, *The Destruction of the Greek Empire*, 153–54, and Vaughan, *Europe and the Turk*, 46.

[21] In September 1423 Venice took over Thessalonica at the invitation of Despot Andronikos Palaeologus, a son of Manuel II, who had been paying tribute to the *Serenissima* since 1415. By 1429 the defense and provision of Thessalonica proved too expensive for Venice, as the annual costs had risen to 6,000 ducats. On Sunday, March 26, 1430, Murad began the siege. The

civitatem, antiquitate, amplitudine, au<c>toritate, pulchritudine, amoenitate, religione, opibus, opportunitate situs, tum terra tum mari, celebritate populi, praestantia dignitateque civium imprimis insignem, vi captam oppugnatamque penitus diripuit. Templa pulcherrima et ditissima expilavit, sacra profanavit, opes ornamentaque perantiqua exhausit. Hac tantae urbis victoria auctus, Epirum et Aetoliam non obscuras provincias in deditionem suam redegit et reliquo regno addidit. Illyriorum agros vastavit, oppida multa vi cepit et expugnavit, alia in deditionem compulit, quaedam funditus evertit. Triballos paene subegit, adversus Pannonios (quos nostra aetate Hungaros vocant) saepe acie instructa conflixit et dum primis copiarum congressibus facile victus ipse videretur et fusus, quo pacto nescio, victor demum evadere poterat in calamitosa illa Var<n>ensi pugna, rege inclyto Ladislao Christianum ducente exercitum, fusae prius fugato Amurate sunt copiae, ne primum quidem Hungarorum impetum sustinere potuerunt. Ubi vero rex ipse castra et Amuratis iam exercitum non regno modo, sed vitae quoque ipsi timentem optimatum ac procerum agmen movens, utpote victor, invadere penitusque opprimere perrexit, damno sui capitis et // Christianae rei ingenti iactura et vulnere manu ipse hostili oppressus et interemptus

for her antiquity, extent, power, beauty, charm, holiness, wealth, and geographical location (both on land and by the sea), populous and eminent with dignity, and especially noted for her citizens' nobility. He plundered the most beautiful and wealthiest churches, he polluted shrines, and he took away her riches and very ancient decorations. Inflated by his great victory over such a city, he brought under his control and added to his kingdom Epirus and Aetolia, the renowned provinces. He devastated the countryside of the Illyrians [= Albanians]; he captured and besieged many towns; some he forced into submission and others he razed. He almost subjugated the Triballians [= Serbs] and launched frequent organized expeditions against the Pannonians (whom our own age knows as "Hungarians"); while often he appeared to have been defeated in battle and was about to be routed, somehow he managed to emerge victorious, as was the case with that famous battle of Varna: at the head of the Christian army was the renowned King Ladislas; Murad was already in flight and his troops were in disarray, unable to withstand the impact of the Hungarians. In pursuit of their army the king himself reached the camp and Murad began to fear not only for his kingdom but for his very life and for his noblemen and courtiers; the king in triumph attacked and wreaked havoc everywhere but he was attacked, was wounded, and was killed by an enemy; the loss of his life resulted in an enormous loss of the Christian cause.[22] An unexpected and glorious victory was offered to

---

main assault was launched on March 29 and the fortifications were stormed. During the early stages of the sack, the Venetian authorities embarked on their ships and sailed to Negroponte/Euboea, abandoning the city to its fate. On the siege and fall of Thessalonica, cf. Momcilo Spremic, "Harac Soluna u XV veku," *ZRVI* 10 (1967): 187–95; Paul Lemerle, "La Domination vénetienne à Thessalonique," in *Miscellanea G. Galbiati*, Fontes Ambrosiani 27 (Milan, 1951), 3: 219–25; Vaughan, *Europe and the Turk*, 47; *LCB*, 365–67; and *MP*, 373. In addition, there exists now a collection, in translation, of Venetian archival documents dealing with Thessalonica in this crucial period: John R. Melville-Jones, *Venice and Thessalonica 1423–1430: The Venetian Documents*, Archivio del Litorale Adriatico 7 (Padova, 2002).

[22] Under Ladislas III the kingdoms of Hungary and Poland were united. Ladislas III and the legendary warlord Janos Corvinus Hunyadi of Transylvania became the leader of a coalition comprised of Hungarians, Serbs, and Wallachians. This crusade set out from Hungary in July, 1443. The Christian army advanced and seized Sofia and, early in 1444, inflicted a severe defeat on an Ottoman army near Kunovica. By February, 1444, the Christians returned to Buda. In the summer of 1444 it was decided to follow up the earlier successes and the westerners moved to Varna, where they encountered the Ottoman army. A long battle ensued on November 10, 1444. The turning point in the battle was the death of Ladislas; his head was displayed on the battlefield by the Turks and, at the sight of the king's head impaled on a lance, the crusaders lost heart and the battle was lost. This defeat dealt a severe blow to European plans to drive the Turks out of the Balkans. All Christian captives were put to death after the battle. On this crusade, whose failure heralded the end of Balkan independence and the beginning of the end for Greco-Byzantine Constantinople, see Oskar Halecki, *The Crusade of Varna: A Discussion of Controversial Problems* (New York, 1943); Steven Runciman, *A History of the Crusades* (Cambridge, 1954), 3: 465 ff.;

est. Victis iam debellatisque hostibus neque sibi ullam futuram salutem sperantibus improvisam et illustrem victoriam pr<a>ebuit. Paulo post Amurates Corinthiacum Isthmum summa vi penitus expugnavit et diruit. Peloponnesum inde ingressus ingentem ac detestabilem calamitatem Graecis invexit, oppida multa cepit concessitque militi diripienda, praedam maxima egit, muros Isthmi funditus demolitus ingressum patefecit et Peloponnesum ipsam peninsulam terrestribus copiis illac invadendam perviam fecit. Proinde Graecis vix tolerandam pecuniam imperavit pacisque conditiones illis ex sententia praescripsit. Demum inde

our enemy who had been defeated and vanquished while he had not expected to survive. A short time later Murad besieged and destroyed the Corinthian Isthmus[23] with a large force. Then he entered the Peloponnese and brought upon the Greeks an enormous and execrable destruction; he captured many towns and allowed his soldiers to plunder them; he amassed enormous booty, razed the walls at the Isthmus, and opened up the peninsula of the Peloponnese to future invasions, as he thus rendered it permeable to land forces. He ordered the Greeks to pay an impossibly high sum and he dictated peace terms,[24] as he

---

Joseph Gill, *The Council of Florence* (Cambridge, 1958), 329–33; *MCT*, 26–40; *LCB*, 378–81; Franz Babinger, "Von Amurath zu Amurath. Vor- und Nachspiel der Schlacht bei Varna," *Oriens* 3 (1950): 229–65; F. Pall, "Autour de la croisade de Varna: la question de la Paix de Sezeged et sa rupture," *Bulletin d'histoire de l'Académie Roumaine* 22 (1941): 114–58; idem, "Un moment décisif de l'histoire du Sud-Est européen: la croisade de Varna," *Balcania* 7 (1944): 102–20; Vaughan, *Europe and the Turk*, 58 ff.; and Deno J. Geanakoplos, "Byzantium and the Crusades, 1354–1453," in *A History of the Crusades*, ed. Kenneth M. Setton and Harry W. Hazard, vol. 3: *The Fourteenth and Fifteenth Centuries* (Madison 1975), 69–103.

[23] The fortified Isthmus was known as the Hexamilion at the time. For modern archaeological researches in the area and for the evidence that has survived, cf. Timothy E. Gregory, *The Hexamilion and the Fortress*, Isthmia 5 (Princeton, 1993).

[24] In 1444 Constantine Palaeologus, the despot of the Morea (since 1443) and brother of the Greek emperor John VIII, rebuilt and strengthened the defenses at the Isthmus of Corinth, the Hexamilion, in order to render his territories impregnable to Turkish attacks. Constantine had been in close touch with the crusaders, with Ladislas III, with Venice, and with Pope Eugenius IV, and had even launched his own offensive north of the Isthmus of Corinth, and his troops even penetrated as far as Phocis. The sultan then decided to put an end to all ambitious plans that Constantine might have formed and brought his forces against him. The sultan also transported heavy artillery pieces, which used gunpowder. Murad's troops easily routed Constantine's forces and stormed the Hexamilion on December 10, 1444. Murad then raided the territory of Corinth and plundered Vasilika (Sicyon), Vostitza (Aigion), the environs of Patras (without capturing the actual town), and Glarentza. After Constantine sued for peace, the sultan withdrew from the Morea, leading away thousands of Greek captives who were later sold in the slave markets of the Orient. All lands that Constantine had subjugated north of the Isthmus then reverted to Ottoman control. The tribute exacted by Murad also made an impression; the anonymous Barberini Chronicle also refers to it, p. 59: "... they arranged a peace treaty, agreeing to pay a specified amount of yearly tribute. And so started the yearly tribute of the Morea, which had not existed previously." On the Morea under Constantine, see *OGN*, 169–80. On these events, see *MCT*, 47 f.; *OGN*, 179; and *LCB*, 380–82. For the Ottoman artillery of the period, cf. J. R. Partington, *A History of Greek Fire and Gunpowder* (Cambridge, 1960), and Carlo M. Cipolla, *Guns, Sails and Empires: Technological Innovation and the Early Phases of European Expansion 1400–1700* (New York, 1965). In addition, cf. two more recent investigations: Kelly DeVries, "Gunpowder Weapons at the Siege of Constantinople, 1453," and Alan Williams, "Ottoman Military Technology: The Metallurgy of Turkish Armor," in *War and Society in the Eastern Mediterranean 7th-15th Centuries*, ed. Yaakov Lev, The Medieval Mediterranean: Peoples, Economies and Cultures, 400–1453, 9 (Leiden, 1997), 343–62, and- 362–98, respectively. In addition, cf. Philippides, "Urban's Bombard(s), Gunpowder, and the Siege of Constantinople (1453)."

reversus navales copias et maritimos apparatus exauxit, domesticum cultum et regiam supellectilem ampliorem latioremque reddidit. Vita denique defunctus subditis atque genti pertriste sui desiderium reliquit.

IX.   Mahumetus subinde filius, qui in praesentia rerum potitur gubernacula imperii ex voto adeptus, instituta totius regni pro ingenio correxit. Leges ipse suas domi forisque attulit, aerarium locupletavit, nova vectigalia excogitavit, copias auxit. In proceres et aulicos saevire contumeliarique coepit, expeditionem adversus Constantinopolim diu animo volvens castellum iuxta litus ad ostium Bosphori paulo ab urbe remotius, aliud simulans, incredibili celeritate extruxit atque munivit. Bellum inde urbi non indixit, // sed contra inita foedera, contra iusiurandum, simul atque intulit et gerere coepit. Innumeris demum

pleased. He then returned home and augmented his naval forces and his armada and enlarged his internal government and his court possessions. When he finally died, he left behind sadness, as his people missed him.²⁵

9.   Mehmed [II], his son, then assumed control of the ship of state, as he had hoped to do, and arranged the entire realm in accordance with his inclinations.²⁶ He spread his laws at home and abroad, he enriched his treasury, he invented new taxes, and he increased his forces. He began to show cruelty and contempt to his nobles and courtiers; for a long time he planned an expedition against Constantinople and he erected and fortified, with incredible speed, a castle at the shore by the mouth of the Bosphorus, very close to the city, but he concealed his real purpose.²⁷ Without a declaration of war upon the city, against the existing treaty, and against his oath, he began the war and initiated hostilities.²⁸

---

²⁵ After the raid in the Morea, Murad abdicated in favor of his son Mehmed and retired to Asia Minor but he was subsequently recalled by his viziers, who had no trust in the abilities of the thirteen-year-old Mehmed to deal with Hunyadi and his Wallachians, who were preparing another attack upon the Turks. For other events in Murad's reign, cf. *MCT*, 53 ff., and *LCB*, 382–83. Murad stopped campaigning in 1449, after he defeated Hunyadi once more; he spent the rest of the year in Adrianople, in the company of poets and intellectuals. In 1450 he and his son and heir Mehmed II attacked Albania but failed to seize the capital. Murad II suffered an attack of apoplexy during a drinking bout (*MCT*, 61) and died on Wednesday, February 4, 1451.

²⁶ Mehmed II was born on March 30, 1432. The identity of his mother remains a mystery; she was probably a slave of Christian origin (as her name, Hatun bint Abdullah, suggests that her father had been a convert to Islam). Later stories and folk tales would have us believe that she was a French princess or an Italian lady. See Franz Babinger, "Mehmeds II., des Eroberers Geburtstag," *Oriens* 2 (1949): 1–5; idem, "Mehmeds II., des Eroberers Mutter," *Beiträge zur Slavenkunde: Festangabe für Paul Diels* (Munich, 1957), 3–12; *MCT*, 11–12.

²⁷ On April 15, 1452, Mehmed II began the construction of a fortress at the narrowest point of the Bosphorus, across from the Anatolian castle (Anadolu Hisar) erected by Bayezid I. Work on the new castle (known variously as Rumeli Hisar, Boğaz-kesen ["throat-cutter"] Baş-kesen ["head-cutter"], Λαιμοκοπίη ["throat-cutter"], or Νεόκαστρον ["new castle"]) was completed by the end of August, 1452. A garrison was instructed to board all ships bound for Constantinople and to exact tolls. On this fortress, whose ultimate contribution was of a psychological nature, as its physical threat was effectively neutralized on every occasion that was by-passed by expert captains who refused to submit to inspection by the Ottoman garrison, cf. *MCT*, 75–79; *FC*, 65–67; *LCB*, 396; and Tursun Beg (to cite one contemporary Turkish source), *The History of Mehmed the Conqueror*, trans. Halil Inalcik and Rhoades Murphey (Minneapolis and Chicago, 1978), 33–34; the most extensive modern study of this fortress is provided in Ekrem H. Ayverdi, *Osmanli Mı 'marısında Fatih Devri* IV, Istanbul Enstitüsü 69 (Istanbul, 1974), 626–62. In addition, see below, Chapter 3, n. 2.

²⁸ The siege, fall, and sack of Constantinople in 1453 have been told in eyewitness accounts, in narratives that claim to be authoritative, and in texts written by authors who claim to be eyewitnesses (and are, in fact, secondary documents composed by writers who lived a long time after the events). Most eyewitness accounts are composed in Latin, Italian, Slavonic, and French. Some primary sources are included in *CC* 1 (and some early secondary narratives in *CC* 2 and in *TIePN*). Translations of various sources into English include: Melville Jones, *Siege*, including

p<a>ene coactis undique copiis, mirabili apparatu, formidoloso animi impetu, terra marique aggressus eam cuniculis, ac latentibus fossis altissime actis, aggere late edito, ponte (quia mare, versus Peram oppidum, muros alluit urbis) longitudine ad duo milia passuum raptim exstructo, turribus ligneis eo usque erectis, ut muros urbis, qui altissimi erant, excederent. Machinarum tormentorumque multiplici adhibito genere, post quartum et quinquagesimum diem summa vi et extrema pugna cepit, imperatore ipso ingressu hostium confosso atque extincto. Principes optimatesque captos crudelis et sanguinarius carnifex foede misereque

Finally he summoned his vassal troops from everywhere, and, with an admirable expeditionary force that brought terror to the mind,[29] he attacked the city from land, sea, and underground: he secretly dug deep mines, constructed wide ramparts, quickly built a bridge[30] (to span the gap from the town of Pera[31] to the walls of the city) that measured two miles in length, and erected wooden towers that were taller than the highest spots of the city walls. There were all sorts of artillery engines and cannon. Finally, in a last mighty, battle he captured the city after fifty-four days of siege; the emperor himself was wounded and was killed, as the enemy poured in. He [Mehmed II] ordered his cruel, bloody executioner

the narratives of Tetaldi, Leonardo, Khalkokondyles, Doukas, "Riccherio" (i.e. the sixteenth-century French scholar Richer; see Philippides, "*Urbs Capta*"), Languschi-Dolfin, and Angelo Giovanni Lomellino; [Melville] Jones, Nicolò Barbaro; Charles T. Riggs, *History of Mehmed the Conqueror by Kritovoulos* (Westport, CT, 1970); *The History of Mehmed the Conqueror by Tursun Beg*, trans. Inalcik and Murphey; Harry J. Magoulias, *Decline and Fall of Byzantium to the Ottoman Turks by Doukas* (Detroit, 1975); Marios Philippides, *The Fall of the Byzantine Empire: A Chronicle by George Sphrantzes, 1401–1477* (Amherst, 1980), which includes the sixteenth-century elaboration of the siege section by Makarios Melissourgos-Melissenos; idem, *Byzantium, Europe, and the Early Ottoman Sultans*, idem, *Emperors, Patriarchs and Sultans of Constantinople*; and Hanak and Philippides, *The Tale of Constantinople (of its Origin and Capture by the Turks in the Year 1453) by Nestor-Iskander*.

[29] The army of Mehmed II consisted of his European contingents, his Anatolian forces, and a Serbian contribution of 1500 horsemen and professional sappers to mine the walls. Greek historians and contemporary chroniclers have undoubtedly overestimated the size of the Turkish army; by contrast, Turkish authors may have underestimated it. A summary of possible numbers can be found in Doukas, *Decline and Fall*, trans. Magoulias, n. 236. OGN, 193–94, suggests that, if we take into account the irregulars and the various Christian renegades, the total number could not have exceeded 250,000. MCT, 84 f., estimates the effective force at 80,000. There were numerous non-combatants, as well, such as mullahs and dervishes. In addition, Mehmed's expert miners and sappers from Serbia may not have counted as soldiers; for further details, cf. the notes that accompany the texts of Tetaldi and Pius II.

[30] Descriptions of this bridge are provided in numerous sources (cf. the summary in FC, III, n. 1). Languschi-Dolfin, 13, describes this bridge as follows: "Et fece construir uno ponte longo 30 stadij sono miglia ... dal mare fino alla ripa de la terra, fatta la zatra fermata sopra le botte ligate per diuider el porto, per lo qual ponte exercito poteua correr apresso el muro de la cita, apresso la giesa, imitando la potentia de Xerxe el quale de Natolia in Grecia tradusse lo suo exercito per lo stretto de Hellesponto. Non restua adoncha saluo la cathena de le naue ne quella impiua tutta la bocha a prohibir el transito de l'intrar al armata."

[31] Pera (or Galata[s]) was a suburb of Constantinople across the Golden Horn, granted to the Genoese by Emperor Michael VIII in the treaty of Nymphaion (1261); thus Genoese merchants had been extended the privilege of establishing themselves in the neighborhood of the Greek capital and the privilege of trading, free of duty, throughout the ports of the Greek empire. During the siege of 1453 Pera remained officially neutral, even though individuals did assist in the defense of the Greek capital; Pera's *podestà*, Angelo Giovanni Lomellino, had received instructions from Genoa to avoid any direct confrontation with the Turks. Furthermore, merchants from Pera supplied the sultan's army with provisions.

iug<u>lari iussit. Quis satis pro dignitate tantae urbis casum tantopere deflendam calamitatem, tot tantoque ab hoste rabido in sacra atque profana, in viros ac mulieres per immanitatem ac scelus passim patrata facinora vel memorare verbis, vel lacrimis prosequi, vel oratione complecti queat? Peram subinde illustre e regione urbis oppositae situam oppidum opulentissimum et claram Ianuensium coloniam tantae urbis clade, tam improvisa calamitate, tam vicino excidio territam et deiectam per deditionem cepit, eiusque demolitus pulcherrimos muros, templa spoliari, sancta violari, reliquum ornatum civitati adimi, cives alio qui t<a>etre et indigne vexari permisit.

X.   Quibus ad hanc diem (proh // scelus!) nequiter ac nefarie dominatur, hac felicitate, hoc prospero rerum cursu vehementer elatus, magna adversus Christianos moliri videtur, magna versare animo, formidanda minari, nefanda appetere, permagna denique sibi et genti suae promittere non verebitur, su<a>eque audaci<a>e et impetenti cupiditati, nisi Christiani nostri peculiari et domestica gravitate au<c>toritate illustri, singulari prudentia, freti armis, consilio, opibus terra marique praepropere occurrere animum induxerint, vehementer utique dubitandum est et rebus (horret animus dicere!) timendum summopere. Quid enim per immortalem Deum non assequetur dominandi libidine et ambitione inflatus iuvenis gloriae et novarum rerum percupidus animus, fortuna armis, opibus domesticis et quidem non facile contemnendis fretus, si

to slaughter the captive princes and lords dishonorably and miserably.³² Who can provide an adequate lamentation for the misfortune experienced by such a dignified city?³³ Who can put into words, into tears, or into speech the numerous, inhumane acts and crimes committed by the rabid enemy upon the sacred and profane and upon men and women everywhere? Then he accepted the surrender of the town of Pera (situated across the region of the city), the famous, very rich colony of the Genoese, which had become terrified and dejected at the unexpected misfortune of such a city, at the destruction of her neighbor. He ordered the dismantling of her most beautiful walls, the plunder of her churches, the violation of her shrines, and the destruction of all her ornaments; he allowed her citizens to be treated in an undignified and objectionable manner.³⁴

10.   On that day (what a crime!) when he became their execrable and wretched master and rejoiced with the happy outcome of events, as he seemed to accomplish great deeds against the Christians, he turned his attention to great projects, produced formidable threats, conceived an appetite for atrocity, and promised greatness to himself and to his tribe with audacity and endless cupidity and, unless our side, the Christians, pay special attention, with seriousness, to their domestic affairs and hasten to take up arms for an extensive expedition over land and sea, it must not be doubted (my mind shudders to state it) that there will be cause for great fear. In the name of God: What if the young man [Mehmed], inflated by the desire and ambition to conquer and by the passion to upset the established order, as well as relying on his good fortune in war and on

---

³² The victims of Mehmed II's wave of executions that followed the sack included the Venetian *bailo*, Girolamo Minotto; the Catalan consul; and the grand duke of Constantinople, Loukas Notaras, with two of his sons.

³³ There is a large corpus of lamentations on the fall of Constantinople. On popular dirges, cf. Hans-Georg Beck, *Geschichte der byzantinischen Volksliteratur* (Munich, 1971), 163 ff.; Georgios Megas, "La Prise de Constantinople dans la poésie et la tradition populaires grecques," in *Le Cinq-Centième Anniversaire de la prise de Constantinople (L'Hellenisme Contemporain)* (Athens, 1953), 125–33; Gerhard Podskalsky, "Der Fall Konstantinopels in der Sicht der Reichseschatologie unter den Klageliedern," *Archiv für Kulturgeschichte* 57 (1975): 71–86. For a translation and commentary by Avedis K. Sanjian of an Armenian elegy composed by Abraham Ankiwrac'i [= of Ankara], *Elegy on the Capture of Constantinople*, see Avedis K. Sanjian. "Two Contemporary Armenian Elegies on the Fall of Constantinople, 1453," *Viator* 1 (1970): 223–61. In western texts one encounters the inevitable comparison between the sack of Constantinople and the sack of Troy, especially since the Turks were thought to be the descendants of the Trojans, who in 1453 avenged the sack of Troy; on this matter, see my comments in the Introduction. In connection with the humanistic climate of Italy, see Hankins, "Renaissance Crusaders."

³⁴ Pera surrendered to the sultan immediately after the fall of Constantinople. The formal document specifying the status of the Genoese has survived; it is an *aman-name*, an imperial decree and not a treaty (as it is usually stated). Cf. Theodore C. Skeat, "Two Byzantine Documents," *British Museum Quarterly* 13 (1952): 71–73, and the translation of this document into English by Melville Jones, *The Siege*, 136–37. Also see below, Appendix II for the Greek and Italian texts of the *aman-name* granted to Pera by Sultan Mehmed II Fatih.

ignavos insuper, si inertes, sopori et desidiae deditos, si saluti suae minus prospicientes hostes offenderit? Quid enim non fuerit facile aggredi et sine magno negotio vincere penitusque opprimere, nemine repugnante? Sed de his hactenus neque enim de istis mihi differendum proposui et satis superque iam a plerisque graviter et prudenter oratum est. Quotidie enim hac de re pulcherrima verba fiunt, quibus vel qui natura hebetes et languidi sunt excitari protinus debeant et ad arma pr<a>ecipites haud iniuria procurrere. Verum iam non verborum egemus nec oratio amplius, sed facto opus est. Quid enim attinet in verbis apte struendis et expolienda orati//one tempus nequicquam consumere, ubi res ipsa acriter urgere videtur, ubi circumstrepentia hostis arma adeo instant ut stimulos nobis iniicere et faces quodammodo admovere debeant, quibus vehementissime lacessitis ex<s>urgere animis ad operam navandam, ad arma capienda, ad vires exercendas, opes effundendas, vitam denique ipsam fortiter expondendam et quibusvis periculis obiectandam deberemus. Ubi videlicet cervicibus impendens calamitas, argutius garrire, diutius agere, verbis indulgentius insistere, non permittit. Ubi hostis ipsius acerrimum studium, assidua meditatio vehemensque cupiditas, magis in dies adversus nos molientis, excogitantis, struentis, fabricantis, periculi futuri nos commonefacere et sopore altoque somno pressos expergefacere posset, nisi vecordes prorsus aut stolidi simus et insania penitus atraque bile laboremus. Dii talem pestem avertite terris!

XI. Equidem, pater reverendissime, ut tibi obsequerer, ut voluntati tuae gererem morem, ut tuis tandem mandatis obtemperarem, mearum partium munus exile quidem, incomptum ac tenue fateor et te tuisque auribus parum dignum, libenter tamen atque impigre sum executus. Hinc itaque facile percipi potest, quam celeri cursu, quam brevi rerum curriculo execranda et barbara ista gens, Otthomano principe obscuris peregrinisque exorta primordiis, quorsum tandem evaserit, quot quantasque res apprehenderit, quos teneat occupetque // quibus indigne ac spurcissime dominetur, quibus immineat, quo iam ire, quo se insinuare impudentissime pergat. Verum si ab Otthomano domus huius au<c>tore incipere vis, his omissis qui nullo herede superstit decessere, reliquos ordine recensendo Orchanem invenies secundum, Amuratem maiorem tertium, Baiazetem quartum, Mahumetum superiorem quintum, Amuratem minorem sextum et Mahumetum hunc postremo septimum, qui utinam et postremus et ultimus sit omnium, neve pestis haec ulterius serpens t<a>etra colluvione aut lue reliquias decoris ac pulchritudinis Christianae foedare ac inquinare possit. Qui utinam cruce triumphali, viribus fidelium ac virtute oppressus prosternatur et ex<s>tinguinatur et horrendum monstrum detestandum, et exitiale prodigium, Christi nostri salvatoris et Dei veri insuperabili auxilio tollatur funditus et radicitus ex<s>tirpetur.

* * * * *

considerable domestic resources, were to attack enemies who, as an additional advantage for him, were cowardly and lazy, corrupted by inactivity and intrigue, and failed to look towards their own salvation? With no one standing in his way, what can he fail to conquer or overwhelm easily? Enough said: it is not my intention to speak of these matters any longer; after all, many others have pronounced serious and thoughtful speeches. Many beautiful words have been daily produced over this subject and should immediately wake up those who are lazy and slow to act by nature, who should now rush to arms to prevent further harm. Yet it is not words nor long speeches we are in need of; we need to act. For while time is being consumed in well-constructed phrases and polished orations, we find ourselves overwhelmed by the circumstances and our enemy has completely surrounded us, as he rattles his armor; all this should move us and provoke us into action; we must awaken our spirits to the task; we must take up arms; we must flex our muscles; we must make use of our resources; and we must risk our very lives in the present danger. As destruction hangs over our heads, we can no longer afford to argue, to delay, or negotiate at leisure. Our enemy's careful plans and extreme desire are daily pressing against us; we are not fighting back, are not making plans, and are not vigilant; we are not aware of the common danger and we are not likely to wake up from our deep sleep and inactivity, unless we remain in our present silly and sluggish state, working with a taste of bitter bile in our mouths. May the Gods protect the earth from such pestilence!

11.   And so, most reverend father, I beg you, so that I keep within your good will and obey your instructions (as I poorly struggle to perform my duty); I admit this is not worthy of you to hear but I have enthusiastically tried my best. One can easily understand how swiftly, in what short time since its origins that execrable and barbarous tribe, under the leadership of Osman, rose from obscure nomadic beginnings, which it soon abandoned, and came to its present state of unworthy and foul domination and pushes itself most shamelessly onward. If you wish to begin with the originator of the dynasty, Osman, and omit those who left no heirs, you will find that Orhan was the second to follow, that Murad I was the third, Bayezid the fourth, Mehmed I was the fifth, Murad II was the sixth, and this reigning Mehmed [II] the seventh; how I wish he were the last of them, with no other foul snake bringing filth and pestilence to pollute and foul what is left of Christian decorum and beauty! How I wish that the cross could triumph and this horrible, execrable monster and destructive creature would be destroyed, wiped out, and totally and irrevocably exterminated and annihilated by the strength of the faithful, with the irresistible help of our God and Savior, Jesus Christ!

* * * * *

Catalogus Turcarum ab Otthomano
usque ad Soleimanum,
qui nunc maximis triumphis
potenter regnat

Ottomanus: Inter reges Turcarum primus monarchiam hanc invasit anno Domini 1300. Hic regulis Turcicis passim trucidatis, ac excuso Caliphe Sultani iugo, regem se constituit Turcarum. Obtinuit B<i>th<y>niam et Cappadociam, Alberto primo imperante.

Orchanes: Patri in regno successit anno 1335. Is Galatiam et omnem terram usque ad Hellespontum imperio adiecit, et Brussae sedem tyrannidis posuit, qui locus adhuc hodie sepultura Turcarum celebris est.

Amurates: Tertius Turcarum imperator regnum occupavit anno 1363. Qui a Graecis dissidentibus evocatus, primus ex Asia in Europam traiecit, Calliopolin et Chersonesum occupavit, per Bulgariam, Thraciam, et Mysiam maximas praedas fecit, imperante Carolo quarto.

Baiazetes: Regnum ingressus est anno 1386. Pulcherrimas Thraciae partes, Phocidem et Bulgariam cum multis aliis bello vicinis eripuit. Captus a Tamerlano Tartaro, ac postea dimissus mortem obiit.

Calepinus: Quintus huius familiae tyrannus filius superioris Sigismundum imperatorem Romanum maxima clade in Bulgaria affecit, et Ioannem Burgundiae ducem ad Nicopolim magna nobilitate comitatum cepit anno 1369 et M<o>esiae partem sibi subiecit.

Moyses: Anno 1400 monarchiam Turcicam accepit. Orchani nepote vitam et imperium eripuit. Ipse quoque sine magna laude hanc sedem reliquit.

Mahumetus: Rebus Turcicis gerendis anno 1408 se praeparavit, moxque fratre Moyse vita functo sceptrum excepit. Daciam, Serviam, Illyriam, totam denique Bosn<i>am, partim Gr<a>ecorum imperatoribus, partim Hungariae regibus vectigalem vi cepit, primusque Turcarum Danubium transgressus, Valachiam ingenti manu populatus est.

Amurates 2: Sceptrum Turcicum anno 1412 accepit. Ep<i>rum, Aetoliam, Achaiam, Boeotiam, Atticam, Thessalonicam armis vendicavit. Vladislaum Poloniae et Hungariae regem in bello 1444 cum proceribus et nobilibus Hungariae interfecit. M<o>esiam depopulatus est. Ioannem Hunniadem nequicquam resistentem magna clade in campo Merulae profligavit.

[ADDITIONS BY JOHN RAMUS:]
*A List of the Turks: from Osman
to Suleyman,
who currently reigns with power
and with the greatest triumphs*

OSMAN: He was the first to establish this monarchy among the kings of the Turks in 1300 AD. He slaughtered the Turkish kings everywhere, was set free from the yoke by the Caliph-Sultan, and established himself as the king of the Turks. He annexed Bithynia and Cappadocia during the reign of Albert I.

ORHAN: He succeeded his father and ascended the throne in the year 1335. He added Galatia and the entire region, as far as the Hellespont, to his empire; he made Prousa the capital; to this day this city functions as the celebrated cemetery of the Turkish rulers.

MURAD I: He was the third Turkish sultan to ascend the throne, in the year 1363. He was summoned by a dissenting faction of the Greeks and was the first to cross from Asia into Europe; he occupied Kallipolis and the Chersonese and launched great raids throughout Bulgaria, Thrace, and Mysia during the reign of Charles IV.

BAYEZID I: He took over the kingdom in the year 1386. He devastated the most beautiful regions of Thrace, Phocis, and Bulgaria and attacked his neighbors. He was captured by Tamburlaine the Mongol and died soon thereafter.

CELEPI: He was the fifth son to become tyrant of the dynasty; he defeated Sigismund, the Holy Roman Emperor, in a disaster in Bulgaria and captured John the duke of Burgundy and the nobles in his extensive retinue in the year 1369 and subjected a part of Moesia.

MUSA: He took over the Turkish monarchy in the year 1400. He killed Orhan, his nephew, and assumed control of the empire. He lost his throne without winning fame.

MEHMED I: He prepared to assume control of the Turkish government in the year 1408 and took over the throne soon after the death of his brother Musa. From the emperors of the Greeks and from the king of Hungary he exacted tribute over Dacia, Serbia, Illyria, and all of Bosnia and was the first Turk to cross the Danube and devastate Wallachia with a huge force.

MURAD II: He ascended the Turkish throne in the year 1412. By force of arms he seized Epirus, Aetolia, Achaea, Boeotia, Attica, and Thessalonica. In battle he put to death Ladislas king of Poland and Hungary with nobles and magnates of Hungary in 1444. He devastated Moesia. In a great disaster he routed John Hunyadi who had opposed him in vain in the Field of the Blackbirds [= Kossovo polje].

Mahumetus 2: H<i>c imperium gubernandum accepit anno 1451. Constantinopolim expugnavit anno 53 die 27 Aprilis. Negropontum, Capham, Macedoniam, Peloponnesum, Bosn<i>am, et universium Graecum Trapezuntinumque imperium Christianae reipublicae orientali ademit. Victus semel a Valacho Stephano, iterum ab Hunniade in Belgrado letali vulnere sauciatus anno 1456 die 22 Iulii. Infestissimae excursiones sub eo factae sunt a bassis in Croatiam, Carniolam et Styriam.

Baiazetes 2: Patrem in imperio secutus est anno 1481. Magnam Graeciam Hydronto expugnato, et quod reliquum adhuc erat Graeciae ditionis maiorum suorum pr<a>edis adiecit, et primus Hungarorum regna bello aggressus est. Croatia in fidem accepta, Sclavoniaque, Carniola, Styria, et foro Iulii usque Tarvisium depopulatis. Methonam in Morea expugnavit anno 1499 die 12 Augusti. Moritur anno 1512, imperii vero sui tricesimo.

Selimus: Homo impietatis scelere inquinatissimus, imperium accepit anno 1512, Ismaelem Persarum regem supra Araxim ultra Armeniam armis aggressus est, ubi primum Ustaoglum ducem cruenta admodum victoria superavit. Mos ab Ismaele victus in Amasiam Cappadociae fugit. Sultanum Aegypti ferentem suppetias Pers<a>e aggreditur subacta Syria et Hierusalem, sultanos duos vicit et occidit, et totum imperium Aegypti et Arabiae vendicavit anno 1516. Moritur anno Domini 19, imperii vero sui septimo.

Soleimanus: Imperator Turcarum duodecimus mox a patris morte regnum gubernandum sumpsit. Belgradum totius Christian<a>e Europae propugnaculum armis sibi subdidit anno 1521. Et inexpugnabilem Rhodum semestri obsidione exhaustam occupavit ipso die nativitatis Christi, anno 1523. Expugnavit Varadunum. Ludovicum regem Hungariae in proelio vicit et occidit. Budam diripuit et incendit anno 1526, die 29 Augusti. Viennam Austriacorum non semel obsidione frustra tentavit. Huic Deus ad suorum salutem omnia in contraria vertat.

MEHMED II: This man took over the throne in the year 1451. Constantinople fell to him on April 27 [*sic*], in the year [14]53. Negroponte, Caffa, Macedonia, the Peloponnese, Bosnia, and the entire empire of the Greeks as well as that of Trebizond he took away from the Christian Oriental Commonwealth. Once he was defeated by Stephen of Wallachia and then a second time by John Hunyadi at Belgrade, when he was seriously wounded on July 22, 1456. His pashas launched most hostile raids into Croatia, Carniola, and Styria.

BAYEZID II: He succeeded his father in the year 1481. He attacked Magna Graecia and occupied Otranto; he added to his ancestral realm whatever was still left in the hands of the Greeks, and he was the first to attack the kingdom of the Hungarians. Croatia came to him by treaty, and he devastated Sclavonia, Carniola, Styria, and Forum Juli, as far as Tarviso. He attacked and conquered Methone in the Morea on August 12, 1499. He died in the year 1512, in the thirteenth year of his reign.

SELIM [YAVUZ]: He was stained by impious crimes; he ascended the throne in the year 1512. He attacked Ishmael, the king of the Persians, above the [river] Araxes, beyond Armenia, where he defeated Lord Ustaoğlu in a bloody victory. Shortly thereafter he was defeated by Ishmael and fled to Amasia in Cappadocia. He attacked the sultan of Egypt who was sending aid to the Persian; he subjugated Syria and Jerusalem, defeated and put to death two sultans, and won for himself the entire empire of Egypt and Arabia in the year 1516. He died in the year [15]19 of our Lord, in the seventh year of his reign.

SULEYMAN [THE MAGNIFICENT]: He assumed control of the government shortly after the death of his father; he was the twelfth Turkish ruler. He subjugated Belgrade, the bulwark of all Christian Europe, in the year 1521. On Christmas Day, 1523, he occupied the impregnable city of Rhodes after it became exhausted in a six-month siege. Varadunum fell to him. He defeated in battle and put to death Louis the king of Hungary. He pillaged and burned Buda on August 29, 1526. More than once did he attempt to seize Vienna, the city of the Austrians, by siege, but it was all in vain. Our Lord God turned his former prosperity into adversity.

CHAPTER III

A BRIEF TREATISE ON THE CAPTURE OF CONSTANTINOPLE BY POPE PIUS II

PII SECUNDI PONTIFICIS MAXIMI
DE CAPTIONE URBIS CONSTANTINOPOLIS
TRACTATULUS

I.　　　Mahumetes <igitur> defuncto Amurate gubernacula regni ex voto adeptus<,> instituta maiorum pro ingenio correxit; leges ipse suas domi forisque tulit; aerarium locupletavit; nona vectigalia excogitavit; copias auxit. In proceres et aulicos saevire contumeliarius cepit.¹ Dicet ille² Mahumetes qui Constantinopolitanis <(ut supra innuimus)> bellum intulit, de quo nunc referre quae³ accepimus haud alienum fuerit. voluerat [ille] iam pridem <animum> Mahumetes<,> quonam modo Constantinopolim sibi subigere posset. Aeque⁴

----

¹ saevire contumeliarive coepit.
² Hic est ille
³ ut
⁴ neque

A BRIEF TREATISE ON THE CAPTURE
OF CONSTANTINOPLE
BY POPE PIUS II

1.   After the death of Murad Mehmed assumed control of the ship of state,[1] in accordance with his wish, and he recast the ancestral form of government to agree with his own inclinations: he personally promoted his laws at home and abroad; he enriched the treasury; he instituted the ninth form of taxation; and he enlarged his forces. He began to treat his nobles and courtiers with cruel insults. This Mehmed, who (as I noted above) attacked the inhabitants of Constantinople, now thinks of nothing other, I hear, than immediate war. That has been Mehmed's state of mind and has guided him in his recent conquest

---

[1] Murad II died on Wednesday, February 4, 1451 (MCT, 61–63). His death was kept secret, as Mehmed, Murad's son, had proved unpopular with the janissary corps in the past. The first vizier, Halil Candarlı, secretly informed the prince of the sultan's death. Mehmed II was enthroned in Adrianople on February 18, 1451. The young sultan confirmed Halil as his first vizier (even though he seems to have disliked him intensely), and raised Zaganos Pasha (who was a convert to Islam, of Greek or Albanian extraction, who had risen through the ranks of the *devşirme*) from the post of third vizier to that of second (FC, 57– 58; MCT, 65). Mehmed then put to death his own brother, Kücük Ahmed Çelebi, who was eighteen months old, thus formally introducing the fratricide law in the Ottoman dynasty, which was still practiced three hundred years later; its aim was to put a firm end to civil wars, which had plagued the succession in the past, by eliminating all possible contenders. Mehmed II faced no other opposition, as his only other distant relative, Orhan (probably a grandson of Bayezid I; see MCT, 70), had sought sanctuary with the Greek emperor in Constantinople and was destined to assist in the defense of the Greek capital in 1453. Immediately after his enthronement, Mehmed turned his attention to foreign policy and renewed the existing peace treaties with Serbia and Venice and further arranged a truce with Janos Hunyadi, the legendary warlord and defender of the Christians in the Balkans. The Greek emperor of Constantinople, Constantine XI Dragaš Palaeologus (1449–1453), congratulated Mehmed on his accession and requested a renewal of the peace treaty between the Porte and the Greek court; Mehmed granted his petition immediately and further offered an annual payment of 300,000 aspers for the upkeep of his relative, Orhan. At the same time he may have renewed another peace treaty with the Greeks of Trebizond. His eagerness to renew treaties of friendship with his neighbors probably created the erroneous impression that this young sultan was inexperienced, timid, and generally amiable, and would pose no further threat (LCB, 394–395). Once he renewed these treaties and he had nothing to fear from his Christian neighbors, Mehmed dealt swiftly with the rebellious Ibrahim of Karaman (OGN, 88; FC, 64; MCT, 70) and with an insurrection of his own janissaries, who demanded a *donativum*; Mehmed acceded to this demand. His grant established a dangerous precedent, as similar *donativa* were subsequently demanded at the accession of sultans. Once the corps had been pacified, Mehmed dismissed their aga, Kazancı (Kurtcu) Doğan, and replaced him with Mustafa Beg; he then proceeded to reorganize his army (MCT, 71).

ad suam gloriam pertinere arbitrabatur, urbem in medio Turchorum⁵ sitam esse, quae suo imperio non pareret<,> tantoque maius inde nomini suo decus accedere<,> si eam urbem expugnaret, quanto progenitores sui idem conati turpius acceptis⁶ destitissent. Cum paucis igitur participato consilio, castellum iuxta litus ad ostium Bosphori paulo ab urbe remotius<,> [et] aliud dissimulans incredibili celeritate extruxit ac⁷ munivit; bellum deinde urbi non modo induxit<,> sed contra multa f<o>edera, contra iusiurandum, intulit<,> simul et gerere cepit.

II.   Senserant eius animum Graeci<,> diffidentesque suis viribus ad Latinorum opes confugerant lacrimis [ac fletibus] auxilia expetentes.⁸ Surdae, pro pudor, nostrorum principum aures fuere, caeci oculi, qui cadente Graecia<,> ruituram Christianae religionis reliquam partem non viderunt, quamvis privatis

---

⁵ Turcarum
⁶ a ceptis
⁷ atque
⁸ expectantes.

of Constantinople. This project would bring him glory and, equally important, the city was located in the middle of the territory of the Turks but was then not his possession; accordingly, the conquest of the city would surpass the glory of his own forefathers who had incurred shame when they failed to succeed in this undertaking. And so he consulted a few individuals and erected a castle on the shore that is next to the mouth of the Bosphorus, not too distant from the city; he pretended that his objective was something else and with incredible speed he constructed and fortified it.[2] Then he did not even bother to declare war upon the city; on the contrary, his hostile actions violated numerous treaties and sworn pacts.

2.   The Greeks sensed his mental state and because they had no faith in their own strength, they turned to the Latins and sought help with wails and tears. It is shameful to admit it but the ears of our princes turned deaf, their eyes turned blind, as they failed to realize that the fall of Greece heralded the imminent destruction of what remained of the Christian religion and I believe that

---

[2] On April 15, 1452, Mehmed II began the construction of a fortress at the narrowest point of the Bosphorus, across from the Anatolian castle (Anadolu Hisar) erected by Bayezid I. Work on the new castle, named Rumeli Hisar, was completed by the end of August, 1452. A garrison of 400 men under the orders of Firuz Beg was instructed to board all ships bound for Constantinople and to exact tolls. For scholarly literature on this castle, see above, Chap. 2, n. 27. Nicolò Barbaro, an eyewitness of the siege, who compiled a precious diary of the days of the siege, provides a concise description of the fortress of doom, and of its first victims, 1 (CC 1, with improved text, 8–9): "Mille quattrozento e cinquanta do de marzo, Machomet bej turco dè prinzipio a fabricar uno castello belitissimo, luntan mìa sie de Costantinopoli verso la boca de Mar Mazor, el qual castello hanno tore quatordexe, de le qual quatordexe, ne sun cinque principal coverte de piombo, e sono maxize ... El primo colpo che trè la bombarda grossa de questo castelo afondò la nave de Antonio Rizo che vignia de Mar Mazor ... el patron de quela sì fo piado in aqua ... e in cavo de zorni 14 el signor el feze impalar suxo un palo, e uno fio che fo de ser Domenego di Maistri, el suo scrivanelo, lol mese in nel suo seraio, e alguni marinari lo i dè lizentia che i dovesse venir a Costantinopoli; altri fece tagliar per mezzo ...." This castle eventually attracted the attention of the Venetians and spies produced at least one drawing of its defenses; it survives in a manuscript (Cod. Mediol. Trivult. lat. N 641 [I 95], fols. 39ᵛ–40ʳ); see Franz Babinger, "Ein venedischer Lageplan der Feste Rümeli Hisâry (2. Hälfte des XV. Jhdts.)," *La Bibliofilia* 58 (1955): 188–95; the plan is further reproduced in *MCT* as pl. IX. This Venetian sketch is the earliest depiction of the fortress in existence. Most impressed, among Greek writers, was Kritoboulos, who devoted a large section of his narrative to the construction of the castle (1.11.1.2), the speed of its erection (1.11.3), its plan and specifications (1.11.4,5), and the deployment of artillery on the towers (1.11.6,7). The architect of this castle was a certain Muslih ed-Din, a Christian renegade in all likelihood (CC 1: 345, n. 3). In the last century the Greek scholar Paspates was able to tour the castle and inspect the *quattrocento* remains of it before extensive renovations were carried out; during the inspection he noted various Greco-Byzantine architectural elements in its structure: see Paspates, Πολιορκία καὶ Ἅλωσις, 80–81.

quemque aut odiis aut commoditatibus occupatum, salutem publicam neglexisse magis crediderim.

III.   Mahumetes interea coactis [vim] undique copiis<,> mirabili apparatu formidando animo <et> impetu<,> terra marique regiam urbem aggressus<,> cuniculis ac latentibus fossis altissimis actis<,> aggere late edito<,> ponteque[9] Peram oppidum versus mare muros alluit urbis, longitudinis ad duo millia passuum raptim extructo<,> turribus ligneis eo usque erectis, ut muros aequis[10]

---

[9] ponte, qua
[10] quamvis

their private feuds and short-term convenience forced them to neglect the commonwealth.³

3.   Meanwhile Mehmed grew in power and assembled his conscripted forces from everywhere; he attacked the city by land and sea with admirable preparations, with terrifying spirit, by means of mines and deeply hidden tunnels,⁴ with a high siege mound, and with a bridge crossing the sea, whose waves reached all the walls of the city, opposite the town of Pera; it was built suddenly and measured two miles in length;⁵ in addition, he constructed such wooden

---

³ Venice was the principal, perhaps only active, ally of Constantine XI in 1453. In fact, in February 1453 Venice despatched a fleet to the relief of Constantinople, under Giacomo Loredano, but, due to inevitable delays, this armada reached the Aegean after the sack. Isidore, the papal legate in Constantinople, had brought to the Greek capital 200 crossbowmen recruited at the pope's expense. Individual companies of volunteers also offered their services to the beleaguered city; among them were the Bocchiardi brothers, who brought, at their own expense, a small company of warriors, and Giovanni Guglielmo Longo Giustiniani, the *condottiere*, with a band of 700 well-armed professional soldiers who became the nucleus of the defense. For the diplomatic efforts of the Greek emperor to secure western aid, see Rodolphe Guilland, "Les appels de Constantine XI Paléologue à Rome et à Venise pour sauver Constantinople," BS 14 (1953): 226–44; and Constantin Marinescu, "Notes sur quelques ambassadeurs byzantins en Occident à la veille de la chute de Constantinople sous les Turcs," *Annuaire de l'Institut de Philologie et l'Histoire Orientales et Slaves* 10 (1950): 419–28.

⁴ See above, Chap. 2, n. 29. The soldiers in the Turkish camp were accompanied by numerous non-combatants, such as mullahs and dervishes. In addition to his other forces, Mehmed II had imported expert miners from Serbia; see Languschi-Dolfin dependent, to a large extent, on the eyewitness account by Leonardo, 10 (fol. 315): "Et per questo el Turcho deluso penso no cessar dal continuo trazer, ma ancora cum piu forte cura de caue subterranee furar la terra, et per questo lauor li fossor delle miniere, che lauoraua a Nouobordo fece uenir." This testimony finds an echo in the eyewitness account of Tetaldi (French version, XIII [1821]): "Du costé de la terre, Sengampsa Albanois [= Zaganos Pasha] renié, qui so siege tenoit, avoit plusieurs hommes accoustumez de miner l'or & l'argent, mina en quatorze lieux soubs le lieu de la ville, pour le tallier, & commença ses mines bien long du mur." The forces of the sultan heavily outnumbered the defenders, whose effective strength was, according to one testimony (Sphrantzes 25.6), 4773 Greeks and 200 (almost certainly a scribal error for 2000) foreigners. FC, 85, estimates that there were 7000 active defenders; OGN, 193, cites 8,000 Greeks and 2000 foreigners. Constantinople's harbor was defended by a heavy iron chain that stretched across the Golden Horn and denied entry to the Turkish armada and by Venetian vessels which had been detained in the capital to reinforce the available resources.

⁵ See above, Chap. 2, n. 30. Descriptions of this bridge are provided in numerous sources (see the summary in FC, III, n. 1). Tetaldi, VII (790), supplies some information in his Latin version (repeated in the French version, XIV [1821]). Tetaldi speaks of one such tower, which he had undoubtedly seen with his own eyes; cf. (French version) XIV (1821): "Le dit Sengampsa fist un chastel de bois si hault & si grant, qu'il seignourissoit le mur, ... & plusieurs instruments de bois, desquels il povoit estre sans estre blechié: & si l'y avoit tours de bois tres-haultes, grandes & ligieress." Tetaldi's Latin version repeats the same details (VII [790]): "Praefatus autem Sangambassa fieri constituit fortalitium castri lignei, magni ampli firmi & alti: adeo ut

altissimos excederent, machinamentorum tormentorumque multiplici adhibito genere oppugnata est urbs<,> defensaque summis utrinque viribus non paucis diebus.

towers that they surpassed the height of the tallest walls.⁶ The city was bombarded with missiles propelled by numerous kinds of engines and cannon.⁷ A general, strong defense was maintained for quite a few days.

....

murorum civitatis celsitudinem excedere videretur ... Multas quoque machinas sua adinventione atque industria fabricari mandavit & diversa carpenta sive stallagia ad repugnandum altitudinis & latitudinis non minimae." The artillery of Mehmed II and his monstrous bombards cast by westerners and renegades in his pay did not make much of a difference in military terms; the effects of the Ottoman artillery were psychological. The most succinct description of Mehmed's artillery can be found in Benvenuto's eyewitness report (*TIePN*: 4, and Pertusi, "The Anconitan Colony in Constantinople and the Report of its Consul, Benvenuto, on the Fall of the City," 199–218; a translation of this document appears in Philippides, *Byzantium, Europe, and the Early Ottoman Sultans*, Appendix B, 197–99; the Latin text is quoted below, Chap. 5, n. 2). Early in the summer of 1452 a Hungarian expert in the manufacture of cannons by the name of Urban(us) or Orban(us) in the employ of the emperor asked Constantine XI for a raise in his salary; the emperor was unable to pay the requested amount and Urban/Orban then left Constantinople and entered the service of the sultan; he was responsible for the artillery that Mehmed placed on Rumeli Hisar and then went on to cast Mehmed's bombards for the siege. His masterpiece, the *basilica*, made a deep impression on the participants (see its detailed description in Kritoboulos, trans. Riggs, 1.125–143). This must be the bombard that Benvenuto described. The *basilica* was positioned on the hill of Maltepe in front of Mehmed II's tent and was aimed at the sector of Saint Romanus, the weak spot of the fortifications; subsequently, the area bombarded by the *basilica* became known as Top Kapı, "the Gate of the Cannon." See Pears, *The Destruction of the Greek Empire*, 245 ff.; *MCT*, 80–82; *FC*, 77–78; and *LCB*, 403. In addition, see DeVries, "Gunpowder Weapons at the Siege of Constantinople, 1453," and Williams, "Ottoman Military Technology: The Metallurgy of Turkish Armor." For a thorough evaluation of this topic, see Philippides, "Urban's Bombard(s), Gunpowder, and the Siege of Constantinople (1453)."

⁶ For operations involving towers of antique designs, cf. the analysis in Philippides, "Urban's Bombard(s)."

⁷ Constantinople was protected by a moat and by a formidable triple line of fortifications; the moat measured approximately 60 feet in width; immediately behind the moat stood a low wall that had been erected by Alexios Apokaukos in 1341. Behind this rampart an open enclosure stretched to a distance of 54 feet all the way to the first line of fortifications, the so-called Outer Wall erected by Emperor Herakleios (610–641); being approximately 12 feet thick, this Outer Wall was reinforced by square towers standing at intervals of 50–100 yards. Behind this line of defenses was a second enclosure averaging 50 feet in width; it stretched to the inner, Great Wall standing an average of 52 feet in height. The Great Wall was about 8 feet thick and was reinforced by square and octagonal towers at intervals of approximatelly 154 feet; the towers rose to a height of 96 feet. In 1422 when Murad II (Mehmed II's father) had besieged Constantinople the defenders manned the Outer Wall and their strategy had been successful, as the Turks proved unable to breach the defenses. John VIII and Constantine XI had strengthened and repaired the Outer Wall. In 1453 the numbers of the defenders were too low and there was no question of manning both Outer and Inner Walls. Necessity forced the defenders to man the Outer Wall and hope for the best. After the sack, Bishop Leonardo, who had participated in the defense and had survived a short captivity, declared that the strategy had been wrong and that the Inner Wall should have been manned. Yet the bishop should have realized that the defenders were too few to man adequately all towers of the Inner Wall. By the end of May, the incessant

IV.   Ad extremum[11] voce praeconis castris inclamatum est v kalendas[12] Maii milites omnes ieiunium sanctificent<,> sequenti[13] die in armis assint<.>[14] Urbem extremis viribus oppugnaturi triduo civitatem militum direptioni futuram<,> constituta die ieiunium ad noctem usque servatum. Exin lucentibus stellis invitationes ac convivia passim habita, ut[15] quisque amicum propinquum notumque habuit<,> cum eo hilaris epulatus est; atque ubi satis adhibitum<,> tanquam se deinceps nunquam visuri essent<,> amplexati<,> exosculatique simul ultimum vale dixerunt.

V.   In urbe autem sacerdotes sacras ferentes imagines<,> sequente populo<,> urbem lustrare<,> auxilium de caelo petere, affligere corpora ieiuniis<,> atque orationibus universe[16] cives intendere. Subsecuta nocte<,> ad sua quisque loca defendenda redi<e>re. Erant muri urbis et altitudine et crassitudine toto orbe celebres<,> sed ob vetustatem et Graecorum incuriam pinnis ac propugnaculis nudi. Antemuralia vero opportune communita. In his Graeci salutem posuere. Armati milites inter muros et <ante>muralia pugnam sustinere decreverunt. Triangularem paene urbis formam fuisse tradunt<.> Duas partes alluit mare. Nec muri desunt ad [pro]pulsandos navales impetus idonei. Quod

---

[11] Non paucis diebus ad extremum
[12] quinto Calen.
[13] sequente
[14] adsint
[15] et
[16] universi

4. At last the crier announced throughout the camp that on May 28 all soldiers were to purify themselves with a fast in order to prepare themselves for the general attack scheduled for the following day; after their victory they could plunder the city for three days; the fast would be maintained all day, until nightfall. When the stars could be distinguished banquets were held and invitations were dispatched widely, so that friendship and camaraderie could be established with feasting and in good cheer. At the end they embraced, kissed each other, and said their last farewell, as if they would never see each other again.[8]

5. In the city, by contrast, the priests brought out the sacred icons and asked help from Heaven by holding processions, with the people in tow, throughout the city, by punishing their bodies with fasts, and by trying to protect the citizens with never-ending public prayer sessions. When night fell, each man returned to his assigned post on the walls. The walls of the city were famous throughout the world for their height and thickness, but battlements and defenses were absent because of old age and of the neglect displayed by the Greeks. The outer line of defense was sufficiently fortified nevertheless. The Greeks had placed all hope of salvation on this line. Armed soldiers had been posted between the first line and the walls to bear the brunt of the attack. They say that the city has an almost triangular shape, whose two sides are washed by the sea. These are defended by

---

bombardment of the sultan's batteries had reduced the Outer Wall to rubble in numerous sectors; the heaviest damage had been inflicted in the area between the Gates of Adrianople and Saint Romanus, the Achilles heel of the defense, as is still evident in the ruins of the walls, in sections where the Outer Wall has simply vanished. Kritoboulos, trans. Riggs, 1.148, states that the defenders had raised a stockade in this area that had to be reinforced constantly. In the areas where walls had disappeared and stockades were being improvised, the role of cavalry seems to have assumed important dimensions, as we seem to infer from statements in our sources. Thus minor cavalry charges and hand-to-hand combat in the enclosures may not be ruled out at this late stage of the siege. On the fortifications of Constantinople in 1453, see Van Millingen, *Byzantine Constantinople*, 237 ff.; FC, 87–92; and OGN, 193–94. The topography of the land walls and the problems they present in regard to the siege are discussed by Philippides and Hanak in *The Pen and the Sword: Historiography, Topography and Military Studies on the Siege of Constantinople in 1453*, chap. 6.

[8] The Turks usually observed a three-day period of ritual cleansing and fasting before a final assault was launched. This three-day period seems to have been observed at this time also. Barbaro, an eyewitness, also refers to the "celebrations" in the Turkish camp, 48 [with improved text in CC 1: 27]: "A dì vinti sie pur de questo mexe de mazo a una hora de note, Turchi se fexe per tuto el suo campo una gran luminaria de fuoghi, li qual fuoghi ogni pavion che iera in nel campo, si feva do fuoghi, i qual fuoghi si iera grandenisimi, e per grando calor de queli, pareva che fosse de zorno chiaro; questi teribeli fuoghi si durò in fina a la meza notte. Questi fuoghi el signor Turco sì i fexe far per el campo, per alegra' el puovolo del campo, perché el se aprossimava la destrution de la puovera zitade, per dare la dura bataia." Bishop Leonardo is more laconic but supplies essentailly identical information, CC 1: 138: "triduo luminaria Deo accendunt, ieiunant die nihil usque ad noctem gustantes."

reliquum est<,> ad terram vergens post alta moenia et antemuralia <(>quae annotavimus<)>, ingenti clauditur fossa.

VI.   Coeptum est proelium paululum ante lucem, cum miles Turcus periculi quam mor<a>e patientior esset<,> ac vulnera et sanguinem praedarum dulcedine pensaret<,> pugnatum est in tenebris maiori Turcorum[17] pernicie, in quos tela superne lib[e]rabantur. At postquam illuxit<,> dato signo undique<,> non solum Constantinopolis<,> sed <etiam> ipsa quoque Pera<,> ne quid auxilii Graecis praestaret<,> oppugnari coepta est<.> Sua cuique legioni murorum pars<,> ac portarum attributa, ut discretus labor fortes atque ignavos distingueret, et ipsa contentione decoris militum virtus magis ac magis acce<n>deretur. Pari modo et navales socii attributas partes invadere iussit. Admoventur urbi ligneae turres. Convectant milites dolabras, falces<,> scalasque. Et iam elatis super capita scutis<,> densa testudine succedunt Graeci saxorum pondera provolvunt, disiectam fluitantem[que] testudinem lanceis contisque perscrutantur, donec soluta com<p>age scutorum exangues lacerosque prosternunt<,>[18] fit strages<.> Et iam Turci[19] deficientibus animis<,> languidius pugnant. Sed adest Mahumetes fortissimum quenque nominatim vocitans<,> utque in proelium redeant adhortatur; hos praemiis allicit, illos minis deterret. Instauratur ex integro certamen. Turci[20] rursus subruere murum<,> portasque quatere innixi humeris<,> et super iteratam testudinem scandentes<,> pr<a>ehensare hostium tela brachiaque nituntur. Iterum integri cum sauciis<,> semianimes cum expirantibus evolvuntur. Cernitur varia pereuntium forma<,> et plurima mortis imago.

---

[17] maiore Turcarum
[18] prostraverunt
[19] Turcae
[20] Turcae

walls, which can resist naval assaults. The remaining part, the land side, is protected by high walls, the outer line of defenses (which I have already noted), and an immense moat.

6.   The battle began a little before dawn,[9] as the Turkish soldiers did not delay but were eager to risk danger, loss of blood, and wounds with the sweet prospect of booty before them. During the fight under cover of darkness the Turks suffered greater slaughter, as all sorts of missiles were thrown against them from above. But after dawn broke the signal was given for a general attack against all sectors, not only against Constantinople but also against Pera so that no aid should be dispatched to the Greeks; so the battle was joined. Every sector of the fortifications was assigned to legions; every gate area was similarly covered so that the task at hand could separate the strong from the coward and so that the contest itself would keep on testing the bravery of the soldiers. He [Mehmed] also ordered his naval forces to attack picked sections. The wooden towers moved towards the city. The soldiers carried axes, grappling hooks, and ladders. They protected their heads with their shields and arranged themselves densely into a tortoise formation as the Greeks were throwing heavy rocks upon them; the tortoise was attacked with lances and pikes until the shield formation broke; butchered, they lost their lives and fell in the slaughter. By now the Turks were losing heart and were fighting rather weakly. Then Mehmed addressed each of his bravest warriors by name and urged them to rejoin battle. To some he promised rewards and others were checked by his threats. Once more the contest began in earnest. The Turks attacked the wall again; they pushed against the gates with their shoulders, reformed their tortoise as they tried to climb on the walls, and strove to protect themselves against the missiles and pikes of the enemy. Once more those who were not injured mixed with the wounded and the dying with the dead. Death took on all sorts of forms and death appeared in many shapes.

---

[9] The general assault seems to have been launched after midnight but before dawn; skirmishes had been going on during the evening and night of May 28 to keep the defenders busy. The condition of the Outer Wall was deplorable, with improvised stockades, while each standing tower was inadequately and irregularly manned by no more than two or three individuals. Excepting the band of Giustiniani, the defenders were badly armed (OGN, 189). The first wave of the assault consisted of the *bašıbazuk* irregulars, which included numerous Christian renegades and adventurers from Serbia, Hungary, Germany, Transylvania, and Greece; they were supervised by the sultan's military police. This wave was easily turned back by the defenders. The second wave consisted of the regular Anatolian regiments of the sultan, who launched an orderly attack but were also repelled. Before the defenders could recover, the third wave came upon them with deadly precision: the dread janissaries who advanced in formation. This was by far the most serious assault but the defenders managed to hold out until Giustiniani was wounded; then the defense collapsed and the improvised defenses at the Saint Romanus sector, i.e. the modern area of Sulu Kule, were overrun by the enemy, while the defenders were busy trampling each other in a hasty retreat to seek shelter behind the Great Wall.

VII.   Ioannes Iustinianus apud Genuam Ligurum metropolim nobili loco natus, qui superioribus diebus solus urbem defendisse videbatur, in hoc certamine vulneratus<,> ubi <fluitare> sanguinem suum animadvertit, ne c<a>eteros deterreret<,> medicum quaerens, clam sese pugnae subtraxit. Sed imperator ut abesse Iustinianum cognovit, quo ierit percunctatur.[21] Inventumque

---

[21] percontatur

7.   Giovanni Giustiniani, who had been born a nobleman in Genoa, the capital of the Ligurians, had seemed, in the previous days, to be the sole defender of the city, but he was wounded in this battle; when he saw himself bleeding, he searched for a physician and secretly withdrew from the battle, without deterring anyone else from doing so.[10] When the emperor discovered that Giustiniani

---

[10] Giovanni Guglielmo Longo Giustiniani, a *condottiere* in the service of the Greek emperor, came to Constantinople in January 1453, bringing a well-armed band of 700 professional soldiers. He was immediately appointed πρωτοστράτωρ/*dux militiae*, or commander-in-chief, by the emperor, and his band provided the nucleus of the defense throughout the siege. Leonardo, trans. Melville Jones, 30, reports that the sultan was so impressed with Giustiniani's defensive measures and skill in combat that he arranged to bribe the Genoese warlord, but Giustiniani would have nothing to do with treason (*MCT*, 91). The wound(s) that Giustiniani received during the third wave of the final assault was indeed the turning point of the battle. The exact circumstances of the incident and its aftermath are not clear. According to Barbaro, trans. Jones, 65, the warlord abandoned his post (and a hand other than the author's, that of Marco Barbaro, "il genealogista," added in the margin of the manuscript: "because he had been wounded," "per esser ferito de frezza"); Barbaro then exhibits Venetian bias against the Genoese, 55 (CC 1: 33): "... e questo Zuan Zustignan, l'imperador si lavea fato capetanio da tera; e scampando questo che iera capetanio, vignando el dito per la tera criando: 'Turchi son intradi dentro da la tera;' e menteva per la gola, che ancora i non iera intradi dentro." Tetaldi (French version), trans. Melville Jones, 8, states that Giustiniani was wounded by a culverin and went to look for a physician. Leonardo, trans. Melville Jones, 36, reports that Giustiniani was wounded by a firearm in the arm; Languschi-Dolfin repeats the same statement, 29: "Zuanne Zustignan capitanio uien ferito de freza ... lo quale come inexperto zouene subito ueduto el sangue pauido de perder la uita ... ascosamente per medicarse se parte da la sua statione, che el hauesse posto un altro in suo loco, la salute de la patria non periua." Tursun Beg, *History of Mehmed the Conqueror*, trans. Inalcik and Murphey, 36, asserts that he was wounded in the belly by a Turk. Nestor-Iskander adds that Giustiniani was wounded twice, 60–61 (74–77): и ударивъ Зустунѣа по персѣмъ, и разрази емы перси. И паде на землю" and 62 (76): "... прилетѣвшу убо склопу, и удари Зустунѣа и срази ему десное плечо, и наде на землю аки мертвъ. И надоша надъ нимь боляре его и людіе, крыча и рыдаш, и поношаше его прочь, тако и Фрягове вси пойдоша за нимъ. That the warlord received two wounds finds confirmation in another source, Sekoundinos (CC 2: 134): "duobus acceptis vulneribus." The departure of Giustiniani and his troops created confusion that could be easily observed by the attacking Turks. The warlord retreated from the stockade and had a gate opened to let himself into the Great Wall and the city. The remaining defenders, feeling abandoned, rushed to get through the same gate themselves and panic ensued. Giustiniani and his band proceeded to the harbor at the Golden Horn, boarded their ship, and sailed to Chios. Giustiniani died on the way to the island and was eventually buried in the church of San Domenico. The inscription on his tomb was recorded, in various forms, in the last century; but the actual stone and all traces of his monument have disappeared. One of the versions of the text of the inscription runs as follows: "Hic iacet Ioannes Iustinianus, inclitus vir ac Genuensis patricius Chiique maonensis, qui in Constantinopolis expugnatione a principe Turchorum Mehemet, serenissimi Constantine Orientialium ultimi Christianorum imperatoris magnanimus dux, lethali vulnere icto interiit, anno a partu Virginis M.III.L.VIII [sic] Kal. Augusti." See Philippides, "Giovanni Guglielmo Longo Giustiniani, the Genoese *Condottiere* of Constantinople in 1453."

rogat ne pugnam deserat. Ille nihilo magis flexus<,> aperiri portam iubet, qua curaturus vulnus in urbem redeat. Era<n>t enim obseratae urbis ianuae, quibus ad antemuralia patebat iter, ne qua fugiendi faculta militi esset<,> ac propterea fortius hosti resisteret<;> fit interea remissior defensio, quod Turci[22] a<nima>dvertentes<,> acrius incumbunt. Et quoniam pars muri iam tormentis aeneis disiecta, fossam magna ex parte oppleverat, per ruinas ipsas scandentes, antemurale conscendunt, Graecosque loco deturbant.

VIII.   Porta quae Ioanni patuerat omnibus aperta, fugam profusiorem reddit. Tunc imperator non ut regem decuit pugnando<,> sed fugiens in ipsis portae angustiis cum [ce]cidisset<,> oppressus calcatusque obiit. In tanta multitudine pugnatorum duo tantum reperti sunt<,> qui se viros ostenderint<,> alter

---

[22]Turcae

had left, he tried to locate him. He found him and asked him why he retreated from the battle. But his mind was made up, and he gave an order to open the gate so that he could take care of his wound within the city. The gates of the city to the outer defenses had been barred in order to deny the defenders an avenue of retreat so that they would fight against the enemy more forcefully. Meanwhile the defense became lax, a fact that did not go unnoticed by the Turks, who attacked with greater force. And since part of the wall had already been demolished by the bronze cannons, and the moat had been partly filled, they climbed over the very ruins, overran the outer defenses, and forced the Greeks to flee.

8.   The gate, opened for Giovanni, now gave access to everyone and created a headlong flight. The emperor perished,[11] not by fighting (which would have been appropriate for a king) but when he fell in the narrow passage to the gate, where he was trodden on and was trampled to death. There were only two individuals who proved themselves to be men in this great crowd of warriors:[12] one

---

[11] Reports of the death of Constantine XI are mostly fictitious; apparently no one in the vicinity of the last stand escaped and consequently no one ever recorded what he had actually seen. Thus there are no dependable accounts of the emperor's last minutes. The reports that exist can be divided into two camps. One camp (by far the majority) seeks heroization, if not actual canonization, for the last emperor and assigns a heroic death to him. Another group, the minority, simply states that the emperor joined the fleeing troops and perished in the ensuing press at the gate. Pius's report belongs to this latter group. The fact, nevertheless, remains that the emperor probably had no wish to survive a successful final assault of the sultan, as Mehmed was notorious for dealing harshly with his prisoners. When Constantine launched his counterattack, accompanied by a few individuals, two of whom are named by Pius, he took care to discard all his imperial regalia (such as a possible tabard or surcoat bearing the coat of arms of the Palaeologi) in order to avoid identification and capture. The plain fact is that details of his death were not known to survivors and in time tales were created (even indicating the spot where the emperor lost his mount during the final assault). One of the earliest reports, that of Benvenuto, has an honest, simple statement: "Item: quod audivit <sc. Benvenutus> ab uno trumpeta quod Imperator Gr<a>ecorum fuit interfectus et eius caput super lancea Turcorum domino pr<a>esentatum." Tursun Beg, *History of Mehmed the Conqueror*, trans. Inalcik and Murphey, 36–37, speaks of the emperor's death as well and states that he was retreating towards the Golden Horn in order to board a ship when he was intercepted and killed by a group of *azabs* (= irregulars). On this matter, cf. FC, 139–40; LCB, 409; OGN, 199; and Pears, *The Destruction of the Greek Empire*, 353–54. The most important article on this topic was written in the beginning of the twentieth century and, despite its numerous eccentricities, it remains the most thorough modern study of the issue: Xenophon A. Siderides, "Κωνσταντίνου Παλαιολόγου Θάνατος, Τάφος, καὶ Σπάθη," Ἡ Μελέτη 2 (1908): 65–78, 129–46.

[12] Most sources are agreed as to the names of these two individuals, who seem indeed to have perished in the vicinity of Constantine XI; they were certainly among those who participated in the last stand. The name of Giovanni Schiavo is variously rendered through Latinization and Hellenization as "Schiavo," "Sclavo/Sclavus/Sclavos," or as "Illyricus." Pseudo-Sphrantzes [= Makarios Melissourgos-Melissenos] added, in his sixteenth-century elaboration of Sphrantzes' authentic work, another individual, Don Francisco de Toledo, who, he claims, was a distant kinsman of Constantine XI. This personality was invented by Pseudo-Sphrantzes

Graecus, alter Dalmata<,> Theophilus Paleologus<,> et Ioannes Sclavus, qui fugere turpe putantes, cum diu Turcorum[23] impetum sustinuissent<,> multosque obtruncassent<,> denique non tam victi quam vincendo fatigati<,> inter cadavera <hostium> occubuere. Iustinianus in Peram cum divertisset<,> inde Chium navigavit<,> ibique seu vulnere seu maestitia morbum incidens<,> inglorius vitam finivit<.> Felix [si] in ipsis Byzantii moenibus animam ex<h>alasset. In ingressu portae octigenti circiter milites ex Latinis Graeci[bu]sque periere, partim vulneribus a tergo confossi, partim concursione[24] oppressi. Et iam hostis superiorem murum tenebat<,> saxaque in cives devolvens<,> ingredientibus suis[25] auxilio erat.

IX. Tum subito capta urbe<,> caesis omnibus qui resistere ausi sunt<,> in rapinas est itum. Erat victorum infinitus numerus<,> in libidinem<,> [ac] saevitiam corruptior<,> non dignitas, non aetas, non sexus quenquam protegebat. Stupra caedibus<,> caedes stupris miscebantur. Senes exacta aetate, feminas

---

[23] Turcarum
[24] conversione
[25] suo

was a Greek, Theophilus Palaeologus; the other was a Dalmatian, John Sclavus. Both deemed flight shameful and kept up the fight against the onslaught of the Turks for a long time, put many to the sword, and finally were overcome not so much by defeat but by fatigue; they fell in the midst of the enemy corpses. Giustiniani went to Pera and then sailed to Chios; there he ended his life without glory, either because of his wound or because of sadness.[13] He would have been a happy man had he given up his spirit on the walls of Byzantium [= Constantinople]. In the passageway of the gate about eight hundred Greek and Latin soldiers perished; some of them bore wounds on their backs and others were overcome by the congestion of the fleeing men. And so the enemy assumed control of the higher wall and began to throw rocks against the citizens below, bringing aid to their entering troops.

9. Suddenly the city had fallen; all those who dared to offer resistance were slain; and the troops turned to plunder. Infinite was the number of the victors who began to look for their pleasure: their cruelty could not be checked by anyone's dignity, age, or sex. Orgies mixed with slaughter, slaughter mixed with orgies. In jest did they drag both old men who were at death's threshold and

---

in order to flatter an influential Spanish family of Naples, the forger's residence; cf. Khasiotes, Μακάριος, Θεόδωρος καὶ Νικηφόρος οἱ Μελισσηνοὶ (Μελισσουργοί), 176. The forger is not the only individual to invent personalities in this incident. Stacton, *The World on the Last Day*, 236, adds to this company another individual, "Demetrius Cantacuzenus." The only *quattrocento* source to mention a Kantakouzenos is Khalkokondyles, ed. Darkó, 395B, who, however, does not cite his Christian name, nor does he state explicitly that he was a member of the heroic group in the last stand; he only reports that he and the emperor addressed each other before they died. Moreover, this personality of Demetrius [Palaeologus] Kantakouzenos seems to have been tampered with in the suspect *Maius*, the forgery of Pseudo-Sphrantzes; see now the meticulous study by Ganchou, "Le Mésazon Démétrius Paléologue Cantacuzène," who concludes his study with the following observation (271): "Le mésazon Démétrius Paléologue Cantacuzène n'a jamais participé au siège de Constantinople en 1453, pour la bonne raison qu'il était mort plus tôt, peut-être de maladie."

[13] This comment ultimately derives from the report of an eyewitness, the source of most *quattrocento* accounts of the fall, Leonardo (CC 1: 40–43; PG 159: 940, 941): "Refugit capitaneus in Pera, qui post Chium navigans ex vulnere vel tristitia inglorium transitum fecit." Languschi-Dolfin, 28–29 (fol. 320), repeats in the vernacular: "tutti li compagni et le forze fono indebilide et seguitorno el suo capitaneo al tuo camariero le chiaue de la porta, la quale aperta se sforzano de passar et fugissene in Pera lo qual dapoi nauigando a Chio de la ferita o piutosto da tristitia morite senza gloria." Pseudo-Sphrantzes paraphrased the gist of this passage into Greek (with a slight modification, as he believed that Giustiniani died at Pera), 3.9.7, 284b [426]: ἀλλ᾽ ἐν τῷ Γαλατᾷ περάσας αἰσχρῶς ἐκεῖ τελευτᾷ ἐκ τῆς πικρίας καὶ περιφρονήσεως. More faithful to the the text of Leonardo is the anonymous Barberini 111, whose author has paraphrased the same passage into the spoken idiom (28–29 [fol. 58ʳ]): Ἀμμὴ ὁ καπετάνιος ἔφυγε καὶ ἐδιάβη εἰς τὸν Γαλατᾶ· καὶ ἀπὸ κεῖ ἐδιάβη εἰς τὴ Χίο λαβωμένος, καὶ ὑστέρου ἀπόθανε μὲ ἐντροπή.

viles ad praedam in ludibrium trahebant<;> ubi adulta virgo<,> aut quis forma conspicuus incidisset in manus rapientium divulsus<,> ipsos postremo direptores in mutuam perniciem agebat<.> Dum pecuniam vel gravia templorum dona sibi quisque traheret<,> maiore aliorum vi truncabatur. Cumque in exercitu maximo ac dissono<,> ex civibus sociis atque externis conflato<,> diversae linguae, varii mores, atque cupidines essent<,> et aliud cuique fas<,> nihil illicitum toto triduo in Constantinopoli fuit<.> Templum Sophiae Iustiniani Caesaris opus<,> toto orbe famosum, [et] cui comparari alterum nequeat<,> nudatum sacrum supellectile<,>[26] ad omnes spurcitias patuit. Ossa martyrum<,> quae fuerant illa in urbe pretiosissima<,> canibus obiecta et suibus. Sanctorum imagines aut luto foedatae<,> aut ferro[27] deletae<.> Altaria diruta. In templis ipsis aut lupanaria meretricum facta<,> aut equorum stabula.

X.   Coacti sunt servi verberibus ac tormentis dominorum abdita scrutari ac [defossa] eruere; inventi non pauci thesauri, quos in ipso belli principio infelices suffoderant[28] cives. Quibus si pro defensione urbis usi fuissent, suam fortasse vitam<,> et patriae libertatem servassent. Sed avaro in aurum nulla potestas; captivi omnes in castra deducti<,> pudet dicere Christianos dedecus<,> dicam tamen et posteritati tradere non verebor<,> quando persuasum mihi est futuros aliquando et fortasse antequam moriar, qui tantam salvatori nostro illatam ignominiam ulciscantur. Simulacrum crucifixi quem colimus<,> et verum Deum esse fatemur<,> tubis et[29] tympanis praeeuntibus raptum ex urbe<,> hostes ad tentoria deferunt<,> sputo<,> lutoque foedant<,> et ad nostrae religionis irrisionem iterum cruci affigunt.

XI.   Exinde[30] pileo quem sarculam[31] vocant<,> capiti eius imposito, corona undique facta<,> hic est <(>inqu<i>unt<)> Christianorum Deus<.> Tum lapides<,> lutumque iactantes, miris dehonestant modis. Sed nihil haec obsunt

---

[26] sacra suppellecte
[27] torro
[28] suffoderunt
[29] ac
[30] Ex in
[31] sartulum

common women as their booty. If a virgin of age or anyone endowed with beauty fell into the hands of looters, it was a cause for mutual destruction among the plunderers. Anyone could snatch up wealth or the heavy dedications of the churches, but then he was slaughtered by others who were stronger. This enormous, inharmonious army (as there were both subjects and allies in it who spoke all sorts of languages, and displayed different customs and desires) turned to unbridled acts and Constantinople was subjected to lawlessness for three days. The church of [Santa] Sophia (erected by Emperor Justinian), famous throughout the world, since it has no match, was stripped of its holy apparatus and admitted pollution. All the precious bones of the martyrs which were housed in that city were offered to dogs and swine. The images of the saints were covered with clay or were destroyed with implements. Altars were plundered. The churches themselves functioned as brothels or were turned into stables for horses.

10.   They compelled the slaves (with beatings and torture) to identify and dig up their masters' hidden property. Quite a few treasures were discovered, which the unhappy citizens themselves had buried in the very beginning of the war. Had they been used for the defense of the city, perhaps their own lives and their ancestral homeland would have been saved. Yet greed possesses no character. All prisoners were led to the camp; it shames me to recount the disgrace of the Christians but I will speak, nevertheless, and will record it for posterity, as I am convinced that in the future perhaps even before I die, there will be revenge for this ignominy that our own Savior has suffered. The enemy snatched the very image of the crucified one whom we worship and declare to be the true God, and brought it to his tents (to the accompaniment of trumpets and drums); he spat upon it; he polluted it; and to make sport of our faith, he crucified it again.

11.   He placed upon it a hat, which they call *zarcula*,[14] and a crown around it and said, "this is the God of the Christians." Then they defiled it in various ways, by throwing rocks and dirt upon it. Yet this means nothing to our God who

---

[14] *Zarcula*, or more properly in Turkish *zerkulah*, refers to the peculiar white headdress worn by the Ottoman janissaries of the period, a well-known item that distinguished these regiments of the sultan. It was also known to Leonardo, who referred to it, in his description of the sack of Constantinople in 1453, as *pileum theucrale* (CC 1: 166; PG 159: 942): "... sputis, blasphemiis, obprobriis iterum processionaliter crucifigunt, pileum theucrale, quod *zarchula* vocant, capiti superponentes deridendo clamabant: Hic est Deus Christianorum!" Barbaro in his *Giornale* of the siege of Constantinople identifies the janissaries as "the sultan's slaves" and comments on their headgear, as well as on the distinguishing costumes of the other Ottoman regiments (CC 1: 17): "per niun modo non se poceva veder tera, che zà la iera cuverta da lor Turchi, massimante de janissari i qual sono i soldadi del Turcho, che sono i più valentomeni che abia il Turco, etiam ne iera assaissimi schiavi del signor, i qual se cognose ai capeli bianchi, e i Turchi natural si porta i capeli rossi, i qual se chiama axapi [= azab] ...."

Deo nostro caelum tenenti<.> Nec maiestatem eius quoquo modo imminuere possunt, cuius ea gloria, ea sublimitas est, ea beatitudinis perfectio, ut nec laudibus humanis extolli<,> nec humiliari vituperiis ullis possit. Animos[32] ista laedunt atque confundunt, qui per ignaviam atque desidiam<,> dum veri Dei cultum perire sinimus<,> <et> in hoc saeculo bonum nomen et in altero spem salutis amittimus.

XII. Post haec convivatus Mahumetes<,> cum forte plus solito adhibuisset<,> ut sanguinem mero adderet, principes optimatesque civitatis captos<,> crudelis est sanguinarius carnifex foede misereque iugulari iussit. Kirelucas qui

---

[32] nos

controls the heavens.¹⁵ They cannot diminish His majesty in this manner; His glory, His magnificence, the perfection of His beatitude can neither be extolled with human praises nor be brought low by any abuse. Such behavior hurts and confuses our souls, as we, through cowardice and sloth, allow the worship of the true God to perish and in this age we have forfeited our good name and in the world to come our hope of salvation.

12.   After these events Mehmed celebrated even more opulently than he had been accustomed to, and so that he could mix blood with his wine, the savage and bloody executioner ordered the miserable execution of the captive princes and noblemen of the city. Lord Loukas [Notaras],¹⁶ whose opinion was

---

¹⁵ Again this statement derives from the narrative of Leonardo, who was a prisoner of the Turks and who could have witnessed such an incident before he was ransomed and was taken away from the occupied quarters of Constantinople to the suburb of Pera across the Golden Horn. He may have seen such a procession that could have been improvised by the elated conquerors. It is one of those details that seem to derive from reality. Moreover, it just this sort of event that would have offended an ecclesiastic, who would not understand why Providence would have allowed the "infidels" to act in such manner. Cf. Leonardo [CC 1: 166, omitted by CC 1:] "O Dei patientiam! Bene videris iratus, bone Iesu, ut pro peccatis nostris tantas iniurias iterum toleres indignatus!" Not surprisingly, the same passage of Leonardo is echoed in Languschi-Dolfin, 31 (fol. 321): "Dapoi tolseno Christo crucifixo, et cum timpani et tamburli cum sputi et blasfemie derisorie posto sopra el capo xarcula ditto sessa turchescha cridando diceuano; questo e dio de Christiani, O patientia de dio, ben pari corozado bon Jesu, che per li peccati nostri tanta iniuria toleri."

¹⁶ Most of our surviving sources have treated Loukas Notaras, the last grand duke of Constantinople and chief minister of Constantine XI, unkindly, unfairly, and unevenly. Pius's summary is probably the most factual report. The most condemning account is provided by Melissenos's forgery of the authentic text of Sphrantzes. For unknown reasons the forger was hostile to the grand duke and wrote with extreme prejudice; cf. Pseudo-Phrantzes, trans. Philippides, 132–33. A short but prejudiced version of his execution is also found in Languschi-Dolfin, 32–33 (fol 322): "Et chiamato a se Chir [= Κύρ, the spoken abbreviated form of κύριος] Luca Notara mega duka [= μέγα δοῦκα] et altri baroni greci, represe quelli che non persuadesse a lo Imperator, o inclinarsi a domandarli pace, o hauerli data libera la citade. Alhora Chirluca [= Κὺρ Λουκᾶ<ς>] che cerchaua mettersi in gratia del Signor, et in disgratia Uenetiani et Genoesi de Pera, li qual fono quelli che dauano consilio, armi et militi in li qual uoltaua ogni colpa, et per star in sua gratia lo imperator faceua resistentia, uogliando quello misero che sempre cerchaua gloria cum mendacio et scisma hauer mazor gratia ... Ma Chirluca non scapolo la pena de la malitia sua, che nel suo conspetto fece occider do grandi sui fioli, laltro impubere zouenetto reservo a sua luxuria et lui in ultimo cum sui baroni fu decapitato." At any rate, why Mehmed II ordered the executions of Notaras and his relatives remains a mystery, especially in view of the fact that the conqueror seems to have treated the grand duke with kindness at first and even gave the impression that he had intended to make use of him, in some administrative position, in his new capital. OGN, 200, seems to point an accusatory finger at the powerful Osmanli nobility (which included a large number of Christian renegades); the courtiers of the Porte had opted for the total elimination of the Greek potentates, at whose expense they had hoped to profit,

apud imperatorem plurimum poterat<,> caeso ante oculos maiori filio, altero ad illicitos usus reservato, securi percussus est. Duo alii eius[33] filii in bello ceciderant.[34] Isidorus cardinalis in eo tumultu captus, cum veste mutata[35] non fuisset cognitus<,> tricentis asperis sese redemit<, id est genus pecuniae admodum levis>. Multi <et> Veneti, et Ianuenses<,>[36] et Latinorum<,> alii gladio caesi sunt, quidam multi[37] redempti auro. Insignis hic annus fuit expugnatione[m] Constantinopolitana[m]<,> tam Christiano populo foedus ac lugubris quam

---

[33] Duo eius alii
[34] occiderant in bello.
[35] mutato
[36] Genuenses
[37] multo

valued the most by the emperor, witnessed with his own eyes the execution of his older son, while the second was reserved for sexual purposes, and he was then felled with the ax. Two of his sons had perished in the war. Cardinal Isidore was captured in the confusion but was not recognized, as he had changed his garments; he was ransomed for three hundred aspers (so cheap was the price!). Many Venetians, Genoese, and Latins were put to the sword but quite a few were ransomed with gold.[17] For all Christians this year, marked by the siege and fall of Constantinople, proved foul and mournful; for the Turks it was joyful and

---

especially through the forfeiture of property; in this way, possible future rivals were also eliminated. *MCT*, 97, expresses the opinion that Notaras was executed precisely because he was reputed to be extremely wealthy. Ultimately, the execution of the grand duke was dictated by a combination of numerous factors, which included pressure from the Porte's nobles, personal friction between Notaras and Mehmed's grand vizier, Halil Candarlı (whose own days were also numbered, as he was arrested and executed within a month after the fall of Constantinople), and considerations of practical matters (*FC*, 153). Before the beginning of the siege Notaras had managed to send his daughters away to safety in Italy, where he had made major financial investments. Before his execution Notaras observed the decapitation of his son and that of his son-in-law. His youngest son, Jacob, was reserved to satisfy the pederastic tendencies of the sultan and was confined to the seraglio, as Languschi-Dolfin correctly reports. In time he escaped from the sultan's harem, found his way to Italy, and joined his sisters. He became a modest merchant and never returned to the Levant. On this important family and its survivors in Italy, see G. Cecchini, "Anna Notara Paleologina: Una principessa greca in Italia e la politica senese di ripopolamento delle Maremma," *Bollettino Senese di Storia Patria* 9 (1938): 6–27; Spyridon P. Lampros, "Ὁ Κωνσταντῖνος Παλαιολόγος ὡς Σύζυγος ἐν τῇ Ἱστορίᾳ καὶ τοῖς Θρύλοις," *NH* 4 (1907): 417–66; idem, " Ἡ Ἄννα Νοταρᾶ ὡς Κυρία Κώδικος," *NH* 5 (1908): 485–86; Manoussos I. Manoussakas, " Ἡ Πρώτη Ἄδεια (1456) τῆς Βενετικῆς Γερουσίας γιὰ τὸ Ναὸ τῶν Ἑλλήνων τῆς Βενετίας καὶ ὁ Καρδινάλιος Ἰσίδωρος," *Θησαυρίσματα* 1 (1962): 109–18; Konstantinos D. Mertzios, " Ἡ Διαθήκη τῆς Ἄννας Παλαιολογίνας Νοταρᾶ," *Ἀθηνᾶ* 53 (1953): 17–21; Donald M. Nicol, "Anna Notaras Palaiologina," in idem, *The Byzantine Lady: Ten Portraits 1250–1500* (Cambridge, 1994), 96–109; and Klaus-Peter Matschke, "The Notaras Family and Its Italian Connections," *DOP* 49 (1995): 59–73.

[17] The victims of Mehmed's wave of executions included Girolamo Minotto, the Venetian *bailo* (and a conspicuous hero of the spirited defense in 1453); Minotto's son; and the Catalan consul (*FC*, 150). Languschi-Dolfin provides the following information, 31: "Essendo redutto in Pera M. Hieronimo Minotto, bailo de Uenetiani, cum la moier et fioli et cum mercanti nobeli et citadini, el Turco per hauer quelli in le man fece proclamar che tutti quelli che hauea case in Constantinopoli, douesse uegnir a demonstrar qual fusseno, che a quelli faria consegnar ... Et all prima fece decapitar el bailo de Uenetiani cum altri nobili, et lo consule taraconiense cum do altri." Ubertino Pusculo, the eyewitness poet of the siege (and a captive of the Turks at the time), has some information on this subject, in *Constantinopolis*, 4.1075–1079 (82): "Baiulus Venetum, cum nato ut victima campo / truncatur. Venetique omnes, qui forte reperti / in Galata fuerant, quinis sex millibus auri / nummorum vitam redimunt. At caetera turba / venditur, et dominos distracta est passa superbos." Languschi-Dolfin, 33 (fol. 322), cites the appropriation of property

Turcorum[38] genti faustus laetusque, qui ab ortu salvatoris Christiani secundus et quinguagesimus supra millenum quadrigen<te>simumque concurrit.[39] <Perenses vetus colonia Genuensium, qui et Galata nuncupantur, cognita Byzantiorum clade, priusquam rogarentur, Mahumeti deditionem fecere. Muri urbis diruti, multorum bona contra foedus direpta, feminae puerique ludibrio habiti.>

Finis.

---

[38] Turcarum
[39] cucurrit.

propitious: it was the 1452nd [sic] year since the birth of Christ, our Savior. The Perenses (who inhabit the old colony of Genoa, also known as Galata) surrendered to Mehmed before they were asked, as soon as they realized that Byzantium [Constantinople] had fallen. The walls of their city were demolished, the goods of many citizens were appropriated (in opposition to the treaty), and the women and children were treated with utter scorn.[18]

---

in connection with the wave of executions: "Per tal proclama tutti Franchi et Greci compareseno demonstrando hauer caxe. Alhora el Turco quelli fece retegnir per farli morir .... Alhora queli che se tolseno taija de recatarsi scapolarono la uita, et fono redempti n°. 24. et piu che per mille, chi 1500 ducati, et chi per due millia tre millia chi piu chi meno tutti zentilhomeni et boni citadini uenetiani."

[18] For Mehmed's *aman-name* which was granted to Pera, see the Latin-Italian text embedded in Languschi-Dolfin, 34 ff. (fol. 322), under the title *Come el gran Turco fece un priuilegio a Genoesi per hauerli data Pera*; for the Greek text (i.e., the official Turkish version, as the Porte employed Greek in its diplomatic documents with westeners), see Lampros, "Ἡ Ἑλληνικὴ ὡς Ἐπίσημος Γλῶσσα τῶν Σουλτάνων," and Skeat, "Two Byzantine Documents." For a translation of the Greek version into English, see Melville Jones, *Siege*, 136–37. For the Greek and Italian texts, see below, Appendix 2. For some observations on this document's phraseology, see above, Introduction, n. 111.

CHAPTER IV

THE FALL AND SACK OF THE CITY OF CONSTANTINOPLE BY THE TURKS IN THE YEAR [14]53 BY MASTER HENRY OF SOEMMERN

MAGISTER HENRICUS DE ZOMERN
QUALITER URBS CONSTANTINOPOLIS ANNO LIII°
A TURCIS DEPREDATA FUIT ET SUBIUGATA

I.   Imperator Teucrorum, adolescens ferocissimus et, ut dicunt, in pactis perfidus, Christiani nominis persecutor acerrimus et Machometicae pravitatis zelocissimus ampliator, qui et ipse Machometa\<e\> nomen habet et a suis magnus amira dicitur, aestate praeterita, scilicet quae istam praecessit, cum exercitu maximo Constantinopolim obsedit et omnibus castris et munitionibus, quae in circuitu erant, expugnatis et captis in eisque plurimis suorum dimissis, in mense Augusti ad patriam suam rediit. Et post septem menses rediit cum CCCm armatorum inter pedites et equites, habens praeparatas galeas inter parvas et magnas CCXX.

II.   Bombardas plures quam mille adduxit, inter quas erant tres generales. Prima enim proiciebat lapidem \<un\>decem palmatarum in circuitu, qui MCCCC libras ponderabat, secunda lapidem decem palmatarum et MCC librarum, tertia novem palmatarum et M librarum. Habuit et alias magnas et colubrinas infinitas. Per has autem bombardas tres maiores LI diebus sine intermissione Constantinopolim oppugnavit; similiter et per alias infinitas et infinita ingenia. Per illas autem tres maiores, quibus bene VIIc lapides contra diversas partes muri urbis proiecit, in diversis locis muros rupit et deiecit. Insuper alia egit, quae incredibilia et vix humano ingenio possibilia viderentur.

III.   Fuit enim tempestive provisum quod portus Constantinopolitanus catena fortissima clauderetur, ne Teucrorum naves introirent et ad custodiam catenae ordinatae fuerunt illic quinque galeae Venetorum et XII magnae naves cum instrumentis, armis et custodibus necessariis. Quod videns imperator Teucrorum fecit de navibus suis LXXX extrahi de mari et eas super ligna rotunda, quae ad hoc fieri praeceperat, et substerni, per montes et colles circumeundo urbem plus quam per tria milliaria duci fecit, erectis etiam velis et vexillis et cetera ac si super mare ducerentur. Et ita deduci fecit citra Constantinopolim, absque hoc quod transirent catenam. Istud facilius intelligunt qui viderunt situm portus. Deinde construxit pontem ligneum super mare, qui adhuc manet, fecitque CCC turres ligneas, quarum aliquae quodam ingenio ab armatis intus existentibus movebantur, quas ad muros urbis, quos in altitudine excedebant, applicabant. In aliquibus autem partibus repletis fossatis turres terrae infixit.

THE FALL AND SACK OF THE CITY OF CONSTANTINOPLE BY THE TURKS IN THE YEAR [14]53 BY MASTER HENRY OF SOEMMERN

1. The emperor [= sultan] of the Turks (a most fearsome young man and, as they say, treacherous in his pacts) is a persecutor of the name of Christ and a most enthusiastic follower of the perversity of Mohammed; his very name is Mohammed and his people call him "grand emir"; he is endowed with astute cleverness, which evidently served him so well that he laid siege to Constantinople with an enormous army; he attacked, stormed, and seized all fortifications and defenses around the city; then he dismissed his army and returned to his home in the month of August. Seven months later he returned with three hundred thousand warriors, cavalry and infantry; he brought along two hundred and twenty small and large galleys, which he had outfitted for the siege.

2. He deployed more than one thousand bombards, among which were three major pieces. The first cast a stone measuring eleven palms in circumference and weighing fourteen hundred pounds; the second cast a stone measuring ten palms and weighing twelve hundred pounds; and the third bombard cast a stone measuring nine palms and weighing one thousand pounds. He had many other pieces and innumerable colubrines. It was mainly through the three major bombards that he bombarded Constantinople, without a break, for fifty-one days; similarly he deployed his other innumerable pieces and countless engines. It was the three major bombards, nevertheless, which fired well over seven hundred stones against sections of the city walls; in several places he destroyed and demolished the walls. In addition, he had other incredible machines, which hardly seem imaginable to the human mind.

3. The harbor of Constantinople was closed before the siege with a very strong chain, to deny entrance to the ships of the Turks; five Venetian galleys and twelve large ships with artillery, men at arms, and the necessary guards were stationed there. When the emperor of the Turks saw this, he pulled eighty ships from the sea and transported them on top of round logs (prepared for this purpose) over the mountains and hills around the city [= the Genoese suburb of Pera] to a distance of over three miles, with spread sails and standards as if they were traveling over the sea. And so he brought them around Constantinople and in this way he bypassed the chain. Those who have seen the harbor can easily understand it. Next he constructed a wooden bridge over the sea (which still stands); he erected three hundred wooden towers, which could be moved by the soldiers within by means of an internal mechanism; they positioned them opposite the walls of the city, which they surpassed in height. In other areas he erected other, well-fortified stationary towers.

IV.   Et ita undique urbem ipsam LI diebus sine intermissione expugnavit. Scalas etiam habuit innumerabiles quae hamos habebant ter factos, qui, quando adhaerebant muro, si ullum defensorum haberent inferius, deici non poterant; et erant scalae istae velatae tabulis a sursum usque deorsum, quod poterant ascendere sine vulnere ac laesione usque ad supra murum. Per has autem scalas et ex his turribus, quas applicare fecit ad partes muri diruptas, LIIa die quae fuit XXIXa dies Maii novissime praeteriti, cum tota die ac nocte praecedenti insultus factus fuisset asperius nostrique prae labore defatigati fuissent, Teucrorum exercitus augeretur et innovaretur momentis singulis, Turci violenta manu per murorum rupturas urbem victores intraverunt et post innumerabilem Christiani sanguinis effusionem reliqui omnes qui superfuerant capti sunt.

V.   Inter quos eos qui nobiles fuerant, quorum erat magna multitudo, licet eis dixisset quod servaverit eis vitam, in conspectu suo una cum filiis et uxoribus suis fecit occidi crudelissime. Nam primo uxores et filios in praesentia parentum et maritorum fecit occidi et postea viros ipsos, eo videndo, fecit in frusta minutatim conscidi feminasque virgines et moniales violari et inhumanissime tractari, qualiter nec pecudes tractarentur. Plurimos autem de parvulis ac puellis popularibus vendidit et totam urbem infra paucos dies fere omni habitatione evacuavit. Mechanicos autem et praesertim fabros ac constructores navium vivos reservavit et eos sibi operari instituit. Dum itaque coram eo sanguis Christianus ita funderetur, apportata sunt in conspectu eius in tribus lanceis per tres Turcos tria capita, quorum unum erat imperatoris Constantini, aliud cuiusdam militis Turci qui contra Turcos cum Christianis urbem defenderat et tertium erat cuiusdam senis barbati monachi de ordine Sancti Basilii, quod eidem dicebatur esse caput cardinalis Rutheni, licet in veritate non fuerat, qui qualiter ex illo excidio evaserat postea dicam.

VI.   Quae autem nefanda commiserunt in sacras ecclesias, reliquias et sanctorum imagines, horribile est dicere. Nam omnia templa urbis spoliaverunt et imaginem quamdam beatae virginis manu beati Lucae factam, quae in maxima veneratione habebatur, detractis gemmis, argento et auro, quae erant in circuitu, per civitatem ignominiose traxerunt eamque sordidis pedibus conculcantes tandem in frusta confregerunt, corpusque beatae Theodosiae virginis, quod illic maximis miraculis crebro claruit, omnesque alias sanctorum reliquias, quae paene innumerabiles erant, laniantes peciatim canibus tradiderunt et in lutum proiecerunt. Ecclesiamque illam insignem Sanctae Sophiae, cui parem non habet nostra religio, imperator sibi in moscheam, ut suo utar vocabulo, <fecit>. Paramenta altarium, stolas et tapetas, in quibus depicta erant miracula Christi vel Christus aut beata virgo pedibus conculcabant et permingebant et alias foedissime pertractabant, deridentes nostram fidem; crucemque quae erat in

4. He besieged the city for fifty-one days, with no respite. He had countless ladders; each had three hooks attached, so it could be affixed firmly to the walls; after they were affixed to the walls they could not be thrown off by any of the defenders below. These ladders were protected with covers, above and below, so that they could ascend unharmed and untroubled as far as the top of the walls. With these ladders and by means of the towers, which he deployed at the demolished sectors of the walls, he launched his major nightly assault that lasted into the next day, on the fifty-second day (it was the twenty-ninth of last May). Our side was worn out by work, while the Turkish army kept receiving reinforcements and was augmented constantly by individuals. By force of arms the victorious Turks entered through the breaches of the walls and after a great deal of Christian blood was poured out, the survivors were captured.

5. There was a multitude of nobles among them; he ordered those who had survived to come before him and he commanded that they, together with their sons and wives, be executed most cruelly. First he had the wives and sons executed before their parents and spouses and then the men themselves after they had witnessed the previous executions; then he commanded that they be dismembered; for women, virgins, and nuns he commanded the most inhuman treatment, such as you would not use even to cattle. He sold many young boys, girls, and townspeople and within a few days he emptied the entire city of almost all its inhabitants. By contrast, he preserved the lives of engineers, architects, and shipbuilders and issued orders that they be put to work for him. And so Christian blood was poured out freely; three Turks brought him three heads affixed to three lances: one of the three was the head of Emperor Constantine; the second belonged to a Turkish soldier [= Orhan, a distant relative of the sultan, in the care of the Greek emperor] who had defended the city on the side of the Christians; the third was the head of an elderly monk of the order of Saint Basil, which was said to be the head of the Russian cardinal [= Cardinal Isidore]; of course, in reality it was not; how the cardinal escaped from that destruction will be my subject later on.

6. It is distasteful to give an account of their criminal behavior towards the holy churches, the relics, and the images of the saints. All churches in the city were looted; a certain icon of the Blessed Virgin, painted by the hand of Blessed Luke, which was the object of extensive veneration, was stripped of the precious stones, silver, and gold that surrounded it; then it was dragged throughout the city irreverently and was trampled by their sordid feet; at long last it was smashed to pieces. The body of Saint Theodosia, the virgin, which was famous for many miracles, and all other countless relics of saints, they dismembered, offered the pieces to dogs, and threw them away in the dirt. That legendary, renowned Church of Santa Sophia (whose equal our religion does not possess), their emperor turned it into his personal mosque, to use his own term. The cover of the altars, the drapery, and the tapestry, on which the miracles performed by Christ, the figure of Christ, or the Blessed Virgin were depicted, were trampled

sublimitate templi deicientes confregerunt. Flamines etiam eorum in sacra altaria ascendentes <Machometam ipsum hymnis et laudibus extollebant> et ut maximum prophetarum et Christianae fidei destructorem praedicabant. Quae etiam nefanda egerunt in monasteriis monachorum <et> monialium, in hospitalibus et variis locis est indicibile.

VII. Venetos etiam, Ianuenses, Arragonenses, quorum illic plurimi erant, fere omnes fecit occidi cum filiis et uxoribus; paucos passus est redimi. Denique post, in fine Iunii, Peram, civitatem fortissimam, prope Constantinopolim sitam, quae partium Ianuensium, similiter expugnavit et muros eius solo coaequavit turrimque magnam, in cuius vertice crux erat, funditus deiecit et Christianos ibi superstites in summa tenet servitute, ita quod non possunt pulsare campanam in elevatione corporis Christi. Coegitque nonnullos Christianos, quos vidit robustos, negare fidem et contra Christianos secum ad bella procedere. Gabellas autem et tributa omnibus civitatibus tam Graecis quam Latinis totius Maris Magni, quod Archipelagus vocatur, imponit gravissima, intenditque ista aetate subiugare sibi omnes insulas Archipelagi. Et de facto circa medium Iulii inter magnas et parvas galeas de Galeopoli (quae est quaedam civitas sua, ad quam capta Constantinopoli divertit ad exercitum suum reparandum), C et L galeas bene armatas misit ad Mare Aegaeum (quod et Archipelagus dicitur) ad subiugandum illas insulas et principaliter contra Negropontem, Chium, Rhodum, Lemnum et Candiam. In quibus omnibus insulis immensus populus qui moratur in campestribus et aliis oppidis parvis una cum rebus suis fugierunt ad urbes fortiores et eas omni diligentia munierunt et servant.

VIII. Tremit totum mare ab inhumanitate istius Turci et iam de facto plures insulae circa finem Iulii ad eum miserunt offerentes eum recognoscere in dominum et solvere tributum, salvo quod eos dimitteret vivere in religione sua et pristino vivendi modo, dubitantes se non obtenturas quod petunt. Quid autem illis responderit, nescitur hic. Parat autem et alias CL galeas et XX grossas naves ad expugnandum tres urbes fortes circa Danubium, quarum una dicitur Perister, alia Fenderobum, tertia Bellogradus, et ita totam transcurrere Hungariam, ut neminem retro se impeditorem habeat. Quia ipse publice dicit et iactat se aestate futura venturum Romam et subiugaturum Italiam et exterminaturum fidem Christianam, et quod quasi se iam certum tenet. Ad quod habet iam paratas CCC galeas et XX grossas naves, bombardas et ingenia infinita restauravitque exercitum CCCm armatorum. Nec putat orbem terrarum sibi resistere posse. Habetque iste saevissimus tyrannus tantum odium contra Christianos quod, quando videt aliquem Christianum, statim oculos abluit quasi ex hoc foedaretur.

underfoot and were soiled. As they derided our faith, they treated other sacred vestments most arrogantly. The cross that topped the Church was thrown down and was smashed. Their priests ascended our sacred altars and chanted the praises of Mohammed himself in hymns and songs, declaring him the greatest prophet and destroyer of the Christian faith. It is impossible to enumerate the crimes that they committed in monasteries, in convents, in hospitals, and in other places.

7. He ordered the execution of almost all the numerous Venetians, Genoese, and Aragonese who were there, together with their sons and wives. He allowed a few to be ransomed. Finally, at the end of June, he similarly seized by siege Pera of the Genoese, a very strong city situated near Constantinople; he leveled its walls and totally demolished a great tower, which bore a cross on its apex; he led the remaining Christians into such wretched servitude that they are not allowed to sound bells at the elevation of Christ's body. He compelled those Christians he judged to be strong to reject their faith and fight with him in his wars against the Christians. He exacted heavy payment and tribute from all states (Greek and Latin) in the Greater Sea (which is called "Archipelago") and he intends to subjugate all the islands of the Archipelago at this time. In fact, it was in the middle of July that he directed his large and small galleys — one hundred and fifty well equipped galleys from Gallipoli (one of his cities, to which he sent his troops to recover after the fall of Constantinople), to the Aegean Sea (which is also called "Archipelago"), to subjugate those islands, and especially Negroponte, Chios, Rhodes, Lemnos, and Crete. In all these islands the inhabitants of the countryside and of small towns have fled, with their goods, to the stronger cities, which they have fortified and guard diligently.

8. The entire sea trembles at the savagery of that Turk; already, around the end of July, most of the islands have actually offered to acknowledge him as their lord and to pay tribute, because he will thus allow them to keep their religion and their ancestral ways, but they doubt that he will grant their petitions. His actual answer to them is not known here. However he has equipped another one hundred and fifty galleys and twenty large ships in order to lay siege to three mighty cities around the Danube: one is called Perister, the other Siderovia, and the third Belgrade; he wants to overrun Hungary so that no one will stand in his way. He himself states publicly that in the future he will come to Rome to subjugate Italy and to exterminate the Christian faith; and he is certain of this. For this project he has equipped three hundred galleys and twenty large ships, with countless bombards and engines and has amassed an army of three hundred thousand warriors. He does not think that the whole world can stop him. This most cruel tyrant nourishes such hatred for Christians that when he lays eyes on a Christian, he immediately washes his eyes as if this sight has polluted him.

IX.   Cardinalis autem Ruthenus, natione Graecus, qui per papam anno iam elapso Constantinopolim missus fuit ad inducendum Graecos ut ipsi primatum ecclesiae Romanae etiam quoad iuridictionem <super> omnes ecclesias orbis recognoscetur (quod et fecit, qui et infra octo dies Romae expectatur), evasit. Per hunc Machometam capta quidem urbe, prope ecclesiam Sanctae Sophiae accessit, putans illic esse armatos aliquot qui Turcis resisterent. Cum autem nullos inveniret resistere paratos et omnes fugerent, bonus pater voluit Turcis obviam procedere et pro Christi fide sanguinem fundere. Unde per aliquos servitorum suorum coactus, fugit in ecclesiam, ubi captus est a Turcis et tanquam incognitus mansit tribus diebus in magno exercitu Teucrorum. Et erat ei praesidio quod famabatur et ab imperatore Turcorum credebatur occisus. Tandemque cardinalis ipse redemptus est pro C ducatis et vectus est in Peram mansitque absconditus VIII diebus fugiendo de domo in domum occulte; sed postquam percepit Turcos accepisse Peram, iudicavit non esse tutum ibi remanere et cum, non posset per loca Christianorum fugere, intravit galeas Turcorum, in quibus mansit tribus diebus incognitus. Obvolutus enim erat in facie pannis eo quod in facie sagitta vulneratur fuerat. Intravit Prusas in galeis Teucrorum, quibus in partibus finxit se esse quemdam pauperem captum redemptum quaerentem filios suos redimere captos Constantinopoli. Et sic paulatim quodam Turco semper associatus est usque ad quemdam locum dictum Focis. Deinde, pertranseunte ipso cardinali, quidam Ianuenses eum agnoverunt et eum inadventer manifestare coeperunt. Unde timens plurimum, quia patria illa Turcorum erat, ingressus quamdam parvulam navem devenit Chium, inde Cretam, in qua stabat, mediocriter valens, VIIIa Iulii novissime prateriti.

X.   Hanc totam seriem rei gestae collegi fideliter ex diversis epistolis scriptis ad diversos de ista materia. Quarum una scripta est domin<i>o Venetorum per dominum Iacobum Lauredanum, generalem capitaneum eorum super mare; alia per ducem Venetorum scripta est domino papae tribusque aliis cardinalibus; <alia domini cardinalis> Ruthenis, qui de hac re unam papae, aliam domino cardinali Firmano; tertia<m>que patens erat omnibus Christifidelibus. Et ex duabus aliis scriptis domino Firmano (quorum unam scripsit ipse agens, familiaris et domesticus dicti cardinalis Rutheni, aliam vicarius ordinis minorum provinciae Candiae). Quarum omnium copias habeo, ex copiis domini Firmani.

XI.   Quando autem tantae cladis fama Romam venit, vehementer animo consternatus est sanctissimus dominus noster et tota curia cum eo statimque ordinavit mittere legatos ad pacificandum Italiam. Ad quam rem misit <ad> Florentino<s> cardinalem Firmanum, ad Venetos autem et Mediolanenses ac ad Florentinos et Senenses cardinalem Sancti Angeli, qui <non> lenti commisso

9.   The Cardinal of Russia, a Greek by birth, who was sent by the pope last year to Constantinople in order to induce the Greeks to accept the primacy of the Church of Rome and recognize his jurisdiction over all the churches in the world (which he did; he is expected to come to Rome within the next eight days) has escaped. When this Mehmed captured the city, he approached the Church of Santa Sophia, as he thought that he would find there a number of armed men to resist the Turks. When he could locate no one prepared to offer resistance (and all were in flight), the good father expressed the wish to advance against the Turks and to pour out his blood for his faith in Christ. Some of his own servants checked him and he fled into the Church, where the Turks captured him; without being recognized, he remained in the extensive Turkish camp for three days. What preserved him was the rumor (to which the emperor of the Turks gave credence) that he had been killed. Finally the Cardinal was ransomed for one hundred ducats and was conveyed to Pera; he remained hidden eight days, as he secretly fled from house to house. But after he heard that Pera would surrender to the Turks, he concluded that it would not be safe for him to stay any longer and, as he could not flee through Christian territory, he boarded a Turkish galley and stayed on board three days; he was not recognized, as his head was covered with bandages because he had been wounded by an arrow on the face. The galleys of the Turks brought him to Prousa; he pretended to be an impoverished man who had been captured and then ransomed, seeking to ransom his sons who were captured in Constantinople. Gradually he attached himself firmly to a Turk, with whom he reached a place called Phocaea. Then, as the Cardinal was traveling, certain Genoese recognized him and inadvertently revealed his identity. He became anxious, because this region belonged to the Turks, and boarded a very small boat which brought him to Chios; next he went to Crete, where he was still in residence, trying to recover somewhat, as of last July 8.

10.   I have been able to piece together a reliable series of these events from many letters that we sent to numerous individuals in regard to these matters. Lord Giacomo Loredano, their captain general over the sea, dispatched one to the doge of Venice. Another was written by the doge of Venice and was sent to our lord, the pope, and to three other cardinals; another was written by the lord Cardinal of Russia, who sent one report to the pope and another to the lord cardinal of Firmano, while another letter of his was addressed to faithful Christians; there were also other letters sent to the cardinal: one he wrote himself, another was written by a close friend of the Cardinal of Russia, and a third one at Candia by the vicar of the Order of the Minorites. I have copies of all of them, from the copies that belong to the Firmano cardinal.

11.   When the news of the terrible disaster reached Rome, our most holy lord [= the pope] became extremely upset and the entire curia shared his concern; he immediately issued orders to dispatch legates in order to establish peace in Italy. For this purpose he sent the Firmano cardinal to Florence and the Cardinal of San Angelo to the Venetians, the Milanese, the Florentines, and the

eis negotio ita profecerunt quod rex Aragonum et Florentini et Veneti et dux Mediolani contenti sunt se, quoad determinationem materiae occasione cuius inter eos quaestio vertebatur, determinationi Romani pontificis submittere et suo arbitrio pacem facere et habere. Et expectantur dictarum partium ambasciatores de die in diem, qui mandatum habent se determinationi papae submittendi. Dicitur quoque iam in consistorio conclusum esse passagium generale et decimam omni clero imponendam; immo dicunt alii de dupli<ci> decima. Quid fiet, novit Deus. Unum scio, quod totam Italiam terret iste Turcus. Fertur tamen quod ille praefatus capitaneus Venetorum, cum Turci vellent intrare Negropontem insulam, ut praetermittitur, classem eorum expugnavit et XXVII grossas naves et undecim galeas accepit; cuius rei occasione nostri aliquantulum spei atque fiduciae resumpserunt.

Raptim, ex urbe Romana, XIa Septembris,
per magistrum Henricum de Zomern.

Sienese, who will accomplish their tasks quickly, as the king of the Aragonese, the Florentines, the Venetians, and the duke of Milan are satisfied that, the solution to their problems can be entrusted to the bishop of Rome and they can thus establish peace among themselves. Any day now embassies are expected to arrive with instructions to submit their problems to the discretion of the pope. It is also said that in the Council it was decided to proclaim a general crusade and to impose a tithe on the clergy; there are those who talk of a double tithe. God knows what will happen. I know one thing: that Turk has terrified all of Italy. It is also said that the aforementioned captain general of the Venetians was sent and defeated the armada of the Turks and captured 27 large ships and eleven galleys, when the Turks attempted to seize the island of Negroponte; this report gave some encouragement and a bit of faith to our side.

    In haste, from the city of Rome, September 11.
    Master Henry of Soemmern.

CHAPTER V

TETALDI:
A TREATISE ON THE FALL OF
CONSTANTINOPLE

TETALDI
TRACTATUS DE EXPUGNATIONE URBIS CONSTANTINOPOLIS

Incipit prooemium
in tractatum de cladibus Constantinopolitanae civitatis, quae
nuper anno a Nativitate Domini 1453 fuit a Turcis expugnata et a
Christianis ablata.

Ob honorem Domini et notitiam posteriorum atque cautelam in futurum, dignum duxi recitandum sub brevitate, qualiter nuper temporibus nostris ab iniquo Turcorum principe, diaboli utique membro, capta sit et expugnata nobilis illa civitas Constantinopolitanae, totius quondam Europae imperium gerens et principatum; quae pro certo pristinis diebus omnium fuit laudibus extollenda. Nunc vero "quia sedet sola civitas plena" pridem "populo" Christiano, "principesque provinciarum facta est sub" Turcorum "tributo": non incongrue a fidelibus eius miseria nunc est dolenda, ac iugi lacrimarum imbre merito deflenda. Igitur priusquam de recenti ipsius loqui atque tractare incipiam calamitate, in qua nunc est, et praecipue clades per quas ad hanc devenit: praeconia ipsius sub brevibus ruminans, situm et qualitatem eius scire cupientibus fideliter intimabo, ut tanto maior habeatur compassio de ipsius, in qua nunc est, miseria, quanto notior fuit pristina eius commoditas et gloria.

O, inquam, civitas Constantinopolitana! Quanta, quam nobilis, quam iucunda, quam delectabilis, quam speciosa, quamque referta es prae cunctis aliis urbibus mundi, ecclesiis et palatiis miro opere fabricatis rutilans ac resplendens! O quae spectacula, quae mirabilia, quae artificiosa opificia ex aere et marmore caelata continentur in te! Cingit te mare ex uno latere murusque inexpugnabilis; ex altero quidem murus immensae magnitudinis turresque in circuitu tuo, vallis et fossa duplex. Denique Trinitatis cultor, Constantinus Augustus, te constituens esse triangularem, nomen scilicet et decorem addidit; omni praeterea tempore frequenti navigio necessaria victus civitatibus paene cunctis abundanter administrans. Cyprus, R<h>odus, Mytilene atque Corinthus, innumerae quoque insulae, tibi quasi matri officiosissime famulantur: Athena et Bulgaria, una cum tota Graecia subsunt providentiae tuae atque dominio, optima quaeque bona ad te dirigentes. Praeterea ex Asia Romaniae civitates et Europa atque Africa huic nobilissimae civitati donaria mittere non cessarunt. In ea Graeci, Bulgari, Alani, Comani, Veneti, Romani, Pygmatici, Italici, Daci, Angli, Malfetani, Turci quoque atque alii gentiles multi. "Iudaei etiam et proselyti, Cretes et Arabes" omniumque nationum quotidie in ea conveniunt multitudines.

Heu! "Quomodo nunc obscuratum est aurum, mutatus est color optimus, dispersi sunt lapides sanctuarii in capite omnium platearum." Nunc bene poteris

TETALDI:
A TREATISE ON THE FALL OF CONSTANTINOPLE

*This is the Beginning of the Treatise
On the Disaster that Recently Befell the City of Constantinople
In the 1453rd Year Since Our Lord's Birth; She Fell to the Turks
And Was Lost to the Christians.*

For the honor of our Lord, for a memorial to posterity, and for future warning, I thought that it would be worthwhile to give a short account of how that famous city of Constantinople (which long ago used to command an empire throughout all of Europe) was besieged and fell recently, in our own days, to the evil prince [= sultan] of the Turks, the very instrument of the devil; to be sure, in antiquity the city had been praised by all. But now the city that had been formerly populated by Christians stands desolate and its lords and provinces pay tribute to the Turks. It is only fitting that her wretchedness be lamented by the faithful, whose tears can only come down in downpours. And so I will begin my account and narration of the disaster that she now finds herself in and the extraordinary misfortune that fell upon her. In presenting this brief public notice, I will give an accurate account, for those who wish to know, of her geographical position and situation; one will feel greater compassion about her present misfortune if one is made aware of ancient glory and fame.

O City of Constantinople: Oh, what a city! How large, how noble, how pleasant, how delightful, and how large you are, surpassing all other cities, throughout the world, with your palaces and churches that were erected in admirable manner, gleaming and glittering! Oh, those sights, those marvels, so artfully made of bronze and marble that are hidden within your territory! You are surrounded by sea and, on one side, by an impregnable wall; on the other side there is a wall of an enormous size with towers throughout the periphery, as well as a double moat. It was the worshipper of the Trinity, Constantine the Augustus, who gave you your triangular form, your name, and your beauty, taking care that you, more than any other city, will be abundantly provided with necessities by numerous sea voyages at all times. Cyprus, Rhodes, Mytilene, and Corinth, in addition to so many other islands, worshipped you and regarded you as their reverend mother. Athens, Bulgaria, and all of Greece exist in your dominion as provinces that ship to you their best products and goods. Furthermore, Asia, the states of Romania, Europe, and Africa take care to send gifts to the noblest city. In that city there are Greeks, Bulgars, Alans, Comans, Venetians, Romans, Pygmatics, Italians, Dacians, Englishmen, Malfitans, Turks, and so many other nations. Daily even Jews and converted persons, Cretans, Arabs, and throngs from all nations flock to her.

Alas! Now the gold cannot be seen; the most beautiful color has been changed; dispersed are the sanctuary jewels throughout all squares and streets.

dicere illa quondam opulenta et illustrior universis: "Nolite me vocare Noëmi (id est pulchram) sed Mara (id est amaram), utpote quam adeo humiliavit Dominus et afflixit Omnipotens." Igitur de talis tantaeque urbis captione locuturus ac vastatione, precor ut nulli sim onerosus; nam omnibus tollere cupiens causam taedii, brevitati operam dare contendam, quatenus auribus tardioribus, quod lectio brevis compendio collectum est, quamquam non comoediam, sed potius tragoediam aggrediamur texere, id quod scripturi sumus, intimamur utrumque et accommodum et utile.

Explicit Prologus

Incipit Tractatus loquens de certificatione transmissa
per Franconem de Twayr, venerabili patri
domino cardinali Avinionensi,
de cladibus et expugnatione praeclarae urbis
Constantinopolitanae per Turcos.

CAPUT I: De obsidione urbis Constantinopolitanae
et de numero adversariorum eius.

1. Anno ab incarnatione Domini 1453., quarta die mensis Aprilis, princeps Turcorum spiritu diabolico agitatus et nimia ambitione repletus praeparavit se ab obsidendum, expugnandum, et obtinendum praeclaram, egregiam, nobilem, ac famosam, omniumque praeconio dignissimam urbem Constantinopolitanam. Sequenti vero die illuscente (id est quinta Aprilis) praefatus princeps exercitu suo pompose satis et ambitiose praeparato, circumcingens eam obsedit cum

She may now be justly called a realm that has lost her ancient splendor and riches: "Do not call me Noëmi (that is to say 'beautiful') but Mara (that is to say 'bitter'), as the Almighty Lord has destroyed me and brought me down." And so as I am about to speak of the fall and sack of such a city, I pray that I will not prove boring to anyone. I so desire to avoid the creation of boredom and I will make my task brief, because a short approach is to be preferred over a long discourse. What I am proposing to do has utility and brings benefit, even though I am not attempting to write comedy but tragedy.[1]

End of Prologue

Here Begins the Treatise Containing the Report Transmitted, through Franco de Twyr, to the Reverend Father, the lord cardinal of Avignon, about the Fall and Sack of the City of Constantinople by the Turks.

CHAPTER I: The Siege of Constantinople and the Numbers of her Adversaries.

1.   In the year 1453 since the incarnation of our Lord, on the 4th day of April, the prince [= sultan] of the Turks was moved by the devil's spirit and, inflated with ambition, prepared himself to lay siege, attack, and seize the famous, excellent, noble, legendary, and by any report most precious city of Constantinople. At dawn of the following day (that is, the fifth of April), the aforementioned prince with his army (prepared in a pompous and ambitious manner) surrounded her and began the siege with a rather large army, indeed an

---

[1] Tetaldi's prologue contains a number of allusions to the Bible, which I have indicated in the Latin text by placing the appropriate items within quotation marks. Among them, the most obvious are the following, as was acutely noticed by one of the anonymous referees of my manuscript:

  1. "sedet sola civitas plena pridem populo Christiano, principesque provinciarum facta est sub Turcorum tributo," "the city that had been formerly populated by Christians stands desolate and its lords and provinces pay tribute to the Turks," echoes Lamentations 1:1, "sedet sola civitas plena populo . . . princeps provinciarum facta est sub tributo."

  2. "Iudaei etiam et proselyti. Cretes et Arabes," "even Jews and converted persons, Cretans, Arabs," echoes Acts 2:10,11: "Judaei et proselyti, Cretes et Arabes."

  3. "Quomodo nunc obscuratum est aurum, mutatus est color optimus, dispersi sunt lapides sanctuarii in capite omnium platearum," "now the gold cannot be seen; the most beautiful color has been changed; dispersed are the sanctuary jewels throughout all squares and streets," echoes Lamentations 4:1: "quomodo obscuratum est aurum, mutatus est color optimus; dispersi sunt lapides sanctuarii in capite omnium platearum."

  4. "Nolite me vocare Noëmi (id est pulchram) sed Mara (id est amaram), utpote quam adeo humiliavit Dominus et afflixit Omnipotens," "Do not call me Noëmi (that is to say 'beautiful') but Mara (that is to say 'bitter'), as the Almighty Lord has destroyed me and brought me down," echoes Ruth 1:20.

populo non pauco immo copioso. Fuerunt enim in eius exercitu viri ducenta millia, e quibus fere sexaginta millia praecellentis erant roboris et virtutis, ad pugnam doctissimi et in armis bellatores validissimi.

2.   Porro circiter triginta quinque seu quadraginta millia equestris erant ordinis, diverso modo armati, quorum quaedam pars loricis seu constipatis diploidibus utebatur; quaedam vero more nostrorum plenis armis erat munita; quaedam vero ad modum Hungarorum seu quorundam aliorum bellatorum pileis ferreis quos galeas vocamus sese tuebatur et balistis, arcubus, gladiis et diversi generis instrumentis defendere se videbatur. Residua vero pars eiusdem diabolici exercitus erat fere inermis, hoc excepto, quod quidam aut scuta ferebant aut peltas seu umbones, ut Turcis moris erat; quorum filiorum Belial multi erant mercatores et mechanici exercitum secuti plus ut bellum viderent seu propter lucrum; quemadmodum histriones, adulatores, trutanni vel ribaldi.

CAPUT II: De copioso apparatu instrumentorum bellicorum.

1.   Erant in exercitu praenominato valde multa fundibula et colubri (sive serpentes) aliaue perplurima huiusmodi instrumenta. Inter quae praeeminebat unus bombardus aereus et fusilis, integer et indivisus emittens ex se (quod dictu mirabile est!) lapides habentes in circumferentia rotunditatis undecim palmorum et trium digitorum mensuram. Pondus vero tormenti huius fere mille octingentarum extitit librarum.

enormous host. In his army there were two hundred thousand men; sixty thousand of them were of excellent strength and fighting spirit, well trained for battle and mighty warriors.

2. Moreover, the cavalry amounted to about thirty-five or forty thousand; they were armed variously: some of them used breastplates or thick doublets. A certain part of our side was also well supplied with weapons. Others were equipped in the Hungarian fashion with iron hats or other (which we call "helmets") and were seen to protect themselves with crossbows, with harquebuses, swords, and weapons of various sorts. But the remaining part of that devil's army was almost unarmed, if one excepts the fact that some carried shields, animal hides, or bucklers in accordance with the Turkish custom. There were many sons of Belial, merchants and engineers, who followed, attracted by war or by the prospect of booty. There were actors, sycophants, moneychangers, and offensive individuals.[2]

CHAPTER II: The Variety of Siege Engines.

1. There was in that army a great variety of artillery, of colubrines (or serpentines), and of many other engines of that sort. They were all surpassed by one bronze fire bombard, made in one piece, without any segments, which fired (it is hard to believe!) stone projectiles of eleven palms and three digits in overall circumference. The weight of that engine was almost one thousand and eight hundred pounds.

---

[2] The impression of the defenders was that the Turkish army was immense. All sources comment on its size, but Tetaldi is one of the few eyewitnesses to realize that the army of Mehmed II could be divided into elite regiments, irregulars, camp followers, renegades, etc. However, the numbers that he reports may not reflect reality, as they are unquestionably exaggerated. In addition, it is quite possible that the "elaborator" of Tetaldi's original report was familiar with some form of the letter composed by Bishop Leonardo, as the phraseology of both accounts is similar (as both share an identical explanatory note about Myrmidons; cf. Leonardo [CC I: 128–30, with Italian translation; PG 159: 927]: "Excitatus itaque in furorem Deus misit Mahomet regem potentissimum Teucrorum, adolescentem quidem audacem, ambitiosum, temulentum, Christianorum capitalem hostem, qui Nonis Aprilis ante Constantinopolis prospectum, cum tercentis et ultra millibus pugnatorum, in gyro terrae castra papilionesque confixit. Milites maiore numero equestres, quamquam omnes pedites magis expugnabant. Inter quos pedites ad regis custodiam deputati audaces, qui ab elementis Christiani aut Christianorum filii, retrorsum conversi, dicti Genizari, ut apud Macedonem Myrmidones, quasi quindecim milia. Ad tertium autem diem, captato urbis situ, machinas innumeras carticulasque ex virgultis viminibusque contextas circummuralis vallum quibus pugnantes tegerunt, fossatis admovit. Initium confusiones hoc nostrum fuit, ut qui telis machinarumque lapidibus iuxta datum ordinem eminus repellendi erant, neglectis singulis, cominus proximare permiserunt. Tantum eorum ordinem instruendis machinis, tantam promptitudinem, tantam acierum providentiam, quidam aut Scipio aut Hannibal aut moderni belli duces admirati fuissent. Sed quis, obsecro, circumvallavit urbem? Qui, nisi perfidi Christiani, instruxere Turcos! Testis sum, quod Graeci, quod Latini, quod Germani, Pannones, Boetes, ex omnium Christianorum regionibus Teucris commixti opera eorum fidemque didicerunt, qui immanius fidei Christianae obliti urbem expugnabant. O impii qui

2. Insuper illic fuerunt decem aut duodecim fundae pensantes mille ducentas et octo libras in pondere; singulis diebus praeparatae ad iaciendum lapides, octoginta sive centum vicibus qualibet die; et hoc 50. diebus continue. Quamobrem pro vero asseritur fundibularios huius modi singulis diebus consum<p>sisse circiter mille libras quotidie in pulveres, qui ad iaciendos lapides requiruntur; quarum summam si colligere volueris, invenies quinquaginta millia librarum huius modi pulveris.

2.   Furthermore, there were ten or twelve artillery pieces which cast projectiles weighing two hundred and eight pounds; the stones were prepared for firing day by day, eighty or one hundred per day, on any given day in turn. And this went on for 50 days. Accordingly, it is said that the artillerymen, who were employed to fire these projectiles, used up about one thousand pounds of gunpowder daily; should you require adding up the total, you will find that it comes to fifty thousand pounds of this gunpowder.[3]

Christum abnega<vi>stis! O satellites Antichristi, damnati gehennatibus flammis! Tempus hoc vestrum est. Satagite augere vobis poenas, quas luatis aeternas." In addition, Niccolò Tignosi (da Foligno), who wrote before November 1453, also uses similar phraseology to describe the assault troops (*TIePN*, 108–10): "Tria sunt quae non modo interritos sed audacissimos ferunt hostes: primum ab oppidanis omnino desperatum subsidium, secundum defensorum paucitas, tertium ipsorum multitudo quae excreverat <ita> ut Achillis Mirmidones viderentur...". Similar is the businesslike account presented in the *aviso* of Benvenuto, the Anconitan consul in residence and, as he proudly points out, a number of times, "a baron of the emperor" [Pertusi, "The Anconitan Colony in Constantinople," 207; English translation of this document in Philippides, *Byzantium, Europe, and the Early Ottoman Sultans*. Appendix B, 97–199; Latin text, with Italian translation also in *TIePN*, 1–6]: "In primus, quod quarta die Aprilis inperator Turcorum venit cum exercitu suo noctis tempore ante civitatem Constantinopolis et die sequente complete fuit exercitus et terram et mare collocatus. Item quod fuerunt pavlioni 60.000 per terram, idest sexaginta milia. Item quod fuerunt inter galeas et fustes per mare 300 <per> tria milia. Item quod inter omnes erant homines per terram 300.00 <idest> tercenta milia hominum. Item quod fuerunt per mare homines 36.000 <idest> triginta sex milia." Cardinal Isidore, in his letter (dated July 8, 1453) to Pope Nicholas V [CC 1: 94], provides his estimate: "Et in mense sexto exercitum pedestrium et equestrium ultra numerum trecentorum milium et triremes magnas et parvas ducentas et viginti praeparavit...." Leonardo [CC 1: 128–30; *PG* 159: 927] agrees with Isidore and makes further mention of the dread janissary corps, the elite regiments of the sultan, as quoted above. It should be noted that Isidore also speaks of the janissaries as "Myrmidons"; it is quite possible that Isidore and Leonardo had exchanged views earlier, while they were both residents and defenders of Constantinople. We shall have occasion to remark on other similarities between the two writers that seem to go back to the days of the siege (cf., e.g, below, n. 5, and their comparison between Mehmed and Xerxes, as well as between Mehmed and Alexander the Great [below, n. 27]).

[3] While the artillery of Mehmed impressed all contemporaries and eyewitnesses, Tetaldi is the only source to provide estimates on the consumption of gunpowder. His measurements of the dimensions of the Turkish artillery pieces and projectiles can be compared to those encountered in other sources:

Benvenuto: "Item, quod erat una bombarda quae simul emittebat tres lapides inaequales. Item, quod lapis maior erat ponderis 1300 librarum. Item, quod lapides alii duo erant ponderis 600 librarum pro quolibet 300 librarum.'

Eparkhos (if that is the correct form of his name; his testimony with that of Diplovatatzes [?] has survived in a contemporary German translation: see above, Chap. 1, n. 77. For the surviving text of the document, see *NE* 2: 514–18 [Italian translation, without the German text in CC 1: 234–39]): "Item: ein ander Pfort, hat geheissen Salgaria; do haben sie fur gelegt IIII Puchsen, 3 gross und clein, und haben aber hinter ein Polberck funff Locher gemacht und hin zu gegraben und haben daz unterpolczt. Nu haben sie in der Stat auch ein Loch gemacht, und wolten

CAPUT III: De divisione exercitus Turcorum et eorum capitaneis.

1. Tali ordine suum princeps Turcorum disposuerat exercitum ut una eius pars infestaret civitatem a terra, altera a mari. Ad portum autem qui est ad latus civitatis fuerunt circiter sedecim galeae, sexaginta octo circiter galiotae

CHAPTER III: The Division of the Army of the Turks and their Captains.

1. The prince of the Turks deployed his army in the following way: one part of it besieged the city on land and another by sea. At the harbor, however, which is situated along the side of the city there were sixteen galleys, and about

herauss zu in, und sind kumen, daz die Locher an ein ander komen; nu prachten die Turcken vil Puchsen und Dings; also namen dis auss der Stat und wurfen Feur darein und verprenten ir etwann gar vil."

Cardinal Isidore, in his letter (dated July 6, 1453, from Candia) to his friend and fellow Greek, Cardinal Bessarion, writes as follows [for the entire Latin translation of a lost Greek letter (with some prosopographical problems ignored), see Georg Hofmann, "Ein Brief des Kardinals Isidor von Kiew an Kardinal Bessarion," *OCP* 14 (1948): 405–14; for a more recent, but partial, edition of the text, with Italian translation, cf. *CC* 1: 64–80]: "Inter cetera vero infinita tormenta, catapultas sive bombardas, tres erant, quarum prima quatuordecim talentorum lapidem proiciebat, altera duodecim, tertia decem. Cum autem reliquas omnes minores densitas et fortitudo murorum substinerent, vires illarum trium et verbera crebro et assidue concutientium m<o>enia tollerare non poterant. Ad secundum enim ictum maxima pars deiecta est atque decussa murorum cum ipsis turribus."

Leonardo (in his famous letter to the pope [*CC* 1: 130; *PG* 159: 927–28]): "Horribilem perinde bombardam, quaquam maior alia. quae confracta fuit, quam vix boum quinquaginta centum iuga vehebant, ad partem illam murorum simplicium, quae nec fossatis nec antemurali tutabatur, Calegariam dictam, figentes lapide, qui palmis undecim ex meis ambibat in gyro, ex ea murum conterebant. Erat tamen murus perlatus fortisque, qui tamen machinae tam horribili cedebat . . ." [not in *CC* 1, but in *PG* 159: 928:] "Sclopis, spingardis, zarbathanis, fundis, sagittis dies noctesque muros hominesque nostros vexabant mactabantque."

Languschi-Dolfin [the basic edition remains that of Thomas, "Die Eroberung Constantinopels," as the selections that appear in *TIePN* are too slim and too vexed by numerous typographical errors to be of use and will not be cited here], with his colorful mixture of the vernacular with Latin, seems to follow Leonardo at this point, 9 (fol. 315): "Accade che la bombarda grande al principio se rompette, la qual um faticha era tirata da 150. para de boui da quella parte chel muro era simplice, ne uaeua fosse ne antemurale, dicta la Calegarea, la qual trazeua pietra, uoltua XI. palmi. Et cum quella ruinaua el muro el qual era largo, et forte, el qual tamen a tanta horribil machina cedeua . . . Et cum altre minor machine se sforzaua per ogni banda ruinar i muri, ne manchaua schiopetti, spingarde, zarbattane, funde, sagitte, el di et la notte a uexar li muri et li homeni mazar."

Bishop Samuel, whose testimony [Grossen Gruess von dem Hawbt zw der Erden Samile dem Bladick (oder Bischoff) vnd von dem andern Bladick (oder Bischoff) von Constantinopolis yecz und zusam gefügt in der Walachay] also survives in a contemporary German translation (dated August 6, 1453): Geben an dem sechsten des Mönäts Augusti, anno Domini MoCCCCoLIIJo; German text in *NE* 4: 65–68; Italian translation without the German text in *CC* 1: 228–31): "Sunder es wa Nyemant der do Rat oder Helf gab vns durfftigen vnd verdebten, vnd dye Turkken vmbgaben vnser Stat zu Landt vnd zw Wasser uberall vnd zy Ryng umb ringen sy uns; sy hetten funffczig gross Püchsen vnd funff hundert kleyner Püchsen vnd ayne die aller grost, dy was in der Gross als ein Kueffen oder ain Vass zw sybenczehen Emern vnd XX Spann lank. Und, do sy mit der grossen Püchsen wurffen sy dirwhundert vnd Llj Stayn zu der Stat, sunder mit den funffhundert klaynen Puchsen schussen sy stätes an Vnderloss auf das

atque decem et octo seu viginti alterius generis naves, quas scaphas vocare possumus pro transvehendis hominibus, seu pallandiones pro traducendis equis; aliorumque generum naves et naviculae non paucae.

2. Capitaneus exercitus qui erat infra constitutus dicebatur Sagambassa, consiliarius et secretarius principis, cui maior in belli exercitio potestas et fidei sinceritas inesse putabatur. Hic sagacitate suaque industria transduci et transportari fecerat per terram viribus Turcorum in spatio duorum vel trium milliariorum, circiter septuaginta quinque galeas aliasque naves ad locum nuncupatum Mandagarim, secus civitatem Peram situm. Alioquin non valuissent Turci

sixty-eight light galleys, as well as eighteen or twenty ships of a different kind, which we may call transport ships, as they were designed to carry men, and barges to ferry horses. There were many ships and vessels of other kinds.

2. The captain of the army that was constituted in this manner was called Sagam [= Zaganos] Pasha; he was a councilor and a secretary of the prince, who, it was thought, commanded considerable power in military affairs and possessed true loyalty. This man made use of his acumen and energy and managed, with his Turkish forces, to transport and convey over land about seventy-five galleys and other ships to a place called Mandagarim [= Mandrakion] (a distance of two or three miles), situated outside the city of Pera.[4] As the Turks

---

Volckh, das Nyemant ein Aug mocht aufgehaben vnd sich beschirmen, vnd an solicher Wer mochten sy nicht zu rechten."

Lauro Quirini, in a letter from Candia dated "1453 Idibus Julii" (Agostino Pertusi, "Le Epistole Storiche di Lauro Quirini sulla Caduta di Costantinopoli e la Potenza dei Turchi," in *Lauro Quirini Umanista*, ed. P. O. Kristeller, K. Krauter, A. Pertusi, G. Ravegnani, and C. Seno [Florence, 1977], 163–259; selections with Italian translation: *TIePN*, 62–94), brings a classical flavor to the siege engines: " . . . admiranda quaedam mechanica composuisse, scalas, balistas, catapultas, testudines, . . . Verum enim vero bombardam unam posuisse admirandae magnitudinis, qualem nulla unquam aetas vidit — lapis enim erat, quem facile proiciebat, mille trecentarum librarum —, quam in Handrinopolim [= Adrianople] confectam magna cum difficultate ductam testantur quingentis videlicet hominibus et viginti curribus, in cuius iactum terram et mare per quatuor milia passuum diu tremuisse asserebant. Hanc bombarda muros Civitatis mira arte fabricatos facile conquasse humique prostrasse."

On Ottoman artillery, see Philippides, "Urban's Bombard(s)."

[4] This notable achievement of the sultan receives praise in all accounts. The last stages of this operation were probably planned at the sultan's naval headquarters at Diplokionion (Two Columns) in the vicinity of Pera by April 21. Construction of the roadway behind Pera, from Diplokionion and Tophane through present-day Taksim Square to Kasim Pasha, had probably begun early in April (FC, 105). During the last stages of the construction a continuous bombardment prevented detection. By April 21 the project had been completed and the transfer of about 70 vessels to the Golden Horn took place on Sunday, April 22; the boom/chain of the defenders was thus bypassed. The presence of the enemy flotilla in the Golden Horn contributed greatly to the demoralization of the defenders and thinned out the available forces further, as the harbor walls had to be fully manned. Antonio Ivani (*TIePN*, 54) claims that the sultan decided to bring his vessels into the harbor after he discovered that Venice was about to send a fleet (see below, n. 24) to the beleaguered capital of the Greeks: "Interea litterae Venetorum ad imperatorem ab hostibus intercipiuntur, <in> quibus nostri commonebantur quindecim naves futuro mense praesidio venturas. Quam ob rem, suum praesidium aberat, regi visum est acrius oppugnationem fore parandam; sed cum vidisset urbem a se frustra obsideri nisi mari etiam oppugnaretur, novum atque arduum consilium inire cepit. Nam cum ob ligneam compaginem in portum classem deducere minime posset, statuit, si secus fieri, nequiret naves curribus per terram devehere." See FC, 105 ff.; OGN, 196; MCT, 88; Pears, *The Destruction of the Greek Empire*, 269–76; and Georgios T. Zoras, Περὶ τὴν Ἅλωσιν τῆς Κωνσταντινουπόλεως (Athens, 1959), 100–12.

pertransire ac civitati Constantinopolitanae appropinquare, praesertim propter obstaculum cuiusdam pontis per Christianos compositi et compacti de navibus,

were not strong enough to cross and approach the city of Constantinople, they put together a real obstacle to the Christians: a bridge supported by boats, by

Eparkhos talks of this significant event: "Item: dar nach hat er das Gepirge ob Pera eingenumen und hat gross Schif hin auff lassen zihen, 2200 Galeen und Fusten, auf Waltzen unf mit Puffeln und Aurochsen und mit gewoppentem Volck, untz auf die Höch der Perg, und haben die widen ablassen schissen, von der Höch piss in daz Mer, zwischen Petra und Constantinopel, in ir Lantwer auf der wasser." Bishop Samuel was also impressed but his estimate of the Turkish boats that were transferred is too high: "Czwissen Galatham [= Pera] vnd Constantinopel auf ainem Tayl des Mers das do flewsset czwischen den Steten, do prachten sy czway hundert Galeyns, grosse Scheff, auff dem grossen Mer, vncz zu dem Landt; do sy ir für bass nicht mochten füren auf dem Mer zu der Stat, do czugen sy dy czway hundert Galeyn auf dem Landt mit jren aygen Henden, wol czwo Meil Wegs lanck, vnd liessen sy in das Tayl des Mers czwischen den vorgenanten Stetten . . . .." It was also evident to some eyewitnesses that Mehmed II could not have accomplished such an engineering feat if he had not been assisted by western experts. Leonardo was explicit about this, PG 159: 930 (not in CC 1): "At cum Teucrus tribus iam in locis concussos lapidibus muros machinis <delere> desperaret, memoratu cuiusdam infidi Christiani, ex colle biremes intromittere iurat. Est enim portus ille ... in longum angustumque protractus, cuius orientalem plagam colligatae naves et catena muniebant; inde hostibus aditus impossibilis erat. Quare, ut coangustaret circumvalleretque magis urbem, iussit invia aequare exque colle, suppositis linitis vasis, lacertorum vi ad stadia septuaginta trahi biremes, quae ascensu gravius sublatae, post hac ex apice in declivum ad ripam levissime sinus introrsum vehebantur. Quam novitatem, puto, Venetorum more, ex Gardae lacu is qui artificium Teucris istud patefecit didicerat." As usual, Leonardo is followed faithfully by Languschi-Dolfin, who adds a number of new details, including the names of the engineers, who had managed a similar transfer of boats overland in Italy a few years earlier, 12 (fol. 315): "Ma el Signor Turcho disperandose dato che da tre porte cum bombarde hauesse dirupato el muro, gli fu ricordato da uno falso Christiano per sopra quelli colli tragettaria in el porto de Costantinopoli che e longo et stretto, tutte fuste del armata perho che la faca del porto oriental cum la cathena facta delle naui era in tutto serata a gli inimici. Et per coangustar, et circumuallar piu la terra, commando fusse spianato le uie, et supra i colli messi in terra i uasi a forza de brazze ... per 70. stadij che sono circa miglia ... introdusse le fuste nel mandrachio le qual per ... miglia con faticha se tirauano in suxo, poi leziere perueniuano all riua del mandrachio. La qual nouita fu trouata da Nicolo Sorbolo, et Nicolo Carcauilla comiti di gallia quando per l Adese condusseno gallie 5. per la campagna de Uerona in lago di Garda in l anno 1438. pth <sic> 240. Et questo artificio da Uenetiani fu insegnato a Turci." Cardinal Isidore also spoke with the authority of an eyewitness in his letter to Cardinal Bessarion (CC 1: 70–72): "Primum quidem cum validissimis catenis portus esset accinctus et clausus a parte montis Galat<a>e [= Pera] usque ad portam Pulchram triremes Venetorum quinque cum duodecim aliis onerariis sive rotundis navibus et quidem maximis portui et catenis mire Turcorum introitum prohibebant. Turci vero cum se illic frustra consistere animadvertent, in Dipplocioniam stationem se cum eorum navibus transtulerunt, ubi et classem instruxerunt. Paucis vero post diebus viam montanam trium milium passuum et ultra sterni iussit Turcus ad transiendas ab una parte montis Galat<a>e in alteram biremes et soliremes nonaginta duas, quas cum in portu eo modo traiecisset, portu potitus est et eius totaliter factus est dominus." Cardinal Isidore discussed the same subject in another letter (dated "anno a nativitate Domini M.CCCC. quinquagesimo tertio, die octava Julii" and addressed to Pope

vasis et similibus, a Constantinopoli usque ad Peram, auxilii mutuo conferendi gratia opemque ac succursum sibi invicem administrandi.

barrels, and by other such things, which stretched from Constantinople to Pera, in order to bring help and aid to their forces on both sides.⁵

Nicholas V), CC 1: 96: "... amira [= emir, i.e., sultan] ... statuit iter super colles et juga fieri per tria miliaria et ultra; iussit quoque suis triremibus stantibus foris ligna sustinere et simul ea colligare per quae biremes LXXII numero deduceret; quas adeo per colles et juga currentes perduxit ac is super mare ducerentur verto frequenti, habentes remos externos, vexilla et tentoria, ut de suo more est super mare portare; quas ad portum tandem deduxit."

⁵ Descriptions of this memorable bridge are also encountered in most sources. Cardinal Isidore expressed admiration for Mehmed's bridge in his letter to Cardinal Bessarion (CC 1: 72): "Aliud iterum mirabilius est machinatus, quod et Xerxes quondam fecisse memoratur: pontem siquidem construxit et fabricavit maximum a mari Sanct<a>e Galatin<a>e usque ad m<o>enia Cynegi, quod duplo maius est spatium quam illius Hellespontiaci olim pontis a Xerxe fabricati, per quem non modo pedites verum etiam equites multi simul traducebantur." Leonardo has similar information and also compares this bridge to Xerxes' fording of the Hellespont in 480 B.C. It is not a question of Isidore and Leonardo copying from each other's text, as they wrote their letters unaware of each other's work. The comparison to Xerxes must therefore derive from their conversations during the siege and from their classical education; in addition, cf. their similar phraseology in describing the janissaries as "Myrmidons," above, n. 2. The two ecclesiastics were close friends and Leonardo was in awe of Isidore; cf. Leonardo (CC 1: 138; PG 159: 931): "Proinde hoc ingenio non contentus Teucrus aliud quoque, quo nos terreret magis, construxit, pontem videlicet longitudinis stadiorum circiter triginta, ex ripa urbi opposita maris qui sinum scinderet, vasis vinariis colligatis, subconstructis confixisque lignis, quo exercitus decurreret ad murum prope urbis iuxta fanum, [non in CC 1, but in PG 159: 931:] imitatus Xerxis potentiam, qui ex Asia in Thraciam Bosphoro exercitum traduxit. Non restabat ergo nisi navium catenaque diametralis initio, quae transitum ingressumve classi prohibebat." Leonardo is followed faithfully by Languschi-Dolfin, as we have had occasion to note, 12 (fol. 315): "Non contento perho de queso inzegno, el Turcho per altro modo cercho spauentarne. Et fece construir uno ponte longo 30 stadij sono miglia ... dal mare fino alla ripa de la terra, fatta la zatra fermata sopra le botte ligate per diuider el proto, per lo qual ponte exercito poteua correr apresso el muro de la cita, apresso la giesia, imitando la potentia di Xerse el quale de Natolia in Grecia tradusse lo suo exercito per lo stretto de Hellesponto." Bishop Samuel's impressions were recorded in German translation: "... vnd liessen sy in das Tayl des Mers czwischen den vorgenanten Stetten, vnd mochten da ein Pruck von aynem Tayl zu dem andern, darinnen leyten sy grosse Vas; vnd darauf leytten sy Püchsen vnd Füessewt ein grosse Menig, vnd auff die selben Vass mochten sy aber ayn Pruck vnd mochten ein zwifächtige Wer auf das Wasser...." Similarly, Eparkhos and Diplovatatzes spoke of this operation and of its effects on the defenders: "Item: als er pei Petra auf daz Wasser ist kumen in ir Lantwer, do hat er alle Fesser genumen, die er mocht zu Wege pringen, und haben die an ein ander gepunden, und haben dar auf gepruck, und auf dem Wasser gestritten sam auf dem Land, und haben do gehabt mit ein 1000 Leittern, die wurffen sie an die Mauren; auch war ein Loch geschossen, ein gross Loch, in die Statmaur, sam Sant Sebolds Kirchhof; dez haben sich die Genuessen unterwunden, sie wollens wol hervaren mit iren Schissen, - die dann hetten vil Schif; es was auch geboten in des Turcken Here bor finfzehen Tagen daz ein itlicher solt ein Leittern tragen, auf dem Wasser und auf dem Land." Cardinal Isidore also spoke of this bridge in his letter to the pope (July 8), CC 1: 96: "Deinde pontem super mare, qui usque ad hodiernum diem manet construxit: habet enim distantiam de terra firma in Constantinopoli per miliare unum et tertium."

3. Igitur exercitus aquatici extitit capitaneus quidam nomine Albitangoly, quem in palaestra sive duello submerserunt quatuor naves Ianuenses proeliantem cum populo sibi subiecto contra Christianos. Illo igitur mortuo princeps Turcorum alterum capitaneum navali exercitui praefecit. Sic igitur patet dispositio bipertita exercitus, a terra videlicet et a mare.

3. The captain of the sea forces was someone called Albitangoly [= Baltaoğlu], whom four Genoese ships submerged in the wrestling ground (or battlefield) while he was fighting with his forces against the Christians. After his death the prince of the Turks placed another captain in charge of the naval forces. And so the army was deployed on two sides, on land and by sea.⁶

⁶ This paragraph seems to be an allusion to a naval battle that was fought on April 20, i.e., two days before the transfer of the Ottoman fleet to the Golden Horn. In fact, this transfer and the subsequent construction of the pontoon platform/bridge seem to have been accelerated by the success of the Christian boats against the entire Turkish flotilla. Some ships came to Constantinople from the west: the exact number remains uncertain; Leonardo and Barbaro speak of three Genoese ships and of one imperial transport. Khalkokondyles and Tursun Beg, however, mention two Genoese vessels and one imperial transport. The Genoese ships had been equipped and provisioned by the pope; the imperial vessel had bought grain in Sicily (with the permission of Alfonso of Aragon). As soon as the Christian ships had been sighted, Mehmed's *kapudan* pasha, Baltaoğlu, launched his attack. After an hour of fighting, the Christian ships were immobilized when the wind dropped; nevertheless the current slowly pushed the big boats towards the shore. The Italian sailors fought off all attacks until late in the day, when the wind picked up and brought them to the vicinity of the boom. It was a major Christian victory that enraged the sultan. Baltaoğlu did not perish in the battle, despite Tetaldi's statement; he lost an eye, either during the battle or during his ordeal after the battle at the hands of the janissaries, to whom he had been delivered by the sultan. Mehmed II was so angry with him that he had him deposed, confiscated his property, and left him to spend his final days in poverty and disgrace; he was replaced by Hamza Beg. On this naval battle and its aftermath, see *FC*, 100–104; *MCT*, 87; *OGN*, 196; the most detailed description and meticulous analysis remain those of Pears, *The Destruction of the Greek Empire*, 263 ff.

Leonardo and his followers [Languschi-Dolfin in Italian; in Greek: Pseudo-Phrantzes, and the Anonymous Barberini 111] have provided the most detailed version of these events; cf., e.g., Languschi-Dolfin, 13–14 (fol. 316): "In questo tempo mezo da Chio uenne in soccorso nostro tre naui genoese armate condutte cum formento. Una del imperator che de Sicilia ueniua carga del formento, le qual essendo uedute aproximar alla citade da l armada turcha, che staua alla guarda de fuora, leuate subito cum strepito de nachare tambure et trombe sonante verso loro andono nui uedando, fenzendo uoler expugnar la naue del imperador. Unde el signor de i monti de Pera staua a guardar lo euento de la fortuna, fano cridori grandi le gallie, se accostano alle naui, et cerchano pigliar quella del imperador, et deffessa da le Genoese cum piu audacia la combatteno, comenzada la pugna cum bombarde et cum fuogi et cum nibule de freze, fanno pugna atrocissima. Alincontro de Mauritio Cataneo, capitaneo de Genoesi alincontro repugna, cui Domenico da Nouara, et Batista Feliciano patroni de bellanieri genoesi forti sieguono la pugna cum balestre datorno, et dardi grossi. Et da le chabie de le naue piere grandeet spesse in l armata turcha demandano. Egregiamente se deffende la naue imperiale alla qual socorre Francesco Lacauela patron, le bombarde resonano, li cridi uano in ciel, se rompe i remi, et Turchi senza remision sono feriti et morti." Furthermore, Leonardo (but, curiously enough, not Languschi-Dolfin) is aware of the fate that befell the sultan's *kapudan* pasha; see e.g. Leonardo (CC 1: 140; PG 159: 931): "Rex contra classis praefectum Baltoglum oppido indignatus, precibus baronum concessa eidem vita, sententiam tulit quod officio et bonis omnibus privaretur."

CAPUT IV: De fortitudine civitatis Constantinopolitanae.

1. Antequam huius inclytae civitatis recitemus lamentabile excidium, de ipsius robore et munitione ac fortitudine pauca loquamur. Constantinopolis itaque fortis est valde, formam in se continens figura triangularis; occupans in circumferentia laterali versus terram sedecim milliaria Lombardica, quinque vero versus mare et quinque similiter versus portum, ubi est communis applicatio navium et statio earum, et quinque apud locum qui Goulfa vocatur. Muri eiusdem civitatis versus terram spissi sunt valde ac versus caelum altitudine praestantes, speculas (seu vigilum domunculas) et foramina pro fundis iaciendis in se plurima continentes. A foris vero muri principales, minoribus et brevioribus muris ad munimen circumcinguntur, qui et ipsi fossatis circumsepti et vallati sunt.

2. Muri principales possident altitudinem viginti circiter passuum; latitudinem vero in quibusdam suis locis septem; in aliis autem octo passuum continent. Minores vero muri super aggestum terrae constabiliti altitudinem sedecim circiter aut quatuordecim cubitorum occupant. Terra vero de subter eminens et a reliqua planitie elevata protenditur viginti duobus cubitis. Latitudo fossatorum praescriptorum viginti quinque tenet cubitos; profunditas vero decem, ut ait quidam; alii vero censent haec fossata viginti quinque circiter passus possidere in latitudine: et decem in profunditate sive altitudine.

CHAPTER IV: The Strength of Constantinople.

1. Before I turn to my report on the lamentable destruction of this famous city, I will say a few words in regard to her strength, her fortifications, and her might. Constantinople is very strong and possesses a triangular shape. The entire periphery over land measures sixteen Lombard miles: five face the sea; similarly another five constitute her port (where there is a common area for ships to dock and be moored); another five at a place called Goulfa. The land walls of this city are very thick and rise up to the sky; they contain watch-towers (or small barracks for the sentries) and numerous fields extending before the defenses. To add strength the main walls are surrounded by gates and by lesser and lower walls, which are also enclosed within moats and ditches.

2. The walls reach to a height of about twenty feet; in certain places they are seven feet thick and in other eight. The lesser walls above a solid earthen rampart reach a height of seventeen or eighteen cubits. The land rises and, elevated from the rest of the plain, extends to twenty-two cubits. The width of the aforementioned ditches measures twenty-five cubits; the depth, as some say, comes to ten; others reckon that these ditches measure about twenty-five in width and ten in depth or height.[7]

---

[7] On the fortifications and defenses of Constantinople, see above, Chap. 3, n. 7. See, in addition, the brief statement of Eparkhos and Diplovatazes: "Item: Constantinopel ist so gross daz einer auf ein Pfert ein gantzen Tag nicht hin umm greiten mag. Item: sie haben vermugt streitpar Man ... on Weib und Kinder. Item: die Stat Maur hat 10.000 Zinner gehabt. Item: sie hat zwifach Maur gegen dem Lande und eine gen Wasser. Item: die Rinck Maur hat 1.100 Thuren gehabt." For the moat in 1453, see Philippides and Hanak, *The Pen and the Sword*, chap. 6. The only Greek source to speak of the moat that existed and of the condition of the fortifications in 1453 was a survivor, who composed a lamentation on Contantinople's fate; see Andronikos Kallistos, Μονῳδία κῦρ Ἀνδρονίκου τοῦ Καλλίστου ἐπὶ τῇ δυστυχεῖ Κωνσταντινουπόλει, ed. Spyridon P. Lampros, "Μονῳδίαι καὶ Θρῆνοι ἐπὶ τῇ Ἀλώσει τῆς Κωνσταντινουπόλεως," NH 5 (1908): 208: Μήκει μὲν οὖν ἡ πόλις πάσας τὰς ἑῴας ἁπλῶς ὑπερεῖχε, κάλλει δὲ καὶ τὰς τῆς ἑσπέρας. τείχη δ᾽ οὕτως ἰσχυρὰ καὶ τοῖς ἐναντίοις ἀνένδοτα οὐκ ἂν εὕροιτό τις συγκρινόμενα πρὸς αὐτά. ἦν μὲν γὰρ ἡ τάφρος εὐθὺς καὶ πλάτει καὶ βάθει καὶ πλίνθοις ὀπτοῖς κατωχυρωμένη, ποταμός τις ἄλλος τοῖς παριοῦσι δοκοῦσα, τεῖχος δὲ εὐθὺς μετ᾽ αὐτὴν ἰσχυρόν, εὔρει τε καὶ ὕψει στερρόν, ἕτερον δὲ μετ᾽ αὐτό, μεῖζον τοῦτο πολύ, ὥστε καὶ θαυμάζειν ποιοῦν τοῖς ἀτενίζουσι πρὸς αὐτό. For the complete text of this monody, the sentiments of which match those expressed by Tetaldi in the opening passages of his *Tractatus* ("The Beginning"), see Lampros, "Μονῳδίαι," 203–18. In a report on the fall of Constantinople, which was written in Italy in 1453 (and which has been rather neglected by modern scholarship, even though it presents us with interesting evidence on the events and further shows some dependence on Barbaro's *Giornale* and on Languschi-Dolfin) and has found its way to Stefano Magno's *Cronica* (extracts in NE 3: 295–301), we encounter the following statement: "É la cittade in forma triangolare, due in mare, con muriazi a propulsar l'empito navale, et quello da terra, dapoi i muri et antemurali, da una grande fossa e terra." Magno's text, in relation to other sources on the fall, deserves a fresh look and should prove fertile ground for further scholarly investigation. Also, see above, Chap. 3, n. 7.

CAPUT V: De numero virorum bellatorum et ordine ipsorum.

1. Fuerunt in hac nobili et famosa civitate viri circiter viginti quinque seu triginta millia; sex autem vel septem millia expediti ad pugnam et ad bellandum fortissimi. Ad portum autem pro catena custodienda deputatae fuerunt triginta naves et novem galeae. Videlicet duae piratarum ad depraedandum, tres Venetorum ad mercandum, tres ex parte regis Constantinopolitani et una quae extitit cuiusdam generosi armigeri qui stipendiarius erat imperatoris Constantinopolitani et ab eo capitaneus constitutus fuerat Graecorum, qui vocabatur Ioannes Iustini<anus>.

CHAPTER V: The Number and Deployment of Warriors.

1. In that noble and renowned city were about twenty-five or thirty thousand men; however six or seven thousand were fit for battle and very strong for combat.[8] At the harbor, however, there were thirty ships and nine galleys deployed to guard the chain. Two were raiding vessels belonging to pirates; three were Venetian merchantmen; three belonged to the emperor of Constantinople; and one was the property of a warlord who had been hired by the emperor of Constantinople and had been appointed by him to the post of captain of the Greeks; his name was Giovanni Giustiniani.[9]

---

[8] We are not well informed as to the numbers or armament of the defenders. What remains certain is that they were heavily outnumbered by Mehmed II's forces. The number of the actual defenders was a closely guarded state secret, precisely because they were so depressingly few; Sphrantzes, a member of the imperial administration and a personal friend of Constantine XI, was charged with providing a census and concluded that there were about 4773 Greek and 200 foreign warriors (Sphrantzes, 25.6; "200" is probably a scribal error for "2000"). Modern estimates also vary. Thus FC, 85, suggests 7,000; OGN, 193, estimates 8,000 Greeks and 2,000 foreigners. For the condition of the Greek army at this time, see Margaret G. Klopf [Carroll], "The Army in Constantinople at the Accession of Constantine XI," Byz 60 (1970): 385–92, and, in general terms, Benedikt S. Benedikz and Sigfús Blöndal, *The Varangians of Byzantiium: An Aspect of Byzantine Military History* (Cambridge, 1978), chap. 7. For a more recent investigation, see Mark C. Bartusis, *The Late Byzantine Army and Society, 1204–1453* (Philadelphia, 1992). Aid came to the city "haphazardly and unintentionally" (PL 2: 111). In his opusculum Niccolò Tignosi (da Foligno) (who wrote before November 1453) mentions this problem (TIePN, 108): "Qua defatigione defessi, confossi, ad tantam paucitatem defensores redacti sunt, ut non modo totam urbem, quae triangularis XVII milibus passuum incircum vergitur, <defendere non potuerint>, verum nec aperte X <milia> hostium potuerint coercere. Quisque tamen suis viribus utitur, sed ultra posse nihil." Nicolla della Tuccia, who wrote his *Cronaca di Viterbo* in October/November of 1453, supplies some information (TIePN, 97): "Essendo la città così assediata, tanto affano avevano li poveri Cristiani, che più non si potevano difendere, perchè la città aveva 11.000 merli nelle mura, a difesa delle quali non ci erano se non 7000 soldati . . .." For the most detailed analysis of the defending forces, including ships securing the harbor, see PL 2: 110–12, and notes 9, 10, and 11.

[9] This *condottiere*, Giovanni Guglielmo Longo Giustiniani, was appointed *dux militiae* of Constantine XI and thus became the emperor's commander-in-chief. He and his disciplined, well-armed troops formed the nucleus of the defense in 1453. He was a member of the Longo family of Chios, which had joined the *albergo* (an "association" of families; cf. Philip P. Argenti, *The Occupation of Chios by the Genoese and Their Administration of the Island, 1346–1566*, vol. 1 [Cambridge, 1958]; Robert S. Lopez, *Storia delle colonie genovesi nel Mediterraneo* [Bologna, 1938], 336–345; Jacques Heers, *Gênes au XVe siècle. Activité économique et problèmes sociaux* [Paris, 1961], 385 ff.; and Geo Pistarino, "Chio dei Genovesi," *Studi Medievali* 19 [1969]: 3–68, esp. 56 ff.) of the Giustiniani, and may have also been related to the Genoese Doria family; cf. below, n. 20. He arrived in Constantinople on January 29, 1453. His life before the siege is neither well documented nor well known. The following is a partial list of documents that may deal with his activities prior to the siege (or alternatively may have something to do with other individuals of

CAPUT VI: De pugna et conflictu utriusque partis et primo a parte maris.

1. Civitate igitur Constantinopolitana sic undique terra marique firmiter vallata et obsessa, illi qui intus erant suo modo prout poterant alacriter se defenderunt et viriliter resisterunt de longe ac de prope arcubus manualibus ac balistis, fundis atque aliis diversis armis bellicis repugnantes diebus quinquaginta.

CHAPTER VI: The Battle and Struggle on Both Sectors; at Sea, to Begin With.

1. And so Constantinople was firmly surrounded and was besieged on all sides: land and sea. The people within defended themselves to the best of their ability and vigorously; they courageously resisted, at close and long range, with harquebuses, hand guns, crossbows, artillery, and other war engines; they fought

....

the same name, as it is impossible to identify them further): *Lib. Diversor. reg.* 31, of the Genoese State Archives, May 7, 1442 (reported in *NE* 3: 88), mentions a Giovanni Giustiniani Longo, son of the late Daniel, in connection with a purchase of a house; *NE* 3: 88, n. 6, suspects that he may be Constantine's *condottiere*. *NE* 3: 259, summarizes a letter of May 2, 1450, addressed to Giovanni Giustiniani, the "consul of Caffa." It is possible that Giustiniani the *condottiere* had served in the post, but it is not certain that we are dealing with the same individual. In a letter dated December 15, 1452, it is reported that a Giovanni Giustiniani and his ship captured a "Saracen" vessel transporting merchandise from Alexandria (*NE* 3: 277); it is possible that Giustiniani was preying on Moslem shipping, as the sultan seems to have referred to him as a "pirate" and a "corsair," which seems to be implied in a phrase of Leonardo (*CC* 1: 132: "mare decursitans forte veniens"), and in the narrative of Barbaro, who is not impressed with Giustiniani (*CC* 1: 12; Cornet, ed. *Giornale* [see below], 13): ".. vene in Costantinopoli Zuan Zustignan Zenovexe e de corser de una nave . . .." Furthermore. another contemporary seems to think of "pirates" included among defenders; see the testimony of Niccolò Tignosi (da Foligno) (before November 1453, *TIePN*, 104): "quoniam Bizantium praeter quosdam piratas [Giustiniani ?] Italosque mercatores nullos habere potuit defensores." The State Archives of Florence (*Dieci di Balia, Carteggio responsive, reg.* 22, fol. 125) contain a letter from Genoa (April 1452) by Soderini mentioning a Giovanni Giustiniano, the captain of three ships, who wishes to buy provisions; the pertinent section (*NE* 2: 464) states: "et fà pensiero andare in Levante et Romania et poi andarsi a porre nel golfo di Vinegia con queste tre o con quelle averse guadagniate, o dove voute, faccendo più danno a vostri nimici." To this document one may add another letter, which announces Giustiniani's secret departure with 700 men on board (*NE* 2: 477–78). Of all the statements that one encounters in modern scholarship in regard to his career, the most suspect, in my view, seems the claim that Giustiniani had served as the *podestà* of Caffa. I have been unable to find any document that can validate this view; as far as I can see, the first time that it was voiced by any modern authority is the simple (undocumented) statement that is encountered in the nineteenth-century *editio princeps* of Barbaro's *Giornale*, the editor of which, Enrico Cornet, *Giornale dell' assedio di Costantinopoli 1453 di Nicolò Barbaro P. V. corredato di note e documenti* (Vienna, 1856), asserted (13, n. 2): "Giovanni Giustiniani Longo era stato due anni prima podestà in Caffa." This note is omitted in the selections of *CC* 1. Leonardo (*CC* 1: 160; *PG* 159: 940), who had closely observed the *condottiere* in Constantinople at the time of the siege, points out that he was young and inexperienced in battle, "inexpertus iuvenis," a statement that has been largely overlooked by scholarship: the same description is repeated in Languschi-Dolfin, 28 (fol. 320): "come inexperto zouene." Youth and inexperience may argue against the view that Giustiniani had ever been the *podestà*/consul of the important outpost of Caffa. The evidence is ambiguous and slim; one must regret the fact that we still need a prosopography of the defenders of Constantinople; in spite of the wealth of archival material and a plethora of evidence supplied by our sources, no study has thus appeared, except individual articles. See., e.g., Philippides, "Some Prosopographical Considerations"; Ganchou, "Le Mésazon Démétrius Paléologue Cantacuzène"; and idem,

Intra hoc temporis spatium firmam Christiani fiduciam conceperunt sperantes cum Dei adiutorio sua praevisatione ac subtilitate posse se faciliter incendio tradere naves Turcorum cum ponte quem composuerant.

2.   Ascendit itaque capitaneus galeae Christiani exercitus subtilem quamdam galeam, quatenus facilius et convenientius ad Turcorum cuneum pervenire valeret et naves illorum concremare. Instigabat autem eum ad haec maxime audacia suorum commilitonum, pleno corde auxiliari sibi cupientium. Sed eorum conatus per adversarios est frustratus: nam illorum mox galeam Turci fundis dissipantes, quosdam Christianorum illic repertos huiusmodi naufragio peremerunt. Quosdam vero comprehendentes horribili supplicio discerpserunt, et hoc ad terrorem aliorum Christianorum. Nam eos crudeliter et immaniter laniantes a subteriore parte ventris usque ad summum eius secantes, et more pecudum aut piscium exenterantes visceribus inhumaniter patefactis Christianorum obtutibus probrose praesentaverunt, ut ipsis hoc modo contumeliam facerent ac de illis suas iniurias quas in congressibus saepius sustinebant, insultus eorum perferendo sese vindicando talionem expeterent.

back for fifty days. During this interval the Christians displayed their faith, in the hope that, with God on their side and through their own efforts, they would easily burn the ships of the Turks together with the bridge that they had put together.

2.   The captain of a galley of the Christian army boarded a certain light galley in order to reach the line of the Turks easily and comfortably and burn their ships. He was incited to do this by the immoderate audacity of his fellow soldiers who desired with all their hearts to be of assistance. But their adversaries frustrated their attempt: the Turks quickly destroyed their galley with artillery fire and captured some Christians whom they found in the wreckage. They executed their prisoners in a horrible manner, to instill terror among the other Christians. They butchered them cruelly and savagely, as they slashed them from the lowest area of the belly to the highest point, and disemboweled them, with their entrails exposed, as if they were fish or sheep, which they shamelessly displayed to the Christians, to mock them in this way, paying them back for the injuries that they had received so often in battle and seeking revenge for the insults that they had endured.[10]

"Sur quelques erreurs." A fuller study will appear in Philippides and Hanak, *The Pen and the Sword*, Chap. 10. On the death of Giustiniani, see above, Chap. 3, n. 10.

Already by the sixteenth century very little was known about Giustiniani's early career, which can be summarized in the work of Hieronimo Giustiniani, who may have used some documents (or, more likely, some oral traditions that had been in circulation) at Chios to provide the following account: Hieronimo Giustiniani, *Istoria di Scio Scritta nell'Anno 1586* (modern edition: Philip P. Argenti, ed., *Hieronimo Giustiniani's History of Chios* [Cambridge, 1943]), 412–20, and, for the quotation, 412: Ioanne Giustiniano magnanimo et esperto capitano, andò in Costantinopoli con una grossa nave, in compania di quella dello Imperatore, la qualle in dispetto dell' armata nemica salvò nel porto di esso luogo, insieme con la sua, il qual per la sua prodezza, fu eletto generale di latini dallo Jmperatore Constantino, ultimo, in diffesa dello imperio et della città, assediata all'hora dal tiranno Mehemet Jmperatore de' Turchi. Questo Giustiniano, dicono le historie, era tanto valoroso, che per gli suoi maravigliosi fatti et stratagemati di guerra, facea maravigliosamente stupire l'infideli. Per la qual cosa Mehmet solea dire, che ne facea più di conto del Giustiniano solo, che del tutto il resto della città. Havea ei in sua compania trecento huomini valorosi genovesi, et una banda de scioti. Et tutti questi bravi soldati, trovandossi sempre in tutte le fattione, faccendo cose, che agl' infideli eranno tenute per impossibile, onde a que' soli l'animo fusse tanto forte, volerne far testa a tanta potenza turchesca et con il solo nome et la sola vista loro, all' hora non solamente harrebbeno spaventato quel poco numero ma tutto il mondo certo haveanno sempre fatto. Che udendo i christiani il nome turco, sgomentati et attoniti molto longi fugivansi per salvarsi, tanto gli era horrendo, nondimeno il Giustiniano facendo ufficio di buon capitano, in tutte le zuffe non perse mai animo, essortando et ammonendo di continuo gli suoi portarsi valorosamente." On Giustiniani and Constantinople, see Philippides, "Giovanni Guglielmo Longo Giustiniani."

[10] This was one of the last, if not the very last, naval operations to be undertaken by the defenders; after its failure, the defense conceded the Golden Horn to the Turkish flotilla, while the better equipped and far superior Christian vessels were under no immediate threat by the light vessels of the Turks that were sailing in the waters of the harbor. After the transfer of the

CAPUT VII: Qualiter in fodiendo subterranea loca civitatis
Christiani et Turci obviaverunt sibi.

1.   Ab altera parte civitatis versus planiciem terrae obsessa multitudini Turcorum praeficitur capitaneus, ut praemissum est, Sangambassa Albanensis, apostata vilis, qui pridem Christianus existens Catholicam fidem abnegaverat, qui in exercitu suo plurimos habuit viros gnaros diversi generis metalla fodiendi

CHAPTER VII: The Encounter of Christians and Turks in Subterranean Mines.

1.   In another part of the city the Albanian captain Sagam [= Zaganos] Pasha, a worthless renegade, who had been born a Christian but had renounced his Catholic faith, ordered a crowd of Turks to dig into the earth, as there were many experienced metal miners of all sorts in his army. They were incited by

---

light vessels overland to the Golden Horn, the Christian defenders were forced to thin out their forces, as they had to maintain a constant alert over the sea walls; while this sector had been neglected in the past (when the Golden Horn was under Christian control), the arrival of the light vessels meant that regiments had to be transferred from the land walls to the sea walls, straining the available manpower. While the Christian ships in the harbor had nothing to fear from the small Turkish vessels, the assault upon the sea walls became a possibility. Thus a decision was made to burn the Turkish vessels in the harbor, in order to re-assign troops back to the critical land sector. The naval operation discussed by Tetaldi took place on April 28, two hours before dawn; it had first been planned for April 24 but was then postponed in order to allow the Genoese to play a part in it, as originally it was only the Venetians who intended to attack. In the interval of four days the operation that was about to take place was reported to the sultan; it appears that the plan had been leaked to the Turks through individuals from Pera. One source, Barbaro, even names the supposed traitor (Cornet, ed., *Giornale*, 30 [CC 1: 20]): "El nostro capetanio, aldando queste oferte si romaxe contento de dover induxiar a una altra note, e quando Zenovexi vete esser zorno, e abiando lor paxe con el Turco, aprì una de le porte de Pera, e mandò fuora uno al Turco, el qual ha nome Faiuzo, e questo Faiuzo, siando al pavion del signor Turco, e a quelo lo i fè asaver come Venitiani, la notte passada, se mise in ordene de andar a cazar fuogo dentro de l'armada del mandrachio de Pera." Languschi-Dolfin also departs from his source, Leonardo (who clearly does not wish to name names, as he asks rhetorically [CC 1: 144; PG 159: 933]: "Sed quid dicam, beatissime pater? Accusarene quempiam licet? Silendum mihi est"); Languschi-Dolfin's departure is unusual but he does cite a name, 15–16 (fol. 316): "Et questo intrauenne per che tal deliberation fu pre Anzolo Zacharia de Pera fato sape al Signor Turco dato segno che, quando se moueranno da riua farano segno de fuogo da le mura de Pera." What is of further interest here is that the same individual is also named by another primary source composed by an eyewitness of the siege, the Brescian scholar Ubertino Pusculo, who had gone to Constantinople to learn ancient Greek and extend his humanistic education and who was destined to become the epic poet of the siege, after he was ransomed from the victorious Turks (cf. above, Chap. 1, n. 123). No edition of this work, taking into account all the available manuscripts, exists; thus the old edition, based on one manuscript, Ven. Marc. lat. XII.73, remains our guide: Adolph S. Ellissen, *Analekten der mittel- und neugriechischen Literatur* (Leipzig, 1857): 12–83 (which follows, without changes the older edition, G. Bergantini, *Miscellanea di varie operette* (Venice, 1740), 1:225–447; for this quotation, see Ellissen, 4.585–588 (72) (not included in CC 1): "Sed raro in multis sunt fida silentia. Furtim / detulit accelerans Machmetto nuntius audax / Angelus ex Galata Zacharias, atque suorum / consilia expandit, manebat quae incendiant naves.' As we have had occasion to remark, Languschi-Dolfin is dependent on Leonardo for the most part. Pusculo wrote his poem sometime after Languschi-Dolfin and it is probable that he had never consulted this chronicle. It is quite possible that both reports derive from some oral tradition identifying the traitor as Angelo Zacharia. One eagerly awaits a complete, reliable edition with an *apparatus criticus* of Pusculo's poem, one of the most

ex terra. Hi ergo capitanei sui sagacitate et calliditate inducti subtus muros civitatis fodere coeperunt per spatium fere viginti quatuor milliariorum ad deiiciendum ac destruendum et annihilandum ipsos muros; sed Christianis intra

their captain's cunning and intelligence, and began to dig under the walls of the city to a distance of almost twenty-four miles in order to reach, undermine, and destroy the very walls. But the Christians in the city attempted to do the same

important eyewitness sources on the siege and fall. No Neo-Latin scholar has studied this poem or its author, and an investigation into Pusculo's career in general is long overdue.

For Venetian seamanship, in general, see John E. Dotson, "Foundations of Venetian Naval Strategy from Pietro II Orseolo to the Battle of Zonchio, 1000–1500," *Viator* 32 (2001): 113–25. The Italian volunteers in this operation were commanded by the Venetian Giacomo Coco. For this defeat of the Christians, see *FC*, 107–11; *MCT*, 89 (which, however, presents an eccentric interpretation, as it is suggested that this operation took place before the transfer of the Turkish vessels to the Golden Horn); and *PL* 2: 118–20. Coco was a capable sailor, as he had successfully by-passed the bombards of the sultan's fortress, the Rumeli Hisarı, in December 1452. He was not so lucky in this operation, which may have been betrayed to the sultan. The events are described in Barbaro's journal, ed. Cornet, 30–31 (not included in CC 1): "A dì vinti otto pur de questo mexe de april ... do ore avanti zorno, cun el nome de spirito santo, se mosse le do nave del porto, le qual nave se iera tutte investide de sacchi de lana, e de sacchi de gotoni, e in compagnia de quelle, si iera la galìa de misser Gabriel Trivixan, e la galìa de misser Zacaria Grioni el cavalier, tutti do armatori al golfo, e ne iera tre fuste de banchi vinti quattro l'una, le qual fuste iera stade armade per i tre patroni de le galìe de Romania cun le sue zurme, i qual patroni si fo questi nominadi, ser Silvestro Trivixan de ser Nicolò, ser Jeruolemo Morexini fo de ser Bernardo, ser Jacomo Coco el grando ... ma el meschin anemoxo de misser Jacomo Coco patron de la galìa de Trabexonda volse esser lui el primo feridor in questa armada in questa armada per aquistar honor in questo mondo. Siando tuta la nostra armada per mezo el mandrachio, dove che iera l'armada soa del turco ... ma misser Jacomo Coco patron de la galìa de Trabexonda, come homo volonteroxo de aquistar honor in questo mondo, non volse aspetar che le nave fosse le prime de investir, anzi el sora dito misser Jacomo volse esser el primo feridor in la predita armada del turco; el dito misser Jacomo fiò una vuoga batuda, e andò inverso quela armada, e quando che el fo per mezo l'armada del turco, i turchi si desserò una delle sue bombarde, e dè arente la pope, e nula i fe', daposa ne desserè una altra, e dege in nel mezo de la fusta, e passòla da una banda al altra; quela fusta non potè star de sora quanto che saria a dir diexe paternostri, subito l'andò con tuti i homeni che iera suxo ... e prima misser Jacomo Coco patron de quella."

Pusculo, in his hexameters, assigned a more theatrical death to Coco, ed. Ellissen, 4.601–654 (73–74) [not included in the selection of CC 1]: "Ast Italisque triremis / credita cui fuerat major, muniverat ipsam / egregius Jacobus Cocchus, generosa propago, / spectatamque manum juvenum dux ipse regebat. / Atque huic cum celsa, stipato vellere tutum / saxa latus contra monstranti puppe Joannes / sese offert primum Genuensis, vulnera forti / velle rate excipere jactorum turbine multo / saxorum. tacite incendunt hoc agmine naves ... / Cocchus vix castra subibant [sic !] ... / haud procul a fluctu socios hortatur, et inquit ... sic fatus corripit ardens / incensam laeva taedam, dextraque coruscat / ensem fulmineum atque cruci dedit oscula .... / Cocchus summis stans fluctibus alta / voce rogat scapham remo suffultus adire, / innixus quo certat aquas superare; sed illum / clamantem frustra auxilium rapuere gravatum / arma imum ad fundum; 'natosque (extrema loquentem) / commendo, o cives, morior, carosque, deoque / hanc animam, nostrae quaeso miserescite sortis.' / talia vociferans Neptuni tractus ad imam est." The Venetians clearly felt that Coco had acted heroically, as after the fall they attempted to help the survivors of the Coco family in Venice. A note (dated "1453 a dì 18 luglio") by the hand of Marco Barbaro on the journal of his relative makes this clear: ed. Cornet, 65 (not included in CC 1): "Fu preso parte, che li provediitori de sal, debbano dar alli figli di messer Jacomo Coco,

urbem ex adverso longe a muris identidem attentatibus et eis obviantibus contigit eos interdum insimul convenire aliquando multosque Turcorum fumo et foetore cadaverum periclitari et extingui et vita sub terra privari. Interdum etiam aquae violentia nostri illos ad interitum compulerunt et sic conatum eorum impedierunt.

thing with a long counter-mine, and it so happened that they came upon them and destroyed many Turks, whom they deprived of their lives with fumes and with the stench from cadavers. Meanwhile our side eliminated them with a flood and put obstacles to their task.[11]

---

che era patron di una galia al viaggio di Romania, qual morse, come apar in questo a carte 31, Ducati 60, per il suo viver per uno anno prossimo, et fra questo anno sian obligati comprar, tanti imprestedi che sia per Ducati 600 d'oro de boni denari, et li facian scriver alla figlia del ditto ser Jacomo, per il suo maritar, et vadi pro sopra cavedal fino si mariterà, et se la morirà anzi il maritar, siano di suo fratello, et fra il termine antedito debban comprar altrelanti imprestedi da esser scritti a suo figlio."

A wave of executions with atrocities seems to have followed this disaster. The Turks may have been excessively brutal in the execution of their prisoners, the survivors from the night operation, mainly crew members of Coco's vessel. Exact numbers of executed prisoners and method of execution remain uncertain. FC, 108, states that ninety Christian sailors were despatched and that two hundred and sixty Turks were executed in retaliation. For other figures, cf. MCT, 89. Pusculo also wrote of these grim incidents (ed. Ellissen, 4.672–674 [p. 74]; not included in the selections of CC 1): "Hos cogunt qui sint fari prius, inde trucidant / ipsorum ante oculos socium quos Cocchus in illa, / qua periit, secum fidos delegerat atre / nocte." Languschi-Dolfin uses similar phraseology, 16 (fol. 316): "Et nostri che uoleuano danifichar Turci fono in prima loro tutti desfatti. Alcuni che erano senza arme nudando in terra, da Turchi fono prexi deducti in exercito in conspecto di nostro fono a mode de pecore tagliati a pezi. Et mossi da ira nostri alcuni Turchi prexoni, che haueuano menati sopra le mure in conspecto de Turchi amazadi fono precipitati. Le naui a questo facto deputate ritornorono al loco doue erano uscite."

[11] The mines of the Turks had targeted the area north of the Gate of Saint Romanus and were concentrated on the sector defined by the Kaligaria Gate (Turkish Eğri Kapı). Cardinal Isidore mentions other locations also, in his letter to Cardinal Bessarion (CC 1: 70–71): "Subvertit itaque muros circa portam Sancti Romani et pr<a>eterea eam partem qu<a>e inter portas Fontis et Auream nuncupatas et antiquam Ventur<a>e portam erant et alteram qu<a>e Caligariorum appellabatur ... Alium et tertium modum aggressus contra urbem versus portam Caligariorum a longe cuniculos quinque et subterraneos dolos effodit, per quos in urbem aditus pateret. Cumque ad murorum usque ac turri<u>m fundamenta applicuissent atque ipsa iam excidere conarentur, nostri pariter intus ex amussim de directi correspondentes cuniculos effoderunt. Sicque hostes ea parte fugati sunt atque depulsi et de melioribus multi sunt interempti cessatvitque illius partis oppugnatio." Eparkhos and Diplovatatzes state that there were five main mines in the Kaligaria sector: "Item hinter der Katzen haben sie sich verporgen und haben gegraben unter der Erden piss an die Stat Maur; do haben se ein Dach gemacht mit Holtz und ein Schut mit Lochern, do durch sie schussen und, wenn einer neur uber die Maur sach, so schussen sie in zu Tod." See also above, n. 3. Quirini in a letter from Candia (dated "Idibus Iulii [= July 15] 1453") adds an interesting detail: the sultan's miners were a mixed lot of experts, Serbs and Turks (TIePN, 68–70): "Habuisse enim affirmabant artifices ex Serbia argentifodinarios et Teucros aerifodinarios sed his similiter machinamentis nihil urbi nocuisse." Leonardo agrees and further identifies the miners as Serbs from Novobrdo; more importantly, he identifies the engineer, John Grand (or is it Grant, a Scot? see FC, 84), Giustiniani's lieutenant from Germany, in charge of counter-mining, whose efforts were ultimately crowned with success, as the Turks did not achieve anything with their mines (CC 1: 134; PG 159: 928): "Minerarum fossores quos ex Novo Brodo conduxerat magistros accersiri iussit. Lignis instrumentisque

CAPUT VIII: De castro et ponte per Sangambassa<m> constructis.

1. Praefatus autem Sangambassa fieri constituit fortalitium castri lignei, magni, ampli, firmi et alti, adeo ut murorum civitatis celsitudinem excedere videretur. Similiter et pontem mira ingeniositate fabricati fecit de vasis, afferibus,

CHAPTER VIII: The Castle and Bridge Erected by Sangam [= Zaganos] Pasha.

1. The aforementioned Sangam Pasha decided to construct a strong wooden castle: large, wide, steady, and tall enough to surpass the height of the city walls.[12] Similarly, he had a bridge made with marvelous skill; it was put

---

advectis solerti cura, ut imperatum, actum est, ut mox per cuniculos tentarent fundamenta suffodere penetrareque omnifarium urbis murum. At cum fundamentis (o rem mirabilem!) primum iam vallum et antemurale mirando cum silentio subcava<vi>ssent, Ioannis Grande Allemani, ingeniosi militis, rerum bellicarum doctissimi, quem Ioannes Iustinianus militiae dux centurionem conduxerat, industria et sagacitate opus detectum est exploratumque id firmatum relatione animos omnium commovit." Languschi-Dolfin agrees and follows Leonardo's text closely in his paraphrase, 10 (fol. 315): "Et per questo el Turcho deluso penso non cessar dal continuo trazer, ma ancora cum piu forte cura de caue subterranee furar la terra, et per questo lauor li fossori delle miniere, che lauraua a Nouobordo fece uenir, li quali posto i muri in ponte de legno adimplino el comandamento, et per tre ua tentauano penetrato i muri passar in la citade. Habiando adoncha passado sotto le fosse, el antimurale, et le mirabili fundamente de la terra cum gran silentio cauato, alhora per opera industria, et sagacita de Joanne Grando Alemano dotto in cose bellice, el qual Joanne Longo Zustigran capitanio condusse descusion, fu descoperto, et per sua relation fu confermato hauer explorato, et per questo l animo de ognun commosse." A modern search carrying out minor excavations, in the Kaligaria area, should identify some of those mines; no archaeological investigation in regard to the siege operations has ever been carried out and is long overdue.

According to Barbaro, the last mine was detected in the Kaligaria sector as late as May 25; clearly the sultan had placed some confidence in this approach, which, in the final analysis, did not prove successful; cf. Barbaro (ed. Cornet, p. 48; not in CC 1): "A dì vinti cinque pur de questo mexe de mazo, a hora de vespero fo travada una cava pur in quel medemo luogo de la Calegaria a presso le altre prime cave, e questa cava si iera forte e dubioxa de pericolo, e questo perchè i avea messo uno pezo de muro in punte, che dado fuogo che i avesse, el saria caduto per tera questa sua cava, e caduda che la fose stà questa cava, subito questi turchi si saria intradi dentro de questa zitade, e avariala abuda a man salva, senza contrasto niuno. Questa cava si fo l'ultima che i fexe, e l'ultima che fosse trovà, ma questa si iera la più dubioxa cava che fose trovà."

[12] The wooden tower mentioned by Tetaldi was one of the more aggressive siege engines produced by the sultan's engineers. Christian renegades with experience in western technology. Eparkhos and Diplovatatzes seem to have the same tower in mind: "Item: dar nach ist er gezogen fur daz Tor gennant Ventura, und hat gemacht ein Polberg same ein Thurn mit Holtz, und mit Leder und Heutten behangen, und daz genetzt daz man kain seiner dar ein mocht schiessen, und unter dem Polberk haben sie angefangen ein Loch, daz ist gangen unter dem Graben und unter der Maur untz in die Forstat. Item: dar nach haben sie gelegt ir Puchssen. Daz hat gehabt ein Thor gegn der Stat; wenn man die Negel zog, so ging daz Thor auf und, wenn der Schuss verging, so vil daz Thor wider zu." Cardinal Isidore, in his letter to Cardinal Bessarion, speaks of a number of those towers, which were evidently mobile, and takes this opportunity to make mention of Archimedes, a reference that his fellow humanist would have appreciated, as it evoked images of ancient Syracuse under siege by the Romans; cf. Hofmann, "Ein Brief des Kardinals Isidor" (with the exception of the first sentence [p. 74], CC 1 has not included this paragraph in its selections): " ... castella pra<e>terea

trabibus et plancis, mille habentem passus in longitudine et septem in latitudine, ut sui ad nostros pertingere possint super mare ex transverso ambulantes et civitatis muris appropinquantes. Multas quoque machinas sua adinventione atque industria fabricari mandavit et diversa carpenta (sive stallagia) ad repugnandum altitudinis et latitudinis non minimae.

2.   Egit etiam paene singulis diebus multos ac diversos contra nostros insultus, in quibus multi ab utraque parte per subitaneam et improvisam mortem sublati sunt demio. Sed ubi unus de civitate inventus est mortem incurrere, e diverso centum de Turcis extra urbem interierunt.

CAPUT IX: De Christianis qui serviebant Turcis et de certificatione mutua eorum, quae contigerunt et acta fuerunt apud eos.

1.   Fuerunt praeterea in exercitu Turcorum multi ex Graecia et aliis partibus mundi, qui quamvis forent sub Turcorum dominio constituti, non tamen coacti sunt deserere fidem suam sed cultum Christiani dogmatis exercere permittuntur. Erant insuper in praefato exercitu quidam Turcorum capitanei qui ad invidiam et contem<p>tum ipsius Sangambassa<e> ipsos nimium aggravantis cum tanta praeavisatione decreverunt populo Christiano qui in civitate obsessus tenebatur, modis quibus poterant notificare consilia sive tractatus atque commenta quae fiebant in secretario principis eorum et hoc per litteras (seu epistolas) fundis immissas seu arcuum sagittis admixtas, quas hoc modo

together with barrels, beams, and planks; it measured one thousand feet in length and seven in width, so that his soldiers could reach our side over the sea across and could walk up to the city walls.[13] He also ordered the construction of many engines that he had designed and issued instructions that they be produced with diligence, in addition to other timber projects (or structures) for combat, of no smaller height and width.

2.   Almost daily he led many assaults of different sorts against us, in which many on both sides were killed in sudden, unforeseen ways. But when a single individual from the city died, one hundred Turks perished outside the city.

CHAPTER IX: The Christians in the Service of the Turks; their Mutual Arrangement; Events and Incidents.

1   Besides, there were in the army of the Turks many individuals from Greece and from other parts of the world, who lived in the realm of the Turks but had not been compelled to abandon their faith and were allowed to practice the rite of the Christian dogma.[14] Furthermore, there were in the aforementioned army certain captains of the Turks who nourished envy and hatred for Sangam Pasha, whom they found absolutely insufferable; they decided with some forethought to notify, by any means possible, the Christian army under siege in the city, of the decisions, activities, and councils in the headquarters of their prince. These they communicated to our side through letters (or epistles) projected by artillery or bows, fastened to arrows; and with such cunning they

---

vastissimorum lignorum erexit, turres urbis exteriores ex<s>uperantia. Aliam insuper machinam excogitavit inauditam quidem at nostris temporibus numquam visam; forma enim quadranguli et solidissima, intus vacuam, domui cuipiam similem, et arte interna hominum inclusorum et rotarum cuilibet angulo suppositarum funibusque illigatis et aliis instrumentis volubilibus mobilem atque mire conduibilem, super quam scal<a>e imposit<a>e deferebantur, qu<a>e res opus effingebat Archimedis et Heronis, quod de per se et a casu moveri videbatur. Scal<a>e autem summitates murorum ac turrium <a>equantes tot<a>e erant tabulis circumquaque vallat<a>e, ne offendi posse<n>t ascensores ab his, qui m<o>enibus insidebant."

[13] This is a reference to the bridge that Tetaldi has already discussed earlier; also see above, Chap. 3, n. 5.

[14] Leonardo (CC 1: 130; PG 159: 927) was also upset by the presence of the numerous Christian warriors in the Turkish army and uses colorful language to give vent to his anger, reproduced above, n. 2. As usual, there is an echo, without the ecclesiastical lore, in Languschi-Dolfin, 9 (fol. 314): "Ne altri circumuallo Costantinopoli saluo perfidi Christiani, che insegnorono a Turci in fra li quali erano Greci, Latini, Germani, Ungari, Boemi insieme cum Turci." Quirini adds that the elite of Mehmed's army had the benefit of western armor (*TIePN*, 72): "cum veteranis militibus more iam Italico armatis." The contribution of Christian regiments to the sultan was immense; cf. *PL* 2: 121: "It would be interesting to know how many Greeks, Italians, Germans, Hungarians, and other Christians, especially technicians, were serving in Mehmed's army and in his fleet. Not all Christians were laboring 'for the honor of God and Christendom.'"

in civitatem miserunt talique arte adinventa secretius eas ad nostros direxerunt. Interea urbici ita edocti sunt per huiusmodi prudentissimam audacissimamque

secretly dispatched them to our side.[15] In the meantime, the townspeople were well and reliably informed through their shrewd, bold, ingenuity, that the prince

[15] E.g., Halil Candarlı was a member of an old, prestigious Anatolian family; on Halil, see above, Chap. 3, n. 16. Throughout his career, under Murad II and Mehmed II, Halil (and other member of the Anatolian nobility) gradually saw their influence at the Porte decrease and faced the enmity of the aggressive faction that had risen through the ranks as former Christians who converted to Islam through the *devşirme*, the infamous child tribute that the Christian subjects of the Turks had to pay to the sultan; see above, Chap. 2, n. 7. Halil assumed the post of first vizier when his predecessor, Işak Pasha (who was probably of Greek extraction), was demoted to the post of second vizier in 1439. The third vizier, Zaganos Pasha, was also of Greek or Albanian extraction, a typical product of the *devşirme*. On the janissaries, the Ottoman *yeni çeri* troops [= "the new army"] rendered by Rizzardo as *giannizzeri* and known in Greek as γενίτσαροι, originating in the "child tribute" (*devşirme* in Turkish and παιδομάζωμα in Greek), see among others, OGN, chap. 6, esp. 72 ff.; Vryonis, "Seljuk Gulams and Ottoman Devshirmes" and "Isidore Glabas and the Turkish Devshirme;" and Papoulia, "*Knabenlese*" with review by Vryonis; see above, Chap. 2, n. 7.

On the early career of Halil and on the Candarlı family, see MCT, 44–46, and OGN, 151–52. Mehmed II disliked his father's first vizier intensely but kept him in office through the siege of 1453. That Halil and a faction at the Porte disapproved of the siege was not a secret, and it was widely rumored that Halil was in the pay of the Greek emperor. It is doubtful, however, that the impoverished Greek emperor of Constantinople had the funds to bribe the sultan's first vizier, who was immensely wealthy. If Halil informed the Greeks of the sultan's deliberations (as numerous sources insist that he did), he must have done so because he was convinced that it was the proper course of action and not because he had sold his services, as the Greeks could not have met his price. Halil and his faction were clearly opposed to the siege, even at this late date; at least such was the opinion of Leonardo (CC 1: 154; PG 159: 937): "Christianis favens, regi semper dissuaserat ne urbem Constantinopolim molestaret, eo quod fortitudine situs, rerum fertilitate providentiaque non tam Graecorum quam Latinorum munita, inexpugnabilis erat, quae proavorum patrisque guerras annis multis tolerasset." Tetaldi is also correct when he names Zaganos as Halil's opponent; Leonardo agrees (CC 1: 156; PG 159: 937): "Zaganos, iunior, secundus consularis baro, Christianorum hostis, tum praecipue Calil Basciae aemulator." He was the leader of the "hawks" at the Porte, in favor of launching an attack upon Constantinople. Zaganos's allies included two influential members of the Turkish nobility, Turahan and Şihabeddin; both of them had befriended Mehmed when he was a young man and had supported him and his claim to the throne. After Mehmed's enthronement in 1451, the hawks became powerful and supported the young sultan's plan to besiege the Greek capital. Soon after the fall of Constantinople, Mehmed had Halil executed. Halil's career is aptly summarized by Eparkhos and Diplovatatzes: "Item: mit Machmet was Hellus Pascha, ein Furst, der sprach er gewunne der Stat nicht; sprach der Keisser der Turcken: 'Gewine ichs, wie sol ich dir thun?' Er sprach: 'Slag mir das Haupt ab.' Daz geschacht." It is possible that after the sack the sultan acquired the evidence (in form of letters, perhaps, or simply through testimony of the Greek survivors) of Halil's treason, and had him executed. For the political climate at the Porte and for an discussion of the date of the vizier's execution, cf. the review article of MCT by Halil Inalcik, "Mehmed the Conqueror (1431–1482) and His Time," *Speculum* 35 (1960): 408–27; Inalcik concludes that the execution took place in August or September of 1453, while MCT, 102,

ad inventionem atque ad notitiam eorum certissime devenit, principem Turcorum iniisse consilium adversus eos per spatium quatuor dierum cum primoribus et baronibus atque comitibus suis.

of the Turks had activated a war council;[16] it lasted four days and he consulted with his foremost advisors, his barons, and his companions.[17]

suggests that Halil was put to death on July 10, 1453, ten days after his arrest. Theoharis Stavrides, *The Sultan of Vezirs: The Life and Times of the Ottoman Grand Vezir Mahmud Pasha Angelović (1453–1474)*, The Ottoman Empire and its Heritage 24 (Leiden, 2001), 51–56, also discusses these events and finds himself in agreement with Inalcik.

[16] This important meeting of the sultan's council took place on Saturday, May 26 (*FC*, 124; *MCT*, 91, implies an earlier date as it is claimed that the sultan proclaimed the day of the assault on May 24). On Friday, May 26, the sultan formally asked the Greek emperor to surrender, through an emissary, Ismail Isfendiyaroğlu, in order to observe the religious obligations imposed by Islamic law: a formal proposal for surrender must precede a general assault. See the comments in Halil Inalcik, "The Policy of Mehmed II toward the Greek Population of Istanbul and the Byzantine Buildings of the City," *DOP* 23/24 (1969/1970): 231–49. As Tetaldi and other sources suggest, Halil was disappointed when Zaganos' advice prevailed and reported to the Greeks the sultan's decision; also see Leonardo (*CC* 1: 156; *PG* 159: 937): "Itaque ut Calil Bascia [= Halil Pasha], senior consularis, complacuisse regi Zagani, aemulatoris sui, consilium intellexit definitumque esse certamen, clam internuntiis admodum fidissimis uti amicus imperatori cuncta denuntiat hortaturque ut non expavescat temulentissimi adolescentis insaniam, nec terreri minis eorum qui magis timuissent nec indoctiore multitudine commoveri; custodes sint et vigiles et pugnam perseverantes exspectent. Frequentes enim epistolae ad imperatorem ex Calil Bascia portabantur." The same text is paraphrased in the vernacular by Languschi-Dolfin (24 [fol. 319]).

[17] Most sources are in agreement as to the preparations of the Turks for the final assault. A general fast was ordered and bonfires were lit throughout the camp. Magno briefly alludes to the activities in the camp: "Dapoi molte pugne, etc. ad extremum per voce preconia fò esclamà adì 18 mazo tutti i militi ieiunio sanctifichi, et il dipoi siano in arme per combatter la cittade; la quale per dì tre futura sia a militi in preda.' Cardinal Isidore, in his letter to Bessarion, adds the interesting detail that the sultan had consulted astrologers and had cast horoscopes for the day of the assault; this detail is not encountered in any other source, but Cardinal Isidore was interested in astrology, in prophecies, and the occult (*CC* 1: 74): "Inter haec quinquaginta et tres dies Turcus consumpsit Constantinopolim obsidens nec quicquam perfecit. Sed cum omnis cognitionis illud difficillimum est, quod futurum est, nobis oculos mentis occ<a>ecavit, illi vero ita aperuit, ut Martem potentissimum ac diem et horam eius accuratissime observaverit; habet enim diligentissimos astrologos Persas, quorum consiliis ac iudicio fretus summa qu<a>eque ac maxima sese consecuturum sperat." Following Leonardo (sporadic selections in *CC* 1: 156, 158; complete text in *PG* 159: 938), Languschi-Dolfin describes the preparations in detail, 24–25 (fol. 320): "Adonchia de comandamento del Signor Turcho fu fatta proclama generale, che a quatro calende de mazo zoe marti adi 28. mazo se dara la battaglia. Et per tre di auanti acceso le lampade inuocauono dio che per uno zorno stagano abstinenti et parati tutti siano a dar battaglia general alla citade. Et cum altissima proclama dice esser uolunta del Signor Turco uoler dar Costantinopoli a sacho zurando per dio Immortal, et per 24. millia sui profeti per Macometto per lanima del padre, per li figlioli, per la spada che zinge. Tutti homini et femene, thesori, substantia de la terra liberamente donaua al exercito, ne mai tal commandamento uoltera. Tutto lo exercito audito tal comandamento del Signor comincio a far festa et alegreza cridando li alla Macometh rossollola, cioe dio, e dio sara et Macometto e seruo de dio, cum grand stupore. Et per tre di accessено tutte

CAPUT X: De consilio Colymbassa\<e\>
qui suggessit principi a obsidione discessere et ad propria redire

1.   Erat in hoc Turcorum consilio quidam generosus vir nomine Colymbassa qui principem suum nitebatur pro posse suo ad hoc inducere quatenus obsidionem civitatis dissolvi iuberet et cum toto suo exercitu ad propria remearet allegans pro se discretas ac rationabiles causas ad haec inducentes et deservientes, haec vel similia verba proferendo:

2.   Ecce, praestantissime domine mi: id quod facere debuisti et potuisti, fecisti nec amplius, ut mihi visum est, facere praevales, cum satis sit, servato honore tuo magnifico, id egisse quod egisti. Vel iam ergo ab incoepto desistere moneo Excellentiam tuam, ne honorem quem huc veniendo amplexa\<ve\>ris ulterius progrediendo perdere coga\<ve\>ris. Fecisti enim adversus hanc civitatem tot insultus, in quibus, ut cernis, tot sunt millia hominum de nostris interem\<p\>ta et illa manet immobilis et indemnis. Sed in hoc etiam inferam: videsne urbem hanc nimiae magnitudinis et populosam atque, ut ita dixerim, inexpugnabilem? Experimento nempe veraci et certo didicimus, quod quanto plures accumulantur ad exterminium huius famosissimae civitatis procurandum, tanto eorum globus minuitur et pauciores redeunt. Fuerunt ex nostris plerique

CHAPTER X: The Counsel of Colym [= Halil] Pasha, Who Suggested that the Prince Give Up the Siege and Return to His Realm.

1. There was in that council of the Turks a nobleman by the name of Colym Pasha who urged, with all his power of persuasion, his prince to dissolve the siege of the city and to return home with all his forces, bringing up different, reasonable arguments in favor of his suggestion; he offered a speech of this sort:

2. "Behold, my most distinguished lord: You have done what you should have done and what was in your power to accomplish; in my opinion, there is nothing more to be accomplished. Enough: your magnificent honor has been preserved, as you have done what needed to be done. From the start of this undertaking I have been warning your Excellency, not to attempt to increase your glory by following this route, in case it has the opposite effect. Indeed, you have launched so many assaults against this city, in which, as you see, many thousands of our soldiers have perished while the city remains unhurt and is still standing. And so I will say: do you see that this city is immense, that she has many inhabitants, and that she is impregnable? We have certainly learned this in our attempt, as many attacked the borders of this renowned city only to see their numbers decrease; few returned. Many of our soldiers recently tried to

---

lampade, jejurno el zorne niente gustando fino alla notte, luno con l altro alegrandose insieme conuiuando, et insieme baciandose. Noi uendendo tanta religion dio propiador cum abundante lachrime pregauemo, le sancte imagine in procession atorno el uallo e la citade pentidi et compunti portando homini et femine a piedi nudi et ogni turba sequente Idio propitio deprecauamo, gemendo cum penitentia cordial, che la sua heredita perire non permettesse, et se degnasse a suoi fedeli in tanto certamine porger l' aiuto de la sua man dextra che solo lui et non altri per Christiani poteua resister, si che riposta ogni nostra speranza in lo auxilio de Dio, el constituto di de la battaglia cosi confortati piu uigorosi aspettauamo. Et per questo chiamati tutti li baroni in conseijo capitanij et condutieri dal imperator fece tal ringha." It is interesting to note that Leonardo records an almost faithful rendering of the formula *la illaha illa 'i-Allah Muhammad rasul Allah* and further translates it as "quod Deus est semper et semper erit et Mahometus est servus eius" (CC 1: 154–156; his translation of this formula is interesting, as "he is and always will be" is perhaps influenced by Exodus 3:14); his follower Languschi-Dolfin renders the phrase into a passable Italian phonetic approximation. The sixteenth-century translator of Leonardo into Italian, Francesco Sansovino, *Gl'Annali Turcheschi overo vite de Principi della casa Othomana di M. Francesco Sansovino ne qvali si descrivono di tempo in tempo tutte le guerre fatte dalla natione de Turchi in diuerse provincie del Mondo con molti particolari della Morea et delle case nobili dell Alabania, & dell' Imperio & stato de Greci* (Venice, 1573), Chap. IX (108), produced the following approximation: "Illalla, Illalla, Maumeth russollala, cioè che Dio è, & sempre sarà, & Macometto è suo seruo." Similar is the situation with Leonardo's Greek followers. Thus Melissenos-Melissourgos (3.7.10) translates this passage as ʽΑλλά, ἀλλά, Μεεμέτη ῥεσούλ ἀλλά, τοῦτ᾽ ἔστιν ὁ θεὸς τῶν θεῶν καὶ ὁ Μαχούμετ ὁ προφήτης αὐτοῦ, and the author of the Barberini Chronicle (25) as ʽΙλαλά, Ἰλαλά, Μουχαμὲτ ρουσοὺλ Ἀλλά. Θέλει νὰ εἰπῇ· Θεός, Θεός, ὁπού ἔναι πάντα, καὶ ὁ Μουχαμέτης, ὁπού ἔναι δοῦλός του. For some observations on Ottoman oath formulas, see above, Chap. I, n. III.

qui nuper conscenderunt muros eius sed suae audaciae poenam luentes celeri praecipitatione repercussi sunt in ultionem tantae praesumptionis.

3.   Audeo denique et hoc superaddere, quod si verum est tu ipse iudicato: nullum praedecessorum tuorum civitati huic in tantum appropinqua<vi>sse quemadmodum tu fecisti! Nec aliquis eorum praesumpsit ad tam vicina eius loca accedere, uti te fecisse dies probavit hesterna et simul hodierna! Idcirco cadat deprecatio mea in conspectu tuo et quod suggero dignanter ausculta. Sufficiat, obsecro, tibi laus et honor praesens potius potentiae omnibus promulganda magnitudine, quam habitatores loci huius nusquam melius experti sunt, quam in tam propinqua appropriatione moderna. Est quippe honor si sane sapis non minimus tibi de huiusmodi tuo adventu cito per universum orbem dilatandus; qui etiam si ab ampliori terrae huius vastatione ac populi eius vexatione desisteris, tibi sufficiens permanebit in aevum.

CAPUT XI: Quod princeps Turcorum his auditis deliberavit cum suis redire in terram suam.

1.   Haec et his similia prosequente Colymbassa non insipienter ad hoc iam princeps exercitus Turcorum inductus erat, ut paene decrevisset ab obsidione inchoata discedere et cum suis ad propria remeare, cum proposito nullatenus redeundi; statuens firmiter et mente concipiens constituere in loco ad quem fortunatissime devenerat, columnas duas aereas perpetuis temporibus duraturas in memoriam videlicet in posterum. Et ob recordationem futuri temporis atque in signum praesentis eventus quatenus omnes et singuli transeuntes per viam illam easque conspicientes memoriae commendantes haec facta reminiscerentur ipsum dudum talia peregisse qualia nec quisquam suorum praedecessorum, ne dicam actitare, sed nec attentare quidem praesumpsit. Nusquam enim aliquis Turcorum princeps hanc audaciam sibi assumpsit, ut tali tantaeque civitati, veluti praefati sumus, in tantum praesumeret ullatenus approximare. Hoc ergo fuit sentimentum Colymbassa<e>, quod supra retulimus, quod tantum valuit apud principem Turcorum, quod si non intercessisset aliud, protinus manda<vi>sset illud executioni.

CAPUT XII: De consilio Sagambasa<e> pessimi capitanei.

1.   Porro Sagambassa erat alterius sentimenti et opinionis, ut ex sequentibus patet et rei docet eventus, nam cum eius quoque consilium requireretur super hac re, fertur tale ad principem de cordis sui fastu et superbia dedisse responsum:

2.   O inclyte ac praepotens dominator; domine, ostendisti veraciter hic maximam tuae virtutis probitatem. Ecce magnas de hac civitate hinc inde murorum pecias conterens deiecisti et iam intento tuo pro media parte consecuto desperatione mentis turpiter victus de cetero cessare deliberans, id quod laudabiliter coepisti magnanimiter consummare detrectas? Certe dimidium facti qui bene coepit habet. Audi ergo meum consilium, obsecro, pro tua clementia et quod suggero dignanter ausculta. Ecce enim parati sumus in perficiendo quod restat tibi viriliter assistere et annihilatione et confractione reliquae partis murorum quae remansit inde sinenter tibi collaborare.

surmount her walls but were punished for their audacity with swift destruction; this was the penalty for such effrontery.

3.   "I will boldly add one more consideration; you yourself judge its validity: none of your predecessors ever came so close to this city as you have. Not a single one of them was bold enough to approach her environs, as you have done; yesterday and today prove it. And so I present my prayer to you and I beg to you to give it due consideration. Your present honor and praise will be sufficient to spread your magnificence everywhere, which the inhabitants of this place have had occasion to observe, as you have come so close to the city. To be sure, your extensive fame from this undertaking will swiftly reach the end of the world; if you refrain from plundering this land and from vexing her inhabitants, your fame will become immortal."

CHAPTER XI: Having Heard this Speech, the Prince of the Turks Considers, in his Council, a Retreat to his Realm.

1.   Colym Pasha continued with his prudent advice and with other, similar considerations; the prince of the army of the Turks was inclined to follow his suggestions and he almost issued orders to begin a retreat from the siege and to lead his forces back to his realm and to embrace the proposal advocating a retreat. He determined, in accordance with an idea of his, to erect two bronze columns on the spot where he had experienced his successes, evidently as a monument of his achievement for posterity. This conspicuous monument would serve as a reminder, to all future travelers through this area, of his accomplishments and of the fact that he had surpassed (so he claimed, I dare not say that he actually did it) the achievements of all his predecessors; no other prince of the Turks had conceived such audacity, such effrontery, as to attack this city, as I have earlier mentioned. And so the opinion of Colym Pasha, as I have reported, would have persuaded the prince of the Turks, if something else had not intervened to annul this course of action.

CHAPTER XII: The Advice of Sagam Pasha, the Most Terrible Captain.

1.   Next Sagam Pasha expressed a different opinion and consideration, as the subsequent event and the course of events reveal. When he was asked for his sentiments on this matter, he is said to have offered, from his heart, the following haughty and arrogant advice to the prince:

2.   "Renowned and mighty Master: you have truly shown, my lord, the strength of your honesty and courage. You have clearly destroyed the great walls of this city with your bombardment and yet are you considering a shameful retreat in a desperate state of mind, proposing to abandon the task that you began in such a laudable and spirited manner? Certainly well begun is half done. So listen to my advice, I implore you: give due consideration to my proposal. Behold: we are ready to complete the task before us; we will assist you and we will work together courageously to destroy and level whatever section of the walls remains standing.

3. Conscendamus ergo forti animo adhuc semel et omni timore procul pulso saltem unica demum vice super civitatem insultum faciamus. Et si quidem valuerimus eam debellando superare merito gloriosior tibi ascribetur triumphus. Si quo vero minus tibi in hac parte fortuna quam placuerit arriserit et non potuerimus eam ad votum obtinere, faciemus cum ipsa pacem aut dabimus ei treugas, eo pacto quo placuerit tibi.

CAPUT XIII: Qualiter princeps Turcorum huius consilium est secutus.

1. His auditis princeps commendavit sentimentum et suggestionem huius capitanei et satis credulus fidemve verbis eius adhibens et approbans per omnia id quod proposuerat; tandem consentiendo iussit ita fieri quemadmodum ille suggesserat. Interim praeavisati his satis fuerant, qui erant intra civitatem ab hostibus obsessi et informati per litteras cautelose, ut est praedictum, intromissas intra civitatem de tractatu habito inter principem Turcorum et eius capitaneos et de conclusione finali, qualiter videlicet adhuc unicum insultum sustinerent urbici. In quo is subsistere ac invicti remanere possent, absque dubio hostes ab obsidione recedere congerentur.

2. Confortantes igitur et cohortantes se mutuo, ut viriliter se opponerent ac resisterent parti adversae, saltem per spatium duorum vel trium dierum. Post quas exercitus Turcorum, ut sperabant, dissipari deberet et obsidionem solvere atque singuli quique hostium ad terram propriam redire.

CAPUT XIV: De ieiunio Turcorum.

1. Hic igitur erat ordo congressus quem princeps Turcorum observare disposuit ante futuram murorum conscensionem ac civitatis iteratam et ultimam debellationem, secundum datum sibi consilium per nequam illum acerrimumque secretarium, quem saepe diximus, Sagambassa\<m\>, et sequitur in hunc modum. Itaque die sequenti, videlicet triduo ante dispositum insultum, indixit princeps Turcorum exercitui suo solemne devotumque secundum exigentiam suae legis ieiunium, in honorem scilicet ac reverentiam solis, quem pro Deo colebant, amplectens afflictionem et abstinentiam cum omni populo suo tribusque diebus continuis usque ad solis occubitum nihil omnino cibi corporalis degustans. In fine vero cuiuslibet diei corpora largioribus epulis et potibus reficiebant ea intentione, ut fertur, ne nimia famis inedia debilitati, in congressu belli ac succumbere cogerentur.

2. Tempore vero nocturno ignem copiosum construentes accenderunt luminaria quoque ac faculas et ligna secum habentes de per se arte, ut creditur, diabolica contra communem naturae regulam in mari simul ardentia et in terra. Sonitu tympanorum et aliorum instrumentorum musicorum ipsum mare quodammodo tinnire faciebant. Tubis enim numquam vel raro utebantur, quia earum copiam non habebant.

3. "And so let us be strong, put away all timidity, and attack together in order to overwhelm the city. If we are successful in combat you will earn a well-deserved, more glorious triumph. But if this be not pleasing to Fortune and we prove unable to prevail, then we will initiate talks and conclude a treaty with the city, as you wish."

CHAPTER XIII: The Advice Embraced by the Prince of the Turks.

1. After these opinions were heard, the prince praised the sentiments and the suggestion of his captain; he trusted his words, displayed faith in them, and approved all his proposals. Finally, he ordered a fast to be observed and to put into action that captain's plan. The besieged people within the city were given sufficient warning, as they were carefully informed by letters dispatched into the city (as I have earlier stated), which revealed the deliberations before the prince of the Turks by his captains and the final decision, which meant for them that they would have to face a general assault. If they proved able to survive this attack, without doubt the enemy would lift the siege and depart.

2. So they encouraged and urged each other to fight bravely and resist the enemy, at least for two or three days. After this interval the army of the Turks, they hoped, should break up and should lift the siege, as each soldier would return to his homeland.

CHAPTER XIV: The Fast of the Turks.

1. The deployment of the forces that the prince of the Turks ordered before the assault against the walls was launched and the last battle to seize the city commenced followed the advice offered during the council by that most cruel secretary, Sagam Pasha (whom we have mentioned a number of times); this is what occurred: On the following day, evidently three days before the final assault, the prince of the Turks proclaimed a solemn, devotional fast, in accordance with their rites, throughout the army; evidently it was in honor and reverence of the sun, which they worship as if it were a god; this fast, he decreed, had to be observed and was enforced by penalties throughout his army for three successive days; until sunset no substance at all could be eaten. At the end of the day they could recover by eating and drinking, so that they would not, it is said, become weak by the lack of food and succumb in the ensuing combat.

2. At night they burned numerous bonfires and had a festival of lights, with small torches and wood that they carried on them; with this diabolical magic, it is believed, they can oppose the general rules of nature over sea and land. With the sound of drums and other musical instruments they made even the sea emit sounds. Trumpets, however, were seldom used because they did not have many of them.[18]

---

[18] Tetaldi's misapprehension about solar worship in Islam and his opinion on light magic deserve future investigation in relation to folklore current among his contemporary Christians. Tetaldi's statement about the use of musical instruments finds an echo in Barbaro, who claims

CAPUT XV: De ordinatione exercitus ac lento congressu Turcorum.

1. His ita sese habentibus utitur princeps deliberatione permaxima haesitans intra se quali ordine conscendere valeret convenientiori modo quo posset nitendo ad expugnationem et captionem civitatis. Cives autem, ut praediximus, invicem sese hortabantur viriliter agere et magnanimiter se defendere sagaciter facientes praeparamenta ad resistendum. Princeps vero Turcorum super omnia cautus paulatim occulte lenteque civitatem aggredi incipiens, in sero vigesimae octavae diei mensis Maii ordinavit suum exercitum sub modo et forma sequentibus.

2. Biglardi dux exercitus Turcorum ordinatus et constitutus erat cum viginti millibus bellatorum ad portam civitatis vocabulo Pichi, ubi maximus putabatur instare resistendi insultus. Colymbassa vero consiliarius principis (amicus tamen et fautor Christianorum), Sagambassa quoque secretarius eiusdem, fere, cum tertia exercitus parte constituti fuerunt ad portam S<ancti> Romani, quae distabat per spatium fere unius milliarii a porta Pichi. Ebigleobet quoque generalis capitaneus Graecorum erat deputatus ad latus Caligarae, in opposito videlicet regalis palatii, ubi hostes (sicut superius dictum est) sub terra fodere coeperant ante hunc congressum; qui locus distat a porta Pichi Romani duobus fere milliaribus. Sagambassa vero Albanensis, Christianae religionis praevaricator, erat constitutus in mari, versus civitatem Peram, cum abnegationis suae sociis et Mahometicae sectae sequacibus, qui cum eo fidem Christi abdicaverant prae timore Turcorum.

CHAPTER XV: The Deployment of the Army and the Slow Assault of the Turks.

1. In this situation the prince, after listening to a very long debate, decided to deploy his forces in the best manner possible in order to capture and seize the city. The citizens, however, encouraged each other, as I have stated, to fight bravely and to defend themselves boldly; they made preparations to resist. The prince of the Turks, being careful in all stages, decided to begin a slow assault against the city, under cover; so in the evening of May 28 he drew up his army in consecutive waves.

2. Biglardi [= Beglerbeg ?], who was appointed lord of the army of the Turks, deployed his twenty thousand warriors at a gate of the city called Pege, where, it was thought, the assault would meet with the greatest opposition. Colym Pasha, the councilor of the prince (who was a friend and a supporter of the Christians), Sagam Pasha, his secretary, with one-third of the army would attack the Gate of Saint Romanus, which was almost one mile away from the Gate of Pege. Ebigleobet [= Beglerbeg ?] was appointed captain general of the Greeks by the side of Caligarea, evidently facing the imperial palace, where the enemy (as I have mentioned earlier) had begun the subterranean mines before the assault; this place is almost two miles distant from the Gate of Pege-Romanus. The Albanian Sagam Pasha, the shameless double-dealer and Christian renegade, was in charge of the assault by sea, against the city of Pera, with his associate renegades and the followers of the Moslem sect, those who had renounced their faith in Christ because they feared the Turks.[19]

---

that the general assault was proclaimed by the sound of the trumpet; cf. Barbaro, CC 1: 27–28 (ed. Cornet, 49): "A dì vinti otto pur de questo mexe de mazo el signor Turco sì fexe far uno comandamento a son de trombeta per tuto el suo campo, che soto pena de la testa tuti i suo bassà ei i suo subasì e tuti altri suo capetani, e d'ogni condition se sia, che abia Turchi a so governo, si debia redurse per tuto questo zorno a le suo poste, e questo perché doman el signor Turco vuol dar doman la bataia zeneral a questa dolente città ... Turchi si andava sonando trombe per el campo e nacare e tamburli per alegrà el puovolo del campo ...."

[19] The deployment of the Turkish forces for the final assault is well known. The first wave of the assault consisted of the irregulars, and of the ill-trained troops, as well as of the adventurers who had joined Mehmed's forces through the prospect of booty. The main thrust was directed at the ruined fortifications at the valley of Lykos. This attack was easily repelled by the defenders. The second wave consisted of the Anatolian regulars, while bombardment of the walls continued; this second attack was also repelled. The janissaries, without allowing any respite to the defenders, then launched their deadly, precise, and orderly assault at carefully selected points in the periphery of the walls. No time had been allowed to effect repairs on the improvised defenses of the besieged and the numerous stockades, fences, and barricades were in ruins. Cardinal Isidore pointed out that the main thrust came upon the vulnerable sector, the Gate of Saint Romanus (CC 1: 74): "Vigessimo itaque nono die mensis Maii proxime peracti aurora illuscente, solis etiam radiis nostros oppugnantibus, mari ac terra urbem invadentes Turci ad eam partem maxime semiruptam circa Sanctum Romanum assiluerunt, ubi multi erant fortes viri Latini et Gr<a>eci absque tamen rege ac imperatore ipsorum." Magno emphasizes

CAPUT XVI: De hostium aggressu, conscensu, et insultu valido.

1. Ordinatione bellatorum ita expedita restat iam ut succincte de hostium invasione loquamur. Hi perinde qui se in civitate, prout poterant, tuebantur, resistere viriliter; sed locus versus portam S<ancti> Romani, quia nimium bassus erat parumque obinde munitus, faciliorem adversariis praebebat transitum. Illic quoque muri minus erant fortes, quorum non minima pars diebus praeteritis fuerat ab adversariis comminuta. Itaque specula quaedam illuc iactu fundae ad terram prostrata est; media quoque pars murorum illius lateris per spatium fere ducentorum passuum deiecta. Erant quippe illic tot fundae atque colubri in aere volitantes, in tanta copia, ut sua densitate aerem viderentur obnubilare.

CHAPTER XVI: The Enemy Charge, Attack, and Strong Assault.

1.   Such was the arrangement of warriors, or, to be more accurate, the assault of the enemy. Those in the city defended themselves, in accordance with their abilities; they resisted bravely, but the sector around the Gate of Saint Romanus offered a better approach to the enemy, because it was low and inadequately fortified. There the walls were weak and in the past days the enemy had destroyed a great section. And so some sections there had been bombarded and leveled to the ground; furthermore, the middle area of that section of the walls had been demolished to a distance of almost two hundred paces. To be sure in that sector numerous artillery pieces and colubrines were firing into the

the deplorable condition of the defenses: "Erano i muri de grande altezza, ma, per vetustà et puocha cura de Greci, nudi di propugraculi, ma de antemurali oppurtunamente puunida [? previda, provveduta ?], nelli quali Greci messero la sua salute et armadi militi infra i muri et antemurali sostegnir decrevettero. È la cittade in forma triangolare, due in mare, con muriazi a propulsar l'empito navale, et quello da terra, dapoi i muri et antemurali, da una grande fossa e terra." Quirini is probably the earliest source to provide us with a concise deployment of Mehmed's forces [*TIePN*, 70–72]: "Ordinem vero belli huiusmodi fuisse affirmant: terrestres copias in tres diuisisse partes, quarum uni praefecit Beilarbeim (totius Graeciae praefectum) [= the Beglerbeg of Rumeli], alteri Sarazanum bassa [= Saraca Pasha], ipsum vero Teucrum mediam cepisse partem cum Chalil bassa [= Halil Pasha]; quem locum magna illa terribilisque bombarda diruisse paulo ante diximus. Ex parte quoque maris maritimas copias ordina<vi>sse ita ut undequaque et terra et mari civitas oppugnaretur. Omnibus itaque dispositis die vigesimo octavo Maii, prima noctis hora, ex parte terrae incepisse proelium gregariis praemissis militibus pugna<vi>sseque per totam noctem. Verum enim illuscente tandem die ipse ille terribilis pestis Teucer cum aurato curru prope moenia veniens cum veteranis militibus more iam Italico armatis auream sagittam in urbem emisisse civitatemque diripiendam pollicitum fuisse. Quo viso auditoque tanto et clamore et alacritate ardoreque animi hostium concitati et scopetorum et sagittarum infinito paene numero ita repente moenia expugna<vi>sse dicunt, ut instar avium muros evolaverint."

Another report (from autumn or early winter of 1453) comes from the pen of Antonio Ivani, who adds a few more details not met in other sources (cf., e.g., his statements as to the plan of the defense and his comments on the role of Constantinople's women and children in the last battle and the use of boiling oil as a deterrent to the enemy), *TIePN* (with Italian translation), 146–65; here 158: "Sex milibus Graecorum totidemque auxiliarium ab ea parte qua hostium castra erant oppositis, quinque milia delectorum militum in media urbe collocat, qui quo eos clamor advocasset eo utique ad resistendum occurrant, reliquam multitudinem navali pugnae resistere iubet ... Rex omnibus copiis ad oppugnandum paratis, duabus circiter ante diem horis, imminente luna, naves moenibus admoveri iubet, ipse quoque tripartito exercitu pluribus simul in locis ancipiti terrore urbem aggreditur quam terrestri navalique proelio undique corona cingit, inque locis ubi moenia diruta sunt ad murum subeunt, alii ignem, alii scalas, alii alia, quibus Graecos terreant, important, quibus multo labore lassis alteri itidem illico succedebant; mari etiam naves prealtis propugnaculis in proram erectis missilibus et sagittis acerrime impugnabant, Graeci iaculis, sagittis, saxis fortiter obsistunt, igne etiam plerumque aqua et oleo fervido hostem submovebant. Tum feminae puerique sedulo adsunt oppugnantibus, tela ministrant, saxa gerunt; quare saepe a muris repellebantur Teucri."

Illi vero qui de civitate erant, prout poterant, muros suos reparando erigebant obstruentes eos terra et vasis ac lignis; quibus resarcitis per aliquod tempus sese defendebant secundum possibilitatem suam, ea cautela et modo ac practica, quas quiverant in tali necessitate constituti excogitare.

CAPUT XVII: De nobili domino Ioanne Iustinensi et opere atque industria eius.

1.   Erat hoc in loco intra civitatem constitutus capitaneus quidam nomen erat Ioannes, vir nobilis, natione Ianuensis, qui eo tempore imperatori Constantinopolitano deservivit sub tributo. Hic se in omnibus exhibuit audacem et virilem velut alter Machabaeus, in cuius potestatis praeeminentia totus cuneus bellatorum omnem spem suam et fiduciam post Deum prae cunctis mortalibus illius aevi statuerat. Qui ostensurus potentiam suam et industriam qua callebat ad faciendum quod cogitavit et valuit, duobus vexillis paratis ac decem millibus virorum fortium electis pro custodia corporis sui, propter nimiam violentiam et copiam adversariorum iuxta castellum ligneo compactum opere (de quo supra tractum est), illic procuravit et adesse iussit sedes et ligna atque stallagia aliaque instrumenta ad repugnandum necessaria coepitque moenia et fossas quae deintus erant replere ac pontibus aequare reliquae terrae, quatenus absque impedimento posset cum suis hostibus occurrere ex adverso venturis.

CAPUT XVIII: De eiusdem domini Ioannis vulneratione
et civitatis ab hostibus devastatione.

1.   His ita se habentibus, praefatus dominus Ioannes Iustiniensis congressu cum hostibus iactu colubri cuiusdam graviter vulneratus est; qui statim letalis quodammodo vulneris ictu sequestrans se ab exercitu cui capitaneus fuit deputatus, ad medicandum ocius properavit suam commendans custodiam et populum sibi subiectum duobus aliis viris nobilibus Ianuensibus. Et ecce dum unius

air so often that the dense smoke seem to cloud over the air. The citizens made the necessary repairs to their walls and re-erected them with earth, containers, and logs; they defended their patchwork for some time, in accordance with their abilities, as they were determined to think up practical ways required in such necessity.

CHAPTER XVII: The Accomplishments and Zeal of Lord Giovanni Giustiniani.

1.   At that place in the city was a certain man who had been appointed captain; his name was Giovanni; he was a nobleman and a Genoese by birth,[20] who at that time had offered his services to the Constantinopolitan emperor for hire. This man proved bold and brave in every operation; he was like another Maccabee, in whose strength the entire phalanx of our warriors had placed all hope and loyalty, after God but before all other mortals of that time. He was about to display his strength and zeal (which he cultivated in order to bring into completion all his plans with determination) and prepared two standards and chose ten thousand strong men to be his bodyguards, as there were very violent confrontations with many adversaries near the castle that had been constructed with timber (as I have indicated above); he assumed command of that area and ordered timber logs, beams, and other tools necessary to fight back, and began to fill in the walls and the ditches and to reach the remaining areas with bridges in order to hinder the enemy who was advancing from the opposite side.

CHAPTER XVIII: The Wound of Lord Giovanni and the Devastation of the City by the Enemy.

1.   In this situation the aforementioned Lord Giovanni Giustiniani was seriously wounded by a missile from an enemy colubrine; as soon as he received the impact of the lethal wound he separated himself from the army, in whose charge he had been placed, and hastened swiftly to take care of his wound, entrusting the defense and his subordinate warriors to two other Genoese

---

[20] On Giovanni Guglielmo Longo Giustiniani and his early career, see above, n. 9. For his coat of arms, see Carl Hopf, *Les Giustiniani dynastes de Chiòs étude historique*, trans. Henri Vlasto (Paris, 1888), 174: "Les armoires des Giustiniani de Chios étaient de gueules à la fortresse d'argent, surmontée de trois tours de même, maçoncées de sable, au chef d'or chargé de l'aigle de l'emprie couronnée, à une tête regardant à dextre, qui leur avait été concédée par Sigismond. Cet écusson est ancore parfaitement visible aujourd'hui sur des marbres, sur de palais et des tours de Chiòs presqu'en ruines, comme aussi sur l'ancien palais de la Maona, à Gênes, dan la contrada de Giustiniani." In n. 1 of the same page, Hopf discusses the original form of this coat of arms: "Les armoires primitives des Giustiniani étaient une fortresse d'argent surmontée de trois tours de même, maçonées de sable, sur champ de gueules." For surviving examples in Chios, see Frederick W. Hasluck, "The Latin Monuments of Chios," *Annual of the British School at Athens* 16 (1909–1910): 137–84, esp. 147, and fig 5. In addition, see Philippides, "Giovanni Guglielmo Longo Giustiniani."

mortis causa sollicitatur, plurimorum salus periclitatur, ut ex his quae sequuntur evidenter comprobatur. Denique dum haec aguntur, intempesta nocte iam lucis

nobles.[21] And thus, while there was concern over the cause of the death of one individual, the safety of the majority was in danger, as becomes clear from the

[21] There is no doubt that the wound of Giustiniani and his departure constituted the turning point in the assault. Thus far the defenders had sustained two major attacks and it looked as if they would be able to maintain the vigorous defense successfully, when the incident involving the warlord occurred and the defense degenerated into a rout. The nature of his wound remains in doubt, as there is no agreement among our sources, since they were not present in the sector of Saint Romanus, where practically all defenders perished in the ensuing rout. The following is a list of early and contemporary sources that discuss the incident in various degrees of detail:

(i) Leonardo (CC 1: 160; PG 159: 940): "Inter haec, malo fato urbis, heu!, Johannes Justinianus sagitta sub assella configitur, qui mox inexpertus iuvenis sui sanguinis effusione pavidus perdendae vitae concutitur et ne pugnatores, qui vulneratum ignorabant, virtute frangantur, clam medicum quaesiturus ab acie discessit." As usual, Leonardo is followed closely by Languschi-Dolfin, 28 (fol. 320): "In fra el combatter per mala sorte de la citade, oyme, che Zuane Zustignan capitanio uien ferito de freza sotto asella del scajo, lo qual inexperto zouene subito ueduto el sangue pauido de perder la uita, et acio li combattanti che non sapeua quello fusse ferito rompesse la uitu, ascosamente per medicarse se parte da la sua statione . . . ." Leonardo's (and Languschi-Dolfin's ?) statements found their way into an immensely popular printed version in the next century in Sansovino's Gl'Annali Turcheschi, 110 (a printer's error; it should read 111, in the rare copy of the Gennadius Library in Athens): "Et mentre ch'egli animaua i suoi a questo modo, ecco he per mala sorte della città, vien ferito Giouanni Giustiniano da vna saetta sotto l'ascelle, il quale comme giouane non pratico, vedendosi tutto bagnato del suo proprio sangue & temendo di perder la vita, si sbigotti tutto. Et accioche i combattenti che non sapeuano che fosse ferito, non rimettessero la virtù loro, i partì ascosamente dalla zuffa, per farsi medicare."

(ii) Pusculo (CC 1: 212; ed. Ellissen, 4.212 ff.): "Lucifer aurorae venientis pallidus ortum / ducebat, portans ubi casumque diemque. / Joannes abiit percussus glande lacertum / ac se subripuit pugnae navesque petivit, / sive metu Teucrum, seu vulnere abactus."

(iii) Barbaro (CC 1: 33; ed. Cornet, 55): "Vedando questo, Zuan Zustignan, zenovexe da Zenova, se delibera de abandonar la sua posta [in margine: per esser ferito de frezza] e corse a la sua nave, che iera stà messa a la cadena; e questo Zuan Zustignan, l'imperador si l'avea fato capetanio da tera; e scampando questo che iera capetanio, vignando el dito per la terra criando: 'Turchi son intradi dentro da la tera,' e menteva per la gola, che ancora i non iera intradi dentro. Or aldando il puovolo queste parole da questo capetanio, che Turchi se iera intradi dentro da la tera, tuti si se comenza a meter in fuga, e subito tuti abandona le sue poste, e cazase a corer verso la marina, per poder scampar con le nave e con le galìe." See above, Chap. 3, n. 10, where part of this passage is quoted.

(iv) Eparkhos and Diplovatatzes (NE 2: 514–18): "Item: der Genuessen Haubtman, der daz Loch inen het, er stellet sich sam er erschossen wer, und ging wek, und als sein Volck ging mit im hinwek; do daz die Turcken sahen, do stellen sie da selbst hin ein."

(v) Benvenuto (207; TIePN, 4): "Item quod, donec Justinianus Longus, custodiens simul cum inperatore Costantinopolitanam et suis nobilibus locum fractum per bomberdas, affugit cum 360 hominibus civitatis, egregie fuit civitas per inexistentes defensata ad modum ut ex custodientibus civitatem solum 40 persone interfecte fuerunt et ex Turcis 7000. Item quod XXVIII Maii de nocte incepit bellum per mare et per terram circumcirca civitatem, et resistebant optime inexistentes ipsi Turco, sed postquam dictus Justinianus affugit adveniente die XXIX Maii media hora die<i> capta fuit civitas Constantinopolitana."

initia vix attingente, ex improviso Turci muros civitatis alacriter conscendunt,

subsequent events. Finally, as these events were occurring, the stormy night was about to end and the early light of dawn had appeared, when suddenly the Turks

....

(vi) Ivani (*TIePN*, 160–62): "Longus Iustinianus, Ianuensis vir bellicae disciplinae haud indoctus, qui ubi plurimum periculi videbatur praepositus erat, e loco cedit sive quod impetum sufferre non posset, sive quod salutem sibi fuga quaereret, cuius exemplo auxiliares milites ad naves confugiunt ac maxima pars sese fugae mandat, pleraeque naves, quae in portu erant, simul tot hominum quot capaces erant complentur, fugam arripiunt."

(vii) Angelo Giovanni Lomellino (the Genoese *podestà* of Pera) (CC 1: 42): "In summo mane Ioannes Iustinianus cepit <vultus tremendum?> et portam suam dimisit et se tiravit ad mar<e> et per ipsam portam Teucri intraverunt, nulla habita resistentia."

(viii) Tursun Beg, *History of Mehmed the Conqueror*, trans. Inalcik and Murphey, 36, states that "the enemy commander" was wounded in the belly.

(ix) Stefano Magno (probably echoing Leonardo and/or Languschi-Dolfin), NE 3: 296–97: "accedete che all' hora sopra li antemurali fù ferido Zuanne Zustignan da Pera, che i superiori zorni solo pareva havesse diffeso la cittade et, abbondandoli il sangue, cercando il medico, acciò gli altri non si spavissero, ascosamente si levò; mà lo imperator, consciuto mancar il detto, cerca dove andava; trovado, pregò non abbandonar la pugna; mà quello, nihilo magis flexo, avrir la porta commandò, quia curaturus vulnus nella città ritorni... essendo la porta che era stà aperta a Zuanne Zustignan a tutti aperta, fuga profusior reddette."

(x) Nikolaos Sekoundinos (in a popular work of his, as it survives in eighteen manuscripts) delivered a speech in the presence of Alfonso of Naples on January 25, 1454; selections in NE 3: 316–23; selections in CC 2: 128–41; complete text based on an inferior manuscript can be found, with numerous errors, in Makušev, *Monumenta Historica Slavorum*, 295–306; cf. CC 2: 134 [NE 3: 319–20]: "Januensis quidam Joannes Longus, vir profecto magni pretii, cum ducentis circiter nautis —nam onerariae navis praefectus, stipendio imperatoris conductus, partem illam moenium suscepit tutandam, cui maximum videretur periculum impendere, quave hostis, postquam crebris tormentorum ictibus moenia demolitus solo propemodum adaequasset, sibi aditum patefacere studio ardentissimo temptaret— is, inquam, Joannes, ubi vidit hostem acrius solito urgere et invalescere, propugnatores vero contra sensim deficere, quippe quorum alii interempti, nonnulli saucii, reliqui perterriti et fugati, salutem urbis desperare coepit duobusque acceptis vulneribus, imperatorem adiit, cui tristissimum attulit nuntium et devolvendum nihil virium amplius, nihil spei esse relictum, pro hostis impediatur, quin Urbem vi capiat et victoria potiatur, polliceri se proinde imperatorem ipsum navi sua incolumem ad locum devecturum salutis." This account agrees with the version that Giustiniani received two wounds, as it is reported in the Slavonic text of Nestor-Iskander, 60–61 (74–77):...но прилетѣвъ исъ пушкы ядро каменное на излетѣ, и удари въ Зустунѣа по персѣмъ, и разрази емы перси. И паде на землю, едва его отсльяша и отнесоша и въ домъ его.... Врачеве же чресъ всю оную нощь тружахуся о поможеніи его, и едва исправиша ему грудь, вшибленое мѣсто отъ удара, and 64 (76–79): ...прилетѣвшу убо склопу, и удари Зустунѣа и срази ему десное плечо, и паде на землю аки мертвъ. И надоша надъ нимъ боляре его и людіе, крыча и рыдаш, и поношаше его прочь, тако и Фрягове вси пойдоша за нимъ.

(xi) A Venetian chronicle in Milan's Ambrosian library, R 113, Sup., fols. 185^v–186^r (extract in NE 3: 301, note 1): "Adì 29 mazo ... et circa do hore avanti zorno fuo ferido da una freza el patron genoese, capetanio a la guardia de lo riparo, e se parti. Visto la soa zurma restar senza capo, se abandonorono detto riparo et fugite verso le soe nave."

videntibus his qui intra civitatem erant, custodientes vigilia noctis. Absente igitur praefato domino Ioanne Iustiniensi qui curationis necessitate diverterat ab exercito suo, hi qui subtractionis eius causam ignorabant putantes eum fugae metusve occasione declina<vi>sse ac praesentiam suam subtraxisse fugae praesidium et ipsi quaesierunt, non praeavisati se defendere contra insultus adversariorum, absente capitaneo suo.

began to mount the walls of the city in lively fashion, in full view of those who were inside the city and keeping the night watch. And so with the departure of the aforementioned Lord Giovanni Giustiniani, who was forced to leave the army in order to take care of his wound, those who were unaware of the reason for his withdrawal formed the impression that he was fleeing or that he had succumbed to fear and thus took himself out of the conflict; they themselves looked for a reason to flee, as they had not been forewarned that they would have to defend themselves against the enemy assault without their captain.[22]

(xii) Adamo di Montaldo ("Adae de Montaldo, *De Constantinopolitano excidio*," ed. Hopf, Dethier, and Desimoni, 325–54; and few selections in *TIePN*; 335–36): "Johannes Justinianus, non minoris multo praestantiae, cum deficere jam pugnantes circumquaque intueretur, seque mortaliter percussum, relicto hostio urbis trans solitum invalescere hostem videbat, peremptorum summis jam moenium cumulum coaequatis, pro laesione vulnerum gravi, copiaque tormentorum et pugnantium, a proelio, pro se altero substituto, abscessit."

(xiii) Hieronimo Giustiniani, 417: "A pena il Giustiniano havea finito a mezzo il raggionamento, i fu costretto disponersi a diffendersi, il qual mentre che combateva strenuamente hebbe una ferita mortale ... Il Giustiniano nondimeno cascò in terra trasmortito, il qual subito ne fu trasportato da' suoi negli allogiamenti. Gli soldati havendo visto il capo quasi morto stetero attoniti et mezzo persi."

[22] The conduct of Giustiniani has been debated since 1453. And it is clear that he was mortally wounded, as he died within a month after the event. Numerous survivors placed the blame for the loss of the city squarely on his shoulders. As is evident in the previous note, it is not clear whether he was accompanied by his troops when he left his post. Some sources suggest that the problem was that no one was left in charge. Others state that he took his band with him and that the critical section of the walls was left totally defenseless. It is practically impossible to reconstruct the actual sequence of events. Charges against him appeared early on. George Scholarius, the opponent of the church union and the first patriarch of the captive Greeks under Mehmed II, spoke of a possible "act of treason" but avoided any mention of Giustiniani's name (ed. Louis Petit, Xenophon A. Sidéridès, and Martin Jugie, *Oeuvres complètes de Gennade Scholarios* [Paris, 1930], 1: 279–80 [the Ἐπιτάφιος on his nephew]): Ὁ πόλεμος ἐνεστήκει, καὶ μόνος ἡ κομιδῇ σὺν ὀλίγοις ὑπολειφθείς, οὕπερ ἐτέταξο, πολλοῖς τραύμασιν, ἃ ταῖς χερσὶν ἐδέξω καὶ τῷ προσώπῳ, αὐταῖς ταῖς κλίμαξι τοὺς δι' αὐτῶν ἐπὶ τὸ τεῖχος ἀνελθεῖν, πεπειρωμένους συγκατεσπάσατε, ἕως ὑμεῖς μὲν ὑπὸ θαλάττης οὐδὲν παρήκατε πράττειν ὧν ἐπεθύμουν, οἱ δὲ ἀπὸ τῆς γῆς, δι' ἐρήμου κατεληλυθότες τοῦ τείχους, πάντα ἐσκύλευον, φυγῆς προδεδωκότων τῶν φυλάξειν ὑποσχομένων. At first Cardinal Isidore seems to have entertained doubts about the conduct of the warlord and he seems to have held him responsible for the fall; thus in his letter to Cardinal Bessarion he refused to talk about the incident but seems to imply that there was something suspicious going on (CC 1: 74): "Erat autem cum imperatore illo ductor quidam nomine Ioannes Iustinianus, quem multi incusant primam fuisse causam tant<a>e captivitatis et excidii: sed omittamus." Cardinal Isidore hastens to add that the particular sector was practically indefensible: "Facilis autem erat in ea parte ad m<o>enia ascensus, quia, ut dictum est, quasi tota erat bombardis illisa ac prope decussa, propter quod et facile hostes in urbem irruperant, nemine illic invento, qui hostium impetum reprimeret aut eam partem defenderet." Pusculo (CC 1: 212) speaks of desertion: "deseruitque locum, trepidantiaque agmina liquit."

2. Sic ergo Turci nocte civitatem Constantinopolitanam (pro dolor!) intraverunt per muros scandentes circa auroram vigesimae octavae diei mensis Maii;

2.   So the Turks entered the city of Constantinople (alas!) at night; they scaled the walls around dawn on the twenty-eighth day of the month of May;

Moreover, early on it was reported, at least by Greek sources, that it was a defender who had wounded Giustiniani. Thus in the early, anonymous Ἔκθεσις Χρονική, composed in the Patriarchate in the sixteenth century, we encounter the rumor (30, [47]): Ἐφημίσθη οὖν ὅτι ἔνδοθεν τοῦ κάστρου δέδωκαν αὐτόν, ἀλλὰ οὐκ οἶδέ τις ὅπως γέγονεν. Another source also reports the same rumor, namely the verse chronicle by Hierax, an official of the Patriarchate; see Sathas, Μεσαιωνικὴ Βιβλιοθήκη, 265 (ll. 636–646):

Πρὸ πάντων δὲ ἦν πρόμαχος αὐτὸς ἐν ταῖς χαλάστραις,
ὡς ἔδει τε ἐμάχετο στερρῶς ἐν τῷ πολέμῳ·
ἀλλά γε βάσκανος ἀνήρ τις διὰ τουφεκίου
βάλλει ἐπὶ τῷ ἥρωι καὶ πλήττει τὸν γενναῖον,
καὶ φόνον ἐπροξένησεν εἰς ἄνδρα τηλικοῦτον.
Λέγεται δὲ ἐκ τῶν ἐντὸς Ῥωμαίων ἦν ὁ δράσας
τοῦτο τὸ ἐπιβούλευμα κατὰ τοῦ Γενοβίου,
φθόνῳ τρωθείς, ὡς εἴθισται, πάντοτε τοῖς βασκάνοις.
Εἰς δὲ τὰς νῆας εἰσελθὼν ἀπῆλθεν εἰς πατρίδα,
πνέων ἔτι ὁ δυστυχὴς τὰ λοίσθια θανάτου.

During the early hours of May 29 the situation at the sector of Saint Romanus must have been chaotic; a stray arrow, bullet, or missile of some sort, perhaps from the inside of the Great Wall, cannot be ruled out; neither can treachery, as Giustiniani had been the right hand of the emperor and must have made scores of enemies, especially among the anti-union and pro-Turkish fifth column within the city. Reports of an unlucky accident even reached the west, as shown in Richer-Riccherio whose account used to be thought to have been composed by an eyewitness, while modern scholarship has demonstrated that it was composed in the 1540s; see above, Chap. 1, notes 23, 29. See Richer, *De rebus Turcarum* (Paris, 1540 [actually 1543]), 94–95: "Accidit ut inter pugnandum cum irrumpenti hosti fronte, advera obsisteret, telo suorum infoeliciter in hostem misso, graviter incautus vulneratur. Cruoris exemplo e dorsi vulnere manentis abundantiam intuitus, nolens ut, demum praedicabat, commilitonibus perturbationi interpellationique esse, si quempiam eorum accersitur medicum dimitteret, clanculum se praelio subduxit." One of Richer's sources was undoubtedly Leonardo, as becomes clear from the phraseology, 97: "Iustinianus verò percepta hostium victoria paeram continuò diffugit: mox illinc haud satis confirmatus, Chium insulam Ioniae adnauigat: vbi aut vi vulneris, aut dolore confectus, quòd importunè praelio excessisset, paucis diebus comparata primùm nominis gloria incredibili orbatus, animam egit; vno certè foelix futurus, si in armis egregius propugnator ad muros Constantinopolitanos mori potuisset." It was in the same century that the first detailed defense of Giustiniani's conduct appeared in print, with scholarly references; see Hieronimo Giustiniani (418–420):

Hora, acciochè ogni uno sappia l'intentione degli historici di quanto sopra ciò per il Giustiniano hanno scritto addure per la giustificatione di tanto grand personagio contra la malvagia invidia d'alcuni le ragione in questo luogo. Laonico Chalcocondila, famoso historico, facendo mentione del Giustiniano adduce queste parole. Arivò in Costantinopoli un personagio genovese, chiamato Giovanni Giustiniano, il qual pervienne in soccorso della città con una grosa nave et con trecenti soldati, al quall'Jmperatore dette a guardare il luogo, nel

omnes interficientes a minimo usque ad maximum, qui eis resistere ac se defendere tentare aussi fuerunt; quodque execrabilius est et horribilius sonat in auribus

all who offered resistance and dared to defend themselves were put to the sword, from the youngest to the oldest. What is more sacrilegious and creates horror

> quale il Gran Turcho con i gianizzari volea dare lo assalto, sforzandossi guagliardamente opponere a loro, non molto discosto dallo Imperatore, il qual ancora lui fortissimamente si deffendeva. Et più sotto dice, che i genovesi dalla gran forza de' turchi furono mossi da loro luogo per forza, et il Giustiniano loro capitano ne fu ferito in una mano da un colpo d'artigliaria, gli altri armati non potendo resistere dalle ferite, a pocco a pocco abbandonando il luogo, i genovesi si salvavanno, i quali i turchi seguitando ammazzavanno. Et rittirandossi il Giustiniano gli soldati lo seguitavanno. Ma lo Jmperatore intesa la retirata de' genovesi corse prestamente verso loro, riccercando, dove ci andavanno. Al qual il Giustiniano respose, che se n'andava in quel luogo, nel quale Iddio apriva la porta a' turchi. Ma la Historia Politica racconta d'un' altra maniera. Capitò a quei tempi, dice, un personagio nobile genovese, il cui nome era Giustiniano, con due grosse nave, il qual considerando il male dal quale i Costantinopolitani eravanno afflitti, et che nessuno de' gentil'huomini della città ardiva opponersi al nemico, et fugendo l'uno et l'altro di qua et di là dalla paura senza volerne combatere, ei sen' appresentò dallo Imperatore et prencipi, et disse, co'l agiuto d'Iddio stare in questo luogo et ribattere l'impeto del nimico, et resistere all sua violenza nelle rovine delle mura, per l'honore et nome di Christo, et questo disse lo voglio fare a spese mie, con nutrire i mei soldati, al qual fu grandemente rigratiato da tutti. Diffese dunque il valoroso personagio molti giorni et i turchi che guagliardamente sforzavanno intrar nella città dalle rovine regittava. Ma il peccato fu cagione che Iddio gli abbandonò. Perchioché mentre combatteva valorosamente contra il nemico fu ferito da un colpo d'artegliería nel piede destro, et dal gran dolore cascone in terra si lasciò per morto. Sichè gli suoi lo portorno via di là et condutolo nelle sue navi, fecero vela et partirno dalla città, et subito che arivò in quel luogo, fu sparso il romore che fusse ferito da qualche d'uno della città, ma non si è potuto nai sapere la verità. Ecco quanto scrissero questi dui historici per il Giustiniano, però diversamente, perciò lasciaremo alla volontà di ciascuno credere quello che li piace.

Giustiniani's spirited defense had become necessary; Sansovino's immensely popular work had advertised the flight of the warlord, whose conduct was then held responsible for the fall; see Sansovino, 110 (not 111): "Et certo s'egli hauesse lasciato qualch' vn' altro in suo luogho, la salute della patria nonsarebbe perita." An Italian report (entitled *Della gran città di Costantinopoli*) found in a seventeenth-century manuscript from Naples was published by Lampros, "Μονῳδίαι καὶ Θρῆνοι," 259–60: "... La qual presa fu che hauendo Constantino messa la miglior gente di fuori a diffendere i barbareni sopra il quali era un caualliere genovese chiamato Giustiniano nel cui valore tutti greci di dentro s'appogiauano, ma essendo ferito abbandono; il loco per andara a curarsi, il che veduto da suoi cominciorno a indebolirsi, et appertagi una porta perche dentro entrasse i suoi si persero d'animo, il che sentito il Turco rinforzo; con maggior empito l'assalto, et gli Christiani per saluarsi si misero in fuga per la porta doue et entrato il genouese, et hauendo i Turchi preso il muro si mescolarono con loro, et entrono nella Città." For some other early testimonies, see Pertusi, "La Lettera di Filippo da Rimini," esp. 145, n. 84. Da Rimini has provided the earliest and perhaps sharpest criticism of Giustiniani and his Genoese, 156: "Superiores erant nostri profecto in Genuensibus excubiis credita statio temere corruisset. Eius enim gentis praefecto saucio et sese a proelio avertenti cedi vigor voluit ex illius vestigia et abitionem eius legio sequeretur, nullis pugnatoribus per manum tradita loci custodia;

piorum, abutentes reliquiis sanctorum, tamquam insani et rabidi canes, insuper iniuriam, contumeliam et irreverentiam maxima exhibuerunt ligno vivificae crucis Domini nostri Iesu Christi simulque imagini sanctae atque intemeratae genetricis eius gloriosaeque virginis Mariae; quam etiam effigiem velut bestiae pessimae in lutum furibunde atque ignominioso proiicientes pedibus suis abominabiliter et despectissime calcaverunt, quod nullo dubio scelus nullo modo patietur is qui patientiam longanimiter in hominum peccatis exhibet inultum remanere, licet ad tempus silere parumper videatur.

CAPUT XIX: De Civitate Pera et pacto eius cum Turcis.

1. Expugnata igitur ac depopulata tam inclyta civitate et redacta sub manu hostili, Pera urbs fortis, quae est vicina Constantinopoli, nullum adhuc insultum sustinuerat ab hostibus; quin immo maior pars populi erat tunc in Constantinopoli, cum daretur in manu hostili ut auxilium ferret illi. Hi vero qui remanserant in urbe Pera necdum cum mobilibus suis bonis et utensilibus melioribus quae possidebant fugam captantes alicubi confluxerant sed nimio terrore percussi intra sua moenia sese hactenus recolligebant. Qui cum se manus Turcorum evadere posse desperarent, initio prudenti consilio, praesertim cum ne viribus praevalere adversus eos valuissent, in hoc unanimiter consenserunt, ut principi Turcorum claves civitatis suae transmitterent eique sese suosque atque

among the pious who may hear of it, they abused the relics of the saints, as if they were mad and rabid dogs; their blasphemous acts went beyond the limits of injury, harm, and irreverence that they displayed to the life-giving wooden cross of our Lord Jesus Christ, and to the holy image of His stainless Mother, the glorious Virgin Mary; like the lowest form of rabid beasts, they kicked dirt on Her effigy and abominably and detestably trampled it. No doubt this crime cannot be allowed to go unpunished, even by one who is accustomed to exhibit endless patience with human sins, even though there might be a time when one must hold one's tongue.

CHAPTER XIX: The City of Pera and her Pact with the Turks.

1. That legendary city was seized, was depopulated, and was plundered by the enemy. The enemy had not attacked Pera, a strong city in the vicinity of Constantinople, thus far. But most of her army was then in Constantinople when it fell to the enemy; they had gone to assist her. Those who had remained in the city of Pera with their property, their goods, and the essential necessities that they possessed turned to flight and went somewhere, but they became terrified and gathered again within their walls. They were desperate to find a way and evade the Turks; at first, following a wise advice, especially since they were not strong enough to defeat them, they all agreed to send the keys of their city to the prince of the Turks and to entrust themselves and their own people to him

---

sic deserta statione portae, sic vacuis pugile moenibus, nullo reluctante, foribus iam ferro et flamma correptis locis iis capitur."

One modern authority absolves Giustiniani of all charges of cowardice and questionable conduct: *PL* 2: 128. The withdrawal of Giustiniani created confusion, which could be observed from the Ottoman line (Tursun Beg, *History of Mehmed the Conqueror*, trans. Inalcik and Murphey, 36). The janissaries assumed control of the makeshift defenses in the sector of Saint Romanus; then they formed a column which proceeded in an orderly fashion to wipe out all pockets of resistance systematically; by now most of the defenders were dead or had retreated to the city. The janissaries opened the Gate of Saint Romanus; at the same time another regiment opened the Gate of Adrianople. Other gates were opened also, while the inhabitants of the district Petrion (which was surrounded by its own palisade) surrendered belatedly in a pathetic effort to spare their neighborhood from harm (*FC*, 140, and Appendix 2). In addition, the districts of Stoudios and Psamathia offered no resistance (*FC*, 141). The greatest amount of slaughter took place in the early hours of the sack because the Turks were under the impression that an army within the city had been kept in reserve; the bloodshed subsided after a few hours, as the Turks realized that there would be no organized resistance. Kritoboulos, trans. Riggs, 1.25.5, reports that 4000 individuals perished in the siege and the sack; more than 50,000 were enslaved. It should be remembered, nevertheless, that in 1453, before the siege, Constantinople was a dying city with a dwindling population; see A. M. Schneider, "Die Bevölkerung Konstantinopels im XV. Jh.," *Nachrichten der Akademie der Wissenschaften in Göttingen, philos.-hist. Klasse* 9 (1949): 234–44. See also Klaus-Peter Matschke, "The Late Byzantine Urban Economy, Thirteenth – Fifteenth Centuries," in *Economic History of Byzantium*, ed. A. E. Laiou (Washington, D.C., 2002), 454–86.

sua sponte ac prom<p>te recommendantes, ipsius voluntati atque bene placito una cum civitate offerent ex<s>pectantes ac sperantes in hoc magis divinum auxilium quam humanum. Istud nempe saepe fallit, illud vero tribulatis semper adesse novit. In hac quippe civitate fuerunt circiter septem millia virorum, qui sicut avisaverunt, ita et fecerunt. Venit nihilominus fugere coacta necessitate magna pars virorum ac mulierum navigio de civitate Ianuensi et insuper vidit Iacobus Tetaldi praenominatus navem eminus venientem, alteram mulieribus plurimis onustam a Turcis nequiter et callide praedatam.

CAPUT XX: De morte regis Constantinopolitani et evasione Iacobi per mare natantis.

1. Interea rex Constantinopolitanus ad extrema devolutus mortem invenit (narrantibus de illo quibusdam), quod capitis detruncatione vitam fini<v>erit, aliis vero dicentibus quod in transitu portae dum fugere tentaret, hostibus occurrentibus, morte praeoccupatus defecerit. Et revera utrumque rationabiliter credi potest, ut in porta primo sit interceptus et postea decollatus.

willingly and promptly, offering good will and peace together with their city,²³ even though their hopes and expectations had focused on divine, not human, help. The latter often fails, though the former is always present to those in trouble. In this city were about seven thousand men, who did exactly as they had been told. A great crowd of men and women were compelled by necessity to flee; the aforementioned Giacomo Tetaldi saw a ship approach from far away, and another, loaded with many women, eagerly and shamelessly plundered by the Turks.

CHAPTER XX: The Death of the Emperor of Constantinople; Giacomo Escapes by Swimming through the Sea.

1.   Meanwhile the emperor of Constantinople met his death (as some people recounted), being decapitated and thus ending his life; others, however, said that he attempted to flee through the passageway of the gate, with the enemy at his heels, and that he died in the press. In actuality, both reports may be accurate, as he may have at first been intercepted at the gate and been subsequently beheaded.²⁴

---

²³ For the *aman-name* granted to Pera with the signature of Zaganos, see above, Chap. 3, n. 18, and Chap. 2, n. 34; for the Greek and Italian text of this document, see below, Appendix II. Angelo Giovanni Lomellino, the *podestà* of Pera, had not yet recovered from the shock of the fall, when he was forced to hand over Pera to avoid a sack and, moreover, was personally concerned about his own nephew who had joined the defenders and had become a prisoner of the Turks. He discusses his actions in regard to Pera; see CC 1: 46: "Fuimus in maximo periculo. Pro evitari tantam furiam, fuit opus facere quod voluit, ut pro introclusa videbitis. Omnia facta fuerunt sub nomine burgensium. Ego me in aliquo intromittere non disposui, bona de causa. Fui postea ad visitandum dominum, qui bis hic fuit; dirui fecit omnia; burgos et partem fossorum de castro dirui fecit; turrim Sanctae Crucis dirui fecit, partim unius cortine intra barbicanae, omnia moenia maris restari; cepit omnes bombardas et intendit capere omnes munitiones et omnia arma burgensium qui de hic recesserunt dicendo: si revertant, restituantur; et si non recesserunt, facta erunt domino."

²⁴ No author of any source was in the vicinity of the sector of Saint Romanus and none had the opportunity to observe the last moments of Constantine XI, who perished either fighting against the attackers or in the press, fleeing with his troops to the safety of the Great Wall. At any rate the following is a summary of the reports:

Benvenuto: "Item, quod audivit ab uno trumpeta quod imperator Graecorum fuit interfectus et eius caput super lancea Turcorum domino praesentatum." See above, Chap. 3, n. 11.

One author of one of the earliest letters was honest enough to state that he was dealing with rumors: Paolo Dotti, who wrote from Crete on June 11, 1453 (CC 2: 16): "De olim Constantinopolitano imperatore est fama eum fuisse in defensione supradictae civitatis ab hostibus interfectum cum aliis paucis Latinis et Graecis."

Eparkhos and Diplovatatzes: reproduced above, Chap. 1, n. 78.

Cardinal Isidore (in his letter to Cardinal Bessarion, CC 1: 74; cf. above, n. 19): "Vigessimo itaque nono die mensis Maii proxime peracti aurora illuscente, solis etiam radiis nostros oppugnantibus, mari ac terra urbem invadentes Turci ad eam partem maxime semiruptam circa Sanctum Romanum assiluerunt, ubi multi erant fortes viri Latini et Gr<a>eci absque tamen rege

2. Interea galeae quaedam Venetorum ad terram sanctam properantes et aliae multae praestolantes in mari a mane usque post meridiem in tuto loco se

2.   In the meantime some Venetian galleys that were on their way to the Holy Land, many others equipped to set sail remained in a safe area next to

ac imperatore ipsorum, qui iam ab hostibus vulneratus ac trucidatus fuerat eiusque caput Turco postea dono datum est, qui eo viso plurimum ex<s>ultavit atque illi petulanti ludibrio improperavit et continuo in Andri<a>nopolim triumphandum misit." In another letter ("composita per ser Pasium de Bertipalia" and dated "ex Candida insulae Cretae pridie Nonas Julii MCCCCLIII"; the text of this letter has never been edited in its entirety from the fifteenth-century manuscript Ven. Marc. lat. 496 [1688], fols. 330^r–331^r), Cardinal Isidore simply tries to place the emperor among the martyrs who have suffered for the faith (CC 1: 60): "Illa enim die anima dicti ultimi Constantini Romanorum imperatorum, impensato martyrio coronata non dubitatur ad superos evolasse cum alia Christianorum multitudine copiosa qui cum eo impie occisi fuerunt."

Barbaro provides an honest report, stating that there was nothing definite that could be discovered (CC 1: 35): "De l'imperador mai non se potè saver novela di fatti soi, ní vivo, ní morto, ma alguni dixe che el fo visto in nel numero di corpi morti, el qual fo dito, che el se sofegà al intra' che fexe i Turchi a la porta de san Romano."

Leonardo (CC 1: 162–64; PG 159: 940): "Imperator insuper, ne ab hostibus capiatur, o quispiam, inquit, valens tyro propter Deum, ne maiestas vafris viris succumbat mea, gladio me transfigat? Inter haec Theophilus Palaeologus, vir Catholicus, iam perdita urbe me, inquit, vivere non licet, Teucrorumque pondus aliquamdiu sustinens et decertans securi discinditur. Ita Ioannes Sclavus Illyricus, veluti Hercules se opponens, multos prius mactat, deinde gladio vitam finivit hostili. Se invicem post nostri, ut portam ingrediantur, compressi pereunt. Quibus innexus imperator cadens atque resurgens relabitur et compressione princeps patriae e vita demigrat." Languschi-Dolfin follows Leonardo closely, 29–30 (fol. 320): "Lo Imperator acio non fusse prexo da Turci, o qualche ualente homo de nui, disse, acio la maiesta imperial non uegna in man de Turci cum suo gladio me occida. Ueduto Theophilo Paleologo, homo catholico perduta la cita disse non me e licito piu uiuer, per bon spacio combattando cum Turchi fu morto, similmente Joanne Schiauo, come Hercules combattendo, prima che fusse morto, occise molti Turchi, li nostri nobili et Latini uolendo intrar in la porta, oppressi da la calcha molti perino, in fra li qual messedato lo Imperatore, cazando, et poi leuando recazette, et da la chalcha de le gente el principe de la patria finite la uita." The following observation, however, owes nothing to the text of Leonardo, 31 (fol. 321): "Postremo faciandosse grande inquisition per commandamento del Signor fra i corpi morti fu trouato el misero capo del Constantino Imperator et portato al Signor lo qual comosso de tanto crudel spectaculo disse ala multitudine circumfusa: questo manchaua, comilitoni mei a darme cumulata gloria de tanta uictoria." Leonardo and Languschi-Dolfin were further used by the sixteenth-century Richer-Riccherio, as becomes clear from his phraseology. Specifically, the mention of "Dalmates" is interesting, as Leonardo also calls him "Sclavus," repeated in Languschi-Dolfin as "Schiauo." Richer, however, interprets the word, which meant "slave" in medieval Greek, and Dalmatas thus becomes a "servant," which probably does not reflect reality; see Richer, 96–97: "Sed Imperator Constantinus vt suos fugere intuetur, sui officii ac dignitatis oblitus, nec eius quod tantum principem decebat satis memor, esse scilicet imperatorium suis fusis pulchram vulneribus mortem oppetere, terga quoque ipse ipse dat, & praeceps recta in portam post suos fertur. Ob cuius angustiam multitudine offensus, atque indiscriminatim abeuntium impetu successus humi procubuisset, miserrime; proculcatus interiit ... Graecus erat Theophilus Palaeologus ... alter Ianus quidam natione Dalmata, seruus conditione." Leonardo and Languschi-Dolfin are also the probable sources of Sansovino, 112: "Et l'Imperadore per non esser preso, chi sarà, disse egli, colui che m'vccida per l'amor di

servabant iuxta urbem devastatam, desiderantes vitam Christianorum servare incolumem et illaesam. Venerunt autem ex illis fere quadringenti fugitivi, intra

the plundered city from morning until midday, desiring to save Christians and keep them from injury and harm. Four hundred refugees departed on board;

Dio, con la mia propria spada, accioche la Maestà mia non si sottoponga al vituperio de Turchi? In questo mezo Theophilo Paleologo huomo cattolico, essendo già perduta la città, io diss'egli, non voglio piu viuere, & sostenendo vn pezzo la faria de Turchi & combattendo, fu diuiso per lo mezo da vna accetta. Cosi Giouanni schiauo Dalmata, opponendosi quasi come vn'altro Hercole, ammazzò prima molti Turchi & poi finì la vita. E molti de Greci nel voler vscir della porta s'ammazzarono nella calca, tra qual li cacciatosi l'Imp. cadendo, & poi rileunadosi, ricadde, & calpestato dalla faria morì."

Pusculo (ed. Ellissen, 4.1007–1016 [81]; not in CC 1): "Rex ut forte caput galea nudatus inani / Inclinans oculos intra tentoria fessos / Carpebat somnum, magno clamore citatus / Exilit, eque fuga cives revocare laborans / Ense petit nudo Teucros, solusque repugnans / Increpitat socios, tres ipsoque aggere truncat / Janizaros. Tandem media inter tempora grandi / Vibrato cecidit gladio. Caput abstulit unus / Ex humeris: regem, ut novit, pro munere caesum / Attulit atque duci Machmetto, et dona recepit."

Tignosi (da Foligno), *TIePN*, 114, first speaks of the emperor's state of mind: "Dragas, oppugnatorum fortissimus imperator, imminentem mortem cognoscens, quod tamen pulcherrimum mortis genus est in periculo – pulchro † et terribili pro patria mori, ut fortem decet, bonam sibi spem proponit," and then briefly speaks of his death (*TIePN*, 118): "Et diu egregieque pugnantes occisis Turcorum plurimis – defensique multitudini non volentes † resistere unanime conglobati in hostes concurrunt et interficientes ab hostibus obtruncatur, nec nisi imperator, qui denominabatur Dragas, captus ab Othomanno visus est decapitari."

Sekoundinos (CC 2: 136): "Imperator, ubi hostem ruinas iam occupare moenium victoriaque potiri certissima vidit, ne caperetur vivus, sibi ipsi quidem proprias iniicere manus et hoc pacto consciscere mortem, tametsi animus minus deerat, nefas tamen duxit et Christiano principe per religionem indignum, suos, cui pauci aderant, hortari coepit, ut se occiderent; sed, cum tantum facinus audere voluisset nemo, imperatoriis insignibus depositis et abiectis, ne hostibus notus fieret, privatum <se> gerens stricto ense in aciem irruit fortiterque pugnando, ne inultus abiret, princeps immortalitate dignus hostili manu tandem est interemptus ruinisque urbis ac regni casui regium immiscuit cadaver.'

Magno (*NE* 3: 297) reports the death in negative terms, but his information may be related to the reports of Leonardo and Languschi-Dolfin: "All' hora lo imperatore, non, come a rè conveniva, pugnando, mà fuggendo, nelle angustie di essa porta però caddè oppresso et, calcado, morì et, in tanta moltitudine de pugnanti che fù, che huomini si monstrorono, uno Theofilo Paleologo, Greco, l'altro Zuanne Schiavo, Dalmatino, quali a fuggir turpe pensando, longamente sostennero lo empito de Turchi, et, cum multi havessero ottrocando, nella fine, non tanto vinti, quanto inter vincendo defatigati, infrà i cadaveri de nemici accumbeteno... Constantino Dragasi Paleologo, imperator de Constantinopoli, como dicuni alcuni, fù tagliado a pezzi in habito incognito; però de quello non se seppe cosa alcuna, nè nelli corpi morti fù trovado alcuno fosse cognossudo per quello."

Di Montaldo (*TIePN*, 196): "Ubi vero a postremo imperator occupatas iam domos, iam vicos, iam palatium respexit, quin in se ensem converteret, vix abstinuit sed dolori atque infamiae rationem, salutem damnationi praeferens, animos vicit suosque adhortari trepidabundos incepit, ut pro ipso Deo morerentur, qui pro nobis gratissimis mori dignatus esset. Positis deinde insigniis princeps Christianissimus et pius, ne cognitus videretur, ex desperato moribundus in barbaros frustra nudo ense prorupit. Nec multo post inter victores hostes, parum

quos erat ille Iacobus Tetaldi nobilis Venetus qui duabus fere horis super muros civitatis sese cum populo sibi subiecto viriliter defenderat post introitum Turcorum. Tandem refluxum maris adeptus exspoliavit se vestibus et misit se in illud, natando pertingens usque ad praedictas galeas et petens ut ab eis assum<p>tus posset aliquatenus perduci illaesus ad ripam: quod et factum est.

CAPUT XXI: De navibus a Turcis submersis et captis et quibusdam intempestive venientibus.

1. Turci vero devastando submerserunt navem quamdam octoginta ductorum diripientes insuper circiter quatuordecim naves alias, quarum tres continebant sexcentos bottos, reliquae vero erant ducentorum vel trecentorum bottorum, inter quas erant galeae et gall<i>otae quae fuerant eo missae ad defensionem et resistentiam deputatae. Hae praecedenti die ante civitatis vastationem mare legentes ad locum cui vocabulum est ad Pontem Magnum applicuerunt. Omnes

among them was Giacomo Tetaldi, a Venetian nobleman, who bravely kept up the defense on the walls of the city with the men under his command for almost two hours after the entry of the Turks. Finally, he came to shore, took off his clothes, and plunged into the sea; he swam until he reached the aforementioned galleys and asked to be taken on board and be conveyed to shore; this was done.

CHAPTER XXI: Ships Sunk and Captured by the Turks and Certain Untimely Arrivals.

1.   The Turks plundered and sank a certain ship [with a capacity] of eighty *ducti*; in addition, they plundered about fourteen other ships, three of which had a capacity of six hundred *botte*; the rest had a capacity of two hundred or three hundred *botte*; among them were galleys and galliots which had been instructed to offer resistance and had been set aside for defense. On the day before the city's fall, they wandered through the sea and came to a place called Big Bridge.[25]

---

pro senio demolitus, extra sequentium visum prolapsus est; eisdem a copiis pressum, aliis sic excessisse e vita, aliis iugulatum, nonnullis trucidatum fuisse relatum est, ceteris, quos secum accerserat, pari exitio datis." He returns to this subject once more, when he speaks of the corpse of the emperor (Hopf et al., 338]; *TlePN*, 198): "Deinde cum imperatoris reliquias, si reperiri possent, habere avide vellet, oblatum tandem a quodam manipulari, auro false donato, caput hominis defuncti, imperatoris simillimum, et forte inventum, per civitatis vicos hasta, jubente rege, longissima praelatum est."

The anonymous report *Della gran città di Costantinopoli*, 259–60: "i Turchi ... entrono nella Città, doue fecero grande uccisione de Christiani, et l'Imperatore fù ucciso hauendosi l'habito mutato per non essere conosciuto, et i̇ suo corpo fù preso, et troncatogli la testa, et postala sopra lancia fù portata per il campo."

[25] Tetaldi's "Big Bridge" is probably Khalkis in Euboea, which in the vernacular of the period was called Negroponte; the change from "Negroponte" (or, more probably, its Latinized form *Nigrum Pontem*) to "Magnum Pontem" can be attributed to an error in the manuscript or perhaps to a misunderstanding of Tetaldi's words. The fact is that an armada from Venice to relieve Constantinople was on its way and encountered the refugee ships from Constantinople at Khalkis. Ivani (above, n. 4) claims that the sultan captured a letter from the doge to the emperor, which announced the imminent departure of the relief column. The Venetian fleet, however, had not left by May 7, when Loredan received his commission as captain-general (cf. PL 2: 122, n. 45) over the fleet that the Doge was about to send to Constantinople, NE 3: 283–85: "ob reverentiam Dei, honorem Christianorum, et conservationem civitatis Constantinopolis paravimus." The fleet did not reach Negroponte before June 3, where it finally met the refugees from the sacked city. Languschi-Dolfin treats these events, 36 (fol. 323): "Le gallie tre de Romania et le do gallie sotil Treuisana et Zacharia Grioni de Candia cum le naue de Candia tirate fuora del porto circa a mezo di feceno uela et in 4. zorni preueno a Negroponte doue trouono M. Jacomo Loredan capitano zeneral cum otto gallie che aspettauano tempo de andar a dar soccorso a Constantinopoli, et per quella sapeno Constantinopoli esser prexo dal Turco adi 28. Mazo 1453 al leuar del sole." From the same source we discover that the captain-general remained in the Aegean, 37 (fol. 323): "Adi 4. luijo fu de mercore da matina zonzeno a Uenetia le tre gallie grosse de Romania desfortunate capitano ser Aluise Diedo zenza leuar San Marcho ne altra

vero naves fuerunt fere num ducentae quadraginta Venetique miserant obsessis in auxilium novem galeas et viginti naves alias grandes bene provisas, quas applicuerunt ad Magnum Pontem sequenti die vastationis saepedictae civitatis. Occubuerunt autem seu perierunt in praefatis navibus seu alio quovis modo nobiles Veneti circiter triginta quinque et alii plebei viri numero quadraginta, quorum animae sempiternam mereantur requiem invenire.

CAPUT XXII: De praeda Turcorum ex Constantinopoli et damno aliarum civitatum.

1.   Fertur quod praeda quam Turci de capta civitate diripuerunt valebat quadraginta millia ducatis, damnum vero quod perpessi sunt Veneti in hoc excidio fuit fere quadraginta millium ducatorum, non minus vero damnum Ianuensium fuisse creditur. Florentini quoque viginti millia ducatos amiserunt; Anchonenses vero quindecim. Anchona nostra civitas est amoena et pulchra supra littus maris sita, in qua dominus Pius papa secundus communis naturae debitum solvisse dicitur. Haec autem sunt armamenta seu casa bellica, quae Veneti praedicatae civitati Constantinopolitanae pro defensione mutuaverunt et perdiderunt: octoginta fundibulae magna, 7000 brigandi, 4000 colubri, 4000 quadrigae cum balistis, 7000 fossoria, 7000 igniferas patellas, 12000 uncos, 2000 secures, 7000 mallei, 40000 situlae, 7000 vasa vinalia pro potibus, 7000

There were almost two hundred and forty ships, and the Venetians had sent to help the besieged nine galleys and twenty other large ships with good provisions; they reached Big Bridge the day after the destruction of the aforementioned city. About thirty-five Venetian noblemen and other commoners, as many as forty, fell or perished on board the aforementioned ships and in other ways. May their souls deserve to find eternal peace.

CHAPTER XXII: The Booty Acquired by the Turks in Constantinople and the Losses of Other Cities.

1. They say that the booty that the Turks plundered from the captive city came to the sum of forty thousand ducats; but the losses suffered by the Venetians in this sack came to almost forty thousand ducats; the losses of the Genoese are believed to have equaled that sum. The Florentines also lost twenty thousand ducats. Ancona lost fifteen thousand. Ancona, our city, is pleasant and beautiful situated by the coast of the sea, where our Lord Pope Pius [II] is said to have paid the common debt we owe to nature. Here is a list of the weapons and instruments of war that the Venetians had provided, and lost, for the defense of the aforementioned city of Constantinople: eighty large artillery pieces; 7,000 brigands; 4,000 colubrines; 4,000 mobile catapults; 7,000 excavators; 7,000 fire-bearing vessels; 12,000 grappling hooks; 2,000 axes; 7,000 hammers; 40,000 urns; 7,000 vessels for drinkable wine; 7,000 team-drawn wagons;

---

insegna senza trombe et pifari, cum ogni segno de mestitia disse hauer lassato M. Jacopo Loredan a Negroponte cum 12. gallie. Poi adi 6. luijo fu fatto soracomito Piero Rimondo era auditor uecchio. Et cum frequentia mandato a trouar M. Jacomo Loredan che era a Negroponte et aspettaua mandato de quello hauesse a far o de andar verso el stretto, o de far altra cosa." Francesco Foscari, the doge of Venice, in a letter dated "datum in nostro ducali palatio die 27. mensi Iulii indictione prima 1453," states that the relief column encountered the refugee ships in the Aegean; see Wolkan, *Der Briefwechsel des Eneas Silvius Piccolomini*, no. 139, 260: "Haec si quidem nova, utinam tam falsa essent quam nimium vera sunt! Nam ea accipimus a capitano galearum nostrarum nuper huc regresso, qui ad illud viagium Constantinopolis et Romaniae cum nonnullis nostris triremibus more mercatorio profectus erat, quive cum eisdem galeis ad tutandam urbem illam usque ad ultimum eius excidium constans permansit, ita ut magna pars hominum triremium earundem male perierit. Nam partim trucidati, partim in miserabilem captivitatem deducti sunt. Multi quoque nobiles, cives et mercatores nostri, qui in ea urbe aderant, cum facultatibus et bonis suis magni valoris aut gladio perierunt aut ad servitutem ipsam crudelissimam devenerunt nec absque magno aere redimi poterunt. Praeterea subinde nuntiatum est, Teucrum ipsum occupa<vi>sse civitatem Perae et quaedam alia loca finitiam cum magno Christianorum excidio, de qua tamen re aliam certiorem notitiam nondum accepimus." From Negroponte the Cretan ships broke off and eventually reached Candia; cf. a Greek note published by Browning, "A Note on the Capture of Constantinople in 1453;" see above, Chap. 1, n. 40. Magno (*NE* 3: 297) also speaks of the activities of Venice's captain-general: "Jacomo Loredan, capitanio zeneral nostro, per tempi contrari non pote arrivare alla detta città de Costantinopoli, noma doppo presa trovò nave venti della preda de Turchi, delle quali ne prese due."

bigas, 4000 ligones, et alia instrumenta plusquam 40000. Item 6000 equestres et 16000 pedestres et 400 galeae solutae pro integro anno.

CAPUT XXIII: De aetate et conditione principis Turcorum.

1. Narrantibus his qui cum principe Turcorum aliquando conversati sunt et eius statum optime noverant constat illum fuisse tunc temporis viginti trium circiter annorum. Ferunt quoque ipsum plus quam dici vel cogitari possit, delectari in humani sanguinis effusione. Propter quod invenitur anhelo pectore quotidie stragem sitiens, ambitioni indefesse studens, damnationes ardenter affectans, bella continue desiderans, discordias infatigabiliter fovens, triumphos modibus omnis amans, principatum totius orbis affectuosissime diligens, immo plusquam Alexander Magnus, Iulius, vel Augustus, vel alii quique potentes imperatores huius mundi. Aestimat denique maiorem et ampliorem virtutem et potentiam se habere quam omnes qui fuerunt ante ipsum; quapropter coram se recitari facit annales historias temporum antiquorum, quatenus ex his posset latius de

4,000 hoes; and other tools in excess of 40,000. Also 6,000 knights and 16,000 infantry with 400 galleys that are sent forth for a whole year.[26]

CHAPTER XXIII: The Age and Condition of the Prince of the Turks.

1.　Those who have, at some point, conversed with the prince of the Turks and know his circumstances very well are in agreement that he is about twenty-three years old. They also say that more than can be expressed or thought of, he delights in shedding human blood. And so it is concluded that he eagerly thirsts for slaughter daily, that he is full of ambition, that he enthusiastically applies punishment, that he constantly desires war, that he thrives on stirring up strife, that he loves triumphs of all sorts, and that he wants to create a world empire that will surpass those of Alexander the Great, of Julius [Caesar], of Augustus, or of any other powerful emperors throughout the world. He thinks that his power and strength surpass those of all who have preceded him. Accordingly, he has historical annals from antiquity recited in his presence, as he wishes to be

---

[26] The estimates of Languschi-Dolfin differ, 37 (fol. 323): "Questo danno fu extimato a la ciota de Uenexia ducati CC°. millia. A nostri feudati et citadini Candioti ducati C° millia. Et e uero che parte di nostre fece piu opinion de saluar el suo in gallia, et questi fono salui, parte de saluar in la terra reputando quella pio segura che le gallie le quale erano ualor de ducati CCC°. millia. Le qual dapo prexa la cita rotte la cadena, cargando tutto quello poteno cargar et aleuar per la occasion che haueruano che Turci attendeuano a depredar la cita, et non haue impazo da la armada Turchescha che era in porto." The humanist Quirini was more interested in the loss of ancient manuscripts and books, which he found unbearable; as he states, some of this information was passed on to him by Cardinal Isidore (*TIePN*, 74): "Ultra centum et viginti milia librorum voluminia, ut a reverendissimo cardinali Rutheno accepi, devastata. Ergo et lingua et litteratura Graecorum tanto tempore, tanto labore, tanta industria inventa, aucta, perfecta peribit, heu peribit! Ecquis vel adeo rudis rerum est vel adeo ferreus, ut se a lacrimis possit abstinere? Illae litterae pereunt, quae orbem universum illustraverunt, quae salutares leges, quae sacram philosophiam, quae reliquas bonas artes adduxerunt, quibus vita humana exculta est." Leonardo became a prisoner of the Turks but was quickly ransomed and joined the hunt for manuscripts, which could be bought from the conquerors. He provides no details on his liberation, which, unlike that of his friend and patron, may have taken place early on, as we learn elsewhere that he was able to buy items that the conquerors were selling on the very day of the sack; had he been forced into a long hiding period, similar to the one experienced by Cardinal Isidore, his books would have been a serious hindrance (Reg. 401, f. 47b, Secret Archives of the Vatican, Pope Nicholas V, 10/18/53 [= Ludwig Pastor, *The History of the Popes from the Close of the Middle Ages*, ed. F. I. Antrobus, vol. 2 (7th ed.; London, 1949), App. 22, pp. 524–25]): "Et sicut eadem petitio subjungebat venerabilis frater noster Leonardus archiepiscopus Methalinensis ord. fratrum praedicatorum professor in Constantinopoli et Pera publice dicere praesumit, quod omnes de preda a Teucris rapta etiam sciente vero domino et contradicente licite emere possunt nec data etiam pretio Teucris soluto restituere tenentur, ipseque archiepiscopus duo missalia et unum breviarium et nonnullos alios libros dicte librarie deputatos emere non dubitaverit."

singulis informari, ut tandem pervenire posset ad Venetos et Romanos et notitiam de duce Mediolanensi ac eius potentia haberet.

2   Versatur namque, sicut praefati sumus, principalis intentio sua circa belli negotia pugnaeque victorias dicitque se velle statuere solium suum regni apud Constantinopolim constructurum se illic affirmans miro opere pontem,

informed in detail about individual events, with the objective of extending his power to Venice and Rome and also to be noticed by the duke of Milan.[27]

2. As I have said, he is well informed; his principal occupation is the conduct of war and victories in battle, and he says that he will make Constantinople the capital of his empire; he asserts that there he will build a bridge, great,

---

[27] The comparison of Mehmed to Alexander the Great is not original; numerous such comparisons appeared immediately after the sack; his troops, we have seen (above, n. 2), were already compared by such eyewitnesses as Leonardo and Isidore, to Alexander's "Myrmidons." Some of the earliest comparisons of Mehmed II to Alexander the Great include:

Cardinal Isidore in his letter of July 6 to Bessarion (CC 1: 78) mentions Mehmed's admiration for Alexander: "Alexandri siquidem vitam quotidie audit arabice, graece et latine"; a letter from the Knights of Rhodes, addressed to the margrave of Brandenburg, "datum Rodi, in nostro Conventu, die ultimo mensis Junii, anno 1453"; a short extract appears in NE 2: 520–21; and a longer extract, with Italian translation, in *TIePN*, 54–57: "magnus Teucer ... exaltavit namque cor suum et gloriatur se magni Alexandri Macedonis gesta aequiparaturum vel superaturum. Minatur etiam quod Alexander numquam se ad Ytaliam et partes occiduas armis et potentia sua penetravit se experiturum an sibi fortuna faveat, quemadmodum per haec orientalia expertus est."

Quirini in a letter of July 15, 1453, used the same comparison (*TIePN*, 80): "Quam ob rem sese principem orbis terrarum gentiumque omnium, idest alterum Alexandrum, et sese dicit vult. Unde et Arrianum, qui res gestas Alexandri diligentissime scripsit, quotidie ferme legere consuevit."

Tignosi (da Foligno) in November 1453 uses similar phrases (*TIePN*, 108): "Quasi novus Caligula terrorem respicientibus incutit moribusque dicitur antiquorum studere (in) historiis et illorum facinora cum admiratur, se Alexandrum Macedonem superaturum aestimat, et Caesarem Octaviumque imitaturus firmissime credit se posse toto orbe potiri."

Languschi-Dolfin (5 [fol. 313]) employs the same comparison and speaks of Mehmed's favorite authors, who are read to him by no other than Cyriacus of Ancona (an impossibility, since the indefatigable Cyriacus had died in 1452, as has been discussed in the Introduction): "El Signor Maumetho gran Turco ... aspirante a gloria quanto Alexandro Macedonico, ogni di; se fa lezer historie romane, et de altri da uno compagno d.° Chriaco d'Ancona, et da uno altro Italo, da questi se fa lezer Laertio, Herodoto, Livio, Quinto Curtio, Cronice de i papi, de imperatori, de re di Franza, de Longobardi."

Di Montaldo also uses a similar comparison (ed. Hopf et al., 330; not in *TIePN*): "Horum trium virorum opera historiarum veterum novam quidem habere cognitionem perplacuit. Lacedaemonios et Carthaginenses resque celebriter ab eis gestas exigui pendens, Cai Caesaris atque Alexandri Magni morem, modo bellandi animo, non eodem tamen ingenio nec virtute, complectitur. Quos prope consequi fallacis spei victoriae tamdiu est deservit. Amborum gesta in asiaticam linguam converti voluit, sibi vehementer ac suis observanda. Subinde animi cupiditate pro acquirendis more maiorum regnis parem utrique se evasurum arbitratur. Quanto magis, dum Alexandrum tam parva manu adeptum facile triumphos adversus tot reges et finitimos orbis provincias bello contemplatur ... Is enim pro obtenta armis victoria ante invictae maioribus suis civitatis, superba quadam petulantia, persuasione duorum augurum, datum ei de superis, falso putat, exemplo Alexandri Magni, suae potentiae terrarum totius orbis non fore defuturum imperium." He returns once more to a citation of Alexander which he included in a speech supposedly delivered by Mehmed himself (ed. Hopf et al., 349; not in *TIePN*): see the text reproduced above, Chap. 1, n. 12.

qui magnus erit et fortis, longus et latus. Ex quo verisimiliter propenditur nullum incolarum illius loci de ipsius adventu fore gavisurum, ipso praestolando, sed potius malle sibi transmittere civitatis claves priusquam appropriet, maxime cum violentia et potentia sua obtinuit famosissimam fortissimamque civitatem quae pro certo tanti dicitur fuisse roboris, ut vix umquam aestimaretur ab ullo principe, duce vel rege posse obtineri.

CAPUT XXIV: Qualiter audaciae Turcorum possent Christiani facillime resistere.

1.   Licet exercitus Turcorum copiosus sit et immensus, subtilis, audax atque strenuus in rebus bellicis, ob mundi huius favorem sese mortis discrimini passim dando, possent tamen Christiani eidem obniti, ac etiam praevalere per modum qui sequitur. Nam apparet quod princeps eorum aestate perita nihil aliud fecit quam quod proinde quieti operam dedat: deliberans ad civitatem Constantinopolim venire ac residentiam illic facere quatenus hoc modo circum adiacentes provincias et civitates absque bello et congressu pugnae obtinere posset. Sed in ei rei veritate nulli sit dubium, quin sagacissime cauteque in contrarium se ipsos praeparabunt Turci terra marique futuris temporibus. Christiani vero si confisi in eo qui assolet se invocantibus promptus plusque semper auxiliator existere, viriles se reddiderint: non fugarent eos ab inde tam cito extra terminos quos

mighty, long, and wide. It will bring no joy to any natives that it would reach, once it is completed; they will choose to surrender the keys of the city to him before he sets out, as he has seized the most renowned and strongest city (her might was legendary) with such inestimable violence and power as have never been associated with any prince, lord, or king.

CHAPTER XXIV: How the Christians Can Most Easily Resist the Audacity of the Turks.

1. Even though the army of the Turks is large, even immense, and exhibits intelligence, audacity, and persistence in wars, as they are not afraid of taking serious risks, nevertheless the Christians can apply themselves and prevail if they pursue the following suggestion. It appears that their prince does nothing all summer long and is interested only in remaining quiet. He is deliberating whether he should go to the city of Constantinople and establish his residence there or how he can annex, by war and battle, the adjacent provinces and cities. There is no doubt whatsoever that the Turks are making cautious and careful land and sea preparations for the future.[28] Yet if the Christians rely on Him, who has always provided prompt, plentiful assistance, by means of their prayers, they will prove themselves valiant. They will not flee from those whom they

---

[28] It is in the early reports on the fall of Constantinople that we encounter the claim that Mehmed II was aiming at world domination. Thus Lomellino stated (CC 1: 48): "Concludendo, de captione Constantinopolis tantam insolentiam cepit, que videtur se facturum in brevi dominum totius orbis, et large dicit non transibunt anni duo que intendit venire usque Romam; et per verum Deum, nisi per christianos providetur et cito, faciet mirabilia." Cardinal Isidore also raised the alarm at least three times in writing; in his letter (translated into Latin by Bertipaglia and dated July 6, 1453) to Pope Nicholas V (CC 1:62): "Ceterum intellege, beatissime pater, et considera huius perfidi terrenam potentiam et innatam superbiam, qui non obstante quod glorietur se genus et nomen Graecorum delevisse, sua barbara saevitia comminatur omne christianum nomen radicitus excerpere et tuam Romanam Urbem et imperii christianorum sedem vi et armis sibi in brevi subiugare." He repeats this opinion in his letter to Cardinal Bessarion (CC 1: 78): "Cum autem in Italiam Turcus omnino transire deliberat cum fortissima manu exercituque maximo, trecentas enim triremes ... implevisse dinoscitur ... pedestrem etiam exercitum et equestrem numero infinitum, et haec tu quidem vera puta, ego futura non dubito." He becomes more specific and rings the alarm bell in his letter addressed to all Christians (CC 1: 88): "et sic proponit totam transcurrere Ungariam eamque perdere et delere, ut neminem habeat retro se impeditorem, quoniam in Ytaliam anno futuro transmigrare decrevit ... et sic a Durachio transire ad Brandicium disponit. Haec omnia non solum agere disponit, verum incipit facere."

These reports intensified by the fall of 1453. Thus Franco Giustiniani in Chios wrote to Genoa on September 27 to point out the naval preparations of the Turk (CC 2: 104): "Contremiscunt etiam omnia Christianorum loca ipsis Teucris finitima, et eo maxime quia noviter praeparare fecit, ut fertur, in Gal<l>ipoli classem ducentum fustarum, triremium, biremium et uniremium, et dicitur infram mensem erit ordinata et parata; quae quo itura sit ignoramus. Dominus sit nostrum custos et defensor!" Furthermore, Leonardo Benvoglienti in a letter dated

apprehenderunt; quin immo usque in saecula sempiterna terras alias copiosas, bonas et spatiosas fertilesque adepturi sunt ipso Deo propitio sed modus quo id facilius posset agnoscatur qui sequitur.

2.   In primis putamus necessarium fore quod ante omnia bonum pacis inter Christianos principes firmetur, sine quo nil boni procul dubio constat posse usque in finem firmari. Necessarium igitur esset quod Veneti, Mediolanenses, Florentini ceterique principes Italici inter se mutuo compaginarentur et exhiberent exercitum viginti millium equitum. Habeant quoque ii sic uniti bonos et electos capitaneos qui eos traducant usque in Albaniam versus partes Christianorum, quia notum est illic fore optimam fertilemque terram, ubi sine dubio securi essent. In brevi tempore multiplicandi per additamentum Albanorum et Sclavorum aliorumque circumcirca, qui libentissime Christianorum legi defendae sese promptissimos exhibuerent.

Hoc autem exercitu sic ordinato ac disposito iam rursus alium maritimum exercitum conveniret provideri per regem Aragonensiem seu Avinionensem, et Venetos, Ianuenses et Florentinos ac per alios insulis magnis sitos. Essent namque ii satis potentes ad expugnandum, invadendum, fugandum et disperdendum Turcorum exercitum, saltem si non excederet murum ante Constantinopolim congregatum. Et iste navalis exercitus pergere deberet versus Nigrum Pontem ad obtinendum Sagripolim aliasve urbes sub Turcorum dominio constitutas et hoc ad impediendum transitum eo de Turcia in Graeciam. Optimum denique videretur, quatenus Caesar cum Hungaris atque Bohemis et circum adiacentibus populis in hunc modum procederet, ordinabiliter constituendo concordem aciem pergentem versus Graeciam per Andrinopolim reliquaque loca sub Turcorum protectione constituta. Servent insuper modum hunc atque ordinem singuli exercitus, ut sint in determinatis locis, ut valeant sibi invicem notificare suos eventus.

CAPUT XXV: Quod multi Christiani coacti servire Turcis mallent, si possent, ab eodem liberari et nostris adhaerere.

1.   Princeps Turcorum hoc in tempore vires quas valuit exercere curavit; habet in exercitu suo parum plusquam ducenta millia bellatorum, connumeratis etiam ineptis, inter quos tamen multi Christiani reperti sunt, qui sequuntur eum coacti et inviti, omni desiderio praestolantes Christianorum auxilium futurum, qui eis succursum et iuvamen ferre possent, quatenus a Turcis liberari et ad propria redire possent. Iste praefatus princeps Turcorum bella exercens, pro consuetudine

encounter outside their borders; on the contrary, they will take over and will possess forever immense, wide, and fertile territories, with the approval of God; they will accomplish this easily by paying attention to what follows.

2. First of all, it will be necessary, in my opinion, that before all else the benefit of peace be firmly established among the Christian princes; without peace nothing can be brought to completion, without doubt. Necessarily the Venetians, the Milanese, the Florentines, and the other Italian princes must conclude pacts among themselves and supply an army of twenty thousand soldiers. United in this manner, let them elect good captains who will conduct them to Albania's Christian regions, as it is known that there are good, fertile lands there, where they will be secure, without any doubt. In a short time their numbers will be multiplied by the additions of Albanians, Slavs, and other neighboring people, who will be very glad and ready to take up the defense of Christians.

3. So much for the arrangement and order of the army. Another naval force must be provided by the king of the Aragonese, Avignon, the Venetians, the Genoese, the Florentines, and by others from large islands. These are the strong ones who must combat, invade, rout, and disperse the army of the Turks, if it does not exceed the numbers that had been mustered before the wall of Constantinople. That naval force should travel to Negroponte [= Khalkis in Euboea] to take charge of Sagripolis and other cities currently under the Turks in order to impede the passage from Turkey to Greece. It will also seem best if the Caesar [= the Holy Roman Emperor] with the Hungarians, the Bohemians, and the neighboring people were to advance in an orderly manner and lead this harmonious force against Greece through Adrianople and the other regions that have been subjected to the Turks. The individual armies will thus proceed in the manner and arrangement and will reach their prearranged objectives; thus they will be able to keep one another informed as to how matters turn out.

CHAPTER XXV: The Numerous Christians Forced to Serve the Turks Will Desert Them, if They Are Given the Chance, and Will Join our Side.

1. The Prince of the Turks is careful to apply the strength available to him; he has, in his army, more than two hundred thousand warriors, if we are to include the irregulars, among whom there are many Christians, who follow him unwillingly and by coercion; they are eager to bring help to the Christians in the future, as they are able to provide assistance and aid, provided that they escape from the Turks and return to their own regions. When that aforementioned

---

November 22, 1453, expresses similar fears (CC 2: 109–10): "El quale dela grandissima potentia et inmanissima crudeltà del Turche contra de christiani et suoi grandissimi thesori, et de l'affirmata volontà sua del venire in Italia et degli inmensi pericoli <che> si corrono per li christiani se presto non si provede ... Et che intende presto venire in Italia facendo transito ad Silla [= Scylla] in nel fine del gholfo a la ponta di Calabria."

habet in nulla civitate vel castro pro tunc residere sed sequenter aut in campis aut in pratis cum populo suo constitere.

2.   Ex quoper penditur eius de facili debilitari posse potentiam, maxime quia Christiani ab eodem angariati ad nostros occasione inventa confugientes ipsis essent in hostes, nobis autem in praesidium et firmamentum. Caramaym quoque vir magnus ac praepotens ac validus inimicus eidem principi Turcorum, si eum per nostros certificari contingeret de Christianorum adventu, permaximum inferret illi damnum atque de facili nostrae fidei adhaereret.

CAPUT XXVI: Quod princeps Turcorum faciliter decipi possit, et nisi id fiat, periculum imminet Christianis.

1.   In Graecia vix aliquis reperiri posset, qui Turcis ministrare victualia dignaretur et sic Turcia fame laborans a militia de R<h>odos citius vastaretur. Insuper Christiani Graeci terras suas sub Turcorum imperio sitas manu armata eos expugnando requirerent et obtinerent; sicque nostris paulatim appropriantibus ab omni parte, nulli dubium quin Turcorum potentia in brevi deficeret prae stipis inopia. Si saltem hae quae protulimus cum diligentiae cautela per providentiam vestram, Domine, iuberentur actitari.

2.   Si vero hosti nostro tribuatur loci et temporis opportunitas, interveniente incuria, desidia et negligentia nostra; qua percepta, sibi de omnibus necessariis provideat terra marique, veraciter fateri cogemur, solum restare nos omnes mercenarios et servos, venditos, infelices et miseros futuros. Quos autem ipse dignetur qui suos in praesenti a malo dignatus est eripere, et in bono sua gratia semper conservare atque post hanc caducam et miseram vitam futura pollicetur praemia se daturum, peracto certaminis labore: Iesus Christus, Dominus noster, qui est super omnia benedictus in saecula saeculorum. Amen.

3.   Ego igitur Simon de Ympegem filius quondam Reuneri de Ympegem hanc certificationis scedulam domino cardinali Avinionensi transmissam per Franconem de Tyvvayr ad finem usque produxi in civitate Pisiensi, in monasterio Beati Ioannis Lateranensis, anno Domini millesimo quadringentesimo quinquagesimo tertio, in solemnitate Purificationis Beatae Mariae Virginis.

Explicit historia de cladibus
civitatis Constantinopolitanae.

prince of the Turks is waging war customarily uses no city or fortified town as his headquarters but resides with his host out in the fields and countryside.

2. Accordingly, to weaken him will prove an easy task, especially because the Christians who owe him service will desert him, given the opportunity, and will become his enemies, while they will assist us and add further troops to our numbers. Caramaym [= Karaman], a great man, is a powerful and mighty enemy of the prince of the Turks; should he be informed by our side of the advance of the Christians, he will bring the greatest injury upon him and will easily convert to our faith.

CHAPTER XXVI: The Prince of the Turks Can Be Easily Deceived; If Not, He Will Be a Menace to the Christians.

1. In Greece one can hardly find an individual willing to supply provisions to the Turks and Turkey would swiftly be devastated by famine in a war with the Rhodians [= the Knights of Saint John at Rhodes]. Furthermore, the Greek Christians will take up arms and reclaim and recover their lands that have been included by conquest in the realm of the Turks. So gradually, as we will draw near from every side, without doubt the power of the Turks will quickly collapse, especially through lack of resources. May my careful, cautious proposals be enacted through Your providence, my Lord.

2. Should our enemy be granted the advantage of choosing the ground and the time, through untimely lack of caution, negligence, or lack of foresight on our part, he will evaluate the situation and make preparations over land and at sea, and we will be forced to confess that all of us will be betrayed and become unhappy and wretched mercenaries and slaves. But may Jesus Christ, our Lord, who is blessed above all forever, who has deigned to rescue His own from the present evil and to keep them ever by His grace in the good, and who promises that He will bestow future rewards after this fleeting and wretched life, Himself have mercy on us once the hard work of the struggle is over. Amen.

3. And so I, Simon de Ympegem, the son of the late Renier de Ympegem, put together this notification, carried by Franco de Tyvvayr to its destination, for the lord cardinal of Avignon; in the city of Pisa, at the Monastery of Saint John Lateran, in 1453 A.D. [sic],[29] during the feast of the Purification of Blessed Mary, the Virgin.

The End of the History of the Destruction
of the City of Constantinople

---

[29] As it is pointed out to me by one of the anonymous referees of my manuscript, this date must be a scribal error, since the feast of Purification falls on February 2; therefore the year should have been cited as 1454 A.D.

CHAPTER VI

THE SIEGE AND DESTRUCTION OF NEGROPONTE,
BY GIACOMO RIZZARDO, SECRETARY OF THE REVEREND
LORD LORENZO CONTARINI,
COMMANDER OF A LARGE GALLEY OF FLANDERS

CASO RUINOSO DELLA CITTADE DI NEGROPONTE INTESO PER MI IACOMO RIZZARDO SCRIVAN DELLO SPETTABIL UOMO MESSER LORENZO CONTARINI SOPRACOMITO DI UNA GALIA GROSSA DI FIANDRA

1.   Adì 15 giugno giunse l'armata del signor Turco a ore otto di giorno a Millemoza e al Burchio. Adì 16 di mattina discese in sull'isola di Negroponte alla parte di Santa Marina, all'incontro della terra al Rivellino del Burchio con bombardiere assaissime nelle quali furono giannizzeri tutti e azappi e turchi, e solamente lasciò i cristiani sull'armata; e venne al Rivellino del Burchio sopra il fosso. I nostri

THE SIEGE AND DESTRUCTION OF NEGROPONTE COMPOSED BY ME, GIACOMO RIZZARDO, SECRETARY OF THE REVEREND LORD LORENZO CONTARINI, COMMANDER OF A LARGE GALLEY OF FLANDERS[1]

1.   At 8:00 am on June 15 the armada of the Lord Turk[2] put in at Millemosa and Vourkos.[3] In the morning of the 16th they disembarked an artillery contingent on the island of Negroponte [= Euboea], in the region of Santa Marina, opposite the mainland, to Rivellino of Vourkos, with artillery of the janissary corps, *azab* troops,[4] and Turks. Only the Christians were left on board. They came to Rivellino of Vourkos to the moat. Our side made a sortie from the walls,

....

[1] The command of Lorenzo Contarini is also mentioned in the Chronicle of Stefano Magno, which still remains in manuscript form: *Cronaca Magno*, vol. 1, Cod. Marc. Class. VII, no. DXIII, marca CVIII, 6: see above, Chap. 2, n. 28. The pertaining extract was published, however, by Cicogna as *Documento A* in the Appendix to Rizzardo's text, 29–33: "Ordene eposte deputade per el magnifico mis. Nicolo da Canal cap. general per andar ad expugnare la desolata et misera terra de Negroponte . . . Fato far barbote 20 de barche et de lauti (liuti) de naue dele qual ha fato 2 capitanj, uno ser Baxeio boter homo de consegio de ser Lorenzo Contarini galia grosa de fiandra." Rizzardo and Magno are the only sources that mention this Lorenzo Contarini, and there is no additional information on him. Magno evidently used Rizzardo's narrative: cf. Carl Hopf, *Chroniques Gréco-Romanes inédites ou peu connues publiées avec notes et tables généalogiques* (Paris, 1873; repr. Brussels, 1966), 206: Fol. 415 r. seq. "De capta Negreponte insula. recepit Magnus in annales suos quae de excidio insulae Rizzardus enarravit, quasi verbotenus."

[2] By "Lord Turk," *il signore Turco*, or simply "lord," *il signor*, Rizzardo consistently refers to Mehmed II, the Conqueror; he never mentions his actual name or his proper title, "sultan." This is a wide usage of the title; cf., e.g., the anonymous sixteenth-century Ἔκθεσις Χρονική, which refers to Mehmed II consistently as ὁ αὐθέντης, a term that was taken up by the Turks and eventually reaches us as "the effendi."

[3] Milemoza (also known as Khilionodion to the Byzantine Greeks) is an island to the south of Khalkis, near Aulis. In the Ottoman period it was known to the locals as "Pasha's Island." Long ago I was told by a local that, according to regional tradition, the Turks who fell in the siege were buried in a mass grave in Milemoza. "Vourkos," as the name signifies, indicates a swamp that no longer exists. Much of the topography has changed since the fifteenth century and few remains from the Venetian period can be identified. For the surviving evidence, cf. the comments of Maria Georgopoulou, *Venice's Mediterranean Colonies: Architecture and Urbanism* (Cambridge, 2001), 100–3. Individual structures from the Venetian era can still be identified in the modern city; thus near the *palazzo* of the *bailo*, there is a house that is still known to the locals as "the pasha's house." Upon inspection, it became evident to me that some parts of this bulding go back to the medieval period. On the various stages of this structure, see Anastasios Kalatheres, "Ἀρχοντικό στή Χαλκίδα," Ἑταιρεία Εὐβοϊκῶν Σπουδῶν 16 (1970): 149–81.

[4] The *azab* were irregulars in the Ottoman army; they were badly equipped and were considered expendable. On the janissaries and the Ottoman "child tribute" or *devşirme*, see above, Chap. 5, n. 15, and cross-references.

usciron fuora e furono alle mani con Turchi per ispazio di ora una e mezza nella quale fu ammazzato un Turco; e portarono la testa dentro la terra, e così allegri si rinfrescarono e tornarono ancora a scaramuzzare: alla quale scaramuzza ferirono giannizzeri e azappi e dei nostri furono feriti da freccie uomini quattro, cioè Nicolò Canuta e Demetrio Zabondarno da Negroponte, e due balestrieri della Canea; e i detti tornarono dentro dalla terra.

2.   Adì 17 di mattina i nostri usciron della terra a scaramuzzar; e dalle mura con spingarde furon morti Turchi dieci, dei quali dai nostri furono tagliate le teste: dal che venne tanta furia di canaglia addosso i nostri, che presero uno dei nostri balestrieri della Canea; e i nostri tornaron dentro dalla terra a rinfrescarsi. Onde unitisi quaranta giovani, i quali si baciarono in bocca, usciron fuora alla scaramuzza; ma venne a loro tanta furia di canaglia che lor convenne gittarsi all' acqua e nelle fosse. Ed uno di quelli che si nomava Zanino Spagnuolo, cittadino di Candia fece testa, ed ebbe sopra lui più di venticinque scimitarre; ed essendogli offesa di più colpi la targhetta e la celata, menò una botta, e tagliò tutte le due gambe a un giannizzero. Raunatisi de' nostri andarono in aita dello Spagnuolo; e i nemici rinculando, il detto Zanino entrò nella terra ferito da una lancia nella schiena con certe ferite sul braccio della targa.

3.   Adì 18 di mattina i nostri usciron fuori della terra alla scaramuzza contra la volontà del Reggimento e le pene e le scritture fatte; ond' è che i nostri ferirono assaissimi de' nemici. Ma rincularono nella terra poichè adì detto a mezzogiorno dalla parte di terraferma alla via di Struez videro venire il campo del Signor Turco con innumerabil moltitudine di gente, e veniva verso il ponte della città dove stette per ispazio di ore due, e poi si partì, e venne alla parte di San Marco, e subito fece menar palandarie assai e fece un ponte sopra palandarie quarantacinque largo quanto eran lunghe le palandarie, tutte di passa dodici, e

and attacked the Turks, and during this engagement that lasted one and a half hours a Turk was killed and his head was brought back to our territory. This success raised morale, and without losing time our side made another sortie and hand-to-hand combat ensued. In the course of this skirmish numerous janissaries and *azab* soldiers were wounded. Four of our own men were wounded by the enemy's arrows, namely Nicolò Canuta, Demetrios Zabondarno from Negroponte, and two crossbowmen from Candia. They returned to our territory.

2.   On the morning of the 17th our side made another sortie. Ten Turks were killed by spingard fire from the walls and were then beheaded. In a counterattack, the rabble fell upon us with such rage that one of our crossbowmen from Candia was captured; our side returned to our territory to recover. Thereupon forty young men gathered, kissed one another on the mouth, and launched an attack. The rabble met them with such fury that they were forced to jump into the water and the moat. One of them, Zanino Spagnuolo by name, a citizen of Candia, fought against twenty-five swordsmen and avoided their blows behind his shield while he managed to cut a janissary's both lower legs. The rest ran to assist Spagnuolo, and after the retreat of the enemy Zannino returned to our territory, wounded on the shoulder by a lance and with cuts on his arm from the shields.

3.   On the morning of the 18th of this month our side made yet another sortie from our territory, without the approval of Headquarters and without taking into account penalties and written orders. Consequently, the enemy wounded numerous soldiers. But they returned to our territory on that day, about noon, when they saw the main army of the Lord Turk approaching from the land side, from the road to Struez [= Styra, or more likely Stives, i.e., Thebes];[5] there was a countless multitude from many nations and they were heading for the bridge of the city, where they halted for two hours and then moved to the region of San Marco.[6] Without delay, he ordered the transportation of many *parandarie* to put together a floating bridge on top of forty-five *parandarie*;[7] in width it measured the breadth of twelve *parandarie* put together; in length it covered the distance

---

[5] There seems to be a bit of confusion here. Styra (Rizzardo's "Struez") is located in southern Euboea; indeed its citadel was attacked by the Turkish armada before it entered the straits of Khalkis, but it seems to be out of place at this point in the chronicle. The sultan led his army over the mainland from Boeotia. It is quite possible that in Rizzardo's manuscript the original word was "Stives" or "Estives" (i.e., the Venetian corruption of the name of the city of Thebes, echoed in Fra Iacopo's narrative [6] as "Stius," through the phrase [εἰ]ς τὶς Θῆβες) was corrupted to "Struez."

[6] More properly the region was known as *Bocca di San Marco*, "Mouth of San Marco"; it refers to the narrows south of the Channel of Khalkis, better known as the "Straits of Aulis."

[7] A *parandaria* was a small vessel propelled by oars, usually involved in the transportation of troops during assaults against cities by sea; they were also used in the siege of Rhodes, as is related by Caoursin; cf. below, Chap. 8, xviii.

lungo quanto è dall' isola a terraferma. Onde circa all'ora dell'Avemaria passò il terzo di loro sopra il ponte, e distese assaissimi padiglioni verso la Montagna della Calogrea e di Santo Elia.

4.   Adì 19 passò la mattina la persona del Signor Turco con lo sforzo del suo esercito dove era Santa Chiara. A San Franscesco distese il padiglione il figlio del signore; e i padiglioni del Signor Turco furono posti alla parte del commercio, cioè alla franchigia, con tutti suoi giannizzeri con dodici carri delle sue donne coperti di veluto cremesino. I suoi bazzari duravano per sette strade dove si vendevan e comperavan tutte cose. Essi continuavano da San Giovanni del Curco fino alla vigna di ser Antonio Venier: e gli azappi erano alloggiati nella parte del borgo, più prossimi al getto di spingarda al fosso della terra e delle mura: dichè alloggiò ogni sua gente con tanto ordine, e con grandissima quantità di padiglioni, i quali copriano per tutto.

5.   Adì ... Volle essere Maometto Bassà a parlamento co' suoi, e con Domenico Demunessi, il qual fuggì per avanti con una sua fusta, e andò a Gallipoli. Il qual Domenico condusse adì sette marzo vele sessantacinque a Stalimene allo assedio del Cocchino. E Maometto Bassà Capitanio dell'armata fece parlare in franco al detto Domenico Demunessi, e con buone parole disse: Chiamatemi il vostro bailo, che qui gli vogliamo parlare da parte del nostro Signore. Rispose Fiorio soldato di ordine del bailo, che gli stava accanto; e disse: Che volete dal nostro bailo, poichè ho licenza da lui che mi diciate quello vi piace. Rispose Domenico Demunessi in italiano: abbiamo comandamento dal nostro Signore di parlare al bailo. E Fiorio rispose e disse: Se tu vuoi dir niente, dì quello ti piace, ch' egli non è per veni qua. — Va, e digli da parte del nostro Signore, che gli debbi dar la terra perch' egli è disposto di mai non si partire, s' ei non ha la terra; e faria sagramento e fede di non far dispiacere ad alcuna persona di che condizione si sia al mondo; e di farvi esenti per anni dieci da tutti carichi; e a' gentiluomini che avranno

from the island to the mainland. Next, about the time of Ave Maria [= the afternoon Angelus], a third of the Turkish army crossed the floating bridge and pitched their tents on the Mount of the Nun [= Kalograia] and of Saint Elias.[8]

4. On the 19th, as morning was passing, the Lord Turk with his forces pushed on to Santa Chiara. In the meantime the son of the Lord Turk pitched his tent at San Francesco; he erected his own tents in the region of the marketplace, that is to say at Franchigia, with all his janissaries and twelve wagons covered with crimson velvet for his wives. His baggage and equipment filled the entire space of seven streets, which used to be, in its entire length, a market for various commodities. Specifically, his equipment covered the entire area from Saint John Kourkos all the way to the vineyard of Sir Antonio Venier. The *azab* troops were ordered to make camp as close to the own as possible, in order to harass, with their spingards, the moat of our territory and the walls. He put order among his men and so many tents were pitched that they covered the entire vicinity.

5. On . . .[9] Mahmud Pasha called a council with his associates, and with Domenico Demunessi, who had deserted with his own single *fusta* and had gone to Gallipoli. He is the same Domenico who had led sixty-five sailboats to Stalimene [= Lemnos] on March 7, to the siege of Kokkinos. Mahmud Pasha, the *Kapudan* Pasha [= admiral] of the armada, wished to speak frankly with Domenico Demunessi and began politely: "Summon your *bailo*, as we wish to hold talks on behalf of our lord." Fiorio, a soldier of the contingent of the *bailo*, answered as he was commanded by the *bailo* standing next to him: "What do you wish to say to our *bailo*? Tell me, as I have authority to hear all your terms." Domenico Demunessi replied in Italian: "We have been ordered by our lord to speak with the *bailo*." Fiorio answered: "If you wish to say something, tell me because he cannot come here." "Go tell him, on behalf of our lord, that he must surrender the territory; our lord is determined not to move before he has conquered it. He pledges no discomfort to anyone, no matter what his social class may be. He promises to exempt you from all imposts for ten years. He promises, to any noble-

---

[8] The manuscript of Rizzardo actually records the word *Caloriza*; there is no error involved here. In colloquial Greek it must have been referred to as Καλογρίτσα, and as such it passed on in the narrative. More formally, it was known as Kalograia, *Calogrea*, and *Calogreta*. The term probably derives from a convent that was in the area. Nowadays the neighborhood is called Velimbaba. Saint Elias, as is usually the case in Greece, refers to a chapel on the summit of a hill. Though the chapel does not exist today, ruins from it were still evident in the nineteenth century, when it had been incorporated within the surviving Turkish fortress on top of the hill known as Karababa.

[9] As with all the dates that follow in the text, the manuscript simply omits the number. We do know from other sources that it was June 25, the day of the first battle; cf. *MCT*, 281, *PL* 2: 301, and the older, authoritative study by Fincati, "La Perdita di Negroponte," esp. 292–93.

una villa ne darà due. E la magnificenza del bailo e Capitanio li farà come signori se vorranno star quì; se non, darà loro grande stato a Costantinopoli; perch'ei sa bene che non avranno accetto a Venezia. Fugli risposto per lo detto Fiorio di licenza del bailo, che là presente era: Dì al tuo Signore, e' si vadi a negar, che la Signoria di Venezia ha fatto questa terra per se: Ma digli che perfino dieci giorni ovvero dodici e' saprà se la vorrà tegnir per se o darla, al vostro Signore: sperando in Dio, che noi vi brucieremo l'armata, e torremo vostri padiglioni; e non saprete dove andarvi nascondere; con tanta vergogna ve ne partirete di qua! E quelli delle mura tutti gridavano. E disse: dì al tuo Signore che vada a mangiar della carne di porco, e poi venga a contrastar al fosso, ch' e' vedrà se potrà aver questa terra. E giunto con la risposta al Signore, e detto quello che gli era stato detto ad incarico e vituperio della sua Signoria, quella notte medesima fece metter le sue bombarde alle poste, cioè, alla Porta di Cristo bombarde tre e uno mortajo; a la Porta del Tempio bombarde quattro e uno mortajo; a San Giorgio in terraferma una bombarda; al Figher una bombarda; e incontro alla casa dello Scanielo una bombarda, ed una alla strada di Struez che buttava verso l' Arsenale e il Burchio. Dal Portello fino al Rivellino altre quattro bombarde, con uno mortajo a Santi Appostoli; e a Santo Stefano sopra la fornace un mortajo.

6. Le quali tutte bombarde e mortaj buttavano una pietra medesima, la qual pietra volgeva palmi quattordici di tondo. Ancora due bastardelle che gittavano una pietra di libbre cento in cima della Montagna di Santa Marina; le quali cascavano a ruina delle case della terra; e fecero queste due bombarde quanto danno s'ebbe nella terra, e ne fecero molto più delle grosse che traevano di fuori alle mura, perchè al continuo lo dì e la notte ne venivan tratte pietre centoventi da tutte bombarde e morteri; i quali mai non fallirono di non dar nella terra, e sempre fecero grandissimo danno.

7. Adì ... giugno di notte essendosi messi i villani a raccoglier rovinaccio ruinato dalle mura del Portello del Patriarcato, il qual rovinaccio veramente buttava verso la marina, i detti villani furon messi alla guardia de' soldati di Tommaso Schiavo, sì perchè non fuggissero, come anche alcuno non venisse a far loro danno. E pare che da Tommaso Schiavo fosse mandato in detta notte fuora al campo del Turco Luca da Curzola; e di presente la mattina fu sentito che questo

man who owns a villa, another one. He promises to appoint your magnificent *bailo* and your captain to great positions and grand honors in Constantinople. He knows well that they will never be able to return to Venice." The same Fiorio replied once more, after he was granted leave by the *bailo* standing next to him: "Tell your lord to jump in the lake. Venice is in charge of this territory. Go tell him that in ten or twelve days Venice will decide whether to keep her own territory or surrender it to your lord. We hope to God that we will set your armada on fire and will tear apart your tents. You will have no place to hide. You will depart in shame!" In the meantime those present on the walls were also raising the war cry and he said: "Go tell your lord to go eat pork; then he can come for a meeting by the moat; then he will see whether he has the strength to seize our territory." He returned to his lord and communicated what he had been told, including the insults to his authority. On the same night he commanded the deployment of the bombards: three bombards and a mortar against the Gate of Christ; four bombards and a mortar against Gate of the Church; one bombard against the Church of Saint George on the mainland; one bombard against Figher;[10] one bombard against Scagnelo's house; and one bombard on the road to Struez [= Thebes][11] towards the Arsenal and Vourkos. From Portello as far as Rivellino there were another four bombards with a mortar against Holy Apostles. In addition, one more mortar against San Stefano, on top of the kiln.

6.   All these bombards and mortars fired a stone that measured 14 palms in diameter. In addition, on top of Santa Marina Mountain they deployed two *bastardelle*: each one fired a stone weighing one hundred pounds; these stone missiles were destroying the houses within the territory, and they caused a great deal of damage within the territory. Indeed the great bombards acted similarly; day and night, without respite, all bombards and mortars fired one hundred and twenty stone missiles that fell within the territory and always created much destruction.

7.   On the night of the ... of June[12] the serfs were directed to gather the debris from the ruins that had collapsed near the walls by Portello of the Patriarchate and throw it into the sea. The serfs were under the supervision of Tommaso Schiavo, who made certain that they were safe and that no one was given an opportunity to desert. In the course of that night, it appears, Tommaso Schiavo dispatched Luca da Curzola as his emissary to the Turkish camp.[13] At

---

[10] "Figher" is most likely a corruption of Furcae; it is referring to the hill of Karababa, on the mainland, across from the modern city of Khalkis.

[11] See above, n. 5. It must be again a reference to Thebes.

[12] Most likely it must be the night of June 26 or 27.

[13] The anonymous author of the Barberini Chronicle suggests that Schiavo indicated the weak spots of the defense and advised the Turks in their deployment of their forces, 117: Καὶ ἔνας Θωμᾶς [= Tommaso Schiavo], λομπαρδιάρης, καλὸς τεχνίτης, εἶπε τοῦ σουλτάνου: "Ἀφέντη, τὴν ὀδεῖνα μερέα νὰ πολεμοῦμε, ὁποῦ εἶναι τὸ τειχίο ἀχαμνότερο." Καὶ ἐπολέμα γεμᾶτα. Very little is known about this individual and the conspiracy in which he

tale Luca da Curzola era andato, perchè nol si trovava per la terra. Onde si mossero assai cittadini e andarono dal bailo, e dissero: Noi abbiamo sentito, magnifico messer lo bailo, come è andato questa notte uno uomo fuora di questa terra:

daybreak, however, it became known that Luca da Curzola had departed and was not to be found within our territory. Consequently, many inhabitants went to the *bailo* and said: "Most illustrious Lord *Bailo*: we must find out, at all costs

....

was involved. In fact, our sources differ as to the details of the entire incident that seems to have culminated in some sort of a massacre of the conspirators within the city. Yet, as we shall see, in Caoursin's account, betrayal from within was probably more feared than the assaults of the enemy and, at the slightest suggestion or hint of any treason, severe measures were immediately adopted. Domenico Malipiero, "Annali veneti dall' anno 1457 al 1500," *Archivio storico italiano* 7.1 (1843): 56–58, narrates an interesting event in connection with Schiavo: Malipiero states that the secretary of Schiavo, Antonio Moriani, persuaded a soldier to report that Negroponte was still holding out as late as July 15 in order to collect Schiavo's salary, and in the same story it is further reported that Schiavo had a wife, on whose behalf Schiavo's salary should be collected. There is another notice on Schiavo in the Archivio di Stato di Venezia, Sen. Mar. Reg. 9, fol. 2ᵛ (*PL* 2: 302, n. 112). Another chronicle by Girolamo Savina includes the following notice of the incident and its aftermath, as quoted from the manuscript (car. 436) by Filippo-Luigi Polidori, in his edition of dalla Castellanas account, *Due Ritmi e Una Narrazione in Prosa intorno alla Presa di Negroponte*, 437, n. (2): " ... avendo gran speranza in Tomaso Schiavon da Livorno, qual haveva una bona compagnia di 500 fanti italiani, dell quali molti la notte fuzivano et andavano al campo de' Turchi. Ancora il detto capitano fu trovato de notte alle mura esser a parlamento con Turchi; et ultimamente Luca da Cortulia nepote del detto Tomaso si callò una notte zoso dalle mura, e andò al Gran Turco con lettere secrete de suo zio. Il povero populo vedendo tanti strani segni comenzò a temer, havendo anche altre sospicion, et apertamente dissero che la sua patria era per esser tradita dal detto Tomaso; il qual vedendo che li citadini di mal animo lo guardavano, fecce meter un zorno tutta la sua compagnia in arme, et venendo alla piazza tuto furiado, a tuti li homeni e donne che scontrava della terra, el dava la morte, e de vituperio minazzavali. Il Bailo con parole e promesse simulate placò l' ira dell' infuriata fiera, e pigliandolo con serena fronte per la mano, con un solo suo compagno lo menò in pallazzo, invitandolo a disnar con lui; e zonto in salla, da alcuni citadini (chè così era l'ordine) con pugnali el fu ferido a morte; et avanti ch'ei compisse de morir, el fu appiccado ad una fenestra. E fu messo in suo luoco Fiorio da Nardon, il quale de li a pochi zorni andò al Gran Turco, avisandolo che mettendo l'artillaria grossa contra la terra dalla parte del Burchio, qual se trovava vecchia e cadeva, piglieria la città; e cusì fu fatto per Maumeth. La torre che menazzava ruvina, poche percosse aspetò, che tuta cascò verso il campo de' Turchi, empiendo li fossi, e alzando el terren de fuori contra città."

So famous was the incident involving Schiavo that it found its way into the popular poetry of the period. In the second lamentation that Polidori published along with Fra Iacopo's narrative, we encounter the following lines (stanzas 28 and 29 [= Polidori, *Due Ritmi*, 416]), which echo the information supplied by Fra Iacopo also:

> Poi al Gran Turco se ne fo andato,
> Dicendo como la terra può avere,
> Come — Tomaso Schiavo è aparechiato
> Di dover rizare le vostre bandiere;
> La porta di Cristo vi sarrà dato,
> E dentro intrar potrete con piacere. —
> Quando il Gran Turco intese tal novella,

E' bisogna ad ogni modo intender per che cosa è stato mandato, e cui l' ha mandato: perchè se questa cosa non si chiarisce, e' v' ha risico che vegniamo assassinati, e che non intendiamo a che modo. Avanti che 'l Turco abbi la terra vogliamo ne tagli a pezzi, acciò traditori nè Turchi ne tagli. A quello rispose il bailo, e disse: Figliuoli miei carissimi: Vi avete gran ragione: pertanto andate per ogni via e modo d' intendere cui ha mandato questo tale fuora della terra.

8.   E perchè nella terra era uno fratello di questo Luca da Curzola il quale aveva nome Francesco da Curzola, fu mandato per lui, e menato al palazzo (e per avanti egli era stato ferito) volle il bailo metterlo al tormento, e disse il detto Francesco: Magnifici Signori: io vi dirò il vero: La verità si è che messer Tommaso Schiavo ha mandato mio fratello di fuora questa notte. Gli fu domandato per che cagione. E' rispose ch' ei non sapea: ma se volete intender la cagione prenderete il cancelliere ed il trombetta; e di presente furon presi i detti. Il trombetta, senza alcun tormento disse: Prima prego le Signorie vostre che mi facciano prima confessare, e comunicare perchè tutti siamo nemici della Cristianità, e prima disse di uno Andrea Albanese che già anni sette era spione del Turco, e sempre da lui ha avuto danari; dichè questi sette anni mai non è stato fatto cosa nè provvigione alcuna a Venezia nè a Negroponte, nè in alcun nostro altro luogo, nè parlamento alcuno, che a tutti egli non si trovasse: Perchè il detto Andrea Albanese praticava in casa di tutti i rettori, e di tutto quello che l' intendeva sempre dava notizia al Signor Turco; il quale Andrea fu preso e messo in prigione, e saccomannato tutta la sua casa, dove e' furon trovate tre freccie scritte sopra in turchesco ed in grechesco. La prima diceva in greco: io son tuo schiavo, e sì mi raccomando alla tua Signoria; e quello io t' ho promesso è apparecchiato alla tua Signoria; la qual freccia aveva apparecchiato per traggerla fuora della terra al Turco. Le altre due dicevan queste parole in turchesco: Fa quello tu hai a far, e che hai promesso al Signor, perchè lui è venuto quì per tue parole, e star quì non può più: quello tu hai a far fallo come tu hai promesso; le quali freccie erano state tratte dal campo del Turco, e dirizzavansi al detto Andrea, e a Tommaso Schiavo, perchè tutti due erano una medesima cosa.

9.   Circa un' ora andò ad orrechie di Tommaso Schiavo la ritenuta di questi tali. Il dettto Tommaso Schiavo montò a cavallo e andò alla volta della piazza

and by all means, his mission and the man who issued him his orders. If we do not get to the bottom of this, we are risking betrayal and death, something we wish to avoid. We would rather die fighting than be captured, through betrayal, and be cut to pieces by the Turks." The *bailo* replied: "Dearest children: you are of course quite right. Use all available means and ways to determine the individual who ordered that man out of the city."

8.   There was in the city a brother of this Luca da Curzola, named Francesco da Curzola: he was summoned to the palace; he had recently received a wound. The *bailo* threatened him with torture and the aforementioned Francesco spoke: "Most illustrious gentlemen: I will tell the truth. It is true that Sir Tommaso Schiavo sent my brother out of the city last night." When he was asked for what reason, he replied that he did not know: "If you wish to discover the reason, summon the scribe and the trumpeter." The two men were arrested and escorted. The trumpeter spoke without the application of torture: "I beg your Excellencies, to allow me first to confess and take communion, as we are all enemies of Christendom." At first he named a certain Andrea Albanese who had been a spy of the Turk for seven years and had been enriched by him. In the course of these seven years he did not fail to attend negotiations and deliberations that had taken place in Venice, in Negroponte, and in other places of ours. This Andrea Albanese frequented the houses of all the public orators and always sent all intelligence information he gathered to the Lord Turk. This Andrea was arrested and thrown into prison, and his house ransacked; there they found three arrows with messages written in Turkish and in Greek. The first message was written in Greek and read: "I am your slave and entrust myself to your lordship; I will act as I have promised your lordship." He had intended to send the arrow from the territory to the Turk. The other two included the following information in Turkish: "Perform your task, as you promised the lord. He came with here relying on your promises and he cannot wait any longer. Act as you have pledged." These two arrows had been sent from the Turkish camp to the aforementioned Andrea and to Tommaso Schiavo, as both individuals were in total agreement.

9.   In one hour, more or less, Tommaso Schiavo heard the details of these incidents. The aforementioned Tommaso Schiavo mounted his horse and, with

> Impromise a lui gran tesoro e castello.
> Dentro a la terra fo adpalesato
> Como Tomaso Schiavo è traditore,
> Per uno rigazzo suo fu rivelato,
> E morto in piaza fo ad gran forore;
> E si fo dicollato e squartato,
> Con ogni vituperio e disonore.
> Ciascun quarto nelle bonbarde fo cacciato,
> E nel campo del Turco fo scaricato.

con circa uomini cento, dicendo: Io voglio veder chi è stato questo che ha preso i miei uomini. Io gli voglio tagliare il naso. Ma avanti il Reggimento aveva mandato per lui, e aveva messo in ordine tutti i gentiluomini di Venezia e cittadini di Negroponte, e tutti i balestrieri di Candia, e tutti stesi attorno le piazze, per li campi, e chiese, e botteghe, e case. Venuto che fu il detto Tommaso Schiavo trovò il bailo che passeggiava per piazza con gentiluomini e cittadini, e col capitanio nuovo e vecchio, e ser Alvise Dolfin e ser Neri Zorzi, e suo fratello, e ser Zuanne da Molin, e ser Geremia Gradellon, e ser Polo di Berti, e molti altri gentiluomini che erano in ordine per volerlo amazzare. E vedendo i loro rettori che il detto Tommaso era con tanta gente, disse il bailo: Che vuol dire, messer Tommaso, che venite con tanta gente; e avete lasciato le poste, onde leggermente potressimo aver vergogna. Voi vedete che abbiamo il campo attorno.

10.   Il detto non pensò più sopra, e diede licenza a tutte sue genti, e smontò da cavallo, e disse: Comandate Signore. Il bailo rispose e disse: Noi abbiamo mandato per voi per far qualche buona fantasia per riparare quel muro del Burchio; ed e' rispose: In buon' ora andiamo dove vi piace. E andò a sentar sotto la loggia, e così il bailo fece d' occhio a tutti i soprascritti ch' eran con lui non dovesero far movimento alcuno; solo andava passeggiando per loggia insieme con detto Tommaso Schiavo, e questo per non mettere la terra a romore. Stati che furono un poco d'ora, Tommaso si levò e andò a casa del bailo, e di presente entrato che fu nella porta della scala del bailo, messer Alvise Dolfin li cacciò un pugnale nel collo in giù verso la spalla. Poi subito gli furon cinquanta spade addosso e passaronlo tutto. Avanti el fusse morto ei disse: Omè, Dio, non più. E morto l'appiccarono per uno piede alle colonne del palazzo del bailo sopra la piazza, e con lui ancora il cancelliere e il trombetta e il suo ragazzo alle dette balconate per li piedi; ed in quel giorno ne furon morti della sua compagna venticinque, e la notte annegati altrettanti di questi traditori; dichè la terra stette in gran doglia,

about one hundred men, went to the main square, declaring: "I wish to see who arrested my men; I wish to cut his nose off." In the meantime, headquarters had made preparations and had dispatched men with orders: all the Venetian noblemen, the townspeople, and all the crossbowmen from Candia; all had taken their stations at the piazzas, the squares, the churches, the shops, and in the houses. Then the aforementioned Tommaso Schiavo found the *bailo* strolling through the main square with noblemen and townspeople, with Sir Alvise Dolfin, with Sir Neri Zorzi, with his brother, with Sir Zuanne da Molin, with Sir Geremia Gradellon, with Sir Polo di Berti, and with many other noblemen who had been given orders to kill him. As soon as the orators encountered the aforementioned Tommaso Schiavo, the *bailo* said: "What do you have to report, Sir Tommaso, you who come here with such an escort, leaving your posts unguarded; you should be ashamed of it. You know how our territory has been surrounded."

10. Without further concern, Tommaso dismissed his contingent, dismounted, and said: "Your orders, sir." The *bailo* replied: "We summoned you here to form a plan and repair the walls at Vourkos." He answered: "In good time we will post ourselves wherever you wish us to be." He walked on under the loggia and the *bailo* made a sign with his eye to his escort to make no sudden movements. The purpose of this short stroll through the loggia with the aforementioned Tommaso Schiavo was to avoid alarm through the territory. They were together for a short while and then reached the house of the *bailo*, and were about to go through the door and climb the staircase of the *bailo*[14] when Sir Alvise Dolfin stabbed him with a dagger in the neck. Without further delay, another fifty swords pierced his body. Before he died, he cried out: "Woe is me! My God, no more!" After he died, they hanged his corpse by one leg from the columns of the palace of the *bailo* above the main square. With him they also hanged (by their feet, from the balconies) his scribe, his trumpeter, and his page. On the same day they put to death twenty-five men from his contingent, and they choked to death another fifty at night. Our territory became very upset

---

[14] Nowadays in modern Khalkis there still survives a house that has traditionally been known as the "House of the *Bailo*" and in the immediate neighborhood are also located the remnants of the loggia; cf. Georgopoulou, *Venice's Mediterranean Colonies*, 102: "The piazza that still forms the core of the old city of Chalkis, the square of the Unknown Soldier, must have been the backbone of the Venetian settlement ... Located across from the church of Saint Mark (now a mosque), the residence of the bailo delimited this central square ... In the fifteenth century this palace was preceded by a colonnade, probably a covered portico. Traditionally a large structure across from the church of Hagia Paraskeve has been known as the "house of the bailo." The structure rests on an early Christian foundation, possibly the baptistery of the church, and displays a Venetian lion above its door. The other public structure on the piazza was ... the loggia ... the loggia also housed the government chancellery." Georgopoulou also provides black-and-white photographs of the "house of the *Bailo*" and of the Venetian lion: Figs. 69 and 70 (101).

e molto smarriti sì per la morte di detto, come *etiam* per lo sminuir della gente; e quel giorno non fu dato battaglia alcuna alla terra.

11.   Adì ... a ore quattro avanti dì cominciò il Turco a dar battaglia al Burchio e al Tempio e a la porta di Cristo: la qual fu battaglia generale, e durò perfino a ore quattro di dì, giudicando il Turco (che non sapeva della morte di Tommaso Schiavo) che detto Tommaso fosse al detto Rivellino del Burchio; il quale aveva promesso dargli la terra da quella parte. Nel detto giorno ne furon morti de' Turchi diecimila, e questi furono delle fosse, rive, e campagne; a delle galee fuste, e palandarie un altro gran numero. Vedendo quelli della terra avere avuto quel giorno vittoria stettero con grandissima allegrezza, benchè furon morti uomini sette alla posta di Giacomo Alemanti, e furono feriti molti della terra: e morirono detti sette da un colpo di bombarde. Et in questo giorno medesimo andò messer Giovanni Bondomier per la terra co' balestieri candiotti, cercando il resto della compagnia di Tommaso Schiavo, e tanti quanti lì ne trovava, senza dir niente altro, venivano tagliati a pezzi, e così si consumavano alla giornata; perchè il bailo se ne doleva dicendo, che non era ben fatto far questo omicidio ancora che fossero traditori, per non esser cui traesse schioppetti, nè *etiam* cui supplisse alle poste: chè pur mancava la gente alla giornata: onde questi di Tommaso Schiavo ogni giorno cercavano di fuggire in campo del Turco, e questo perchè come venivan trovati tagliati a pezzi e malmenati.

12.   Adì ... vedendo messer Giovanni Bondomier esser mancata e distrutta la compagnia di Tommaso Schiavo, e che non eran schioppettieri, andò nell'Arsenale, e trovò schioppetti cinquecento; e di presente mandò per il gastaldo, e fece fare una grida per la terra, che tutti i garzoni da anni dieci in su debban venire all'Arsenale; e lì mise uno monte di tornesi sopra una tavola, e sì vennero

with these events and the entire camp was disturbed over the death of the aforementioned man and over the diminution of the forces. On that day there was no fighting anywhere in the territory.

11.   On ... at four o'clock, the Turks commenced an attack against Vourkos, the church, and the Gate of Christ. It was a general attack that lasted until the fourth hour of the day. The Turk (who knew nothing about Tommaso Schiavo's death) was under the impression that Tommaso Schiavo was present at his sector in Rivellino of Vourkos, where he had promised to let them seize the territory. On that day ten thousand Turks fell in the course of that battle, at the ditches, at the banks, and the in countryside. A great number of them perished in the galleys, *fuste*, and *parandarie*. When this battle was over and our side realized that they had achieved a great victory that day, they began celebrations and merrymaking, in spite of the fact that seven men, at the sector of Giacomo Alemanti, had fallen and many had been wounded in our territory; the aforementioned seven were killed by a bombard missile. On the same day Sir Giovanni Bondomier,[15] together with Cretan crossbowmen, searched for the rest of Tommaso Schiavo's company. He cut to pieces all those he encountered without explanation to anyone. The entire day was spent in this manner. The *bailo* felt sorry for this slaughter and kept saying that it was not right to murder so many men, even if they were traitors, since our gunners were being wasted and there were no others to take up their defensive positions. Consequently, Tommaso Schiavo's men were trying all day long to find means to desert to the camp of the Turk, since they were certain that they would be put to death and cut into pieces if they were found.

12.   On ... Sir Giovanni Bondomier saw that Tommaso Schiavo's contingent had been massacred and destroyed and that there were no gunners; so he went to the Arsenal and found five hundred guns. Then he instructed the public crier to make a tour of the territory and summon all boys ten years and older to the Arsenal. More than one thousand boys came, and he selected five hundred older ones; he gave each one a gun and two hyperpers,[16] as wages for one month.

---

[15] Giovanni Bondomier was one of the ten *provveditori* at Negroponte, as appears in Cicogna's *Documento E*, published as an Appendix to Rizzardo's text: "1466 Zuanne Boudumier fu di Antonio." His massacre of Schiavo's company is not reported in other texts. The numbers of the slain, in general, are of course highly exaggerated and not reliable in this chronicle. The same holds true of most accounts. Fincati, "La Perdita di Negroponte" (for which PL 2: 302, and 303, n. 118, reserves high praise), estimated (297–98) the population within the walls at about 2500, to which he added 300 refugees; in terms of active defenders, Fincati calculated 400 mercenaries, 500 (under Schiavo), and 300 crossbowmen from Crete, concluding that they could not have exceeded 4000; in addition, Fincati estimated that the Ottoman forces could not have been more than 20,000, which, he added, was still an exaggeration. In addition, see PL 2: 302.

[16] The ὑπέρπερα/*perperi*/*iperperi*,' hyperpers were the 20-carat gold Byzantine coins introduced at the end of the eleventh century; cf. P. Grierson in *ODB* 2: 964–65; they were supposedly still in use even though Constantinople had earlier fallen to the Turks. The exact value of this coin cannot be calculated. The aspers (referred to in the next paragraph of Rizzardo) were Turkish silver coins of very low value; see idem, "Asper," *ODB* 1: 211.

circa da putti mille più, e tolse cinquecento de' maggiori, e diè loro uno schioppetto per uno e iperperi due per paga di mese uno: ai quali per alcuni schioppettieri veniva monstrato il trarre; dichè in poche ore tutti furon maestri; e quelli che furon d'avanzo, i quali non avevano schioppetti, piangevano, e conveniva aver pazienza. E di quelli cinquecento che avevano schioppetto furon fatte poste duecento dal Tempio fino al Burchio. Quelli dal Burchio traevano verso il Tempio. Quelli dal Tempio traevan verso il Burchio: dichè non fu mai tale e bell'ordine.

13.   Vedendo questo il Reggimento con tutti della terra rimasero contenti, e con allegrezza di tal cosa: dichè il bailo a cagion che stessero alle poste e che sempre traessero, volle che a cadauno di quelli garzoni che ammazzeria un Turco e ch' ei mostrasse solo una testimonianza, fossero dati due aspri per cadaun Turco che avesser amazzato: dichè ogni giorno di sera il bailo si aveva esborsato a questi tali garzoni da aspri trecento in cinquecento: dichè Turchi stavano molto maravigliati, dicendo: che schioppetti son questi che prima mai non avevan tratto, e che ora fanno tanto male? dove possano essere entrati si davano gran maraviglia. Perlochè il Signor Turco mandossi per Luca da Curzola, e Fiorio soldato che per avanti era fuggito della terra dappoi Luca da Curzola, e domandonne i detti, che schioppettieri eran quelli che traevano, e che faceano tanto male. Rispose Fiorio ultimamente fuggito, come tutti i schioppettieri che avevano eran della compagnia di Tommaso Schiavo, i quali tutti erano stati tagliati a pezzi dentro dalla terra; perchè ancora il detto Fiorio disse che il bailo aveva mandato nelle parti di Napoli con lettere al Capitanio cinque uomini, ma quello avesse scritto non sapeva. Il Turco notò le parole di Fiorio e subito mandò a dimandare alle mura alla posta di Filippo Zuparo, che schioppettieri erano quelli traevano sì forte. Rispose il detto Filippo, e disse, come in quella notte erano entrati schioppettieri settecento da Napoli per la via del ponte; e disse come le nostre galee e navi veniran domani, e sì vi faran lasciare i vostri padiglioni, e brucieran la vostra armata. Quegli ch' eran venuti a domandare degli schioppettieri andarono al Signore e riferirono tali parole. Perlochè egli mandossi per uomini 44 che erano alla guardia del ponte a cagione che nullo entrasse nè uscisse, e a tutti fece tagliare la testa; e con tutto ch' egli intendesse essere entrati detti schioppettieri, mai non restava di dì nè di notte di dar battaglia. E ogni giorno dimandava la terra tre fiate, e per il simile tre fiate la notte per parte del Signore colle promesse

Other gunners showed them how to handle their guns and they became experts in a few hours. In the meantime, those boys who were not given guns began to cry and were asked to be patient. The five hundred boys equipped with guns were posted in two hundred positions, covering the distance from the Church to Vourkos. Those deployed at Vourkos aimed towards the Church and those along the ramparts of the Church directed their aim towards Vourkos. They were deployed in excellent order.

13. The rest of the regular army and all the people in the territory saw this and remained content with high morale. In order to encourage the boys to maintain their positions strongly and to keep up constant fire, the *bailo* announced an award of two aspers to each boy who was proven (with only one testimony) to have killed a Turk. Each day the *bailo* took out of his wallet three to five hundred aspers and distributed them to the boys. The Turks were truly amazed, wondering: "What kind of gunmen are these? At first they did not even fire and now they are causing so much damage!" They were at a loss and were wondering whether reinforcements had entered the city. So the Lord Turk summoned Luca da Curzola and the soldier Fiorio (who had earlier also deserted to the Turks) and asked: "Who are these gunmen who cause so much damage?" Fiorio, who had recently abandoned the city, replied that all the regular gunmen were in Tommaso Schiavo's contingent, and all of them had been subsequently massacred in the territory. The aforementioned Fiorio added that the *bailo* had dispatched letters to the region of Naples[17] with five men but that he did not know their contents. The Turk noted this information and immediately sent his men to the vicinity of the post held by Filippo Zuparo to discover the identity of those gunmen who maintained such effective fire. The aforementioned Filippo replied that seven hundred gunmen had arrived from Naples the night before and that they had entered the territory through the bridge. Then he added: "Tomorrow we expect the galleys and our ships; we will tear apart your tents and will burn your armada." With this reply the emissaries returned to their lord and reported the matter. The Lord Turk then summoned forty-four men who had been guarding the bridge with orders to allow no one in or out, and ordered their decapitation. And so they were under the impression that gunmen came as reinforcements. Nevertheless, they kept up the war day and night without respite, three times per day and three times per night. On behalf of their lord

---

[17] I am not certain that this is a reference to Naples in Italy. In the Frankish period the city in the Peloponnese known as Nauplion was also called *Napoli*. It is possible Rizzardo is referring to Nauplion. This *Napoli* appellation must have originated in popular speech, as in spoken Greek Nauplion was referred to as "Anapli." Cf. Hopf, *Chroniques gréco-romanes*, 238, who quotes (pseudo-)Dorotheus: . . . Καὶ ἦτον καὶ εὐρίσκετο ὁ αὐτὸς Φραντσέζος ἀφέντης τοῦ Ἀναπλίου . . . . and again, 240: "Noi Gui d'Anguiano Signor di Argues et di Napoli." "Anapli" to Napoli/Naples is an easy mistake/transition in pronunciation.

fatte per avanti. Adì ... tre dì e tre notte sempre da ogni banda ebbe la battaglia generale, e sempre domandandogli la terra *ut supra*.

14.   Adì ... apparse l'armata nostra, dalla parte di sopra per modo che'l Signor Turco cominciò a piangere, e fece chiamare tutti i suoi familiari, e disse loro: L' è una nostra gran vergogna che già mesi tre siam fuora di casa nostra con tanta armata, e tanto esercito; e che ora sien venuti i Franchi, e che ne tolgan questa terra dalle mani che si può dire esser nostra! Perlochè i familiari risposero, e dissero: Signor, comanda quello che ti piace. Noi anderemo alle fosse e sì

they made promises. On . . . there was a general assault with all their forces, lasting three days and three nights, and they kept making the previous demands.

14. On . . . appeared our fleet coming from the north.[18] At this the Lord Turk began to wail, and summoned all his trusted men and said:[19] "It is our great shame; three months we have been away from our home, escorted by a large fleet and a great army. Now the Franks are coming to take this territory, which we have almost seized." His trusted men replied: "Lord, command what you deem best. We will go to the ditches, we will cut our heads off, and we will thus

---

[18] Cicogna has appended, as *Documento A* (29–35), an extract from Magno's *Cronaca*, which mentions the strength of da Canale's fleet, the various commanders, and his orders for the operation to save Negroponte. The first paragraph lists da Canale's instructions and strategic plan: "Ordene e poste deputade per el magnifico mis. Nicolo da Canal cap. general per andar ad expugnare le desolata et misera terra de Negroponte ordenandose come qui soto, et prima. Fato far barbote 20 de barche et de lauti [= liuti] de naue dele qual ha fato a capitanj, uno ser Baxeio boter homo de consegio de ser Lorenzo Contarini galia grosas de fiandra, ser Piero de Uersi comito de ser Hieronimo Morexini galia grossa de fiandra; e ditj dieno esser primi a intrar ala ponta de san marcho luno di qual uadj a dretura ale ponte et . . . parte a pasar i molini dela terra ferma forzandosi de ruinar el ponte uier dala terra ferma ala foreteza de la zita siche schorso da terra ferma non posi per quela uia nela terra intrar et molestar dala parte sopra del ponte." The manuscript continues, and points out that a second contingent of two galleys were to follow the first assault in order to attack the fortress of the bridge: " . . . le qual a galie dieno far forza intrar tra la forteza del pont et i molini con i gati et altri edificij fati e quella cerchar expugnar e rumper el ponte che ua ala terra et comparir li driedo i molini per la porta che ua soto la tore et che ua in la terra tra do muri et con questi etiam è 2 belengieri." A third contingent had the objective of attacking the area around the arsenal. A fourth contingent was to attack the Gate of the "Fisheries" ("porta dela pescharia") in the attempt. A fifth assault was also planned against the Gate of the Giudecca. A sixth contingent was to attempt to attack an important sector: " . . . a la ponta de san Marcho smuntar driedo Milemoa uerso el Burchio et die andar a romper el ponte a la porta X.º e quela del Tempio ouer brusar per o.iar che la zente de lisola no uegni a socorso dela terra." For the Venetian navy, see Dotson, "Foundations of Venetian Naval Strategy from Pietro II Orseolo to the Battle of Zonchio, 1000–1500."

[19] That Mehmed had overestimated the Venetian fleet and its commander's abilities has never been doubted by scholars, who believe that the sultan even summoned a council of his officers to re-evaluate options and even consider withdrawal (cf., e.g., MCT, 282). Such an event, however, may add more pathos to any general narrative of a siege. We hear of similar concerns at the last stage of the siege of Constantinople in 1453; when rumor invaded the Turkish camp of western aid approaching the beleaguered city, the sultan considered withdrawal and summoned a war council; cf., e.g. Leonardo (PG: 937 [CC 1: 154, provides a truncated extract of the council]): "Vox inter haec ex castris exploratorum relatu fit, quod triremes navesque aliquot in subsidium ab Italia mitterentur, et Joannes [= John Corvinus Hunyadi] Pannonum dux exercitus, Biancus vulgo nuncupatus, ad Danubium contra Turcum congressurus adventasset; qua concitatus exercitus disciditur." During the ensuing council Mehmed II was dissuaded from withdrawing by the war faction of his Porte, headed by Zaganos.

taglieremo le nostre teste, e sì faremo mura e scale da entrar nella terra per sopra le nostre teste. Rispose il Signore: Andate, e datemi la terra; e tutto quello ch' è dentro, cioè oro, e perle, e tesoro, schiavi, e schiave, tutto sia vostro. Mandò subito il suo marobato per suso le fosse della terra facendo la grida, a sacco a sacco, e per tutto il campo sì per darne avviso al suo esercito, come *eziam* acciò gli assediati intendessero, a cagion che dessero la terra, e venissero a patti: ma niuno della terra stimava i lor gridi solo per la speranza che avevano dell'armata. Erano fuora alla parte di sopra navi e galee forti da Santa Chiara fino alla Politica; e ricordovi che tutto il campo aveva abbandonata la terra per sentire la nostra armata esser venuta da quella parte: perchè dubitava non li venisse a investir il ponte che era di palandarie trentanove. E la notte montaron sopra questo ponte schioppettieri 1000 di Turchi a defensione di quello; e anche passò assaissima gente sulla Turchia, dichè eran fornite tutte le rive dalla banda della Turchia, e dalla banda dell' isola, ed ave<v>an girato le bombarde che giacevano alla porta del Tempio, e sempre stavano attenti tementi che il ponte fosse investito, e che l'armata andasse a soccorrere la terra come si doveva fare: perocchè quelli della terra sempre speravano tale ajuto: e Dio gli perdoni, per chi mancò, a modo che 'l merita.

15.   Onde passate ore cinque di notte, che l'armata non aveva investito per mancamento di animo, il Turco lasciò la marina ed il ponte, e buttossi alla disperata alle mura, e tolsele. E a due ore di giorno prese la terra, e mise i suoi familiari suso le mura, e tanti quanti li venivan per mezzo, tanti tagliava a pezzi. Il perchè

build towers and ladders for you to climb over our own heads and enter the city."
The Lord Turk replied: "Go and give me this territory. Whatever is within, gold, pearls, treasure, male and female slaves, are all yours." Next he directed his public crier to the moat of the territory, to make a tour and proclaim: "Plunder! Plunder!" He toured the entire camp shouting out his threats, in order to create panic among the besieged, who might then surrender the city under a truce. Yet no one among the besieged paid any attention to his shouting, as they were hoping to receive aid from the fleet. On the upper part, from Santa Chiara as far as Politika, there were ships and strong galleys. I do recall that they abandoned the entire camp to see the approach of our armada from the north, as they were also afraid that the bridge of thirty-nine *parendarie* would come under attack; at night the Turks reinforced it with 1000 gunners. In addition, large sections of the Turkish army that had been stationed across the contingents on the opposite side of the mainland and contingents on the island were transferred to the north, to which vicinity the bombards stationed against the Gate of the Church were also directed. Having taken these measures against assault, the Turks maintained a general alarm, in case the bridge came under attack and then the fleet sailed to the aid of the encircled city; these maneuvers should have taken place as a matter of course. In any case the besieged had placed all their hopes on this aid. May God forgive the individual who failed to perform his duty![20]

15.   When five hours of the night had passed and the armada had not dared to invest the bridge, the Turks left the anchorage and the bridge and desperately attacked the walls;[21] after a desperate struggle they finally climbed on the walls. And on the second hour of the day he seized the territory and placed

---

[20] This is a direct reference to da Canale, the captain general of the Venetian fleet. The extract from Giustiniani's book (presented below, Appendix IIIB) supplies more explicit details about his indecision, inability, and unsuitability for command. In addition, cf. *PL* 2: 303: "... da Canale suddenly appeared in the channel of Talanda, having rounded the northern end of the island. By coming this way he had added two days to his voyage from Crete, and he had avoided contact with the Turkish fleet ... Canale's route suggests timidity rather than tactics." As I have noted above in the Introduction, da Canale was eventually found guilty for his (in)action at Negroponte and was sentenced to perpetual exile and confinement at Portogruaro in Friuli; he spent the rest of his life there, even though the pope attempted to intercede with the doge on his behalf a number of times. At the same time Francesco Filelfo, the humanist and philhellene, also attempted to defend da Canale, a fellow scholar, in his correspondence (*MCT*, 283). On the nature of the penalty imposed on da Canale, see *PL* 2: 307: "By the standards of the times Canale's punishment was hardly severe. Mehmed II was as likely as not to execute an incompetent or unsuccessful commander."

[21] The weakest point in the city walls was indicated by Fiorio di Nardone, the deserter (*MCT*, 282), on whom Fra Jacopo dalla Castellana has supplied extensive information. In addition, Savina makes mention of him (Fiorio da Nardon) in his account of the Schiavo incident; cf. the extract quoted above, n. 13.

dentro dal ponte eran ridotte molte donne di gentiluomini, e di cittadini, e puttini assaissimi; e tenevansi forte al ponte levato. Perlochè montò sopra il muro del Rivellino dei Molini quel traditor di Domenico Demunessi insieme con Maometto Bassà, che per il Signore era mandato in quel luogo; il quale ebbe a parlar col capitanio del ponte, dicendo: Non vedete che la terra è perduta, e vi volete tenere? Sarete tagliati a pezzi tutti come questi della terra: per lo che il capitanio del ponte sì gli disse: fate salvocondotto le persone. Il Bassà e Domenico Demunessi gli promise di lasciar loro la vita, ma che sarebbero schiavi. Rispose, che erano contenti. Ed il Bassà entrò, e andò la nuova al Signore ch' egli aveva fatto l'entrata in quell' ora nella terra, e dimandò quel che faceva il capitano del ponte. Gli fu detto che 'l Bassà era entrato; e subito il Signor Turco mandò per Maometto Bassà; il quale aveva dato la fede al capitanio perchè s' aveva tenuto parecchie ore. Il Signor Turco gli rispose, e disse: se avete dato la fede, non sapete il sagramento? Fugli risposto per il Bassà: Tu sei Signor, comanda. E di presente mandò per tutte quelle anime ridotte nel ponte, e fece tagliar tutte a pezzi fino i putti ai petti, chè non ne scapolò uno il gran tagliare.

16.   La carnificina fatta in Negroponte è stata tanto grandissima, ch' e' non c'è persona cui si potesse dar ad intendere la gran crudeltà, e male azioni fatte dai perfidi Turchi. E tutto è stato per le male parole usate verso di lui da quelli delle mura quando domandavano la terra a patti. Veniva molto dispregiato il Signore ed ingiuriato lui e la sua gente, e se n' è voluto ricordare. E quand li venivan riportate le male riposte detteli per quelli della terra, li dolea molto; il perchè tra sè e' fece sagramento, che se l' entrava in quella terra, gliele faria ricordare. E come la terra fu presa il Signore andò di presente cavalcando con suoi figliuoli, e col Bassà e con altri assaissimi signori Turchi sopra, guardando se alcun giannizzero ovvero azappo menava alcuno di quelli della terra via per trafurarli; e tanti quanti ne trovava tutti li faceva tagliar a pezzi lì davanti alla chiesa de' SS. Apostoli. Alla

garrisons on the walls. Whoever came before them was killed. Many wives of noblemen and of townspeople with crowds of children had assembled behind the bridge to hold out with the drawbridge lifted. The traitor Domenico Demunessi and Mahmud Pasha, who had been ordered by the lord to that place, had climbed over the wall of Rivellino of the Mills. They spoke with the captain of the bridge:[22] "Can't you see that the territory has fallen? You will be slaughtered like those in the territory." The captain of the bridge replied: "Pledge safe-conduct to all persons." The pasha and Domenico Demunessi promised to grant their lives but they would be enslaved. The captain of the bridge answered that they were satisfied. The pasha entered and reported the news to the lord, who at that moment was about to enter the territory; he asked what was done with the captain of the bridge. He was told that the pasha had entered and that Mahmud Pasha[23] had promised the captain that he would spare their lives. The Lord Turk said: "If you promised to spare their lives, I believe that you have forgotten my oath." Mahmud Pasha replied: "You are the lord; command!" Immediately orders were issued to put to death all those souls, except the boys and the infants; no one else escaped from the great massacre.

16.   The slaughter that ensued within the city was so great that no human being can adequately convey the bloodshed and the savagery committed by the Turks. This great slaughter took place because the Turks had been enraged by the insults that the townspeople had been hurling at them, when they had asked them to surrender. In truth, both the Lord Turk and his army had been humiliated and when they had reported to him the insults offered by the besieged he had been extremely upset and had taken an oath from the bottom of his heart that, when he took this city, they would regret it. And so, after the fall of the city, the Lord Turk, mounted on his horse and escorted by his sons, by the pasha, and by a crowd of Turkish officials, patrolled the main square in case a janissary or an *azab* dared to guide one of our men to safety. All those whom he encountered were ordered to be sawn asunder, in front of the Church of the Holy Apostles.

---

[22] Rizzardo seems to be confused at this point. The "captain" of this castle midway in the channel was the *bailo* of Negroponte himself, Paolo Erizzo; indeed Mehmed violated the pledge and had the *bailo* tied between two boards and sawn in half (PL 2: 302). Rizzardo speaks of Erizzo's execution in paragraph 20. Evidently he confused two different individuals. According to Giovanni (Gian) Maria Angiolello from Vicenza, who was enslaved at Negroponte and spent a long time with the Turks before he returned to Italy to write his memoirs, it was July 13 when Mehmed began his organized massacre by first rounding up all prisoners (about 800 of them) who wore beards and having them decapitated; Angiolello was an eyewitness to this massacre (PL 2: 302, n. 115; MCT, 284–85).

[23] On Mahmud Pasha, Mehmed II's Grand Vizier and Beglerbeg, and his controversial role during the siege of Negroponte and its aftermath, see the observations of Stavrides, *The Sultan of Vezirs*, 168–72.

marina del Burchio e' si aveva ridotto per far tale crudeltà, e la prima fiata nel detto luogo fece tagliar persone 280; e andò alla volta della porta del Tempio, e lì trovò ch' e' ne veniva menati da circa 400, i quali fece menar a Santa Chiara dove erano i padiglioni; e tutti quelli fece tagliare a pezzi come fece gli altri; e andò a desinare. Giunto ch' e' fu al padiglione fece mettere in cima di quello per allegrezza uno stendardo d' oro e molto ricco. Fece toccar tutte sue tamblacane e pifari e trombetti nel levar di quello.

17.   Vedendo giannizzeri ed azappi tanta crudeltà fatta per il Signore di tagliare a pezzi ogni uno, si ingegnarono nascondere tutti gli schiavi avevano ricuperati per metter le loro vesti per le fosse. Subito fu riportato alle orecchie del Signore di questo nascondere. Desinato ch' ei ebbe montò a cavallo, e andò per li padiglioni onde si trovavano assaissimi; e di presente li faceva tagliare a pezzi nei luoghi dove si trovavano; e fu da persone mille e più. Ancora fu accusato al Signore, come Caracasin stratioto, che per avanti stava a Napoli, era nascosto al padiglione di un familiare; il quale era con anime 500 tra putti, e femmine e uomini assai; il Signore andò a quel padiglione, e trovò il detto Caracasin con le anime soprascritte; le quali anime e' fece menare a San Giovanni Boccadoro, e grandi, e picoli tutti e' fece andar per lo fil della spada.

18.   Vedendo il Signore che Turchi, e giannizzeri, e azappi con altre sue genti li face van di queste truffe di trafurar Franchi, deliberò d' andar per tutta l'armata, e tanti quanti e' ritrovava sulle galie, fosse, e palandarie che Franco fosse tratto di Negroponte, di presente lo faceva tagliare; e nientedimeno pur ne veniva trafurato qualcuno secreto. E ancor questo fu riportato al Signor Turco il quale fece far una grida per tutto il campo e l' armata: se ci fosse alcuno di che condizion esser si voglia che avesse Franco alcuno; e che quello non menasse di presente al padiglione del Signor Turco, e fosse dappoi trovato alcun Franco, li faria tagliar le testa al medesimo e allo schiavo; in modo che pochi Franchi sono scapolati di quelli della terra.

19.   In questo giorno si trovarono due almadari, cioè due appaltatori, l' uno di allumi, e l' altro di sale della sua signoria, i quali avevano nascosto dieci Franchi in uno de' loro padiglioni; i quali erano per metà, cioè 5 per uno, e fu riportato al Signor Turco. Mandò per loro, e fece loro levar il *zargolla* di testa e mise loro cappelli ungareschi in testa; e feceli menar sul ponte, e lì furon tagliate le teste ai detti appaltatori insieme con quelli dieci cristiani; i quali appaltatori davano di utilità alla sua signoria ogni anno cadauno aspri 500 m. e tolse loro tutto il suo avere, chè cadauno di loro aveva gambeli 100; ed altre facoltà che valevan aspri 600 m. per cadauno di loro.

The same acts of cruelty he repeated in the marina of Vourkos, where he put to death 280 individuals; then he directed himself to the Gate of the Church, where he discovered that about 400 individuals had been hidden; he had them brought to Santa Chiara, where the tents were; he had all of them killed like the others. Afterwards he went to dinner. When he came to his pavilion, full of joy, he set aside for himself a standard of gold and many other riches. He had all his tocsins, fifes, and trumpets sounded as he had it lifted up.

17.   Seeing the cruel acts perpetrated by the lord, who was massacring all, janissaries and *azab* troops attempted to hide by the moat all the slaves that they had captured, by dressing them in their own clothes. Immediately the disguise was brought to the attention of the Lord Turk. After dinner he mounted his horse and went to the tents where he found a great crowd; he ordered all of them, more than 1000, to be slaughtered right there where they were discovered; there were more than one thousand. In addition, the Lord Turk was informed that the soldier Karakasin, who had previously lived in Naples, was hidden in a tent of an acquaintance, together with 500 souls, children, women, and many men. The lord went to his tent and found the aforementioned Karakasin with the souls I just mentioned. He commanded that they be taken to Saint John Boccadoro [= Chrysostom], where, all of them, young and old, were put to the sword.

18.   And so the lord realized that the Turks, janissaries, *azab* troops, and others of their nation were inventing ways to steal Franks, and decided to inspect the entire armada. All those discovered hidden in the galleys, in the ditches, and in the *parandarie* that stretched to Negroponte were executed. So no one could secretly conceal anyone. Again the Lord Turk received further reports and made a tour throughout the entire camp and the armada announcing that if anyone, no matter what his social class, failed to present his prisoner to the tent of the Lord Turk, both he and the prisoner would lose their heads. So very few Franks survived in the territory.

19.   That day two *almadari*, i.e. contractors, were discovered, one in charge of alum and the other in charge of salt pans, from his own staff. They had concealed ten Franks (i.e. five each), in one of their tents. This matter was reported to the Lord Turk. He summoned them before him, removed their *zarcula*[24] and placed Hungarian caps on their heads. Then they were conducted to the bridge and, together with the ten Christians, were decapitated. These contractors had proved very useful to his lordship, if one takes into account that each man's annual salary amounted to 500 thousand aspers, minus each man's own fortune (as each one possessed 100 camels) and other wealth that amounted to 600 thousand aspers.

---

[24] On this peculiar white headdress worn by the janissaries, cf. above, Chap. 3, n. 14.

20.   Vedendo questo ciascheduno di loro si spaventò molto, in modo ch' e' si conta che della terra di Negroponte e' non sia campato che uomini da otto anni in giù: il resto tutti tagliati a pezzi. Dappoi ebbe fatto tagliare le testa ai detti appaltatori, fece fare un' altra grida, che tutti quelli che avessero garzoni d'anni dieci in suso, che potessero portar corazza, tutti fossero menati alla sua presenza; e tanti quanti ne furon menadi, di presente lor faceva tagliare la testa: e questo perchè aveva inteso come quelli erano quelli che traevano i schioppetti dalle mura, i quali avevano morto grandissima quantità de' lor Turchi. Essendo sopra questo di far morire di questi poveri garzoni, pare che venisse uno schiavo delle parti di Ungheria con una freccia bruciata, con una camicia sanguinata, con il collare d' oro, dicendo: Signor, provedi che il tuo figlio Emarbei è in grandi affanni. Subito il giorno di presente si è levato colla gente dalla terra; ma s' e' non fosse stata questa nuova e' voleva metter in ordine di far conciar la terra, e far forti le punte. Lasciò tutto, e solo fece provvigione; e prima lasciò nella detta terra giannizzeri 300 e azappi 300 con uno familiare nell'isola con cavalli 1500. Questa è quanta guardia e provvigione e' lasciò alla terra e all' isola di Negroponte; ed anche licenziò l'armata con ordine dovesse andar più presto fosse possibile a Gallipoli.

21.   Il partire del Signor Turco fu adì ... luglio; e andò a Struez, dove e' trovò che alcuni giannizzeri avevan condotto lì ser Bortolomio Bocharan, e ser Marco Venier di messer Antonio. Il Signore venne a sentar, e messer Bortolomio Bocharan fu tagliato a pezzi, e di ser Marco Venier non si sa nulla quel che di lui è seguito. Si giudica per esser in compagnia del Bocharan, il quale aveva con lui ducati dieci mila in suso, il detto ser Marco con quelli si riscattasse. E in detto luogo il Signor Turco trovò messer Polo Erizzo bailo di Negroponte, onde che colle sue propie mani il Signor Turco lo scannò, e lavossi le mani e'l volto del suo sangue.

20.		Much terror resulted from the slaughter he brought about; it was said that in the territory of Negroponte only chilren under the age of eight survived; the rest were put to the sword. After he beheaded the aforementioned contractors, he issued another edict and summoned to his presence all boys, ten years and older, who could wear armor. Then he ordered the decapitation of all these boys brought to him because he had discovered that boys like them had been shooting from the walls and had put to death many Turks. While he was ececuting the poor boys, it was heard that a slave had arrived from the region of Hungary, bearing a scorched arrow and wearing a bloody shirt and a gold collar. He said: "Lord, I inform you that your son, Amar Beg, is in great danger." On the day he received the news he put an end to his activities. If the news had not come, he would have wished to fortify the territory and strengthen the bridges. He abandoned everything but made some provisions to protect the territory and to fortify his position: he first ordered three hundred janissaries, three hundred *azab* troops, and an intimate friend of his with fifteen hundred horsemen, to guard the aforementioned territory. After this garrrison was provisioned and put in command, he left the territory of the island of Negroponte. He issued orders to his armada to proceedto Gallipoli as soon as possible.

21.		And the departure of the Lord Turk took place on ... of July.[25] He went to Struez [= Styra],[26] where he was informed that some janissaries had concealed there Sir Bortolomio Bocharan and Sir Marco Venier, the son of Sir Antonio. It came to the attention of the lord, and Sir Bortolomio Bocharan was put to death while no one knows what happened to Sir Marco Venier. Perhaps he is with Bocharan who had with him ten thousand ducats; this sum may have saved Sir Marco's life. In the same place the Lord Turk discovered Paolo Erizzo, the *bailo* of Negroponte, whom he put to death with his own hands, which, together with his face, he washed in his blood.[27]

---

[25] Angiolello, in the entourage of the sultan as a prisoner, carefully noted down the itinerary of Mehmed from Negroponte to Constantinople. He reached Thebes/Stives [i.e., Rizzardo's Struez/Styra] on July 28; he was in Athens next day and then moved through Boeotia passing through the main cities of Leivadia, Salona (Amphissa), Boudonitza, and Zeitouni (Lamia); by August 9 he reached Domokos in Thessaly, and he proceeded through Larissa and Platamon; he reached Thessalonica on August 11 and moved eastward through the rest of Macedonia, passing through Serres (August 13) and through Philippi (August 15), Kavalla (August 16), Komotini (August 19), Didymoteikhon (August 22), and Adrianople (August 25), where the sultan remained, rested, and ordered the gruesome public execution of an official of his Porte, Nasuh Beg, on the mere suspicion that he was a friend of his Asiatic enemy Uzun Hasan. He finally left on September 5 and entered Constantinople on September 9. On this itinerary based on the detailed information supplied by Angiolello, see *PL* 2: 302, n. 115, and *MCT*, 285.

[26] Rizzardo does not mention the return of the fleet or the operations that followed. These are treated in the extract from Giustiniani's history, which are provided below, Appendix IIIB. Da Canale followed the fleet at a considerable distance and avoided any engagement; Mahmud Pasha, in charge of the Ottoman fleet, ther joked that the Venetians were providing him with an escort; cf. Stavrides, *The Sultan of Vezirs*, 168.

[27] See above, n. 22.

CHAPTER VII

THE LOSS OF NEGROPONTE
BY BROTHER JACOPO DALLA CASTELLANA

PERDITA DI NEGROPONTE,
SCRITTA PER FRATE IACOPO DALLA CASTELLANA

1. Nelli anni Domini del nostro Signore Iesu Cristo MCCCCLXX, a-dì v del mese di giugno, usci fuori dello streto l'armata del Turco, cioè treciento vele, infra galee e fuste e parandarie, cioè marani. L'armata della Signoria,[1] cioè xxxiii galie, si trovava allo Tenedo quando usci fuori la detta armata del Turco, all' insula del Nembio, là dov'era rettore messer Bernardo da Ranatale; ellì prese lo castello dove era rettore messer Marco Zane; e ellì el bassà, cioè il capitano dell'armata del Turco, fecie tagliare a pezi il rettore, con tutti quelli de numero di ccc anime, s<e>nza[2] li putti, ch'elli mandò a Costantinopoli[3] per ischiavi.

2. E a dì x del detto mese, andò la detta armata del Turco alla insula di Stalimini, là dove era stato rettore messer Bartolomeo Barba<r>o,[4] e al presente era rettore messere Antonio de Capoppo; e lì conbattè il Poliocastro cinque dì e cinque notti, e *tamen* non potè fare niente, per essere forte el castello; e de lì si partio la detta armata del Turco, e andò all insula de Schiro, e sì abrusò il borgo, e al castello non potè fare niente, per esser forte. E l'armata de' Viniziani rimase a Schiotto e Schopilo, ellì prese xviii fuste de' Turchi e due galee, senza anima, per essere iscampate in terra ferma; essì prese una caravella da Scio, con cinque mila ducati, e ciento braccia di scarlatto, che mandavano quelli da Scio per trebutto allo Granturco a Nigroponte.

3. A dì XV del detto mese, cioè il dì di Santo Vito, andò la detta armata dello Turco a Nigroponte dalla banda di Carasto e de Porto Leone; e sì entrò dentro dal canale, e surse allo ponte di Santo Marco, di lungi da terra tre miglia. In quello medesimo dì, in quella ora, giunse il Granturco in persona, e venne per terra con treciento migliaia di uomini, non contando quelli dell'armata, chessi estimavano essere sessantamilia, che volea dire ccclx milia persone per mare e per terra.

4. E a dì xxv del detto, el Turco fecie fare uno ponte di lengniame sopra le parandarie,[5] cioè marani; da terra ferma alla insula era lungo passa ciento, e era largo passa quaranta; e era allo ponte di San Marco, dove era surta la sua armata: e da sopra allo ditto ponte passò el Granturco in persona, e il suo figliuolo minore, e lo bassà della Romania, perchè lo bassà della Natulia era capitano generale dell'arma-

---

[1] Ms: Singnoria
[2] Ms: sanza
[3] Ms: Gonstantinopoli
[4] Ms: Barbao
[5] Ms: palandrie

THE LOSS OF NEGROPONTE
BY BROTHER JACOPO DALLA CASTELLANA

1.   In the year of our Lord Jesus Christ 1470, on the 5th day of the month of June, the Turkish armada (three hundred sails, beyond galleys, *fuste*, and *parandarie* [i.e., boats]) exited the straits. The fleet of the *Signoria*, i.e., thirty-three galleys, was at Tenedos at the moment that that the aforementioned Turkish armada sailed by the island of Nembio, whose commander was Sir Bernado da Ranatale. They conquered the fortress commanded by Sir Marco Zane; and the pasha, i.e., the captain of the Turk's armada [= *kapudan* pasha], executed the commander along with three hundred souls, without counting the infants ordered to Constantinople as slaves.

2.   On the 10th day of the same month the aforementioned armada of the Turk came to the island Stalimini [Stalimeni/Lemnos], whose commander had been Sir Bartolomeo Barba[r]o; the present commander was Sir Antonio de Capoppo. They attacked Palaeokastron for five days and five nights without results, as the fortress was strong. Then the armada of the Turk departed and came to the island of Skyros. There they burned the town, as they could achieve nothing against the castle that was strong. The armada of the Venetians remained at Skiathos and Skopelos; there it captured eighteen Turkish *fuste*, two galleys by land, immobilized by lack of wind, and one caravel that was sailing from Chios carrying five thousand ducats and one hundred arm lengths of scarlet cloth, which the inhabitants of Chios had dispatched as their tribute to the Grand Turk at Negroponte.

3.   On the 15th day of this month, i.e. on the feast day of San Vito, the armada of the Turk reached Negroponte by the region of Karystos and the harbor of Porto Leone [Piraeus] and entered the channel, approaching the Bridge of San Marco that measures three miles from the mainland. On the same day and hour came the Grand Turk himself over land with three hundred thousand men (not counting the men of the fleet who amounted to sixty thousand); *in toto* there were 360,000 individuals with the army and navy.

4.   On the 24th day of the aforementioned month the Turk ordered that a wooden bridge be built over boats; it measured one hundred paces, i.e., it was as long as the distance from the mainland to the island. Its width measured forty paces. It was positioned in the area near the bridge of San Marco, by the army's bivouac. From the same spot passed the Grand Turk and his youngest son, as well as the pasha of Romania [= Rumeli], as the pasha of Anatolia was the general captain of the armada [= admiral]. The Grand Turk passed into the island

ta. E essendo passato il Granturco in sulla insula con qualche dugiento cinquanta milia persone, tutte a cavallo, riservato qualche xiiij milia Tanengarii, cioè Cristiani rinnegati.

5.   E si fecie mettere il suo padiglione sotto Santa Clara, di lungi da terra mezo miglio; e era lo detto padiglione in un bassetto a fronte colle Forche, che erano in terra ferma. E lì misse una bombarda[6] sopra la montagniuola, che buttava alla porta de Cristo. Questa porta è de qua alle bande della beccaria inverso levante. El bassà misse el suo padiglione dentro a San Francesco arente alla fontana; e lì erano xxx m<o>rtali,[7] cioè bombarde,[8] tanto larghe quanto longhe, e mettevano su all'erta quando le volevano buttare; e la petra di ciascuna dugiento rotoli, che monta libre siecento, e butavano in aere, e al cascare cascavano entro la terra; le quale guastavano molte case, e amazavano dimolte zente. Il suo figliuolo minore misse el suo padiglione sotto la Falegriza, cioè Santa Maria sopra 'l monte; e da lì alla fontana, cioè dreto a San Francesco, era pieno di tende de' Turchi, sicchè l' una toccava l'altra, cioè per ispazio di cinque miglia.

6.   Alle Fornaci, cioè dentro del borgo a mano sinistra in verso austro, elli erano due bombarde[9] grossissime del Turco che buttavano alla porta del Templo, spezialmente quella che fecie fare il capitano passato, cioè meser Bondinieri; e queste doi bombarde[10] che stavano alle Fornaci, eragli un grande reparo advante le bombarde,[11] acciò che quelli della terra nogli potesse danneggiare. In terra ferma, cioè dalle Forche insino alla Ficara, dov'era la fontana, tutto era pieno di tende e padiglioni di Turchi. Buttava sopra lo canale alle mura in fra li ponti e la porta di Cristo; ciò è quello muro dove era dipinto ad ogni merlo San Marco dalla banda di Turchia. El Granturco misse dieci bombarde,[12] in su quello poggietto alla via de Stius, che buttavano sopra lo mare, e buttavano alla Iudeca allo Burchio, ciò è allo Archenale: e le ditte dieci bombarde[13] buttavano dì e notte xxiiij colpi per una.

7.   L'ultimo dì del predetto mese, el Granturco vedendo che la terra non si voleva arrendere, mandò per dispetto tre milia cavalli collo stendardo per la insula, per insino al Rio, tagliando a pezi ognuno, uomini e femmine.[14] E' putti da xv anni in su li mandava in Costantinopoli per ischiavi, e li puttini di culla in

---

[6] Ms: bonbarda
[7] Ms: mertali
[8] Ms: bonbarde
[9] Ms: bonbarde
[10] Ms: bonbarde
[11] Ms: bonbarde
[12] Ms: bonbarde
[13] Ms: bonbarde
[14] Ms: fenmine

with two hundred and fifty thousand individuals to the island; they were all horsemen, outside of 14,000 *Tanengarii* [= janissaries], i.e., Christian renegades.

5.   He had his tent erected below Santa Chiara, half a mile's distance from the city. This tent was erected on a low spot, opposite Furcae on the mainland. There he deployed a bombard over the hill, which pounded the Gate of Christ. This Gate is the middle of the regions of Becaria, facing east. The pasha erected his tent within the area of San Francesco, by the fountain. There were deployed thirty mortars, i.e., bombards, which have the same width and length and are placed upright when they are about to be fired; they cast stone missiles of two hundred *rotoli* each weighing six hundred pounds, which they fired into the air so they could tumble down into our territory. They damaged many houses and killed many people. His young son, who was not yet an adult, erected his tent under Falegriza [= Kalograia], i.e., in Santa Mari[n]a, on top of the hill. From there to the fountain, that is to say within San Francesco, the entire region was full of the tents of the Turks, stretching, from one side to the other, to a distance of a five miles.

6.   At Fornaki, i.e., within the city, at the left side to the south, two very large bombards of the Turk were deployed and bombarded the Gate of the Church, specifically the very gate that had been repaired by the former commander, Sir Bondinieri [= Bondumier]. The two bombards against Fornaki were protected by a huge rampart in front of them, and could not be destroyed by those within our territory. On the mainland, i.e. the region from Furcae to Figher, where the fountain is located, the territory was covered by the tents and pavilions of the Turks. This section is situated above the channel and near the walls, between the bridges and the Gate of Christ; on this wall San Marco is depicted, facing Turkish territory [= Boeotia]. The Grand Turk deployed ten bombards on top of that small hill, on the road to Stives [= Thebes], that fired their missiles over the sea against the Giudecca and Vourkos, i.e. the arsenal. These ten cannons fired 24 missiles each, day and night.

7.   On the last day of the aforementioned month, the Grand Turk realized that the city was not going to surrender and dispatched three thousand horsemen with his standard throughout the island, as far as Rio, and they put everyone, men and women, to the sword. Boys, up to the age of 15, were sent to Constantinople

fascie sì li facie shioppare come uno cagnuolo.[15] E quelli detti tremilia cavalli presono uno castello per tradimento, che aveva nome la Tuppa; e lì erano dentro lo ditto castello tremilia Cristiani, ciò è Greci. Tutti furono tagliati a pezi inanti le mura di Nigroponte, che quelli della terra li vedevano: e questo facievano acciò che la terra si arrendesse per terrore.

8.   In quello dì venne uno marano, ciò è uno navilio carico di munizioni e di soldati, da Vinegia per soccorso della terra, e sì entrò in lo canale dalla banda ove era l'armata del Turco, non credendo fosse lì; e così lo Granturco fecie pigliare li detti soldati e marinari, e fecieli tagliare a pezi tutti inanzi alla terra. In quello dì, il nostro giovinetto bombardiere,[16] cioè era in Negroponte, amazò colla bombarda[17] due bombardieri[18] del Turco, li migliori che avesse.

9.   A dì v del mese di luglio, el Granturco fecie empiere le fosse de fascine là dove aveva rovinato le mura, ciò è dalla parte del Tempio insino alla porta di Cristo; e pieni che furono li detti fossi, incominciò a dare la battaglia per volere entrare drento nella terra: e quelli della terra buttarono polvere da bombarda[19] sopra le dette fascine; e entrat<i>[20] che furono li Turchi dentro nel fosso, quelli della terra buttarono fuoco drento le fascine; e a quella prima battaglia sì abrusciarono e anegarono più di xiiij milia Turchi: e questo fu saputo per uno schiavo, che'l bassà facciendo la mostra, trovò manco li detti Turchi. E a dì viij del detto mese, el Turco dalla banda della insula incominciò a dare la seconda battaglia; e dando la battaglia, quelli della terra missono una bandiera del Turco in sulle mura ruinate per ingannarli, acciò che dovessino entrare drento le fosse. Esso Granturco vedendo la sua bandiera in sulle mura ruinate, si credette che fussono quelli del trattato, ciò è Tommaso[21] Ischiavo: e il Granturco buttò il suo bastone de argiento; che se intendeva la terra a sacco. E data ch'elli ebbe la terra a sacco, corsero qualche CC scalie turch<e>[22] alle fosse per entrare drento, credendosi avere la terra; e quelli della terra si difesono realmente. In quella seconda battaglia furono morti xvj milia Turchi; che sono, con la prima battaglia, trentamilia Turchi.

10.   In quello dì medesimo, drento alla terra fu discoperto el tradimento che aveva ordinato la maladetta anima di Tommaso[23] Ischiavo, capitano di cinquecientto soldati; e questo tal tradimento fu discoperto per la femmina[24] del ditto

---

[15] Ms: cangnuolo
[16] Ms: bonbardiere
[17] Ms: bonbarda
[18] Ms: bonbardieri
[19] Ms: bonbarda
[20] Ms: entrato
[21] Ms: Tonmaso
[22] Ms: turchi
[23] Ms: Tonmaso
[24] Ms: fenmina

to be slaves; infants in the cradle were killed, as if they were puppies. The same three thousand horsemen captured, through treachery, a fort named Touppa [La Cuppa]. In that fortress there were three thousand Christians, i.e., Greeks. They were all slaughtered before the walls of Negroponte in order to inspire fear and terror among the besieged and compel them to surrender.

8. On the same day came a vessel, a cargo ship from Venice carrying war supplies and soldiers to the aid of our territory. The ship entered the channel from where the armada of the Turk was, as they did not suspect that it would be there. So the Grand Turk ordered the execution of soldiers and sailors, all of them in full view from our territory. On the same day a young bombardier who was in Negroponte struck with his bombard two bombardiers of the Turk, who were his best.

9. On the 5th day of the month of July the Grand Turk issued orders to fill the ditches with timber on the side that the walls the been destroyed, i.e., from the church to the Gate of Christ. As soon as the aforementioned ditches had been filled, the Turk began an assault, intending to gain entrance into the territory. The defenders poured gunpowder on the aforementioned timber and, when the Turks were in the middle of the moat, the defenders set fire to the timber. In the course of this first battle more than 14,000 Turks were burned or drowned, as we were informed by a slave who managed to escape from the Turks. On the 8th day of the same month the Turks launched their second assault against the island and, during the attack, the defenders erected a Turkish standard on the collapsed walls in order to deceive the enemy and lure them across the moat. The Grand Turk saw his standard on the collapsed walls and concluded that it had been erected by those who advocated surrender, i.e., by Tommaso Schiavo. Then the Grand Turk dropped his silver baton under the impression that the city was already being sacked. As they believed that the city was being sacked, about 200 Turkish regiments hastened to enter. The defenders resisted bravely. In this second battle 16 thousand Turks were killed, i.e., casualties from the first and second battles together amounted to thirty thousand Turks.

10. On the same day the plot engineered within our territory by the cursed soul of Tommaso Schiavo was discovered; he was a captain of 500 soldiers. His treachery was discovered by the wife of the aforementioned Tommaso, who went and revealed it to an old Greek lady. In turn, this old lady went to inform

Tommaso,[25] che lo andò a dire ad una vecchia greca, e la detta vecchia l'andò a dire messer Bailo; e messer Bailo mandò per Tommaso[26] Schiavo e per Fioredinardo conestabile, e per altri conestaboli, e per Giorgio Albanese; e lui confessò la cosa come era. E Tommaso Schiavo[27] vedendo Giorgio Albanese aveva confessato la cosa come era stata senza essere tirato, confessò il detto tradimento, voleva dare la notte la terra al Granturco, per essere lui bassà. E in quello, messer Loiso Dolfini, in presenza di messer lo Bailo, li dette con uno pugnale in lo petto al detto Tommaso;[28] e in quello messere lo Bailo fecie isquartare il detto Tommaso[29] e Fioredinardo e altri, e fecie li quarti buttare nel campo del Turco. E maestro Enrico bombardiere[30] fu ciecato, e maestro Piero Albanese bombardiero[31] si gittò dalli muri, e andò allo Turco.

11.   E a dì ix del detto mese, el Granturco dette la terza battaglia pure a Negroponte dalla banda della insula. In quella terza battaglia furono morti cinque milia Turchi: che vol dire in tutto xxxv milia Turchi. A dì x del detto mese, el bassà volse dare la quarta battaglia, e li furono morti tremila Turchi: in tutto li morti xxxviij migliaia.

12.   A dì xi del predetto mese, el Granturco fecie empiere li fossi di botti e di corpi morti, e incominciò a dare la battaglia avanti dì per la banda della insula (e questo fu il giovedì), là dove aveva rovinate le mura, cioè dalla parte del Templo a quella di Cristo, e per mare. Fecie venire l'oste armata lì dove aveva rovinate le mura, ciò è dalla Iudeca; e quando l'oste armata se acostò a intrare alla terra, el nostro bombardiere,[32] ciò è il zovinetto, rompè trenta galee del Turco.

13.   La nostra armata de' Viniziani entrò dalla banda del canale nel ponte di Santa Clara verso levante, e poteva molto ben dar soccorso alla terra: ma per paura delle quattro bombarde[33] del Turco che traevano arente allo secondo ponte, che era dalla banda de qua, dove era l'armata della Signoria;[34] e lo detto ponte era fatto sopra le fuste del Turco, le quali furono xxx; e feciele passare lo Turco asceso con ingiegni dallo ponte di San Marco fino al ponte di Santa Clara, che è cinque miglia: e inperò la Magnificenzia del Capitano Generale[35] errò, ciò

---

[25] Ms: Tonmaso
[26] Ms: Tonmaso
[27] Ms: Tonmaso
[28] Ms: Tonmaso
[29] Ms: Tonmaso
[30] Ms: bonbardiere
[31] Ms: bonbardiero
[32] Ms: bonbardiere
[33] Ms: bonbarde
[34] Ms: Signioria
[35] Ms: Gienerale

the lord *bailo* of the plot. The lord *bailo* then summoned Tommaso Schiavo and Commander Fioredinardo [Fiorio di Nardo], along with the other commanders, including Giorgio Albanese, who confessed the reality of the conspiracy. When Tommaso Schiavo realized that Giorgio Albanese had revealed the whole plot without the application of torture, he was forced to admit his treacherous plans, according to which he was going to surrender the territory at night to the Grand Turk and so become a pasha. Then Sir Loiso Dolfini [= Alvise Dolfin], in the presence of the lord *bailo*, stabbed Tommaso in the chest with a dagger; then the *bailo* ordered that the aforementioned Tommaso and Fioredinardo be quartered and the sections thrown into the camp of the Turk. Master Enrico, the bombardier, was blinded and his scribe Master Petro Albanese was thrown off the walls but managed to go over to the Turks.

11. On the 9th day of the same month the Grand Turk launched his third assault upon Negroponte from the side of the island; it was a Thursday. In this third battle five thousand Turks perished; I mean to say that *in toto* 35,000 Turks had been killed. On the 10th day of the aforementioned month the pasha launched the fourth assault, in which three thousand Turks perished; *in toto* 38,000 had been killed.

12. On the 11th day of the aforementioned month the Grand Turk issued orders to fill in the ditches with barrels and with corpses. He then began a frontal attack upon the island, where he had destroyed the walls, i.e., from the region of the Church, from the region of Christ, and from the sea. He commanded his fleet to approach the same parts from the sea, where the walls were in ruins, i.e. from the Giudecca. When the fleet approached the city to enter our territory, our bombardier, a young man, struck thirty Turkish galleys.

13. Our fleet from Venice entered from the part of the channel by the Bridge of Santa Clara [Chiara] to the east and was in good position to help our territory. But they were apprehensive of the four bombards of the Turk that had been deployed on the second bridge, which was on the side of the armada of the *Signoria*. This bridge had been constructed over 30 *fuste* of the Turk; it offered a passage to the Turk and his engines from the Bridge of San Marco to the Bridge of Santa Clara [Chiara], i.e., a distance of 5 miles. His Magnificence, the Captain General Nicolo da Canale, made an error, as His Magnificence would not

è messer Nicholò da Canale, perchè la sua Magnificenzia lassava andare quelle navi de' Genovesi che aveva preso in Candia, a ortare e investire lo ponte; e ionseli due galie de Cipri, due da Rodi, che se ofersoro andare a dare soccorso alla terra: la sua Magnificenzia nolli volse lasciare andare; la causa perchè non se sa; e per questo non soccorrete la terra. E noi della terra vedendo non avere soccorso, conttuttociò conbattemmo valentemente per insino a ore due del dì; perchè a due ore del dì li Turchi erano signori[36] di tutti e' muri di Nigroponte, e a mezo dì conbattero la piazza. E dalla porta dove se levava San Marco alla porta del Tempio, le strade erano sbarrate de travi e con botte. Le donne da su le finestre con aqua bollita e con calcina e coppi amazarono gran quantità di Turchi. E in quello dì fu pigliato Nigroponte, ciò è tutta la terra, riservato el ponte, el quale ebbe poi el sabato.

14.   Elli fecie tagliare a pezi tutti quelli s'erono trovati in Nigroponte, uomini e femmine[37] da quindici anni in su; e li fanciullini de fascia li facieva ischioppare a modo de cagnolini. El Granturco fecie fare la mostra della sua giente, quanti ne era morti in quella ultima battaglia. Trovò mancati xxxviiij migliaia di Turchi; che vole dire, con quelli altri, lxxvij milia Turchi. El capitano generale[38] de' Viniziani fecie fare la discussione, che possevano essere morti de' Cristiani xxx milia, infra grandi e picolini.

15.   Stato e Scopulo e l'Orto e lo Carasco aveano mandate le chiave alli Turchi. Dolimbro et de Castalimoni e lo Fittilto se ragionava che avevano mandate le chiavi al Turco.

16.   In quello dì arrivò il vecie capitanio de' Viniziani messer Lorenzo Lor<e>dano[39] con xvj galie e cinque navi e doi galeazi; e anco vi arrivò messer Iacopo Veneri, capitano gienerale delle nave, con xij nave e quattro galeaze: in somma, lassai a Porto Leone lxxviiij vele.

Io frate Iacomo dalla Castellana vidi tutte queste cose,
e scampai in sulla insula per sapere la lingua turchesca e grechesca.

---

[36] Ms: signiori
[37] Ms: fenmine
[38] Ms: gienerale
[39] Ms: Lordano

allow some ships of the Genoese that had been enlisted in Candia to attack and besiege the bridge or the two galleys from Cyprus and two galleys from Rhodes that volunteered to sail to the aid of the city. His Magnificence would not issue permission to attack. The cause of this is not known but, consequently, our territory received no assistance. We within the territory realized that we were not going to receive any help; yet we fought on bravely until the second hour of the day. By the second hour of the day the Turks assumed command of all the walls of Negroponte; at noon the fighting went on in the main square. From the Gate that bore the image of San Marco to the Gate of the Church the streets had been barricaded with beams and barrels. The women put to death a large number of Turks by pouring boiling water and lime on them from windows. On that day Negroponte was plundered, i.e., the entire territory, with the exception of the bridge that fell the following Saturday.

14. Those found in Negroponte, men and women 15 years and over, were slaughtered; the infants in swaddling clothes were killed like puppy dogs. The Grand Turk called a general assembly to see how many of his men had perished in the last battle. They discovered that 39,000 Turks had fallen; I mean to say that together with the others 77,000 Turks perished. The Captain General of the Venetians announced that about 30,000 Christians had perished, young and old.

15. Stato, Scopulo, Orto, and Carasco dispatched their keys [surrendered] to the Turks. It was also said that in a similar way Dolimbro, Castalimoni, and Fittilto also surrendered their keys to the Turk.

16. On that day arrived the vice-captain of the Venetians, Lorenzo Loredano, with sixteen galleys, five ships, and two *galeazi*. Also came Sir Giacomo Veneri, the Captain General of the ships, with 12 ships and four *galeaze*. In sum, 59 ships set sail from Porto Leone.

I, Brother Jacopo dalla Castellana, saw all these events,
and escaped from the island because I speak both Turkish and Greek.

CHAPTER VIII

A DESCRIPTION OF THE SIEGE OF RHODES
BY GUILLAUME CAOURSIN, THE VICE
CHANCELLOR OF THE RHODIANS
[HOSPITALLERS]

GU\<G\>LIELMI CAO\<U\>RSI\<N\>I RHODIORUM VICE CANCELARII
OBSIDIONIS RHODIAE URBIS DESCRIPTIO

I.   Rhodiae urbis obsidionem descripturus, causas in primis narrare institui, quae Turcorum tyrannum Mahum\<m\>etum potissime impulerunt ut tanto

A DESCRIPTION OF THE SIEGE OF RHODES BY GUILLAUME CAOURSIN, THE VICE CHANCELLOR OF THE RHODIANS [HOSPITALLERS][1]

1.   As I am about to begin my description of the siege of the city of Rhodes, I will first give an account of the causes which so very strongly compelled Mehmed,

....

[1] The Order of the Hospital, dedicated to Saint John the Baptist, was founded in Jerusalem in the eleventh century to take care of pilgrims. Two centuries later the Moslems expelled the Knights from the Holy Land and they sought residence in Cyprus, where Guy de Lusignan granted them some privileges. They took over Rhodes in 1306 or 1309 from the Genoese Vignolo de Vignoli, even though their island formally belonged to Constantinople. In time they occupied several neighboring islands such as Cos, Leros, Nisyros, and Kalymnos, and further erected on the nearby shore of Asia Minor the fortress of Saint Peter near ancient Halikarnassos. Formally they were under the authority of the pope but they maintained their own autonomy and laws. Their Order in Rhodes was organized in "langues," *linguae* or tongues, which reflected the languages that were spoken by the members; thus they were a multi-ethnic order, whose official language was Latin (but, as *PL* 2: 349, n. 12, observes, "[a]t Rhodes, as long as the Knights were there, French was the chief language of administration and of high society"); the Knights were headed by their Grand Master (*Magister Magnus*) and his officers. There were seven langues: Provence, Auvergne, France, Italy, Aragon (divided into Castile and Aragon in 1461), England, and Germany. In addition to numerous lands that they possessed in the Morea, the Order gained a great deal of income through piracy and the slave trade, as they consistently preyed upon Moslem merchantmen and upon Christian ships that transported Moslem traders. Since the fall of Constantinople, they had been involved in a number of incidents with the Porte, Venice, and Egypt. With Egypt, however, there was a thirty-one-year truce, as the Mamluk sultan had no wish to see the Turks take over Rhodes. The following is a list of the Grand Masters of the Order, their langues and dates, since their arrival in the island of Rhodes:

Foulques de Villaret (Provence), 1308–1319 Robert de Juillac (France), 1374–1376
[Revolt in 1317 by Maurice de Pagnac] Juan de Heredia (Aragon), 1376–1396
Hélion de Villeneuve (Provence), 1319–1346 Philibert de Naillac (France), 1396–1421
Dieudonné de Gozon (Provence), 1346–1353 Antonio Fluvian (Aragon), 1421–1437
Pierre de Corneillan (Provence), 1353–1355 Jean de Lastic (Auvergne), 1437–1454
Roger de Pins (Provence), 1355–1365 Jacques de Milly (Auvergne), 1454–1461
Raymond de Berenger (Provence), 1365–1374 Raymondo Zacosta (Aragon), 1461–1467
Gian Baptista Orsini (Italy), 1467–1476
Pierre d'Aubusson (Auvergne), 1476–1503

The Knights (*milites*) of the order were noblemen; below them were the chaplains (*cappelani*), the priests, arranged in three grades: clerics, chaplains, and priors, with the highest grade being the prior of the Saint John of the Collachium. The sergeants (*servientes armorum*) were the sons of freemen but were not noblemen. The high command under the Grand Master included a number of officers, while supreme authority was exercised by the *Capitulum Generale* (whose decisions had the force of law) and the *Capitulum* or *Conventus*, which advised the Grand Master.

conatu Rhodios aggredetur. Licet enim cum Turcis non parva dissidia Rhodii habuerint, tamen cum eo, qui nunc imperat, post Constantinopolis expugnationem gravia gessere bella. Inimicus quidem in dies vires augens insolentior traditur. Cumque quattuor ac viginti annorum curriculo complures sibi vicinas urbes subegisset, animo inflatus aegre admodum tulit Rhodiam urbem Hierosolymorumque equitum ditionem finitimam eius imperio liberam absolutamque esse, maxime quod diverso tempore quattuor classibus instructis castella et Rhodiorum agros invaserit, obsederit, oppugnaverit, ex quibus ignominiam, discrimen et cladem reportavit: ex Turcis nanque multi trucidati, palo suffixii, furcis suspensi, sagittis affecti, lapidibus caesi, calamis praeustis suffissi, gladiis obiecti, membratim discerpti perierunt. Terra marique hostes succu<m>buerunt.

II.   Conspecta igitur Rhodiorum militum generositate, quod vi assequi non potuit, dolo versutiaque tentare decrevit. Saepius enim submissis Graeculis, qui sibi parent, studuit confoederationem // cum Rhodiis inire aequa conditione permissa, dummodo quippiam tributi titulo concederetur. Cum vero reiectum vectigal saepenumero videret, arte pacem tractat; eam ratam habet, si tacita tributi conditione orator Hierosolymorum cum munusculis tribunal suum adeat. Arbitratus quidem munera tributi titulo accepturum, quae Rhodiorum magistri munera vocitaret, fallitur quoque hostis hoc commento: nec Rhodii conditionem accipiunt eique coniungi contemnunt, qui fidem Christi persequitur, quam ex professionis voto tutantur, defendunt, iuvant. His de causis rabidus hostis odium contra Rhodios inexorabile concipit menteque destinavit urbem, si posset, prodere et Rhodiorum nomen penitus delere.

the tyrant [= sultan] of the Turks, to attack the Rhodians with such great force. After the fall of Constantinople there was considerable enmity between the Rhodians and the Turks; there were serious engagements fought against their reigning lord. Daily he augmented his strength and grew more insolent. In the course of twenty-four years he brought numerous neighboring states under his control and became so arrogant that he could hardly endure the fact that Rhodes and the Knights of Jerusalem, his immediate neighbors, were free and independent, especially since he had put together four armadas which had attacked the towns and the fields of the Rhodians; he laid siege and launched raids but reaped only danger and slaughter, as many Turks perished when they were butchered, were impaled, were hanged from the gallows, were pierced by arrows, were pelted by stone projectiles, were dispatched with pikes hardened in fire, were put to the sword, and were dismembered. On land and sea the enemy perished.

2.   When he saw that he could not overcome the bravery of the Knights of Rhodes by force, he decided to use deception and cunning. Frequently did he send his subject Greeklings[2] to ask the Rhodians for an alliance between equals, demanding only nominal tribute. Just as often his proposal was turned down and he handled peace with skill, as he thought that an unspoken state of tribute existed if the orator of [the order of the Knights of] Jerusalem came to his court [= Porte], bearing a few gifts. Under the impression that the gifts were equivalent to tribute, which he often called "due honors from the [Grand] Master of the Rhodians," our enemy was deceived once more: the Rhodians had not accepted his terms and had only contempt for an alliance with him; their avowed aim was to pursue, defend, and assist the Christian faith. Driven to madness by such considerations, our enemy conceived inexorable hatred for the Rhodians in his mind and intended, if it were within his power, to occupy the city and wipe out the name of the Rhodians once and for all.[3]

....

On the Order, see among others, Giacomo Bosio, *Dell'Istoria della sacra religione et illustrissima militia di S. Giovanni di Geroselimitano*, 3 vols. (Venice, 1594); Aubert René Daubef de Vertot, *Histoire des Chevaliers Hospitaliers de S. Jean de Jérusalem, appelés depuis le Chevaliers de Rhodes et aujourd'hui les Chevaliers de Malta*, 5 vols. (Paris, 1772) [= English translation: *History of the Knights Hospitallers of St. John of Jerusalem, Styled Afterwards the Knights of Rhodes, and at Present the Knights of Malta* (Edinburgh, 1757)]; Joseph Delaville le Roulx, *Les hospitaliers à Rhodes jusqu'à la mort de Philibert de Naillac (1310–1421)* (Paris, 1913); Nicolae Iorga, *Rhodes sous les hospitaliers* (Paris, 1931); Berthold von Waldstein-Wartenberg, *Die Vassallen Christi. Kulturgeschichte des Johanniterordens im Mittelalter* (Graz, 1988); and Kollias, *The Knights of Rhodes: The Palace and the City*. In addition, see the various studies of Anthony Luttrell assembled in idem, *The Hospitaller State on Rhodes and its Western Provinces, 1306–1462* (Aldershot, 1999).

[2] On *Graeculus*-Greekling, cf. M. Dubuisson, "Graecus, Graeculus, Graecari: l'emploi péjoratif du nom des Grecs en latin," in *ΕΛΛΗΝΙΣΜΟΣ: Quelques jalons pour un histoire de l'identité grecque*, ed. Suzanne Saïd (Leiden, 1991), 315–35.

[3] Since the election of d'Aubusson, the prior of Auvergne, as Grand Master (1479), the knights had been expecting an attack upon their island, but the Turkish assault was delayed by the sultan's war with Venice which lasted until 1479. Towards the end of 1478 Giovanni Dario,

III.   Impulsus quoque est quorundam persuasionibus, qui ad Turcos defecerant abditaque urbis cogno<ve>rant; inter quos primum locum obtinuit vir nefarius et prodita ingenii, Antonius Meligalo<s> Rhodius non infimo loco natus qui rem domesticam iampridem dilapidaverat. Is rei domesticae penuria ductus diutius cogitans quonam modo Rhodiis infestus esset et patriae cladem afferet, urbis propugnacula, turres, moenia, abdita loca, munitiones diligentius speculatus civitatisque situm aedificia describens ad Turcum traiecit. Constantinopoli quoque degens, vanae pollicitationis, spe urbis potiundae data, quendam bassam Graeculum ex nobili Palaeologorum familia natum ad nefandum facinus // allexit. Secutus est huius vestigia Euboicus quidam Demetrius Sophiana vir quidem superstitiosus et maleficus qui post Euboicam direptionem ad Turcum defecit; aliquondam quoque Rhodii habitavit et postea nuntii nomine de pace tractavit; hic etiam suasor obsidionis extitit.

3. He was further persuaded by the arguments offered by certain individuals who had defected to him and knew our city intimately; most prominent among them was an execrable man, a traitor by nature: the Rhodian Antonios Meligalos, born to a family of modest rank, who long ago had ruined his family fortune at home. Because of his destitution, he became an enemy of the Rhodians and often pondered ways to bring disaster upon his homeland; so he took careful notes of the city's defenses, towers, walls, secret places, and fortifications, made observations, and produced a description of the layout of the town and its buildings, and sent it to the Turk. He came to Constantinople, and created the hope that he would hand the city over; it was a false promise; yet he attracted to his unspeakable crime a certain pasha, a Greekling, who had been born to the noble family of the Palaeologi. His steps were followed by Demetrios Sophianos from Khalkis, a tiresome man of evil character, who had defected to the Turk after the sack of Khalkis [Negroponte/Euboea]. He had also lived in Rhodes and had later paid a visit, pretending to be an envoy for the peace treaty; this man also added his support to the arguments in favor of the siege.[4]

....

the secretary of Venice, was sent to the Porte with instructions to secure a peace treaty that would protect Venetian commerce in the Levant; the treaty was concluded on January 25, 1479. Its terms specified that Venice would cede to the Porte Scutari (Valona/Avlona), the island of Lemnos, and Mani in the Morea; moreover, Venice would renounce all claims to Negroponte/Euboea in Greece and Krüje in Albania. In return, Mehmed II restored the Venetian possessions that he had seized in Dalmatia, Albania, and the Morea; see *MCT*, 374–76. After peace was concluded, it was obvious that the attack upon Rhodes was imminent. Meanwhile, d'Aubusson had taken advantage of the Porte's preoccupation with Venice to strengthen the fortifications of Rhodes, to build up supplies, and to recruit mercenaries from the west. His renovation program of the defenses is further attested by his coat of arms (*d'or à la croix ancrée de gules*) on the fortifications, which, by one count (*PL* 2: 346), appears almost fifty times. As the sultan needed time for his preparations, he concluded a truce with Rhodes by the late summer of 1479. For the negotiations between Rhodes and the Porte, see L. Thouasne, *Djem-sultan fils de Mohammed II, frére de Bayezid II (1459–1495)* (Paris, 1892), 12–18.

[4] Antonios Meligalos and Demetrios Sophianos are typical examples of their age. Meligalos, a Rhodian, simply desired a better life and there were more opportunities offered by the Turk, in whose service, as we have seen in regard to the siege of Constantinople, were numerous European engineers, soldiers of fortune, and adventurers. Sophianos entered the service of the Porte after his hometown in Negroponte was sacked by the troops of Mehmed II (July 12, 1470). Meligalos and Sophianos had joined the circle of a German engineer, also a renegade, in the service of the sultan; the three renegades then attached themselves to the circle of Mesih (or Misac) Pasha, yet another Greek renegade, with ties to the imperial family of the Palaeologi. What exactly Mesih's relationship to the last imperial family was has been an annoying problem for scholars (e.g. *PL* 2: 348, n. 8: "I do not know what relation Mesih Pasha was in fact to the imperial family." Cecil Torr, *Rhodes in Modern Times* (Cambridge, 1887), thinks he was the 'son of the last despot of the Morea and nephew of the last emperor of Constantinople,' which seems unlikely . . ."). Mesih Pasha seems now to have been finally identified with a certain Doukas Palaeologus Megethos from Mistra, on the strength of a note in a silver bull from the reign

IV.   Exactis itaque his in oriundis suadendisque annis tribus, tandem res bassae placuit. Profuit ad id inducendum apostatarum plurimorum, qui fidem abnega<ve>runt, iniquitas, qui perversorum suasus proba<ve>runt. Asserebat proditor Antonius urbem, nonnullis locis veteribus, muris vetustate collapsis, facile inimico patere ac paucos cives defensoresque adesse et plerumque commeatuum triticique penuria laborare; subsidia quoque a longinquis regionibus Rhodiis ex<s>pectare, quae tempori adesse non poterunt. Idem testatur Demetrius; id quoque sequaces astipulantur. His iactis fundamentis suadebant facinus aggredi oportere.

4. After three years of debate and arguments had passed, the pasha finally agreed to the proposed undertaking. The perverse character of numerous renegades who had rejected their faith and approved the favorable arguments of the wretches proved instrumental. Antonios, the traitor, maintained that the city, which was in a dilapidated condition with its ancient walls in ruins, would prove an easy prey to an enemy, that there were few citizens and defenders present, and that for the most part it would suffer through lack of food and grain; in addition, the assistance expected by the Rhodians to come from distant places could not arrive in time. Identical was the testimony of Demetrios; their sycophantic associates went along also. With these fundamental assumptions they persuaded him to embark upon this project.

....
of Constantine XI Palaeologus: Ἄνωθεν προσθήκη: Κῦρ Θωμᾶς Πυρόπουλος εἶχεν γυναῖκα τὴν ἀδελφὴν τοῦ Μισιχπασιᾶ τοῦ Δούκα Παλαιολόγου Μέγεθου ἐκ τὸν Μυζηθρᾶν. For the entire document and a translation into English, see Marios Philippides, *Constantine XI Dragaš Palaeologus: A Biography of the Last Greek Emperor*, forthcoming, Appendix II. On Pyropoulos and his connections with the Greco-Italian Spandugnino family, see Klaus-Peter Matschke, "Zum Anteil der Byzantiner und der Bergbauentwicklung Südosteuropas im 14. und 15. Jahrhundert," *BZ* 84/85 (1991/1992): 49–71. esp. 67, n. 120; idem, "The Notaras Family and Its Italian Connections," 71–72, n. 75; and Kharalambos Bouras, "Τὸ Ἐπιτύμβιο τοῦ Λουκᾶ Σπαντούνη στὴ Βασιλικὴ τοῦ Ἁγίου Δημητρίου Θεσσαλονίκης," in *Η Ἐπιστημονικὴ Ἐπετηρὶς τῆς Πολυτεχνικῆς Σχολῆς. Τμῆμα Ἀρχιτεκτόνων* 6 (1973): 1–63. During the war with Venice, Mesih had been involved in a strange incident, as he had offered for a price to surrender the Ottoman fleet and the Dardanelles to the Venetians, who, however, thought that his price was too high and had turned down his offer. Apparently, Mesih had ambitions to become the lord of the Morea; see *MCT*, 290. The anonymous author of the Barberini Chronicle III also speaks of these events and persons but has slightly changed the names, 120: Καὶ ἔβαλε εἰς τὴν ἀρμάδα καπετὰν πασᾶ τὸν Παλαιολόγο, τραχτικὸν ἄνθρωπον, Τοῦρκον. Καὶ ἐδιάβησαν εἰς τὸν σουλτάνο ἕνας Δημήτριος Ὀθωνίας καὶ ὁ Ἀντώνιος Μελιγάμπος, ἐκάμανε ἀθιβολὴ τὴν Ρόδο καὶ τὴν ἐδώσανε τοῦ σουλτὰν Μεχεμέτη ὅτι: "Ἂν θέλῃς νὰ πάρῃς τὴν Ρόδο, ἀπὸ τὸν τάδε τόπον παίρνεται." Καὶ ἔστερξε ὁ σουλτάνος καὶ τοὺς ἐτίμησε τοὺς δημηγέρτες, οἱ ὁποῖοι ἤτανε ὁ ἕνας ἀπὸ τὴν Ρόδο καὶ ὁ ἄλλος ἀπὸ τὴν Ἔγριπον. During the siege a number of Christian renegades defected from the Ottoman camp and were admitted into Rhodes. It was never easy for the Knights to separate the genuine defectors from the "plants" and double agents that were sent into Rhodes by the Ottoman high command. Among the renegades was the German engineer of the sultan. His name was Meister Georg of Saxony but his last name is variously recorded in contemporary texts as Frapan, Frapant, Frepand, and in Latinized form *Frapanus*. There is no doubt that the two had carried out intelligence work for the Porte in the days before the siege but their maps and plans of the fortifications were outdated by the time the Ottoman expedition set sail. See Brockman, *The Two Sieges of Rhodes*, 63; *SOC*, 127; and *MCT*, 397. The Knights had also availed themselves of the services of individuals with questionable background. There is evidence to suggest that the "Langues d'Espaigne" in particular had recruited a number of condemned criminals who had their sentences commuted provided that they defended Rhodes. After the siege d'Aubusson wrote two letters asking Isabella of Castille to pardon Fernando de Vergonde and Pedro Pignera, in view of their services during the siege; for details cf. *PL* 2: 362.

V.   Dum haec Byzantii agitarentur, Rhodiorum clarissimus princeps et magister Petrus Daubus<s>on, vir quidem magno excellentique ingenio ac prudentia, illustri familia apud Galliam Celticam natus, quem ea non latebant, divino instinctu ductus vetustiora urbis loca delapsa et minus munita toto triennio magnifice erexit, munivit, ampliavit excogitavitque frumenti vim magnam et commeatuum copiam comparare religiososque ac mercenarios milites accire, quo urbem tueretur. Pro quibus // devehendis et conducendis epistolas mandatorias ad diversas orbis provincias destinavit. Ita, nutu Dei et magistri opera, civitas munitur, commeatus comparantur; naves, milites ad tuitionem accedunt.

VI.   Proditor Antonius, horum inscius, arbitratus omnia negligentius apud Rhodios praeteriri, instigat bassam ut properet et rem memoratu dignam aggrediatur. Id ipsum suadere conatur Demetrius. Quo effectum est ut bassa ad Turcum ea ex ordine referret. Saepius quoque inter Turci satellites re agitata de Rhodiae urbis expugnatione consultatur. De qua varia oritur sententia. Quibusdam asserentibus rem penitus inanem esse, ne id posse facile consequi

5. While these developments were taking place in Byzantium [= Constantinople], the most glorious lord and Grand Master [of the Knights of Saint John], Pierre d'Aubusson, a highly talented and most resourceful man, who had been born to a noble family in France,[5] kept a watchful eye on the situation; inspired by divine guidance, in the space of only three years he splendidly erected, fortified, and enlarged the older sections of the city, which had collapsed and were rather weak, further sought out means to acquire a large quantity of grain, and also summoned the knights of the order and mercenaries to defend the city. Accordingly, he dispatched letters to all the different parts of the world. And so, with the will of God and the efforts of the Grand Master, the town was fortified, provisions were collected, and ships and soldiers came to see to the defense.

6. Antonios, the traitor, was unaware of these events and was under the impression that the Rhodians were not being careful; he urged the pasha to make haste and embark upon an undertaking that would secure for him a place in the annals of memory. Demetrios also pressed him to do so. Consequently, the pasha brought this matter to the Turkish tyrant [sultan]. The matter of the siege of Rhodes had been often raised and debated by the servile ministers of the Turk but there had been no agreement; some had declared that it was of no importance and that the conquest would not be feasible, on account of the city's

---

[5] Pierre d'Aubusson was born in La Marche, his family's estate, in 1423; the family had been nobles, semi-independent seigneurs, controlling their estates from their capital Guéret. His first military action was with Louis XI, who, as the dauphin, had campaigned against the Swiss in 1444; he had also served with Charles VII before he came to Rhodes and joined the langue of Auvergne. After the fall of Constantinople, which alarmed the Knights greatly, he was sent by the Grand Master, Jean de Lastic, to Europe to seek aid for the Order. His efforts brought 100,000 *scudi* from Charles VII to Rhodes, a sum that was much needed. Under the orders of de Lastic's successor, d'Aubusson defended the island of Cos (1457). Through his efforts and advice, and at the expense of Duke Philip of Burgundy, the knights built Fort St. Nicholas to secure the main harbor; this fort was destined to play an important part in the siege. It was under the Italian Orsini that d'Aubusson began a serious renovation of the defenses and the moat. In 1470 he had commanded the ships that the order had sent to aid Negroponte against the Turkish siege. As Orsini's health was failing, a great deal of responsibility fell on the shoulders of d'Aubusson, who pressed on with the renovation of the fortifications, supervising the construction of new towers and preparing a boom for the chain that would protect the commercial harbor from the Turkish armada, a project similar to the one that Venetians had carried out during the siege of Constantinople in 1453. He was elected to the post of Grand Master at Orsini's death. The most detailed biography of d'Aubusson remains that of Père Dominique Bouhours, S.J., *Histoire de Pierre D'Abusson Grand-Maistre de Rhodes* (Paris, 1676); it has been translated into modern Greek by P. Boutsina, with handsome illustrations and some *marginalia*, under the title *Pierre d'Aubusson: Μεγάλος Μαγίστρος της Ρόδου Πολιορκία 1480–'Αλωση 1522* (Athens, 1996). This biography by Bouhours was commissioned, in all probability, by François d'Aubusson, the bishop of Embrun (to whom it is dedicated). On the composition of this work, see G. Rossignol, *Pierre d'Aubusson, ... le bouclier de la chrétienté, ... Les Hospitaliers à Rhodes* (Paris, 1991), 36 ff.

ob urbis magnificentiam et militum generositatem, qui Asiaticis pares censeri non debent, quibus mortem potius oppetere quam aliquid turpiter imbecilleque agere animo est. Aliis rem facile causis assertis affirmantibus nec tam parvo tempore quibusvis magistrum providisse; quare, si cum celeritate et diligentia exercitus maritimus atque terrestris comparetur, urbem haud dubio expugnatum iri putant.

VII.   Accersiuntur ad hanc consultationem diffiniendam machinarum viri periti; inter quos numeratus est Georgius, vir vafro et subtilique ingenio, qui ex Chiis ad Turcum dudum defecerat Constantinopolique quoque degens uxorem et liberos nutriebat, a Turco dilectus et plurimis gratiis dotatus. // Is aliquandam Rhodi fuerat urbemque tabula designaverat sed tunc non tam munita fuit; praeterierant na<n>que anni viginti ab eo tempore quo eam viderat. Descripserunt et Turci iussu plures egregii artifices Rhodiae urbis situm sed Georgius cunctos superavit.

VIII.   Magnis itaque rationibus adductis vicit tandem sententia ut urbis oppugnatio magna vi fieret, hoc fundamento inhaerentes nullos tam crassos mures esse, qui machinarum impetu demoliri non queant magnamque Turci esse potentiam, qui duo imperia, duodecim regna, tot provincias totque urbes subegit. Hostem quoque non parum movit Rhodiae urbis situs ad comparandas classes aptissimus insulaeque celebritas magnis laudibus ab antiquis praedicata quam ob loci magnificentiam, aeris salubritatem et ad Orientis provincias subigendas commoditatem. Potentes quondam Romani benevolam et sibi amicam reddidere putatque si hanc potitus fuerit, finitimis subactis ditionibus, fines suos per Aegeum Ioniumque pelagus facile perlaturum. Resistentibus itaque quibusdam bassis atque in sinistrum praesagientibus, classis instauratur exercitusque comparatur. Decretum est ut milites terrestre iter faciant traiectoque Hellesponto per Asiam in Lyciam (quae Rhodiorum insulae adiacet) pergant et per fretum Lycium a Phisco antiqua continentis civitate duodeviginti mil<l>ibus passuum distante Rhodium navigent; reliquos vero machinarum et belli // ingeniorum apparatus cum parte copia<r>um classe devehi<an>t.

IX.   Bassa Palaeologus expeditionis praefectus classem conscendens Antonium perquiri iubet, quem paulo ante morte turpiter obiisse comperit. Arcessito igitur Demetrio satellitem adhibet. Tunc passim rumor exiit classem et copiosum exercitum Rhodios parari. Turcus, ut haec res nos lateret, aditus portus passus custodit prohibitque ne quis nuntium deferat; sed non valuit eius astutia magistri solertiam prohibere, qui assidue litteris et nuntiis ex Turcia apparatum intellegit. Nonnulli quoque ex nuntiis in dolo versati sunt; nam cum exercitus in Lycia degeret classem operientes affirma<ve>runt vita excessisse et aliis ex

magnificence and the bravery of the Knights, who should not be thought an equal match for their Asiatic counterpart, since they preferred death over shame and cowardice. Others presented arguments and claimed that the Grand Master could not have taken adequate measures in such short time and they thought that, if the naval and land forces were to be mustered quickly and carefully, the city would undoubtedly be conquered.

7. Three men, experts in artillery, were summoned to conclude the deliberations; among them was George, a man of vain yet sharp intellect, who had, a long time ago, defected to the Turk from Chios; he now made Constantinople his home and had a wife and children to care for; he was valued and was loaded with marks of distinction by the Turk. This man had been to Rhodes long ago and had made a sketch of the city, which had not been heavily fortified back then. Twenty years had passed since he had seen it. Many other expert engineers had provided descriptions by order of the Turk, but George surpassed them all.

8. After weighty arguments were heard, it was finally decided to conquer our city with great force, under the basic assumption that there existed no walls so thick to be able to withstand the impact of cannon [projectiles] and that the power of the Turk, who had subjugated two empires, twelve kingdoms, and so many provinces and cities, was great. The enemy was equally attracted by the geographical position of the city of Rhodes, well-suited for equipping armadas, by the fame of the island, sung in great praises by the ancients on account of its magnificence, by its healthy air, and by its suitability to bring the eastern provinces to submission. Long ago the powerful Romans had courted her good will and won her friendship. So he thought that, if he assumed control of her, with her neighbors already under his command, he would easily extend his own borders through the Aegean and the Ionian Seas. Even though some pashas remained unconvinced and were predicting a bad turn of events, an armada was prepared and the army assembled. It was decided that the soldiers would make their way over land, would cross the Hellespont into Asia and reach Lycia (which is adjacent to the island of Rhodes); from Phiskos (an ancient town, eighteen miles away) they would then sail through the Lycian straits to Rhodes. The artillery and the other war engines would be ferried, together with a part of the army, by the armada.

9. As he was about to embark, Pasha Palaeologus, the commander of the expedition, issued an order to locate Antonios, who, he discovered, had died in shame a little earlier. And so he summoned Demetrios, who became his associate. Then a rumor spread far and wide, that the Rhodians were preparing an armada and an enormous army. So that we might not discover the truth, the Turk closed under guard the approach to his harbor to prevent anyone from sending a message. His cunning was no match for the talents of our Grand Master, who was kept informed of the developments by a barrage of letters and by messengers from Turkey. In addition, some of the messengers were skilled in deception: once the army reached Lycia, those working in the armada maintained that he had

causis exercitum illic adesse. Dum hic rerum status esset, summa cura princeps noster hostium dolos acute prospiciens cuncta disponit et de praesidiis Langonis, castelli Sancti Petri, Pheracli, Lindi, Monolithi ordinat, quae loca defensoribus, commeatibus, machinis et ceteris bello aptis muniuntur. Omnis plebs cum supellectili Rhodum et oppida intrat; hordei quod maturum fuit colligitur quantocius. Frumentum crudum (non dum messis tempus aderat), quod urbem circumdabat, prout cuique facultas fuit, populus eradicat, elegit et in domos portat.

X. Dum haec magno cum tumultu agerentur, vigil qui in specula montis qui ad Occidentem vergit sacello Sancti Stephani sacri nuntiat classem apparere extensisque velis navigare. Magna quippe populi frequentia ad hoc spectandum concurrit. Tota civitate trepidatur populique clamore cun//cta resonant. Classis

died and that the army was there for other purposes. In this situation, our lord saw through the tricks of the enemy and arranged everything with the utmost care: he established the garrisons of Lango [= Cos], of the castle of Saint Peter, of Pheraklos, of Lindos, and of Monolithos; all these places were strengthened with defenders, supplies, artillery, and the necessities for war.[6] All the people, with their possessions, came into Rhodes and into the towns. As swiftly as possible, the grain that had matured was harvested; the wheat that was still green (as it was not yet harvest time) around the city was pulled out by the people, was collected, and was carried into houses.[7]

10. In the midst of this great commotion, the sentinel stationed in the holy chapel of Saint Stephen to the west announced that he saw the armada moving under full sail. Large throngs of our people ran out to see the spectacle. The entire town was in confusion and resounded with the noise that people made.

---

[6] The Grand Master's pleas for assistance in the west did not bring forth an outpouring of support for his island in the face of the Turkish menace. Very few knights traveled to Rhodes. The greatest assistance came in the form of financial support from France, whose king, Louis XI, entrusted the funds to d'Aubusson's brother; thus Antoine d'Aubusson brought 2,000 mercenaries to Rhodes in the spring of 1480. The total defending force of Rhodes could not have exceeded 600–700 knights and men-at-arms (regular members of the Order) and Antoine's mercenary regiments; to these we must add the local inhabitants, who assisted greatly in the defense of the walls. For a lower estimate of the defending forces, cf. Brockman, *The Two Sieges*, 65. In addition, the knights had the services of Johann Berger of Nordlingen, an experienced gunsmith, who was enrolled for life in the Order in May of 1480 (see *PL* 2: 350, and n. 15 for documentation): "Considerantes igitur vestram in rebus bellicis experienciam presertim circa tormentorum seu machinarum vulgo nuncupatorum bombardarum et culvinarum usum artemque propriam"). During the spring the Grand Master had made preparations for the expected attack, by securing the castle at Kos [= Lango] and at Halikarnassos, ten miles away on the Asiatic shore. In addition, he had fortified the coast fortress of Pheraklos [= Feraclo], Lindos, and Monolithos in Rhodes. However, he had been forced to abandon the castle on Mount Phileremos [= Fileremo] with the Church dedicated to the Virgin Mary; this chapel was the successor to an ancient shrine dedicated to another divine virgin, the ancient goddess Athena, whose temple stood in the immediate vicinity. D'Aubusson, however, ensured that the icon of the Virgin, reputed to be miraculous, had been brought to the city to assist in the defense against the infidel. The icon accompanied the knights to their new home in Malta, when Rhodes was finally surrendered to Suleyman the Magnificent in 1523, and eventually found its way to Russia in 1799. See *PL* 2: 349–50.

[7] Caoursin has neglected to treat the preliminary hostile action, which had broken out in the winter of 1479/1480, when Mesih Pasha had attempted to establish a base in Rhodes by landing a party of raiders on the northern coast near the fortress of Phanes [= Fane]; his raiders moved inland but his approach had been detected and the population had sought shelter in the various local fortresses. The raiders were attacked by the grand prior of Brandenburg and were forced back to their ships; Mesih then attacked the island of Telos but the knights fought back and the Turks retreated with heavy losses; the raiding party then moved to Phiskos [= Marmara Limani, see next note]. For these events, see Bosio, *Dell'Istoria*, 317–19; Bouhours, *Histoire de Pierre D'Abusson* (1806 ed.), 84–86; *PL* 2: 348–49; Brockman, *The Two Sieges*, 64; and *MCT*, 382.

Phiscum navigare properat ut milites qui terrestre iter fecerant conscendant et Rhodiorum freto transito repente velis conversis ad nostra declinat littora. Appulit itaque ea classis velorum centum decimo Kalendas Iunii, anno incarnationis Verbi Divini MCCCCLXXX, militeque in terra exposito. Primum in vertice montis Sancti Stephani et circa eius montis colles castrametati sunt. Machinas quoque et bellica ingenia in littus exonerant eo in loco, quem ab ipso monte defluens fons abluit, qui a Rhodiis obice collis spectari non potuit. His peractis pars classis ad devehendum terrestrem exercitum Phiscum navigat. In classis adventu quidam Turci equestres pedestresque versus urbis moenia audacia quadam freti irruunt. Eruptione autem a nostris facta hostes fugantur, funduntur; quidam quoque ex eis trucidantur. Postea, dum nostri commensarentur, altera eruptione facta, Turci propelluntur caduntque nonnulli. Ex nostris vero miles unus periit, qui incautius manum conserebat, cuius spolia et cadaver nostri sibi vendicant. Turci, capite abscisso, illud lancea suffigunt; ad suos quoque cum plausu revertunt.

XI.   Postridie eius diei qua classis appulit, hostis tres ingentes machinas in hortis ecclesiae Sancti Antonii, vicinis arboribus omnis generis fructuum consitis, collocat; turrim quoque Sancto Nicolao dicatam in vertice molis sitam oppugnare conant aerisque machinas lignearum munitionum // propugnaculis operiuntur

The armada hastened to Phiskos[8] to take on board the troops that had made their way over land, and then changed course, transversed the Rhodian straits under full sail, and headed for our shores. And so that armada of one hundred ships arrived and the troops disembarked ten days before the Calends of June [= May 23], in the year 1480 after the incarnation of the Divine Word. First of all they made camp on the top of Mount Saint Stephen and around the neighboring hills. They also unloaded their artillery on a spot washed by the waters of a spring flowing down from the same mountain; blocked by a hill, it could not be seen even from the highest point of [the city of] Rhodes. After these activities the armada sailed to Phiskos to bring the land forces. With the arrival of the armada some Turkish horsemen and infantrymen, armed with audacity, attacked the walls of the city. Our side made a sortie, put the enemy to flight, and chased him away; some of them were slaughtered. Later, while our side was eating supper, there was another skirmish and the Turks were repelled with some casualties; from our side a knight was killed, who had rather carelessly gone into combat; our side recovered his corpse and his weapons. The Turks had cut his head off and placed it on a lance; to the sound of applause they returned to their side.

11.   On the day following the arrival of the armada the enemy deployed three enormous cannons in the gardens of the Church of Saint Anthony, whose neighborhood had been planted with trees bearing all sorts of fruit; they tried to attack the tower named after Saint Nicholas, situated at the very end of the quay;[9] they operated and protected their wooden engines and bronze cannon

---

[8] Phiskos, Physkos, or Fisco, the ancient Lycian Limyra, is situated on the shores of Asia Minor across from Rhodes. It is further known as Marmara/Marmaris and as the bay of Phenike. The chapel of Saint Stephen is the acropolis of the ancient city of Rhodes; this site became the headquarters of Mesih Pasha (and was destined again to be the encampment of the Ottoman invasion force in 1522).

[9] The Tower, or Fort, of Saint Nicholas had been erected by the Grand Master Pedro Ramon Zacosta in 1455. Its successor still stands, clearly dominating and protecting the entire harbor of Rhodes, which was later known as the Port of Commerce. The fortifications of Rhodes were in good order to withstand the siege. Fort Saint Nicholas became the focal point of the Turkish attacks and bore the brunt of the Ottoman bombardment. The overall strategy of Mesih Pasha is clear at this point: he wished to assumed control of the harbor, imitating the actions of Mehmed II during the siege of Constantinople in 1453; after Mehmed had assumed control of the Golden Horn the defenders could no longer hold out as they had to resist assaults from two sides. If Mesih Pasha assumed control of the Mandraki, the forces of the defenders would have to be thinned out and the Turks would have a better chance in their attacks against the land walls. After the siege was lifted the Grand Master observed that the Fort had been almost demolished after the impact of about three hundred missiles. The commencement of hostilities was reported in d'Aubusson's 1480 encyclical ("datum Rhodi in nostro conventu die XXVIII mensis Maii"); see *PL* 2: 350–51, n. 17: "Itaque nuper ingenti classe velorum CLX vel circiter parata contractisque undique copiis ex provinciis Rhodo vicinis quas ex continenti terraque firma devexit traicitque insulam nostram, Rhodiorum agros ac urbem nostram potenti

defenduntque. Nostri vero munimentis (quae repara vocantur) conspectis, tria tormenta (quae bombardae vocantur) ad hostium dextera in hortuculo palatii militum Averniorum statuunt. Eiusque diei diluculo Georgius machinarum egregius artifex — de quo supra habitus est sermo — repente ad fossae ripam, quae magistri palatium munit, visus est. Amice omnes salutans clamitansque ut introducatur ab rerum ignaris paene confoditur, defenditur ab aliis exemploque ad magistrum producitur. Vir enim erat corpore procero, forma eleganti, satis eloquentiae, magna astutia, cui Germania patria est. Rogatus de causa adventus respondit caelo fidei compulsus et publico Christianae religionis commodo suasus ad nostros defecisse. Placide excipitur laudaturque propositum, si in eo persistat. De hostis exercitusque habitu, dispositione, qualitate consultus, constanter, prudenter intrepideque respondit: inter cetera edocet numerum militum omnis generis centum mil<l>ia vel circiter adesse, classem eam (quam diximus), machinas sexdecim ingentes devexisse, quarum longitudinis dimensio palmorum duorum et viginti fertur, quae vehementissimo, velocissimoque iactu globos saxeos rotunditatis palmorum novem plerosque undecim torquent. De huius viri defectione variae quidem sententiae suboriuntur. Quidam exploratorem affirmabant et fugam commento asservisse ut Rhodios fallat. Nonnullorum assertio // fuit eum callidum et maleficum virum esse multaque olim effinxisse. Quibusdam aliis sentientibus et in bonam partem defectionem interpretantibus cumque prudens esset et poenitens errati, id fecerit lapideque intelligeret haec Rhodiis machinari non posse, ubi tam prudentem principem et expertissimos milites intelligit degere. Augent suspiciones epistolae ex castris inimicorum in civitatem missae quae Georgium insimulant et ab eo cavendum esse dictitant. Magister ingenio solers et perspicax Georgium arcta custodia servari iubet sex robustissimis comitibus adhibitis in his quae machinarum iactum et belli ingenia spectant ipsius arte caute utitur.

XII.   Omni igitur conatu Turci ad expugnationem turris et molis Sancti Nicolai incumbunt. Si huius potiantur, putant urbem in suam potestatem facile

with covers. Our side saw their fortifications (called "defenses") and deployed three cannon (called "bombards") in the small garden of the Knights from Auvergne. At dawn that day George,[10] the expert manufacturer of cannon (of whom mention has been made earlier) suddenly appeared at the bank of the moat that fortifies the palace our Grand Master. He greeted everyone amiably and asked to be taken to our Grand Master. He was an impressive man, elegant, sufficiently eloquent, very talented, whose homeland was Germany. He was asked why he had come and answered that his faith in the divine and in the public good of the Christian faith made him defect to our side. He was received in peace and his motives were praised, especially if they persisted in his heart. He provided reasonable, credible, and fearless answers when he was consulted about our enemy's equipment, deployment, and quality; among other things he revealed that their total number was about one hundred thousand, that their aforementioned armada had transported sixteen enormous cannon measuring eighteen palms in length, it was believed, which fired, with immense force, round stone projectiles of nine palms (but most measured eleven). In regard to his defection there were various opinions. Some claimed that he was a spy and maintained that he had faked his defection to deceive the Rhodians. Others suggested that he was a clever man but malevolent who had formulated this plan a long time ago. Yet others believed his defection to be sincere and felt that he was a prudent man who had come to regret the error of his ways and had come to realize that he could not intrigue against the Rhodians, when he saw that they were led by such a prudent prince and were themselves such experienced knights. The suspicions were magnified by letters, which were sent to our city from the camp of the enemy, which charged George with treason and urged us to keep an eye on him and his activities. Our Grand Master, with his sharpness and common sense, ordered six very strong individuals to accompany and guard George to keep an eye on the way he used his skill in regard to his cannon trajectories and his war engines.

12.   The Turks proceeded with a strenuous attack[11] upon the tower and quay of Saint Nicholas; after its capture, they reckoned, the city would easily

---

manu X Kal. Iunii aggressus est, obsedit et circumdat. Comportavit ad urbem nostram oppugnandam tormentorum, machinarum, bombardarum lignearumque turrium ingeniorum bello aptorum grandem numerum suntque in castro in nos collocatis hostes circiter LXX^m qui non assiduis insultibus petunt, invadunt, obpugnant."

[10] On Meister Georg of Saxony, see above, n. 4. There were numerous defectors to the Christian cause but all were viewed with suspicion by the Knights, especially by the Grand Master. Cf. the summary in *SOC* (which is largely based on Caoursin), 127–28. After the siege was over about sixty defectors were shipped by the Knights to Rome so that the inquisition might make inquiries and separate the sincere individuals from the Ottoman spies. Cf. *PL* 2: 355.

[11] Our sources do not specify a date for the first assault upon Fort Saint Nicholas. We know that the Ottoman fleet arrived on May 23; if one week is allowed for the encampment and the deployment of artillery, bombardment could have commenced early in June. By the beginning of the second week of June the Turks would have been ready to launch their first attack.

venturam. Est enim moles ipsa trecentorum circiter passuum in mare protensa miro artificio ab antiquis manufacta, quae suo progressu portum triremibus aptum a parte Occidentis efficit, cuius introitus cautibus concluditur ut triremis introire vix possit. In molis quidem vertice Septentrionem spectante arx (de qua sermo est), magnifice nostra aetate erecta est, ubi priscis temporibus Colossus ille ingens Rhodius, unus de septem mirabilibus mundi, positus erat, qui, post tres et quinquaginta annos quo structus est, terrae motus corruit osque portus Rhodii spectat. // A machinis quoque illic collocatis sublimes quidem turres quae portum claudunt valide oppugnari ac dirui naves quoque ne portum subeant, prohiberi haud difficile possunt. Loci igitur et turris opportunitate hostis allectus omni conatu arcem aggreditur, quatit, oppugnat iactuque trecentorum lapidum sphaericorum diruit eam praesertim partem quae Occidentem spectat. Ruina quidem turrim munit; licet enim suo pondere ictuumque vehementia saxa ingentia ex quibus aedificata erat laberentur, tamen materia calce harena et lapillis immixtis confecta adeo demoliri non potuit quin turris potior pars staret, ex quo facilis ascensus hosti negatur. Terrori fuit tanti aedificii lapsus. Multorum enim annorum opus illustre temporis momento ruit; praeter quoque plurimorum opinionem ingentes et impetuosae machinae illam arcem lacerant, deturpant, devastant. Cum autem turris labefacta vix vitabilis videretur, statuit magister industria, ingenio, vigilantia roboreque militum eam arcem tutari, quae murorum crassitudine defendi non potuit. Adhibitis viribus summa cura parantur quae turri et moli praesidio sunt. Milites igitur in primis strenuissimi deliguntur, qui locum defendant vallumque ex lignis efficitur, quod turrim claudat fossamque cautibus excisis circumducunt. Collocatur in turri praesidium validum pro loci capacitate. // Turris nanque iussu magistri qui assiduo cogitatu tuitioni loci invigilans non formidat, cymba vectus diruptam arcem inscius, dum machinae lapides torquerent, calce et lapide oppletur ut locus vix commilitonum

succumb. The quay itself measures about three hundred steps and extends into the sea; it had been built by the ancients with admirable skill to create a harbor in the west, suitable for triremes; its entrance is so small that it hardly accommodates a single galley. At the very end of the quay (towards the north) there stands the aforementioned fort, which was magnificently erected in our own age on the very spot occupied by the famous, enormous Colossus (one of the world's Seven Wonders) in antiquity; an earthquake brought it down five hundred and three years after its construction and its watch over the harbor of Rhodes.[12] The artillery placed on the lofty towers that enclosed the harbor bombarded and scattered the ships, easily denying them entrance. Attracted by the advantageous position of the area and the tower, the enemy strenuously attacked, shook, and pounded the fort with a bombardment of three hundred round stone projectiles, and reduced the western part to rubble. Although the heavy impact brought down the enormous stones that had been used in its construction, nevertheless the mixture of gravel, sand, and pebbles could not be demolished; on the contrary, a section of the tower stood firmer and denied easy access to the enemy. The collapse of such a structure caused terror. In one moment the famous work that took so many years to accomplish was demolished. Contrary to the expectation of numerous individuals, those enormous, powerful cannon devastated, damaged, and wrought havoc upon the fort. When the collapse of the tower appeared imminent, our Grand Master determined to defend that fort with the energy, cleverness, talent, vigilance, and might of the knights, as it could no longer be defended by the thickness of its walls. With the greatest care a strong band was put together to defend the tower and the quay. The strongest of our knights were chosen to defend the place; they constructed a stockade, which enclosed the tower and surrounded the moat with sharp rocks. The tower was manned with a strong garrison, as many men as there was room. So there was no fear for the tower, which was defended energetically and thoughtfully by order of our Grand Master; he was not aware of the collapse of the fort and he came over in a boat; while the cannon fired their stone projectiles, they filled the area with gravel and rocks so that the place could not accommodate more comrades

---

[12] All contemporary sources that deal with the siege devote a few passages to the antiquities of Rhodes. This interest in the past is yet another indication of the humanistic interest that has begun to pervade the southern Europeans at this time. Even later Dominique Bouhours, in his 1676 *Histoire de Pierre d'Aubusson Grand-Maistre de Rhodes*, begins the third book of his narrative with a digression on Rhodes's past. Yet Caoursin is wrong to think of the Colossus as standing on the quay of Fort Saint Nicholas. The statue probably stood further back on what is now the shore of the harbor, the Mandraki. On the other hand the misconception that the Colossus stood on the quay has persisted, along with the erroneous notion, so popular in the Renaissance, that the ancient wonder straddled the entrance of the harbor. As late as the past decade divers announced that pieces of the Colossus were located on the bottom of the sea near Fort Saint Nicholas. Of course there was no truth to these stories, but such wishful thinking did capture the popular imagination and the story was sustained for some time in the local press.

capax reddatur. Constituit et aliud praesidium equestrium et pedestrium in antemurali, quod a turri Sancti Petri ad inferiorem Mandracii partem protenditur, qui transitum Turcis prohibeant. Humile nanque mare et vadosum illic transiri potest, ubi et vegetum munitiones paratae et tabulae clavorum infixione infestae in profundo fixae sunt, quae impedimento hosti vadenti. In vallo autem radicis molis milites electissimi locati sunt, qui pugnantibus nostris praesidio sunt, ubi magister insignis armis auroque fulgens facinori clarissimo intendebat. Disponuntur ea parte murorum urbis bombardae et tormenta quae triremes et Turcorum navigia expugnent perfrigantque; prope quoque cautes eius arcis cymbae combustibilibus oppletae stationem habent, quae in oppugnatione incendantur et hostium classi incendium afferant. His rebus magno subtilique ingenio dispositis fiunt vigiliae; praestolatur hostium invasio.

XIII. Demum exhorto Lucifero, dum Zephyri placide flarent, Turcorum triremes a littore cautium montis Stephani solvunt superatoque Saburrae promontorio navigant eamque turrim propugnant. Primo congressu, antequam in terram // descendatur, ingenti clamore et tympanorum sono voces edunt ut terrori multitudo sit. Nostri autem in armis dispositi praesto adsunt. Cum enim triremes turrim propugnant, machinae saxa iaciunt. Praesidium quod in turri locatum erat armorum vi, balistis iactuque lapidum hostem propulsat. Pelluntur Turci, fugantur, trucidantur. Ea in pugna (quemadmodum postea a perfugis relatum est) septingenti Turci interiere, multi vulnerati, quidam desiderati. Victoria potitus princeps insigni equo vectus illustri comitatus phalange urbem more triumphantis intrat sacellumque <in> quo imago sacratissimae Virginis Philer<e>mi montis miraculis percelebris posita erat visitans gratias agit et demum ad restaurandos animos militum domum revertitur. Perdita tunc spe

in arms. He also placed another garrison of horsemen and foot soldiers in the outer wall, which extended from the tower of Saint Peter to the inner section of the Mandrakion, to deny passage to the Turks; there the sea was low and one could wade across, but defense works were put together and planks studded with nails had been fixed on the bottom to impede the approach of the enemy. In the stockade, however, at the root of the quay our outstanding knights were stationed to protect our fighters; at this spot our Grand Master, visible in armor shining with gold, watched over the most glorious work. In this section of the city walls bombards and artillery pieces were deployed to attack and destroy the galleys and vessels of the Turks; near the rocks of that fort boats loaded with combustible material were stationed, to be set afire during the battle and burn the enemy's armada. And so the guards were deployed with great and expert skill; the enemy prepared his assault.

13.   Finally, as Lucifer rose and westerly breezes blew softly,[13] the galleys of the Turks left the shore by Mount Saint Stephen, passed the promontory of Saburra, and attacked the tower. During the initial approach, before they landed, they cried out loudly and beat their drums to inspire terror in our multitudes. Our soldiers, however, were ready in arms. When the galleys began the attack upon the tower, the cannon spewed forth their stone projectiles. The garrison in the tower repelled the enemy with force of arms, catapults, and the impact of stone projectiles. The Turks were pushed back, put to flight, and slaughtered. In this battle (as we were subsequently told by the deserters) seven hundred Turks perished; there were many wounded and some missing. On horseback our victorious leader, accompanied by a notable cohort, entered the city in triumph, and paid a visit to the chapel in which the icon of the most sacred Virgin of Phileremos, the Mount of the famous miracles, had been deposited; he gave thanks and returned home to raise the morale of the soldiers.[14] After the Turks lost hope of

---

[13] This second major assault was launched on the night of June 10 and lasted well into the next day. By late morning they were forced to withdraw. At this point the Ottoman command had to reconsider its plans, as it became evident that the fort could not be taken. Mesih Pasha then decided to concentrate his efforts on the land side and attack the formidable fortifications of the Knights. See Ernle Bradford, *The Knights of the Order* (New York, 1972), chap. 13.

[14] The eyewitness and participant in the defense, Mary Dupuis (in de Vertot, *Histoire des Chevaliers*, II: 608) states: "a Dieu et a Nostre Dame de Philerme et a Monseigneur saint Jehan Baptiste, de la grace que Dieu leur fasoit de obtenir victoire a lecontre de leurs enemis." Also see *PL* 2: 354. The Knights' Church of Our Lady of Phileremos (*domina omnium gratiarum/ Madonna di Tutte le Grazie*), near the classical remains of the Acropolis of Ialysos and next to an ancient temple of Athena, was restored in 1931 and was even given a tower; nearby is a castle of the Knights, in a dilapidated condition. The entire area was thickly settled from Mycenaean times onwards. The chapel of the Knights housed a miraculous icon of the Virgin. After the fall of Rhodes to the Turks in 1523, this icon was taken by the Knights to Malta and then was taken to Russia in 1799 when Czar Paul I became the Grand Master (see above, n. 6). During the siege of 1480 this icon was paraded on the walls. For this story of the image and its connection with pagan antiquity, see *PL* 2: 349–50.

arcis molisque potiundae visoque valido praesidio Turci grandioribus viribus arcem aggredi aliaque loca oppugnare, moenia diruere student ut defensoribus distractis uno momento molem et loca dirupta invadant, ne vires nostrorum unitae essent et dum diversas partes tutari cogitaremus negligentius in mole res ageretur. Sequenti igitur nocte magno clamore virorum onera subeuntium cuncta resonant. Machinas ad moenia Hebraeorum revehunt. Ante hos muros octo ingentes machinas collocant, quae munitionibus defensa in moenia // saxa grandia iaciunt. Aliam machinam prope radicem molis, quae Septentrionem vergit, <ei> qui damnati sunt extremo afficiunt supplicio ponuntque in turrim verticis molis molendinorum et molendina supra molis aedificata globos saxeos torquent. Hostium proposito agnito magister solita prudentia cuncta dirigens divinis supplicationibus cum populo et commilitonibus innitens munitiones ad interiora urbis parat. Iudaeorum aedes quae in pomerio erectae erant diruunt. Vallum paratur, fossa cavatur et murus fossae summa arte et diligentia obiicitur. Interdiu noctuque operi intendentur; non magister, nec baiulini, nec priores, non milites, nec cives, nec negotiatores, nec matronae, nec nuptae, nec virgines opere vacant: lapides, terram, calcem portant humeris. Auro, argento suppellectili nec parcitur ut publicae saluti consulatur.

XIV.   Machinae hostium vehementissimo impetu moenia quatiunt et faciem egregiorum lapidum diruunt. Tanta enim erat iactus violentia tormentorum ut omnibus admirationi fuerit nullus quoque Rhodi degens (ubi ex omni natione Latini nominis nonnulli versabantur) compertus est, qui nec affirmaret ullo unquam tempore tales machinas vidisse aut audivisse. Id quoque Georgius perfuga affirmavit et nusquam terrarum tam grandes inveniri asserit. Dum enim saxa sphaerica iaciunt in lapidis exitu sonus ingens editur, qui tonitrui instar resonat fumusque tanquam nubes crassa diuturno tempore in aere vento fertur; quorum // sonus plerumque ab oppidanis castelli Rubei auditus est, quod a Rhodo centum mil<l>ibus passuum Orientem versus distat. Ipsaeque machinae mirabilius quoddam efficiebant. Machinarum posteriora in munitionem, quae palis terrae affixis fabricabatur, tam grandem impetum reddebant ut (instar motus terrae) aedificia urbis paululum hoc impulsu moverentur. Spe igitur moenium tuitione perdita totis viribus, vallo, fossa et munitionibus interioribus tutamen constituimus nec ea hosti sufficiunt. Aggreditur quippe alio terrore vexare urbem: collocat enim omni ex parte tormenta et mortaria quae ex transverso aedificia urbis verberent, diruant mortales quoque conterant et tormenta (mortaria dicta) interdiu noctuque saxa in aera sublime iaciunt. Erat quippe populo ingenti terrori, qui in aere tam grandes globos saxeos conspiciebat. Non enim parvam anxietatem id nostris incussit; plus tamen noctu quam interdiu terroris attulit: nullus in privatis domibus tutus videbatur. Quilibet latebras quaeritabat; verum ei vulneri mens humana medetur. Iussu magistri mulieres, infantes et omnis imbecilis aetas in

taking by force the tower and the quay and after they saw how strong the garrison was, they launched attacks upon other sectors, eager to destroy the walls so that the defenders would focus their attention elsewhere; then, at one specific point, while we would be busy with defense of other places and neglect the quay, they would invade the tower and the ruined sector. And so next night all places were filled with noise made by men toiling. They deployed their artillery against the walls of the Jewish quarter. Before those walls were eight enormous cannon, which fired large stone projectiles against the reinforced walls. Men condemned to death deployed, near the base of the quay (which extends northward), and operated another cannon against the tower at the peak of the quay; they fired stone projectiles against the mills. When our Grand Master realized what they were trying to do, he responded with his customary prudence and with prayers to God; together with the help of the townspeople and his comrades in arms he directed inner defenses to be prepared for our city. The houses of the Jews, built in the defense perimeter, were demolished; a stockade was erected, a ditch was dug, and a wall was thrown over the ditch, built with the utmost skill and care. Night and day did the workers toil; everyone participated: our Grand Master, our baileys, our priors, our knights, the citizens, the merchants, older women, brides, and virgins. They carried stones, soil, and pebbles on their shoulders. Nothing was spared that could be of help to the commonwealth: gold, silver, or possessions.

14. The cannon of the enemy shook our walls with the mighty impact [of the projectiles] and destroyed their outer stone surface. So great was the force of their impact that all the inhabitants of Rhodes (which also hosts a number of Latins) declared that such cannon had never been seen or heard of anywhere. George, the defector, was of the same opinion and asserted that nowhere on earth could such enormous pieces be found. The firing of their round stone projectiles is accompanied by a loud noise like a thunderclap, and by smoke like a thick cloud in daytime which is carried about by the winds. Their roar was heard by most inhabitants of the city of Rubeum one hundred miles away, to the east. The cannon themselves produced miraculous results. The posterior sections of the cannon were protected and were fixed with stakes on the soil; consequently, their recoil shook the earth like an earthquake and made the buildings of our city tremble for a while. When we lost all hope of saving the walls, we decided to build a stockade, a ditch, and an inner fortification with all our strength to impede the enemy, who proceeded to terrorize our city in a different manner: he deployed some engines and mortar pieces to pound the buildings of the city at an angle and to wipe out human beings; day and night the engines called "mortars" fired their stones high up into the air. This caused great terror among the people, who saw the large stone projectiles up in the air. Our side thus became greatly anxious, but the terror was more intense at night than in the day, as no one seemed safe in his own home and sought hiding places. The human mind found a remedy for this affliction. By order of our Grand Master the women, infants, and

pomerio collocatur et crassa trabe protegitur. Ea nanque ingenia raro illic decidat. Ad urbis quippe frequentiora loca diriguntur ut mortales conterant domosque quatiant. Iuvenes vero et robusti qui interdiu saxa suspiciebant tor//menta facile vitabant. Noctu autem quidam caveas subterraneas, quidam valvas crassissimas, quidam fornices et sacras aedes quaerentes sub eis trepidum somnum carpebant. Hoc quoque miraculo fuit nutuque Dei factu<m> esse haud aliter creditur, qui publicis supplicationibus assidue ecclesiis et altaribus exorabatur ut, cum plura saxa machinae torquerent, pauci tamen mortales et quaedam bruta eorum iactu interierunt, quae potius domorum ruina iactu lapidis collaps<o>rumque saxei globi pondere attrita sunt. Hostes quoque id parum arbitrati duas machinas ex grandioribus in eminentiori loco qui ad Hesperum vergit, ex quo urbs prospicitur, collocavit, quae assidue in urbem et loca aedificis frequentiora saxa torquent. Nec ipsae machinae licet terrori essent damnum insigne ediderunt, nec mortales occiderunt, praepeditae (non ambigo) orationibus quae Deo, eius genitrici intemeratae et beato Ioanni Baptistae fiebant.

XV.   Bassa vero principis nostri vigilantiam et ingenium conatibus suis inficere coniectans magistrum dolo interficere aggressus est submissis quibusdam qui defectionis praetextu eum adorirentur. Quo eventu arbitratur rerum facile potiturum hoc quidem nefandum facinus perfuga quidam veneno perficere statuit comite accito qui postridie cum toxico urbem intraret; his perfugis bassa grandia pollicetur <ut> facinus perficiant. Qui prior ingressus est // examini prudentum, ut ceteri<s> subicitur, contrariis sermonibus deprehenditur crimenque ultro pandit monetque ut caveat princeps quia plurimae in eum sunt paratae insidiae. Damnatus perfuga securique percussus interiit. Cum vero sceleris comes venenum gestans ad nos transiret, a quibusdam vix confoditur; unde perterritus ad Turcum revertitur.

those rendered infirm by old age were taken to the defense perimeter and were protected by thick walls, which were seldom hit by this bombardment. Their fire was directed at the more crowded sections in order to kill people and weaken houses. The young and the strong, who could see the cannon in the daytime, easily avoided their projectiles. At night they slept uneasily in basements and sought shelter in well-protected places, covered archways, and churches. That there were few human and animal casualties (crushed by the weight of rubble when houses collapsed and not by the impact of the projectiles), despite the heavy bombardment, was universally counted an undisputed miracle, performed by God's will and effected through incessant public prayer in churches and by the altars. The enemy then transferred two of his heavier cannon to a higher spot in the western sector, from which he could view our city, and initiated a constant bombardment, the projectiles of which fell upon the city and its thickly settled neighborhoods. These cannon did not cause terror and did insignificant damage; they caused no one's death, impeded, no doubt, by our prayers to God, to His pure Mother, and to John the Baptist.

15. Faced with our leader's vigilance and talent, the pasha tried to kill our Grand Master with a trick: some individuals volunteered to fake their defection and eliminate him. In this manner he thought he would achieve his objective; a deserter decided to attempt the horrible crime; he chose an accomplice to bring him the poison, when he would enter the city on the following day. To those deserters the pasha promised important rewards upon their success. When the first one defected we thought it prudent to interrogate him; he was tortured and was caught contradicting himself; he confessed and warned us that they had made many plans against our leader. The deserter was condemned and dispatched with the ax. When his associate in crime came to our side next day, carrying the poison, he was almost killed and in terror returned to the Turk.[15]

---

[15] Bouhours, *Histoire de Pierre D'Abusson*, in Book III, supplies further details on this plot. He claims that one of the assassins was from Dalmatia while the other was Albanian. According to Brockman, *The Two Sieges*, 80, the Dalmatian name's was Gianni and the Albanian Epirote was called Pizzio; they were both men of substance and were even acquainted with Italian humanists. In addition, the two renegades spread alarming information, thus engaging in psychological warfare. They stated that Mehmed II was on his way with reinforcements. This information complicated matters for the knights, as a few Spaniards and Italians were alarmed and formed a conspiracy to surrender the city; when the conspirators attempted to contact a knight by the name of Philelpho (perhaps it should have been cited by Bouhours as "Filelfo"), the plot was revealed to the Grand Master. D'Aubusson then had a harsh talk with the malcontents and managed to change their minds. The conspirators were not arrested, as the knights could hardly afford any losses, but were shamed into performing their assigned duties. The Albanian assassin also contacted Philelpho, who feigned interest in the plot until details were revealed. The Albanian was subjected to torture and revealed the plan of the assassination and named his accomplice, the renegade from Dalmatia, who had managed to gain access to the Grand Master's kitchen. He was also arrested. The two individuals were then condemned to death, the Dalmatian by

XVI.   Dum hostis Italiae stationis moenia oppugnat, nocte ad ripam fossae munitionem ac repara diligentius erigit. Hostibus munimentis fossae adhibitis conspectis, de his dirimendis consilia ag<un>tur. Deliguntur fortissimi iuvenes quinquaginta, quibus miles ordinis praeficitur egregius. Eruptione itaque facta per fossam occulto nostri vadunt. Ubi ad partem munitioni obiectam ventum est, scalis erectis ripam fossae extemplo conscendunt sagittis, gladiis et saxis hostes persequuntur, fugant, trucidant. Ea in pugna Turci decem gladio caesi sunt; munitio fracta. Egregii iuvenes victoria potiti quattuor capitibus hastis affixis urbem ovantes intrant oppidanorum ingenti plausu excipiunt. Magister victores muneribus donat ad incitandum iuvenum animos et alios ad quoque egregie obeunda alliciendos.

XVII.   Paucis diebus interiectis Turci turris potiundae desiderio compulsi superiorique repulsa accensi arceque Sancti Nicolai grandiori conatu, arte et ingenio aggrediuntur; munimenta quoque et propugnacula iactu machinarum demoliuntur. Quod perterritur; summa // diligentia restituitur. Parant ad conflictum ligneum pontem qui ex sacello Sancti Antonii Turcis in molem transitum praebeat. Pons autem ex lignis variis vegetibus connexis, quibus asseres clavis confixae erant, construitur. Latitudo sex militum aequo gradu fronteque dimicantium capax fuit. Longitudo vero tanta erat, qua e littus utrumque contingeret. Pontem in mare Turci ad ripam molis traducere ingenio proponunt: ancoram enim rudenti alligatam quo fune pons religatus erat circa molem hostes in mare devehunt ut fracto fune ancoraque mordaci dente renitente pons in ulteriorem molis ripam natare compellatur. A nostris arte cognita nauta quidam rerum maritimarum non ignarus noctu undis se obruit, ancoram solvit fune cautibus remissius alligato, qui parva vi dissolvatur. Egregium facinus ad magistrum detulit qui aureo munere donatus gaudens comitum plausu ad stationem molis revertitur.

16. While the enemy was attacking the walls of [the langue of] Italy, he was by night erecting fortifications and defenses at the bank of the ditch. When we observed that breastworks had been applied to the ditch, we held councils to find a way to eliminate them. Five hundred very strong youths were chosen; an outstanding knight of our Order was placed in charge of them. They made a sortie and secretly charged through the ditch. When they reached the newly constructed breastworks, they placed ladders and without delay proceeded to climb on top and pursue, put to flight, and slaughter the enemy with arrows, swords, and rocks. In this battle ten Turks were put to the sword and their fortifications were broken up. The victorious, outstanding young men entered the city triumphantly, bringing four heads fixed on lances, to the enormous applause of the townspeople. Our Grand Master distributed gifts to the victors to reward their spirit and to encourage others to perform their duties in an outstanding manner.[16]

17. A few days later the Turks realized that they had to assume control of the fort of Saint Nicholas (from which they had been earlier repelled) and eagerly launched an attack with skill and talent; they bombarded the fortifications and the outer defenses with their cannon. They caused a great deal of terror but the damage was repaired with the greatest energy. They prepared for their assault a wooden bridge to provide a passageway from the chapel of Saint Anthony to the quay. The bridge was put together from various kinds of timbers, which were nailed together. Its width could accommodate six fighting soldiers advancing together; its length was such that it connected both shores. The Turks intended to float the bridge into the sea and to reach our quay with a clever device: an anchor connected to the bridge with a rope; in the vicinity of our quay they would sink the anchor which would be fixed in the bottom and keep the bridge in place, its end touching the quay. One of our sailors, a known expert swimmer, dove at night and easily cut the rope to which the anchor had been attached loosely. His outstanding performance was reported to our Grand Master who rewarded him with gold; rejoicing, he returned to his post at the quay, to the applause of his comrades.[17]

---

decapitation and the Albanian by hanging, but neither one seems to have made it to the place of execution, as on the way they fell into the hands of the mob. It should be noted that Caoursin's version of the events differs, as he states that the second accomplice managed to escape.

[16] Caoursin is very diplomatic in his account. We have already noted that he made no mention of the malcontents and their intention to come to an understanding with the enemy (cf. the previous note). From Bouhours, again, we find out that among the outstanding warriors involved in this incident were the very malcontents that the Grand Master had shamed into the performance of their duties and that they made this attack in order to exonerate themselves. The Grand Master publicly praised the malcontents.

[17] It seems that the Turks turned their attention to Fort Saint Nicholas after their setback in the sortie. Mesih Pasha seems to have centered his plan of attack on a floating bridge, about 600 feet long, across the Mandraki harbor. His plan became known to the knights and a sailor

XVIII. Turci, comperto dolo, cum primum pontis devectionem experiuntur, decepti statuunt scapharum remigio pontem ad ripam transvehere. Hostis quoque tantae rei intentus ad oppugnationem triremes triginta parat bene quidem munitas et ad conflictum ornatas. Praeter has quoque adiiciunt nonnulla oneraria navigia (parandarias vulgo dictas), ex quibus quaedam machinis et saxeis globis tormentis adaptatis onustae fuere ut, si turris victoria potirentur re// pente ex eo loco portum, turres moeniaque diruerent, prosternerent, demolirentur. Nec praetermittunt celeriores cymbas disponere, quae Turcorum strenuissimos quosque ad molem devehant, qui primi nostros aggrediantur et cum eis manus conserant; quibus proeliantibus ceteri ex ponte et triremibus in molem discendant imponuntque triremibus et parandariis non parvas machinas quibus nostros prosternere possint. Grandes quoque machinae quae turrim diruerant ad tempus ineundi conflictus officio frangantur.

XIX. Princeps vero noster summe invigilans subtilique ingenio et solerti mente cuncta diiudicans fretus strenuissimi cuiusque commilitonis sententia, qui ex Occidentali natione aderant. Nec defuerunt plerique indigenae Graecique ingenio manuque prompti; summa cura arcis defensioni consulit. Suspicati enim post primam pugnam quod contigit, turris et moles propugnaculis, fossa valloque abundantius munitur accersitis operariis fere mil<l>e qui interdiu noctuque cautibus excissis rupibusque demolitis, quod expetitur conficiunt. Nec impensarum sarcinis parcitur. Praesidia quoque in turris ruina collocantur. Pariter alia praesidia in radice molis disponuntur, quae nostris casu urgente opitulentur. Rebus sic ad pugnam paratis subditavere nostri ne Turci duobus locis urbem eodem momento aggrederentur, ut vires partirentur et quod cupiunt facilius conficiant. Cui inco//mmoditati et periculo magistri prudentia providet; praesidia quippe robustissimorum in moenibus Iudaeorum ac Italiae stationis, quae iam iactu machinarum partim demolita erant, statuit, qui tuitioni intendant, nec suo iniussu discedant; non est qui sane diiudicaret ac sentiret nostram salutem in turris tuitione collocatam esse, quod fit ut uno ore omnes tamque fidei veri athletae eius tuitioni consulerent et ut commune Christianorum domicilium servarent. In quo plurimorum equitum Hierosolymorum ac nobilium infimorumque Latinorum pariter Graecorum Rhodiorumque virtus et animositas emicuit, qui concordi audacia et animositate asylum et tutissimum Christianorum refugium Rhodiam urbem tutantur. Duo mercenarii iuvenes qui turris praesidio a<d>scripti sunt comprehenduntur arma in pelagus deiecisse, qui facinore perpetrato ad Turcum deficere proponunt; crimine damnati capitis supplicio afficiuntur.

18. So their trick was discovered, and since the Turks could not be conveyed through the bridge, they decided to row the bridge with boats to the shore. Eager to launch such an important assault, the enemy prepared thirty galleys, fortified and well arrayed for the attack. In addition, they were joined by some cargo boats (commonly called *parandarie*); a number of them were loaded with cannon and engines modified for stone projectiles to assume control of the tower; at once out of this spot they would attack, ruin, and demolish the harbor, the towers, and the walls. They also deployed very fast boats to convey to the quay the strongest Turks, who would be the first ones to engage our side in hand-to-hand combat; during this fight others would land on the quay from the bridge, the galleys, and the *parandarie*, to deploy large artillery pieces to wipe out our side. They also prepared heavy cannon to demolish the tower during the assault.

19. Our leader was extremely watchful and made arrangements for all possibilities with his subtle talents and his accomplished mind; he also relied on the opinion of his most forceful comrades, who had come from the west. There were also many indigenous Greeks ready to assist with their advice or with action. He meticulously sought advice for the defense of the tower. After the first assault, they had expected that this attack would come and they had summoned almost one thousand workers, who had labored to cut stones day and night and had abundantly reinforced the tower and the quay with battlements, a ditch, and a stockade. Heavy loads were added. A garrison was stationed at the collapsed tower. Similarly, others were stationed at the base of the quay, to provide urgent assistance to our cause. So our side prepared to resist, in case the Turks attacked our city in two places at the same time; our forces were divided to achieve their purpose easily. Our Grand Master's foresight countered the threat and danger; he established garrisons of very strong men to guard the walls of the Jews and of Italy, which had been brought down in part by the bombardment; they would not leave their assigned stations without orders to do so. Everyone realized and felt that our safety rested in the fate of the tower and all were asked to contribute to its defense, like true athletes of faith about to preserve the common shelter of Christians. The courage and brave spirit of most Knights of Jerusalem, of the high- and low-born Latins, and, similarly, of the Rhodian Greeks shone, who defended the city of Rhodes the safest asylum and refuge of Christians. Two young mercenaries who were assigned to the tower's garrison were caught as they were throwing their weapons into the sea; after this crime had been committed, they were going to desert to the Turk; they were condemned for this crime and were executed.

---

named Gervais Roger (Bouhours states that he was an Englishman) was able to dive underwater and separate the floating bridge from its anchor, rendering it useless to the enemy. The Turks attacked the fort on all three sides that were exposed to the sea. The attack commenced at midnight on June 19.

XX.   Ad turris demum oppugnationem Turci tertio decimo Kalendas Iulii intempesta nocte terra marique summo silentio accedunt. Ubi vero pugnam inire conantur grandi cum clamore et tympanorum sono invadunt, nostri quidem arrectis auribus hostium impetum comperientes, ubi eos adesse comperiunt, gladios stringunt balistis et tormentorum iactu hostes lacessunt deturbantque hostium triremes ne cymbae littoribus adhaereant; pons quoque tradducitur, // quo conscenso hostes transeunt. Nostrae quidem machinae muris collocatae globos saxeos torquent; pons natans frangitur; Turci merguntur; quattuor quoque triremes et navigia tormentis onusta iactu machinarum prosternuntur et undis obruunt. Turci frequentes qui ex cymbis et triremibus in molem descenderant a nostris caeduntur trucidanturque. Ignis etiam in classem solutis lintribus immittitur; nec Turci impigri bombardis repondent: ignes iaciunt; sagittas impetuosissimas ex balistis et catapultis torquent magna vi in obscuro; nisi dum ignes iaculati lucem plerumque praebent, acriter pugnant et media nocte usque ad horam decimam diei sequentis durans pugna propulsis hostibus victisque dirimitur. Vidisses toto triduo hostium cadavera littore iacentia auro, argento insignique veste fulgentia et complura mari fluctuantia qua pelagi aestus (ut natura solet) in superficie ferebat; quorum spoliis complures potiti sunt et ex his non parum commodi vendicant. Insignis quidem haec pugna fuit morte clarorum virorum qui Turcis praeerant; quorum interitus maerorem et luctum hosti attulit. Praesertim generi Turci viri quidem strenuissimi a Turcoque dilecti mors magno fuit maerori, cuius cadaver post triduum mari ebulliente in molis littoris devectum reperitur eiusque spoliis quidam ex nostris potitur. Perfugae qui post // proelium ad nostros defecerunt edocent exercitum magnam cladem accepisse Turcosque ea in pugna duo mil<l>ia quingenti cedisse, ex eoque bassa ingentem maerorem concepisse, qui tres dies intra papiliones frequentia commilitonum prohibita se continuit et stragem Turco celerius nuntiat; eo quoque magis mens eius roditur, quod post tantam ruinam turri illatam arce potiri non potuerit et quod tantam in eius oppugnatione ignominiam acceperit existimans Turcensem numerosum exercitum invalidum esse, qui turrim diruptam expugnare non valuerit.

XXI.   Cum autem Turci spem turris expugnandae perdidissent, conatum, studium, industriam omnesque vires ad civitatem omni experte oppugnandam convertunt et licet ad moenia Iudaeorum ac Italiae stationis animum potissime convertant, non cessant tantum circum quoque muros verberare et demoliri.

20.   The Turks finally launched their assault on the thirteenth day before the Calends of July [= June 19] at the dead of night and silently made their approach by land and sea. Then they launched their attack to the accompaniment of yells and the sound of drums; our side had kept an ear open and knew that we were about to come under attack; when they realized that the enemy had come close, they drew their swords and attacked and decimated the enemy with catapults and artillery fire; they put the enemy galleys to flight so that their boats could not approach the shore. They [= the enemy] dragged the bridge to use it as a passageway. But our cannon deployed on the walls fired their stone projectiles; the floating bridge broke up and the Turks fell into the sea; in addition, four galleys and cargo boats were destroyed by our cannon fire and sank in the waves. Throngs of Turks landed on the quay from the galleys and the boats, only to be slaughtered and butchered by our side. We let loose our skiffs and sent them to set fire to their fleet. The Turks responded eagerly with their bombards; they used flame throwers; they released very powerful bolts from their engines and catapults in darkness; but their artillery fire provided light for the most part; there was a fierce battle that lasted from midnight until the tenth hour of the following day when the enemy was pushed back in defeat. For three days one could see their corpses lying on the shore; they were shining with gold, silver, and bright vestments; most of them were being pushed by the ebb and flow of the sea, as nature usually dictates. Many took spoils and gained a great deal. In this battle many distinguished Turkish leaders fell. The Turk considered the death of an outstanding nobleman a great loss; three days later his corpse was brought by the swelling sea to the shore of the quay and someone from our side found it and took the spoils. The deserters who came to us after this battle said that the Turkish army had suffered a disaster and had sustained in that engagement two thousand and five hundred casualties, which had sent the pasha into such great mourning that he kept himself away from his comrades and remained within his tent for three days; he quickly announced the disaster to the [Grand] Turk. He was also worried because he was not able to assume command of the tower, despite the fact that it was utterly ruined, because he had only reaped shame, despite the fact that he had launched such an attack against it, and because he reckoned that the huge numbers of the Turkish army lacked the strength to conquer a ruined tower.

21.   After the Turks lost hope of conquering the tower, they turned their zeal, efforts, enthusiasm, energy, and might to the siege of the city; even though they paid special attention to the walls of the Jews and of Italy,[18] they continued to launch attacks throughout the periphery and to destroy our walls. The

---

[18] Specifically the Turks deployed eight of their sixteen large cannon to the southeast of the city before the Rhodian *Giudecha* (also cited as "Juifrie" in our sources), opposite the defenses of the langues of Italy and Provence; these civilian quarters and the neighboring defenses were then subjected to a savage bombardment.

Hostis coeptum opus continuat assiduoque conatu aggreditur propositum conficere. Excogitant itaque Turci urbem ingenio occulto propinquare: fossas labyrinthi persimiles effodiunt, quas lignis arborum ramusculis contextis aedificant terraque operiunt ut latenter ad fossas urbis accedant. Propugnacula quoque multis in locis cratibus de viminibus contextis aedificant, ex quibus assiduo sagittant. Colubrinis quoque ac serpentinis nostros deturbant, fatigant; pensitant quoque eis conducere et aliquam partem fossae, qua moenibus adiacet, opplere. // Opera itaque ab hoste adhibita lapides congerere non cessant et occulto in fossam iaciunt. Operis assiduitate pars fossae oppletur, antemurali quoque aequatur, ex quo et murorum ruina in dorsi formam redacta facillimus conscensus in moenia efficitur.

XXII. Praecellentissimus princeps noster, Rhodiorum magister, his conspectis divino quodam ingenio agendis incumbens nil praetermittere decrevit, quod saluti urbis conducere videatur maturitateque ac solita modestia utens militibus ad contionem vocatis conatus et discrimina graviter ac pudenter explicat. Adhaerebat enim lateri nobilissimus eius frater excellens miles Antonius Daubusson dominus de Montelio ad vicecomitem. Vir quidem consilio et armis clarus, qui paulo ante ex Gallis robustis comitatus viris in Orientem Sancti Sepulchri visitandi gratia cupiens summopere tam glorioso certamini interesse transfretarat. Is enim a fratre patrum decreto ob fidei integritatem, agendorum experientiam artisque militaris disciplinam commilitonum dux et urbis capitaneus designatus magnanimi et prudentis capitanei ruina obiit et rerum summae consulit. Aderant non pauci equites Hierosolymorum, praecellentes baiulini, priores senatorii ordinis, praeceptores et fratres nobilibus familiis in Occidentali plaga nati. Affuerunt negotiatores prudentia pollentes ac Rhodii cives Graeci quoque ingenio praediti qui unanimi consensu de // tutanda urbe consultant. Excelluit

enemy was determined to bring his project into successful completion. And so the Turks devised a hidden way of coming close to the city: they dug out trenches to look like a labyrinth, which they reinforced with timber and tree branches; they secretly removed the soil so that they could come close to the ditches of the city. They also built battlements out of wine barrels, from which they incessantly released arrows. They annoyed and fatigued our side with bombardment from their colubrines and serpents; they also thought that it would benefit them to fill up another part of the ditch adjacent to the walls. And so our enemy piled up stones and secretly took up stations in the ditch. A section was soon filled by the strenuous efforts of the laborers and equaled in height the first line of defense; from this spot, whose ruins resembled the shape of buttocks, they could very easily make their way into our walls.

22. Our outstanding leader, the Grand Master of the Rhodians, had figured out what was going on (assisted by his almost divine intuition) and issued orders to exercise extreme vigilance; he summoned, with his usual seasoned modesty, the knights to the assembly and in a serious tone he wisely explained the danger and the measures likely to save the city. His most noble brother, the excellent knight Anthony d'Aubusson, the lord from Montelium assigned to the Viscount, was always by his side.[19] He had already demonstrated his worth in councils and in war, and while he had earlier, accompanied by strong men, left France for the east to visit the Holy Sepulcher, he changed his plans and came to participate in the glorious battle. This man's true faith, experience, and skill in warfare compelled his brother to appoint him, by decree of the fathers, commander of the comrades and captain of the city; he was a great captain and a valuable counselor.[20] Also present were quite a few knights of Jerusalem, outstanding baileys, priors of the senatorial rank, preceptors, and brothers with noble lineage, born in the west. Also present were businessmen to offer their wise advice, Rhodian citizens and talented Greeks who in unison offered their advice to save the city.

---

[19] Antoine d'Aubusson, the older brother of the Grand Master, had been given financial aid and a force of 500 knights and 2,000 volunteer men at arms by Louis XI to assist in the defense of Rhodes. By far this was the largest contingent that had come from Europe to assist the Knights. For the efforts of the papacy and the other Christian powers to assist in the defense, see *PL* 2: 355–56. As with the siege of Constantinople, Europe was slow to act and the Knights were more or less forced to rely on their own resources in the defense. Antoine was sixty-seven years old when he came to assist his brother. Bouhours, *Histoire de Pierre d'Aubusson Grand-Maistre de Rhodes*, in Book III, cites a number of French noblemen who came to Rhodes in his retinue; among them, the following names are listed: Louis de Craon, Guillaume Gomare, Matthieu Brangelier, Claude Colomb, Charles de Roy, and Louis Sanguin.

[20] Bouhours, *Histoire de Pierre d'Aubusson*, Book III, also supplies an interesting detail: Antoine d'Aubusson was personally involved in a skirmish at this time; his band confronted a Turkish detachment that was being led by Demetrios Sophianos, the renegade who lost his mount, in the engagement, and was trampled to death by the other horses. Bouhours comments that it was an appropriate death for such a renegade and traitor.

profecto plurimorum cuiusque generis astantium probitas, generositas, virtus ac magnanimitas, quorum sententiis discussis principis nostri solertia quod optimum, diiudicatum est elegit.

XXIII. Nostri vero cuiusdam experti suasu machinam vers<at>ilem (quod tribucum vocant, ingentia saxa in munitiones et hostium fossas torquens) erigere statuunt. Aedificatur quoque celeriter machina periti viri sententia, nautarumque et architectorum opera, quae ubi erecta est, vir peritus gravia saxa in hostes iacit multosque conterit, munimenta diruit damnaque intulit non parvi pendenda. Excogitatum quoque est eam partem fossae, quae lapidibus a Turcis oppleta erat, evacuare sed, cum id palam effici non possit, cuniculo in pomerio effosso exitum sub lapidibus nostri habent et clam lapides in urbem comportant. Sentiunt profecto Turci qui fossae propinqui erant lapidum congeriem minui et ascensus opportunitatem adimi, nisi quam citius quod cupiunt efficiant. Atroci enim murorum ruina conspecta statuitur munitionibus inniti, quae impetum machinarum sustineant. Murorum igitur lapsui munimenta et repara nostri obiiciunt, quae in hunc facta sunt modum: murus crassitudinis palmorum duorum in pomerio ex opposito moenium ducitur palique ex robustissimo ligno terrae infinguntur gladiis, ramusculis, fruticibus quoque intermixti intus; ponitur assiduoque attritu insula, a qua firmant densaturque; provident insuper ingeniis hostes in ipso //

Actually the advice, generosity, courage, and spirit of the majority proved outstanding; our leader considered their proposals and chose, with his cunning, the best advice.

23.   Our side was persuaded by the advice of an expert and decided to build a versatile engine (called "trebuchet")[21] that could hurl enormous rocks against the defenses and ditches of the enemy. Through the instructions of the expert the engine was put together swiftly by sailors and construction workers; it was positioned and a specialist directed its bombardment of heavy rocks which killed many of the enemy, destroyed their fortifications, and created panic for their lives. We also considered various ways of emptying that part of the ditch that had been filled in by the Turks; when we could not do it openly, we dug mines in the defense periphery, which ended under the stones that had been piled up, and we secretly transported the stones into the city. The Turks who were stationed in the vicinity of the ditch realized that the heap of stones was decreasing in size and that they would not be able to make the ascent unless they accomplished what they desired in the very near future.[22] It was decided to provide cover from the bombardment under the extensive ruins. Our side created defenses and fortifications by utilizing the ruins of the walls in the following manner: a wall, two palms thick, was built into the defense periphery, opposite the walls; the stockade was firmly planted and it was reinforced with swords, branches, and timber. An island was placed and was strengthened and reinforced

---

[21] The term that Caoursin uses for this engine, *tribucum*, is a clear reference to the old trebuchet, the formidable siege engine of the Middle Ages, which at this time of gunpowder must have looked like a relic. It is, in fact, the last documented usage of the trebuchet in warfare. The word that Caoursin used was also very close to the Latin *tributum*, or "tribute," and the word-play must have caused amusement at the time. By the time Bouhours wrote, both he and his readers were unfamiliar with this engine and he simply calls it "tributet," as the term trebuchet had been forgotten. Bouhours speaks of the engine in admiring terms, clearly unaware that it had been a standard weapon in the Middle Ages. For this trebuchet, see Brockman, *The Two Sieges*, 83. For a recent review of this weapon (and for some modern experimentation with it), see Jim Bradbury, *The Medieval Siege* (Woodbridge, 1992), 239–70. In addition, see Paul E. Chevedden, "The Invention of the Counterweight Trebuchet: A Study in Cultural Diffusion," *DOP* 54 (2000): 71–116.

[22] Mines and counter-mines were a recognized form of siege warfare and defense in the *quattrocento*. Mines had been used widely but unsuccessfully by the Turks and their Serbian sappers during the siege of Constantinople in 1453. Ultimately this method derives from Roman warfare and is even discussed by Vitruvius (Book II). The most advanced form of this method was employed by the Turks against the Knights during the siege of Malta in 1522. The objective was to undermine the foundations of a wall or a tower by excavating directly under the structure, which would then collapse into the tunnel. To detect counter-mines the defenders would usually place vats full of water on the fortifications and watch for water movement as a suitable warning. If a mine had been detected a counter-mine would be dug by the defenders; if the enemy mine were encountered, it would then be destroyed, while sometimes battles were fought underground by the opposing parties. For this method of fighting, see Bradbury, *The Medieval Siege*, 270–74.

congressu propellere et propulsare. Ignes itaque artificiosos parant variis modiis reconditos cadis pice, sulphure combustibilique materia repletis ac sacculis laminis ferreis pulvereque machinarum refertis, quae ingenia exitio hosti futura sint. Ingens propterea cylindrorum copia affertur; in hostes ruant eosque proterant. Varia quoque propugnaculorum forma editur, quae Turcis impedimento, nostris sint adiumento. Delectabant conspicientes virorum ingenia, qui remedia excogitabant ac plaudebant.

XXIV. Adducitur Georgius proditor forti comitatus caterva ad custodiam data. Consultus de his quae tuitioni futura sint remissius tardiusque respondet nec de se experimentum ab eo expectatum praebet, quemadmodum pollicitus erat. Sperabat quippe vir iniquus et callidus videns murorum iacturam et facilem ascensum per ruinam civitatem in hostium potestatem futuram. Quaedam tunc protulit ut eius astutiam occultaret. Suadet machinam parari, quae in machinas hostis iaceat; quod ut factum est, Turcus machinae ictus ex adverso dirigit murumque non parum laedit. Dum haec agerentur, epistolae ex castris in urbem sagittis diriguntur, quae Georgium insimulant. Nec Georgius licet urbis discrimen videret verbis procacibus se abstinet, quae, ut ad notitiam deveniunt, vehemens suspicio in eum oritur. Quibus ex causis vinculis et carcere arcetur deputantque <eos> qui virum examinent et causas defectionis perquirant. // Examinatus contradictoriis ac coniecturis sufficientibus convictus torquetur. In tormento et extra rogatus ultro fatetur iussu Turcorum tyranni ad Rhodios defecisse ut urbem, si posset, proderet quemadmodum plura oppida prodidit. Sin minus Rhodi persinistre versaretur, cuncta diligentius acutiusque perquireret et specularetur moresque status et conditiones incolarum et religionis intelligeret ac domum, si classis non vinceret, ad Turcum reverteretur edocturus quae ad urbis expugnationem conducerent. Proponebat namque Turcus hanc urbem in suam ditionem redigere, quod ut conficeret multis pollicitationibus ac pluribus donis allectus

by the widespread ruins. On top of this the enemy deployed cannon to assist them in the assault. They also prepared incendiary devices[23] of all sorts: buckets filled with pitch, sulfur, and combustible material, as well as sacks filled with gunpowder and metal fragments to destroy the enemy. They also transported a plethora of cylinders to attack the enemy and to protect themselves. There were various forms of battlements prepared by our side to help us and to hinder the Turks. They were amazed to look upon the talents of those whose defensive devices they applauded.

24.   George, the traitor, was summoned; he was accompanied by the guards who had been ordered to follow him. He was consulted about our defenses but his answers came slowly and carelessly and he was unable to produce the results that he had promised; the unjust, wily man had seen the ruinous state of the walls and he hoped that the enemy would easily climb over the ruins and take over the city. And so he only offered pieces of advice that would hide his cleverness. He persuaded us to construct an engine that would destroy the engines of the enemy. After it was put together, the Turk directed his artillery bombardment crosswise but could not inflict an equal amount of damage on the wall. In the midst of all this, we received letters from their camp, fired into the city by arrows, which charged George with treason. In spite of the danger to our city, George made some unguarded remarks, which, when they came to our attention, created suspicion. Consequently, he was put in irons and jailed; then he was summoned to face his examiners who questioned him about his motivation to defect. Under examination he was convicted to our satisfaction by his contradictions and conjectures. Both freely and under torture he was questioned further and admitted that he had defected to the Rhodians by order of the tyrant [sultan] of the Turks, so that he might, if possible, betray the city, as he had betrayed numerous other cities. If he proved unable to accomplish his mission at Rhodes, he was to make careful note of everything, to observe and assess the morale, the condition, and the spirit of the inhabitants and of the Order, and, if the armada failed to prevail, to return to the Turk and suggest means of taking the city. The Turk meant to bring this city under his power and George proposed to accomplish this, seduced by many

---

[23] Combustibles of all sorts were widely used in siege warfare. The Turks seemed to have inherited the famous Greek or Liquid Fire in the Levant, and they seem to have used various forms of it against the Knights (see above, § 20). While the composition and the use of Greek Fire still remain largely controversial and debatable, most of the evidence is summarized in Theodoros K. Korres, " Ύγρὸν Πῦρ": Ἕvα Ὅπλο της Βυζαντινής Ναυτικής Τακτικής, 2nd ed. Ἑταιρεία Βυζαντινῶν Ἐρευνῶν 6 (Thessalonica, 1989); J. R. Partington, *A History of Greek Fire and Gunpowder* (Cambridge, 1960), esp. 1–41; and J. Haldon and M. Byrne, "A Possible Solution to the problem of Greek Fire," *BZ* 70 (1977): 91–99. Other devices that were used included fire wheels (hoops dipped in combustible liquid and rubbed with oil and gunpowder). The threat of fire was so common that normally barrels of water were placed on fortifications so that individuals whose clothes had caught fire could jump into them. For such devices, cf. Bradbury, *The Medieval Siege*, 277–78.

Georgius extitit. Crimine convictus supplicio capitis damnatur et in propatulo spectante populo fune furcae religato Georgius suffocatur. Ut animam exhalavit, populus cum plausu ad privatas stationes revertitur laetus et gaudens de nece proditoris Christianae religionis, qui tot animas perdere voluit et ad iugulationem et fidei orthodoxae ad negationem tot praeclaros viros castissimasque matronas sacrasque virgines et plebem Christianam perducere studuit. Luit tandem poenas sceleri debitas.

XXV.   Vir perfidus vigilans et semper aliquid cogitans Turcensis classis praefectus bassa alteras litteras in urbem iacere studet, quae Graecos indigenas et cives Latinos ad deditionem hortantur: vita et supellectili salva promissa multam immunitatem // polliceretur; solum urbis ditionem expostulat et interitum militum ac perniciem religionis Hierosolymorum affectat; si secus rebus suis consulant ad unum omnes interituros affirmat. Putavit vir nefarius populum infidum invenire et qui metu terreretur vel muneribus alliceretur sed reperit orthodoxae fidei plebem devotam ac ordini Hierosolymorum fidam consilioque et armis mutua equitum et Latinorum et nostrorum conversatione experta. Ea igitur in vanum tentante alio utitur commento: mittit ad ecclesiam Beatae Mariae Virginis Eleimonitrae Graeculum (qui dudum ad Turcos defecerat), qui vigiles alloquens ait bassam oratorem ad principem nostrum velle destinare dummodo tutus aditus pateat. Respondetur ut illuc ad ripam fossae nuntium mittat aderitque in bolevardo qui nomine magistri respondeat. Affuit postridie bassae orator qui nostris prius salutatis ait praefectum classis non parum immo vehementer admirari, quod tam potenti principi resistere audeamus, qui duo imperia, tot regna, tot urbes, tot provincias totque potentatus subiugavit; quare suadet ut nostrae urbi et agris indoleamus nec patiamur tam crudelem facinus perpetrari nec urbem diripi et ad iugulationem viros et mulieres ad raptum et ignominiam duci; bellum an pax praestiterit dicamus. Pollicetur quippe brevi

promises and numerous rewards. He was convicted and sentenced to death; publicly, as the people watched, George was brought to the gallows and was hanged until he suffocated. After he expired, the people applauded and returned home in joy, delighted with the death of the traitor to the Christian faith, who wanted to destroy so many souls, and to force so many noblemen, respected women, nuns, and the Christian populace to slaughter and to the denial of the Orthodox faith. He finally paid a just penalty for his crime.[24]

25.   The commander of the Turkish fleet, the pasha, was a faithless man who always came up with something, and he desired to send letters into the city in order to urge the native Greeks and the Latin citizens to surrender; he promised them their lives, their property, and extensive immunity; he demanded only control of the city, the death of the soldiers, and the destruction of the Order of Jerusalem; if they went against his wishes, he asserted that they would all die, to the last man. The wretch thought that he would find a faithless people who could be controlled with terror or could be intimidated by rewards; instead he found a group devoted to the Orthodox faith, loyal to the Order of Jerusalem, ready to offer advice or weapons to the knights, and familiar with the Latins and with our side. And when this attempt came to nothing, he tried another trick: he sent a Greekling (who had defected to the Turks a long time ago) to the Church of the Blessed Virgin Mary Eleimonitra; he addressed the sentries and said that the pasha wished to dispatch his representative to our leader, if we would allow passage. He was told to send the messenger to the bank of the ditch and he would meet our Grand Master's representative in the avenue. Next day the representative[25] of the pasha came, greeted our side, and said that the commander of the armada was amazed that we dared to oppose such a powerful prince, who has conquered two empires, so many kingdoms, cities, and provinces, and so many states. He accordingly wished to persuade us to spare our city and countryside and not to allow such a cruel fate to fall upon us: the plunder of our city, the slaughter of our men, the shameful rape of our women; we should declare whether we opt for war or peace. He promised that, if we chose peace swiftly

---

[24] On Meister Georg, see above, n. 4, and 10. As *PL* 2: 355, has concluded: "D'Aubusson suspected all those who deserted the crescent to join him in those weeks of peril, *tant Turcs que Chrestiens*, of whom there were said to be about sixty . . .." On his death, see Brockman, *The Two Sieges*, 81.

[25] Bouhours, *Histoire de Pierre d'Aubusson*, Book III, supplies a name for this emissary: Suleyman, who, he adds, was an old man. *MCT*, 398, provides the motivation for such an offer of peace: "This was in keeping with Ottoman military law, which required that before a fortress was stormed the adversary be given an opportunity to profess Islam. But in the case of the Palaeologus Mesih Pasha, another consideration played a part. He calculated that if the Knights of St. John should lay down their arms, the rich spoils of the city would not fall into the hands of the army and that he would be able to claim them for the sultan and himself." A similar offer to Constantine XI, the emperor of Constantinople, was made before the final assault of May 29, 1453 by Mehmed II. On this point, see above, Chap. 5, n. 16.

forma et compendio pacem si libuerit se praestiturum et nos possessores urbis et agrorum // permansuros. Aliter minas addens promittit prope diem civitatem in suam potestatem transituram direptionique praebituram et omne genus crudelitatis ex<s>ecuturum. Qui principis nostri vice aderat edoctus respondet: Non possumus satis non admirari vos qui cum classe et impetuosis machinis castrorumque copia urbem nostram circumdatis nos ad pacem hortari, cum id a militantium officio alienum videatur; verum figmento agere videmini ut animos tentetis. Sciatis nec pollicitationes nec munera vestra nos movere aut ad aliquid indecens conficiendum allicere; nec profecto minae vestrae nos terrent. Sumus enim unanim<i> nec discrimen est inter Latinum et Graecum. Christum enim colimus una fide et firma mente, pro quo pugnare parati sumus et mortem prius oppetere quam Mahumm<e>to coniungi, sicut facessant promissa et minae quibus nos movere conamini. Cum vestra classis domesticos lares reviserit, si oratores de pace tractaturos mittetis de re consultabimus. Cum armati et exercitu praecincti estis, officium bellantium perficite et vobis, Deo propitio, constanti animo respondebimus. Cognoscetis quoque non cum Asiaticis et effeminatis viris contendere sed cum Catholicis fortissimis manum conserere. Quo dicto Turci vultu demisso extemplo discedunt.

XXVI. Dum Turcis maiori conatu, ingenio arteque resistitur, ipsorum insania incenditur. Pudet quippe eos, tantum exercitum, // iugulandos et qui vivi capti essent palis quos ad id ex<s>equendum mil<l>ia octo paraverant cruciandos civitatis ditione Turcorum tyranno reservata. His divulgatis properant Turci civitatem aggredi. Priusquam id moliantur, Mahum<m>etum suo more invocant, corpus lavant, purgantque, sacculos ad rapinam parant, funiculos ad captivos religandos conis connectunt. Pridie quam pugna iniretur totaque nocte diei continue ac diluculo quo mane quo pugnatum est praecessit octo machinae muris obiectae saxa ingentia assidue torquent, quod loco propugnaculorum adhibitum erat diruunt. Vigiles quoque ac custodes et moenium praesidia partim occidunt ut muris quisquam superstare vix possit nisi summo astu occultaretur et scalas ad signum campanae paulum descenderet et demum conscenderet. Nec tempus

and without delay, we could keep possession of our city and our countryside. Otherwise, he pronounced threats and promised that, on the day the city fell into his hands, he would plunder and commit all kinds of cruel acts. Then the man who had been chosen to speak for our leader[26] came forth and responded as he had been instructed: "We can only express our admiration for you, who have first surrounded our city with an armada, with powerful cannon, and with a large army, and are now urging us to peace; such intentions do not seem to agree with a warring faction. We think that you are only pretending to test our spirit. Know that neither your promises nor your gifts can move us; nothing will force us to commit anything indecent; your threats do not terrify us. We are unanimous in this and there is no distinction between Latin and Greek. We firmly worship Christ in one faith, for whom we are prepared to wage war and would rather die than join Mohammed, as you are urging us to do with promises and threats. Arm yourselves and your soldiers and do the duty of warriors; God willing, we will respond with firm spirit. Know that you are not fighting against Asiatics and effeminate men but against very strong Catholics." At this response, the Turks immediately departed in dejection.

26. While we resisted the Turks with greater determination, talent, and skill, their madness raged on. It shamed them that they, such a large army, were put to the sword; so they prepared eight thousand stakes to impale their prisoners, once the city came under the control of the tyrant of the Turks. The Turks spread this news and hastened to attack the city. Before the assault, they invoked Mohammed in accordance with their custom, and they washed their bodies, purified themselves,[27] and prepared sacks for their booty, and ropes to tie batches of their prisoners. Eight cannon, deployed before the wall on the day before the attack, directed their concentrated bombardment of enormous stone missiles to destroy the sector where battlements had been erected; it lasted all day and all night, and continued during the dawn of the day of the assault. They killed some sentries, watches, and guardians of the walls, so that one could hardly stand on the wall, unless one hid oneself very cleverly, by climbing down the ladder at

---

[26] The representative of the Grand Master was the castellan of Rhodes, Antoine Gaultier (Brockman, *The Two Sieges*, 81: "Fra Antoine Gaultier").

[27] Such preparations, with ritual overtones, were standard in the Turkish armies of the period before a final assault was launched. See above, Chap. 5, nn. 16 and 17. The Knights must have been well aware of the fact that such festivities were the prelude to the *certamen generale*. For similar activities in the Turkish camp before the final assault on Constantinople, cf. Leonardo's eyewitness testimony (discussed above, Chap. 5, n. 17), CC 1: 156–58: "Ergo proclamatum est in castris edicto, ut quarto Kalendis Maii, die videlicet Martis, praeviis diebus tribus quibus luminaria Deo accendant, Deum invocent, integra die abstineant, parati sint omnes ad proelium, daturi Christianis generale certamen, altissimaque voce praecones voluntate regis urbem triduo ad saccum esse bellatoribus donatam ... O si audivisses voces ad caelum illatas "Illala, Illala, Machomet Russullala," scilicet est et semper erit et Machometus est servus eius, quidem obstupuisses! Sicque factum est: triduo luminaria Deo accendunt, ieiunant die nihil usque ad noctem gustantes."

datum est propugnacula denuo instaurandi, cum bombardarum ictus frequentiores essent; ita ut tam parvo tempore trecenta vel circiter saxa iacta sint. Turci vero iactu machinarum peracto ad signum iactus mortarii (quod pridem eo in loco constituerunt) confertissimi magno impetu quam celeriter quinto Kalendas Augusti ruinam orto sole conscendunt. Erat namque facilis (ut diximus) ei<s> ascensus, immo facilior quam nostris per scalas superiora quoque murorum loca // occupant trucidato quod illic erat praesidio, quod primum tanto impetui resistere nequivit. Antequam subsidia nostra scalas conscenderint et illic hostilia signa statuunt. Idem quoque faciunt ad turrim Italiae, cuius verticem oppugnant. XXVII. Clamor undique oritur; manus quoque viriliter conseritur magnaque vi pugnatur. Nostri quoque a dextro sinistroque cornu fortiter hosti resistunt. Ubi affuerunt gloriose dimicantes, miles praestantissimus dominus de Montelio capitaneus armis pollens, baiulini quoque et equites Hierosolymorum ac negotiatores non paucique indigenae et cuiusvis nationis strenui, quorum quidam inter confertissimos hostes acriter dimicantes cecidere; alii multis vulneribus acceptis vitam servavere. Scalis quoque (quae quattuor erant), quibus in vicum Iudaeorum descendatur una iussu princips noster perfracta, qua Turci descendere coeperant extemplo conscensus clar<i>ssimus magister et princeps noster Petrus Daubusson praeclara comitatus cohorte magno fortique animo hosti se

the signal of the bell, and then climbing back up. No time could be found to repair the battlements, as the bombardment increased. In a short time about three hundred stones were fired. After the cannon had completed their task, the signal was given by a mortar (which they had earlier deployed in this sector) and the Turks strongly advanced as swiftly as possible to the ruins in large numbers, as the sun rose on the fifth day before the Calends of August [= July 28].[28] As I have stated, it was easy for them (easier than for our side) to climb on ladders, slaughter the garrison, and occupy the higher places of the walls, as it proved impossible to resist such forceful assault at first. Before we could send help up the ladders, the enemy planted his standards on this spot and at the tower of Italy, whose summit they occupied.

27.   The din rose everywhere. There was brave, strong hand-to-hand combat. Our side bravely resisted the enemy's right and left horns. The outstanding knight, the brave lord and captain from Montelium, the baileys, the knights of Jerusalem, the merchants, quite a few of the natives, and the strong from every nation were present in the most dangerous sectors, some of whom fell fighting against the thick waves of the enemy; others survived with multiple wounds.[29] The Turks descended by ladders (there were four) into the quarter of the Jews; by order of our leader, a ladder was brought to the spot where the Turks were making their descent; without delay our glorious Grand Master and leader, Pierre d'Aubusson, escorted by a strong company, bravely threw himself against

---

[28] The date, as is well known, is problematic, since our sources differ considerably. According to d'Aubusson himself, the battle took place "VII Kalen. Augusti" and a near-contemporary German translation of this work gives the date as "am XXV. tag des monats Julii." D'Aubusson's letter of September 15 to Sixtus IV specifies July 28. In later years d'Aubusson set the day of July 27, the feast of Saint Pantaleon, as the memorial day of his victory, and Pope Innocent VIII in the bull *Redemptor noster* (May 31, 1485), made the same day a perpetual thanksgiving feast. The problem is discussed (with all the evidence) in *PL* 2: 357–58 n. 36 and 37. Bouhours, *Histoire de Pierre d'Aubusson*, Book III, accepts July 27. *MCT*, 399, without discussion of the problem, accepts "Friday, July 28."

[29] Good relations between the Knights and the local Greek population contributed to the success of the defense (cf. above, § 25). This situation contrasts sharply with the defense of Constantinople in 1453, in which the Greek population, the Venetians, and the Genoese mercenaries of the Greek emperor were at odds with one another, as the Orthodox and the Catholics never fully cooperated, to the detriment of the defense. The Knights in Rhodes provide a better example of cooperation by Christians against the Islamic threat. This situation is further analyzed in Christodoulos I. Papachristodoulou, Ἱστορία τῆς Ῥόδου ἀπὸ τοὺς Προϊστορικοὺς Χρόνους ἕως τὴν Ἐνσωμάτωση τῆς Δωδεκανήσου, 2nd ed. (Athens, 1972), 167. The contribution of the locals was recognized by the Knights. After the battle, a local resident by the name of Antonio Palapanno, who had lost his right arm in the defense, was granted an annual pension; see *PL* 2: 358, n. 38: "Anthonius Palapanno in die aggressionis Turcorum, ad muros Iudeorum viriliter pugnavit et tutatus est murum in quo casu pugn<a>e perdidit manum dexteram."

obiicit scalamque conscendit hostemque viriliter oppugnat, propulsat quosdamque trucidat; nec aliter ipse suique commilitones, quibus comitatus erat, pro fide Catholica et republica Christianorum pugnavere quam olim gloriosi Macabei pro cultu divino et Hebraeorum libertate proeliati sunt; nec haud secus quam plerique Ro//mani principes pro tutanda patria dimicavere, qui ob servatam rempublicam meruerunt patres patriae appellari. Hos enim praecellentissimos viros imitatus princeps et magister noster discrimina non formidans vulneribus quinque in corpore exceptis (quorum unum letale censebatur nisi medicorum cura remedium attulisset), Rhodiorum rempublicam tutatus est, servavit, restituit. Ob quod praeclarum quidem facinus pater patriae optimo iure appellandus est.

XXVIII.   Turci enim perpulchre armati duo mil<l>ia quingenti super muros erant confertissimi nostros secum manus conserentes armorum vi propellere nitebantur. Primorum tamen virtus invicta persistens divino praesidio suffulta nequaquam loco cessit. Sequebatur quoque Turcos qui muris potiti erant ingens Turcorum multitudo quae totum campum adiacentem, ruinam, vallum et fossam expleverat ut terra vix conspici posset. Affirmant perfugae quadraginta mil<l>ia Turcorum invasioni adesse. Pugnatum est duabus horis ambigua fortuna, modo ad nostros modo ad Turcos victoria inclinante. Tandem divina clementia principis et nostrorum virtutem favente Turci funduntur, propulsantur, caeduntur tantoque impetu et celeritate terga vertunt ut sibi ipsis necem et vulnera afferent. Spectaculo nobis fuit, quod a nostris inter pugnandum gestum est conspicere. Ex Turcis quippe qui nostros fortiter lacessebant super muros stantes trecenti a nostris // in vicum Iudaeorum praecipites trahuntur et impelluntur. Erat namque muri altitudo ad intra fere pedum XX. Hi omnes ad unum trucidati sunt et cadavera vulneribus deformia passi<m> iacentia intra urbem visa sunt. Cum Turci pedem referrent et ad castra tenderent, nostri eos consecuti sunt et complures intra munitiones occiderunt, quorum spoliis ac insigni tyranni vexillo auro argentoque ornato, quod tantae victoriae monumentum extitit, potiti magno cum plausu urbem per murorum ruinam intrant. Cecidere ea in pugna Turci tria mil<l>ia quingenti, quorum cadavera intra urbem, super moenia, <in> fossa munitionibusque hostium et mari reperta sunt et postmodum ad luem vitandam, quae passi<m> deformia et lacera iacebant combusta. Interiere prout perfugae divulga<ve>runt, qui cum exercitus a bassa recenseretur aderant, ex Turcis obsidionis tempore novem mil<l>ia vulneratique sunt mil<l>ia quindecim magisque incommoditatibus exercitum affertum affirmant.

the enemy, climbed on the ladder, and courageously fought, repelled the enemy, and put some to the sword. Both he and his escort fought for the Catholic faith and the Christian commonwealth as if they were the ancient Maccabees, who had waged war on behalf of God's worship and for the freedom of the Hebrews. In a similar manner so many Roman princes had fought to protect their homeland, who were then appropriately assigned the title "fathers of the fatherland." Our leader and Grand Master imitated those outstanding men; he disregarded the danger, even though he had received five wounds[30] on his body (one of which would have proved lethal if the care of the physicians had not been applied), and preserved, protected, and saved the commonwealth of the Rhodians. Because of his extraordinary deed, he was most justly called "father of the fatherland."

28. Two thousand five hundred superbly equipped Turks attacked our side in close waves and proceeded to fight a hand-to-hand battle. The courage of our first rank remained undefeated and, with the support of God, we yielded nowhere. A huge multitude of Turks from the nearby camp followed the Turks who had assumed command of the walls and inundated the ruins, the stockade, and the ditch; one could hardly see the ground. The deserters asserted that forty thousand Turks had participated in the assault. Two hours passed and the battle was not decided; at some points the Turks seemed victorious, at others we won the upper hand. Finally, God showed pity for the courage of our leader and the Turks fell into confusion, fell back, and were put to the sword; swiftly and forcefully they turned tail and inflicted casualties and injuries to their own side. We witnessed a spectacle, as in the midst of the battle we saw what was happening. Three hundred Turks, who had seriously hurt us and were standing on the walls of the Jewish sector, were attacked and engaged by our side. The height of the wall on the interior was almost twenty feet. They were all slaughtered to the last man and their corpses, deformed by wounds, were seen lying everywhere in the city. As the Turks were retreating and were on their way to the camp, our side gave chase and killed many within the fortifications; our side took spoils and a conspicuous standard decorated with gold and silver, belonging to their tyrant, which became the trophy for our great victory, and to the sound of applause entered the ruined walls. Three thousand five hundred Turks fell in that battle; their bodies were found in the city, on the walls, in the ditch, within the enemy defenses, and in the sea; to avoid pestilence, the deformed and butchered bodies that were lying everywhere were then burned. As the deserters, who were present in the camp when the pasha took the census, made clear, during the siege nine thousand Turks were wounded and fifteen thousand more were incapacitated.

---

[30] As *PL* 2: 358, n. 38, points out, d'Aubusson was seriously wounded in the assault and in the second siege of Rhodes in 1522 his body was paraded on the walls along with his armor and his red velvet tunic with the white cross that still bore the bloodstains from that battle. Perhaps it should also be noted that there may be a Christ-like parallel of five wounds involved in Caoursin's prose.

XXIX. Fama satis constans est palam a perfugis vulgatur Turcos visionis miraculo exterritos tanta trepidatione loco cessisse ac pedem retulisse. Aiunt enim cum vexilla Domini nostri Iesu Christi ac Virginis Mariae ac Sancti Ioannis Baptistae religionisque Hierosolymorum in conflictu iussu principis erecta sunt, crucem auream in aere splendidissimam hostes vidisse; apparuisse insuper candidissimam virginem clipeum et hastam gestantem ac hominem vili veste obsitum // splendidissimo comitatu stipatum praesidio adesse. Quae visio tantum terrorem eis incussit <ut> nullo pacto progredi ausi sint. Fatendum quoque est hanc victoriam caelo demissa esse. Quomodo tam parva militum nostrorum copia hosti potentissimo tam muris potito resistere potuisset nisi divinum praesidium affuisset? Quomodo tam parva temporis morula tanta hostium manus cecidisset nisi angelus Dei victoriam attulisset et inimicos trucida<vi>sset? Erant enim tot occis<s>orum cadavera et ita perpulchre ordinata ut non horarum sed dierum opus esse videretur et id potius divinitus quam humanitus contigisse putetur.

Quis hostem moenia possidentem iamque victoria lascivientem et ex<s>ultantem terruit?
Deus clementissimus.
Quis hostem ne scalis descenderet antequam subsidia conscendentur prohibuit?
Deus fortissimus.
Quis eorum mentes obcaecavit ut post primam pugnam non aggrediuntur nostros et multis vulneribus oppressos et defatigatos oppugnentur?
Deus clementissimus.
Quis tam potentem hostem qui tot et tanta regna subiugavit prohibuit ne hunc Hierosolymorum principatum mediocrem quidem ac ceterorum comparatione tenuem post Constantinopolitanae urbis excidium suae ditionis faceret?
Deus sapientissimus.
Agamus igitur gratias de tanto benefici ei qui nos ab impiorum manibus praeservavit.

29.   A persistent rumor was spread by the deserters that a vision terrified the Turk who then yielded and retreated. For they say that when the standards of our Lord Jesus Christ, of the Virgin Mary, of Saint John the Baptist, and of the Order of Jerusalem were brought out during the assault by order of our leader, the enemy saw a most splendid golden cross in the air; moreover, the enemy saw the appearance of a virgin, all in white and carrying a shield and a spear, and of a man wearing shabby clothes, accompanied by a guard, a most splendid band. Facing this vision, they were struck with such terror that they could advance no farther. One must confess that this victory was heaven-sent. How could this small band of our knights have resisted the enemy's powerful multitudes unless divine protection had played a part? How could such a large enemy force perish in such a short time, unless an angel of God brought victory and butchered our foe? There were so many corpses of the slain, who had been so well equipped (preparing themselves for days, it would seem, not hours), that our victory could be achieved only though divine, and not through human, means.

Who could have terrified our enemy, who had assumed control of our walls, had
already been gloating in victory, and was rejoicing?
Our most clement God.
Who prevented the enemy from climbing down his ladders before help came?
Our most powerful God.
Who blinded the enemy's mind to such a degree that after the initial assault they
failed to attack our side, hard pressed by wounds and fatigue?
Our most clement God.
Who stopped our most powerful enemy, who had already conquered numerous
large kingdoms after he sacked Constantinople, from seizing the principality of
the knights of Jerusalem, a mediocre state by comparison?
Our most wise God.
Let us give thanks for His kind act, which saved us from the hands of the impious
[Turks].[31]

---

[31] Similar rhetoric over a miraculous outcome of a battle is encountered elsewhere. When Murad II besieged Constantinople (June 10 – September 6, 1422) a miracle of the same sort occurred during the Turkish *certamen generale* (August 24) and was described by the eyewitness reporter, Ioannes Kananos, in very similar terms: Ἰωάννου τοῦ Κανανοῦ, Διήγησις περὶ τοῦ ἐν Κωνσταντινουπόλει γεγονότος πολέμου κατὰ τὸ ἔτος 1422, in *Georgius Phrantzes, Ioannes Cananus, Ioannes Anagnostes*, ed. Immanuel Bekker, CSHB (Bonn, 1838), 478–79: ἀμὴ ἡ γυναῖκα ἐκείνη ἡ ὀξέα φοροῦσα καὶ περιπατοῦσα τοῦ κάστρου καὶ τῶν προμαχιόνων ἐπάνω ἀφόβως τοῦ πολέμου τὴν ὥραν, ἐκείνη ἀντέπραξε τὰς δυνάμεις τῶν ἄστρων καὶ τὴν τέχνην τῶν ἀστρολόγων ... καὶ τὰ στρατεύματα πάντα τῶν Τούρκων ἐνεμαρτύρουν ἐνόρκως ... καὶ ἐδιηγοῦντο ... ὅταν ἔφθασαν εἰς τὰ τείχη τοῦ κάστρου ... τότε εἶδον γυναῖκα ὀξέα ροῦχα φοροῦσαν καὶ περιπατοῦσαν ἐπάνω τῶν προμαχιόνων τοῦ ἔξω κάστρου. καὶ ταύτην

XXX. Turci enim spe potiundae urbis ducti quaeque crudelitatis genera // exercere proponebant sed nefando optatu frustrati tanquam pecudes trucidantur, propulsantur, vincuntur. Extemplo ponunt commissa ad primum lapidem castra et papiliones Turci collocant machinas ad littus maris devehunt et navigiis onerariis vulneratos et quos ex Lycia traiecera<n>t multos dies usque ad eorum discessum in Turciam cum omni eorum supellectili revehunt. Hortos, vineas, praedia, si quae intacta illaesaque remanserant, vastant, depopulantur, incendunt, ingenti pecudis multitudine abacta. Dum haec Turci molirentur et discessum pararent, apparuere subsidiariae naves quas praecellentissimus Siciliae rex Ferdinandus fidei Catholicae devotissimus Rhodiis mittebat, quae ad auram post meridiem Turcis conspicientibus et Rhodiorum plausu et gratiis Altissimo datis portum intrare non formidant. Hostis machinas quas ad hoc paraverat in eas dirigit; iactu machinarum una detrimentum malo excipit, altera incolumis evasit. Ancoris ante aditum portus naves subnixae vi tormentorum et maris aestu fervente paulum ab aditu discedunt. Hespero adiiciente et procella ingruente navis quae laesa fuerat portum intrat; altera vela ventis dare compellitur. Postridie eius diei cum ea navis portum subire niteretur, vento deficiente, dum placidum reditur mare, nec longius a classe Turcensi distaret; triremes Turcorum viginti exercitu et Rhodiis conspicientibus nav<e>m ag//grediuntur et oppugnant; qui navi devehuntur viriliter se tutantur. Horis vero tribus navali proelio machinarum iactu pugnatum est. Tandem nostri victores evasere. In qua pugna triremium praefectus occiditur. Hac quoque incommoditate accepta ad

30. When the Turks still retained hope of conquering our city, they had proposed to inflict horrible acts of cruelty; their criminal wishes were frustrated, the goal was not realized: they were put to the slaughter as if they were sheep, were repelled, and were defeated. Without further delay, the Turks struck camp, collected their tents, and transported their cannon and their wounded to the seashore; it took many days for them to depart on their heavy transports and return to Turkey from Lycia with all their belongings. They plundered, devastated, destroyed, and burned whatever gardens, vineyards, and fields had remained untouched; they took an enormous flock of sheep. While the Turks were so engaged and were making preparations to depart, there appeared the ships that His Excellency, the most Catholic King Ferdinand of Sicily, had sent to the aid of the Rhodians, which after midday, with a favorable breeze, boldly headed for the harbor, under the eyes of the Turks and to the enormous applause of the Rhodians who were thanking God. The enemy deployed cannon against them and commenced firing; one ship suffered damage when she was struck, by bad luck; the other escaped unharmed. The ships dropped anchor at the entrance of the harbor but were forced by the bombardment and the heavy seas to move a little farther from the entrance. The west wind picked up and under a heavy sea the ship that had sustained damage entered the harbor. The other was forced to move on under full sail. Next day, when that ship attempted to enter the harbor, as the wind died down and the sea became calm again, she found herself rather close to the Turkish armada. Twenty galleys of the Turks moved and attacked her, while the Rhodians and the enemy army watched. The sailors defended themselves and their ship bravely. The naval battle and the cannonade lasted three hours. Finally our side emerged victorious. In this engagement the admiral of

ἰδόντες, σκότος καὶ ζάλη καὶ τρόμος καὶ φόβος ἄφνω εἰς τὰς ψυχὰς εἰσῆλθε τῶν πάντων, καὶ πρὸς φυγὴν ἔβλεψαν ... τῆς γυναικὸς γὰρ ἐκείνης ἔλαβον τὴν δειλίαν καὶ ἠλευθερώθη ἡ πόλις ... καὶ χαίρετε, ὦ φίλοι, χαίρετε τὸ μὲν τὴν ἐλευθερίαν τῆς πόλεως ... τὸ δὲ πανθαύμαστον θαῦμα τῆς Παναγίας ..... Similar stories were in circulation in antiquity, according to which Athena Promachos had saved Athens from the Goths by frightening Alaric away: Kenneth M. Setton, *Athens in the Middle Ages* 3 (London, 1975), 179. For such traditions, in general, see Norman H. Baynes, "The Supernatural Defenders of Constantinople," *Analecta Bollandiana* 7 (1949): 165–77 [repr. in idem, *Byzantine Studies and Other Essays* (London, 1955), 248–61]. While the Turkish force left the island, the Knights were not at all certain that the war was over and remained anxious. When the first ship from the west came to Rhodes in September, its crew had trouble persuading the authorities that they were not enemies in the pay of the Turks. The same ship that was carrying pilgrims to the Holy Land remained in Rhodes for four days and we have an account of the devastation that had been carried out by the Turks. Aside from the obvious destruction carried out by the long bombardment, we are informed that most of the city lay in ruins and that stone projectiles fired by the Ottoman batteries were very much in evidence. Judging by those projectiles that are still in evidence at Rhodes (mixed with the stone projectiles fired by the Turks in the second siege), the modern visitor can form a rough estimate of the widespread destruction. For this incident, cf. the account in *SOC*, 129.

suos hostis revertitur et navis subsidiaria postero die portum plenis velis intrare non formidat.

XXXI. Attulerunt profecto hae naves nuntium, quod Rhodios non parva affecit laetitia. Pontificiae quippe litterae recitant, quae Rhodiorum animos paterna monitione solidant. Subsidia quoque navium parata pandunt, quae propediem ventura erant. Praeterea grandem expeditionem parari nuntiant, quae nedum Rhodios obsidione liberare, verum etiam inimicam classem expugnare ac prosternere possit. Rhodii laeto accepto nuntio clementissimum Romanum pontificem Sixtum quartum miris laudibus tollunt, laudant, praedicant Deoque pro eius felici statu humiles preces fundunt. Hic quoque rumor ad Turcos transit, qui perterriti coeptum discessum accelerant.

XXXII. Exactis igitur novem et octoginta diebus Rhodiorum littore classis solvens Phiscum navigare preparat; illic milites et supellectilem exonerat. Ubi dies XI morata ad domesticos lares cum clade et ignominia revertitur. Qui obsidionis pericula expertus est et rei publico functus officio cognovit.

Ad laudem Dei, Christianae religionis exaltationem,
Rhodiorum gloriam, rerum gestarum commentarium edidit.

FINIS

the [Turkish] galleys perished. With this additional setback the enemy retreated and next day the ship that came to help us boldly entered the harbor under full sail.³²

31.   On board these ships was a [papal] courier, at whose arrival the Rhodians rejoiced greatly. The pontifical letters were read and their paternal advice strengthened the resolution of the Rhodians. They also revealed that ships had been made ready to come to our help. Furthermore, they announced that a great expedition was being prepared which would put an end to the siege of Rhodes and attack and wipe out the enemy armada. The courier was joyfully received and the Rhodians praised, with wonderful comments, the most clement Pope Sixtus IV; they humbly poured out their prayers to God for the happy outcome. The Turks got wind of this information and in terror accelerated their preparations for departure.

32.   The enemy armada that had spent eighty-nine days at the shores of Rhodes left and headed for Physkos; there the soldiers with their belongings landed. Eleven days later it returned home in shameful defeat. He who shared in the dangers of the siege and served as an appointed official knows it.

He produced this
Memoir of the siege
to praise God, to magnify the Christian faith, [and] to glorify the Rhodians and their deeds.

THE END

---

³² Mesih Pasha led his troops back to Constantinople; on the way he attacked the castle of the Knights at Halikarnassos but proved unable to storm it. As a result of his failure at Rhodes, he was demoted from the rank of vizier to *sancak beg*. After the death of Mehmed, Bayezid II restored him to favor and granted him the governorship of Rumeli. Mesih Pasha eventually made the pilgrimage to Mecca and in 1499 rose to the post of Grand Vizier. For a summary of his later career, see *MCT*, 399–400. In the spring of 1481 Mehmed II mustered his troops for another expedition but his true objective remained a secret. Rumors quickly spread that the sultan was going to attack Rhodes personally. While on the march Mehmed fell ill and died on May 3, 1481. Less than a month later, Caoursin pronounced his speech entitled *Oratio in senatu Rhodiorum de morte Magni Thurci habita pridie Kalendas Iunias MCCCCLXXXI*, in which he expressed great joy over the death of his adversary. In the speech, he likened Mehmed to a second Mohammed, to Lucifer, and to the Antichrist. The cause of the sultan's death is not clear, but *MCT*, 404, favors the view that he had been poisoned at the behest of his son and successor, Bayezid II. On these events cf. *MCT*, 400–5; E. Birnbaum, "Hekim Ya'kub, Physician to Sultan Mehemmed, the Conqueror," *Hebrew Medical Journal* 1 (1961): 250–322; Bernard Lewis, "The Privileges Granted by Mehmed II to his Physician," *Bulletin of the School of Oriental and African Studies* 14 (1952): 551–63; and Franz Babinger, "Ja'kub Pascha, ein Leibarzt Mehmeds II.", *Rivista degli Studi Orientali* 26 (1951): 82–113. For the European reaction to the death, see idem, "Eine lateinische Totenklage auf Mehmed II," *Studi Orientali in onore di Giorgio della Vida* (Rome, 1956), 1:15–31, and *MCT*, 408.

CHAPTER IX

LETTERS TO THE POPE AND HOSPITALLERS

I

EPISTOLA AD PAPAM
UNA CUM VEXILLO TURCHINO
MISSA 1480, DIE XVIII NOV.,
DE OBSIDIONE INSULAE, RHODUS, A TURCIS

I.   Beatissime pater, post pedum oscula beatorum. Quae in obsidione urbis Rhodiae et a nobis tutando gestae sunt, non indecens videtur Sanctitati Vestrae significare, cum ad hanc diem pugna ad honorem Christiani nominis felicem exitum, non parvam laetitiam concepturum, cuius subsidiis et favore quicquid aggredimur efficimus, speramusque divina favente clementia, auxiliisque V. R. adiutos victoriam de hoste reportaturos.[1]

II.   Turci, ubi circa urbem castrametati sunt, oppugnationis loca diligentius explorant. Civitatem quoque omni ex parte bombardis diruere proponunt,[2] et quod mente concipiunt, opere demonstrant; ad id quoque exsequendum bombardiis et mortariis, muros circundant, verberant, diruunt, turres IX et belondardos[3] magistratusque palatia concurrunt et prosternunt. Tribus tamen ex partibus commodissimum sibi esse videtur civitatem oppugnare et aggredi, potissime ad rem conficiendam pertinere videtur turris moles Sancti Nicolai expugnatura.[4] Ex qua urbem in suam potestatem facile transituram arbitrantur.

III.   Est enim arx ipsa in vertice molis posita,[5] quae versus Septentrionem in mari prominet. Eoque portus conspicit, et aditum navigantibus qui eam tenent si libet, facile prohibent, ad occidentem Oratorium Sancti Anthonii situm est, fere CC passibus a turre distans, mari interiecto.[6] Conspecta igitur loci opportunitate hostis, potiundae turris avidus, cum conatu incumbit, ut eam in suam redigat potestatem. Ad turrim itaque diruendam, tres ingentes bombardas aeneas devehunt, quarum magnitudo et vehementia incredibilis erat. Saxa quoque sphaerica novem[7] palmarum torquebant, eas quoque apud Sacellum

....

[1] Invictissime ac serenissime Princeps: Quae in obsidione Rhodiae urbis a Turcis expugnando et a nobis tutando gesta sunt, non incongruum vestrae imperiali Maiestati significare, cum ad hanc diem pugnae ad honorem Christiani nominis felicem exitum adeptae sint; et non ambigimus vestrae imperiali Maiestati ex victoriis non parvam laetitiam excepturam.

[2] bombardis quatere et diruere proponunt

[3] et Bolvvardon;

[4] Sancti Nicolai expugnatio, ex qua

[5] molis sita,

[6] prominet, usque ad portum conspicit, et aditum navigantibus, qui eam tenet, si libet, facile prohibet; ad Occidentem

[7] IX

I

LETTER TO THE POPE
TOGETHER WITH A TURKISH STANDARD
CAPTURED FROM THE TURKS DURING THE SIEGE
OF THE ISLAND OF RHODES,
SENT ON NOVEMBER 18, 1480

1. Most Blessed Father: my respects to the blessed. It seems not impolite to relate to Your Holiness the events surrounding the siege of the city Rhodes and our actions in her defense, which battle resulted, thus far, in a resounding victory to the honor of the name of the Christians; it brought considerable joy, as with His help and favor we achieved this and we hope that with divine aid and clemency on our side we will prevail over our enemy.

2. After the Turks made camp, they carefully explored the points to be assaulted. They proposed to destroy the city through total bombardment, and what they conceived in their minds they put into operation; for this purpose they deployed bombards and mortars; they surrounded our walls and bombarded and destroyed nine towers and a boulevard; they attacked and razed the palace of the administration. It seemed to them advantageous to attack and assault the city from three areas, especially because they thought that their purpose would be achieved if they seized the tower and mole of Saint Nicholas, as they were under the impression that the city would easily fall into their hands in this manner.

3. For a fortress is erected on the tip of the mole, which extends northwards into the sea. It looks over the harbor and can easily grant or deny entrance to sailing vessels; to the west, almost 200 steps from the tower (with the sea in between), the Chapel of Saint Anthony is situated, almost two hundred paces away from the tower with the sea in between. In order to demolish this tower, they deployed three enormous bronze bombards, whose length and power were incredible: they propelled round stone projectiles measuring nine palms. They placed these bombards at the Chapel of Saint Anthony. It was a miracle to relate,

Sancti Anthonii collocant. Mirabile dictu, calamitosum visu, opus quidem praecelebre,[8] et quod stabilissimum videbatur sex[9] diebus assiduis CCCtis[10] lapidum ictibus turris pro parte potiori[11] diruitur, prosternitur, laceratur. Hostis ruinam conspiciens[12] exsultat, plausibus quoque aera complet, quae bona[13] gaudia in suum lutum commissa[14] sunt. Nos vero de turris tuitione[15] soliciti grandem horrendamque eius ruinam adspicientes,[16] quod supererat munitione oplere[17] iussimus. Et quia[18] id quoque parum fore visum est,[19] propter ipsius magnum lapsum, constituimus, nedum arcem tutari, sed ne molem ipsam Sancti Nicolai defendere.[20]

IV. Omni igitur vigilantia, cura et ingenio operariis fere mille die noctuque adhibitis totis his diebus[21] fossa in cantibus exorsa,[22] propugnaculis quoque ex lignis aedificatis inverticem[23] ipsius molis circa turrim in media quoque eius radice turrim et molem inexpugnabilem non sine parvo[24] sumptu reddidimus, praesidium[25] quoque fortissimorum commilitonum in ruina turris[26] et munitionibus ac propugnaculis circa eam confectis[27] in radice quoque ac pede eius molis altera praesidia ad Orientem et Occidentem collocamus. Nam illic radix muro clauditur et mare vadosum est, quare observatur defenditurque, ne Turci illic[28] transirent, et nostros a tergo adorirentur,[29] in moenibus urbis bombardas disponi iubemus, quae ad tempus pugnae officio fungantur ignesque[30] cum sulphuris[31]

---

[8] percelebre
[9] sed
[10] CCC
[11] pro potiori parte
[12] Hostis quidem ruinam conspiciens
[13] vana
[14] in luctum suum conversa
[15] de tutione turris
[16] grandem horrendamque ruinam conspicientes
[17] opplere
[18] quia
[19] parum visum est
[20] se molem ipsam Sancti Nicolai defendere
[21] totis diebus
[22] fossa non incassum excisa
[23] in vertice
[24] magno
[25] reclusimus; tum praesidium
[26] molis
[27] confectis collocamus;
[28] illuc
[29] adoriantur
[30] ignes quoque
[31] scaphis

an awesome sight, and a glorious achievement: the tower that seemed so solid after six days and three hundred hits by the stone projectiles was demolished, was razed and leveled, and lay in ruins for the most part. The enemy looked upon the ruins and rejoiced; applause filled the air, even though this joy turned into his utter destruction. Worried over the defense of the tower, we inspected the extensive and fearful ruins ad issued orders to fill out the remains with defensive structures. And since this had not been foreseen, on account of the magnitude of the ruins we decided to give up the defense of the tower, as well as that of the mole of Saint Nicholas itself.

4. And so with all vigilance, care, and resourcefulness almost one thousand laborers were assigned to the task: day and night they dug a ditch and built wooden battlements at the tip of the very mole around the tower; on the middle and its base we had built, at considerable cost, a tower and an impregnable mole and we placed, in the ruins of the tower, a garrison of very strong comrades at arms; the defenses and the completed battlements around he tower and at the foot of the mole to the east and west were manned by other guards. There the base of the mole was enclosed and the sea could be crossed on foot; we took care to defend it so that no Turks could cross at this point and attack our side from the rear; we issued orders to deploy bombards along the walls of the city, which, during battle, would perform the task, with the assigned fire

parantur, quae in classem mittuntur.³² Turci aedificii ruina allecti uno et demum altero proelio turrim invadunt. Primum cum facile ipsam³³ expugnare putarent, mediocribus viribus aggrediuntur ante auroram luce adhuc dubia, triremibus ad hoc paratis arcem oppugnant proelianturque. Nostri quidem tuitioni intenti locum constanter tutantur. Sic hostis victus discedit. Ea in pugna fere VII.³⁴ Turci (prout profugae significarunt³⁵) cecidere.

V.   Interiectis autem diebus accensi priori repulsa, turrim maiori potentia arte et ingenio oppugnant, ac reparatoria³⁶ et³⁷ propugnacula³⁸ iactu bombardarum quatiunt, non nullosque³⁹ conterunt. Nosque⁴⁰ reficimus summa celeritate quod obteritur. Parant ad haec conficienda triremes XXX. bene⁴¹ munitas et ingeniose ad proelium armatas, adiiciunt et magna quaedam oneraria⁴² (*parandarias*⁴³ vulgo dictas), quarum quaedam onustae bombardis et saxis erant, ut locum turris et molis qua se potituros credebant munirent, et ex his urbem lacesserant, dirruerant, oppugnarentque.⁴⁴ Cymbasque quasdam⁴⁵ disponunt ex quibus quinque⁴⁶ Turcorum strenuissimi facile in molem transitum praebent.⁴⁷ Nos enim post primam pugnam suspicati quod evenit abundantius,⁴⁸ dies noctesque circa turris et molis tutamen⁴⁹ vires et ingenium adhibemus, munimenta ampliamus, praesidia augemus, gravissimis non parcemus.⁵⁰ Nam et in ea salutem urbis constitutam consciebamus.⁵¹

VI.   Media igitur nocte grandiori accensi ardore Turci XIII. die Iulii⁵² arcem summo silentio aggrediuntur, omnique ex parte magno⁵³ impetu invadunt.

---

³² mittantur
³³ Primum cum ipsam facile
³⁴ 700
³⁵ significaverunt
³⁶ repatoria
³⁷ ac
³⁸ reparamenta
³⁹ nonnullaque
⁴⁰ Nos quoque
⁴¹ triremes bene munitas
⁴² et navigia quaedam oneraria
⁴³ parendarias
⁴⁴ lecesserent, diruerent expugnarentque.
⁴⁵ Cymbas praeterea quasdam
⁴⁶ quique
⁴⁷ in molem descendant et potem miro artificio aedificiant, qui ex Ecclesia Sancti Antonii turris in molem transitum praebeat.
⁴⁸ Nos enim suspicati quod evenit post primam pugnam abundantius
⁴⁹ tutamenta
⁵⁰ gravissimis impensis non parcimus
⁵¹ coniiciebamus
⁵² XIII Kal. Iulii
⁵³ omnique parte magno

and sulfur [= gunpowder], and attack the fleet. The Turks were attracted by the ruined condition of the structure and attacked the tower once or twice. At first they thought that that they would capture the tower easily and attacked with moderate forces before dawn, at twilight, with the triremes that they had equipped for this purpose; they launched an assault upon the tower and the fight began. Our side defended the spot with intensity and determination. And so the enemy retreated in defeat. In that battle seven <hundred> Turks (as the deserters revealed) fell.

5.   After a few days passed, they became upset over their defeat and attacked the tower with greater strength, thought, and ingenuity. They shook our repaired structures and the battlements with their bombard projectiles and even brought down quite a few. In the highest speed possible we repaired the damaged areas. To complete their design they prepared 30 triremes; they were well fortified and cleverly equipped for battle; in addition, they added a number of cargo boats (commonly called *parandarie*), some of which were loaded with bombards and rocks (to fortify the spot that they believed would come under their control and then assail, beset, and level the city). They deployed certain boats to transfer some very strong Turks to the mole. After the first battle we had a lot of reasons to suspect that this would occur; day and night we applied our strength and resources to provide a defense around the tower and mole: we extended the fortifications, we increased the garrison, and we spared nothing. We believed that the safety of the city depended on this outcome.

6.   On July 13, in the middle of the night, the Turks, burning with higher desire, launched their very strong attack from all places in total silence. Our

Arrectae⁵⁴ etiam erant nostrorum aures, nec dormitabant. Ubi autem adesse inimicos comperitur, machinae saxa iaciunt milites gladiis stringunt, balistis fundis saxorum⁵⁵ iactu ex turri et mole hostem deturbent⁵⁶ et propellunt, pugnatum est summa vi a media nocte usque ad horam decimam. Turci vero quamplures qui ex cymbis et triremibus descenderant in molem⁵⁷ trucidantur. Pons natans Turcis onustus et actu machinarum⁵⁸ frangitur, qui supererant Turci merguntur. Quatuor quoque triremes et ea navigia quae bombardis et lapidibus onusta erant, iactu saxorum ex tormentis perfringuntur et undis obruuntur. Ignis quoque in classem mittitur, qui eam retrocedere compellit.⁵⁹ Sicque discedunt victi Turci. Insignis quidem haec pugna fuit morte clarorum virorum qui Turcis praeerant quorum interitus luctum exercitui praebuit; perfugae⁶⁰ quoque post pugnam introducti affirmant Turcos hac in pugna magnam stragem accepisse ex eis quoque fere MMD⁶¹ cecidisse.

VII. Cum autem Turci spem turris expugnandae perdidissent, industriam, ingenium, vires et omnem conatum ad urbem expugnandam convertunt, et licet tota civitas machinis concuteretur et laceraretur, ut vix forma prioris urbis remanserit, tamen potissimam⁶² murorum partem oppugnare intendunt, quae⁶³ Iudaeorum domos claudunt Orientemque spectant eamque etiam partem, quae ad turrim Italiae ducitur. Ad haec igitur moenia diruenda et diliceranda VIII⁶⁴ ingentes grandissimasque bombardas comportant, saxa circuitus palmarum IX. torquentes, quae assiduo die noctuque verberant muros⁶⁵ nec cessant bombardo et mortaria circa civitatem locata similes lapides torquere, quin immo ad terrorem et detrimentum iactus⁶⁶ multiplicant. Nos ad iactum mortariorum vitandum imbellicem aetatem ac mulieres sub fornicibus, valvis ac pluribus⁶⁷ locis pomerii cohabitare statuimus, quo effectum est, ut pauci hoc tormento interierint.⁶⁸ Usi quoque sunt⁶⁹ alio tormenti genere, quo igneas pilas proiiciebant, ac sagittas ignitas ex balistis et catapultis torquebant,⁷⁰ quo ignem

---

⁵⁴ Erectae
⁵⁵ fundis et saxorum
⁵⁶ deturbant
⁵⁷ in molem descendarant
⁵⁸ machinarum iactu
⁵⁹ compulit
⁶⁰ profugi
⁶¹ IICƆIƆ
⁶² potissime
⁶³ qui
⁶⁴ octo
⁶⁵ muros verberant
⁶⁶ ictus
⁶⁷ et valvis et pluribus
⁶⁸ interirent
⁶⁹ Usi sunt quoque
⁷⁰ torquent

troops had kept their ears open and were not caught napping. As soon as we discovered the presence of the enemy, our knights put into operation the stone-throwing machines, drew their swords, and threw the enemy into confusion with catapult projectiles from the tower and the mole. A multitude of Turks from the boats descended upon the mole and was put to the sword. The moving bridge, loaded with Turks, was broken up by bombardment and the Turks on it were drowned. In addition, the twenty-four vessels loaded with bombards and rocks were destroyed by artillery fire and were submerged into the waves. We met their fleet with fire and they were forced to retreat. And so the Turks perished in defeat. This battle was marked by the death of many famous men, who had been in charge of the Turks; their demise was an occasion for mourning. The deserters who came to us after the battle asserted that fifteen hundred Turks had fallen in the slaughter during the battle.

7. After the Turks lost all hope of seizing the tower by force, they turned their efforts, resources, strength, and all attention to the conquest of the city; their cannon shook and mangled the entire city; the former appearance of our city vanished; they proposed to attack the most powerful section of the walls, which encloses the neighborhood of the Jews to the east and that area which leads to the tower of Italy. For this purpose they deployed eight enormous, very heavy bombards, which ejected stone projectiles of nine palms in circumference; continuously, day and night, they pounded the walls, and similar stone projectiles from bombards and mortars kept falling around the city; their impact enhanced the resulting loss and terror. We ordered those who could not fight because of their age and the women to seek shelter under arcades, doors, and numerous spots within the defensive perimeter in order to avoid the mortar bombardment; after this came into effect, few perished in this annoying bombardment. They also used other engines, which threw fiery round projectiles and released lighted arrows from catapults, which set fire to our buildings. We consulted about the

in aedificia iniecerunt.⁷¹ Nos vero indemnitati urbis consulendi⁷² peritos artis delegimus, qui post casum pilarum magna solertia ignem exstinguerent. His remediis Rhodii a magnis incommodis servati sunt.

VIII.   Excogitant insuper impii Turci urbem⁷³ ingenio occulto propugnare. Fossas itaque tortuosas effodiunt, quas partim viminibus et terra operiunt ut latenter ad fossas urbis accedant. Propugnacula quoque multis in locis aedificant, ex quibus assiduo sagittant, et colubrinis et serpentinis nostros⁷⁴ deturbant fatigantque ac pensitant⁷⁵ et eis esse commodissimum aliquam partem fossae civitatis quae muro Spetionis⁷⁶ adiacet complere, opera itaque ab hoste adhibita lapidis congeriem cessat et occulto in fossam iaciunt. Assiduitate pars fossae opletur⁷⁷ antemurali quoque aequatur, ex quo et ruina in dorsi formam⁷⁸ redacta facilimus⁷⁹ conscensus in moenia efficitur. Nos enim⁸⁰ inimici conatum inspicientes tuitioni urbis invigilamus totiusque urbis et ad muros Iudaeorum et alio se convertunt.⁸¹ Et nos munimentis ac reparationibus⁸² validissimis ruinam murorum⁸³ firmamus palis lignorum humatissimorum⁸⁴ infixis ac terra tenaci fascibus arbustorum⁸⁵ et ramorum interiectis, quo⁸⁶ invicem subtilissime firmissimeque cohaerentes vim machinarum sustinebant et ruinam protegebant, ne muri collapsi intra urbem facilem descensum praeberent, qui a parte urbis nisi cum scalis conscendi potuerunt, licet a parte exteriori ruina facilem ascensum praeberet, etiam loco propugnaculorum palos et vegetes terra repletos⁸⁷ statuimus, quae nostros tutarentur et conscendentibus Turcis impedimento essent. Ignes quoque artificiosos et alia ingenia paramus⁸⁸ quae ad propulsandam Turcorum vim conducere videbantur. Excogitatum quoque est, eam partem fossae quae lapidibus

---

⁷¹ iacerent
⁷² consulentes
⁷³ impii urbem
⁷⁴ colubrinis ac serpentinis bombardis nostros
⁷⁵ Pensitant quoque
⁷⁶ speronis
⁷⁷ oppletur
⁷⁸ formam dorsi
⁷⁹ facillimus
⁸⁰ autem
⁸¹ invigilamus totaque urbe et castello reparatis et munitionibus fossis quoque quam diligenter intendimus. Quod Turci coniectantes desperati ad muro Iudaeorum et alio se covertunt
⁸² reparis
⁸³ Turcorum
⁸⁴ vivacissimorum
⁸⁵ ac terra fascibus arbustorum
⁸⁶ quae
⁸⁷ oppletas
⁸⁸ paravimus

danger that menaced our city and we selected experienced men who were able, with great skill, to put out the fires after the impact of the projectiles. With these efforts the Rhodians were spared great troubles.

8.   In addition, the impious Turks came up with a concealed way to attack the city: they dug up complicated tunnels, which they covered up partly with wicker baskets, and opened up passageways in the ground to approach the ditches of the city in secret. They constructed battlements in numerous spots, behind which they kept up a constant shower of arrows and further hindered and fatigued our troops with fire from colubrine and serpentine artillery pieces; they thought that this ploy would create an advantage for them and they could fill part of the moat of the city, which was adjacent to the walls of the Hospital. And so the enemy gathered a huge mass of rocks, which they secretly threw into the moat. Part of the moat was filled and became level with the area before the walls through their efforts; this and the ruins presenting a flat area created a very easy climb to our walls. We observed the efforts of the enemy and we remained vigilant in the defense of the city; we made repairs throughout the city and diligently repaired the defenses of the citadel and the fortifications of the moat; the Turks realized it and in despair turned themselves to the walls of the Jews and elsewhere. We strengthened the ruins of the walls with repairs and strong supports, with wooden, green stakes fixed to the ground, and with bundles of trees firmly connected to the earth, and we interwove branches in-between; clinging to one another very well and very firmly they sustained the force of the artillery and protected the ruins so that the collapsed walls would not offer an easy passage down to the city; they could only reach parts of the city by means of ladders, even though on the exterior the ruins offered an easy climb; we erected stakes and barrels filled with soil in place of battlements, which shielded our warriors and hindered the downward movement of the Turks. We also put together artificial fire and other traps to push back the force of the Turks. We also decided

a Turcis opleta[89] erat, evacuare. Sed cum id palam effici non posset, cuniculo latente quae fossa in pomerio[90] aedificata exitum sub lapidibus nostri habent et occulto lapides in urbem comportant. Sentiunt profecto Turci qui fossae propinqui erant lapidum congeriem minui et accensus opportunitatem adimi nisi quam citius[91] quod cupiunt efficiant. Itaque his in operibus XXX.[92] diebus consumptis quo in tempore trium milium V.[93] vel circiter ingentium saxorum globi in moenia[94] et urbem iacti sunt, Turci ratione invadendae urbis spectata[95] ne ascensus commoditas auferret[96] accelerant propositum conficere.

IX.   Pridie quam proelium iniretur ac sequenti nocte et diliculo quod mane quo pugnatum est praecessit,[97] VIII.[98] bombardae dictis muris obiectae absque intermissione saxa ingentia torquent, quod loco propugnaculorum adhibitum erat, dilacerant et diruunt, vigiles, custodes et moenium praesidia pro parte potiori occidunt, ut quisquam vix superstare muris[99] possit nisi summo astu occultaretur, et scalas[100] ad signum campanae paululum descenderet,[101] et demum conscenderet,[102] nec tempus datum est propugnacula denuo instauranda, cum semper ictus bombardarum augerentur. Ut eo pauco tempore III.[103] vel circiter saxa iacta sint. Turci vero iactu bombardarum finito ad signum iactus mortarii, quod pridem eo in loco constituerant, confertissimi magno impetu quam celerrime Vto die Augusti[104] conscendunt. Erat namque facilis, ut dicimus,[105] eis ascensus facilior quam nostris esset per scallas.[106] Superiora quoque murorum loca trucidato[107] nostro quo[108] illic erat praesidio, quod primo tantum impetui[109] resistere nequivit, antequam subsidia nostra scalas[110] conscenderant,

---

[89] oppleta
[90] latentique fossa in pomerio aedificata
[91] nisis quantocius
[92] XXXVIII
[93] 3500
[94] ingentium saxorum in moenia
[95] Turci sciliciet occasione invadendi urbis conspecta
[96] auferatur
[97] praecesserat
[98] octo
[99] vix muris superstare
[100] scala
[101] descenderent
[102] conscenderent
[103] CCC
[104] VII Kal. Augusti
[105] diximus
[106] nostris per scalas
[107] eradicato
[108] quod
[109] primum tanto impetu
[110] scalas

to empty the part of the moat that had been filled with rocks by the Turks; but since this could not be carried out openly, we created a hidden mine, which led under the rocks through the perimeter, and we secretly carried the rocks to the city. Actually the Turks who were stationed near the moat realized that the heap of stones was getting smaller and that their chance was being snatched away, faster than they could achieve it. And so thirty days passed with these activities, during which time three to five thousand stone projectiles were fired into the city and against the walls. So that their chance of invading the city by ascent would not vanish altogether, they redoubled their efforts to reach their goal.

9. The day before the battle came and during the following night and the dawn's early light (which preceded the day of the struggle), the eight bombards I have mentioned pounded the wall with enormous stone projectiles and tore apart and destroyed our improvised defenses in place of battlements; the sentries and the garrison of the walls perished for the most part; one could only keep his post on the walls though clever concealment and had to descend slowly at the toll of the bell, then climb up again, and there was no time given to repair the battlements, as the bombardment kept thickening. And in this short period about three [hundred] projectiles were fired. When finally the bombards ceased firing, to the signal of the mortar fire, which had been earlier deployed in the area, the Turks began their very swift ascent in packs; it was August 5. As I mentioned, they did not have to struggle; their ascent was easier than ours, as dictated by the use of ladders. The upper parts of the fortifications were without defenders and garrison (as they had perished), and there was no one to oppose their first assault; before our supporting troops could climb up through the

occupavit,[111] et illic vexilla sua statuit.[112] Idem quoque faciunt ad turrim Italiae, cuius verticem expugnant.[113]

X.   Clamor undique oritur, manus quoque viriliter conserit,[114] magna quoque vi[115] pugnatur, repente nostris se obiicientibus hosti, dextra[116] levaque in murorum[117] superioribus locis inter[118] hostem impugnant[119] et valde[120] deturbant ne moenia discurrerant.[121] Scalae[122] quoque quae quatuor erant quibus in vicum Iudaeorum descendebatur una iussu nostro perfractae,[123] conscensis hostibus nos obiicimus,[124] tutamur, defendimus. Turci vero perpulchre armati duo millia[125] super muros erant confertissimi, qui secum magnam conferentiam[126] armorum vi propellere et loco expellere intebantur.[127] Sed nostrorum turba[128] firma persistens nequaquam loco cessit. Sequebantur enim[129] Turcos qui muros potiti erant. Ingens quoque multitudo[130] Turcorum quae totum campum adiacentem ruinam vallum et fossam appleverat[131] ut terra vix conspici posset. Affirmarunt profugae MMM[132] Turcorum invasioni adesse. Vexillum imaginis Sanctissimae Dominis nostri Iesu Christi et religionis nostrae ante hostis conspectus ereximus. Nostri ex Turcis qui super muro erant CCC. vel circiter in vicum Iudaeorum propellunt, qui ad unum occisi sunt.[133] Summa itaque vi horis duabus pugnatum est. Tandem Turci pressi, fatigati et perterriti,[134] vulneribus

---

[111] occupant
[112] statuunt
[113] oppugnant
[114] conseruntur
[115] magna vi
[116] dextera
[117] levaque murorum
[118] nostri
[119] oppugnant
[120] valide
[121] discurrerent
[122] Scalis
[123] perfracta
[124] hosti nos opponimus
[125] II⊂⊃
[126] confertissimi de nostris secum manus conferentes
[127] nitebantur
[128] virtus
[129] sequebatur vero
[130] ingens multitudo
[131] oppleverat
[132] XI⊂⊃

[133] adesse. Nostri ex Turcis qui super muro erant CCC vel circiter in vicum Iudaeorum propellunt, qui ad unum occisi sunt. Eo in conflicto vexillum Imaginis Sacratissimi Domini nostri Iesu Christi et religionis nostrae ante hostibus conspectum ereximus.

[134] fatigati perterriti

ladders, the enemy had erected his standards there. They same situation prevailed at the tower of Italy, whose summit they seized.

10.   Clamor reigned everywhere, as hand-to-hand combat commenced; our side opposed the enemy; they fought against him, left and right, on the highest areas of the walls and confused him with their strength so that he would not overrun the walls. With one order the four ladders that led to the neighborhood of the Jews were broken and we opposed the enemy. We fought on, and kept up the defense. There was a crowd of three thousand Turks extremely well equipped on top of the walls, who were engaging with force a great force of warriors in their efforts to push them off the walls. But our group persisted with determination and yielded nowhere. They pursued the Turks who had assumed control of the walls. In addition, enormous numbers of Turks (who had amassed in the neighboring camp and occupied the ditch and the moat to such an extent that the ground could not be seen) joined the assault. The deserters assert that there were Turks present in the assault. The standard bearing the image of our Lord Jesus Christ and of our order we raised in the face of the enemy. We had about three hundred men on top of the walls in the vicinity of the Jews; they all fell, to the last man. The hard battle lasted two hours. Finally the Turks were

confossi¹³⁵ terga vertunt et fugam tanto impetu arripiunt, ut sibi ipsis impedimento essent et perniciem afferrent.

XI. Cecidere¹³⁶ ea in pugna tria milia quingenti¹³⁷ vel circiter, quorum cadavera intra urbem ac supra moenia et in fossa¹³⁸ munitionibus hostium et mari reperta sunt, et postmodum ad luem vitandam combusta, quorum spoliis nostri potiti fuere, qui fugientes Turcos usque ad campi planitiem magno animo secuti, eos trucidantes tandem incolumes urbem ingressi¹³⁹ sunt. In proelio quidem ex nostris militibus quam plurimi inter¹⁴⁰ confertissimos hostes constanter pugnantes occubuere nostrique¹⁴¹ commilitones pluribus vulneribus acceptis. Deo gratias acturi, vulneraque curaturi praesidio valido muris imposito dum revertuntur; ne quid¹⁴² profecto sine divino auxilio contingit, qui tantam¹⁴³ cladem a nobis evertit. Misit eum Deus non ambiguus¹⁴⁴ de caelo auxilium, ne plebecula¹⁴⁵ Christum colens Mahometis¹⁴⁶ spurcitiis inficeretur. Paraverantque¹⁴⁷ spe potiundae urbis plures funes¹⁴⁸ ad captivos allegandos,¹⁴⁹ et palorum ingentem multitudinem¹⁵⁰ ad vivos cruciandos decreverunt. Dirruerunt enim¹⁵¹ omnes mortales et feminas¹⁵² supra X.¹⁵³ annorum aetatem trucidare et palis suffigere, teneriorisque aetatis mortales in captivitatem deducere,¹⁵⁴ et ad fidem abnegandam compellere, et ruinae¹⁵⁵ supellectilem in praedam committere,¹⁵⁶ urbis ditione¹⁵⁷ Turco reservata. Sed frustrati sunt nefando¹⁵⁸ optatu, tanquam pecudes occiduntur.¹⁵⁹

---

¹³⁵ vulneribus quoque fessi
¹³⁶ Decidere
¹³⁷ IIIcI⊃Vc
¹³⁸ fossam
¹³⁹ incolumes regressi
¹⁴⁰ militibus et balivis inter
¹⁴¹ occubuere. Nos nostrique
¹⁴² acturi, praesidio valido muris imposito domum revertimur; nec id profecto
¹⁴³ tandem
¹⁴⁴ ambigimus
¹⁴⁵ plebecula
¹⁴⁶ Machometis
¹⁴⁷ Paraverant Turci
¹⁴⁸ urbis funes sibi ad
¹⁴⁹ alligandos
¹⁵⁰ magnitudinem
¹⁵¹ cruciandos. Decreverant enim
¹⁵² mortales, mares, et feminas
¹⁵³ decem
¹⁵⁴ ducere
¹⁵⁵ omne
¹⁵⁶ convertere
¹⁵⁷ ditionem
¹⁵⁸ frustrati suo nefando
¹⁵⁹ ceduntur

overwhelmed in fatigue and terror; having sustained wounds, they turned their backs and joined in such a headlong flight that they impeded each other and destroyed themselves.

11.   About three thousand five hundred of them fell during that battle, whose cadavers were found in the city, on top of the walls, in the moat, and in the defenses and the water; they were afterwards burned to avoid pestilence but our troops won the spoils; they spiritedly chased the Turks to their level camp, put them to the sword, and finally entered the city without losses. Yet in the battle we lost very many of our knights, who sustained many wounds, in the thick of the fight against the enemy. Giving thanks to God, they withdrew in order to see to their wounds and a strong garrison was placed in charge of the walls. The fact that such disaster was averted can only be attributed to divine help. Our manifest God sent help from heaven, so that his Christ-worshipping folk would not be infected with the abomination of Mohammed. As they had hoped to seize the city, they had prepared ropes to bind their prisoners and an enormous number of stakes to impale their live captives. They had decreed that all men and women aged beyond ten years would be slaughtered and impaled; those of a younger age would be enslaved and forced to give up their religion; all property would become their booty and the control of the city would pass to the Turk. But their criminal wishes did not come to fruition and they perished as if they were sheep.

XII. His in pugnis et cinctionibus[160] duobus[161] diebus factis ut appropinquationem prohiberemus et fossam evacuaremus et ageremus quod civitati commodum esset, etiam machinarum iactu in exercitum et viridaria quae incolebant (prout[162] profugae divulgarunt[163]), Turci fere novem millia[164] occisi sunt; ingens quidem multitudo vulnerata inter quos quidem capitanei et primarum bassa[165] et quidem[166] Turci gener occubuerunt.[167] Pugna commissa extemplo Turci remotis castrametantur, machinas quoque ac Turcos, qui ex Lycia transerant cum omni supellectili Phiscum antiquam continentis urbem devehunt, viridaria, agros, vineas, ac praedia vastant, depopulantur, et incendunt omneque pecus fere abigunt. His peractis littori accedunt et in Lyciam transfretant, ubi XI dies stationem habentes tandem cum iactura multa et ignominia ad domesticos lares revertuntur. Quemadmodum diffusius V<estrae> S<anctitati> explicabunt magnificus ac percellens miles Anthonius dominus de Montelio ad vicecomitem primanus noster ac venerandi fratres Ventum de fautonibus prior Capc. et Diomedes de Villagut praeceptor Daliaga, Locumtenens venerandi Seneschali omnes nostri, quibus nonnulla commisimus explicanda V<estrae> S<anctitati> nomine nostro supplicant, ut in dicendis fidem et agendis votivam expeditionem S<anctitati> V<estrae> dare dignetur. Omnipotens Deus V<estrae> S<anctitati> feliciter conservet.[168]

Datum Rhod. die XV Septembris CIↃ CCCC LXXX.
Humiles et devotissimi servuli Magister Hospitalitatis Ierosolymitanae et concilium.[169]

Subscriptio: Sanctissimo clementissimoque Domino nostro D. Sixto, divina providentia pontifici constituto.

---

[160] eruptionibus
[161] diversis
[162] ut
[163] divulgaverunt
[164] IX CIↃ
[165] ac Germanus Balse
[166] quidam
[167] occubuere
[168] Pugna commissa, munimentis prius exustis, ad primum lapidem castra Turci locarunt, ubi supellectili, impedimentis, ac machinis onerandis, ac Turcis in Lyciam revehendis nonnullis diebus consumptis Rhodiorum littore solventes Phiscum continentem urbem antiquam navigant; sic quoque victi cum ignominia recedunt. Omnipotens Deus vestram imperialem Maiestatem feliciter conservet ad vota.
[169] Datum Rhodii die XIII Septembris, anno Redemptoris nostri incarnationis MCCCCLXXX. E. V. Imperii M. Humiles servitores, Petrus Daubusson Magister Hospitalis Hierosolymitani et consules.

12. Two days were spent in these fights and battles; we denied access to the enemy, we cleaned out the moat and did what was best for our commonwealth; during our bombardment the Turks (as the deserters revealed) suffered almost nine thousand casualties dead in their camp and in the gardens that they had occupied. A huge number of them suffered wounds; among them were their captains and their lord pasha; some notable Turks perished. After the conclusion of the battle the Turks broke camp and took away their troops and the engines, which they had transported along with their equipment to Phiscus, the ancient city on the continent. They devastated, pillaged, and burned our gardens, fields, vineyards, and fortresses; they even carried away almost all our flocks. After these events they proceeded to the shore and crossed to Lycia; they remained there eleven days and then they returned to their homeland with no glory and with great loss of life. The magnificent and excellent knight Anthony, the lord of Monteil, our leader, and the reverend brothers, the prior of the Capuchins and Diomedes de Villagut, our preceptor Daliaga, in place of the Reverend Seneschal, will supply details to your Holiness, as they have been charged with this mission and will come as suppliants to your Holiness to declare their faith and see what must be done for the launching of a crusade. May Almighty God preserve your Holiness in happiness.

Given at Rhodes on September 15, 1480.

The humble and most devoted servants: The [Grand] Master and the Council of the Order of the Hospitallers of Jerusalem.

Subscription: To the most holy and most clement Lord Sixtus, our Lord, appointed Lord Pope by divine providence.

II

Frater Petrus Daubusson &c. & nos Conventus &c.
universis & singulis prioribus, praeceptoribus, & fratribus Ordinis
nostri ubilibet constitutis,
ad quos nostrae praesentes literae pervenerint salutem in eo, qui est
omnium vera salus.

I.   Quod in Rhodios Turcorum tyrannus iam pridem machinatus est proficere conatur: concepit olim fidei inimicus in nos, et ordinem nostrum inexorabile odium, quia pro fide Christi sibi resistimus; augeretur quoque eius insanus furor, quod annos quatuor et viginti, quo Constantinopolis expugnata est, nulla ditionis nostrae portione subacta suae tyrannidi, vires opponimus, et censum petitum recusavimus. Itaque nuper ingenti classe velorum CIX, vel circiter parata, contractisque undique copiis ex provinciis Rhodo vicinis, quas ex continenti, terraque firma devexit, traicitque in insulam nostram, Rhodiorum agros, ac urbem nostram potenti manu XV Iuni aggressus est, obsedit, et circumdat; comportavit ad urbem nostram oppugnandam, tormentorum, machinarum, bombardarum, lignearumque turrium, ingeniorumque bello aptorum grandem numerum; suntque in castrum in nos collocati hostes circiter LXX M. qui nos assiduis insultibus petunt, invadunt, oppugnant; his profecto acri, fortique animo resistimus, vires quoque opponimus, et hostium conatus propulsamus, divina pietate atque clementia freti, qui sperantes in se et pro fide Catholica pugnantes non deserit.

II.   Non faciet enim hostes cum imbelli milite manum conserere; aut cum molli Asiatico pugnare: milite, militans certis pacto, ingeniis, bellorum machinis, et bombardis, frumento, ac munitionibus abundamus, quibus hostium vires sustinere possumus et fratrum nostrorum subsidia, auxilia quoque operiri, in quo omnem status nostri tuitionis spem constituimus. Est quoque civitas Rhodia non sine grandi impensa muro, vallo, fossa, turribus munita ornataque; quo effectum est, ut eius potentiam non formidamus, si modo affuerint fratrum nostrorum praesidia in tempore accelerata, quibus fractus hostis discedat, et opinione concepta frustretur. Arbitratur ipse tyrannus obsidionis diuturna protractione commeatus nostros et vires militesque nostros terere, frangere, attenuare; studetque, si quis ex suis bello cadunt, alios ex continenti ducere, et prostratorum loco sufficere; nostris comminutis putat posse rerum potiri: fallitur quippe hic furibundus draco, nec videt Sanctissimi Domini nostri, Romanae quoque Ecclesiae, ac Serenissorum regum Catholicorumque principum auxilia praesto futura, et nobis suffragatura; ignorat quoque fratrum commilitonumque nostrorum in fidem Catholicam ardentissimum zelum, veram obedientiam, integram observantiam, qui nullo pacto caput et arcem ordinis nostri urbem Rhodiam periclitari

II

Brother Pierre d'Aubusson etc. and we the Convent etc.
To all and to each individual prior, preceptor, and brother of our
Order, wherever they may be,
Wherever they receive our letter: health in Him who is the true
salvation of all.

1. The tyrant of the Turks has been making plans for some time and is about to put them into operation: he is an ancient enemy of our faith and maintains implacable hatred for our Order, because we resist him for our faith in Christ. His mad fury has been increasing in the twenty-four years since his occupation of Constantinople, as no part of our dominion has come under his control; we oppose his strength and we reject his petitions to pay him tribute. And so he has put together an armada of about one hundred and nine ships, and has gathered troops from all his provinces that are adjacent to Rhodes; these he has directed to move overland to the continent; he has transported them to our island and on June 15 he launched an attack on the fields of Rhodes, and surrounded and laid siege to our city; in order to besiege our city he transported a huge number of engines, machines, bombards, wooden towers, and siege equipment. The enemy in the camp facing us numbers about seventy thousand individuals, who fight against us with endless attacks, battles, and incursions. We resist them with determination and courage, as we muster our strength and oppose the enemy's efforts; we rely on our piety and on divine clemency, hoping that God will not abandon those who hope in Him and fight for the Catholic faith.

2. It is not the case that the enemy will join battle with an effeminate band of knights; he will not fight against soft people from Asia; we have many knights under contract, artillery, war engines, bombards, provisions, and fortifications, which will enable us to withstand the strength of the enemy; in addition, there is assistance from our brothers and actual help in the operations, in which we have placed all hope for our defense. The city of Rhodes is fortified with a strong wall, with a moat, with a ditch, and with towers; in consequence, we would not fear his strength if the forces of our brothers were to arrive on time; then the enemy would fall apart and his plans would come to nothing. The tyrant himself is under the impression that with a prolonged siege he will wear down, diminish, and destroy our provisions, our strength, and our knights; he is eager, as he can send more troops from the continent to make up his own losses in the war. He believes that he will be the master of the situation, as we lose strength. To be sure, this mad dragon is wrong, as he does not see that our most holy lord [= the pope], the Roman Church, most serene kings, and Catholic princes will soon despatch aid to support us; he is not familiar with the most enthusiastic zeal of our brothers and fellow knights for the Catholic faith, with their total devotion, with their unquestionable willingness to serve; they will see to it that the capital

sinant. Nec intelligit hostis fidei, qui nos oppugnat, aditum portus nostri cuique patere, nec eum prohiberi ab eo posse flante Zephyro aestivo autumnalique tempore, qui navigantes sollicitos et perspicaces, dum fretum Lycium, quod nostram insulam alluit, intrant in eum portum Rhodium prospero cursu impellit.

III.   Fratres dilectissimi, haec sunt quae dudum literis, nuntiis, et mandatis, vestris fraternitatibus significavimus, et ob quae auxilia imploravimus, in quibus praestandis nonnulli fuerunt, et contumaciores, quam putavimus, semper vos monuimus, accersivimus, vocavimus, ut adessetis praesidio, data sunt verba, nec creditum est dictis veracibus; non igitur amplius est praestolandum, nec de obsidione ambigendum: credite factis, qui fidem monitis ac verbis non praestitistis. Hostes fidei Turci immanes nos magno impetu oppugnant, obsidunt, circumdant machinis, bombardis, et ingeniosis bellorum instrumentis invadunt, quibus resistimus, et viriliter ictus repellimus, sed putant diuturnam obsidionem non posse sustinere; prius quoque quam adsint auxilia, credunt victores evadere.

IV.   Fratres praeclarissimi videtis periculum quod instat et imminet amplius: siquidem non est differendum; subvenite ergo atque ei ordini succurrite, qui vos nutrivit, aluit, et ad honores evexit. Oppugnatur Rhodia urbs, caput et arx, decus et honor religionis nostrae, et commune in Oriente Christicolarum refugium, asylum, et domicilium. Etenim haec urbs antiqua priscorum munimentis celebrata, tum loci opportunitate, tum aedificiorum magnificentia, tum ad naviles usus aptissima miris laudibus praedicata. Ne igitur tam grave vulnus, quod Deus avertat, Christiano nomini contigat, omnes, et singulos venerabiles priores, bailivos, praeceptores, et fratres ordinis nostri ubilibet constitutos monemus, hortamur, et si opus sit, in vim obedientiae praecipimus et mandamus, ut quantocius in subsidium Rhodiae urbis a Turco obsessae cum navibus onerariis, milite, frumento, armis, et bombardis, munitis atque suffultis accedant, nec formident obsidionem; ipso namque invito inimico aditum portus nostri subire possunt: si id feceritis, fratres dilectissimi, ultra meritum vitae aeternae, quod inde secuturi estis, ingentem nominis famam et gloriam adipiscamini; qui vero vita post victoriam funguntur, gloriosi et praeclari toti orbi erunt; si qui vero ceciderint, ut belli casus plerumque affert, diademate martyrii coronantur. Quid enim felicius quam fidem tueri Orthodoxam? Quid iucundius quam pro Christo pugnare? Quid praeclarius quam efficere quod verbis in assumptione habitus ordinis nostri pollicemur? Non est enim qui ab hoc tam glorioso certamine excusari possit, nec senex, nec debilis, nec pauper et multominus qui iuvenis, qui robustus, qui opulentus; si ab aliis auxilium imploramus, merito ab his ea requirimus, qui dignitates, qui opes ipsius ordinis possident, qui praesto adesse debent, ut ceteri exemplo allecti quantocius succurrant, accedant, veniant. Ut enim omnibus subsidiorum et auxiliorum, quae imploravimus, vocati fratres nostres subvenire possint, eis licentiam, facultatem arrendandi et afficitandi ad tres annos

and citadel of our order, the city of Rhodes, will not come to harm. The enemy of our faith, who has launched this attack upon us, does not realize that access to our harbor is easy, nor can anyone be prevented from entering, as the west wind blows in the summer and fall and those who had a difficult passage while they were crossing the Lycian straits, whose waters reach our island, sail into the harbor of Rhodes without difficulty.

3. Most esteemed brothers: such is the situation, which I have already explained to your brotherhoods by means of letters, with emissaries, and through messages; so we beg your help; as we face inordinate stubbornness, we have warned you, we have called you, and we have summoned you to assist in our defense; our words have reached you but you have not been persuaded by the truth. There is no time for further preparation: we are under siege, no doubt about it; accept reality, you of little faith in words and warnings. The Turks, the savage enemies of our faith, have launched a great attack upon us: they wage war and lay siege to us; they have surrounded us with machines, bombards, and clever war engines. We resist and oppose their blows in manly fashion but they think that we will not be able to hold out against a prolonged siege; they think that they will be victorious before help reaches us.

4. Most glorious brothers: you see the danger and the serious threat that we face. There must be no delay. Come and help the Order which has sustained you, nourished you, and led you to honors. The city of Rhodes, our capital and citadel, the ornament and glory of our religion and common shelter, asylum, and home of all Christian refugees in the East, is under siege. This ancient city (celebrated because of its ancient monuments) has always received marvelous praise because of its geographical position, the magnificence of its buildings, and the convenience it offers to ships. We ask and urge you not to allow serious danger to threaten our priors, bailiffs, preceptors, and brothers of the Order wherever they may be. If need be, we bid and command you under obiedience to come, with all due haste, to the aid of the city of Rhodes under siege by the Turk, who has attacked us with his cargo ships, his soldiers, his supplies, his bombards, his arms, and his equipment and war gear; they show no fear in this siege. Our side can enter the mouth of our harbor to the chagrin of the enemy. If you were to do this, most esteemed brothers, you would earn eternal life and more: you will win enormous glory to your name and fame. Those who survive the battle after our victory will have won glory throughout the world; as for those who fall in battle (as happens to many through the fortune of war), they will wear the crown of martyrdom. Can there be a better cause than the defense of Orthodoxy? Can there be greater joy than to fight for Christ? What can be clearer than to turn words into action, as we promised to do when we assumed the habit? No one can be excused from this glorious struggle: not the old, not the weak, not the poor, not the very young, not the strong, not the rich. If we ask help from others, we ask them to do their proper duty, as they hold the offices and the wealth of our Order itself; they should be here so that the others will be drawn by their

pecuniis anticipatis praeceptorias, prioratus, baiulias, domos, et membra, salvis iuribus nostri communis tesauri ac dimidias annatas, serie praecensium invicem maturo et deliberato consilio impertimur, concedimus et donamus. In cuius rei testimonium bulla nostra communis plumbea praesentibus est appensa.

Datum Rhodi in nostro conventu, die XXVIII mensis Maii, anno ab Incarnato Christo Iesu Domino nostro MCCCCLXXX.

example and will come to our aid as swiftly as possible. So that our brothers can obey our plea and come to our help and aid, after due deliberations, we extend, grant and donate them funds for three years, from our anticipated proceeds through priories, preceptorial accounts, baileys, properties, and dues which are amassed in our communal treasury yearly. For this pledge we affix our order's lead seal to the present document.

Given at Rhodes, in our Convent, on May 28, in the year 1480 since the incarnation of our Lord Jesus Christ.

APPENDIX I

TETALDI'S FRENCH TEXT

Informations envoyées,
tant par Francisco de Franc, à tresreverend pere en Dieu monseigneur le
cardinal d'Avignon,
que par Jehan Blanchin & Jacques Edaldy marchant Florentin,
de la prinse de Constantinople par l'empereur Turc
le xxix. jour de May MCCCCLIII.
à laquelle ledit Jacques estoit pe<r>sonnellement.

I.   Le iv. jour d'Avril le Turc couru prés de Constantinople, & le v. jour dudit mois posa son siege.

II.   Oudit siege y avoit en tout deux cens mille hommes, desquels il povoit avoir soixante mille hommes de trente a quarante mille chevaux, le quart d'eulx aucuns en y avoit armez à la guise de France, & aucuns en aultre façon, aucuns avoient chapeaulx de fer, les autres avoient arcs & cranequins, les autres gens de fait estoient pour la plûpart sans armes, sauf qu'ils avoient targette & semettaire, qui est espée turque.

III.   Le surplus desdits deux cens mille hommes, estoient robeurs, gasteurs, marchands, artisans, & autres suivant le siege pour gagner.

IV.   Oudit siege s'y avoit plusieurs bombardes & autres instruments pour abatre le mur, & entre les autres une grand bombarde de métal, tirant pierre de neuf espaulx & quatre dois d'entour, & pesant mille quatre cens cinquante-une livres, les autres tirans dix ou douze centenars: lesquelles bombardes tiroient chascun jour de cent à six-vingt coups, & dura cecy cinquante-cinq jours; par quoy on compte qu'ils employerent chascun jour mille livres de poudre de bombarde; & ainsi en cinquante-cinq jours dépendirent cinquante-cinq mille livres, & s'y avoient dix mille coulevrines.

V.   L'armée du Turc estant tant au port que dehors de seize à dix-huit gallées, soixante, ou soixante-dix galliotes, de dix-huit à vingt vans, de saize à vingt barques petites, comme pour porter chevaulx & fustes.

VI.	Le siege posé par terre, de Semgampsa [Zaganos Pasha] conseiller du Turc, & celuy qui a plus d'auctorité entour luy, fit porter de la mer par terre deux ou trois mille, de soixante-dix à quatre-vingt gallées que autres fustes armées, dedens le goufle de Maudraquin [Mandraquin, i.e., Mandrakion], qui est entre les deux citez, ausquieulx est le port de Constantinople, auquel port ne povoit le navire du Turc aller par mer pour l'armée des Chrestiens, & un pont de barques que les Chrestiens avoient fait pour aller de Constantinople à Peyre pour s'entre-secourir. Et de ceste armée fut capitaine un nommé Alingag-oly [Baltaoğlu], lequel quatre nefs Jenevoises rompirent. Lors le Turcs s'y fit ung autre capitaine; & ainsi fut ferme le siege par mer & par terre.

VII.	Constantinople est tres-forte, en figure triangulaire, & a seize mille de tour devers la terre, cinq devers la mer, six devers le port, & le goufle cinq.

VIII.	Les principaux murs sont haults de vingt à vingt deux braches, & gros en cyme, & en aucuns lieux de six, en autres de huit braches, & dehors y a barbequennes, desquelles le derraint est hault de douze braches, & le mur de dessus hault de quatorze braches, & gros de trois braches; les fossez longs de vingt-six braches, & perfons de dix braches.

IX.	En icelle cité ly avoit entour de trente à trente-six milles homines, & six à sept mille combattans, & non plus.

X.	Au port, pour deffendre le havre, avoit des Chrestiens trente-neuf gallées, c'est à sçavoir deux subtiles, & trois marchandes Venitiennes, & trois de l'empereur, une de messire Jean Justinien [Giovanni Guglielmo Longo Giustiniani] Jennevois, aux gaiges de l'empereur.

XI.	Constantinople donc ainsi assiegée par mer & par terre, & battu de bombardes & de traits, se deffendit cinquante-cinq jours.

XII.	Parmy ce temps advint aucunes particularités, semblant aux Chrestiens estre ligier de brûler le navire du Turc; le capitaine de la gallée de Trapesonde [Giacomo/Jacopo Cocco] monta sur une gallée subtile, pour ce faire avecques certains autres ordonnés à ce; mais leur gallée fut enfondrée d'une bombarde du Turc, & les gens noyex, desquieulx les anciens furent prins par les Turcs, qui furent par le fondement affichez sur paulx agus, devant ceux qui faisoient la garde sur le mur.

XIII.	Du costé de la terre, Sengampsa Albanois renié, qui son siege tenoit, avoit plusieurs hommes accoustumez de miner l'or & l'argent, mina en quatorze lieux soubs le lieu de la ville, pour le tailler, & commença ses mines bien long du mur. Les Chrestiens contreminerent, en escoutant le redond, & par diverses fois estouferent les Turcs en leurs mines, adez par fumée, adez par pueur, adez les noyant par force d'eauës, & aucune fois combattant main à main.

XIV.	Ledit Sengampsa fist ung chastel de bois si hault & si grant, qu'il seignourissoit le mur, & ung pont sur bottes, long de mille braches, & large de sept, pour passer la mer à travers le port jusques au pié du mur; & plusieurs instruments de bois, desquels il povoit estre sans estre blechié; & si l'y avoit tours de bois tres-haultes, grandes & ligieres.

XV. Ainsi chacun jour faisant grandes escarmouches, où il mourut moult de gens deça & delà; pour ung qu'il en mourroit dedens, il en mourroit cent dehors.
XVI. Au siege du Turc l'y avoit plusieurs Chrestiens de Grece, & de autres nations; & combien qu'ils soient subgiés au Turc, toutesfois se ne sont-ils pas contraints à renoyer la foy chrestienne, ains arrent & prient, & arrent à leur plaisir; & sy avoit aucuns capitaines & autres puissans Turcs, qui par despit de Sengampsa, qui trop les oppressoit, advisoient que ceux de dedens estoient infourmez de tout ce qu e l'en faisoit au siege par lettres, & autres choses furent advisez, comme le Turc avec tous ses barons, princes, seigneurs, & conseillers, avoit tenu conseil trois jours continuels, entre lesquieulx estoit un capitaine Columbassa [Halil (Candarlı) Pasha], qui conseilloit au Turc à lever le siege, alleguant au Turc: Tu ais fait ton devoir, tu leur as donné plusieurs batailles, & y a tant de jours, où est mort tres-grant quantité de tes gens. Tu vois la cité deffensable & inexpugnable, en maniere que tant plus va de gens à l'assaut, plus en demeure. Ceux qui ont esté sur le mur, ont esté reboutez & tuez. Tes ancesseurs jamais ne vindrent si avant, ce te est grant gloire de avoir fait ce que tu as fait, & te doit suffire, sans vouloir destruire tous tes gens. Et tant fut dit, que le Turc déliberoit de soy lever & de s'en retourner, & de ficher aucunes colompnes, pour nottifier à jamais ce que il avoit fait, & que nul de ses ancesseurs ne se osa approucher de Constantinople. Sengampsa en cette conclusion s'y opposa, disant au Turc: Tu es le plus fort, tu as rué sus une grande piece du mur, nous en ruërons de l'autre; donne leur encore ung assault; & se nous faillons, nous prendrons aprés le party que bon te semblera. Et tant parla, que le Turc se consenty. De tout ce furent advisez ceulx de dedens, & confortez que ils seroient seurs; car le siege s'en iroit sans nul retour.
XVII. Le Turc deliberé d'encore les assaillir, trois jours devant l'assaut commenda solemnpelle jeûne à l'onneur & reverence de Dieu du ciel, lequel Dieu seul il arure [id est: adore], jûnerent luy & tous le siens trois jours continuels, par ainsi que tout le jour ne mangeoient rien, mais seulement de nuit par leur sainte vie. Et de nuit firent infiny luminaire de chandelles, & de bois qui brûloit de soi mesme en mer & en terre, tant qu'il sembloit que la terre ardist, avec tres grands sons de tambours; car de trompettes ne ont-ils point.
XVIII. Estant ces choses en ces termes, & le Turc déliberé d'assaillir, quoyque à pou intencion de vaincre; & ceulx de dedens de bien se deffendre, commença son assault le xxvii. jour de May au soir, & ordonna ses gens en la maniere que ensy.
XIX. Bigliardi [Beglerbeg ?] capitaine general de Turquie avoit vingt mille hommes à la porte de Pigli [Pege], où estoit la grant bastille.
XX. Columbassa conseiller du Turc, amy des Chrestiens, & ledit Sengampsa aussi conseiller du Turc, estoient prés de la terre de l'autre part des gens du siege, à la porte de S. Romain, loing de Pigli entour ung mille.
XXI. Elbigliabée [Beglerbeg ?] capitaine general de Grece, fut mise à costé de Caligaria, à l'endroit du palais de l'empereur, loing de S. Romain deux mille.

XXII. L'assault commencé, ceulx de dedens par-tout se deffendirent vaillamment à S. Romain, & le lieu plus legier à avoir. En la muraille plus faible, de laquelle avoit ja esté abatuë les jours passez, là estoient les bombardes, qui bouterent jus une barbequenne & la montre du mur du meilleu, & en cheut bien deux cens braches. Là aussi sy avoit tant de coulevrines, & de traits, que on ne voyoit point leciel.

XXIII. Tout ceulx de dedens recloirent les braches du mur à botes de bois, terre, & se deffendirent mieulx qu'ils povoient.

XXIV. En ce lieu déffendoit monseigneur Jehan Justinien, & se portoit vaillamment: & aussi toute la cité avoit esperance en sa vaillance.

XXV. A ce lieu pour faire son derrain effort, se approuche le Turc à deux bannieres desployées, avecques dix mille hommes esleus pour la garde de sa personne, & infinis aultres avec le chastel de bois, pont, eschielles, & aultres instruments, & commencerent à emplir les fossez, & getter pons, eschielles, & monterent sur le mur. Là fut monseigneur Jean Justinien blechié d'une couleuvrine, s'en parti pour se faire mediciner, & bailla sa garde à deux gentils-hommes Jennevois. Le gens de garde de dedens voyant les Turcs sur le mur cuidans qu'il s'enfuist, leurs gardes abandonnerent, & s'enfuirent; & ainsi les Turcs entrerent en Constantinople à l'aube du jour, le xxix. jour de May, mistrent à mort tout ce que ils faisoient à eulx resistance.

XXVI. Pesyre n'avoit encore eu nul assault, & estoit la plus grant part des Pesyriens à Constantinople, pour deffendre. Ceulx qui estoient à Peyrre, qui ne avoient rien osté de leurs biens, délibererent de bailler les clefs au Turc, & se recommander à luy, & luy offrir la cité, où il s'y avoit tout six cens de hommes & de femmes; monterent sur une nef de Jennevois, pour s'en aller ensemble audit Jacques, que une accointare chargée de femmes de Peyre fut prise des Turcs.

XXVII. Le cardinal de Russie [Cardinal Isidore] mourut en la presse, aussi mourut l'empereur [Constantine XI Palaeologus]. Aucuns dient qu'il eust la teste taillée, ou qu'il mourut en la presse, s'en voulant s'yssir l'un & l'autre, peut-être qu'il fut mort en la presse, & que puis les Turcs luy eussent taillé la teste.

XXVIII. Les gallées Venitiennes de voyage de Romanie, & de Trapesonde demourerent là jusques à midy, attendans pour sauver aucuns Chrestiens, dont il en est venu ung, entre lesquieulx fut cestuy Jacques Tedaldy, qui estant sur le mur en sa garde de la part où entrerent les Turcs, senti leur entrée bien deux heures aprés. Ainsi gagna la mer, & se dépoüilla, & entra jusques aux gallées, qui le receurent.

XXIX. Le Turc a enfondré une nef Jennevoise de dix-huit cens botes, riche de quatre-vins mille ducas, & a prins de treize à quatorze naves d'environt cinq cens botes chascune, & le reste de deux à trois cens botes, & qu'il a de navire deux cens quarante, que nefs & gallées, que galliotes, &c. dont de la plus grand part est à faire pou d'extime.

XXX. Se l'armée de Venise que menoit messire Jehan Jordono, fust arrivée à Constantinople ung jour avant fust prinse, certes il n'y a nul doubte que la ville

n'eust esté rescousse: laquelle estoit de neuf gallées Venitiennes & vingt naves en tout; mais elle ne vint pas à temps, & arriva à Nigrepont seulement ung jour aprés les gallées fuyes y estoient.

XXXI. On estime que le butin de Constantinople vault aux Turcs quatre millions de ducas. La perte de Venise se estime cinquante mille ducas, que en ceste gallée c'est sauvé vingt mil ducas de Jennevois, & a perte infinie de Florentins, vingt mil ducas d'accointares.

XXXII. On trouve par ceulx qui les fuis du Turc ont cogneu ses condicions & sa puissance, qui est de l'âge de vingt-trois à vingt-quatre ans, plus cruel que Neron, se delectant à respandre sang humain, courageux & ardant de seignourer & converser tout le monde: voire plus qu'Alexandre, ne Cesar, ne aultre vaillant qui ait esté allegué qu'il a plus grande puissance & seignourie que nul d'eulx n'avoit: & tousjours faisoit lire leur histoire, demande où & comment est posé Venise, combien loing de terre ferme, & comme on y puet entrer par mer & par terre. Et tient legier luy seroit faire ung grant pont durant de Margara à Venise: pour pouvoir passer ses gens d'armes. Pareillement deman e de Romme où elle est assise, & du duc de Milan, & de ses vaillans: & d'autres choses que de guerre ne parle. Dit qu'il veult faire son siege à Constantinople; car là il veult faire merveilleux navires. Ainsi ne sera comme il estime en mer & en terre celluy qui ne luy porte les clefs avant que l'attendre: considerant qu'il a prins Constantinople, la plus forte cité de Europe; & si forte, que on cuidoit que jamais combien qu'elle fust grande, le deust surmonter; & que luy & les siens sont hardis & ingenieux en armes, tant que plus faire se peult, & ne sont estimez de leur vie.

XXXIII. On estime que cet Esté le Turc ne fera nul autre grant fait d'armes, mais entendra à ses fais pour venir en Constantinople, ses gens retourner vouldront chacun en sa maison, pour recueillir leurs biens, & reposer; mais on peut bien tenir pour certain, qu'il se apprestera merveilleusement par mer & par terre, pour se mettre sus en temps nommé.

XXXIV. Mais si les Chrestiens y pourvoyent, on dit fermement qu'on le chassera du pays, & conquestera t-on le pays pour jamais. Et la maniere d'y pourvoir sont cestes.

XXXV. Premierement il faut faire paix entre les princes Chrestiens.

XXXVI. Item, fauldroit que les Veniciens, le duc de Millan, les Florentins, & autres seigneurs d'Italie feissent une armée de vingt mil chevaulx, & bien à point & autres bons capitaines, laquelle fust conduite par Albanie, jusques aux conduis des Chrestiens, & là se poser en leur fort en abundance de vivres, & que là ils seroient seurs, & incontinent Albanies, Sclavons, & autres nations Chrestiennes, qui vouluntiers vendroient pour deffendre la foy.

XXXVII. Par mer, oultre l'armée faite, à icelle fauldroit adjoindre une autre du roy d'Arragon, de Veniciens, de Jennevois, de corsaires, & aultres qui sont à la marine, qui suffiroit à vaincre celle du Turc, se elle n'est plus grosse qu'elle n'est à present: laquelle armée s'en alle au port de Negrepont, pour prendre Sacombolin & les aultres lieux du Turc, & obvier au passage de l'Escion, que le Turc veult faire du Turquie en Grece, & de Grece en Turquie.

XXXVIII. Item, fauldroit que l'empereur, les Hongres, les Boësmes, les Pollons, & autres nations dudit pays, avecque Jehan Vamade, tres redoubté au Turc feissent une autre armée, & entrast en Grece par Andrinople, & autres lieux occupez du Turc, & faudroit tenir la maniere que toutes ces armées fussent ung temps ausdit lieux, & eussent bonne intelligence l'un l'autre de ce qui s'ensuiroit en cest effet.

XXXIX.   Le Turc qui à ceste fois a fait tout son effort, n'a que deux cens mil hommes, que bons, que mechans, entre lesquieulx s'y a grant quantité de Chrestiens, & autres ses subgiez qui le suivent mal voulentiers, lesquieulx se ils sentoient l'armée des Chrestiens, l'abandonneroient, & se adjoindroient aux Chrestiens.

XL.   Item, le Turc par nature & usance ne tient point la guerre à cité, ne à ville, ne à chastel; mais tient continuellement aux champs luy & toute sa force, & pour ce se délibera luy & les siens.

XLI.   En oultre, les Chrestiens de Russie & des autres pays se vendroient tous l'armée des Chrestiens.

XLII.   En outre, le Carraman, qui est grand seigneur, & ennemy capital du Turc, se advise que se Chrestiens guerroyoient le Turc, & l'oppressent grandement, il leur fera guerre.

XLIII.   En Grece n'aura marchant, ne laboreur, qui ne porte vivres aux Chrestiens. Les vivres fauldront au Turc en Grece, le pays de Turquie luy sera rompu par la mer; les Chrestiens de Grece vouldront à l'espée recouvrir leurs terres & lieux occupez du Turc. Et aussi se les armées s'approuchent pou à pou l'une de l'autre, il n'est nul doubte que en brief le Turc & son exercite ne soit du tout deffait.

XLIV.   Se on n'y pourvoye diligemment, & que on donne temps & loisir au Turc de se mettre à point à mer & en terre, il n'est nul doubte que il ne face grande esclandre en chrestienté, dont Dieu nous gard.

XLV.   En ceste gallée sont revenus de Constantinople huit citadins Venitiens, & sont là demourez trente-six gentils hommes, & aultres gens de bien prés de Carante. Dieu leur aide, quoyque on les conte en brief pour se despeschier.

APPENDIX II

THE *AMAN-NAME* OF MEHMED II, GRANTED TO PERA (1453)

A. Greek Version

Ἐγὼ ὁ μέγας αὐθέντης καὶ μέγας ἀμυρᾶς σουλτάνος ὁ Μεχμὲτ μπέης, ὁ υἱὸς τοῦ μεγάλου αὐθέντου καὶ μεγάλου ἀμυρᾶ σουλτάνου τοῦ Μουρὰτ μπέη.

Ὀμνύω εἰς τὸν θεὸν τοῦ οὐρανοῦ καὶ τῆς γῆς καὶ εἰς τὸν μέγαν ἡμῶν προφήτην τὸν Μωάμεθ καὶ εἰς τὰ ἑπτὰ μουσάφια ὅπου ἔχομεν καὶ ὁμολογοῦμεν, καὶ εἰς τοὺς ρκδ΄ χιλιάδας προφήτας τοῦ θεοῦ, καὶ πρὸς τὴν ψυχὴν τοῦ πάππου μου καὶ τοῦ πατρός μου, καὶ πρὸς ἑαυτὸν καὶ πρὸς τὰ παιδία μου καὶ εἰς τὸ σπαθὶ ὅπου ζώνομαι.

Ἐπειδὴ ἔστειλαν οἱ καθολικοὶ ἄρχοντες τοῦ Γαλατᾶ πρὸς τὴν πόρταν τῆς αὐθεντείας μου τοὺς τετιμημένους ἄρχοντες, τὸν κύριον Μπαπιλᾶν Παραβᾶν καὶ τὸν κύριον Μαρκέζον Δριφάγκην καὶ τὸν δραγομάνον των Νικόλαον Πελατζόνην, καὶ ἐπροσκύνησαν τὴν βασιλείαν μου, καὶ ἐδεήθησαν τῆς αὐθεντείας μου, καὶ νὰ ἔχουν τὰς νομὰς κατὰ τὴν συνήθειαν τοῦ καθόλου τόπου τῆς αὐθεντείας μου· νὰ ⟨μὴ⟩ χαλάσω τὸ κάστρον των, αὐτοὶ δὲ νὰ ἔχουν τὰ πράγματά των καὶ τὰ ὀσπήτια των καὶ τὰ μαγαζία των καὶ τὰ ἀμπέλια των καὶ τοὺς μύλους των καὶ τὰ καράβια των καὶ τὰς βάρκας των καὶ τὰς πραγματείας των ὅλας, καὶ τὰς γυναῖκας των καὶ τὰ παιδία των εἰς τὸ θέλημά των, καὶ νὰ πωλοῦν τὰς πραγματείας των ἐλεύθερα, καθὼς ὅλος ὁ τόπος τῆς αὐθεντείας μοι, νὰ πηγαίνουν καὶ νὰ ἔρχωνται ἐλεύθερα διὰ ξηρᾶς καὶ θαλάσσης καὶ κουμέρκιον νὰ μὴ δίδουν, μήτε φτιαστικόν, εἰ μὴ νὰ δίδουν χαράτζιον, ὡς καθὼς εἶναι ὅλος ὁ τόπος τῆς αὐθεντείας μου· οἱ αὐτοὶ νόμοι καὶ συνήθειαι νὰ εἶναι οἱ αὐτοὶ ἀπὸ τοῦ νῦν καὶ ἔμπροσθεν, καὶ νὰ τοὺς ἔχω ἀκριβοὺς καὶ νὰ τοὺς διαφεντεύω, ὡς καθὼς διαφεντεύω τὸ πρόσωπόν μου ὅλον.

Τὰς ἐκκλησίας των νὰ τὰς ἔχουν καὶ νὰ τὰς ψάλλουν, μόνον καμπάναις καὶ σημαντήρια νὰ μηδὲν κτυποῦν, ἀπὸ τὰς ἐκκλησίας μαίδιον νὰ μὴ ζητήσω μηδὲ αὐτοὶ νὰ ποιήσουν ἄλλας ἐκκλησίας. Οἱ πραγματευτάδες τῶν Γενουβέζων νὰ πηγαίνουν καὶ νὰ ἔρχωνται ἐλεύθερα, νὰ ποιοῦν τὰς πραγματείας των, παιδία ποτὲ εἰς γιανιτζάρους νὰ μὴ πάρω, μήτε τινὰ νέον, μήτε Τοῦρκοι νὰ εἶναι εἰς τὸ μέσον των, ἀμὴ νὰ εἶναι ἐξόχως, εἰ μὴ νὰ βάλῃ ἡ αὐθεντεία μου σκλάβον νὰ τοὺς βλέπῃ· αὐτοὶ δὲ οἱ Γαλατιανοὶ νὰ ἔχουν ἄδειαν νὰ βάλλουν πρωτόγηρον εἰς τὸ μέσον των διὰ νὰ διορθώνῃ τὰς δουλείας ὁποῦ ἔχουν οἱ πραγματευτάδες. Γιανιτζάροι καὶ σκλάβοι νὰ μηδὲν κονεύουν εἰς τὰ ὁσπήτια των· τὰ κουμέρκια, ὁποῦ χρεωστοῦν, νὰ τὰ μαζώξουν· ἔχουν καὶ χρέος ἀπερνῶντες τὰ ὅσα ἐξώδευσαν, ἔχουν τὴν ἄδειαν νὰ τὰ μαζώξουν ἀπὸ τὴν μέσην τους, διὰ νὰ εὔγουν ἀπὸ τὸ χρέος. Οἱ ἄρχοντες καὶ οἱ πραγματευτάδες των νὰ μηδὲν ἀγγαρεύωνται. Οἱ πραγματευτάδες τῶν Γενουβέζων νὰ ἔχουν ἄδειαν νὰ πηγαίνουν καὶ νὰ ἔρχωνται καὶ νὰ δίδουν κουμέρκιον κατὰ τοὺς νόμους καὶ συνήθειαν.

Ἐγράφη τὸ παρὸν ὁρκομωτικόν, καὶ ὤμοσεν ἡ αὐθεντεία μου ἐν ἔτει ͵ϛξα΄ ἀπὸ κτίσεως κόσμου. Ἐγύρας ἔτος ωνζ΄.

B. Italian Version (in Languschi-Dolfin)

Come le gran Turcho fece un priuilegio a Genoesi per hauerli data Pera.

Che diro del podesta de Pera, o praua et mala deliberatione de Genoexi, che mandano suo legato cum le chiaue a offerir Pera al Turcho. El qual iocundamente quelli accetto per sciaui. Et patizo cum loro li capitoli sotto scripti et constitui uno suo bassa che ministrasse raxon, confisco tutti li beno de fugitiui, comando fusseno ruinadi li muri de Pera, et fu obedito da loro, desprezando el mandato de la comunita de Genoa per saluarsi. Et Genoesi che erano liberi et in pace cum el Signor Turcho, hora sono serui, da la qual seruitu mai se liberarano, saluo da uniuersal union de Christiani la qual Idio per sua misericordia e pieta se degni concieder per liberarne da tanti mali.

Questo e lo priuilegio che fece lo gran Turco Maumeto a Genoesi de Pera in quella hora quando prese Constantinopoli che mandono suo legato alla porta cum le chiaue a darli la cita de Pera etc.

Io grande Signor et grande amiraglio soldan Maumeto, fiolo del grande Signor et grande armiraijo sultan Muratbei, Juro in dio del cielo et de la terra, et nel grande profeta nostro Macometto, et ne li septe precepti che hauemo et confessemo nui musulmani, et in cento et uentitremillia profeti de dio, et in anima del mio auo, et padre mio, et in uita mia, et in uita de mie fioli et in lo gladio che tengo. Da poi che hano mandato tutti li nobili de Galatea Pera a la porta de la mia Signoria li honorabili gentilhomini M. Babilan Palauixin, et Marchio di Franchi et suo interprete Nicoloso Pauizon a inclinarse a la mia Signoria et sottometterse esser mie serui. Et che habiano ogni consuetudine et costume da tutti i loci de mia Signoria et gouernar el castello suo Pera. Et che essi habiano tutti li suo beni caxe magazeni uigne molini, tutte sue naue barche et tutte mercantie, et tutte sue donne fioli et serui in sua uolunta. Et possano far ogni sua mercantia libera, sicome fano in tutti li luoghi de la mia Signoria, et possano andar et uegnir per terra et per mar, et comerchi non pagar, saluo solo el caragio si come pagano tutti li luoghi de la mia Signoria cum la usanza consueta siano etiam questi hora, et per lo auignir a mi charissimi. Et questi deffendero come li altri luoghi mei. Tutte sue chiesie habiano, et canteno, et tamen campane et simandirio non sone, et de le chiese sue sinagoge non faro. Ne etiam questi faciano altre chiese. Li mercanti soi Genoesi, uegna et partase liberi cum sue mercantie, et fioli soi, et quelli mai per Janizari non toro senza uolunta sua, ne che Turchi staga cum loro infra loro ma stagano separati. Et la mia Signoria mettera el schiauo in sua custodia. Et che Perensi habia liberta metter gubernator in fra loro che gouerni le cause de suo mercadanti. Axapi et schiaui non habitarano in le caxe loro. Dacij che doueano hauer da principio scoder possano et possano scoder le spexe fatte in fra loro. Et i nobili mercadanti soi genoexi habia libertade uegnir et ritornar cum merce sue, et pagar i dacij soi si come e de consuetudine sua.

Scripto el presente priuilegio jurato in l anno sexto de la mia Signoria 6 millia 9 cento et sesantauno Indicione prima del mese de mazo di uintinoue, marti damatina in Constantinopoli lo qual suo priuilegio jurato, mai ha obseruato.

APPENDIX III

EXTRACTS FROM PIETRO GIUSTINIANI

EXTRACTS FROM PIETRO GIUSTINIANI, *RERUM VENETARUM AB URBE CONDITA AD ANNUM M.D.LXXV* (ARGENTORATI M. DC. XI)

A. The Fall of Constantinople (1453): Liber Octavus (154–55)

I. Turcarum apparatus in Graeciam

1. Novi quoque ex Graecia bellorum motus exaudiebantur, Mahometum scilicet Turcorum Regem, terra marique arma parare, et iam haud procul a Thracio Bosphoro circa Propontidem castellum munitissimum erexisse: ferebaturque Byzantii Imperium hoc armorum apparatu peti. Quare Nicolaus Pontifex enixe studebat, res Italiae, Christianorumque Principum discordias quantum in se erat, componere. Domestica tamen coniuratione paene oppressus, tunc id praestare non potuit: Nam Stephanus Portius inter Romanos cives nobilitate, et divitiis potens, in eum cum quibusdam facinorosis viris nefarie conspirarat, Pontificiaque oppressa dignitate populo Romano libertatem restituere moliebatur. Sed coniuratione patefacta, Portii conatus irriti fuere, ipseque ad supplicium tractus, meritam mortis damnationem tulit.

. . . . .

II. Jac<obi> Laured<ani> Turcorum terra marique copiae

1. In hoc statu Venetae, Sforcianaeque res erant, quum in Graecia Byzantium terra marique circumvallatum Mahometi arma gravissime premebant, cuius urbis periculo patrum animi vehementer commovebantur. Itaque continuo decem triremes instruuntur ad ipsius urbis presidium, earumque Imperium Jacobo Lauredano demandatur, eundemque navium longarum numerum Alphonsus fuerat pollicitus, ac totidem Pontifex, ut triginta triremium classis esset: quod levissimum in tanto hostilium armorum apparatu auxilium fuit. Othomanus enim cum trecentis bellatorum millibus, et triremibus biremibusque amplius ducentis, minoribusque aliis navigiis prope centum et quinquaginta terra marique ad Byzantium oppugnandum consedit.

2. Tenebat autem tunc Graeciae Imperium Constantinus Palaeologus, Caloioannis filius; munieratque urbem tumultuario opere, ac a vigili cura ad eius defensionem milites, commeatus, armaque paraverat; obiectaque est ad angustias sinus eximiae crassitudinis cathena ferrea, quae a Gallorum turri per longum spatium usque ad Peranae Clarae pontem protendebatur, ubi tres Venetorum triremes ex Pontica negotiatione reversae, ad loci praesidium constiterant.

EXTRACTS FROM PIETRO GIUSTINIANI, HISTORY OF VENICE, FROM ITS FOUNDATION TO THE YEAR 1575 (STRASBOURG, 1611)

A. The Fall of Constantinople (1453): Book 8 (154–55)

I. The Turkish Expedition into Greece

1. News from Greece suggested war movements; evidently Mehmed, the king [= sultan] of the Turks, was preparing his army and navy for war. Soon thereafter he erected a very strong castle [= Rumeli Hisar] on the Thracian Bosphorus around Propontis. It was rumored that he was going to take over the empire of Byzantium [= Constantinople] by force of arms. And so the pontiff, Nicholas [V (1447–1455)], turned his attention, with all his abilities, to Italian affairs and to the wars among the princes of the Christians, to put an end to them. But he proved unable to accomplish his task, because he was almost overwhelmed in a domestic conspiracy [January 1453]. A noble, wealthy, and powerful Roman, Stephen Portius [= Stefano Porcaro], together with some criminals, wrongly conspired against him, as he wished to restore liberty to the Roman people at a time when the dignity of the pontiff had been diminished. But the conspiracy was discovered and the attempt of Portius came to nothing; he himself was subjected to torture and was justly condemned to death for his crime.

. . . . .

II. The Army and Navy of the Turks

1. Such was the situation between Venice and Sforza, when the territory of Byzantium in Greece was surrounded by land and sea and was hard-pressed by the forces of Mehmed. The danger faced by that city became a great concern to the fathers [= senators of Venice]. Immediately ten triremes [= galleys] were equipped to protect that city; Giacomo Loredan was placed in charge. Alfonso [of Naples] was also concerned and promised the same number of warships; the Pontiff did also, so that there would be a fleet of thirty triremes. And yet this was very slight help against the forces that the enemy had assembled: the Ottoman [= Mehmed II] had three hundred thousand warriors and more than two hundred triremes and biremes, in addition to other smaller vessels that numbered almost one hundred and fifty, with which he was besieging by land and sea, and hoped to conquer Byzantium.

2. At the time the emperor of Greece was Constantine [Dragaš] Palaeologus [1449–1453], the son [sic] of John [VIII] the Good [Palaeologus]. He heavily strengthened his city and carefully assembled soldiers, provisions, and armament for the defense. Across the narrow straits of the gulf [= the Golden Horn] a very thick iron chain was stretched, from the Tower of the Galli to the Clara Bridge of Pera (a long distance), and there three Venetian triremes that

Affuit et cethea una Lygustica eximiae magnitudinis, cum quibusdam Grippariis Cretensibus; inde tres aliae Genuensium naves ex Chio advenere, commeatus et virorum fortium plenae, quibus sub ipsum portus ingressum Turcorum aliquot navigia occurrerunt: continuoque pugna contrahitur, in qua foeda untrinque caedes edita est. Demum hoc primo congressu victi Barbari superantur.

III. Io<annes> Iustinian<us>

1.   Accessit postea Ioannes Iustinianus natione Lygur cum duabus cetheis, trecentosque secum ille habebat bellatores, quorum opera Imperator usus, eos ad Romanam portam cum Iustiniano Duce suo constituit. Venetis quoque patriciis, Nic<olao> Mollino, Ioanne Lauredano, et Baptistae Gritto, qui ea temporum novitate Byzantii mercaturam exercebant, quaedam urbis loca tuenda assignata sunt.

2.   Turcae interim complures aeneas machinas terra marique circa moenia disposuerant, quibus ingens murorum, munitionumque ruina facta est: ita terrestribus maritimisque viribus Graeci oppugnati, barbarorum impetum vix sustinere poterant. Nam ubique multitudine sua saevus hostis imminebat: ausus tamen Imperatorius miles, Veneto, Lygureque adiuvante, in Othomanicam classem impetum facere, ea siquidem a Peranis columnis praeter oppidi moenia in sinum traducta fuerat.

3.   Contracto igitur navali certamine Christiani numero hominum, naviumque inferiores Barbaro facile cesserunt, et biremes duae, una Cretensis, altera Veneta, tormento hostili concussae, periere. Tentavit exinde Turca cuniculo urbem irrumpere: sed opportune a Graeco itum est obviam: multique hostium subterranea fovea, subita, voracique flamma sunt ambusti. Ad Romanam, Chersinamque portam interea moenia, turresque late prociderant, quo factum est, ut aperto aditu Turcae urbem semidirutam occupare posse in spem venerant. Itaque terribili clamore, horrendisque vocibus per collapsa moenia vadentes, accerime in Graecos pugnabant. At imperator intus obsequitando suos magnis precibus hortabatur, ut patriam, penates, parentes, liberos, coniuges a Turcorum rabie, armis protegerent, praesentique ope circumsesso Imperio adessent, venisse tempus, dicere, quo si solita strenuitate uti vellent, non solum Orientalis Imperii Maiestas pristinam retineret amplitudinem, sed aucta quoque in altius excresceret fastigium.

IV. Turcorum in urbem irruptio. Palaeolo<gi> Imp<eratoris> memorabile interitus

1.   Durarent igitur, hostisque minas haud timerent, a quo si victi essent, desperata omnino venia omnes ferro caderent. Haec ille moenia circumvectus,

had returned from trading in the Pontus [= Black Sea] were stationed to guard the place. Also present by the chain was an extremely large vessel from Genoa, together with three *grippi* from Crete. In addition, there were three Genoese ships that came from Chios, loaded with provisions and plenty of strong men. All these vessels prevented the Turkish ships from entering the harbor. Battles were fought without respite and both sides sustained horrible casualties. The barbarians [= Turks] were defeated in the first assault.

III. Giovanni [Guglielmo Longo] Giustiniani

1. Then came Giovanni Giustiniani, a Genoese by origin, with two ships and three hundred warriors at his command; the emperor accepted their help and deployed them, together with their leader Giustiniani, at the sector of the Gate of [Saint] Romanus. The defense of some places in the city was entrusted to the Venetian patricians Nicolo Mollino, Giovanni Loredan, and Battista Gritti, who had been trading in Byzantium at that perilous time.

2. In the meantime the Turks deployed numerous bronze machines [= cannon] around the land and sea walls, which greatly damaged the walls and the defenses. The Greeks were assaulted by land and sea forces and could hardly repel the attacks of the barbarians. The savage enemy represented a great threat everywhere with his multitudes. The soldiers of the emperor, assisted by Venetians and Genoese, attacked the Ottoman fleet, which had been transported from the Columns next to Pera [= Diplokionion] to the gulf [= Golden Horn] over against the city walls.

3. In the ensuing naval battle the Christians, whose numbers (men and ships) were inferior to those of the barbarian, were easily defeated and two of their biremes, a Cretan and a Venetian, were hit by cannon fire and sank. Then the Turk attempted to break into the city through a subterranean tunnel but the Greeks, in time, through a counter-mine, burned many of the enemy in the tunnel with a voracious fire. At the land Gates of [Saint] Romanus and of Kharisios [= Adrianople/Edirne] the towers were badly damaged and when this was accomplished the Turks began to hope that they would be able to enter through these ruins and occupy the city that had been almost destroyed. And so with terrible noise and with horrible shouts they attacked the collapsed walls and fought very hard against the Greeks. The emperor within besought, on his horse, all his warriors and urged them on with pleas to protect with their weapons their fatherland, their religion, their parents, their children, and their wives from the rabid anger of the Turks; they should be willing to defend the surrounded empire; he said that the time had come to exert themselves not only to restore the majesty of the eastern empire to its ancient glory but to augment it as well.

IV. The Entry of the Turks into the City. The Memorable Death of Emperor Palaeologus.

1. They endured and did not fear the threats of the enemy; if they were defeated they knew none would be spared. He [= the emperor] toured the walls

suis memorare, sed parum dicta profuere, territis omnibus effera Turcorum rabie, et furore, qui iam ad Romani portam Graecos munitionibus depulerant, ac Iustiniano gravi vulnere affecto, nudato urbs praesidio, Barbarorum irruptioni patebat. Quo viso Imperator cum paucis, quos secum habebat, locum statim subiit; tentavitque vi iam hostem alium post alium muros scandentem repellere, multosque ex barbaris irrumpentes exturbavit, eorumque repressit impetum.

2.   Verum ubi rem perditam vidit, caesisque ac fugatis propugnatoribus paene solum se derelictum cognovit, tum gladio pectus transfigere propria manu voluisse dicitur: Inde quia ipse haud Christianum esse adiudicabat, honestiorem ad mortem viam meditatus, imperatoria deposuit insignia, ac stricto ferro in irrumpentium Turcorum cuneum, furibundumque agmen irruit, fortiterque pugnando Princeps omnibus saeculis memoria dignus hostili ferro confoditur, cadensque simul vitam, et Imperium amisit. Illi postea media caesorum strage iacenti, sanguineque oppleto, Mahometi iussu caput est abscissum, totaque urbe, a castris lancea circumlatum, miserabile omnibus spectaculum praebuit.

3.   In ea trepidatione aliis alio dilabentibus, ingens mortalium concursus ad Divae Sophiae templum factus est. Ibique omnes capti, ac urbs tota direpta est: nec non aedes, araeque Divorum profanatae, infandaque barbarae impietatis exempla aedita. Nam senes, viri caesi; adolescentes, pueri, abducti; matronae, virgines, constupratae, in omnemque aetatem a barbara gente saevissime grassatum . . . .

4.   In hunc modum Constantinopolis nobilissima Graeciae totiusque Europae urbs a Mahometo Turcarum Rege, anno salutis millesimo, quadringentissimo, quinquagesimo secundo capta dicitur; qui statim Paleologi Imperatoris caput cum cura servatum, quadragintaque egregia corporis specie adolescentulos, et viginti puellas a tota praeda delectas in victoriae iactationem per Legatos ad Soldanum Aegypti deferri iussit.

V. Barth\<olomaeus\> Marcellus

1.   Nuntio autem expugnati Byzantii Venetias ad partes perlato, ingenti civitas maestitia affecta est, incredibilis quoque Christianae genti terror incussus. Continuo itaque Nicolaus Pontifex quinque triremes suis sumptibus Venetiis viris armisque instruendas curavit: egit ad haec cum patribus de pace. In tanto Reip\<ublicae\> Christianae periculo, Sforciam quoque ad id hortatus est, omneque studium optimus Pontifex adhibuit, ut Italiae Christianitatisque statum pacaret, futurumque se pacis arbitrum declaravit; quam si quis pervicaci animo detrectarat, fore, ut ille statim diris execrationibus petitus, a piorum coetu excluderetur. Haec Pontifex.

and encouraged his men, but words could accomplish little, as they were all terrified by the savage anger of the Turks and by their fury, with which they already were pushing back the Greeks from the fortifications of the Gate of [Saint] Romanus. Giustiniani received a serious wound, then the city was stripped of its defenders, and the way inside was open to the barbarians. The emperor saw this and, with the few men around him, immediately went to the spot. He tried to push back the enemy, who were climbing in droves up to the walls, and he put to the sword many of the barbarians who were rushing into the interior and checked their access.

2. When he saw that all was lost and realized that he had been left almost all alone, with the defenders either slain or in flight, then, it is related, he wished to kill himself with his own sword. But then he judged this action as non-Christian, and devised a more honest way to die: he threw off his imperial insignia and with naked sword in hand he attacked the incoming formation of the Turks; he rushed against their furious regiment and fought bravely; the prince finally was killed by a sword. He is worthy of eternal memory; thus, as he fell, he lost both his life and his empire. By order of Mehmed his head was cut off after his body was found in the bloody slaughter and the heaps of the slain; it was placed on a lance and was paraded from the fortifications through the entire city. It offered a wretched spectacle to all.

3. In such confusion, as everyone was scattering in all directions, a huge crowd of mortals ran together to the temple of Santa Sophia. There they were all captured and the whole city was plundered. Neither building nor saintly chapel was excepted from sacrilegious treatment. Unspeakable were the examples of barbarous sacrilege. Elders and men were put to the sword; young men and boys were abducted; matrons and virgins were violated, and the barbarous nation dealt most cruelly with every age....

4. In this manner Constantinople, the most noble city of Greece and of all Europe, was plundered by Mehmed the king of the Turks in 1452 [*sic*] A.D. Immediately he ordered that the head of Emperor Palaeologus be preserved with care and despatched it, along with forty especially handsome young men and twenty girls chosen from the entire booty, with his officers to the sultan of Egypt to boast of his victory.

V. Bartholomeo Marcello

1. When the news that Byzantium had fallen came to the territory of Venice, the state went into great mourning and all of Christendom was struck with terror. Immediately Pontiff Nicholas prepared five triremes at his own expense; the Venetians manned and equipped them. He also negotiated with the fathers about peace. The Christian Commonwealth was in such peril that the good pontiff also strongly urged Sforza in his efforts to restore and pacify Italy and Christendom, and he declared himself the future arbiter of peace. With dire threats he excommunicated from the faithful anyone who would dare do otherwise. Such were the activities of the pontiff.

2.   At Veneti de suorum civium salute solliciti, Bart<olomaeum> Marcellum ad Mahometum Constantinopolim mittunt, qui publico nomine suos cives eorumque res bello captas repeteret, omnia benigne impetrata; reversusque Marcellus novam cum Othomano pacem nuntiavit, quam nec probare, nec reiicere patres voluere; rem autem differre tamdiu statuerant, quoad pax foedusve inter Christianos Principes ictum esset. Turpe enim putabant, cum Turca communi hoste pacem habere, quanto cum eodem ceteri Christiani Principes bellum terra marique gererent.

2.   Worrying about the safety of their own citizens, the Venetians sent Bartholomeo Marcello to Mehmed in Constantinople to reclaim, in the name of the Republic, their [captive] citizens and ask for restoration of the property seized in the war; he was granted all requests politely. Then Marcello returned and announced the new peace with the Ottoman, which the fathers wished neither to ratify nor to reject. They decided to postpone the matter, until a treaty or a peace was established among the Christian princes. They believed that it would be shameful to have a mutual peace treaty with the Turk, while the other Christian princes waged war on land and sea.

B. The Fall of Negroponte (1470): Liber Octavus (162–63)

I. Euboeae Insulae descriptio. Chalcidis obsidionis

1. Sedet autem Euboea, ut de situ Insulae pauca subiiciam, Aegeo mari posita, inter duo promontoria, Gerasum ad Atticam vergens, et Caphareum ad Hellespontum, Boeotiaeque avulsa, per centum quinquaginta millia passuum: circuitus autem eius trecenta et sexaginta stadia excedit, multas urbes olim insula habuit, Pyrram, Portamum, Hessum, Cerinthum, Oreum, Dium, Achaliam; nunc tantum Chalcidem, a cuius regione in continenti Aulis sita est, modicusque interfluit Euripus, qui ponte iunctus, transcensum ad insulam ex continenti praebet. Othomanus igitur cum centum viginti millibus Turcorum Byzantio digressus per Boeotiam affuit, copiisque Insulam ponte traductis, ad Divi Marci fanum mille circiter passus a Chalcide castra posuit, innumerisque circa urbem fixis tentoriis, collocatisque pluribus locis ad concutienda moenia bellicis machinis, ter totis viribus Othomanus terra marique urbem oppugnavit, ex qua hostes magna semper caede repulsi sunt.

2. Veneta interea classis dum armis res circa Chalcidem geritur, ex proxime Euboeae statione ad comparandum commeatum in Cretam concessit inde cibariis celeriter expeditis discedens, ac septem Cretensibus onerariis ceterae classi adiunctis, ad pristinam rediit stationem. Fama autem Chalcidicae obsidionis Venetias perlata, ingentem curam ac metum civitati iniecit. Quare patres ad potentissimi hostis conatus repellendos, quotquot triremes expedire, instruereque potuere, alias post alias irrequieto cursu ad Chalcidis subsidium mittendas curarunt. Verebantur enim futurae cladis quasi praescii, ne nobilissimam insulam furens Turca expugnaret, qua occupata omnem brevi postea maritimam Graeciae oram; cunctasque Aegei, Pamphiliique maris insulas usque in Syriam armis subacturus esset.

II. Thomae proditoris caedes. Mahometi Bassa consilium

1. Canalis interim ut suis opem ferret, cum tota classe ad angustias Euripi pervenit, plenisque velis, ventoque, et aquis secundis in hostem ferebatur. Tum vero Chalcidenses recreati, qui iam tricesimum diem pugnando fessi, ferocem hostem pertulerant, proditioque in urbe atrox detecta erat, cuius Thomas Illyricus auctor habebatur. Is igitur perfidiae convictus, magistratuum iussu publice est interfectus. Tot malis Chalcidenses circumventi, in Veneta classe spes omnes suas reposuerant, iam die noctuque in ore habere, Canalis Imperatoris opem implorare, ad eum ex ipsis moenibus supplices manus tendere.

2. Tum quatuordecim ex tota classe triremes viris armisque optime instructae, et onerarie duae sub Bartholomaei Minii viri fortissimi ductu ad mille

B. The Fall of Negroponte (1470): Book 8 (162–63)

I. Description of the Island of Euboea. The Siege of Khalkis [Negroponte].

1. Euboea is situated (so that I may add a few words about its geographical position) in the Aegean Sea, between two promontories: Gerasus that turns to Attica and Caphareus towards the Hellespont. It is separated from Boeotia by a gulf of one hundred and fifty miles. Its circumference exceeds three hundred and sixty stades. The island had many cities long ago: Pyrra, Portamus, Hessus, Cerinthus, Oreus, Dium, and Achalia. Now there is only Khalkis; opposite its territory, on the continent, Aulis is situated; in between flow the waters of the moderate channel Euripos which offers a passage from the mainland to the island with a bridge. And so the Ottoman [= Sultan Mehmed II] with one hundred and twenty thousand Turks left Byzantium and came to Boeotia; he marched his soldiers to the island over the bridge and made camp at the Church of San Marco, about one mile from Khalkis. Around the city they pitched innumerable tents and in many places deployed war machines [= artillery] to demolish the walls. The Ottoman launched three assaults against the city, over land and sea, but his forces were repelled, always with heavy casualties.

2. Meanwhile, the Venetian fleet that was waging war around Khalkis went from the neighborhood of Euboea to Crete in order obtain provisions, and then returned swiftly augmented by seven Cretan cargo ships added to the rest of the fleet; it returned to its former station. A rumor that Khalkis was under siege reached Venice and created great concern and fear in the state. The fathers took immense care to repel the attacks of a most powerful enemy and to equip and outfit as many triremes as possible and to send others the swiftest way to the aid of Khalkis. Some predicted with fear the future disaster, that the rabid Turk would seize in war the most noble island, and with this possession he would then in a short time occupy the shores of Greece and go on to subjugate by force all the islands of the Aegean and the Pamphilian Sea as far as Syria.

II. The Death of Traitor Thomas [Tommaso Schiavo].
The Council of Mahmud Pasha

1. In the meantime, in order to bring aid to his side, da Canale with the entire fleet came to the straits of Euripos, and moved against the enemy under full sail and with a favorable wind and current. Then the people of Khalkis, who had been exhausted in thirty days' fighting against a savage enemy, were revived. A foul betrayal was detected in the city, the originator of which, it was held, was Thomas Illyricus [= Tommaso Schiavo]. He was found guilty of disloyalty and, by order of the magistrates, he was publicly executed. As the people of Khalkis had been surrounded by many misfortunes, they placed all their hopes, as they were saying day and night, on the Venetian fleet. They implored Commander da Canale for help and were extending their suppliant arms to him from the walls.

2. Then fourteen triremes from the fleet, excellently equipped with men and arms, and two cargo boats under the orders of Bartholomeo Mini, a very

passus ponti appropinquarunt, in quem vento et mari secundis agi videbantur, ut eo disiecto, barbarum subito impeto invaderent. Ferunt, Othomanum ad hunc Venetae classis motum exterritum, de fuga cogitare coepisse, conscendisseque equum expeditissimum, ut statim ex insula, donec integrum esset, in continentem abiret: sed a Mahometo Asiaticae orae prafecto, quem Bassam Turcae vocant, admonitus, ne id faceret; fore, ut si inde arrepta fuga abiret, et classis et exercitus, Regis vulgato discessu, uno tempore in summum educerentur discrimen, quia potius urbem ipsam atrocissime terra marique, ad incutiendum maiorem terrorem, sub profundam noctem oppugnatione adoriretur, eamque militi diripiendam regio edicto proponeret.

3.   Mahometi consilium Othomanus sequutus, continuo suos ad novum, ultimumque certamen revocat, ingentiaque proponit praemia, qui primus Othomanica signa in muris statuerit. Sub obscuram igitur noctem oppugnatione et copiae terra, et ex Euripo classis moenibus improviso magis barbarorum clamoribus admota est, pugnaque atroci urbem ex omni parte ferox hostis fatigat, in tanto discrimine Chalcidensibus constitutis, omnes a Venetis triremibus ad Imperatorem conversi, uno ore clamabant, ut suppetias actutum ferri iuberet, paratos se vel vincere, vel fortiter pro sociae civitatis salute occumbere.

III. Chalcis capitur

1.   Picemani fratres Cretenses nobili familia orti, onerariae unius prafecti, primas partes ad erumpendum sibi dari efflagitabant, pontemque impetu navis rescissuros pollicebantur, aut, si fata obstarent, non dubitaturos se, et suos, ut viros fortes decet, morti obiicere. Vetat Canalis Imperator, eos et alios quicquam temere agere, reliquam classem expectandam censet, quae proximo loco ad Politiam subsederat; ac statim mittuntur, qui eam arcserent.

2.   Chalcidenses interim tota nocte dimicandi defessi, aegre iam Turcorum armis resistere poterant: magistratuum praesentia eos non parum confirmabat. Aderat enim Paulus Erizus urbis praetor; Ludovicus Calbus praefectus, Ioan<nes> Bondimerius Legatus, Aloysius Delphinus quaestor, ac plerique alii patricii viri, qui militum oppidanorumque stationes obeundo, singulos hortabantur. At miseri Chalcidenses, amicae classis auxilio destituti, vulneribus, inedia, pervigilioque affecti, quum tota nocte incessanter dimicassent, atque amplius non possent, circa secundam diei horam, propugnacula stationesque deseruerunt. Tum hostes, nudatis defensoribus muris, irruptione subito facta, urbem capiunt, foedissimamque edunt caedem, ac armati, inermesque pariter, obtrucantur, in pubesque usque crudele ferrum districtum, caesi quoque magistratus, alii alio loco.

strong man, approached within one mile from the bridge, against which they seemed to move by a favorable wind and current, in order to dismantle it and launch a sudden attack on the barbarian. They say that the Ottoman was terrified by this maneuver of the Venetian fleet, and began to consider flight, to mount the cavalry quickly in order to leave the island while his force was still undamaged and cross over to the mainland. But he was warned by Mahmud, the prefect of the Asiatic shore [= *Beglerbeg* of Asia], whom the Turks address as "pasha," not to do it; if he left in flight, both the army and the navy (once the departure of the king became known) would be in grave danger and it would be better to attack the city by land and sea at the darkest part of the night to inspire greater terror, and he proposed to hand the city over to plunder by royal decree.

3.   The Ottoman followed the advice of Mahmud and immediately mustered his people for a new, final assault; he promised huge rewards to the man who would first raise the Ottoman standards on the walls. And so in the darkness of the night with all the land and naval forces, including the fleet from Euripos, the attack of the barbarians against the walls began suddenly with great noise. In a desperate struggle the ferocious enemy exhausted the city on all sides, and the people of Khalkis were in such great danger that all the crews of the Venetian fleet turned to their commander [= da Canale] and in unison begged him to issue the order to come to the city's aid, saying that they were prepared either to win to fall bravely in the defense of this allied city.

III. The Fall of Khalkis

1.   The Picemani, Cretan brothers from a noble family, captains of one cargo vessel, were eager to take the first position on a counter-attack and promised to break up the bridge with the their ship's impact, or, if God should will it otherwise, to die, as they should, like brave men. Commander da Canale ordered them and all others not to do anything rash and decided to wait for the rest of the fleet, which was moored nearby at Politia; and immediately sent men to summon the fleet.

2.   Meanwhile, about the middle of the night the people of Khalkis became exhausted in the struggle and were hardly able to resist the attacks of the Turks; but they were greatly heartened by the presence of their magistrates. Present were: Paolo Erizzo, the praetor [= *bailo*] of the city; Ludovico [= Alvise] Calbo, the prefect [= *provveditore*]; Giovanni Bondumier the legate; Alvise Dolfin the *quaestor* [= treasurer]; and many other patricians, who urged them to fight on, as they toured the posts of the soldiers and the townspeople. But the unfortunate people of Khalkis, who did not receive any help from the fleet and had fought all night long without any break, were so affected by wounds, hunger, and lack of sleep, that they could no longer resist. They abandoned the battlements and their stations at about the second hour of the day. The enemy, as the walls were stripped of defenders, launched a sudden assault and seized the city; they began a most foul slaughter. Armed and unarmed men were equally butchered, and even the young were offered the cruel naked sword; the magistrates too and others were slain everywhere.

IV. Magistratus caesi. Turcarum caedes

1. Nam Ludovicus Calbus in foro fortissime pugnans interficitur; Bondimerius Legatus in privatis aedibus Pauli Andreotii, quo confugerat; Erizus autem ex munitione loco ubi se tenebat, sub Othomani fide digressus, ad conspectumque eius adductus, crudelissimo mortis genere interemptus est. Nam cavillatus immanis tyrannus pollicitum se fuisse cervici, non lateribus parsurum, infanda perfidia hominem medium secari iussit, magnaque in omnes crudelitate usus est, in ultionem caedis suorum, circa Chalcidem paucis illis diebus amissorum, quibus obsidionem tenuit. Nam ad quadraginta Turcorum milia Chalcidensium armis caesa dicuntur, et in urbe supra quinque millia ferro Barbarico occubuere. Caesorum capita publice ante Patriarchae aedes et Francisci fanum coacervata, luctuosum horrendumque omnibus spectaculum praebuerunt; cadavera ipsa tam intus, quam foris passim iacentia, ne postea suo foetore caelum inficerent, in proximum Euripum nuda sunt proiecta.

2. Othomanus autem, validissimo ad Chalcidem praesidio relicto, terrestri itinere cum reliquis copiis ex insula excessit, Byzantiumque est reversus. Classis quoque Euboico relicto littore Chium venit, hostemque eo Canalis secutus, ad delendam Chalcidicam ignominiam proelium expetebat. Nam mirifice classa aucta, quae centum habuit triremes, Turcam medio mari aggredi Canalis statuerat, spectabatque hostem posse vincere, quum is ad Venetae classis conspectum fugam meditari coepisset: nam ob turmarum infrequentiam, quorum maior pars ad Chalcidem perierat, certus erat, nullo modi congredi. Verum tanta vincendi occasione Veneti uti nescivere, quibusdam triremium praefectis negantibus, cum victore Turca minime dimicandum esse, ne Resp<ublica> in apertum discrimen coniceretur. Itaque sine ullo certamine Veneta classis ad Caeam insulam iuxta Euboeam, unde venerat, reversa est. Barbarus vero, ubi per speculatorias scaphas cognovit, Venetum recessisse, omniaque pacata esse, navigationis suae cursum in Hellespontum libero mari prosequutus, in tutum abiit. Feruntque, Bosphori angustiis superatis, Barbarae classis prafectum ad suos laeta fronte conversum dixisse: Satis amice se a Venetis habitos fuisse, qui frequenti navium apparatu, hospitalem toto mari comitatum praestitissent.

V. Canalis e classe revocatur

1. Chalcidis interim expugnatione Venetias perlata, tantus luctus, et maeror patribus, ac universae civitati iniectus est, ut nullus maior percipi, afferrique potuisset, omnis uno ordine classis trierarchos, prafectosque odisse, sed in primis Imperatorem ipsum Canalem damnare, detestari, qui nullam obsessae civitati, et miseris Chalcidensibus opem tulisset, ac dum potuisset, hostem facile vincere, elabi eum passus esset. Fit itaque animis accensis statim

IV. The Death of the Magistrates. The Slaughter of the Turks

1. Ludovico Calbo was killed fighting bravely in the forum [= *piazza*]. The legate Bondumier was killed in the private home of Paolo Andreotti, where he had fled. Erizzo barricaded himself in a fortified place but came out, relying on a promise given by the Ottoman; he was led before him and was put to death in a most cruel way. For the execrable tyrant made a joke and said that he had promised him his head but not his waist; with unprecedented treachery he issued orders to saw the man in half and with this act of great cruelty he avenged the death of his men who had fallen around Khalkis. It is related that up to forty thousand Turks were killed in battle by the people of Khalkis and that in the city more than five thousand fell victim to the sword of the barbarian. The heads of the slain were gathered before the patriarchate and the church of San Francesco, and this mournful and horrible spectacle was shown to all. The naked corpses themselves that were within the city and were also lying everywhere in the squares were thrown into the neighboring Euripos so that the corruption would not foul the air.

2. The Ottoman left a very strong garrison to guard Khalkis and with the rest of the army marched out of the island and returned to Byzantium by land. The fleet also left the Euboean shores and went to Chios. Da Canale followed the enemy and offered battle to reverse the shame he had incurred at Khalkis. For his fleet had been augmented admirably: he had one hundred triremes to attack the Turks in the open sea. Da Canale had so decided and saw that he could defeat the enemy, who would consider flight at the sight of the Venetian fleet. Their fleet had thinned out, as the greatest part had perished at Khalkis and it was certain that there had been no reinforcements. But the Venetians missed this opportunity of seizing victory, as some captains said that there should be no engagement with the victorious Turk, lest the Republic come to certain danger. And so the Venetian fleet, without an engagement, turned back from Keos, the island it had put in at. But when the barbarian discovered, through his spy boats, that the Venetian fleet had departed, and that no region was under attack, he continued his course to the Hellespont unopposed through the sea in safety. They say that after they had passed the straits of the Bosphorus, the prefect [= *kapudan* pasha] of the barbarian fleet, turned to his associates and said in joy: "How friendly of the Venetians to offer us a good, hospitable escort with so many ships!"

V. Da Canale is Recalled from the Fleet

1. When the news of the fall of Khalkis reached Venice, there was unprecedented and unheard-of sorrow and mourning among the fathers and the entire city; there was hatred exhibited against the trierarchs [= captains of galleys] and commanders, but most of all there was condemnation, even loathing, against da Canale, the Commander [= Captain-General] himself, who offered no help to the besieged city and the unfortunate people of Khalkis, and allowed the enemy to escape even though he could have easily defeated him. And so, while anger

Senatusconsultum, de imperio ei abrogando, unaque, ut is e provincia revocatus, in vincula coniceretur. Petrus Mocenicus eius loco ad Imperium maris mittitur.

2.   Tentavit interim Canalis, dum haec domi fiunt, atque Othomanica classis abest, an Chalcidem inopinato accessu recipere posset. Classe itaque urbi admota, et expositis in terram militibus, sub Ioanne Trono, Federico Iustiniano, et Nic<olao> Mollino, ducibus, res primum eo die in hostes strenue gesta est. Modico postea temporis intervallo Barbari ex urbe erumpentes, Venetos invadunt, quorum ducenti, et amplius sub moenibus foede obtruncantur, et in his Ioannes Tronus fuit, homo impiger, et cuius virtus pluribus iam pridem in Italia bellis enituit, reliqui in fugam versi, se trepide ad naves reperunt. Ita infecta re ad Aulidem classis relicta Euboea Veneta recessit.

VI. Mocenici verba

1.   Eodem die Petrus Mocenicus novus classis Imperator cum tribus triremibus eo applicuit; cui obviam Canalis progressus, post mutuam salutationem, quid in animo haberet, exposuit, conflasse se centum triremium classem, ut diis bene iuvantibus, Chalcidem recepere, venisseque in spe, his viribus, urbis recuperandae, nisi abrogato imperio sibi decedendum esset, verum non desperare omnino eventurum, ut quae ipse frustra antea tentasset, novus Imperator, fortuna duce, ac sua virtute facile perficeret. Ad ea Mocenicus, qua erat prudentia, Quin age, potius! inquit, et tu, si quid spei recuperanda urbe reliquum est, perge armis agere: nam quod ad me attinet, vel collega, vel comes tua sequar imperia, ne publicum impediatur commodum; nullumque recusabo tecum laborem, nullum periculum, ut extorta e Turcorum manibus victoria, in pristinam res Veneta dignitatem restituatur. Tum Canale negante alienis auspiciis quicquam ausurum, expeditio intermissa est, quae dubia, ac difficilis infelicem eventum protendere videbatur.

VII. Canalis in vincula coniectus. Canalis damnatio

1.   Recepta igitur Mocenicus classe, et Canale, ut mandatum erat, in vincula coniecto, quum iam hibernorum tempus appeteret, in Peloponnesum concessit, eo consilio, ut veris initio in Turcas movens, aliquod praeclarum ederet facinus. At Canalis ubi domum venit, perpetua est in Carnis relegatione damnatus. Qui interrogatus a M<arco> Anto<nio> Sabellico, historiarum scriptore, ut ipse ab eo audisse tradit, qua potissimum ratione patriae desiderium levaret? duplici indagine respondisse dicitur, senatoria et literaria: Nam optimarum artium studia a pueri amplexus, insigni eruditione praeditus erat: Togaque Senator praestantissimus habebatur; sed arma, ac militiam navalem sequutus, quae a Musis abhorret, omnem amisit dignitatem.

commanded everyone's spirit, a *senatusconsultum* [= order of the senate] was issued to strip him of his command, to recall him from the province, and to put him in irons. Piero Mocenigo was sent to replace him as Commander of the Sea [= Captain-General].

2. Such was the situation at home; meanwhile, in the absence of the Ottoman fleet, da Canale attempted to seize Khalkis with an unexpected attack. And so the fleet got under sail and soldiers disembarked on land (under the leadership of Giovanni Trono, Federico Giustiniani, and Nicolo Mollino) to launch an assault on the same day. After a short interval the barbarians burst out of the city and attacked the Venetians; about two hundred of them and even more were horribly put to the sword below the walls. Among them was Giovanni Trono, an energetic man, whose courage had already become famous in previous wars in Italy; the rest turned to flight and in fear returned to the ships. After the conclusion of this incident the fleet went to Aulis, then left Euboea and returned to Venice.

VI. The Words of Mocenigo

1. On the same day Piero Mocenigo, the new Commander of the fleet, arrived there with three triremes; da Canale advanced to meet him, and after they exchanged greetings he communicated his intention and his hope that if he enlarged the fleet by one hundred triremes, with God's help and with these forces he would recover the city of Khalkis, unless his command were to be taken away from him; he did not despair about the future, as the new leader, with good luck, would achieve easily with his courage what he himself had failed to accomplish. Mocenigo responded to these words: "How I wish that the only concern would be to launch an attack and recover the city! My concern, as your colleague, is to follow your orders and ensure that the Commonwealth is not harmed; I will refuse no labor or danger to work with you in order to wrest victory from the hands of the Turks and restore the dignity of Venice to its original status." Then da Canale would not dare anything against the enemy's successes, and the expedition came to an end, as it seemed difficult and with a doubtful outcome.

VII. Da Canale is Put in Irons. Da Canale's Punishment

1. So Mocenigo took over the fleet and da Canale, as had been ordered, was put in irons; as winter was approaching, he departed for the Peloponnese with the intention of moving against the Turks in the spring and performing some illustrious deed. But da Canale returned home and was sentenced to perpetual exile at Carni. He was asked by Marc'Antonio Sabellico the historian (who handed down his words): "By what means do you console yourself over the loss of your homeland?" He replied: "Two factors: politics and literature. Even when I was a boy I embraced the study of literature and I have been endowed with exceptional erudition. In addition, I was considered an excellent senator when I wore the toga. Yet I lost all dignity when I turned to arms and to naval expeditions, pursuits abhorred by the Muses."

BIBLIOGRAPHY

I. Collections of Sources

Belgrano, Luigi T. "Prima Serie di Documenti Riguardanti la Colonia di Pera." *Atti della Società Ligure di Storia Patria* 13 (1877): 229–58.

Déthier, Philippe A., and Karl Hopf. *Monumenta Hungariae Historica. Ser. Scriptores* (Második osztály Írok). Vol. 21, parts 1–2; vol. 22, parts 1–2. Sine loco [Galata/Pera ?], sine anno [1872 ?/1875 ?].

Dölger, Franz. *Regesten der Kaiserkunden des oströmischen Reiches*. Vol. 5: 1341–1453. Munich and Berlin, 1965.

Ellissen, Adolph. *Analekten der mittel- und neugriechischen Literatur*. 5 vols. Leipzig, 1855–1882.

Hopf, Carl [Karl]. *Chroniques gréco-romanes inédites ou peu connues publiés avec notes et tables généalogiques*. Paris, 1873; repr. Brussels, 1966.

Iorga (Jorga), Nicolae. *Notes et Extraits pour servir à l'histoire des Croisades au XVe Siècle*. 6 vols. Paris and Bucharest, 1899–1902, 1916.

Lampros, Spyridon P. "Μονῳδίαι καὶ Θρῆνοι ἐπὶ τῇ Ἁλώσει τῆς Κωνσταντινουπόλεως." *Νέος Ἑλληνομνήμων* 5 (1908): 190–270.

———. *Παλαιολόγεια καὶ Πελοποννησιακά*. 4 vols. Athens, 1912–1930; repr. Athens, 1972.

Ludewig, J. P. *Reliquiae manuscriptorum omnis aevi diplomatum ac monumentorum ineditorum adhuc*. Vol. 5. Frankfurt and Leipzig, 1723.

Melville Jones, John R. *The Siege of Constantinople 1453: Seven Contemporary Accounts*. Amsterdam, 1972.

Melville-Jones, John R. *Venice and Thessalonica 1423–1430: The Venetian Documents*. Archivio del Litorale Adriatico 7. Padova, 2002.

Migne, Jacques-Paul. *Patrologiae Cursus Completus Omnium SS. Patrum Scriptorumque Ecclesiasticorum, sive Latinorum, sive Graecorum*. 160 vols. Paris-Turnhout, 1857–1866.

Miklosich, Frank, and Joseph Müller. *Acta et diplomata graeca medii aevi sacra et profana*. 6 vols. Vienna, 1860–1890.

Pauli, S. *Codice diplomatico del Sacro militare ordine gerosolimitano, oggi di Malta, raccolto de varj documenti di quell' archivio, per servire alla storia dello stesso ordine in Storia in Rodi ed in Malta, e illustrato con una serie chronologica di gran maestri, che lo governarono in quei tempi, con alcune notizie storiche, genealogiche, geographiche, ed altre osservazioni.* 2 vols. Lucca, 1733–1737.

Pertusi, Agostino. *La Caduta di Costantinopoli.* Vol. 1: *Le Testimonianze dei Contemporanei.* Vol. 2: *L'Eco nel Mondo.* Verona, 1976.

———. *Testi Inediti e Poco Noti sulla Caduta di Costantinopoli.* Il Mondo Medievale: Studi di Storia e Storiographia: Sezione di Storia Bizantina e Slava 4 (edizione postuma a cura di Antonio Carile). Bologna, 1983.

Petit, Louis, Xenophon A. Sidéridès, and Martin Jugie. *Oeuvres complètes de Gennade Scholarios.* 8 vols. Paris, 1929–1935.

Polidori, Filippo-Luigi. "Due Ritmi e una narrazione in prosa di autori contemporanei intorno alla presa di Negroponte fatta dai Turchi a danno dei Veneziani nel MCCCCLXX." *Archivio storico italiano* 9 (1853): 397–440.

Sathas, Constantine N. Μεσαιωνικὴ Βιβλιοθήκη: *Bibliotheca graeca medii aevi.* 7 vols. Venice and Paris, 1872–1894; repr. Athens, 1972.

———. Μνημεῖα Ἑλληνικῆς Ἱστορίας: *Documents inédits relatifs à l'histoire de la Grèce au moyen âge.* 9 vols. Paris, 1880–1890; repr. Athens, 1972.

Schreiner, Peter. *Die byzantinischen Kleinchroniken.* Corpus Fontium Historiae Byzantinae 12.1–3. 3 vols. Vienna, 1975.

Taaffe, J. *History of the Holy, Military, Sovereign Order of St. John in Jerusalem, or Knights Templars, Knights of Rhodes, Knights of Malta.* 4 vols. London, 1852.

Thiriet, Freddy. *Régestes des déliberations du Sénat de Venise concernant la Romanie.* 3 vols. Paris and the Hague, 1958–1961.

II. Individual Sources

Abraham Ankiwraċ i [= of Ankara]. *Elegy on the Capture of Constantinople.* Trans. Avedis K. Sanjian. In "Two Contemporary Armenian Elegies on the Fall of Constantinople, 1453." *Viator* 1 (1970): 223–61.

Angiolello, Giovanni Maria. *Historia turchesca, 1300–1514.* Ed. I. Ursu. Bucharest, 1909.

Anonymous. "A Note on the Capture of Constantinople in 1453." Ed. Robert Browning. *Byzantion* 22 (1953): 379–83.

———. *Testi Inediti e Poco Noti sulla Caduta di Costantinopoli,* ed. Pertusi, 214–15.

Barbaro, Nicolò. *Giornale dell'assedio di Costantinopoli 1453 di Nicolò Barbaro P.V. corredato di note e documenti.* Ed. Enrico Cornet. Vienna, 1856.

———. *Nicolò Barbaro: Diary of the Siege of Constantinople.* Trans. John R. [Melville] Jones. Jericho, New York, 1969.

———. Selections (with improved text). In *La caduta di Costantinopoli,* ed. Pertusi, 1: 8–38.

Benvenuto. *Relazione.* "The Anconitan Colony in Constantinople and the Report of its Consul, Benvenuto, on the Fall of the City." Ed. Agostino

Pertusi. In *Charanis Studies: Essays in Honor of Peter Charanis*, ed. Angeliki E. Laiou-Thomadakis, 199–218. New Brunswick, 1980.

———. In *Testi Inediti e Poco Noti sulla Caduta di Costantinopoli*, ed. Pertusi, 4–5.

———. Trans. Marios Philippides. In idem, *Byzantium, Europe, and the Early Ottoman Sultans 1373–1513: An Anonymous Greek Chronicle of the Seventeenth Century (Codex Barberinus Graecus 111)*, 197–99. Late Byzantine and Ottoman Studies 4. New Rochelle, 1991.

Benvoglienti, Leonardo. *Dispaccio da Venezia*. Selections. In *La Caduta di Costantinopoli*, ed. Pertusi, 2: 108–11.

Birago, Lampo [Lampugnino]. *Strategicon adversus Turcos*. "Le Notizie sulla organizzazione amministrave e militari dei Turchi nello Strategicon adversus Turcos di Lampo Birago (c. 1453–1455)." Ed. Agostino Pertusi. In *Studi sul medioevo cristiano offerti a R. Morghen per il 90° anniversario dell'Istituto Storico Italiano (1183–1973)*, 2: 669–700. Rome, 1974.

———. Selections. In *La Caduta di Costantinopoli*, ed. Pertusi, 2:114–25.

Bouhours, Père Dominique, S.J.. *Histoire de Pierre D'Abusson Grand-Maistre de Rhodes*. Paris, 1676.

———. Trans. P. Boutsina. *Pierre d'Aubusson: Μεγάλος Μαγίστρος της Ρόδου Πολιορκία 1480 — Άλωση 1522*. Athens, 1996.

Bosio, Giacomo. *Dell'Istoria della sacra religione et illustrissima militia di S. Giovanni di Gerosolimitano*. 3 vols. Venice, 1594.

Χρονικὸν περὶ τῶν Τούρκων Σουλτάνων (κατὰ τὸν Βαρβερινὸν Ἑλληνικὸν Κώδικα 111). Ed. Georgios T. Zoras. Athens, 1956. Also: *Ἡ Ἅλωσις τῆς Κωνσταντινουπολεως καὶ ἡ Βασιλεία Μωάμεθ Β' τοῦ Κατακτητοῦ (κατὰ τὸν Ἀνέκδοτον Ἑλληνικὸν Βαρβερινὸν Κώδικα 111 τῆς Βατικανῆς Βιβλιοθήκης)*. Athens, 1952.

———. *Byzantium, Europe, and the Early Ottoman Sultans 1373–1513: An Anonymous Greek Chronicle of the Seventeenth Century (Codex Barberinus Graecus 111)*. Trans. Philippides.

Critobulus. See Kritoboulos, Michael (Hermodorus ?).

Dolfin, Zorzi. *Cronaca delle famiglie nobili di Venezia*. Ed. Georg M. Thomas. "Die Eroberung Constantinopels im Jahre 1453 auf einer venetianischen Chronik." *Sitzungsberichte der königlichen bayerischen Akademie der Wissenschaften, philos.-hist. Klasse*, 2 (1866): 1–38.

———. Selections. *In Testi Inediti e Poco Noti sulla Caduta di Costantinopoli*, ed. Pertusi, 169–80.

Doukas, [Michael ?]. *Historia Byzantina*. Ed. Immanuel Bekker. Corpus Scriptorum Historiae Byzantinae. Bonn, 1834.

———. *Istoria Turco-Byzantina (1341–1461)*. Scriptores Byzantini 3. Ed. and trans. (into Romanian) Vasile Grecu. Bucharest, 1958.

———. Partial trans. in Melville Jones, *The Siege of Constantinople*, 56–116.

———. *Decline and Fall of Byzantium to the Ottoman Turks by Doukas. An Annotated Translation of "Historia Turco-Byzantina"*. Trans. Harry J. Magoulias. Detroit, 1975.

———. Selections. In *La Caduta di Costantinopoli*, ed. Pertusi, 2: 162–93.

Ecthesis Chronica and Chronicon Athenarum. Ed. Spyridon P. Lampros. London, 1902.

———. *Emperors, Patriarchs, and Sultans of Constantinople, 1373–1513. An Anonymous Greek Chronicle of the Sixteenth Century*. Ed. and trans. Marios Philippides. The Archbishop Iakovos Library of Ecclesiastical and Historical Sources 13. Brookline, 1990.

Eparchos, Thomas, and Joseph Diplovatazes (?). *Relazione*. In *Notes et Extraits pour servir à l'histoire des Croisades au XVe Siècle*, ed. Iorga, 2: 514–18.

———. Selections. In *La Caduta di Costantinopoli*, ed. Pertusi, 1: 234–39.

Gennadius [Scholarius, George]. Ἐπιτάφιος τῷ Μακαρίῳ Θεοδώρῳ Σοφιανῷ, ἐν τῇ ἱερᾷ μονῇ τοῦ Βατοπεδίου ταφέντι, ὃν εἶπεν ἐξ ὑπογείου ὁ θεῖος αὐτοῦ Γεννάδιος μοναχὸς ἐπὶ τῷ τάφῳ. In *Oeuvres complètes de Gennade Scholarios*, ed. Petit, Sidéridès, and Jugie, 1: 277–88.

Giustiniani, Hieronimo. *Istoria di Scio Scritta nell'Anno 1586*. Ed. Philip P. Argenti. *Hieronimo Giustiniani's History of Chios*. Cambridge, 1943.

Giustiniani, Leonardo. See Leonardo of Chios.

Giustiniani, Pietro. *Rerum Venetarum ab Urbe Condita ad Annum M.D.LXXV. Petri Justiniani Patricii Veneti Aloisi filii, Senatorii ordinis viri amplissimi. Ab eodem Autore denuo revisa & rerum memorabilium additione illustrata, cumque indice locupletissimo ornata. Cui haec Accesserunt Opuscula*. Argentorati/Strassburg, M.DC.XI.

Hierax. Χρονικὸν περὶ τῆς τῶν Τούρκων Βασιλείας. In Μεσαιωνικὴ Βιβλιοθήκη, ed. Sathas, 1: 243–68.

Isidore, Cardinal. "Ein Brief des Kardinals Isidor von Kiew an Kardinal Bessarion." Ed. Georg Hofmann. *Orientalia Christiana Periodica* 14 (1948): 405–14.

———. "Quellen zu Isidor von Kiew als Kardinal und Patriarch." Ed. Georg Hofmann. *Orientalia Christiana Periodica* 18 (1952): 146–48.

———. "Ein zweiter Brief Isidors von Kiew über die Eroberung Konstantinopels." Ed. W. Röll. *Byzantinische Zeitschrift* 69 (1976): 13–16.

———. Letters. In *La Caduta di Costantinopoli*, ed. Pertusi, 1: 58–111.

———. Letters. *In Testi Inediti e Poco Noti sulla Caduta di Costantinopoli*, ed. Pertusi, 16–21.

Ivani [da Sarzana], Antonio. *Anonymi historiola quae inscribitur Constantinopolitanae civitatis expugnatio*. In *Monumenta Hungariae Historica. Ser. Scriptores*, ed. Déthier and Hopf, 21: 71–94.

———. *Expugnatio Constantinopolitana edita per Antonium Ivanum ad illustrem dominum Federicum Montisferetri Urbini ac Durantis comitem*. In *Testi Inediti e Poco Noti sulla Caduta di Costantinopoli*, ed. Pertusi, 146–65.

Kallistos, Andronikos. Μονῳδία κῦρ Ἀνδρονίκου τοῦ Καλλίστου ἐπὶ τῇ δυστυχεῖ Κωνσταντινουπόλει. Ed. Spyridon P. Lampros. In "Μονῳδίαι καὶ Θρῆνοι ἐπὶ τῇ Ἁλώσει τῆς Κωνσταντινουπόλεως." Νέος Ἑλληνομνήμων 5 (1908): 203–18.

Kananos, Ioannes. De Constantinopoli anno 1422 oppugnata narratio. Ed. Immanuel Bekker. Corpus Scriptorum Historiae Byzantinae. Bonn, 1838; repr. in Patrologia Graeca, 156: 151–166.

———. L'assedio di Costantinopoli. Ed. Emilio Pinto. Messina, 1977.

———. "Sulla Διήγησις di Giovanni Cananos." Trans. Emilio Colonna. Università di Napoli, Annali della Facoltà di lettere e filosofia 7 (1957): 151–66.

Khalkokondyles, Laonikos (Nikolaos). Laonici Chalcocondylae Historiarum Demonstrationes. Ed. Eugenius Darkó. 2 vols. Budapest, 1922–1927.

———. Selections. In La Caduta di Costantinopoli, ed. Pertusi, 2: 196–227.

———. Nicoloudis, N. Laonikos Chalkokondyles: A Translation and Commentary of the "Demonstrations of Histories" (Books I–III). Athens, 1996.

Kritoboulos, Michael (Hermodorus ?). Κριτόβουλος: Βίος τοῦ Μωάμεθ Β'. In Monumenta Hungariae Historica. Ser. Scriptores, ed. Déthier and Hopf, 21:1–346.

———. De rebus gestis Muhammetis II. In Fragmenta Historicorum Graecorum, 5: 52–164. Ed. C. Müller. Paris, 1883.

———. The History of Mehmed the Conqueror by Kritovoulos. Trans. Charles T. Riggs. Princeton, 1954; repr. Westport, CT., 1970.

———. Ed. and trans. (into Romanian) Vasile Grecu. Critobul din Imbros din domnia lui Mahomed al II-lea anii 1451–1467. Scriptores Byzantini 4. Bucharest, 1963.

———. Selections. In La Caduta di Costantinopoli, ed. Pertusi, 2: 230–51.

———. Critobuli Imbriotae Historiae. Ed. Diether R. Reinsch. Corpus Fontium Historiae Byzantinae 22. Berlin and New York, 1983.

Languschi de', Giacomo [Langusco de, Giacomo]. See Dolfin, Zorzi.

Leonardo of Chios. De Urbis Constantinopoleos Jactura Captivitateque. In Повѣсть о Царьградѣ, ed. Izmail I. Sreznevskii, 50–68. Saint Petersburg, 1855.

———. Epistola. In Patrologia Graeca 159: 923–953.

———. Epistola. In Monumenta Hungariae Historica. Ser. Scriptores, ed. Déthier and Hopf, 21: 553–616.

———. Epistola reverendissimi in Christo patris et domini domini Leonardi Ordinis Praedicatorum, archiepiscopi Mitileni, sacrarum litterarum professoris, ad beatissimum dominum nostrum Nicolaum papam quintum de urbis Constantinopolis captivitate. In "Prima Serie di Documenti Riguardanti la Colonia di Pera," ed. Belgrano, no. 150: 233–57.

———.Trans. Melville Jones. The Siege of Constantinople, 11–42.

———. Selections. In La Caduta di Costantinopoli, ed. Pertusi, 1: 124–71.

Lomellino, Angello Giovanni. *Epistula*. Ed. S. de Sacy. "Pièces diplomatiques tirées des Archives de la République de Gênnes." *Notices et extraits des manuscrits de la Bibliothèque du Roi* 11 (1827): 74–79.
———. Ed. Luigi T. Belgrano. In "Prima serie di documenti," no. 149: 229–233.
———. Ed. Nicolae Iorga (Jorga). "Notes et extraits pour servir à l'histoire des croisades au XVe siècle." *Revue de l'Orient latin* 8 (1900/1901): 105–08.
———. Trans. Melville Jones. *The Siege of Constantinople*, 131–35.
———. In *La Caduta di Costantinopoli*, ed. Pertusi, 1: 42–51.
Mehmed II, Sultan. *Aman-name*. Ed. Spyridon P. Lampros. "Ἡ Ἑλληνικὴ ὡς Ἐπίσημος Γλῶσσα τῶν Σουλτάνων." *Νέος Ἑλληνομνήμων* 5 (1908): 40–79.
———. *Aman-name*. Ed. and trans. Theodore C. Skeat. "Two Byzantine Documents." *British Museum Quarterly* 18 (1953): 71–73.
———. *Aman-name*. Trans. Melville Jones. *The Fall of Constantinople*, 136–37.
Montaldo, Adamo di. *De Constantinopolitano Excidio ad nobilissimum iuvenem Melladucam Cicaddam*. In *Monumenta Hungariae Historica. Ser. Scriptores*, ed. Déthier and Hopf, 21: 35–70.
———. Ed. Philippe A. Déthier, Cornelio Desimoni, and Carl Hopf. "Della Conquista di Costantinopoli per Maometto II nel MCCCLIII." *Atti della Società Ligure di Storia Patria* 10 (1874): 289–354.
———. Selections. *In Testi Inediti e Poco Noti sulla Caduta di Costantinopoli*, ed. Pertusi, 188–209.
Nestor-Iskander. Повѣсть о Царьградѣ. Ed. Izmail I. Sreznevskii. Saint Petersburg, 1855.
———. Selections. Trans. E. Folco. In *La Caduta di Costantinopoli*, ed. Pertusi, 267–98.
———. *The Tale of Constantinople (of its Origin and Capture by the Turks in the Year 1453) by Nestor-Iskander: From the Early Sixteenth-Century Manuscript of the Troitse-Sergieva Lavra, No. 773*. Late Byzantine and Ottoman Studies 5. Ed. and trans. Walter K. Hanak and Marios Philippides. New Rochelle, Athens, and Moscow, 1998.
Piccolomini, Aeneas Sylvius. *Aeneae Sylvii Piccolomini Senensis, qui post adeptum pontificatum Pius eius nominis Secundus appellatus est, opera quae extant omnia, nunc demum post corruptissimas aeditiones summa diligentia castigata & in unum corpus redacta, quorum elenchum uersa pagella indicabit*. Basel, sine anno [1551 ?]; repr. Frankfurt, 1967.
———. *Cosmographia Pii Papae in Asiae et Europae eleganti descriptione*. Paris, 1509.
———. Ed. R. Wolkan. *Der Briefwechsel des Eneas Silvius Piccolomini*. Fontes Rerum Austriacarum 68. Vienna, 1918.
Pius II, Pope. See Piccolomini, Aeneas Sylvius.
Pusculo, Ubertino. *Constantinopolis libri IV*. In *Analekten der mittel- und neu-griechischen Literatur*, ed. Ellissen, 3: 12–83. Leipzig, 1857.

———. Selections. In *La Caduta di Costantinopoli*, ed. Pertusi, 1: 200–13.
Quirini, Lauro. "Le Epistole Storiche di Lauro Quirini sulla Caduta di Costantinopoli e la Potenza dei Turchi." In *Lauro Quirini Umanista*, Studi e Testi a cura di P. O. Kristeller, K. Krauter, A. Pertusi, G. Ravegnani, C. Seno, ed. Agostino Pertusi, 163–259. Florence, 1977.
———. Selections. In *Testi Inediti e Poco Noti sulla Caduta di Costantinopoli*, ed. Pertusi, 62–94.
Riccherio [Richer], Christoforo. *De rebus Turcarum libri octo*. Paris, 1540.
———. Partial trans. Melville Jones, *The Siege of Constantinople*, 117–24.
Rimini, Filippo da. *Epistola ad Franciscum Barbarum, virum inclitum, procuratorem Sancti Marci dignissimum [Excidium Constantinopolitanae urbis]*. In *Monumenta Hungariae Historica. Ser. Scriptores*, ed. Déthier and Hopf, 21: 656–82.
———. "La lettera di Filippo da Rimini, cancelliere di Corfù, a Francesco Barbaro e i primi documenti occidentali sulla caduta di Costantinopoli (1453)." In Μνημόσυνον Σοφίας Ἀντωνιάδη, ed. Agostino Pertusi, 120–57. Βιβλιοθήκη τοῦ Ἑλληνικοῦ Ἰνστιτούτου Βενετίας Βυζαντινῶν καὶ Μεταβυζαντινῶν Σπουδῶν 6. Venice, 1974.
———. Selections. In *Testi Inediti e Poco Noti sulla Caduta di Costantinopoli*, ed. Pertusi, 127–41.
Saguntino. Cf. Sekoundinos, Nikolaos.
Salamonti, Francesco. *Vita Viri Clarissimi et Famosissimi Kyriaci Anconitani by Francesco Salamonti*. Ed. Charles Mitchell and Edward W. Bodnar, S.J. Transactions of the American Philosophical Society 86.4. Philadelphia, 1996.
Samuel, Bishop. *Epistula*. In *Notes et extraits pour servir à l'Histoire des Croisades au XVe siècle*, ed. Jorga, 4: 65–68.
———. *Epistula*. In *La Caduta di Costantinopoli*, ed. Pertusi, 1: 228–31.
Sansovino, Francesco. *Historia universale dell'origine et imperio dei Turchi: nella quale si contengono la origine, le lege, l'usanze, i costumi, cose religiosi come mondani de' Turchi: oltre cio vi sono tutte le guerre che di tempo sono state fatte da quella natione cominciando da Othomano primo Re di questa gente fino al moderno Selim con le vite di tutti i principi di casa Othomana*. 3 vols. Venice, 1564, 1568, 1571, etc.
———. *Gl'Annali overo le vite de principi et signori della casa Ottomana ne quali si leggono di tempo tutte le guerre particolarmente fatte della natione de' Turchi in diverse provincie del mondo contra i Christiani*. Venice, 1571.
Sanudo Torsello, Marin. *Marin Sanudo Torsello Istoria di Romania: Introduction, Edition, Translation, Commentary*. Ed. Eutychia M. Papadopoulou. National Hellenic Research Foundation, Institute for Byzantine Research: Sources 4. Athens, 2000.
———. *I Diarii (<MCCCCXVI–MDXXXIII> dall' autografo marciano ital. cl. VII codd. CDXIX–CDLXXVII)*. 58 vols. Venice, 1879–1903.

Schiltberger, Johann. *The Bondage and Travels of Johann Schiltberger*. Trans. J. B. Telfer. London, 1879.
Scholarius, George. See Gennadius [Scholarius, George].
Sekoundinos, Nikolaos. *Ad serenissimum principem et invictissimum regem Alfonsum Nicolai Sagundini oratio*. In *Monumenta Historica Slavorum Meridionalium Vicinorumque Populorum*, ed. Vikentii V. Makušev, 1: 295–306. Warsaw, 1874.
———. Selections. In *Notes et extraits pour servir à l'Histoire des Croisades au XVe siècle*, ed. Jorga, 3: 316–23.
———. Selections. In *La Caduta di Costantinopoli*, ed. Pertusi, 2: 128–41.
Soemmern, Henry. *Qualiter urbs Constantinopolis anno LIII° a Turcis depraedata fuit et subiugata*. In *Notes et extraits pour servir à l'histoire des croisades au XVe siècle*, ed. Jorga, 3: 307–15.
———. Selections. In *La Caduta di Costantinopoli*, ed. Pertusi, 2: 82–97.
Spandounis [Spandugnino], Theodorus. *De la origine degli imperatori Ottomani ordini de la corte, forma del guerreggiare loro religione, rito, et costumi de la nationes*. In Μνημεῖα Ἑλληνικῆς Ἱστορίας, ed. Sathas, 9: 135–261.
———. Trans. Donald M. Nicol, *Theodore Spandounes: On the Origin of the Ottoman Emperors*. Cambridge, 1997.
Spandugnino. See Spandounis [Spandugnino], Theodorus.
Sphrantzes, George. *Chronicon Minus. Georgios Sphrantzes, Memorii 1401–1477. În anexă Pseudo-Phrantzes. Macarie Melissenos Cronaca, 1258–1481*. Scriptores Byzantini 5. Ed. and trans. (into Romanian) Vasile Grecu. Bucharest, 1966.
———. *The Fall of the Byzantine Empire. A Chronicle by George Sphrantzes, 1401–1477*. Trans. Marios Philippides. Amherst, 1980.
———. *Georgii Sphrantzae Chronicon*. Corpus Fontium Historiae Byzantinae 29. Ed. and trans. (into Italian) Riccardo Maisano. Rome, 1990.
Tetaldi [Edaldy, Dedaldi, Tedaldi, Tetardi], Jacopo. *Informations envoyées*. In *Thesaurus novus anecdotorum tomus primus, complectens regum ac principum, aliorumque virorum illustrium epistolas et diplomata benè multa*, ed. Edmond Martène and Ursin Durand, 1819–26. Paris, 1717.
———. *Informations envoyées*. In *Monumenta Hungariae Historica. Ser. Scriptores*, ed. Déthier and Hopf, 21: 891–915.
———. *Tractatus de Expugnatione Urbis Constantinopolis*. In *Veterum scriptorum et monumentorum historicorum, dogmaticorum, moralium amplissima collectio*, ed. Edmond Martène and Ursin Durand, 5: 785–800. Paris, 1729.
———. Trans. Melville Jones. In *The Siege of Constantinople*, 1–10.
———. Selections. In *La Caduta di Costantinopoli*, ed. Pertusi, 1: 175–89.
Tignosi, da Foligno, Niccolò. *Expugnatio Constantinopolitana*. Selections. In *Testi Inediti e Poco Noti sulla Caduta di Costantinopoli*, ed. Pertusi, 101–23.
Tursun Beg. *The History of Mehmed the Conqueror by Tursun Beg*. Trans. Halil Inalcik and Rhoades Murphey. Minneapolis and Chicago, 1978.

III. Modern Works

Alderson, Anthony D. *The Structure of the Ottoman Dynasty.* Oxford, 1956.

Andreeva, Marija. "Zur Reise Manuels II Palaiologos nach West-Europa." *Byzantinische Zeitschrift* 34 (1934): 37–47.

Andrews, A. D. "The Turkish Threat to Venice, 1453–1463." Ph.D. diss., University of Pennsylvania, 1962.

Arampatzoglou, Odysseus M. *Ἡ Φώτειος Βιβλιοθήκη.* Constantinople, 1933.

Argenti, Philip P. *The Occupation of Chios by the Genoese and Their Administration of the Island, 1346–1566.* Vol. 1. Cambridge, 1958.

Arnakis, George Georgiades. *Οἱ Πρῶτοι Ὀθωμανοί.* Texte und Forschungen zur byzantinisch-neugriechischen Philologie 41. Athens, 1947.

Aschback, Joseph. *Geschichte Kaiser Sigismunds I.: Sigismunds frühere Geschichte bis auf die Eröffnung des Constanzer Conciliums.* Hamburg, 1838.

Atiya, Aziz S. *The Crusade of Nicopolis.* London, 1934.

———. *The Crusade in the Later Middle Ages.* London 1938.

Ayverdi, Ekrem H. *Osmanli Mı 'marısınde Fatih Devri* IV. Istanbul Enstitüsü 69. Istanbul, 1974.

Babinger, Franz. "Quizil Elma." *Der Islam* 12 (1922): 109–11.

———. *Beiträge zur Frühgeschichte der Türkenherrschaft in Rumelien (14.–15. Jahrhundert).* Südeuropäische Arbeiten 34. Munich, 1934.

———. "Mehmeds II., des Eroberers Geburtstag." *Oriens* 2 (1949): 1–5.

———. "Von Amurath zu Amurath. Vor- und Nachspiel der Schlacht bei Varna." *Oriens* 3 (1950): 229–65.

———. "Ja'kub Pascha, ein Leibarzt Mehmeds II." *Rivista degli Studi Orientali* 26 (1951): 82–113.

———. "Ein venedischer Lageplan der Feste Rûmeli Hisâry (2. Hälfte des XV. Jhdts.)." *La Bibiofilia* 58 (1955): 188–95.

———. "Eine lateinische Totenklage auf Mehmed II." In *Studi Orientali in onore di Giorgio della Vida*, 1: 15–31. Rome, 1956.

———. "Die Quellenwert der Berichte über den Einsatz von Belgrade am 21./22. Juli 1456." *Sitzungsberichte der bayerischen Akademie der Wissenschaften, philos.-hist. Klasse* 6 (1957): 1–69.

———. "Mehmeds II., des Eroberers Mutter." In *Beiträge zur Slavenkunde, Festgabe für Paul Diels*, 3–12. Munich, 1957.

———. "Notes on Cyriac of Ancona and Some of his Friends." *Journal of the Warburg and Courtauld Institutes* 25 (1962): 321–23.

———. "Nicolaos Sagoundinos, ein griechisch-venedischer Humanist des 15. Jahrhunderts." In *Χαριστήριον εἰς Ἀναστάσιον Ὀρλάνδον*, 1: 198–212. Athens, 1964.

———. *Mehmed the Conqueror and his Time.* Trans. R. Manheim, ed. W. C. Hickman. Bollingen Series 96. Princeton, 1978.

Bain, Robert N. "The Siege of Belgrade by Muhammad II, July 1–23, 1456." *English Historical Review* 7 (1892): 235–53.

Barker, John W. *Manuel II Palaeologus (1391–1425). A Study in Late Byzantine Statesmanship.* New Brunswick, 1969.
Bartusis, Mark C. *The Late Byzantine Army: Arms and Society, 1204–1453.* Philadelphia, 1992.
Baynes, Norman H. "The Supernatural Defenders of Constantinople." *Analecta Bollandiana* 7 (1949): 165–77.
———. *Byzantine Studies and Other Essays.* London, 1955.
Beck, Hans-Georg. *Geschichte der byzantinischen Volksliteratur.* Munich, 1971.
Belabre, Fradin Baron de. *Rhodes of the Knights.* Oxford, 1908.
Benedikz, Benedikt S., and Sigfús Blöndal. *The Varangians of Byzantiium: An Aspect of Byzantine Military History.* Cambridge, 1978.
Berchet, Guglielmo. *La Republica di Venezia e la Persia.* Turin, 1865.
Bernicolas-Hatzopoulos, Dionysios. "The First Siege of Constantinople by the Ottomans (1394–1402) and its Repercussions on the Civilian Population of the City." *Byzantine Studies/Etudes Byzantines* 10 (1983): 39–51.
Biazes, Spyridon. "Ἡρωῒς κατὰ τὴν Ἅλωσιν τῆς Χαλκίδος τῷ 1470." *Πανευβοϊκὸν Ἡμερολόγιον* 1 (1916): 8–11.
Bisaha, Nancy. *Creating East and West: Renaissance Humanists and the Ottoman Turks.* Philadelphia, 2004.
Birnbaum, E. "Hekim Ya'kub, Physician to Sultan Mehemmed, the Conqueror." *Hebrew Medical Journal* 1 (1961): 250–322.
Bombaci, Alessio. "Venezia e la impressa turca di Otranto." *Rivista storica italiana* 56 (1954): 159–203.
Bouras, Kharalambos. "Τὸ Ἐπιτύμβιο τοῦ Λουκᾶ Σπαντούνη στὴ Βασιλικὴ τοῦ Ἁγίου Δημητρίου Θεσσαλονίκης." *Ἐπιστημονικὴ Ἐπετηρὶς τῆς Πολυτεχνικῆς Σχολῆς. Τμῆμα Ἀρχιτεκτόνων* 6 (1973): 1–63.
Bowman, Steven B. *The Jews of Byzantium, 1204–1453.* University Park, PA, 1985.
Bradbury, Jim. *The Medieval Siege.* Woodbridge, 1992.
Bradford, Ernle. *The Knights of the Order.* New York, 1972.
Brockman, Eric. *The Two Sieges of Rhodes 1480–1522.* London, 1969.
Braun, Maximilian. *Kossovo. Die Schlacht auf dem Amsefelde in geschichtlichen und epischen Überlieferung.* Leipzig, 1937.
Browning, Robert. "A Note on the Fall of Constantinople in 1453." *Byzantion* 22 (1953): 379–87.
Cecchini, G. "Anna Notara Paleologina. Una principessa greca in Italia e la politica senese di ripopolamento della Maremma." *Bolletino Senese di Storia Patria* 9 (1938): 6–27.
Charanis, Peter. "Internal Strife in Byzantium during the Fourteenth Century." *Byzantion* 15 (1940/1941): 208–30.
———. "The Strife among the Palaeologi and the Ottoman Turks 1370–1402." *Byzantion* 16 (1942/1943): 286–314.
Cheetham, Nicolas. *Mediaeval Greece.* New Haven and London, 1981.

Chevedden, Paul E. "The Invention of the Counterweight Trebuchet: A Study in Cultural Diffusion." *Dumbarton Oaks Papers* 54 (2000): 71–116.

Cipolla, Carlo M. *Guns, Sails and Empires: Technological Innovation and the Early Phase of European Expansion 1400–1700*. New York, 1965.

Cochrane, Eric. *Historians and Historiography in the Italian Renaissance*. Chicago and London, 1981.

Coco, P. *La Guerra contro i Turchi in Otranto. Fatti e persone, 1480–1481*. Lecce, 1945.

Colin, J. *Cyriaque d'Ancône: Le voyageur, le marchand, l'humaniste*. Paris, 1981.

Concasty, Marie-Louise. "Les 'Informations' de Jacques Tetaldi sur le siège et la prise de Constantinople." *Byzantion* 24 (1954): 95–110.

Contamine, Philippe. *War in the Middle Ages*. Trans. M. Jones. Oxford, 1984.

Delaville le Roulx, Joseph. *Les Hospitaliers à Rhodes jusqu'à la mort de Philibert de Naillac, 1310–1421*. 2 vols. Paris, 1886.

Dennis, George T. *The Reign of Manuel II in Thessalonica, 1382–1387*. Orientalia Christiana Analecta 159. Rome, 1960.

———. "The Byzantine-Turkish Treaty of 1403." *Orientalia Christiana Periodica* 33 (1967): 72–88.

———. *Byzantium and the Franks, 1350–1420*. London, 1982.

Dereksen, David. See Stacton, David.

DeVries, Kelly. "Gunpowder Weapons at the Siege of Constantinople, 1453." In *War and Society in the Eastern Mediterranean, 7th–15th Centuries*, ed. Yaakov Lev, 343–63. The Medieval Mediterranean: Peoples, Economies and Cultures 9. Leiden, 1997.

Dölger, Franz. "Ein literarischer und diplomatischer Fälscher des 16. Jahrhunderts: Metropolit Makarios von Monembasia." In *Otto Glaunig zum 60. Geburtstag, Festangabe aus Wissenschaft und Bibliothek*, 25–36. Leipzig, 1936.

———. *Byzantinische Diplomatik. 20 Aufsätze zum Urkundenwesen der Byzantiner*. Ettal, 1956.

Dotson, John E. "Foundations of Venetian Naval Strategy from Pietro II Orseolo to the Battle of Zonchio, 1000–1500." *Viator* 32 (2001): 113–25.

Drizari, Nelo. *Scanderbeg: His Life, Correspondence, Orations, Victories, and Philosophy*. Palo Alto, 1968.

Dubuisson, M. "Graecus, Graeculus, Graecari: l'emploi péjoratif du nom des Grecs en latin." In *ΕΛΛΗΝΙΣΜΟΣ: Quelques jalons pour un histoire de l'identité grecque*, ed. Suzanne Saïd, 315–35. Leiden, 1991.

Dzhagatspanian, E. D. "Мировоззрение Византийского Историка XV в. Георгия Сфрандзи." *Кавказ и Византия* 3 (1982): 45–63.

———. "Некоторые Замечания по Поводу Австорства Болшой Хроники Псевдо-Сфрандзи." *Византийски Времменик* 43 (1982): 299–330.

Edge, D., and Miles J. Paddock. *Arms and Armor of the Medieval Knight: An Illustrated History of Weaponry in the Middle Ages*. New York, 1985.

Estopañan, Sebastian Cirac. *Byzancio y España. La caida del imperio byzantino y los Españoles*. Barcelona, 1954.

Falier-Papadopoulos, Jean B. "Phrantzès est-il réellement l'auteur du grand chronique qui porte son nom?." In *Actes du IVe Congrès international des études byzantines*, 177–89. Известия на Българския Археологически Институт 8; *Bulletin de l'Institut Archéologique Bulgare* 9–10. Vol. 1 (Sofia, 1935–1936): 177–189.

Fincati, Luigi. "La Perdita di Negroponte (luglio 1470)." *Archivio veneto* 22 (1886): 267–307.

Fossati, E. "Dal 25 luglio 1480 al 6 aprile 1481: l'opera di Milano." *Archivio storico lombardo* 36 (1909): 1–71.

Gabriel, A. *Chateaux turcs du Bosphore*. Memoires de l'Institut Français d'Archéologie à Stamboul 6. Paris, 1943.

Ganchou, Thierry. "Le Mésazon Démétrius Paléologue Cantacuzène a-t-il figuré parmi les défenseurs du siège de Constantinople (19 Mai 1453)?." *Revue des études byzantines* 52 (1994): 245–72.

———. "Sur quelques erreurs relatives aux dernier défenseurs grecs de Constantinople en 1453." Θησαυρίσματα: Περιοδικὸν τοῦ Ἑλληνικοῦ Ἰνστιτούτου Βυζαντινῶν καὶ Μεταβυζαντινῶν Σπουδῶν τῆς Βενετίας 25 (1995): 61–82.

Geanakoplos, Deno J. "Byzantium and the Crusades, 1354–1453." In *A History of the Crusades*, vol. 3: *The Fourteenth and Fifteenth Centuries*, ed. Kenneth M. Setton and Harry W. Hazard, 69–103. Madison, 1975.

Gedeon, Manuel. Πατριαρχικοὶ Πίνακες. Εἰδήσεις Ἱστορικαὶ καὶ Βιογραφικαὶ περὶ τῶν Πατριαρχῶν Κωνσταντινουπόλεως ἀπὸ Ἀνδρέου τοῦ Πρωτοκλήτου μέχρις Ἰωακεὶμ Γ΄ τοῦ ἀπὸ Θεσσαλονίκης. Constantinople, 1890.

Gegaj, Athanas. *L'Albanie et l'invasion turque au XVe siècle*. Louvain, 1937.

Georgopoulou, Maria. *Venice's Mediterranean Colonies: Architecture and Urbanism*. Cambridge, 2001.

Gibbons, Herbert A. *The Foundation of the Ottoman Empire: History of the Osmanlis up to the Death of Bayezid I, 1330–1403*. New York, 1916.

Gill, Joseph. *The Council of Florence*. Cambridge, 1958.

Giokhalas, Titos P. Ὁ Γεώργιος Καστριώτης-Σκεντέρμπεης εἰς τὴν Νεοελληνικὴν Ἱστοριογραφίαν καὶ Λογοτεχνίαν. Ἵδρυμα Μελετῶν τῆς Χερσονήσου τοῦ Αἴμου 151. Thessalonica, 1975.

Grecu, Vasile. "Das Memoirenwerk des Georgios Sphrantzes." In *Actes du XIIe Congrès international d'études byzantines* 1: 327–41. Paris, 1963.

———. "Georgios Sphrantzes. Leben und Werk. Makarios Melissenos und sein Werk. Die Ausgaben." *Byzantinoslavica* 26 (1965): 62–73.

Gregory, Timothy E. *The Hexamilion and the Fortress.* Isthmia 5. Princeton, 1993.
Guilland, Rodolphe. "Les appels de Constantine XI Paléologue à Rome et à Venise pour sauver Constantinople." *Byzantinoslavica* 14 (1953): 226–44.
Haldon, John F., and M. Byrne. "A Possible Solution to the Problem of Greek Fire." *Byzantinische Zeitschrift* 70 (1977): 91–99.
Halecki, Oskar. *The Crusade of Varna: A Discussion of Controversial Problems.* New York, 1943.
Hammer-Purgstall, Joseph von. *Geschichte des osmanischen Reiches.* 10 vols. Pest, 1827–1835.
Hanak, Walter K. "One Source, Two Renditions: 'The Tale of Constantinople' and Its Fall in 1453." *Twenty-Eighth Annual Byzantine Studies Conference Abstracts of Papers*, 91. Columbus, 2002.
Hankins, James. "Renaissance Crusaders: Humanist Crusade Literature in the Age of Mehmed II." *Dumbarton Oaks Papers* 49 (1995) [Symposium on Byzantium and the Italians, 13th–15th Centuries]: 111–209.
Hasluck, Frederick W. "The Latin Monuments of Chios." *Annual of the British School at Athens* 16 (1909–1910): 137–84.
Heers, Jacques. *Gênes au XVe siècle. Activité économique et problémes sociaux.* Paris, 1961.
Held, Joseph. *Hunyadi: Legend and Reality.* East European Monographs 178. Boulder, 1985.
Heywood, Colin. *Writing Ottoman History: Documents and Interpretations.* Collected Studies. Aldershot, 2002.
Hookham, Hilda. *Tamburlaine the Conqueror.* London, 1962.
Hopf, Carl. *Les Giustiniani dynastes de Chiòs: étude historique.* Paris, 1888.
Hussey, Joan M., ed. *Cambridge Medieval History.* Vol. 4: *The Byzantine Empire*, Part I: *Byzantium and its Neigobours*; Part II: *Government, Church and Civilization.* Cambridge, 1966, 1968.
Imber, Colin. *The Ottoman Empire, 1300–1481.* Istanbul, 1990.
Inalcik, Halil. "Ottoman Methods of Conquest." *Studia Islamica* 2 (1954): 103–29.
———. "Bursa and the Commerce of the Levant." *Journal of Social and Economic History of the Orient* 3 (1960): 131–42.
———. "Mehmed the Conqueror (1431–1482) and His Time." *Speculum* 35 (1960): 408–27.
———. "The Policy of Mehmed II toward the Greek Population of Istanbul and the Byzantine Buildings of the City." *Dumbarton Oaks Papers* 23/24 (1969/1970): 231–49.
———. *The Ottoman Empire: Conquest, Organisation, and Economy.* London, 1978.
———. "The Question of the Emergence of the Ottoman State." *International Journal of Turkish Studies* 2 (1980): 71–79.

———. *Studies in Ottoman Social and Economic History*. London, 1985.
———. *The Ottoman Empire: The Classical Age 1300–1600*. Trans. Norman Itzkowitz and Colin Imber. Late Byzantine and Ottoman Studies 1. New Rochelle, 1989.
Iorga, Nicolae. *Geschichte des osmanischen Reiches*. 5 vols. Gotha, 1908–1913.
———. *Rhodes sous les hospitaliers*. Paris, 1931.
———. "Sur les deux prétendants Moustafa du XVe siècle." *Revue historique du Sud-est européen* 10 (1933): 12–3.
———. *Byzance après Byzance. Continuation de l'"Histoire" de la vie byzantine*. Bucharest, 1935. Τὸ Βυζάντιο μετὰ τὸ Βυζάντιο. Trans. John Karas. Athens, 1989.
Itzkowitz, Norman. *Ottoman Empire and Islamic Tradition*. Chicago, 1972.
Jacobs, Emil. "Cyriacus von Ancona und Mehemmed II." *Byzantinische Zeitschrift* 30 (1929): 197–202.
Jacoby, David. "La population de Constantinople à l'epoque byzantine: un problème de démographie urbaine." *Byzantion* 31 (1961): 81–109.
Janssens, Emile. *Trébizond en Colchide*. Brussels, 1969.
Jugie, Martin. "Le voyage de l'empereur Manuel Paléologue en Occident (1399–1403)." *Echos d'Orient* 15 (1912): 322–33.
Kalatheres, Anastasios. "Ἀρχοντικό στή Χαλκίδα." Ἑταιρεία Εὐβοϊκῶν Σπουδῶν 16 (1970): 19–81.
Kazhdan, Alexander, et al. ed. *The Oxford Dictionary of Byzantium*. 3 vols. New York and Oxford, 1991.
Khasiotes, Ioannes K. Μακάριος, Θεόδωρος καὶ Νικηφόρος οἱ Μελισσηνοὶ (Μελισσουργοὶ) (16ος - 17ος αἰ.). Thessalonica, 1966.
Klopf [Carroll], Margaret G. "The Army in Constantinople at the Accession of Constantine XI." *Byzantion* 60 (1970): 385–92.
Koch, Hansjoachim W. *Medieval Warfare*. London, 1978.
Kollias, Elias. *The Knights of Rhodes: The Palace and the City*. Athens, 1988.
Köprülü, Mehmed F. *Les origines de l'empire ottoman*. Paris, 1934.
Korres, Theodoros K. Ὑγρὸν Πῦρ · Ἕνα Ὅπλο τῆς Βυζαντινῆς Ναυτικῆς Τακτικῆς. Ἑταιρεία Βυζαντινῶν Ἐρευνῶν 6. Thessalonica, 1989.
Kougeas, Sokrates. "Notizbuch eines Beamten der Metropolis von Thessalonike aus dem Anfang des XV. Jahrhunderts." *Byzantinische Zeitschrift* 23 (1914–1919): 143–63.
Koukoules, Phaidon. Βυζαντινῶν Βίος καὶ Πολιτισμός. 6 vols. Athens, 1948–1957.
Laiou, Angeliki, ed. *The Economic History of Byzantium from the Seventh through the Fifteenth Century*. 3 vols. Dumbarton Oaks Studies 39. Washington, DC, 2002.
Lampros, Spyridon P. "Ἡ Ἅλωσις τῆς Τραπεζοῦντος καὶ ἡ Βενετία." *Νέος Ἑλληνομνήμων* 2 (1905): 324–33.

———." Ὁ Κωνσταντίνος Παλαιολόγος ὡς Σύζυγος ἐν τῇ Ἱστορίᾳ καὶ τοῖς Θρύλοις." *Νέος Ἑλληνομνήμων* 4 (1907): 417–66.

———." Ἡ Ἑλληνικὴ ὡς Ἐπίσημος Γλῶσσα τῶν Σουλτάνων." *Νέος Ἑλληνομνήμων* 5 (1908): 40–79.

———." Ἑλληνικὰ Δημόσια Γράμματα τοῦ Σουλτάνου Βαγιαζὴτ Β΄." *Νέος Ἑλληνομνήμων* 5 (1908): 155–89.

———." Ἡ Ἄννα Νοταρᾶ ὡς Κυρία Κώδικος." *Νέος Ἑλληνομνήμων* 5 (1908): 485–6.

———."Κατάλογος τῶν Οἴκων Κερκύρας." *Νέος Ἑλληνομνήμων* 10 (1913): 449–56.

———." Ἡ περὶ Ἁλώσεως Τραπεζοῦντος Ἐπιστολὴ τοῦ Ἀμηρούτζη." *Νέος Ἑλληνομνήμων* 12 (1915): 276–78.

Lemerle, Paul."La Domination vénetienne à Thessalonique." In *Miscellanea G. Galbiati*, 3: 219–25. Fontes Ambrosiani 27. Milan, 1951.

Lev, Yaakov, ed. *War and Society in the Eastern Mediterranean, 7th–15th Centuries*. The Medieval Mediterranean: Peoples, Economies and Cultures 9. Leiden, 1997.

Lewis, Bernard."The Privileges Granted by Mehmed II to his Physician." *Bulletin of the School of Oriental and African Studies* 14 (1952): 551–63.

Lindner, Rudi P. *Nomads and Ottomans in Medieval Anatolia*. Bloomington, 1983.

Lock, Peter. *The Franks in the Aegean 1204–1500*. London and New York, 1995.

Loenertz, Raymond-Joseph."La première insurrection d'Andronic Paléologue." *Echos d'Orient* 38 (1939): 342–45.

———."Autour du Chronicon Maius attribué à Georges Phrantzès." In *Miscellanea G. Mercati*, 273–311. Studi e Testi 123. Vatican City, 1946.

Lowry, Heath W. *The Nature of the Early Ottoman State*. Albany, 2003.

Lopez, Robert S. *Storia delle colonie genovesi nel Mediterraneo*. Bologna, 1938.

Luttrell, Anthony. *The Hospitaller State on Rhodes and its Western Provinces, 1306–1462*. Aldershot, 1999.

Maisano, Riccardo."Il manoscritto Napoletano II. E. 25 e la storia della tradizione dello pseudo-Sfrantze." *Ἰταλοελληνικά: Rivista di cultura greco-moderna* 2 (1989): 103–21.

Manoussakas, Manoussos."Les derniers défenseurs crétois de Constantinople d'après les documents vénitiens." In *Akten des XI. Internationalen Byzantinischen Kongresses*, ed. Franz Dölger and Hans-Georg Beck, 331–40. Munich, 1958.

———." Ἡ Πρώτη Ἄδεια (1456) τῆς Βενετικῆς Γερουσίας γιὰ τὸ Ναὸ τῶν Ἑλλήνων τῆς Βενετίας καὶ ὁ Καρδινάλιος Ἰσίδωρος." *Θησαυρίσματα: Περιοδικὸν τοῦ Ἑλληνικοῦ Ἰνστιτούτου Βυζαντινῶν καὶ Μεταβυζαντινῶν Σπουδῶν τῆς Βενετίας* 1 (1962): 109–18.

———. "Notes sur quelques ambassadeurs byzantins en Occident à la veille de la chute de Constantinople sous les Turcs." *Annuaire de l'Institut de Philologie et l'Histoire Orientales et Slaves* 10 (1950): 419–28.

Mastrodemetres, Panagiotes D. *Νικόλαος Σεκουνδινὸς (1402–1464) Βίος καὶ Ἔργον: Συμβολὴ εἰς τὴν Μελέτην τῶν Ἑλλήνων τῆς Διασπορᾶς*. Βιβλιοθήκη Σοφίας Ν. Σαριπόλου 9. Athens, 1970.

———. "Nicolaos Secundinòs a Napoli dopo la caduta di Costantinopoli." *Ἰταλοελληνικά: Rivista di cultura greco-moderna* 2 (1989): 21–38.

Matschke, Klaus-Peter. *Die Schlacht bei Ankara und das Schicksal von Byzanz. Studien zur spätbyzantinischen Geschichte zwischen 1402 und 1422*. Weimar, 1981.

———. "Zum Anteil der Byzantiner und der Bergbauentwicklung Südosteuropas im 14. und 15. Jahrhundert." *Byzantinische Zeitschrift* 84/85 (1991/1992): 49–71.

———. "The Notaras Family and Its Italian Connections." *Dumbarton Oaks Papers* 49 (1995): 59–72.

———. "The Late Byzantine Urban Economy. Thirteenth – Fifteenth Centuries." In *Economic History of Byzantium*, ed. A. E. Laiou, 454–86. Washington, DC, 2002.

Megas, Georgios. "La Prise de Constantinople dans la poésie et la tradition populaires grecques." In *Le Cinq-Centième Anniversaire de la Prise de Constantinople*, 125–133. L'Hellénisme Contemporain. Athens, 1953.

Mercati, Giovanni. *Scritti d'Isidoro il cardinale Ruteno e codici a lui appartenuti che si conservano nella Biblioteca Apostolica Vaticana*. Studi e Testi 46. Vatican City, 1926.

Mertzios, Konstantinos D. "Περὶ Παλαιολόγων καὶ Ἄλλων Εὐγενῶν Κωνσταντινουπολιτῶν." In *Γέρας Κεραμοπούλλου*, 335–72. Athens, 1933.

———. "Ἡ Διαθήκη τῆς Ἄννας Παλαιολογίνας Νοταρᾶ." *Ἀθηνᾶ* 53 (1953): 17–21.

Mijatovich, Chedomil. *Constantine Palaeologus: The Last Emperor of the Greeks 1448–1453. The Conquest of Constantinople by the Turks*. London, 1892; repr. Chicago, 1968.

Miller, William. *The Latins in the Levant. A History of Frankish Greece (1204–1566)*. London, 1892; repr. Chicago, 1968.

———. *Trebizond: The Last Greek Empire*. London, 1926; repr. Chicago, 1968.

Mordtmann, Andreas D. *Belagerung und Eroberung Constantinopels durch die Türken im Jahre 1453 nach den Originalquellen bearbeitet*. Stuttgart and Augsburg, 1858.

Mordtmann, Johannes H. "Die Kapitulation von Konstantinopel im Jahre 1453." *Byzantinische Zeitschrift* 21 (1901): 129–44.

Nicol, Donald M. "A Byzantine Emperor in England. Manuel II's Visit to London in 1400–1401." *University of Birmingham Historical Journal* 12 (1971): 204–25.

———. *The Last Centuries of Byzantium 1261–1453.* New York, 1972; 2nd ed. Cambridge, 1993.

———. *The Byzantine Lady: Ten Portraits 1250–1500.* Cambridge, 1994.

Noli, Fan S. *George Kastrioti Scanderbeg.* New York, 1947.

Norman, A. V. B., and Don Pottinger. *English Weapons and Warfare, 449–1660.* Englewood Cliffs, 1979.

Olgiati, G. "Angelo Giovanni Lomellino: Attività politica e mercantile dell'ultimo podestà de Pera." *Storia dei Genovesi* 9 (1989): 139–96.

Paliouras, Athanasios D. Ὁ Ζωγράφος Γεώργιος Κλόντζας *(1540 - ci. 1608)* καὶ αἱ Μικρογραφίαι τοῦ Κώδικος Αὐτοῦ. Athens, 1977.

Pall, F. "Ciriaco d'Ancona e la crociata contro i Turchi." *Bulletin d'histoire de l'Académie roumaine* 20 (1933): 9–68.

———. "Autour de la croisade de Varna: la question de la Paix de Szeged et sa rupture." *Bulletin d'histoire de l'Académie roumaine* 22 (1941): 114–58.

———. "Un moment décisif de l'histoire du Sud-Est européen: la croisade de Varna." *Balcania* 7 (1944): 102–20.

———. "Skanderbeg et Ianco Hunedoara." *Revue des études sud-est européens* 6 (1968): 5–21.

———. "Byzance à la veille de sa chute et Janco de Hunedoara (Hunyadi)." *Byzantinoslavica* 30 (1969): 119–26.

Panarco, G. "In terra d'Otranto dopo l'invasione turchesca." *Rivista storica salentina* 7 (1913): 35–56.

Papachristodoulou, Christodoulos I. Ἱστορία τῆς Ῥόδου ἀπὸ τοὺς Προϊστορικοὺς Χρόνους ἕως τὴν Ἐνσωμάτωση τῆς Δωδεκανήσου. Athens, 1972.

Papoulia, Basilike. *Ursprung und Wesen der "Knabenlese" im osmanischen Reich.* Munich, 1964.

Partington, J. R. *A History of Greek Fire and Gunpowder.* Cambridge, 1960.

Paspates, Alexandros G. Βυζαντιναὶ Μελέται Τοπογραφικαὶ καὶ Ἱστορικαί. Constantinople, 1874; repr. Athens, 1986.

———. Πολιορκία καὶ Ἅλωσις τῆς Κωνσταντινουπόλεως ὑπὸ τῶν Ὀθωμανῶν ἐν ἔτει 1453. Athens, 1890; repr. Athens, 1995.

Pastor, Ludwig. *The History of the Popes, from the Close of the Middle Ages Drawn from Secret Archives of the Vatican and Other Original Sources.* Trans. and ed. F. I. Antrobus. Vol. 2. London, 1949.

Patrinelis, Christos G. "Κυριακὸς ὁ Ἀγκωνίτης: Ἡ Δῆθεν Ὑπηρεσία του εἰς τὴν Αὐλὴν τοῦ Σουλτάνου τοῦ Πορθητοῦ καὶ ὁ Χρόνος τοῦ Θανάτου Αὐτοῦ." Ἐπετηρὶς Ἑταιρείας Βυζαντινῶν Σπουδῶν 16 (1968): 152–60.

———. "Mehmed II the Conqueror and his Presumed Knowledge of Greek and Latin." *Viator* 2 (1971): 349–55.

Pears, Edwin. *The Fall of Constantinople Being the Story of the Fourth Crusade.* New York, 1866.

———. *The Destruction of the Greek Empire and the Story of the Capture of Constantinople by the Turks*. London, 1903; repr. New York, 1968.
Picenardi, G. S. *Itinéraire d'un chevalier de Saint-Jean de Jérusalem dans l'ile de Rhode*. Lille, 1900.
Philippides, Marios. "The Fall of Constantinople 1453: Bishop Leonard and the Greek Accounts." *Greek, Roman and Byzantine Studies* 22 (1980): 287–300.
———. "Σύγχρονες Ἔρευνες στὰ κείμενα τοῦ Σφραντζῆ." *Παρνασσὸς* 25 (1983): 94–99.
———. "An 'Unknown' Source for Book III of the *Chronicon Maius* by Pseudo-Sphrantzes." *Byzantine Studies/Etudes Byzantines* 10 (1983): 174–83.
———. "Patriarchal Chronicles of the Sixteenth Century." *Greek, Roman and Byzantine Studies* 25 (1984): 87–94.
———. "Some Prosopographical Considerations in Nestor-Iskander's Text." *Macedonian Studies* 6 (1989): 35–50.
———. "Early Post-Byzantine Historiography." In *The Classics in the Middle Ages*, ed. Aldo S. Bernardo and Saul Levin, 253–63. Medieval and Renaissance Texts and Studies 69. Binghamton, 1990.
———. "The Value of Christoforo Riccherio's 'Eyewitness' Narrative of the Fall of Constantinople in 1453." *Sixteenth Annual Byzantine Studies Conference Abstracts of Papers*, 36-37. Baltimore, 1990.
———. "*Urbs Capta*: Early 'Sources' on the Fall of Constantinople." In *Peace and War in Byzantium: Essays in Honor of George T. Dennis, S.J.*, ed. Timothy S. Miller and John Nesbitt, 209–25. Washington, DC, 1995.
———. "The Fall of Constantinople 1453: Bishop Leonardo Giustiniani and His Italian Followers." *Viator* 29 (1998): 189–227.
———. "Giovanni Guglielmo Longo Giustiniani, the Genoese *Condottiere* of Constantinople in 1453." *Byzantine Studies/Etudes Byzantines* n. s. 3 (1998 [= 2000]): 13–54.
———. "A 'New' Eyewitness Source and the Prosopography of the Defenders in the Siege of Constantinople (1453)." *Twenty-Eighth Annual Byzantine Studies Conference Abstracts of Papers*, 90–91. Columbus, 2002.
———. "Urban's Bombard(s), Gunpowder, and the Siege of Constantinople (1453)." *Byzantine Studies/Etudes Byzantines* n. s. 4 (1999 [= 2002]): 1–67.
———. "History Repeats Itself: Ancient Troy and Renaissance Istanbul." *İstanbul Üniversitesi 550. Yıl Uluslararası Bizans ve Osmanlı Sempozyumu (XV. Yüzyıl), 30–31 Mayıs 2003*, ed. Sümer Atasöy, 41–69. Istanbul, 2004.
———. *Constantine XI Dragaš Palaeologus: A Biography of the Last Greek Emperor*. Forthcoming.
———, and Walter K. Hanak. *The Pen and the Sword: Historiography, Topography, and Military Studies on the Siege of Constantinople (1453)*. Forthcoming.
Pistarino, Geo. "Chio dei Genovesi." *Studi Medievali* 19 (1969): 3–68.

Podskalsky, Gerhard. "Der Fall Konstantinopels in der Sicht der Reichseschatologie unter den Klagelieder." *Archiv für Kulturgeschichte* 57 (1975): 71–86.

Raby, Julian. "Cyriacus of Ancona and the Sultan Mehmed II." *Journal of the Warburg and Courtauld Institutes* 43 (1980): 242–46.

Radojičić, Dorde S. "La Chronologie de la bataille de Rovine." *Revue historique du sud-est européen* 5 (1928): 136–39.

Reinert, Stephen W. "From Niš to Kosovo Polje. Reflections on Murad I's Final Years." In *The Ottoman Emirate (1300–1389). Halcyon Days in Crete I: A Symposium Held in Rethymnon 11–13 January 1991*, ed. Elizabeth A. Zachariadou, 169–211. Rethymnon, 1993.

Roloff, G. "Die Schlacht bei Angora." *Historische Zeitschrift* 161 (1943): 244–62.

Rothero, Christopher. *Medieval Military Dress, 1066–1500*. Dorset, 1983.

Runciman, Steven. *A History of the Crusades*. Vol. 3. Cambridge, 1954.

———. *The Fall of Constantinople 1453*. Cambridge, 1965.

Sabbadini, Remigio. "Ciriaco d'Ancona e la sua descrizione autografa del Peloponneso trasmessa da Leonardo Botta." In *Miscellanea Ceriani. Raccolta di scritti originali per onorare la memoria di A. M. Ceriani*, 180–247. Milan, 1910; repr. in idem, *Classici e Umanisti da Codici Ambrosiani*, 1–52. Fontes Ambrosiani 2. Florence, 1933.

Schlumberger, Gustave. *Le siège, la prise et le sac de Constantinople par les Turcs en 1453*. Paris, 1914. Ἅλωσις τῆς Κωνσταντινουπόλεως. Trans. E. G. Protopsaltes, Athens, *sine anno*. Κωνσταντῖνος Παλαιολόγος καὶ ἡ Πολιορκία καὶ Ἅλωσις τῆς Κωνσταντινουπόλεως ὑπὸ τῶν Τούρκων τῷ 1453. Trans. Spyridon P. Lampros. Athens, 1914; repr. Thessalonica, 1991.

———. *Un Empereur de Byzance à Paris et Londres*. Paris, 1916.

Schneider, M. "Die Bevölkerung Konstantinopels im XV. Jahrhundert." *Nachrichten der Akademie der Wissenschaften in Göttingen, Philos.-Hist. Kl.* 9 (1949): 233–44.

Schwoebel, Robert. *The Shadow of the Crescent: The Renaissance Image of the Turk (1453–1517)*. Nieuwkoop, 1967.

Setton, Kenneth M. *The Papacy and the Levant (1203–1571)*, 1: *The Thirteenth and Fourteenth Centuries*, 2: *The Fifteenth Century*. Philadelphia, 1976.

Shaw, Stanford J. *History of the Ottoman Empire and Modern Turkey*, 1: *Empire of the Gazis: The Rise and Fall of the Ottoman Empire, 1280–1808*. Cambridge, 1976.

Siderides, Xenophon A. "Κωνσταντίνου Παλαιολόγου Θάνατος, Τάφος, καὶ Σπάθη." *Ἡ Μελέτη* 2 (1908): 65–78, 129–46.

Skeat, Theodore C. "Two Byzantine Documents." *British Museum Quarterly* 18 (1953): 71–73.

Smith, C. "Cyriacus of Ancona's Seven Drawings of Hagia Sophia." *Art Bulletin* 69 (1987): 16–32.

Spremic, Momcilo. "Harac Soluna u XV veku." *Zbornik Radova Vizantijloškog Instituta* 19 (1967): 187–95.
Stacton, David. *The World on the Last Day. The Sack of Constantinople by the Turks on May 29, 1453: Its Causes and Consequences.* London, 1965. Published in the United States under the pseudonym David Dereksen with the title *The Crescent and the Cross: The Fall of Byzantium, May 29, 1453.* New York, 1964.
Stavrides, Theoharis. *The Sultan of Vezirs: The Life and Times of the Ottoman Grand Vezir Mahmud Pasha Angelović (1453–1474).* The Ottoman Empire and its Heritage 24. Leiden, 2001.
Taeschner, Franz. "Beiträge zur frühosmanischen Epigraphik und Archäologie." *Der Islam* 30 (1932): 109–86.
Temperley, Harold W. V. *History of Serbia.* London, 1917.
Thouasne, L. *Djem-sultan fils de Mohammed II, frère de Bayezid II (1459–1495).* Paris, 1892.
Tomadakis, Nikolaos B. Περὶ Ἁλώσεως τῆς Κωνσταντινουπόλεως. Athens, 1953; repr. Thessalonica, 1993.
Torr, Cecil. *Rhodes in Modern Times.* Cambridge, 1887.
Trapp, Erich, Hans-Veit Beyer, et al. *Prosopographisches Lexikon der Palaiologenzeit.* 11 vols. [+ 2 supplements]. Vienna, 1976–1991.
Tsangadas, Byron C. P. *The Fortifications and Defense of Constantinople.* East European Monographs 71. Boulder and New York, 1980.
Vacalopoulos. Apostolos E. *Origins of the Greek Nation: The Byzantine Period, 1204–1461.* Trans. I. Moles. New Brunswick, 1970.
Van Millingen, Alexander. *Byzantine Constantinople: The Walls of the City and Adjoining Historical Sites.* London, 1899.
Vasiliev, Alexander A. *History of the Byzantine Empire 324–1453.* 2 vols. Madison, 1976.
Vaughan, Dorothy M. *Europe and the Turk: A Pattern of Alliances 1350–1700.* Liverpool, 1954.
de Vertot, Daubef René Aubert. *Histoire des Chevaliers Hospitaliers de S. Jean de Jérusalem, appelés depuis le Chevaliers de Rhodes et aujourd'hui les Chevaliers de Malta.* 5 vols. Paris, 1772. *History of the Knights Hospitallers of St. John of Jerusalem, Styled Afterwards the Knights of Rhodes, and at Present the Knights of Malta.* Edinburgh, 1757.
Vryonis, Speros. "Isidore Glabas and the Turkish Devshirme." *Speculum* 31 (1956): 433–43.
———. "Seljuk Gulams and Ottoman Devshirmes." *Der Islam* 41 (1965): 224–52.
———. *The Decline of Medieval Hellenism in Asia Minor and the Process of Islamization from the Eleventh to the Fifteenth Century.* Berkeley and Los Angeles, 1971.

———. *Byzantium: Its Internal History and Relations with the Muslim World.* Collected Studies. London, 1971.
Waldstein-Wartenberg, Berthold von. *Die Vassallen Christi. Kulturgeschichte des Johanniterordens im Mittelalter.* Graz, 1988.
Werner, Ernst. *Die Geburt einer Grossmacht: Die Osmanen (1300 bis 1481). Ein Beitrag zur Genesis des türkischen Feudalismus.* Forschungen zur mittelalterlichen Geschichte 13. Berlin, 1966.
Williams, Alan. "Ottoman Technology: The Metallurgy of Turkish Armor." In *War and Society in the Eastern Mediterranean, 7th–15th Centuries,* ed. Lev, 363–99.
Wittek, Paul. *Das Fürstentum Mentesche: Studien zur Geschichte Westkleinasiens im 13.–15. Jh.* Istanbul, 1934.
———. "De la défaite d'Ankara à la prise de Constantinople." *Revue des études islamiques* 12 (1938): 1–34.
———. *The Rise of the Ottoman Empire.* London, 1938.
Zachariadou, Elizabeth A. Τὸ Χρονικὸ τῶν Τούρκων Σουλτάνων (τοῦ Βαρβερινοῦ Ἑλληνικοῦ Κώδικα 111) καὶ τὸ Ἰταλικό του Πρότυπο. Thessalonica, 1960.
———. "The First Serbian Campaigns of Mehemmed II (1454, 1455)." *Annali* 14 (1964): 837–40.
Zinkeisen, Johann W. *Geschichte des osmanischen Reiches in Europa.* 7 vols. Gotha, 1908–1913.
Zoras, Georgios T. Περὶ τὴν Ἅλωσιν τῆς Κωνσταντινουπόλεως. Athens, 1959.

ILLUSTRATIONS

Illustrations 1 & 2

In the beginning of April, 1452, Mehmed II marched to the straits of the Bosphorus and began the construction of this castle that would become known as the "Fortress of Rumeli" or Rumeli Hisar (Doukas, 34.7:): καὶ δὴ καταλαβὼν μίαν ῥαχίαν κάτωθεν τοῦ Σωσθενίου καλουμένην ἔκπαλαι Φονέαν, ἐκεῖ ὡς ἐν τριγώνῳ σχήματι τὸν θεμέλιον ὡρίσατο πηγνύναι, ὃ καὶ γενόμενον τὴν κλῆσιν τοῦ κάστρου Πασχεσὲν ἐκέλευσε καλεῖσθαι, ἐξελληνιζόμενον δὲ ἑρμηνεύεται κεφαλοκόπτης, ἔχον ἄντικρυ καὶ τὸ φρούριον ὃ ἐδείματο ὁ πάππος αὐτοῦ ["and he (Mehmed II) occupied a cliff below Sosthenion, which had been long ago named 'Phoneus'; there he ordered the foundations to be arranged in the shape of a triangle; after this was done he named the castle Başkesen, which can be rendered into Greek as 'Head-cutter'; across from it was the fortress (Anadolu Hisar) built by his grandfather (Bayezid I)"]. The layout of the fortress, the strength of the walls, and the speed with which it was completed impressed all contemporaries. Thus the sultan finally completed his encirclement of Constantinople and made it as tight as it could be. To the east the Greeks possessed nothing, for all of Asia Minor was occupied by the Turks. To the west, Thrace had come under firm Ottoman rule, with the ancient Greek city of Adrianople as the capital of the sultan. To the north the Greeks still controlled few isolated pockets such as Mesembria and Selybria, which could easily fall to the Turks, as they did soon thereafter; but access to them from Constantinople was now completely denied by the castle on the Bosphorus, which

ILLUSTRATION I
Rumeli Hisar
(Photo: Walter K. Hanak)

further blocked passage to the Black Sea. Thus for the Greeks the only avenue of communication that remained open was the southern channel to the Aegean, and even that waterway was surrounded by Turkish territory on both sides. Beyond the strategic and tactical advantages that the sultan gained with the construction of his fortress, his most significant victory was scored in the psychological domain, as the fort of Rumeli Hisar became a most important pawn in his campaign of psychological warfare that lasted almost six months before the actual commencement of hostilities. The Greeks became convinced that the end was drawing near. Mehmed's fortress of doom with its dread bombards provided a tangible hint of Armageddon. It is no wonder that Greeks surrendered themselves to their fate, as they formed the impression that their ruin had been sealed.

ILLUSTRATION 2
Rumeli Hisar, detail
(Photo: Walter K. Hanak)

Illustration 3

This was the "Achilles heel" in the fortification of Constantinople, as the walls reach their lowest point at the valley through which the stream Lykos flows (as it still does nowadays under the modern avenue *Vatan*). The picture shows the sector between the Adrianople Gate (*Edirne Kapı*) and the Gate of Saint Romanus (*Top Kapı*), where the final assault took place in the early hours of May 29. It was against this sector that the sultan had concentrated his artillery fire; in front of the walls Giovanni Guglielmo Longo Giustiniani and his professional band of Genoese *condottieri* had repeatedly repelled the assaults of the Ottoman troops. He had been stationed just to the north of the Gate of Saint Romanus and the stream Lykos, in the heart of modern Istanbul's *Sulu Kule* neighborhood, while the emperor had his headquarters just south of the Lykos, near the Gate of Saint Romanus.

ILLUSTRATION 3
The *Mesoteikhion* ("Middle of the [Land] Walls") of Constantinople
(*Photo: author*)

Illustration 4

Roughly the middle of the *Mesoteikhion* (see Illustration 3), just to the north of the Lykos and in the heart of the modern *Sulu Kule* neighborhood, there is a small postern gate, known as the "Fifth", in whose immediate region the critical moments of the last battle took place. Before this gate there was no outer wall and the moat did not extend this far north. Giustiniani had erected a makeshift barrier or fence to defend himself and his troops from the Ottoman army. The only access to the Great Wall and to the interior was provided by this gate, which was locked during the final assault to prevent easy access to the interior both to the enemy and to the defenders in case they took matters to their own hands and decided to abandon their posts. After Giustiniani had repelled two major assaults, on the morning of May 29, launched by irregulars and by the regular Anatolian troops of the sultan, he had to face a third assault by the highly disciplined janissaries. As this third assault was about to be repelled, Giustiniani was wounded and opened the *Pempton* Gate to gain access to the city; he withdrew from the battle after a heated quarrel with the emperor. His retreat was soon duplicated by others, who were exhausted and, despite the efforts of the emperor to check a general flight, soon the remaining defenders abandoned their posts and trampled each other to death in their efforts to

ILLUSTRATION 4
The Pempton or "Fifth [Military] Gate"
(Photo: author)

enter through this gate. In front of this gate the emperor made his last desperate attempt and perished. The Turks simply overran this sector and faced no resistance as they went over the defenses, since the gate was congested with corpses of the defenders. A source from the Patriarchate in the early sixteenth century produces the following report, which probably derives from memories from the survivors of the carnage of the sack (Ἔκθεσις Χρονική, 32 [p. 48-49]): καὶ ἀπεπνίγησαν ἐκ τῆς πλησμονῆς μὴ δυνηθέντες εἰσελθεῖν ἐκ τῶν νεκρῶν σωμάτων, γεμισθέντων τῶν πυλῶν ... μέχρις ἀψίδων αὐτῶν. Ὡς καὶ τοὺς αἰχμαλώτους, γυναῖκας τε καὶ παῖδας, μὴ δυναμένους ἐξελθεῖν, ἀλλ᾽ ἐκ τῶν τειχῶν σχοινίοις χαλνῶντες αὐτοὺς ["and they (sc. the defenders) perished in the press; they could not enter because of the dead bodies blocking the entrance ... congested, all the way up to the arches. Later, the captives, women and children, could not be brought out but had to be lowered by rope from the walls"].

Illustration 5

The moat did not parallel the Great Walls throughout their full extent. Its width has been recorded as much as 20 meters and its depth, perhaps at the extreme, at 7 meters. Given the gradual slope downward from the Fourth Military Gate (just south of the Saint Romanus Gate) to the Sea of Marmara, the relatively level terrain provided the best opportunity for the construction and maintenance of a substantial moat that would retain its waters through a series of dams and provide adequate defense. Thereafter, the steep decline of the terrain into the Lykos Valley and the rapid rise of the ground to the heights of the Adrianople Gate posed construction and maintenance problems, because of repeated flooding and earthquakes that caused earth movement, that by 1453 the officials and residents of the city could not address and all but abandoned its upkeep. Therefore, the moat fell short of the Adrianople Gate. Its width has been recorded as much as 20 meters and its depth, perhaps at the extreme, at 7 meters. By the third decade of the fifteenth century the moat and the entire stretch of the land walls were in dire need of maintenance. An anonymous author of an *encomium* on behalf of John VIII Palaeologus, the brother and predecessor of the last Palaeologus, Constantine XI, stresses that particular attention was devoted to the moat that had been neglected for so long, especially since it had become evident that a Turkish siege was imminent (Ἐγκώμιον εἰς τὸν Αὐτοκράτορα [Ἰωάννην τὸν Παλαιολόγον], *Παλαιολόγεια καὶ Πελοποννησιακὰ* 3 [Athens 1926]: 296): Ἐνταῦθα γὰρ αἱ διώρυχες περὶ τὸ τεῖχος καὶ οἱ τάφροι πάλαι μὲν βάθος ὠρύγησαν παρὰ τῶν τηνικαῦτα κρατούντων... χρόνου δὲ προϊόντος ἐν ὥραις χειμερινais τῇ τῶν ὑδάτων ἐπιρροῇ κατὰ μικρὸν τὴν ὕλην ἐπισπωμένων ἐπληρώθησαν ταύτης ἄχρι τῶν ἄνω ["here the channels around the walls and the moat had long ago been dug to some

Illustrations 397

ILLUSTRATION 5
The moat of Constantinople looking southward from the Selybria-Pege Gate
[*Silivri Kapı*]
(Photo: author)

depth by the emperors of old...but with the passage of time, in winters, under the influence of water, gradually the soil was loosened and filled the moat all the way up"]. Given the lack of resources in the Constantinopolitan court, the renovation of the moat was quite an accomplishment and the anonymous author compares John VIII's achievement to the feat of Xerxes who in antiquity had cut a channel through the peninsula of Mount Athos. In the siege of 1453 the moat was functional and the main Turkish assaults occurred in a sector that was not protected by the moat, mainly the *Mesoteikhion* (cf. Illustration 3).

Illustration 6

There is general scholarly agreement that this gate, with an entry width of 3 meters, and an approximate height approaching 5 meters, was the first major target of Mehmed II's cannons, including Urban's monstrous *basilica*, in the early stages of the siege in April 1453, and in the last weeks of the siege the mining activities of the sultan's engineers. Ultimately, Mehmed realized the futility of this bombardment and abandoned this approach because of the steepness of the

ILLUSTRATION 6
The Kaligaria Gate
(Photo: author)

terrain, which in this sector rises abruptly in elevation of the terrain from west to east; consequently, the trajectory of his shots required an extremely high projectile path. Eventually the futility and unproductiveness of this tactic against this sector were realized and the bombard was transferred to the south and was deployed more fruitfully against the Gate of Saint Romanus and the *Mesoteikhion*. In the late stages of the siege the sultan directed his engineers to construct mines under the Kaligaria Gate, as in this area there was no moat separating defenders from besiegers. The topography of this sector, however, did facilitate his mining activities. The absence of a moat and the tactical challenges are attested by Leonardo (*PG* 159: 927 [*CC* 1: 130]), who relates: *ad partem illam murorum simplicium, qua nec fossatis, nec antemurali tutebatur, Calegariam dictam* ["at a portion of that simple wall, designated Kaligaria, on which side there is no ditch (moat) to guard against the wall"]. The bishop further observes in regard to this sector (*PG* 159: 927 [*CC* 1: 130]): *Erat tamen murus perlatus fortisque* ["the wall, nevertheless, is extensive, strong"].

Illustration 7

Urban, the military engineer who transferred his services from the Greek emperor to the Ottoman sultan, cast a monstrous bombard for the siege of 1453, an impressive piece that deeply terrified the defenders and left an indelible mark in our sources. Practically all eyewitness and secondary accounts make mention of it. Cardinal Isidore, the pope's Greek legate and a heroic defender of Constantinople, generally refers to this cannon as *bombarda* a number of times; Isidore's associate and ardent admirer Archbishop Leonardo also often refers to it as *bombarda* (and once as *machina-engine*) and differentiates it from the other artillery by assigning distinctive descriptive adjectives to it: *horribilis*-horrible, *ingens*-huge, and so forth. Tetaldi's Latin account correctly identifies Urban's masterpiece as *unus bombardus aereus et fusilis*, "one bronze and fire bombard," and then the Florentine merchant hastens to specify that it was made in one solid piece, *integer et indivisus*, "whole, without separate parts," while Kritoboulos, who supplies a long and detailed description, claims that it was composed of two separate pieces, a breech-receptacle for the gunpowder and a barrel-chamber for the stone projectile (I.30.1). The exact measurements of the projectile cannot be ascertained, as no missile seems to have survived intact. In the first quarter of the twentieth century there were a few projectiles surviving in the targeted sector of the *Mesoteikhion* as has been often stated in literature as late as 1978 (e.g., *PL* 2: 114: "Such cannon balls more than seven feet in circumference are still to be seen in Istanbul"). In the summer of 1990, in June of 2000, and in June 2001, Professors Walter K. Hanak and Marios Philippides surveyed the land fortifications and recorded their condition before the current program of renovation and restoration of the Byzantine land fortifications renders the topography useless

for those interested in the siege of 1453; in the process we could not identify any stone missiles intact, let alone those from 1453. The only undamaged stone cannon balls currently on display are located within the fortress of the Ἑπταπύργιον (the Ottoman *Yedi Kule* fortress, by the Golden Gate). These balls do not date to the siege of 1453. They are small, perfectly round, and identical to the stone balls fired during the first and second siege of Rhodes still encountered throughout the town (cf. Illustration 17). In June of 2000 we discovered, identified, and photographed one missile in the *Mesoteikhion* area (south of the towers at the Lykos River, a destroyed tower below the Gate of Saint Romanus). In June of 2001 we returned to the same site, measured and photographed this damaged missile: at the face eleven hands in circumference or 148 inches [= 375 cms.]; in height or diameter 39 inches [= 99 cms.]; and in length 41 inches [= 99 cms.].

At the commencement of the siege, Mehmed deployed Urban's masterpiece and other bombards and probably anticipated the total destruction of both the inner and outer walls in the *Mesoteikhion*. This strategy and approach did not yield results. The bombards created havoc and destroyed extensive sections of the outer wall but the defenders, under the command of the brilliant *condottiere* Giustiniani, made effective repairs and erected makeshift defenses and fought with determination, repelling repeated attacks. The inner wall withstood the

ILLUSTRATION 7
Damaged stone missile from Urban's bombard *in situ*
(Photo: author)

relentless bombardment and hand-to-hand combat took place outside, on the ground between the great wall and the hastily erected stockades. Urban's bombards, with the accompanying roar and clouds of smoke, must have terrified the non-combatants and must have contributed to the demoralization of the inhabitants. At the same time Mehmed must have realized the superior quality of Giustiniani's professional band of *condottieri* and the inadequacies of his own artillery and infantry.

Illustrations 8 & 9

Few remains from the Venetian period remain in modern Khalkis and the topography has changed radically since the fifteenth century. The "House of the bailo" stands on the modern square that houses Saint Paraskeve, an Orthodox basilica decorated with arches that has incorporated elements of previous buildings from the fifteenth century within its structure. The house is archaeologically complicated and its foundations indicate that originally it was part of a religious foundation; it was probably in this square that the Venetian loggia was located, in

ILLUSTRATION 8
The "House of the bailo" in Negroponte (Khalkis)
(Photo: author)

which the murder of Schiavo took place. The house displays a relief of the Venetian lion above its main door (cf. Illustration 9). It is not certain that this was actually the residence of the bailo. For the topography and archaeology of Venetian Negroponte, see Johannes Koder, *Untersuchungen zur Topographie und Siedlungsgeschichte der Insel Euboia während der Zeit der Venezianerherrschaft*, Philosophisch-Historische Klasse, Denkschriften, 112. Band (Vienna, 1973). Some of Koder's conclusions have not been universally accepted and numerous topographical problems and puzzles remain unsolved.

Illustration 9
Detail of Illustration 8, the relief of the Venetian lion
(Photo: author)

Illustrations 10 and 11

As with Rhodes, numerous stone projectiles from Mehmed II's artillery survive around the old city. These are a few examples. They all seem to be of the same size, as Mehmed did not employ the enormous type of bombard that he had experimented with in the siege of Constantinople. He seems to have realized the limited potential of Urban's bombard. By the middle of the fifteenth century the era of the big bombard had been over in Europe, anyway, as European engineers had turned their attention to smaller, mobile iron artillery pieces.

Illustrations 403

ILLUSTRATIONS 10 AND 11
Stone projectiles from the Ottoman siege
(Photo: author)

Illustration 12

This square was the center of the Venetian quarter, which must have included most of the administrative buildings. Behind this building one can see the steeple of Saint Paraskeve where the "house of the bailo" is located. San Marco was converted into a mosque soon after the conquest and the mosque's minarets were removed after the liberation of Greece from the Ottoman Empire in the nineteenth century; the remnants of one polygonal minaret are still identifiable.

Illustrations 13 & 14

This fountain was intended for the Moslems to perform ablutions before they entered the mosque for prayers.

ILLUSTRATION 12
This mosque dates from the Ottoman period but it has incorporated Venetian structures, including the Venetian church of San Marco
(Photo: author)

Illustrations 405

ILLUSTRATION 13
Ottoman fountain in front of San Marco dating from the Ottoman period.
(Photo: author).

ILLUSTRATION 14
Detail of 13: Inscription on the Ottoman fountain.
(Photo: author).

ILLUSTRATION 15
The straits of Negroponte (Euripos) separating Euboea from the mainland.
(Photo: author).

Illustration 15

In this area there was a Venetian bridge and a fortress but no traces of either structure remain in evidence; moreover, all traces for the fortifications have disappeared. On top of the hill and on the side of the mainland stands the Ottoman fortress of Karababa, erected in 1686 over earlier structures, including a possible Macedonian fort from the fourth century BC. The remains of the Venetian fortifications guarding this approach to the city were finally demolished in 1896 when Belgian engineers widened the channel to accommodate larger ships.

Illustration 16

Medieval structures still line up this street that leads to the palace of the Grand Master in the modern city of Rhodes and to the Collachium or Castellum, the administrative center and the headquarters of the Knights of Saint John. The style of architecture employed by the Knights of Saint John in Rhodes was a mixture of Byzantine local elements and western design deriving from Provence and the papal court at Avignon. After the siege of 1480 and the destruction that followed a devastating earthquake in 1481, renovations were in order and were carried out by western engineers and architects under the supervision of the heroic Grand Master d'Aubusson.

ILLUSTRATION 16
Rhodes, the "Street of the Knights"
(Photo: author)

Illustration 17

One can easily compare the stone projectiles from Rhodes to those from Khalkis (Illustrations 10 and 11) or to those that are still exhibited in the grounds of the Ἑπταπύργιον/*Yedi Kule*, the "Seven Tower Fortress" behind the Golden Gate at the southern tip of Constantinople's land fortifications. Behind the bombard projectiles, one can see the remnants of ancient Greek temples before the medieval building. Sights of this sort faced the Knights every day and, as Caoursin's narrative demonstrates, the Knights were extremely proud, and rather knowledgeable, of their city's ancient heritage.

ILLUSTRATION 17
Square in Rhodes with stone projectiles from the Ottoman bombards.
(*Photo: author*)

Illustration 18

This gate bears over the lintel the coat of arms for the Knights (on the left) and Pierre d'Aubusson's family coat of arms (right). The tincture is, of course, no longer there. The Knights' coat of arms bears a white cross, the cross of Saint John, on a red field and d'Aubussons bears a red anchry cross (symbolizing hope as Christ's cross) on a gold field.

Illustrations 409

ILLUSTRATION 18
The Gate of Saint John, Rhodes.
(Photo: author)

Illustration 21

This fort was a major objective of the Ottoman army and navy in 1480 and played a key role in the strategy of the besiegers and the besieged. Although the fort was in ruins by the end of the siege, the Ottoman army faced stiff resistance and could not capture it. As it stands now, it displays the repairs that were carried out after the siege of 1480 and after the second siege of 1520. Very little, other than foundations, dates back to the days before the first Turkish assault of 1480.

ILLUSTRATION 19
Section of land fortifications, Rhodes.
(Photo: author)

Illustrations 411

ILLUSTRATION 20
Section of land fortifications, Rhodes.
(Photo: author)

ILLUSTRATION 21
Fort Saint Nicholas, at the tip of harbor quay.
(Photo: author)

INDEX OF PERSONS

Abraham of Ankara, 85n. 33
Achilles, 5
Aeneas, 12
Ajax, 5
Albanese, Andrea, 231
Albanese, Giorgio, 257
Albanese, Petro, 257
Alemanti, Giacomo, 235
Alexander the Great, 11, 12, 14, 141n. 2, 209, 211n. 27, 345
Alexander, tsar of Bulgaria, 63n. 5
Alfonso, duke of Calabria, 43n. 96
Alfonso of Aragon, king of Naples, 14, 151n. 6, 189n. 21, 353
Aliega, d', Preceptor, 47n. 108
Anchises, father of Aeneas, 12
Andreotti, Paolo, 365
Angelović, Mahmud Pasha, 40n. 84, 225, 243, 243n. 23, 247n. 26, 251, 253, 361, 363, 365, 367
Angiolello, Gian-Maria [Giovanni Maria], 34, 243n. 22, 247n. 26
Antenor, 12
Apokaukos, Alexios, 101n. 7
Archimedes, 167n. 12
Arrian, 211n. 27
Aubusson, d', Antoine, 275n. 6, 295, 295n. 19, 295n. 20, 305, 333, 335
Aubusson, d', François, 271n. 5
Aubusson, d', Pierre, 4, 40n. 85, 41, 41n. 86, 42n. 86, 46, 47, 263n. 1, 265n. 3, 267n. 3, 271, 271n. 5, 273, 275n. 6, 277n. 9, 279, 281, 283, 285, 287, 287n. 15, 289, 289n. 16, 291, 295, 297n. 21, 301, 301n. 24, 303, 303n. 28, 307, 307n. 30, 333
Augustus, 209

Baltaoğlu [Albitangly Alingagoly], Mehmed II's *kapudan* pasha, 151, 342
Barbaro, Bartolomeo, 251
Barbaro, Marco, 107n. 10, 163n. 10
Barbaro, Nicolò, 25n. 40, 25n. 41, 49n. 115, 83n. 28, 97n. 2, 103n. 8, 107n. 10, 151nn. 6–7, 57n. 9, 167n. 11, 179n. 18, 187n. 21, 201n. 24
Barr, de, Philippe, 73n. 14
Bayezid I (Yıldırım, "Lightning"), Sultan, 63, 65, 67, 69, 71, 87, 89, 95
Bayezid II, Sultan, 313n. 32n. 1, 97n. 2
Bayezid II, Sultan, 91
Bembo, Petrus, 7
Ben Shabettai Koen Balbo, 27
Benvenuto, Anconitan Consul in Constantinople, 22, 101n. 5, 109n. 11, 141nn. 2–3, 187n. 21, 199n. 24
Benvoglienti, Leonardo, 40, 213,n. 28
Berenger, de, Raymond, 263n. 1
Berger of Nordlingen, Johann, 275n. 6
Berti di, Polo, 233
Bessarion, Cardinal, 8, 143n.3, 147n. 4, 149n. 5, 165n. 11, 167,n. 12, 173n. 17, 181n. 19, 191n. 22, 199n. 24, 211n. 27, 213n. 28
Blanchin [Blancet], Jean [Jehan, Johann], 22
Bocchiardi Brothers, 99n. 3

413

Bocharan, Bortolomio, 247
Bondomier [Bondumier, Bondinieri], Giovanni [Zuanne], 235, 235n. 15, 253, 363, 365
Boucicaut, Jean II le Meingre, 67n. 8, 67n. 9
Bourbon, Jacques, 73n. 14
Boniface IX, Pope, 71n. 13
Bouhours, Dominique, 41n. 87
Brangelier, Matthieu, 295n. 19
Branković, George, Despot of Serbia, 2
Branković, Vuk, 63n. 5

Calbo, Leonardo, 30
Calbo, Ludovico [Alvise], 365
Caligula, 211n. 27
Cambini, Andrea, 15
Canal[e], da, Nicolò, 30, 31, 32, 33, 221n. 1, 239n. 18, 241n. 20, 247n. 26, 361, 363, 365, 367
Candarlı, Halil [Colymbassa, Columbassa], grand vizier, 53, 95, 171n. 15, 173n. 15, 181, 183n. 19, 343
Canuta, Nicolò, 223
Caoursin, Guillaume, 40, 41, 42, 45, 46, 223n. 7, 228n. 13, 263, 275n. 7, 279n. 10, 281n. 12, 289nn. 15–16, 297n. 21, 301n. 24, 307n. 30, 313n. 32
Capistrano, Giovanni, 2, 43
Capoppo, Antonio, 251
Caracciolo, Roberto, 28
Cassandra of Troy, 6, 39
Castellana dalla, Jacopo [Iacopo] Fra, 27, 35, 229n. 13, 251, 259
Cataneo, Mauritio, 151n. 6
Chartier, Jean, 21
Chateaumorand, de, Jean, 67n. 9
Chrysoloras, 6
Coco [Cocchus], Giacomo [Jacopo], 163n. 10, 165n. 10, 342
Colomb, Claude, 295n. 19
Columbi, 23
Constantine the Great, 135
Contarini, Lorenzo, 39, 221, 231n. 1, 239n. 8
Corneillan, de, Pierre, 263n. 1

Cosareno, Marcus, 8
Curti de, Giacomo, 45
Craon, de, Louis, 295n. 19
Curtius, Quintus, 12, 211n. 27
Curzola, da, Francesco, 231
Curzola, da [Cortulia, da], Luca, 53, 227, 227n. 13, 229, 229n. 13, 231, 237
Cyriacus of Ancona, 12, 211n. 27
Cyrus, king of Persia, 5

Dario, Giovanni, 40n. 84, 265n. 3
Demosthenes, 7
Demunes[s]i, Domenico, 225, 243
Diedo, Alvise [Aluvixe, Ludovico], 28n. 50, 205n. 25
Diogenes Laertius, 12, 211n. 27
Diplovatatzes, Joseph, 39, 141n. 3, 149n. 5, 153n. 7, 165n. 11, 167n. 12, 171n. 15, 187n. 21, 199n. 24
Dolfin, Alvise [Dolfini, Loiso], 233, 257, 363
Dolfin, Zorzi, 50n. 115
Döring, Matthias, 40
Dotti, Paolo, 27, 199n. 24
Doukas, Michael (?), 83nn. 28–29
Dupuis, Mary, 44, 45, 283n. 14

Enrico, Master, 257
Eparkhos, Thomas, 39, 141n. 4, 147n. 3, 149n. 5, 153n. 7, 165n. 11, 167n. 12, 171n. 15, 187n. 21, 199n. 24
Erizzo, Anna, 38, 39
Erizzo, Paolo, *bailo* of Negroponte, 30, 37, 38, 225, 227, 229, 231, 233, 235, 237, 243n. 22, 247, 257, 363, 365
Escouchy, d', Matthieu, 40
Eugenius IV, Pope, 8, 79n. 24

Feliciano, Batista, 151n. 6
Ferducci, Lillo Othman, 5
Ferrante [Ferdinand], king of Naples, and Sicily, 42, 44n. 96, 311
Filelfo, Francesco, 4, 5, 6, 8, 17n. 24, 241n. 20
Filelfo, Giovanni Mario, 5, 6
Firuz Beg, garrison commander of Rumeli Hisar, 97n. 2

Fluvian, Antonio, 263n. 1
Foscari, Francesco, doge of Venice, 23, 129, 205n. 25, 207n. 25
Franc, Francisco, 341
Franchi di [Driphange], Marchio [Markezos], 347, 349
Frapan [Frapan{d/t}, Frapanus] of Saxony, Georg, Meister, 53, 271n. 4, 273, 279, 279n. 10, 299, 301, 301n. 24
Frederick III, Holy Roman Emperor, 28, 46

Gaius Caesar, 11, 211n. 27
Gaza, Theodore, 6
Gaultier, Antoine, 303n. 26
Genghis Khan, 71n. 10
Gervais, Roger, 291n. 17
Gholas, John, 23
Gianni from Dalmatia, 287n. 15
Giovio, Paolo, 15
Giustiniani, Federico, 367
Giustiniani, Franco, 213n. 28
Giustiniani, Hieronimo, 159n. 9, 193n. 22
Giustiniani, Leonardo, Archbishop of Lesbos, 17, 18, 20, 48n. 111, 83n. 23, 99n. 4, 101n. 7, 103n. 8, 107n. 10, 111n. 13, 113n. 15, 139n. 2, 141n. 2, 143n. 3, 147n. 4, 149,n. 5, 151n. 6, 157n. 9, 165n. 11, 169n. 14, 171n. 15, 173n. 16, 173n. 17, 175n. 17, 187n. 21, 189n. 21, 193n. 22, 201n. 24, 203n. 24, 209n. 26, 211n. 27, 239n. 19, 303n. 27
Giustiniani Longo, Daniel, 157n. 9
Giustiniani Longo, Giovanni Guglielmo, 23, 54, 99n. 3, 103n. 9, 107, 109, 111, 113n. 15, 117n. 17, 119n. 18, 155, 155n. 9, 157n. 9, 159n. 9, 165n. 11, 167n. 11, 185, 185n. 20, 187n. 21, 189n. 21, 191, 191n. 21–22, 193n. 22, 195n. 22, 197n. 22, 342, 344, 355 357
Giustiniani [Justinianus], Pietro [Petrus], 49, 241n. 20, 247n. 26, 353
Gomare, Guillaume, 295n. 19
Gozon de, Dieudonné, 263n. 1
Gradellon, Geremia, 233
Gradenico, Francesco, 30

Grand [Grant], John, 165n. 11, 167n. 11
Grioni, Zacaria, 163n. 10, 205n. 25
Gritti, Battista, 355

Halil Pasha. *See* Candarlı, Halil [Colymbassa], grand vizier
Hannibal of Carthage, 5, 14
Hamza Beg, Mehmed II's *kapudan* pasha, 151n. 6
Hatun bint Abdullah, mother of Mehmed II Fatih, 81n. 26
Henry IV of England, 67n. 9
Henry of Soemmern, 17, 20, 21, 27n. 46, 123, 131
Herakleios, Emperor, 101n. 7
Hero, 169n. 12
Heredia, de, Juan, 263n. 1
Herodotus, 3, 12, 211n. 27
Hierax, 193n. 22
Homer, 5
Hunyadi Corvinus, John, 2, 43, 77n. 22, 81n. 25, 89, 93, 95n. 1, 239n. 19, 348
Hyalinas [Yalinas], [Antonios], 23, 24, 25

Ibrahim of Karaman, 95n. 1
Innocent VIII, Pope, 305n. 28
Isabella of Aragon, 269n. 4
Isidore, Cardinal, 20, 21, 23, 27, 99n. 3, 117, 125, 129, 141n. 2, 143n. 3, 147n. 4, 149n. 5, 165n. 11, 167,n. 12, 173n. 17, 181n. 19, 191n. 22, 199n. 24, 201n. 24, 209n. 26, 211n. 27, 213n. 28, 344
Isfendiyar of Sinope, 67n. 10
Isfendiyaroğlu Ismail, 173n. 16
Ishmael, king of Persia, 91
Ivani [da Sarzana], Antonio, 145n. 4, 183n. 19, 189n. 22

Juillac, de, Robert, 263n. 1
Jordono, Jehan, 344
Julius Caesar, 209, 345
Justinian I, Emperor, 113

Kallistos, Andronikos, 153n. 7
Kananos, Ioannes, 309n. 31
Kantakouzene, Theodora, 61n. 4

Index of Persons

Kantakouzenos, Demetrios, 111n. 12
Kantakouzenos, John VI, 61n. 4
Karakasin, 245
Kay, John, 46
Kazanci Kurtcu Doğan, 95n. 1
Khalkokondyles Laonikos [Nikolaos], 3, 15, 83n. 28, 151n. 6, 193n. 22
Khortatzes, 24
Klontzas, George, 16, 17n. 24
Kritoboulos [Kritovoulos], Michael Hermodoros, 4, 50n. 115, 83n. 28, 97n. 2, 101n. 5, 103n. 7, 197n. 22
Küçük Ahmed, Çelebi, brother of Mehmed II Fatih, 95n. 1

Laertius. *See* Diogenes Laertius
Lacauella [Lecanella], Francesco, 151n. 6
Ladislas III, king of Poland and Hungary, 77, 79n. 24, 89
Languschi-Dolfin, 11, 12, 20, 52n. 123, 83n. 28, 83n. 30, 99n. 4, 107n. 10, 111n. 13, 113n. 15, 117nn. 16–17, 119n. 18, 143n. 3, 147n. 4, 149n. 5, 165n. 10, 167n. 11, 169n. 14, 173n. 15, 173n. 17, 175,n. 17, 187n. 21, 189n. 21, 201n. 24, 203n. 24, 205n. 25, 209n. 26, 211n. 27
Langusco [Languschi], Jacomo, 12, 50n. 115, 151n. 6, 153n. 7, 167n. 9, 161n. 10
Lastic de, Jean, 41n. 86, 263n. 1, 271n. 5
Lazar of Serbia, 63n. 5
Lazarević, Stephen, 73n. 15, 73 n.17
Leonardo. *See* Giustiniani, Leonardo, Archbishop of Lesbos
Lezze da, Donato, 35
Livy, 12, 211n. 27
Lomellino, Angelo Giovanni, *podestà* of Pera, 49n. 115, 52n. 123, 55n. 126, 83n. 28, 83n. 31, 189n. 21, 213n. 28
Lonicer, Philip, 18n. 26
Loredan[o], Giacomo, [Jacopo], 99n. 3, 129, 205n. 25, 207n. 25, 353
Loredan[o], Giovanni, 355
Loredan[o], Lorenzo, 259
Louis IX, 271n. 5, 275n. 6, 295n. 19
Lusignan, de, Guy, 263

Magno, Stefano, 18, 19, 20, 153n. 7, 173n. 17, 181n. 19, 189n. 21, 203n. 24, 207n. 25, 221n. 1, 245n. 18
Mahmud Pasha. *See* Angelović, Mahmud Pasha
Malipiero, Domenico, 229n. 13
Marcello, Bartolomeo, 9, 29, 357, 359
Mehmed I, Sultan, 71n. 12, 73n. 15, 73n. 17, 75, 87, 89
Mehmed II Fatih, Sultan [Grand Turk], 2, 4, 6, 9–15, 23, 28, 29, 32, 35–41, 41n. 84, 42–44, 47, 48, 53, 63n. 5, 81, 83, 85, 87, 91, 95, 97, 99, 101n. 5, 103n. 7, 105, 109, 115, 119, 123, 125, 127, 135, 137, 139n. 2, 141n. 3, 143, 151n. 6, 155n. 8, 171n. 15, 173n. 17, 175, 179, 183n. 19, 191n. 22, 195n. 22, 201n. 24, 209, 211n. 25, 213, 213n. 28, 215, 221n. 2, 225, 227n. 13, 229n. 13, 237, 239, 239n. 19, 241, 241n. 20, 243, 243nn. 22–23, 245, 251, 253, 255, 257, 259, 263, 265, 267nn. 3–4, 271, 273, 277n. 9, 287n. 15, 293, 299, 307, 313n. 32, 335, 341, 343, 345, 346, 347, 349, 353, 357, 359, 361, 363, 365
Meligalos, Antonios, 53, 267, 267n. 4, 269, 271, 273
Memo, Nicolaus, 7
Melissourgos-Melissenos, Makarios [Pseudo-Sphrantzes], 49 n.116, 50 n.116, 51, 83n. 28, 109n. 12, 111n. 13, 113n. 16, 151n. 6, 175n. 17
Mesih [Misac] Pasha. *See* Paleologus Doukas Megethos [Mesih Pasha]
Milly, de, Jacques, 263n. 1
Mini, Batholomeo, 361
Minotto, Girolamo, *bailo* in Constantinople, 29, 85n. 32, 117n. 17
Mircea the Old, voivode of Wallachia, 65n. 7, 73n. 15
Mocenigo, Pietro [Piero], 30, 31, 367
Moli, da, Zuanne, 233
Mollino, Nicolo, 355, 367
Montaldo di, Adamo, 13, 49n. 113, 191n. 21, 203n. 24, 211n. 27
Monteil, de, Anthony, 46n. 108
Morexini. *See* Morosini

Index of Persons   417

Moriani, Antonio, 229n. 13
Moro, Giovanni, 28
Morosini [Morexini], Hieronimo, 239n. 18
Morosini [Morexini], Jeruolamo, 163n. 10
Murad I, Sultan, 61, 63, 87
Murad II, Sultan, 7, 10, 75, 87, 89, 95,
    101n. 7, 171n. 15, 173n. 16, 309n. 31
Musa, 71n. 12, 73, 91
Muslih ed-Din, architect of Rumeli Hisar,
    97n. 2
Mustafa Beg, aga of Mehmed II's janissaries,
    95n. 1
Mustafa, pretender, 75
Myrmidons, 139n. 2, 141n. 2, 149n. 5,
    211n. 27

Naillac, de, Philibert, 263n. 1
Nardo[ne], da, Fiorio [Fioredinardo], 225,
    227, 229n. 13, 257
Nasuh Beg, 247n. 25
Neri, Zorzi, 233, 237, 241n. 21
Nestor-Iskander, 18n. 26, 50n. 115,
    83n. 28, 107n. 10, 189n. 21
Nevers, de, Jean, comte, 71n. 13, 73n. 14
Nicholas V, Pope, 129, 131, 141n. 2,
    149n. 5, 209n. 26, 213n. 28, 353, 357
Notaras, Anna, 117n. 16
Notaras, Jacob, 117n. 16
Notaras, Loukas, 53, 85n. 32
Novara [Nouara], da, Domenico, 151n. 6

Octavian, 211n. 27
Ömer [Turahanoğlu], Pasha, 37
Onesander, 14
Orbanus [Urbanus], 101n. 5
Orhan, grandson of Bayezid I, 95n. 1, 125
Orhan, son of Bayezid I, 73, 89
Orhan I, Sultan, 61, 87, 89
Orsini, Gian Baptista, 42n. 86, 263n. 1,
    271n. 5
Osman [Othman], 61, 87, 89

Pagnac, de, Maurice, 263n. 1, 203n. 24
Palaeologi, family/dynasty of, 267n. 4
Palaeologus Andronikos, despot of
    Thessalonica, 75n. 21

Palaeologus Doukas Megethos [Mesih
    Pasha], 44, 267n. 4, 268, 269n. 4, 271,
    273, 275n. 7, 277n. 8–9, 287, 289n. 16,
    293, 301, 301n. 25, 313n. 32
Palaeologus, Dragaš Constantine XI, 2, 25,
    29, 39, 40, 54, 79n. 24, 95n. 1, 99n. 3,
    101n. 5, 101n. 7, 107, 109, 113n. 16,
    125, 155, 171n. 15, 183, 195n. 22, 199,
    199n. 24, 201n. 24, 301n. 25, 344, 353,
    355, 357
Palaeologus, John VIII, 75n. 19, 75n. 21,
    79, 81, 353
Palaeologus, Manuel II, 65, 67n. 8, 73n. 17,
    75n. 19, 75n. 21, 79, 81
Paleologus, Michael VIII, 83n. 31
Palaeologus, Theophilus, 17, 18, 19, 20, 111,
    201n. 24,
Palapano, Antonio, 305n. 29
Palauixin [Palavicino, Paravas], Babilan,
    347, 349
Pauison [Pelatzoni], Nicolo [Nikolaos],
    347, 349
Paul I, Czar, 283n. 14
Pausanias, 3
Philelpho [Filelfo ?], 287n. 15
Philip, duke of Burgundy, 42n. 86, 271n. 5
Philip II, king of Macedon, 5, 14
Philomates, [Antonios], 25
Picemani Brothers, 363
Piccolomini, Aeneas Sylvius (See also Pius
    II, Pope), 6, 7, 8, 15, 17, 19, 20, 21,
    29n. 51
Pignera, Pedro, 269n. 4
Pius II, Pope (See also Piccolomini, Aeneas
    Sylvius), 6, 17, 21, 29n. 51, 83n. 24, 95,
    109n. 11, 207, 333
Pizzio from Epirote Albania, 287n. 15
Plutarch, 7
Polani, Alvise, 8
Porcaro [Portius], Stefano, 353
Priam, king of Troy, 4
Pusculo, Ubertino, 52n. 121, 117n. 17,
    161n. 10, 163n. 10, 165n. 10, 187n. 21,
    191n. 22, 203n. 24
Pyropoulos, Thomas, 269n. 4
Pyrrhus, king of Epirus, 5

Quirini, Lauro, 145n. 3, 165n. 11, 169n. 14, 183n. 19, 209n. 26, 211n. 27

Ramusio [Ramus], Giovanni [John] Battista, 15, 71nn. 12–13, 89
Ranatale, Bernardo, 251
Richer [Riccherio], Francesco, 16n. 23, 83n. 28, 193n. 22, 201n. 24
Rimini da, Filippo, 39, 40, 195n. 22
Rimondo, Piero, 207n. 25
Rizo, Antonio, 97n. 2
Rizzardo, Giacomo, 27, 32, 34, 35, 171n. 15, 221, 221,n. 1, 225n. 8, 235n. 16, 237,n. 17, 243n. 22, 247nn. 25–26
Roy, de, Charles, 295n. 19

Sabellico, Marc'Antonio, 367
Samuel, Bishop ["Vladik"], 29, 143n. 3, 149n. 5
Sanguin, Louis, 295n. 19
Sansovino, Francesco, 15, 16, 18n. 26, 19, 20, 175n. 17, 187n. 20, 195n. 22, 201n. 24
Santin, Diana, 34
Sanuto, Marino, 31n. 59
Savina, Girolamo, 229n. 13
Scagnelo, 227
Scanderbeg Kastriota, George, 2, 43
Schiavo, John. See Sclavus [Schiavo] Illyricus, John [Giovanni]
Schiavo [Illyricus], Tommaso, 53, 227, 229n. 13, 231, 233, 235, 235n. 25, 237, 241n. 21, 255, 257, 361
Schiltberger, Johann, 73n. 14
Scholarius George [Patriarch Gennadius II], 191n. 22
Scipio Africanus, 14
Sclavus [Schiavo] Illyricus, John [Giovanni], 17, 18, 19, 20, 107n. 12, 111, 201n. 24, 203n. 24
Sekoundinos [Sagundino], Alvise, 7, 31
Sekoundinos [Sagundino], Nikolaos, 4, 6–9, 12, 14–17, 31, 63n. 5, 67n. 7, 69n. 11, 71n. 12, 73n. 16, 107n. 10, 189n. 21, 203n. 24
Selim (Yavuz, "the Bold"), Sultan, 91
Sforza, Galeazzo Maria, 6

Sgouros, [George], 25
Sixtus IV, Pope, 42, 46, 305n. 28, 313
Sophianos, Demetrios, 53, 267, 267n. 4, 269, 271, 273, 277n. 20
Spagnuolo, Zanino, 223
Spandugnino [Spandounis/Spadounis], Theodorus, 69n. 11, 269n. 4
Sphrantzes, George, 33, 35, 51, 73n. 16, 75n. 20, 83n. 28, 155n. 8
Suleyman Çelebi, 71, 73, 89
Suleyman, emissary of Mesih Pasha, 297n. 22
Suleyman the Magnificent, Sultan, 89, 91, 275n. 6

Tahartar, 69n. 10
Tamburlaine [Timur-i-lenk], 67, 69, 89
Tetaldi [Edaldy, Tetaldy], Giacomo [Jacques], 21–24, 26, 27, 47, 83n. 28, 85n. 29, 99nn. 4–5, 137n. 1, 139n. 2, 141n. 3, 151n. 6, 153n. 7, 161n. 10, 167n. 12, 171n. 15, 173n. 16, 179n. 18, 199, 205, 205n. 25, 341, 344
Theotokopoulos, Domenikos [el Greco], 16
Thucydides, 3
Tignosi [da Foligno], Niccolò, 141n. 2, 155n. 8, 157n. 9, 203n. 24, 211n. 27
Tocco, Leonardo III, Count of Leucas, 44
Toledo, de, Francisco Don, 109n. 12
Trémouille de la, Guy, 73n. 14
Trevisan [Trivixan], Silvestro, 163n. 10
Trono, Giovanni, 367
Tuccia, della, Nicola, 155n. 8
Tursun Beg, 81n. 27, 83n. 29, 107n. 10, 109,n. 11, 151n. 6, 189n. 21, 197,n. 22
Tvrtko of Bosnia, 63n. 5
Twyr [Tyvvayr], de, Franco, 137, 217

Urbanus. See Orbanus [Urbanus]
Ustaoğlu, 91
Uzun Hasan, 15, 247n. 25

Vamade, Jehan. See Hunyadi Corvinus, John
Valentinus, Russian slave of Tetaldi, 23, 26, 27
Veneri, Giacomo, 259

Venier, Antonio, 34, 225, 247
Venier, Marco, 34, 247
Vergil, 4
Vergonde, Fernando, 269n. 4
Versi, Piero, 239n. 18, 241n. 20
Vertot, de, René d'Aubert, Abbé, 45
Vignoli, de, Vignolo, 263n. 1
Villagut, de, Diomedes, 333
Villaret, de, Foulques, 263n.1
Villeneuve, de, Hélion, 263n. 1
Vitruvius, 299n. 22
Vitturi, Lorenzo, 29
Volterranus, Raphael, 17n. 24

Xerxes, Great King of Persia, 141n. 2, 149n. 5

Yakub, brother of Bayezid I Yıldırım, 63n. 6
Ympegem, de, Simon, 217
Ympegem, de, Renier, 217

Zabondarno, Demetrios, 223
Zaccharia, Angelo, 161n. 10
Zacosta, Pedro Ramón [Raymond], 42n. 86, 163n. 1, 277n. 9
Zaganos [Sagan, Sangam, Sengampsa, Semgampsa], Pasha, 47, 95n. 1, 99n. 4, 161, 167, 169, 171n. 15, 173n. 16, 177, 179, 181, 199n. 23, 239n. 19, 342, 343
Zane, Marco, 251
Zorsi, Fantin, 30
Zuparo, Filippo, 237

INDEX OF PLACES

Achaea, 89
Achalia, Negroponte, 361
Adrianople [Edirne], 81n. 25, 95n. 1, 215, 247n. 25, 345, 346
Adrianople [Kharisios, Edirne] Gate, Constantinople, 197,n. 22, 355
Adrianople Gate, 103n. 7
Aegean Sea, 1–3, 26, 27, 33, 41, 99n. 3, 127, 205n. 25, 207n. 25, 273, 361
Aetolia, 77, 89
Afghanistan, 69n. 10
Africa, 14, 135
Ak Şehir, 69n. 11
Albania, 1–3, 40n. 84, 41n. 84, 43, 81n. 25, 267n. 3, 287n. 15
Alexandria, 157n. 9
Amasia, 91
Amasya, 71n. 12
Anadolu Hisar, 81n. 27, 97n. 2
Anatolia, 63n. 5, 67n. 10, 69n. 10, 69n. 15, 73n. 17, 75n. 20, 251
Ancona, 12, 22, 207, 211n. 27
Ankara, 67n. 9, 69n. 11, 71n. 12
Ankarathos Monastery, Crete, 24, 27
Arabia, 91
Aragon, 263n. 1, 345
Argos, 43n. 93
Athens, 15, 17, 34, 46, 135, 187n. 20, 247n. 25, 311n. 31
Attica, 65, 89, 361
Aulis, 221n. 3, 223n. 6, 361, 367
Auvergne, 41, 45, 263n. 1, 279
Avignon, 23, 137, 215, 217, 341
Aydın, 67n. 10

Balkans, 1, 43, 61n. 4, 71n. 13, 77n. 22
Baphaion, 59n. 3
Barcelona, 45
Basel, 17
Becaria, Negroponte, 253
Belgrade, 2, 42, 43, 91, 127
Bithynia, 57, 89
Black Sea, 14, 42, 71n. 13, 355
Boeotia, 65, 89, 247n. 25, 253, 361
Bologna, 28
Bosnia, 43n. 93, 89, 91
Bosphorus, 81, 97, 353, 365
Boudonitza, 247n. 25
Brandenburg, 211n. 27, 275n. 7
Brindisi [Brandicium], 43n. 96, 213n. 28
Bruges, 45
Buda, 77n. 22, 91
Bulgaria, 1, 89, 135
Burgundy, 29, 71n. 13, 89, 273n. 5
Bursa. See Prousa [Bursa]
Byzantium, 4, 65, 75, 111, 119, 157n. 9, 271, 353, 357, 361, 365; See also Constantinople

Caffa, 91, 157n. 9
Cairo, 31
Calabria, 43n. 96, 215n. 28
Caligaria. See Kaligaria Gate [Eğri Kapı], Constantinople
Cambrai, 22
Candia [Candida], Crete, 27, 28, 34, 129, 143n. 3, 145n. 3, 165n. 11, 199n. 24, 201,n. 24, 205n. 25, 207n. 25, 259
Caphareus, Negroponte, 361

Index of Places

Cappadocia, 57, 89, 91, 223, 233
Carasco, 259
Carni, 367
Carniola, 91
Carthage, 5
Castile, 263n. 1, 269n. 4
Cephalonia, 44
Cerinthus, Negroponte, 361
Chersonese, 63, 89
Chios, 107n. 10, 127, 129, 185n. 20, 193n. 22, 213n. 28, 251, 273, 355
Christ Church, Negroponte, 235
Christ Gate, Negroponte, 227, 235, 253, 255, 257
Church Gate, Negroponte, 227, 253, 257, 259
Constantinople, 1, 2, 4, 6–9, 12, 13, 17, 20–24, 26, 29, 34, 35, 40, 41n. 85, 42, 44, 47, 49, 50, 53, 54, 65n. 7, 67nn. 8–9, 73n. 15, 73n. 17, 75, 77n. 22, 81n. 25, 83, 85, 91, 95, 97, 99n. 4, 101n. 5, 101n. 7, 103, 107n. 10, 111, 113, 117, 119, 123, 125, 127, 129, 135, 137, 141n. 2, 151n. 6, 153, 155, 157, 161n. 10, 171n. 15, 173n. 17, 183n. 19, 193, 197, 197n. 22, 203, 205n. 25, 207, 207n. 25, 213, 213n. 28, 215, 239,n. 19, 247n. 25, 251, 253, 263n. 1, 265, 267, 267n. 9, 271, 271n. 5, 273, 277, 297n. 22, 303n. 27, 203n. 29, 309n. 31, 335, 341, 342, 344, 345, 346, 350, 353, 357, 359; *See also* Byzantium
Corfu, 39
Corinth, 79n. 84, 135
Cos [Lango], 263n. 1, 271n. 5, 275, 275n. 6
Costalimoni, 259
Cremona, 12
Crete, 14, 23, 24, 25, 28, 121, 129, 199n. 24, 201n. 29, 235n. 15, 355, 361
Crimea, 43
Croatia, 91
Cyprus, 135, 259, 263n. 1

Dacia, 89
Dalmatia, 31, 41n. 84, 267n. 3, 287n. 15
Dardanelles, 27, 267n. 3
Denmark, 29
Didymoteikhon, 247n. 25

Diplokionion, 145n. 4, 355
Dium, Negroponte, 361
Dobrudja, 71n. 13
Dolibro, 259
Domokos, 247n. 25
Drama, 63n. 5
Durazzo [Durachium], 213n. 28

Egypt, 31, 42, 91, 263n. 1
England, 67n. 9, 263n. 1
Epirus, 5, 44, 77, 89
Euboea, 3, 6, 22, 28, 29, 30, 34, 36, 43, 77n. 21, 205n. 25, 215, 221, 223n. 5, 267, 267n. 3, 361
Euripos, 36, 37n. 41, 361, 363, 365
Euxine, 75

Ferrara, 8, 67n. 9
Fighier [Figher], Negroponte, 227, 227n. 10, 253
Fittilto, 259
Flanders, 221, 221n. 1, 239n. 18
Florence, 8, 23, 129, 157n. 9
Fornaki, Negroponte, 253
Forum Julii. *See* Friuli
France, 12, 34, 44n. 96, 67, 211n. 27, 263n. 1, 271, 275n. 6, 295
Franchigia, Negroponte, 225
Friuli [Forum Julii], 43, 91, 241n. 20
Furcae, Negroponte, 253

Galatia, 57, 89
Gallipoli. *See* Kallipolis [Gallipoli, Gelibolu]
Genoa, 8, 28, 67n. 9, 107, 119, 157n. 9, 213n. 28, 355
Gerasus, Negroponte, 361
Germany, 34, 165n. 11, 263n. 1, 279
Germiyan, 67 n.10
Giudecca, Negroponte, 253, 257
Giudecha [Juifrie], Rhodes, 293n. 18, 306, 325, 329
Glarentza, 79n. 24
Golden Horn, 83n. 31, 99n. 4, 113n. 15, 145n. 4, 151 n. 6, 159n. 10, 161n. 10, 277n. 9, 353, 355
Goulfa, 153
Graz, 28

Index of Places   423

Halikarnassos, 263n. 1, 275n. 6
Hamit, 67n. 10
Hellespont, 61, 63, 75, 89, 273, 365
Hermanstadt, 29
Hessus, Negroponte, 361
Hexamilion, 79n. 23
Holy Apostles Church, Negroponte, 243
Hungary [Upper Pannonia], 1, 63n. 5, 71, 77n. 22, 89, 105n. 9, 127

Ialysos, Rhodes, 285n. 14
Ikonion [Konya], 67n. 10
Iberia [Georgia], 69n. 10
Illyria, 89
India, 69n. 10
Ionia, 57
Ionian Sea, 273
Isthmus of Corinth, 79
Italy, 2, 29, 42, 43, 44, 127, 211n. 27, 213n. 28, 243n. 22, 263n. 1, 289, 193n. 18, 357

Jamurlu, 73n. 17
Jerusalem, 91, 263n. 1, 265, 291, 295, 301, 305, 309

Kaligaria Gate [Eğri Kapı], Constantinople, 167n. 11, 181, 343
Kalograia [Falegriza], Negroponte, 225, 225n. 8, 253
Kallipolis [Gallipoli, Gelibolu], 61n. 4, 63, 89, 127, 213n. 28, 225
Kalymnos, 263n. 1
Karaman [Caramaym], 67n. 10, 95n. 1, 216
Karystos, Negroponte, 251
Kastamonia [Kastamonu], 67n. 10
Kavalla, 63n. 5, 247n. 25
Keos, 365
Khalkis, 3, 7, 22, 28–30, 36, 205n. 25, 215, 221n. 3, 223nn. 5–6, 233n. 14, 267 361, 363, 365, 367
Kokkinos, Lemnos, 225
Komotini, 247n. 25
Kossovo polje, 63n. 5, 91
Krüje, 267n. 3
Kunovica, 77n. 22

Larissa, 247n. 25
Lecce, 43n. 96
Leivadia, 247n. 25
Lemnos [Stalimene, Stalimini], 40n. 84, 75n. 20, 127, 225, 251, 267n. 3
Lepanto [Naupaktos], 6, 43n. 93, 49
Leros, 263n. 1
Lesbos, 3
Leucas [Santa Maura], 44
Lindos, Rhodes, 275, 275n. 6
London, 27, 67n. 9
Lycia, 273, 311
Lykos River, Constantinople, 181n. 19

Macedonia, 5, 11, 12, 63n. 5, 65, 91, 247n. 25
Malta, 47n. 108, 277n. 9, 283n. 14, 297n. 22
Maltepe, 101n. 5
Mani, 40n. 84, 267n. 3
Maritza, 63n. 5
Methone [Modon], 28, 43n. 93, 91
Milan, 5, 33, 67n. 9, 131, 211, 345
Millemosa [Khiliomodion], Negroponte, 221, 221n. 3
Mistra, 267n. 4
Moesia, 89
Monolithos, Rhodes, 275, 275n. 6
Monteil [Montelium], 295, 305, 333
Morea [Peloponnese], 2, 28, 34, 40n. 84, 41n. 84, 43, 67n. 9, 79, 83n. 25, 91, 263n. 1, 267n. 3, 367
Mysia, 89
Mytilene, 135

Naples, Italy, 6, 7, 9, 14, 111n. 12, 189n. 21, 353
Naples [Nauplion, Anapli, Napoli], 237, 237n. 17, 245
Nembio, 251
Negroponte, 3, 6, 22, 29, 30–34, 36, 37, 40, 41, 43, 49, 53, 77n. 21, 91, 127, 131, 207n. 25, 215, 221, 221n. 1, 223, 229n. 13, 231, 235n. 15, 239n. 18, 241n. 20, 243nn. 22–23, 245, 247,n. 25, 251, 253, 255, 257, 259, 267, 267nn. 3–4, 271n. 5, 361

Index of Places

Nicopolis, 67n. 8, 71n. 13, 205n. 25, 345
Nisyros, 263n. 1
Novo Brdo [Novobrdo], 2, 165n. 11, 167n. 11
Nuremberg, 45n. 99
Nymphaion, 83n. 31

Odense, 45
Oreus, Negroponte, 361
Orto, 259
Otranto, 3, 42, 43, 91

Paleokastron, Lemnos, 251
Pamphylia, 57
Pamphylian Sea, 361
Paris, 67n. 9
Parma, 45
Passau, 45
Patras, 79n. 24
Pavia, 67n. 9
Pege [Pigli, Silivri Kapı] Gate, Constantinople, 181, 342, 343
Pelekanon, 61n. 4
Peloponnese. *See* Morea
Pera [Galata(s)], 47, 48, 83, 85, 99, 105, 111, 113n. 15, 119, 123, 127, 129, 145n. 4, 161n. 10, 181, 189n. 21, 197, 199n. 23, 207n. 25, 342, 343, 347, 349, 353, 355
Perister(ion), 127
Persia, 5, 57
Petrion, Constantinople, 197n. 22
Phanes [Fane] Fort, Rhodes, 275n. 7
Phenike, Rhodes, 277n. 8
Pheraklos [Feraclo], Rhodes, 275, 275n. 6
Phileremos [Fileremo], Rhodes, 275n. 6, 283, 283n. 14
Philippi, 247n. 25
Philippopolis [Plovdiv, Filibe], 63n. 5
Phiskos [Physkos, Fisco, Phiscus, Marmara Limani], 273, 275n. 7, 277, 277,n. 8, 313, 333
Phocaea, 129
Phocis, 65, 79n. 24, 89
Phrygia, 57
Pisa, 217

Platamon, 247n. 25
Poland, 89
Politia, Negroponte, 363
Pontus, 57, 355
Portamus, Negroponte, 361
Portello, Negroponte, 227
Porto Leone [Piraeus], 251, 259
Portogruaro, 241n. 20
Portugal, 29, 33
Prousa [Bursa], 59n. 3, 61n. 4, 73n. 15, 89, 129
Provence, 263n. 1, 293n. 18
Psamathia, Constantinople, 197n. 22
Pyrra, Negroponte, 361

Rhodes, 3, 40–42, 44, 45, 53, 71n. 13, 91, 127, 135, 217, 223n. 7, 259, 263, 263n. 1, 265, 267, 267n. 3, 269n. 4, 271, 271n. 5, 273, 275, 275n. 6. 275n. 7, 277, 277n. 8, 305n. 29, 207n. 30, 309n. 31, 313, 313n. 32, 317, 333, 335, 337, 339
Rivellino, Negroponte, 221, 227, 235, 243
Romania, 135, 205n. 25, 207n. 25, 151, 344
Rome, 28, 42, 45, 46, 127, 129, 211, 213n. 28, 279n. 10
Rovine, 71n. 3
Rubeum, Rhodes, 283
Rumeli, 37, 251, 313n. 32
Rumeli Hisar, 81n. 27, 97n. 2, 163n. 10, 353, 390, 391
Russia, 69n. 10, 275n. 6, 283n. 14, 346

Saburra, Rhodes, 283
Sagripolis, 215
Saint Anthony Church, Rhodes, 277, 289, 317
Saint Elias Church, Negroponte, 2255, 225n. 8
Saint George Gate, Negroponte, 227
Saint John Chrysostom [Giovanni Boccadoro] Church, Negroponte, 245
Saint John Kourkos, Negroponte, 225
Saint Mary Eleimonitra Church, Rhodes, 301

Index of Places   425

Saint Nicholas Fort, Rhodes, 41n. 86, 271n. 5, 277, 277n. 9, 279, 279 n. 11, 281, 281n. 12, 285, 289n. 16, 293, 317, 319
Saint Peter Fort, Rhodes, 275, 283
Saint Romanus Gate, Constantinople, 54, 101n. 5, 165n. 11, 181, 181n. 19, 183, 193n. 22, 197n. 22, 199n. 24, 201n. 24, 343, 344, 355, 357; *See also* Top Kapı
Saint Stephen Church, Rhodes, 275
Saint Stephen Mountain, Rhodes, 277
Salona [Amphissa], 247n. 25
Samarkand, 69n. 10
San Domenico Church, Chios, 107n. 10
San Francesco Church, Negroponte, 225, 253
San Marco [Bocca di] Church, Negroponte, 223, 223n. 6, 251, 257, 259
San Stefano Church, Negroponte, 227
Santa Chiara [Clara] Church, Negroponte, 225, 241, 245, 253, 257
Santa Mari[n]a Church, Negroponte, 227, 253
Santa Sophia of Constantinople, 39, 40, 113, 125, 129, 357
Sclavonia, 91
Scutari [Valona, Avlona], 40,n. 84, 267n. 3
Sebasteia [Sivas], 69n. 10
Serbia, 1, 2, 28, 63n. 5, 73n. 15, 73n. 17, 83n. 29, 89, 95n. 1, 99n. 4, 165n. 11
Serres, 63n. 5, 247n. 25
Sicily, 153n. 6, 311
Siderovia. *See* Smederevo [Ferrovia, Siderovia]
Siena, 6, 14
Sinope, 67n. 10
Skiathos [Stato], 251, 259
Skopelos [Scopulo], 251, 259
Skyros, 251
Smederevo [Ferrovia, Siderovia], 2, 127
Sofia, 63n. 5, 77n. 22
Stoudios, Constantinople, 197n. 22
Strasbourg [Argentorati], 45n. 99, 49, 353
Struez, 223, 227, 247
Styra, 223, 247

Styria, 28, 91
Sulu Kule, 105n. 9
Syria, 91, 361

Taranto, 43n. 96
Tarviso, 91
Tekke, 67n. 10
Telos, 275n. 7
Tenedos, 251
Thebes [Stius, Stives], 223, 223n. 5, 227, 247n. 25, 253
Thessalonica, 7, 63n. 5, 75, 89, 247n. 25
Thessaly, 67, 73n. 16, 247n. 25
Thrace, 61, 63, 65, 71, 73n. 15, 75, 89
Tilos, 45
Top Kapı, 101n. 5; *See also* Saint Romanus Gate, Constantinople
Touppa [La Cuppa] Fort, Negroponte, 255, Transylvania, 1, 2, 29, 43, 77n. 22, 105n. 9
Trebizond, 2, 14, 43, 91, 95n. 1, 163n. 10, 344
Troy, 4, 39, 85n. 33
Tunisia, 42

Varadunum, 91
Varna, 77
Valona, 44
Vassilika [Sicyon], 79n. 24
Venice, 9, 14, 15, 22, 23, 28, 29, 30, 34, 40, 41, 43, 45, 46, 49, 67nn. 8–9, 75n. 21, 95n. 1, 99n. 3, 105n. 9, 145n. 4, 163n. 10, 205n. 25, 211, 227, 231, 255, 263n. 1, 267n. 3, 269n. 4, 345, 353, 357, 361, 365, 367
Vicenza, 35, 67n. 9, 243n. 22
Vienna, 6, 21, 91
Vostitza [Aigion], 79n. 24
Vourkos [Burchio], Negroponte, 221, 221n. 3, 227, 229n. 13, 233, 235, 237, 245, 253, 257

Wallachia, 2, 29, 65n. 7, 73n. 15, 89, 91

Zacynthus, 44
Zeitouni [Lamia], 247n. 25

INDEX OF SCHOLARS

Alderson, Anthony D, 75n. 18
Andreeva, Marija, 67n. 9
Andrews, A. D. , 43n. 93
Arampatzoglou, Odysseus, 24n. 40
Argenti, Philip P., 155n. 9, 159n. 9
Arnakis, Georgiadis Georgios, 57n. 1
Aschback, Joseph, 71n. 13
Atasöy, Sümer, 5n. 1
Atiya, Aziz S., 71n. 13
Ayverdi, Ekrem H., 81n. 27

Babinger, Franz, 7n. 2, 42,n. 89, 65n. 7
    79n. 22, 81n. 26, 97n. 2, 313n. 32
Bain, Robert, 42n. 89
Bartusis, Mark C., 155n. 8
Baynes, Norman H., 311n. 31
Beck, Hans-Georg, 25n. 40, 85n. 33
Bekker, Immanuel, 309n. 31
Belgrano, Luigi T., 18n. 26, 49n. 115
Benedikz, Benedikt S., 155n. 8
Berchet, Guglielmo, 14n. 15
Bergantini, G., 52n. 123
Bernikolas-Hatzopoulos, Dionysios, 67n. 7
Biazes, Spyridon, 38n. 76
Birnbaum, E., 313n. 32
Bisaha, Nancy, 5n. 1
Blöndal, Sigfús, 155n. 8
Bodnar, Edward W., 12n. 11
Boissonade, J. F. , 43n. 91
Bombaci, Alesio, 43n. 96
Bosio, Giacomo, 265n. 1, 277n. 7
Bouras, Kharalampos, 269n. 4
Bradbury, Jim, 297nn. 21–22, 299n. 23
Bradford, Ernle, 283n. 13
Braun, M. , 63n. 5

Brockman, Eric, 269n. 4, 275nn. 6–7,
    287n. 15, 297n. 21, 301n. 24, 303n. 26
Browning, Robert, 24n. 40, 207n. 25
Bouhours, Dominique, Père, 41n. 87,
    271n. 5, 275n. 7, 281n. 12, 287n. 15,
    289n. 16, 295nn. 19–20, 297n. 21,
    301,n. 25, 305n. 28
Boutsina, P., 271n. 5
Byrne, M., 299n. 23

Cecchini, G., 117n. 16
Charanis, Peter, 59n. 2, 63n. 5
Charavay, Étienne, 44n. 98
Cheetham, Nicholas, 43n. 94
Chevedden, Paul, 297n. 21
Cicogna, Emmanuelle E., 31n. 57, 32, 34,
    35, 221n. 1, 235 n.15, 239n. 18
Cipolla, Carlo M. , 79n. 24
Cochrane, Eric, 19n. 28, 48n. 113
Coco, P., 43n. 96
Concasty, Marie-Louise, 21n. 32
Cornet, Enrico, 49n. 115, 157n. 9, 163n. 10,
    167n. 11, 187n. 21

Delaville le Roulx, Joseph, 265n. 1
Dennis, George T., 16n. 23, 69n. 12
Desimoni, Cornelio, 13n. 12, 49n. 115, 191n. 21
Déthier, Philippe A, 13n. 12, 18n. 26, 26,
    50n. 115, 191n. 21
DeVries, Kelly, 79n. 24, 101n. 5
Dölger, Franz, 25n. 40, 50n. 116
Dotson, John E., 163n. 10, 239n. 18
Drizari, N., 42n. 92
Dubuisson, M. , 265n. 2
Durand, Ursin, 26

Index of Scholars

Ellissen, Adolph S., 52n. 123, 161n. 10, 163n. 10, 165n. 10, 187n. 21, 203n. 24

Fincati, Luigi, 31n. 57, 225n. 9, 235n. 15
Fossari, E., 43n.96

Ganchou, Thierry, 50n. 116, 54n. 126, 111n. 12, 157n. 9
Geanakoplos, Deno J., 79n. 22,
Gegaj, Athanas, 42n. 92
Georgopoulou, Maria, 221n. 3, 233n. 14
Gibbon, Edward, 52
Gibbons, Herbert A., 59n. 2, 65n. 7, 69nn. 10–11, 71n. 13
Gill, Joseph, 79n. 22
Giokhalas, Titos P, 42n. 92
Godefroy, D., 26
Grecu, Vasile, 50n. 116
Gregory, Timothy E., 79n. 23
Grierson, P., 235n. 16
Guilland, Rodolphe, 99n. 2

Haldon, J., 299,n. 23
Halecki, Oscar, 77n. 22
Hammer-Purgstall, Joseph von, 59n. 3
Hanak, Walter K., 12n. 10, 49n. 115, 54n. 126, 83n. 28, 103n. 7, 153n. 7, 159n. 9
Hankins, James, 7n. 2, 13n. 12, 85n. 33
Hasluck, Frederick W, 185n. 20
Hatzidimitriou, Constantine, 48n. 114
Hazard, Harry W., 79n. 22
Heers, Jacques, 155n. 9
Held, Joseph, 43n. 90
Heywood, Colin, 59n. 3
Hofmann, Georg, 143n. 3, 167n. 12
Hookham, Hilda, 69,n. 10, 69n. 11
Hopf, Carl, 13n. 12, 26, 49n. 115, 185n. 20, 191n. 21, 211 n.27, 221n. 1, 235n. 17

Imber, Colin, 59n. 3
Inalcik, Halil, 57n. 1, 59n. 2, 59n. 3, 61n. 4, 81n. 27, 83n. 28, 171n. 15, 173n. 15, 189n. 21, 197n. 22
Iorga [Jorga], Nicolae, 21, 23n. 38, 38n. 77, 75n. 20, 265n. 1
Itzkowitz, Norman, 57n. 1

Janssens, Emile, 43n. 91
Jireček, C., 63n. 5
Jugie, Martin, 67n. 9, 191n. 22

Kalatheres, Anastasios, 221n. 3
Khasiotes, Ioannes K., 50n. 116, 103n. 7
Klopf [Carroll], Margaret G., 155n. 8
Kollias, Elias, 45n. 103, 265n. 1
Köprülü, Mehmed F., 61n. 3
Korres, Theodoros K., 299n. 23
Kougeas, Sokrates, 75n. 18
Krauter, K., 145n. 3
Kristeller, P. O., 145n. 3

Laiou, Angeliki E., 197n. 22; Laiou-Thomadakis, Angeliki E., 21n. 33
Lampros, Spyridon P., 25n. 41, 43n. 91, 47n. 111, 51n. 120, 117n. 16, 119n. 18, 153n. 7, 195n. 22
Lemerle, Paul, 77n. 21
Leonid, Archimandrite, 50n. 115
Lev, Yaakov, 79n. 24
Lewis, Bernard, 313n. 32
Lindner, Paul R., 57n. 1
Lock, Peter, 43n. 94
Loenertz, Raymond-Joseph, 50n. 116, 63n. 5
Lopez, Robert S., 155n. 9
Lowry, Heath W., 57n. 1
Ludewig, J. P., 46n. 106
Luttrell, Anthony, 255n. 1

MacKay, Pierre, 35n. 68
Magoulias, Harry J., 83nn. 28–29
Maisano, Riccardo, 50n. 116
Makušev, Vikentii V., 10n. 9, 189n. 29
Manoussakas, Manoussos, 25n. 40, 117n. 16
Marinescu, Constantin, 99n. 2
Martène, Edmond, 26
Mastrodemetres, Panagiotes, 7n. 2
Matschke, Klaus-Peter, 71n. 12, 117n. 16, 197n. 22, 269n. 4
Megas, Georgios, 85n. 33
Melville Jones, John R., 11n. 10, 12n. 10, 19n. 29, 22n. 34, 23n. 38, 25n. 41, 26, 47n. 109, 48n. 112, 77n. 21, 81n. 27, 83n. 28, 85n. 34, 107n. 10, 119n. 18

Index of Scholars

Mertzios, Konstantinos D., 24n. 40, 117n. 16
Miklosich, Frank, 47, 109
Miller, Timothy S., 16n. 23
Miller, William, 42n. 89, 43n. 92
Millingen, Alexander Van, 52n. 118, 103n. 7
Mitchell, Charles, 12n. 11
Mizzi, E. F., 45
Mordtmann, Andreas D., 50n. 117
Müller, C., 50n. 115
Müller, Joseph, 48n. 111
Murphey, Rhoades, 81n. 27, 83n. 28, 189n. 21, 197n. 22

Nesbitt, John, 16n. 23
Nicol, Donald M., 67n. 7, 117n. 16
Noli, Fan S., 42n. 92

Olgiati, G, 54n. 126

Paliouras, Athanasios D., 17n. 24
Pall, F., 42n. 92, 79n. 22
Panarco, G., 43n. 96
Papachristodoulou, Christodoulos I., 305n. 29
Papadopoulou, Eutychia E., 30n. 55
Papoulia, Basilike, 65n. 7, 171n. 15
Partington, J. R., 79n. 24, 299n. 23
Paspates, Alexander G., 19n. 29, 51, 97n. 2
Pastor, Ludwig, 209n. 26
Patrinelis, Christos G., 13n. 11
Pears, Edwin, 19n. 29, 26n. 42, 51, 52n. 123, 69n. 11, 101n. 5, 109n. 11, 151n. 6
Pertusi, Agostino, 18n. 26, 19n. 28, 20, 21n. 33, 39nn. 79–80, 47, 101n. 5, 141n. 2, 145n. 3, 195n. 22
Petit, Louis, 191n. 22,
Picenardi, G., 45n. 101
Pistarino, Geo, 155n. 9
Philippides, Marios, 5n. 1, 12n. 10, 16nn. 22–23, 17n. 25, 19n. 30, 22n. 33, 26n. 42, 36n. 72, 37n. 73, 38nn. 74–75, 44n. 97, 50nn. 115–116, 52n. 123, 53nn. 124–125, 63n. 5, 79n. 24, 83n. 28, 101nn. 5–6, 103n. 7, 107n. 10, 113n. 16, 141n. 2, 145n. 3, 153n. 7, 159n. 9, 185n. 20, 269n. 4
Podskalsky, Gerhard, 85n. 33
Pogodin, P. D., 22n. 35
Polidori, Filippo-Luigi, 35, 38n. 76, 229n. 13
Protopsaltes, E. G., 51n. 120

Raby, Julian, 12n. 11
Ravegnani, G., 145n. 3
Radojičić, Dorde S., 65n. 7
Reinert, Stephen W., 64n. 5
Riggs, Charles T., 83n. 28, 101n. 5, 103n. 7, 197n. 22
Roloff G., 69n. 11
Rossignol, G., 271n. 5
Runciman, Steven, 19n. 29, 49n. 116, 50, 51, 77n. 22

Sacy, de, S., 49n. 115
Saïd, Suzanne, 265n. 2
Sanjian, Avedis K., 85n. 33
Sathas, Constantine N., 193n. 22
Schlumberger, Gustave, 51n. 120, 67n. 9
Schneider, A. M., 197n. 22
Schreiner, Peter, 35nn. 70–71
Seno, C., 145n. 3
Setton, Kenneth M., 21n. 32, 51, 79n. 22, 311n. 31
Shaw, Stanford J., 40n. 84, 57n. 1, 63n. 5, 69n. 10
Siderides [Sidéridès], Xenophon A., 109n. 11, 191n. 22
Skeat, Theodore C., 85n. 34, 119n. 18
Spremic, Momcilo, 77n. 21
Sreznevskii, Izmail I., 18n. 26, 49n. 115
Stacton [Dereksen], David, 51, 111n. 12
Stavrides, Theoharis, 40n. 84, 173n. 15, 243n. 23, 247n. 26

Taafe, J., 55n. 106
Taeschner, Franz, 59n. 2, 75n. 18
Talbot, Alice-Mary, 7n. 2
Telfer, J. B., 73n. 14
Temperley, Harold W. V., 63n. 5
Thomas, Georg M., 11n. 10, 49n. 115, 143n. 3

Thouasne, L., 267n. 3
Tomadakis, Nikolaos B., 50n. 116
Torr, Cecil, 267n. 4

Ursu, I., 35

Valsen, Joseph, 44n. 98
Vertot, de, Aubert René Daubef, 265n. 1, 283n. 14
Vigna, A., 20n. 31
Vaughan, Dorothy M., 43n. 93, 65n. 7, 77 n.21, 81n. 27, 83n. 28
Vryonis, Speros, 57n. 1, 65n. 7, 171n. 15

Waldstein-Wartenberg, Berthold von, 265n. 1
Werner, Ernst, 57n. 1, 69n. 11
Williams, Alan, 79n. 24, 101n. 5
Wittek, Paul, 57n. 1, 59n. 3, 71n. 12
Wolkan, R., 29n. 51, 207n. 25
Wright Gilliland, Diana, 47n. 111

Zachariadou, Elizabeth A., 19n. 29, 41n. 88, 63 n.5
Zinkeisen, Johann W., 59n.3
Zoras, George, T., 36n. 73, 37nn. 74–75, 44n. 97, 145n. 4